# Lecture Notes of the Institute for Computer Sciences, Social Informatics and Telecommunications Engineering    561

The LNICST series publishes ICST's conferences, symposia and workshops.

LNICST reports state-of-the-art results in areas related to the scope of the Institute. The type of material published includes

- Proceedings (published in time for the respective event)
- Other edited monographs (such as project reports or invited volumes)

LNICST topics span the following areas:

- General Computer Science
- E-Economy
- E-Medicine
- Knowledge Management
- Multimedia
- Operations, Management and Policy
- Social Informatics
- Systems

Honghao Gao · Xinheng Wang · Nikolaos Voros
Editors

# Collaborative Computing: Networking, Applications and Worksharing

19th EAI International Conference, CollaborateCom 2023
Corfu Island, Greece, October 4–6, 2023
Proceedings, Part I

 Springer

*Editors*
Honghao Gao
Shanghai University
Shanghai, China

Xinheng Wang
Xi'an Jiaotong-Liverpool
Suzhou, China

Nikolaos Voros
University of Peloponnese
Patra, Greece

ISSN 1867-8211          ISSN 1867-822X (electronic)
Lecture Notes of the Institute for Computer Sciences, Social Informatics
and Telecommunications Engineering
ISBN 978-3-031-54520-7          ISBN 978-3-031-54521-4 (eBook)
https://doi.org/10.1007/978-3-031-54521-4

This Springer imprint is published by the registered company Springer Nature Switzerland AG
The registered company address is: Gewerbestrasse 11, 6330 Cham, Switzerland

Paper in this product is recyclable.

# Preface

We are delighted to introduce the proceedings of the 19th European Alliance for Innovation (EAI) International Conference on Collaborative Computing: Networking, Applications and Worksharing (CollaborateCom 2023). This conference brought together researchers, developers and practitioners around the world who are interested in fully realizing the promises of electronic collaboration from the aspects of networking, technology and systems, user interfaces and interaction paradigms, and interoperation with application-specific components and tools.

This year's conference accepted 72 submissions. Each submission was reviewed by an average of 3 reviewers. The conference sessions were: Day 1 Session 1 – Collaborative Computing; Session 2 – Edge Computing & Collaborative Working; Session 3 – Blockchain Application; Session 4 – Code Search and Completion; Session 5 – Edge Computing Scheduling and Offloading; Session 6 – Deep Learning and Application; Session 7 – Graph Computing; Session 8 – Security and Privacy Protection; Session 9 – Processing and Recognition; Session 10 – Deep Learning and Application; Session 11 – Onsite Session. Day 2 Session 12 – Federated Learning and Application; Session 13 – Collaborative Working; Session 14 – Edge Computing; Session 15 – Security and Privacy Protection; Session 16 – Prediction, Optimization and Applications. Apart from high-quality technical paper presentations, the technical program also featured two keynote speeches that were delivered by Christos Masouros from University College London and Michael Hübner from Brandenburgische Technische Universität (BTU).

Coordination with the steering chair, Xinheng Wang, and steering members Song Guo, Bo Li, Xiaofei Liao, Honghao Gao, and Ning Gu was essential for the success of the conference. We sincerely appreciate their constant support and guidance. It was also a great pleasure to work with such an excellent organizing committee team for their hard work in organizing and supporting the conference. In particular, the Technical Program Committee, led by our General Chairs Nikolaos Voros and General Co-Chairs Tasos Dagiuklas, Xinheng Wang, and Honghao Gao, TPC Chairs Christos Antonopoulos, and Eleni Christopoulou, and TPC Co-Chair Dimitrios Ringas completed the peer-review process of technical papers and made a high-quality technical program. We are also grateful to the Conference Manager, Karolina Marcinova, for her support and to all the authors who submitted their papers to the CollaborateCom 2023 conference.

We strongly believe that CollaborateCom provides a good forum for all researchers, developers and practitioners to discuss all science and technology aspects that are relevant to collaborative computing. We also expect that the future CollaborateCom conferences will be as successful and stimulating, as indicated by the contributions presented in this volume.

Honghao Gao
Xinheng Wang
Nikolaos Voros

# Conference Organization

## Steering Committee

### Chair

Xinheng Wang                    Xi'an Jiaotong-Liverpool University

### Members

Bo Li                           Hong Kong University of Science and
                                    Technology, China
Honghao Gao                     Shanghai University, China
Ning Gu                         Fudan University, China
Song Guo                        University of Aizu, Japan
Xiaofei Liao                    Huazhong University of Science and Technology,
                                    China

## Organizing Committee

### General Chair

Nikolaos Voros                  University of the Peloponnese, Greece

### General Co-chairs

Tasos Dagiuklas                 London South Bank University, UK
Xinheng Wang                    Xi'an Jiaotong-Liverpool University, China
Honghao Gao                     Shanghai University, China

### TPC Chair and Co-chairs

Christos Antonopoulos           University of the Peloponnese, Greece
Eleni Christopoulou             Ionian University, Greece
Dimitrios Ringas                Ionian University, Greece

viii      Conference Organization

**Sponsorship and Exhibit Chair**

Christina Politi                     University of the Peloponnese, Greece

**Local Chair**

Eleni Christopoulou                  Ionian University, Greece

**Workshops Chair**

Georgios Keramidas                   Aristotle University of Thessaloniki, Greece

**Publicity and Social Media Chair**

Katerina Lamprakopoulou              University of the Peloponnese, Greece

**Publications Chair**

Christos Antonopoulos                University of the Peloponnese, Greece

**Web Chair**

Evi Faliagka                         University of the Peloponnese, Greece

# Technical Program Committee

| | |
|---|---|
| Zhongqin Bi | Shanghai University of Electric Power, China |
| Shizhan Chen | Tianjing University, China |
| Lizhen Cui | Shandong University, China |
| Weilong Ding | North China University of Technology, China |
| Yucong Duan | Hainan University, China |
| Honghao Gao | Shanghai University, China |
| Fan Guisheng | East China University of Science and Technology, China |
| Haiping Huang | Nanjing University of Posts and Telecommunications, China |
| Li Kuang | Central South University, China |
| Youhuizi Li | Hangzhou Dianzi University, China |
| Rui Li | Xidian University, China |
| Xuan Liu | Yangzhou University, China |

| Tong Liu | Shanghai University, China |
| Xiaobing Sun | Yangzhou University, China |
| Haiyan Wang | Nanjing University of Posts & Telecommunications, China |
| Xinheng Wang | Xi'an Jiaotong-Liverpool University, China |
| Xiaoxian Yang | Shanghai Polytechnic University, China |
| Yuyu Yin | Hangzhou Dianzi University, China |
| Jun Zeng | Chongqing University, China |
| Zijian Zhang | Beijing Institute of Technology, China |

# Contents – Part I

**Collaborative Computing**

Enhanced Sound Recognition and Classification Through Spectrogram
Analysis, MEMS Sensors, and PyTorch: A Comprehensive Approach ......... 3
*Alexandros Spournias, Nikolaos Nanos, Evanthia Faliagka,
Christos Antonopoulos, Nikolaos Voros, and Giorgos Keramidas*

TCP Cubic Implementation in the OMNeT++ INET Framework for SIoT
Simulation Scenarios ..................................................... 18
*Ioannis Angelis, Athanasios Tsipis, Eleni Christopoulou,
and Konstantinos Oikonomou*

Implementation Framework of a Blockchain Based Infrastructure
for Electricity Trading Within a Microgrid ............................. 38
*Milan Todorović, Milica Knežević, Domagoj Ševerdija, Slobodan Jelić,
and Miodrag J. Mihaljević*

Resource Cooperative Scheduling Optimization Considering Security
in Edge Mobile Networks ................................................. 54
*Cheng Fang, Peng Yang, Meng Yi, Miao Du, and Bing Li*

**Edge Computing and Collaborative Working**

DQN-Based Applications Offloading with Multiple Interdependent Tasks
in Mobile Edge Computing ............................................... 77
*Jiaxue Tu, Dongge Zhu, Yunni Xia, Yin Li, Yong Ma, Fan Li,
and Qinglan Peng*

Edge Server Deployment Approach Based on Uniformity and Centrality ...... 93
*Xinghong Jiang, Yong Ma, Yunni Xia, Qilin Xie, and Wenxin Jian*

Budget-Constrained Contention-Aware Workflow Scheduling in a Hybrid
Cloud .................................................................. 111
*Qingliang Zhang, Xinyue Shu, and Quanwang Wu*

A Dichotomous Repair-Based Load-Balanced Task Allocation Strategy
in Cloud-Edge Environment .............................................. 128
*Zekun Hu, Pengwei Wang, Peihai Zhao, and Zhaohui Zhang*

DPIM: Dynamic Pricing Incentive Mechanism for Mobile Crowd Sensing ..... 149
    *Weiwei Xing, Xinwei Yao, and Chufeng Qi*

**Blockchain Applications**

Efficient and Revocable Anonymous Account Guarantee System Based
on Blockchain ........................................................... 167
    *Weiyou Liang, Yujue Wang, Yong Ding, Hai Liang, Changsong Yang,
    and Huiyong Wang*

Computing Resource Allocation for Hybrid Applications of Blockchain
and Mobile Edge Computing ............................................. 187
    *Yuqi Fan, Jun Zhang, Xu Ding, Zhifeng Jin, and Lei Shi*

Blockchain-Based EMR Enhancement: Introducing PMI-Chain
for Improved Medical Data Security and Privacy ......................... 207
    *Bo Cui, Tianyu Mei, and Xu Liu*

BGET: A Blockchain-Based Grouping-EigenTrust Reputation
Management Approach for P2P Networks ................................. 225
    *Yang Peng, Jie Huang, Sirui Zhou, Zixuan Ju, Xiaowen Wang,
    and Peihao Li*

Privacy-Preserving Blockchain Supervision with Responsibility Tracking ...... 243
    *Baodong Wen, Yujue Wang, Yong Ding, Haibin Zheng, Hai Liang,
    Changsong Yang, and Jinyuan Liu*

**Code Search and Completion**

JARAD: An Approach for Java API Mention Recognition
and Disambiguation in Stack Overflow .................................. 265
    *Qingmi Liang, Yi Jin, Qi Xie, Li Kuang, and Yu Sheng*

Enrich Code Search Query Semantics with Raw Descriptions ............... 284
    *Xiangzheng Liu, Jianxun Liu, Haize Hu, and Yi Liu*

A Code Completion Approach Combining Pointer Network
and Transformer-XL Network ........................................... 303
    *Xiangping Zhang, Jianxun Liu, Teng Long, and Haize Hu*

A Code Search Method Incorporating Code Annotations ................... 323
    *Qi Li, Jianxun Liu, and Xiangping Zhang*

CUTE: A Collaborative Fusion Representation-Based Fine-Tuning
and Retrieval Framework for Code Search ............................. 343
    *Qihong Song, Jianxun Liu, and Haize Hu*

## Edge Computing Scheduling and Offloading

Roadside IRS Assisted Task Offloading in Vehicular Edge Computing
Network ......................................................... 365
    *Yibin Xie, Lei Shi, Zhehao Li, Xu Ding, and Feng Liu*

Collaborative Task Processing and Resource Allocation Based on Multiple
MEC Servers ..................................................... 385
    *Lei Shi, Shilong Feng, Rui Ji, Juan Xu, Xu Ding, and Baotong Zhan*

Collaborative Cloud-Edge Computing with Mixed Wireless and Wired
Backhaul Links: Joint Task Offloading and Resource Allocation .............. 403
    *Daqing Zhang and Haifeng Sun*

Dynamic Offloading Based on Meta Deep Reinforcement Learning
and Load Prediction in Smart Home Edge Computing ..................... 421
    *Mingchu Li, Shuai Li, and Wanying Qi*

**Author Index** ....................................................... 441

# Contents – Part II

**Deep Learning and Applications**

Task Offloading in UAV-to-Cell MEC Networks: Cell Clustering and Path
Planning ................................................... 3
   *Mingchu Li, Wanying Qi, and Shuai Li*

LAMB: Label-Induced Mixed-Level Blending for Multimodal Multi-label
Emotion Detection ........................................... 20
   *Shuwei Qian, Ming Guo, Zhicheng Fan, Mingcai Chen,*
   *and Chongjun Wang*

MSAM: Deep Semantic Interaction Network for Visual Question
Answering .................................................. 39
   *Fan Wang, Bin Wang, Fuyong Xu, Jiaxin Li, and Peiyu Liu*

Defeating the Non-stationary Opponent Using Deep Reinforcement
Learning and Opponent Modeling ................................ 57
   *Qian Yao, Xinli Xiong, Peng Wang, and Yongjie Wang*

A Multi-Agent Deep Reinforcement Learning-Based Approach
to Mobility-Aware Caching ..................................... 79
   *Han Zhao, Shiyun Shao, Yong Ma, Yunni Xia, Jiajun Su, Lingmeng Liu,*
   *Kaiwei Chen, and Qinglan Peng*

D-AE: A Discriminant Encode-Decode Nets for Data Generation ............. 96
   *Gongju Wang, Yulun Song, Yang Li, Mingjian Ni, Long Yan, Bowen Hu,*
   *Quanda Wang, Yixuan Li, and Xingru Huang*

ECCRG: A Emotion- and Content-Controllable Response Generation
Model ..................................................... 115
   *Hui Chen, Bo Wang, Ke Yang, and Yi Song*

Origin-Destination Convolution Recurrent Network: A Novel OD Matrix
Prediction Framework ......................................... 131
   *Jiayu Chang, Tian Liang, Wanzhi Xiao, and Li Kuang*

MD-TransUNet: TransUNet with Multi-attention and Dilated Convolution
for Brain Stroke Lesion Segmentation ............................ 151
   *Jie Xu, Jian Wan, and Xin Zhang*

## Graph Computing

DGFormer: An Effective Dynamic Graph Transformer Based Anomaly
Detection Model for IoT Time Series .................................... 173
  *Hongxia He, Xi Li, Peng Chen, Juan Chen, Weijian Song, and Qinghui Xi*

STAPointGNN: Spatial-Temporal Attention Graph Neural Network
for Gesture Recognition Using Millimeter-Wave Radar .................... 189
  *Jun Zhang, Chunyu Wang, Shunli Wang, and Lihua Zhang*

NPGraph: An Efficient Graph Computing Model in NUMA-Based
Persistent Memory Systems ............................................. 205
  *Baoke Li, Cong Cao, Fangfang Yuan, Yuling Yang, Majing Su,
  Yanbing Liu, and Jianhui Fu*

tHR-Net: A Hybrid Reasoning Framework for Temporal Knowledge Graph .... 223
  *Yijing Zhao, Yumeng Liu, Zihang Wan, and Hongan Wang*

Improving Code Representation Learning via Multi-view Contrastive
Graph Pooling for Abstract Syntax Tree ............................... 242
  *Ruoting Wu, Yuxin Zhang, and Liang Chen*

## Security and Privacy Protection

Protect Applications and Data in Use in IoT Environment Using
Collaborative Computing .............................................. 265
  *Xincai Peng, Li Shan Cang, Shuai Zhang, and Muddesar Iqbal*

Robustness-Enhanced Assertion Generation Method Based on Code
Mutation and Attack Defense .......................................... 281
  *Min Li, Shizhan Chen, Guodong Fan, Lu Zhang, Hongyue Wu,
  Xiao Xue, and Zhiyong Feng*

Secure Traffic Data Sharing in UAV-Assisted VANETs ..................... 301
  *Yilin Liu, Yujue Wang, Chen Yi, Yong Ding, Changsong Yang,
  and Huiyong Wang*

A Lightweight PUF-Based Group Authentication Scheme
for Privacy-Preserving Metering Data Collection in Smart Grid .............. 321
  *Ya-Nan Cao, Yujue Wang, Yong Ding, Zhenwei Guo, Changsong Yang,
  and Hai Liang*

A Semi-supervised Learning Method for Malware Traffic Classification
with Raw Bitmaps ....................................................... 341
*Jingrun Ma, Xiaolin Xu, Tianning Zang, Xi Wang, Beibei Feng,
and Xiang Li*

Secure and Private Approximated Coded Distributed Computing Using
Elliptic Curve Cryptography ............................................. 357
*Houming Qiu and Kun Zhu*

A Novel Semi-supervised IoT Time Series Anomaly Detection Model
Using Graph Structure Learning ........................................ 375
*Weijian Song, Peng Chen, Juan Chen, Yunni Xia, Xi Li, Qinghui Xi,
and Hongxia He*

Structural Adversarial Attack for Code Representation Models .............. 392
*Yuxin Zhang, Ruoting Wu, Jie Liao, and Liang Chen*

An Efficient Authentication and Key Agreement Scheme for CAV Internal
Applications ........................................................... 414
*Yang Li, Qingyang Zhang, Wenwen Cao, Jie Cui, and Hong Zhong*

**Processing and Recognition**

SimBPG: A Comprehensive Similarity Evaluation Metric for Business
Process Graphs ......................................................... 437
*Qinkai Jiang, Jiaxing Wang, Bin Cao, and Jing Fan*

Probabilistic Inference Based Incremental Graph Index for Similarity
Search on Social Networks .............................................. 458
*Tong Lu, Zhiwei Qi, Kun Yue, and Liang Duan*

Cloud-Edge-Device Collaborative Image Retrieval and Recognition
for Mobile Web ........................................................ 474
*Yakun Huang, Wenwei Li, Shouyi Wu, Xiuquan Qiao, Meng Guo,
Hongshun He, and Yang Li*

Contrastive Learning-Based Finger-Vein Recognition with Automatic
Adversarial Augmentation .............................................. 495
*Shaojiang Deng, Huaxiu Luo, Huafeng Qin, and Yantao Li*

Multi-dimensional Sequential Contrastive Learning for QoS Prediction ........ 514
*Yuyu Yin, Qianhui Di, Yuanqing Zhang, Tingting Liang, Youhuizi Li,
and Yu Li*

**Author Index** ...................................................... 533

# Contents – Part III

**Onsite Session Day 2**

Multi-agent Reinforcement Learning Based Collaborative Multi-task
Scheduling for Vehicular Edge Computing ............................... 3
    *Peisong Li, Ziren Xiao, Xinheng Wang, Kaizhu Huang, Yi Huang,*
    *and Andrei Tchernykh*

A Novel Topology Metric for Indoor Point Cloud SLAM Based on Plane
Detection Optimization ..................................................... 23
    *Zhenchao Ouyang, Jiahe Cui, Yunxiang He, Dongyu Li, Qinglei Hu,*
    *and Changjie Zhang*

On the Performance of Federated Learning Network ....................... 41
    *Godwin Idoje, Tasos Dagiuklas, and Muddesar Iqbal*

**Federated Learning and Application**

FedECCR: Federated Learning Method with Encoding Comparison
and Classification Rectification ........................................ 59
    *Yan Zeng, Hui Zheng, Xin Wang, Beibei Zhang, Mingyao Zhou,*
    *Jilin Zhang, and YongJian Ren*

CSA_FedVeh: Cluster-Based Semi-asynchronous Federated Learning
Framework for Internet of Vehicles ..................................... 79
    *Dun Cao, Jiasi Xiong, Nanfang Lei, Robert Simon Sherratt, and Jin Wang*

Efficiently Detecting Anomalies in IoT: A Novel Multi-Task Federated
Learning Method ........................................................ 100
    *Junfeng Hao, Juan Chen, Peng Chen, Yang Wang, Xianhua Niu, Lei Xu,*
    *and Yunni Xia*

A Novel Deep Federated Learning-Based and Profit-Driven Service
Caching Method ........................................................ 118
    *Zhaobin Ouyang, Yunni Xia, Qinglan Peng, Yin Li, Peng Chen,*
    *and Xu Wang*

A Multi-behavior Recommendation Algorithm Based on Personalized
Federated Learning ..................................................... 134
    *Zhongqin Bi, Yutang Duan, Weina Zhang, and Meijing Shan*

FederatedMesh: Collaborative Federated Learning for Medical Data
Sharing in Mesh Networks .............................................. 154
   *Lamir Shkurti, Mennan Selimi, and Adrian Besimi*

**Collaborative Working**

Enhance Broadcasting Throughput by Associating Network Coding
with UAVs Relays Deployment in Emergency Communications .............. 173
   *Chaonong Xu and Yujie Jiang*

Dynamic Target User Selection Model for Market Promotion with Multiple
Stakeholders .......................................................... 191
   *Linxin Guo, Shiqi Wang, Min Gao, and Chongming Gao*

Collaborative Decision-Making Processes Analysis of Service Ecosystem:
A Case Study of Academic Ecosystem Involution ........................ 208
   *Xiangpei Yan, Xiao Xue, Chao Peng, Donghua Liu, Zhiyong Feng,
   and Wang Xiao*

Operationalizing the Use of Sensor Data in Mobile Crowdsensing:
A Systematic Review and Practical Guidelines ......................... 229
   *Robin Kraft, Maximilian Blasi, Marc Schickler, Manfred Reichert,
   and Rüdiger Pryss*

Enriching Process Models with Relevant Process Details for Flexible
Human-Robot Teaming .................................................. 249
   *Myriel Fichtner, Sascha Sucker, Dominik Riedelbauch,
   Stefan Jablonski, and Dominik Henrich*

**Edge Computing**

Joint Optimization of PAoI and Queue Backlog with Energy Constraints
in LoRa Gateway Systems .............................................. 273
   *Lei Shi, Rui Ji, Zhen Wei, Shilong Feng, and Zhehao Li*

Enhancing Session-Based Recommendation with Multi-granularity User
Interest-Aware Graph Neural Networks ................................. 291
   *Cairong Yan, Yiwei Zhang, Xiangyang Feng, and Yanglan Gan*

Delay-Constrained Multicast Throughput Maximization in MEC Networks
for High-Speed Railways .............................................. 308
   *Junyi Xu, Zhenchun Wei, Xiaohui Yuan, Zengwei Lyu, Lin Feng,
   and Jianghong Han*

An Evolving Transformer Network Based on Hybrid Dilated Convolution
for Traffic Flow Prediction .............................................. 329
    *Qi Yu, Weilong Ding, Maoxiang Sun, and Jihai Huang*

**Prediction, Optimization and Applications**

DualDNSMiner: A Dual-Stack Resolver Discovery Method Based
on Alias Resolution ...................................................... 347
    *Dingkang Han, Yujia Zhu, Liang Jiao, Dikai Mo, Yong Sun,
    Yuedong Zhang, and Qingyun Liu*

DT-MUSA: Dual Transfer Driven Multi-source Domain Adaptation
for WEEE Reverse Logistics Return Prediction .......................... 365
    *Ruiqi Liu, Min Gao, Yujiang Wu, Jie Zeng, Jia Zhang, and Jinyong Gao*

A Synchronous Parallel Method with Parameters Communication
Prediction for Distributed Machine Learning ........................... 385
    *Yanguo Zeng, Meiting Xue, Peiran Xu, Yukun Shi, Kaisheng Zeng,
    Jilin Zhang, and Lupeng Yue*

**Author Index** ....................................................... 405

# Collaborative Computing

# Enhanced Sound Recognition and Classification Through Spectrogram Analysis, MEMS Sensors, and PyTorch: A Comprehensive Approach

Alexandros Spournias[1]([✉]) [iD], Nikolaos Nanos[1], Evanthia Faliagka[1],
Christos Antonopoulos[1], Nikolaos Voros[1], and Giorgos Keramidas[2]

[1] Electrical and Computer Engineering Department, University of the Peloponnese, Patra,
Greece
a.spournias@esdalab.ece.uop.gr

[2] School of Informatics, Aristotle University of Thessaloniki, Thessaloniki, Greece

**Abstract.** The importance of sound recognition and classification systems in various fields has led researchers to seek innovative methods to address these challenges. In this paper, the authors propose a concise yet effective approach for sound recognition and classification by combining spectrogram analysis, Micro-Electro-Mechanical Systems (MEMS) sensors, and the Pytorch deep learning framework. This method utilizes the rich information in audio signals to develop a robust and accurate sound recognition and classification system.

The authors outline a three-stage process: data acquisition, feature extraction, and classification. MEMS sensors are employed for data acquisition, offering advantages such as reduced noise, low power consumption, and enhanced sensitivity compared to traditional microphones. The acquired audio signals are then preprocessed and converted into spectrograms, visually representing the audio data's frequency, amplitude, and temporal attributes.

During feature extraction, the spectrograms are analyzed to extract significant features conducive to sound recognition and classification. The classification task is performed using a custom deep learning model in Pytorch, leveraging modern neural networks' pattern recognition capabilities. The model is trained and validated on a diverse dataset of audio samples, ensuring its proficiency in recognizing and classifying various sound types.

The experimental results demonstrate the effectiveness of the proposed method, surpassing existing techniques in sound recognition and classification performance. By integrating spectrogram analysis, MEMS sensors, and Pytorch, the authors present a compact yet powerful sound recognition system with potential applications in numerous domains, such as predictive maintenance, environmental monitoring, and personalized voice-controlled devices.

**Keywords:** Sound recognition · Machine Learning · PyTorch · Environmental Monitoring · Spectrogram · Sound Analysis

H. Gao et al. (Eds.): CollaborateCom 2023, LNICST 561, pp. 3–17, 2024.
https://doi.org/10.1007/978-3-031-54521-4_1

# 1   Introduction

The ability to accurately recognize and classify sound plays a crucial role in numerous applications, including predictive maintenance, environmental monitoring, surveillance systems, natural language processing, and human-computer interaction. Traditional methods of sound recognition and classification often rely on handcrafted features and shallow learning models, which can be limited in their capacity to capture complex patterns within audio signals. Consequently, there has been a surge of interest in developing more sophisticated methods that can effectively recognize and classify a wide range of sound types.

In recent years, deep learning techniques have demonstrated remarkable success in various pattern recognition tasks, including sound recognition and classification. These techniques excel in their ability to automatically learn discriminative features from raw data, which has led to significant improvements in recognition and classification performance. In this context, the PyTorch deep learning framework [1] has emerged as a popular choice for researchers, due to its flexibility, ease of use, and strong community support. Spectrogram analysis, which provides a visual representation of the time-frequency characteristics of audio signals, has also been widely employed in sound recognition and classification tasks. The rich information contained within spectrograms enables the identification of distinctive patterns that can be used to differentiate between various sound sources. In parallel, advances in sensor technology, particularly Micro-Electro-Mechanical Systems (MEMS) sensors [2], have facilitated the development of high-quality audio data acquisition systems. MEMS sensors offer numerous advantages over conventional microphones, such as reduced noise levels, low power consumption, and increased sensitivity.

In this paper, the authors propose a novel sound recognition and classification method that includes spectrogram analysis [3], MEMS sensors, and the PyTorch deep learning framework. The primary objectives of this work are to develop a comprehensive approach for sound recognition and classification that leverages the rich information contained in audio signals, and to demonstrate the effectiveness of the proposed method through extensive experimental validation. The remainder of this paper is organized as follows: Section 2 provides a literature review; Sect. 3 an overview of the proposed methodology, including data acquisition, feature extraction, and training- classification stages; Sect. 4 presents the experimental results and performance evaluation; and Sect. 5 concludes the paper with a discussion on future research directions and potential applications.

# 2   Literature Review

The field of sound recognition and classification has attracted significant attention from researchers due to its wide range of applications and the inherent challenges in processing and understanding audio data. This section provides a review of the relevant literature, focusing on sound analysis, spectrogram representations, MEMS sensors, and the application of PyTorch at sound recognition and classification.

## 2.1 Sound Analysis and Spectrogram Representations

Sound analysis techniques play a vital role in extracting meaningful information from raw audio signals. Traditional methods, such as Mel-Frequency Cepstral Coefficients (MFCC) and Linear Predictive Coding (LPC), have been extensively used to capture the spectral characteristics of audio signals (Davis & Mermelstein, 1980 [4]; Rabiner & Schafer, 1978 [5]). However, these handcrafted features often fail to capture complex patterns present in the data.

Spectrogram representations, which display the time-frequency characteristics of audio signals, have emerged as an effective alternative to traditional methods (Fulop & Fitz, 2006 [6]). By converting raw audio signals into spectrograms, researchers can visualize and analyze the spectral content and temporal patterns of sounds, enabling more efficient feature extraction and classification.

## 2.2 MEMS Sensors for Audio Data Acquisition

The quality of audio data acquisition plays a crucial role in the performance of sound recognition and classification systems. Traditional microphones have certain limitations, such as high noise levels and power consumption. MEMS sensors, on the other hand, offer numerous advantages, including reduced noise levels, low power consumption, and increased sensitivity (Koickal et al., 2006 [7]). The use of MEMS sensors in sound recognition and classification tasks has led to significant improvements in data quality and system performance.

## 2.3 Deep Learning and PyTorch in Sound Recognition and Classification

Deep learning techniques have revolutionized pattern recognition tasks, including sound recognition and classification. Convolutional Neural Networks (CNNs) [8] and Recurrent Neural Networks (RNNs) [9] have been widely played a role in this domain due to their ability to automatically learn discriminative features from raw data (Hinton et al., 2012 [10]; LeCun et al., 2015 [11]). The Pytorch deep learning framework has become a popular choice for implementing deep learning models, thanks to its flexibility, ease of use, and strong community support (Paszke et al., 2019 [12]).

Several studies have explored the use of deep learning and Pytorch in sound recognition and classification tasks. For example, Aytar et al. (2016) [13] used CNNs for environmental sound classification, while Zhang et al. (2017) [14] applied Long Short-Term Memory (LSTM) networks for speech recognition. These studies have demonstrated the effectiveness of deep learning models in recognizing and classifying various sound types.

In summary, the literature highlights the potential of combining spectrogram analysis, MEMS sensors, and PyTorch-based deep learning models for sound recognition and classification tasks. This paper aims to develop a novel method that integrates these techniques, aiming to achieve improved performance and applicability across a wide range of domains such as a predictive maintenance and environmental monitoring.

## 3   Methodology

This section describes the proposed methodology for sound recognition and classification, which integrates spectrogram analysis, MEMS sensors, and the PyTorch deep learning framework. The proposed system is quite general and can be adapted for various data sources (e.g. image, video, audio). However, we consider the case where the data we get from the sensors is audio data. A block diagram of our model is shown in (see Fig. 1). The methodology consists of three main stages: data acquisition, feature extraction, and training - classification.

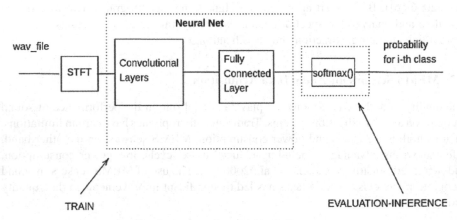

**Fig. 1.** Proposed model block diagram.

### 3.1   Data Acquisition

In the data acquisition phase of the study, the authors employed a Raspberry Pi 4 [15], a Raspberry Pi Pico [16], and an Adafruit MEMS microphone [17] to effectively gather the necessary data. The Raspberry Pi 4, a versatile and powerful single-board computer, served as the central processing unit, managing data acquisition and communication with the Raspberry Pi Pico via a USB connection.

The Raspberry Pi Pico, a microcontroller board based on the RP2040 microcontroller chip, was utilized for real-time signal processing and data transfer. The Pico was connected to the Adafruit MEMS a high-performance and compact digital microphone, responsible for capturing and converting acoustic signals into digital data. The microphone's wide frequency response and low noise ensured accurate representation of the collected audio data (see Fig. 2).

To facilitate communication between the Raspberry Pi 4 and the Raspberry Pi Pico, the authors developed also, a custom data acquisition system using the Python programming language. This system allowed for the efficient coordination and exchange of data between the two devices via the USB connection. The Raspberry Pi Pico was chosen for its affordability, simplicity, and compatibility with the Raspberry Pi 4.

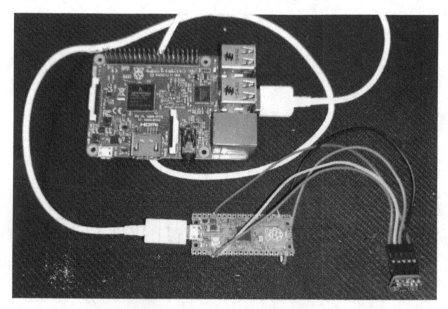

**Fig. 2.** System for Data Acquisition

The Adafruit MEMS microphone, played a crucial role in capturing high-quality audio data. Authors selected the Adafruit MEMS microphone for its impressive performance characteristics and compatibility with the Raspberry Pi ecosystem.

The collected data is focused on four distinct sound classes, namely *Motor_single*, *Motor_gran_no_chain*, *seatrak_all_elements*, and *kinhsh_koble*, which collectively comprise the dataset. Each sound class is represented by a set of WAV files that were recorded within the laboratory environment. To efficiently manage the files, the authors utilized Audacity software [18] to edit the length of each WAV file for every class, subsequently allocating the files into their respective folders (see Fig. 3), including test and valid, based on their corresponding labels.

### 3.2  Feature Extraction

The feature extraction stage involves the conversion of raw audio signals into spectrograms, which provide a visual representation of the frequency, amplitude, and temporal characteristics of the audio data. Spectrogram analysis allows for the identification of salient features that are conducive to sound recognition and classification.

To generate spectrograms, the Short-Time Fourier Transform (STFT) [19], is applied to the preprocessed audio signals, resulting in a time-frequency representation that captures the spectral content and temporal patterns of the sounds. The Short Time Fourier Transform (STFT) is a well-established technique for examining the time-varying frequency content of a signal. The STFT is computed by taking the Fourier Transform of a signal multiplied by a window function that is translated over time. The mathematical formula for the STFT is expressed as follows (Eq. 1):

$$STFT(x(t), w(t), \tau) = X(\omega, \tau) = \int x(t) * w(t - \tau) * e^{-j\omega t} dt \qquad (1)$$

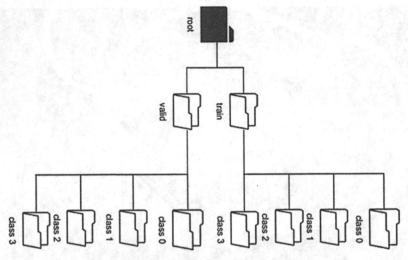

**Fig. 3.** Dir structure of the Wav files

Here, $x(t)$ represents the input signal as a function of time '$t$', and $w(t)$ denotes the window function as a function of time '$t$'. The parameter $\tau$ is the time shift or translation parameter, while $\omega$ is the angular frequency ($\omega = 2\pi f$, with '$f$' being the frequency in Hz). The STFT output, $X(\omega, \tau)$, is a complex-valued function of both angular frequency '$\omega$' and time shift '$\tau$'. Lastly, $j$ is the imaginary unit ($j^2 = -1$).

By varying the time shift parameter '$\tau$', the authors obtain the time-frequency representation of the signal, which offers valuable insights into the frequency content of the signal at different time intervals. In the subsequent figure (see Fig. 4), the authors present a comparative visualization of the previously mentioned fields for a linear Chirp audio signal [20], often referred to as the "linear Chirp."

Employing a sound spectrogram, a technique for visualizing audio signals is elucidated, which affords an understanding of the integral frequencies of the auditory input. Within the spectrogram, the ordinate signifies frequency, while the abscissa corresponds to the temporal aspect. Each individual pixel in the spectrogram discloses the intensity of a distinct frequency at a specific moment, thus granting a thorough comprehension of the time-frequency association present in the audio signal. As previously noted, the gathered data was segregated into four distinct categories, with the corresponding spectrograms exhibited in subsequent Figure (see Fig. 5).

### 3.3 Training - Classification

The training - classification stage employs a custom deep learning model implemented in PyTorch, a popular deep learning framework known for its flexibility, ease of use, and strong community support. The model is designed to automatically learn discriminative features from the spectrograms and effectively classify the sound sources (see Fig. 6).

The proposed model consists of a combination of convolutional and recurrent layers, which enables the simultaneous learning of spectral and temporal features from

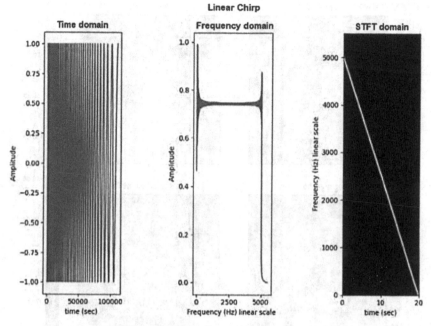

**Fig. 4.** Linear Chirp in different domains

the spectrograms. The spectrogram representation of every individual class undergoes processing through Convolutional Layers to extract features of the input spectrogram. It is anticipated that, following the Convolutional Layers, the problem under investigation transforms into a linearly separable one. Consequently, these features are transmitted to the Fully Connected layers.

Ultimately, the unnormalized Neural Network responses are modeled as probabilities employing the widely recognized softmax non-linearity. The softmax activation function [21], a generalized variant of the sigmoid function, serves as a methodical selection at the output stage of a Neural Network addressing a multi-class classification issue. The attainable values range between [0, 1], with the aggregate of probabilities equating to 1. The element within the output vector exhibiting the highest probability additionally signifies the class of the input waveform. The softmax function is depicted schematically in the subsequent figure (see Fig. 7).

The convolutional layers are tasked with detecting local patterns, whereas the recurrent layers are responsible for capturing long-range dependencies and temporal dynamics. The model undergoes training using a diverse dataset of spectrogram frames, with the aim of minimizing classification error.

During the training phase, the dataset is partitioned into 70% for training, 15% for validation, and 15% for testing. The CNN classifies and subsequently predicts the input, which is a wave file divided into blocks of duration *seq_dur* (5 s), as well as the class it belongs to (out of the four classes). The output of the CNN is a matrix of dimensions *(nb_blocks, nb_classes)*, with each row representing the unnormalized responses for the four classes for one block. The objective function employed for minimization is the

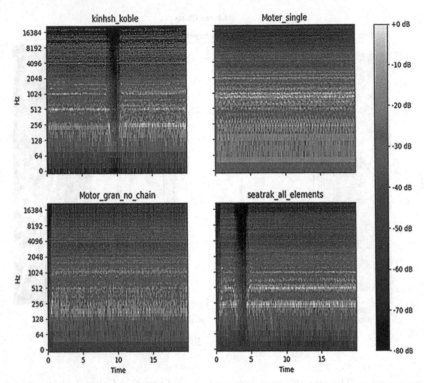

**Fig. 5.** Spectrograms of sound classes

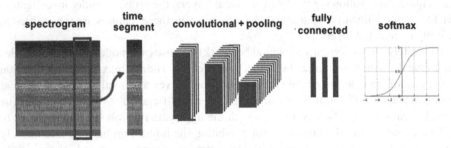

**Fig. 6.** Training – classification

cross-entropy function available in PyTorch's CrossEntropyLoss [22], where weights are also utilized for each class to balance the input, as the dataset is typically unbalanced. The training phase is depicted in the subsequent figure (see Fig. 8).

In the following figure (see Fig. 9), the training error is represented by the blue line, which is considerably small from the second epoch onwards, while the validation error, illustrated by the red line, remains low from the first epoch.

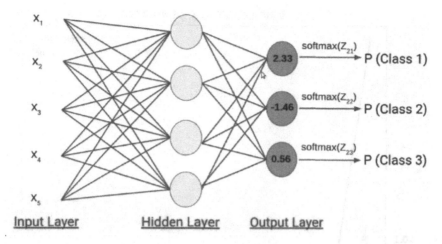

**Fig. 7.** Softmax layers

```
c:\ML1\ML_pipeline_code_multiple_classes_v1>python3 train.py --root c:\ML1\ML_pipeline_code_multiple_classes_v1\Spectrograms_
tst --nb_classes 4 --output c:\ML1\ML_pipeline_code_multiple_classes_v1\Spectrograms_tst\pretr_model --epochs 10
Using GPU: True
the model will be running on cuda device
 3%|                                                                                | 0/10 [00:00<?, ?it/s]=
===========================================================================================
Layer (type:depth-idx)                    Output Shape              Param #
===========================================================================================
Net                                        [16, 4]                  --
├─Sequential: 1-1                          [16, 16, 257, 145]       --
│    └─Conv2d: 2-1                         [16, 16, 257, 145]       416
│    └─BatchNorm2d: 2-2                     [16, 16, 257, 145]       32
│    └─LeakyReLU: 2-3                       [16, 16, 257, 145]       --
├─Sequential: 1-2                          [16, 32, 129, 73]        --
│    └─Conv2d: 2-4                         [16, 32, 129, 73]        12,832
│    └─BatchNorm2d: 2-5                     [16, 32, 129, 73]        64
│    └─LeakyReLU: 2-6                       [16, 32, 129, 73]        --
├─Sequential: 1-3                          [16, 64, 65, 37]         --
│    └─Conv2d: 2-7                         [16, 64, 65, 37]         51,264
│    └─BatchNorm2d: 2-8                     [16, 64, 65, 37]         128
│    └─LeakyReLU: 2-9                       [16, 64, 65, 37]         --
├─Sequential: 1-4                          [16, 128, 33, 19]        --
│    └─Conv2d: 2-10                        [16, 128, 33, 19]        204,928
│    └─BatchNorm2d: 2-11                    [16, 128, 33, 19]        256
│    └─LeakyReLU: 2-12                      [16, 128, 33, 19]        --
├─Sequential: 1-5                          [16, 256, 17, 10]        --
│    └─Conv2d: 2-13                        [16, 256, 17, 10]        819,456
│    └─BatchNorm2d: 2-14                    [16, 256, 17, 10]        512
│    └─LeakyReLU: 2-15                      [16, 256, 17, 10]        --
├─Linear: 1-6                              [16, 4]                  595,884
===========================================================================================
Total params: 1,684,972
Trainable params: 1,684,972
Non-trainable params: 0
Total mult-adds (G): 8.45
===========================================================================================
Input size (MB): 9.52
Forward/backward pass size (MB): 300.87
Params size (MB): 6.74
Estimated Total Size (MB): 317.13
===========================================================================================
Training batch: 100%|████████████████████████| 49/49 [00:00<00:00, 52.70it/s, loss=0.529]
Training batch: 100%|████████████████████████| 49/49 [00:00<00:00, 66.47it/s, loss=0.001]
Training batch: 100%|████████████████████████| 49/49 [00:00<00:00, 66.30it/s, loss=0.001]
Training batch: 100%|████████████████████████| 49/49 [00:00<00:00, 66.73it/s, loss=0.000]
Training batch: 100%|████████████████████████| 49/49 [00:00<00:00, 66.21it/s, loss=0.000]
Training batch: 100%|████████████████████████| 49/49 [00:00<00:00, 66.67it/s, loss=0.000]
Training batch: 100%|████████████████████████| 49/49 [00:00<00:00, 64.87it/s, loss=0.000]
Training batch: 100%|████████████████████████| 49/49 [00:00<00:00, 65.44it/s, loss=0.000]
Training batch: 100%|████████████████████████| 49/49 [00:00<00:00, 66.03it/s, loss=0.000]
Training batch: 100%|████████████████████████| 49/49 [00:00<00:00, 66.50it/s, loss=0.000]
Training epoch: 100%|████████████████████████| 10/10 [00:12<00:00,  1.29s/it, train_loss=0.008143, val_loss=0.0791]
c:\ML1\ML_pipeline_code_multiple_classes_v1>
```

**Fig. 8.** Training phase

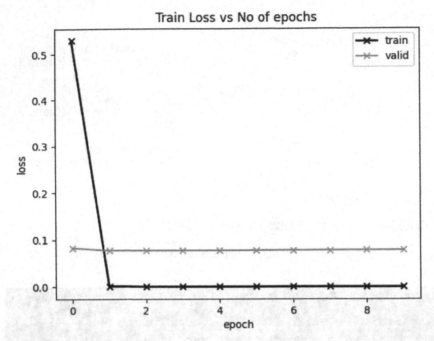

Fig. 9. Training - validation error (Color figure online)

## 4    Experimental Results - Performance Evaluation

The methodology consists of three main stages: Block of input-wav, Overall classification performance of input-wav, Real-time classification performance of a sound.

### 4.1    Block of Input-Wav Classification Performance

In order to evaluate the performance of the proposed model, the network's accuracy in classifying the provided blocks into various classes is assessed. The softmax non-linearity is applied to the unnormalized network response (a 4-element vector corresponding to the number of classes) to determine the class to which a block belongs.

This procedure is executed to transform these unnormalized responses into four probabilities with values ranging from 0 to 1. The index of the highest probability (within the vector) represents the class predicted by the network for the specific batch. The model is then tested on an independent set of spectrogram frames, which have not been utilized during training. A range of performance metrics, including accuracy, precision, recall, and F1-score, are employed to evaluate the model's efficacy in identifying and classifying distinct sound sources. The evaluation phase of a single sound class block *(kinisi_koble)* is depicted in the following figure (see Fig. 10 and Table 1).

### 4.2    Overall Classification Performance of Input-Wav

During the inference stage, to ascertain the class to which the input-wav belongs, the same step as in the evaluation is executed on the network's output. However, the aim

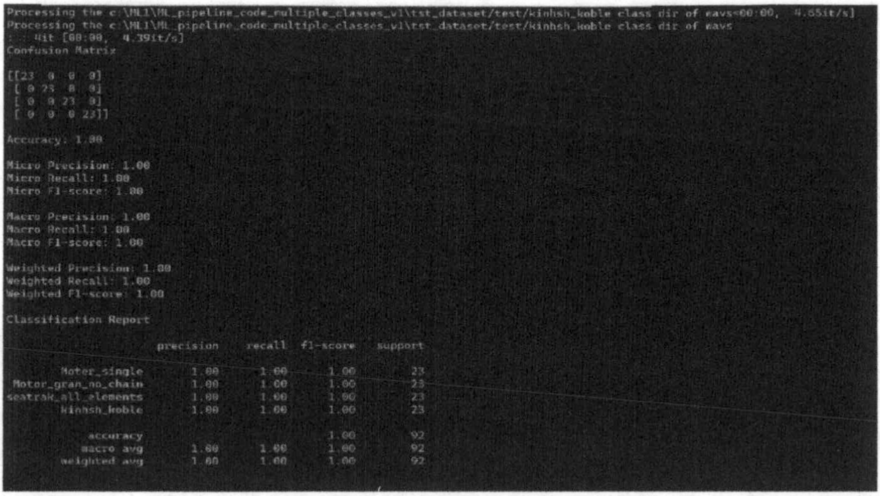

**Fig. 10.** Evaluation phase of a single sound class

**Table 1.** Evaluation performance

| Name of Class | Precision | Recall | F1-Score | Support |
|---|---|---|---|---|
| *Moter_single* | 1.00 | 1.00 | 1.00 | 23 |
| *Motor_gran_no_chain* | 1.00 | 1.00 | 1.00 | 23 |
| *seatrak_all_elements* | 1.00 | 1.00 | 1.00 | 23 |
| *Kinisi_koble* | 1.00 | 1.00 | 1.00 | 23 |

here is to determine the class of the entire input-wav, rather than merely its blocks. Consequently, the decision is made in favor of the class with the most occurrences, akin to consulting a histogram. It could be argued that the class to which a block belongs is a random variable, and the distribution of this variable is calculated through this histogram. The evaluation phase of a whole sound class (kinisi_koble) is depicted in the following figure (see Fig. 11).

## 4.3   Real-Time Classification Performance of a Sound

In the real-time inference process, to determine the class to which the input-wav belongs, the same step as previous in the evaluation is executed on the network's output. However, the goal here is to decide the class of the entire input-wav, not just its blocks. As a result, the decision is made in favor of the class with the most occurrences, as if consulting a histogram (It could be posited that the class to which a block belongs is a random variable, and the distribution of this variable is calculated through this histogram). The evaluation phase of a whole three sound classes in real-time, is depicted in the following figure (see Fig. 12).

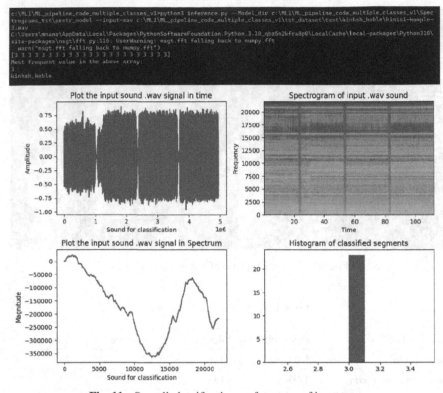

**Fig. 11.** Overall classification performance of input-wav

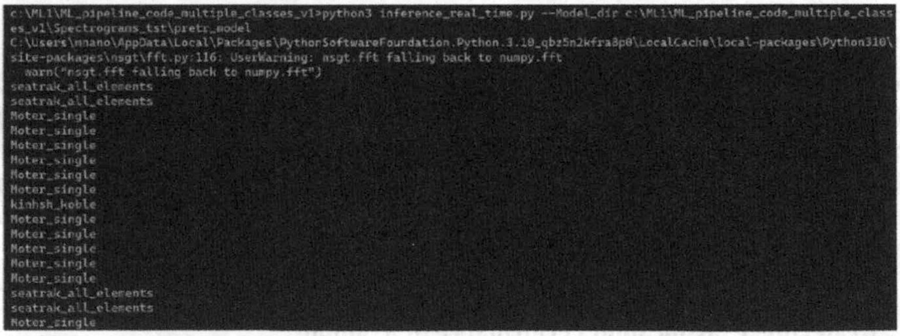

**Fig. 12.** Real-time classification performance

For the experimental process, 15 recognition trials were conducted for each class. The results demonstrated that recognition was highly successful in the class representing a unique sound with a specific pattern. On the other hand, for complex sounds that included a mix of noises from various components, the recognition performance was equally good, despite a slight increase in false recognitions.

In summary, the following graph (see Fig. 13) present the experimental results and performance evaluation of the proposed method, demonstrating its effectiveness in recognizing and classifying various sound types.

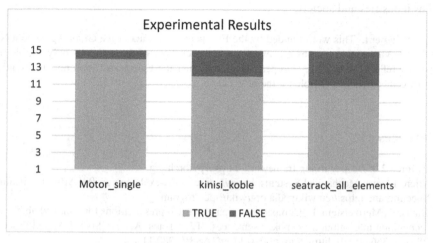

**Fig. 13.** Experimental results.

# 5  Conclusion – Future Work and Potential Applications

In conclusion, this study has demonstrated the potential of machine learning-based classification techniques in sound recognition tasks. The findings indicate that such methods can effectively classify unique sounds and even complex mixtures of noises from various components. However, there is still room for improvement in terms of reducing false recognitions.

Future research directions could explore the incorporation of more advanced deep learning architectures, such as attention mechanisms, to enhance the model's ability to focus on the most salient features within the input data. Additionally, the development of more robust and diverse datasets would contribute to the generalization capabilities of the models, making them more applicable to real-world scenarios.

Potential applications of sound recognition via machine learning classification span across various domains, including environmental monitoring, healthcare, industry, and smart cities. For instance, in environmental monitoring, these techniques could be employed to track and identify the presence of specific species, monitor ecosystems, or detect signs of pollution. In healthcare, sound recognition models could be used for early detection of diseases or monitoring patients' conditions through the analysis of sounds produced by the human body. In industrial settings, these techniques can be applied to monitor equipment performance, identify malfunctions, and predict maintenance requirements. Lastly, in the context of smart cities, sound recognition models could contribute to the optimization of traffic management and the enhancement of public safety by detecting unusual or potentially dangerous events based on sound patterns.

Overall, the advancements in machine learning classification for sound recognition hold great promise for numerous practical applications across diverse sectors. Continued research in this area will undoubtedly contribute to the development of more efficient, accurate, and versatile sound recognition systems, addressing the ever-growing needs of various industries and society.

**Acknowledgment.** This work Funded by the European Union under the Grant Agreement No. 101087257. Views and opinions expressed are however those of the author(s) only and do not necessarily reflect those of the European Union. Neither the European Union nor the granting authority can be held responsible for them.

# References

1. PyTorch 2.0: Deep learning framework. https://pytorch.org
2. Micro-Electro-Mechanical Systems. https://www.mems-exchange.org/MEMS/what-is.html
3. Spectrogram. https://en.wikipedia.org/wiki/Spectrogram
4. Davis, S., Mermelstein, P.: Comparison of parametric representations for monosyllabic word recognition in continuously spoken sentences. IEEE Trans. Acoust. Speech Signal Process. **28**, 357–366 (1980). https://doi.org/10.1109/TASSP.1980.1163420
5. Rabiner, L.R., Schafer, R.W.: Digital Processing of Speech Signals. Prentice Hall, Upper Saddle River (1978). https://ieeexplore.ieee.org/stamp/stamp.jsp?arnumber=1456137
6. Fulop, S.A., Fitz, K.: A Spectrogram for the Twenty-First Century, January 2006. https://www.researchgate.net/publication/243716460_A_Spectrogram_for_the_Twenty-First_Century
7. Koickal, T.J., Hamilton, A., Tan, S.L., Covington, J.A., Gardner, J.W., Pearce, T.C.: Analog VLSI circuit implementation of an adaptive neuromorphic olfaction chip. Circuits Syst. (2007). shorturl.at/qNQW3
8. Convolutional Neural Networks. https://en.wikipedia.org/wiki/Convolutional_neural_network
9. Recurrent Neural Networks. https://en.wikipedia.org/wiki/Recurrent_neural_network
10. Hinton, G.E., Srivastava, N., Krizhevsky, A., Sutskever, I., Salakhutdinov, R.R.: Improving neural networks by preventing co-adaptation of feature detectors. https://doi.org/10.48550/arXiv.1207.0580
11. LeCun, Y., Bengio, Y., Hinton, G.: Deep learning (2015). https://www.nature.com/articles/nature14539
12. Paszke, A., et al.: PyTorch: an imperative style, high-performance deep learning library. https://papers.nips.cc/paper_files/paper/2019/file/bdbca288fee7f92f2bfa9f7012727740-Paper.pdf
13. Aytar, Y., Vondrick, C., Torralba, A.: SoundNet: learning sound representations from unlabeled video. https://proceedings.neurips.cc/paper/2016/file/7dcd340d84f762eba80aa538b0c527f7-Paper.pdf
14. Zhang, Z., et al.: A framework for quantifying the impacts of sub-pixel reflectance variance and covariance on cloud optical thickness and effective radius retrievals based on the bi-spectral method (2017). https://aip.scitation.org/doi/abs/10.1063/1.4975502
15. Raspberry Pi 4. https://www.raspberrypi.com/products/raspberry-pi-4-model-b/
16. Raspberry Pi Pico. https://www.raspberrypi.com/products/raspberry-pi-pico/
17. Adafruit I2S MEMS Microphone Breakout - SPH0645LM4H. https://www.adafruit.com/product/3421
18. Audacity, Free, open source, cross-platform audio software. https://www.audacityteam.org

19. Short-Time Fourier Transform (STFT). https://www.dsprelated.com/freebooks/sasp/Short_Time_Fourier_Transform.html
20. Linear Chirp waves. https://en.wikipedia.org/wiki/Chirp
21. Softmax activation function. https://deepai.org/machine-learning-glossary-and-terms/softmax-layer
22. Cross Entropy Loss. https://pytorch.org/docs/stable/generated/torch.nn.CrossEntropyLoss.html

# TCP Cubic Implementation
# in the OMNeT++ INET Framework
# for SIoT Simulation Scenarios

Ioannis Angelis[1]([✉]) [iD], Athanasios Tsipis[2] [iD], Eleni Christopoulou[1] [iD],
and Konstantinos Oikonomou[1] [iD]

[1] Department of Informatics, Ionian University, 49100 Corfu, Greece
{iangelis,hristope,okon}@ionio.gr
[2] Department of Digital Media and Communication, Ionian University,
28100 Kefalonia, Greece
atsipis@ionio.gr

**Abstract.** TCP is a well-known protocol for reliable data transfer. Although TCP was originally designed for networks with low Round Trip Time (RTT) and low error rates over the communication channel, in modern networks these characteristics vary drastically, e.g., Long Fat Networks are usually attributed a high Bandwidth Delay Product. When considering satellite communications, which are also characterized by high error rates but are considered a driving force for future networks, such as the Satellite Internet of Things (SIoT), it becomes clear that there exists an ever-growing need to revisit TCP protocol variants and develop new tools to simulate their behavior and optimize their performance. In this paper, a TCP Cubic implementation for the OMNeT++ INET Framework is presented and made publicly available to the research community. Simulation experiments validate its expected behavior in accordance with the theoretical analysis. A performance comparison against the popular TCP NewReno is also performed to evaluate TCP Cubic's applicability to satellite environments. The obtained results testify to the latter's superiority in efficiently allocating the bandwidth among the different information flows with vast gains to the overall system throughput, thus, rendering it the better candidate for future SIoT environments.

**Keywords:** INET Framework · Network Simulation · OMNeT++ ·
SIoT · Satellite Communication · TCP Cubic

## 1 Introduction

The Internet of Things (IoT) has impacted our lives in many different domains, from everyday use to industrial appliances [6]. Nowadays, there is a growing talk about how Smart Cities, Smart Agriculture, and Smart Grids can better our lives by installing IoT devices (e.g., sensors) that can collect massive amounts of data from the environment in order to assist decision-making processes and

H. Gao et al. (Eds.): CollaborateCom 2023, LNICST 561, pp. 18–37, 2024.
https://doi.org/10.1007/978-3-031-54521-4_2

enable reduction of costs, object tracking, real-time monitoring, etc. Neverthe-less, the operation of such devices necessitates the preexistence of a suitable network infrastructure that will facilitate their seamless communication, adher-ing to specific and stringent network requirements [30], e.g., low latency and bandwidth utilization.

In remote locations where the network infrastructure is not readily available or is considered expensive to build, satellites can play a key role in providing global coverage and connecting remote regions to the Internet. Moreover, satellite communication has become substantially cheaper today when compared to the previous decade, due to the booming of the space industry [10], thus paving the pay for the Satellite IoT (SIoT).

SIoT, as a natural expansion to the terrestrial networks, is characterized by the combination of conventional IoT technologies with satellite communica-tion [22]. As such, it can be exploited for both industrial and commercial use, offering new ways for enhancing remote connectivity and availability of services and applications, especially in critical or high-risk settings where there is a need for continuous and uninterrupted monitoring of the underlying conditions [13], such as wildfire detection in forest regions, disaster or crisis management in machine-to-machine communications, military applications in remote tactical geographical areas, collaborative services in industrial systems, etc.

Still, the use of satellites as intermediate network nodes has a twofold impact on the network. First, wireless communication over long distances experiences a high error rate. Second, the long distance between the Earth and the satellite unavoidably introduces a high Round Trip Time (RTT) and at the same time exhibits a large Bandwidth Delay Product (BDP). These characteristics affect the operation of transport protocols and hinder the SIoT devices' interoperabil-ity [12], especially when multiple devices must collectively participate in data acquisition and information exchange or collaboratively support the decision-making process and produce actionable outcomes.

One of the most widespread protocols for reliable and orderly communica-tion is the Transmission Control Protocol (TCP) [26]. It is well known that there exist multiple variations (also called flavors) of the TCP depending on the particular environment. However, for any real-world protocol application to be successful, prior to its standardization, it requires extensive and comprehensive experimentation under simulation environments that accurately mimic realistic conditions and acutely capture the intricacies of diverse network settings.

Having this in mind, in the current ongoing work, we consider the TCP Cubic [19] as the TCP flavor more suitable for SIoT environments, in order to test hypotheses and validate use-case scenarios for future SIoT environments. However, to our knowledge, this is the first publicly available implementation for TCP Cubic using the INET Framework for the OMNeT++ simulator. Inspired by the fact that, at the time of writing, no implementation of the TCP Cubic is openly available for the OMNeT++ discrete event simulator [32], which is one of the most widespread simulators available for distributed networking systems, including IoT, we hereinafter present initial results, from both a theoretical and practical standpoint, regarding TCP Cubic's implementation in the aforementioned simulator. Our vision is for the presented implementation to become part of the researchers' technology arsenal, an important collaboration tool for experimentation purposes, and ultimately enrich ongoing and future research endeavors, that study the behavior of the SIoT ecosystem, with valuable insights.

### 1.1  Contribution

Based on the preceding, our contribution to the research community is fourfold and can be summarised in the following aspects:

– Motivated by the current absence of the TCP Cubic flavor in the OMNeT++ simulator, in this paper, its implementation in the INET Framework is presented and made publicly available to the research community.
– An overview of the TCP structure within the INET Framework is also provided to support the logic of our implementation, with detailed descriptions relating to its class, subclasses, and functions, along with an analytical study of its idiosyncrasies.
– Additionally, comprehensive simulation experiments are conducted to evaluate the expected behavior of our model under two different topologies; that is, in point-to-point and dumbbell networks. The results are in accordance with the theoretical analysis.
– Finally, to test TCP Cubic's applicability to satellite topologies (i.e., in SIoT systems), a comparison with the well-known TCP NewReno, which is used as a baseline here, is conducted for a variety of RTT values. The results clearly indicate how the former surpasses the latter, with notable gains in throughput, making it the more suitable candidate for augmenting communication in future SIoT environments.

### 1.2  Paper Structure

The rest of the paper is organized as follows: Sect. 2 includes necessary background information on the TCP, OMNeT++ simulator, and INET Framework; Sect. 3 describes the theoretical behavior of TCP Cubic; Sect. 4 presents the structure of TCP in INET as well as how it is extended with the implementation of TCP Cubic; Sect. 5 demonstrates simulation results of TCP Cubic's performance and provides insights from its comparison against the TCP NewReno in SIoT environments; and, finally, Sect. 6 concludes the paper, summarizing its key findings and providing future research directions.

## 2  Background Information

Following, some background information on TCP and OMNeT++/INET Framework is provided to familiarize the reader with the topics of the current research investigation.

## 2.1   TCP Related Work

TCP Cubic is the default implementation on the Linux kernel, its appearance tracing back to 2008 [17]. As the researchers highlight in their work, a path with a 10 Gbps bandwidth, an RTT of 100 ms delay, and a segment size of 1250 bytes produces a high BDP that standard TCP variations like Reno and NewReno will take approximately 1.4 h when growing their window to the full BDP size, a fact that severely under-utilizes the network path link. When referring to satellite communications, high BDP is to be expected depending on the altitude of the orbit. For instance, low-Earth orbit satellites located 160 km to 1000 km above the surface of the Earth result in RTT smaller than 100 ms. On the other hand, Geosynchronous Equatorial Orbit satellites are positioned at 35.786 km over the ground and hence their RTT can range anywhere between 480 ms to 700 ms.

TCP Hybla, on the other hand, was introduced in 2004 for satellite communications as a variant to the TCP NewReno [19]. Hybla possesses a higher throughput than TCP NewReno given the same values for their BDP and RTT, however, it is unfair to other flows that use the same algorithm [8].

TCP-START [23] is another variation of TCP that has been designed for the Satellite Internet around 2006. The authors proposed three new mechanisms to overcome the drawbacks of the performance of standard TCP in Satellite Environments: 1) Congestion Window Setting: This mechanism helps to avoid the unnecessary reduction of the transmission rate using Available Bandwidth Estimation (ABE) when a bit error causes the data loss. 2) Lift Window Control: As its name suggests, this mechanism increases the cwnd faster using the values of TCP Reno and the ABE. 3) Acknowledgment Error Notification: This mechanism is used to minimize unnecessary timeouts by ACK loss or delay, and avoid the reduction of throughput via mis-retransmission of data. The experimentation of the authors showed to have better throughput from TCP-WestwoodBR and TCP-J in addition to having similar fairness with TCP-WestwoodBR in homogeneous environments and slightly worse results in heterogeneous environments. This TCP variation requires only changes on the sender side.

TCP Peach [4] was designed for satellite networks and uses four algorithms, two of which are Fast Retransmit and Congestion Avoidance. It also introduced two new algorithms, namely the Sudden Start and Rapid Recovery. TCP Peach tries to distinguish the drops emanated by congestion from those originating due to link failures. With the new algorithms, TCP Peach can probe the available bandwidth in one RTT using dummy packets with low-priority service that do not contain new data for the receiver. An improvement to the particular protocol is the so-called TCP Peach+ [5] which replaces the low priory dummy packets with low-priority new data.

TCP Norirdwick [28] was introduced in 2008 as an alternative congestion control algorithm that uses burst base transmission. The researchers in their paradigm use this algorithm to transfer sort web traffic over satellite links. The newest version of this protocol is the TCP Wave [2] which can be used in more network-wide communication scenarios. It is designed with three principles [1]: Burst Transmission, ACK-based Capacity, and Congestion Estimation, and Rate

Control algorithm. This protocol requires dramatic changes to the side of the sender.

In the last years, a new congestion control has been developed, TCP Bottleneck Bandwidth and Round-trip time (BBR) by Google, as an alternative algorithm for TCP Cubic. TCP BBR is used extensively in the servers of Google after 2017 [9]. The algorithm estimates periodically the minimum RTT and the available bandwidth of the path, its main goal being to not build up queues in the intermediate nodes. In a follow-up work [33] it was shown that TCP BBR dominates the TCP Cubic on start-up and steady state in satellite environments. Conversely, in another work [11], TCP Hybla was shown to perform better for small-size downloads (e.g. Web Pages) relative to TCP BBR.

Considering TCP as the prime transport protocol for SIoT environments, the next step is experimenting through simulation. As presented, a lot of interesting TCP flavors have been proposed in the literature for satellite communication that lack, however, implementation within the OMNeT++/INET Framework. This is also the case for TCP Cubic. Given that i) a growing volume of related research uses TCP Cubic as their preferred flavor for SIoT systems; ii) the fact that it is the default variant in the Linux distribution; and iii) there is no such implementation currently publicly available in OMNeT++, our aim in the upcoming sections is to develop one within the INET Framework and make it openly accessible to the research community.

Note that TCP Peach and Peach+, as discussed, are also popular solutions for SIoT systems. However, their functionality necessitates routers to have first implemented some queue priority scheduling disciplines that, in turn, require extensive modifications on the receiver side. In contrast, the implementation of TCP Cubic, as provided here, is embedded seamlessly within the existing TCP family of INET by overriding some of its current TCP classes, thus, making it a more suitable addition to the OMNeT++ simulator.

## 2.2    OMNeT++ and INET Framework

Before proceeding with our proposed implementation, it is necessary to introduce the reader to the selected simulator. Objective Modular Network Testbed in C++ (or OMNeT++[1] in short) is an open-source modular component-based simulator for networks, that increasingly gains momentum in the academic community for diverse networking research agendas [31]. It essentially comprises a discrete, event-driven, and general-purpose simulator that gives the flexibility to simulate different types of networks like peer-to-peer, queuing, ad-hoc, and many more [32].

The INET Framework[2] on the other hand, is a popular open-source library for the OMNeT++ simulator [21]. It provides a variety of protocols and modes to simulate wired and wireless networks. Further, it includes a model for the simulation of the complete Internet stack.

---

[1] Accessible at the web address: https://omnetpp.org/.

[2] Accesible at the web address: https://inet.omnetpp.org/.

One of the protocols, offered by the INET Framework, is that of TCP. Using the modular approach of OMNeT++, INET implements the core functionality of TCP wherein different congestion control algorithms extend the "TcpBaseAlg" according to their needs. With that said, currently, there are implementations for the following algorithms: Tahoe, Reno, NewReno, Vegas, Westwood, and DCTCP. In this paper, aiming to enrich the toolkit of available TCP algorithms, the authors provide the implementation of TCP Cubic as an extension to the TcpBaseAlg, and then present initial results from its application in the SIoT ecosystem.

## 3   Theory of TCP Cubic

The main features of TCP Cubic are scalability, stability, and its proclivity towards fairness in regard to competing flows that use the same path [7]. To do so, TCP Cubic redefines the congestion avoidance algorithm and the computation of the slow start threshold ($ssthresh$) but uses the same mechanisms for Fast Retransmit and Fast Recovery as the TCP NewReno after a package loss. Moreover, in the TCP Cubic new state variables for the computation of the congestion window ($cwnd$) are introduced. In particular, when a loss event occurs the TCP Cubic registers the maximum value of $cwnd$ in the variable $W_{max}$ before the reduction of $cwnd$. After performing multiple decreases of $cwnd$ by a constant factor $\beta$, it enters the congestion avoidance phase when the Fast Recovery phase has ended.

Going into more detail, TCP Cubic uses $epoch\_start$, $t$, and $K$ to track the time from the loss event. The variable $epoch\_start$ is used to register the time when TCP for the first time acknowledges (ACK) new data. The $t$ variable keeps track of the time that has passed from the loss event. $K$ stands for the time when the $cwnd$ reaches the value $W_{max}$, if no further losses occur, and is calculated as

$$K = \sqrt[3]{\frac{W_{max}\beta}{C}}, \tag{1}$$

where $C$ is a constant that regulates the aggressiveness of TCP Cubic.

With the previous variables, Cubic is able to determine the current $cwnd$, according to the following expression:

$$W(t) = C(t - K)^3 + W_{max}. \tag{2}$$

The cubic function in the right part of Eq. (2) is utilized by TCP Cubic for the computation of the window growth function of $cwnd$, relative to $W_{max}$, in the congestion avoidance phase.

Different from most alternative congestion control algorithms to Standard TCP, which increases the $cwnd$ using convex functions, TCP Cubic uses both a concave and a convex profile for the increase of $cwnd$ in the congestion avoidance [17]. The alteration between the two profiles helps the TCP Cubic to achieve higher network utilization and stability. This is done as follows. Before TCP

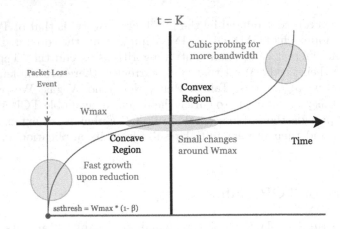

**Fig. 1.** Cubic theoretical growth function depicting its concave-convex profile switching behavior.

Cubic performs multiple decreases due to packet loss, it registers the current $cwnd$ to $W_{max}$. Then it enters the congestion avoidance where the $cwnd$ growth follows the concave profile until it reaches the $W_{max}$ used as a plateau. In this region (i.e., the concave region), $cwnd$ initially grows fast and as it approaches the $W_{max}$ plateau its changes become very small. When it reaches the $W_{max}$, the profile switch takes place whereby the $cwnd$ enters the convex region. In this region, the increase in the growth of $cwnd$ is initially slow, but as time progresses it speeds up in order to probe for more bandwidth.

The aforementioned theoretical behavior of the window adjustment is more accurately depicted in Fig. 1. In the beginning, after the packet loss event occurs, $cwnd$ experiences a fast growth as it has only passed a small amount of time since $epoch\_start$. As time passes and $t$ approaches $K$, the increase to $cwnd$ becomes smaller. At some point when the $t$ will be larger than $K$, the Cubic turns from the concave to the convex profile. In the convex region, the Cubic updates the $cwnd$ growth initially by small values. However, as time $t$ passes, the changes grow continuously larger maximizing in this way bandwidth probing.

When Standard TCP detects a loss event from Retransmission Timeout (RTO) or three duplicate Acknowledgments, it computes the new $ssthresh$ as half of the current $cwnd$ size. This approach is too conservative and dramatically reduces the performance of TCP. In contrast, TCP Cubic reduces the current $cwnd$ by a factor $\beta$ that is smaller than one-half of the one that the Standard TCP uses. Typically, this factor is set to 0.2 or 0.3 [17,27]. Cubic then uses the below expression (3) to calculate the new value of $ssthresh$ as:

$$ssthresh = W_{max}(1 - \beta). \qquad (3)$$

The TCP Reno family, on the other hand, works very well in networks with small RTT and small BDP. TCP Cubic uses the TCP-friendly region to achieve the same throughput as the TCP Reno family for those networks. This is done by computing the theoretical $cwnd$ ($W_{tcp(t)}$) of the TCP Reno family at the reception of each new Acknowledgment in the Congestion Avoidance phase. Next, it compares the $W_{tcp(t)}$ with the current $cwnd$. If $cwnd$ is found to be less than $W_{tcp(t)}$, the protocol sets $cwnd$ equal to $W_{tcp(t)}$ at each ACK reception, where the $W_{tcp(t)}$ is computed by Eq. (4):

$$W_{tcp(t)} = W_{max}(1 - \beta) + 3\frac{\beta}{2 - \beta}\frac{t}{RTT}. \tag{4}$$

TCP Cubic utilizes a heuristic sub-routine to improve the convergence speed. While incoming flows join the same link path, existing flows must release some of their bandwidth shares to accommodate the newly arrived. This is done when TCP detects a packet loss event. In such cases, if the $cwnd$ is smaller than the previous $W_{max}$, then it assigns to the $W_{max}$ a smaller value than the value of the current $cwnd$. Otherwise, the $W_{max}$ registers the actual value of the $cwnd$. The end goal of the fast convergence sub-routine is to give some time to new flows to catch up with the existing $cwnd$ of the other flows within the network.

## 4   INET Implementation

INET Framework is an open souse library that provides simulation models of the Internet Stack for wire and wireless networks. These models follow the modular approach of OMNeT++, wherein smaller basic components build compound and more complex models. For example, INET provides basic queues that can be used to form a buffer for the application. In this section, we will describe the details of our implementation of TCP Cubic using the INET Framework.

### 4.1   TCP Structure on INET

TCP is a complex protocol to simulate due to its mechanisms used to provide for reliable, in-ordered, and error-checked delivery of information. In Fig. 2, the structure of the TCP model in the INET Framework is presented with a UML class diagram.

The TCP class is composed of several (sub-)classes such as TcpSendQueue, TcpReceiveQueue, and TcpConnection. To administrate the incoming and outcoming chunks of information, TCP calls TcpSendQueue and TcpReceiveQueue to manage the corresponding buffers accordingly. TcpConnection follows the functionality guidelines set forth by RFC 793 [26] to implement the state machine that handles all the connections that open and close from the host. If Selective Acknowledgments (SACK) are used, TcpConnection calls the TcpSackRexmitQueue class for the handling of SACK retransmission.

The TcpAlgorithm class is an abstract class that encapsulates all behavior of the transfer state of TCP (e.g., functions for establishing and then closing connections). TcpBaseAlg inherits and extends TcpAlgorithm class, and it is responsible for keeping track of the TCP timers, in addition to restarting them when the need arises, as well as for the collection of appropriate statistics. Finally,

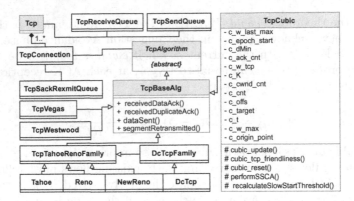

**Fig. 2.** UML diagram of the TCP on the INET Framework along with the TcpCubic class implemented in this paper.

it provides a general implementation for tasks relevant to data sending, to ACKs or duplicate ACKs reception, and to what action must be taken given out-of-order segment retransmission.

Over time, a variety of congestion avoidance mechanisms have been created for TCP that use different strategies to deal with congestion. Some of them adopt the same logic and elements. For this reason, a family class has been implemented in INET that provides the basic utility for those algorithms. The family class is inherited from the TcpBaseAlg class and is used to facilitate the easier management of the corresponding mechanism algorithms. To exemplify this, consider the Tahoe, Reno, and NewReno TCP flavors all of which inherit characteristics from the same family, i.e., the TcpTahoeRenoFamily.

In some cases, the TCP flavors can directly inherit and overwrite the functions of the TcpBaseAlg class, as has been done with TCP Vegas and Westwood. Even though TCP Cubic uses some of the characteristics of TCP NewReno, it was decided to directly inherit and overwrite the TcpBaseAlg class for our INET TCP Cubic implementation, as shown in Fig. 2.

## 4.2   TCP Cubic Implementation

In this section, we will deepen the analysis of our TCP Cubic class implementation, henceforth named TcpCubic, as well as the functions we use to define its behavior. We have used the implementation of Cubic in Linux code as a guideline. The code of Linux uses integer arithmetics and kernel functions for performance tuning. Conversely, the INET Framework is a simulation library within OMNeT++ and not a kernel per se. For this reason, we will not focus on TCP Cubic state variables of the Linux code, although comprehensive documentation on these aspects can be found by other researchers [15, 20]. For dissemination purposes, our TCP Cubic implementation is made publicly available

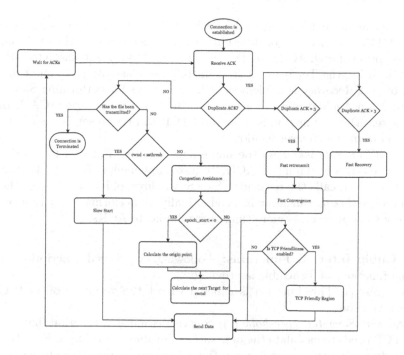

**Fig. 3.** Flow chart of TCP Cubic.

on the Github repository[3] Its flow chart (with the exception of timeouts which are part of the core TCP) is illustrated in Fig. 3 while its functions are discussed thoroughly below.

**TPC Cubic External Functions:** Based on the previously defined TCP Cubic functionality, the TcpBaseAlg class is overridden by the following functions:

*dataSent():* This function is called each time the TCP sends a new segment. It schedules the retransmission timer if it is not running, starts the measurement of RTT, and remembers the last time that data was sent. INET doesn't support TCP timestamps but instead uses a utility class, called TcpSegmentTransmit-InfoList, which stores information about the packet like the first and last time the package was sent and the number of transitions. With this information, we can calculate later the time for the variables $t$ and $dMin$.

*segmentRetransmitted():* This function is called from the TcpConnection class whenever needed, after data retransmission. Similar to the dataSent() function, we need to update the time in TcpSegmentTransmitInfoList when we retransmitting a package.

*receivedDataAck():* This class is called each time the TCP receives an ACK from the data that was sent. The TcpBaseAlg class provides basic functionality

---

[3] Accessible at the web address: https://github.com/GIANNIS-AGGELIS/INET-TCP-CUBIC.

for retransmission handling as well as a PERSIST timer, while leaving to each flavor of TCP the decision of determining the specific action that will happen upon reception of each ACK. For TCP Cubic we extend this function to calculate the *dMin* using the TcpSegmentTransmitInfoList class. At the same time, the action of Fast Recovery is implemented here whereas for performing Slow Start or Congestion Avoidance a call is made to the function performSSCA(). In the end, the sendData() function is called and TCP will try to send a new date if it is allowed from the receiver window.

*receivedDuplicateAck():* As the name suggests, this function is called when the TCP receives a duplicate ACK. It also implements the Fast Retransmit algorithm, which calls the recalculateSlowStartThreshold() function for the calculation of *ssthresh* whenever in need. Finally, it performs the action of Fast Recovery when it receives more than three duplicate ACKs.

**TPC Cubic Internal Functions:** Following, a detailed description of the internal functions of TcpCubic is provided:

*cubic_reset():* This function is called to reset the variables of TCP Cubic during a time-out.

*recalculateSlowStartThreshold():* It constitutes a utility function that is called when TCP needs to calculate the new *ssthresh* value according to Eq. (3). Also, this function includes the implementation of the fast convergence heuristic subroutine.

*cubic_update():* This function is called by performSSCA() each time TCP receives a new ACK in the Congestion Avoidance phase. For its implementation, we have closely followed as a guideline the pseudo-code provided in the original work of Ha et al., [17]. In INET, the default *cwnd* size is represented in number of bytes. Thus, for the calculation of both $K$ and the target window, one must first convert the *cwnd* size into a number of segments in order to properly proceed with its calculation. One observation that we make is that we need to compute the absolute value of $|t - k|$ from Eq. (2).

*cubic_tcp_friendliness():* This function is called at the end of cubic_update() with the aim of computing the theoretical *cwnd* of the TCP Reno family. In the circumstance that *cwnd* is smaller than the $W_{tcp}$, then it uses that as the target window.

## 5   Simulation Results

In this section, we discuss the different simulation experiments that were conducted to validate our INET implementation of TCP Cubic. In all experiments, we simulate an FTP scenario. Two sets of experiments are considered. For the first, we evaluate our implementation under generalized client-server scenarios whereas, for the second, we consider a more specific scenario targeted at the SIoT environments.

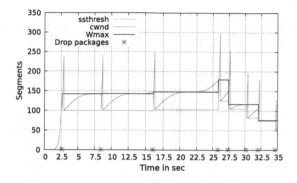

**Fig. 4.** Growth of *cwnd* of TCP Cubic over time.

## 5.1  Evaluation Under Client-Server Scenarios

For the first experiment, we begin with a typical use case by employing two Standard Hosts from the INET library which are connected directly via a wire link in a point-to-point communication. One node represents the Client and the other the Server with the first running a Tcp Session App and the second running a Tcp Sink App respectively. The file size that we wish to transfer is 20 MB, and the maximum segment size is 1024 bytes. The transmission begins at 1.2 s. For link characteristics, we choose a one-way delay at 40 ms, a 5 Mbps of data rate, and as for the error rate, we input a probability of 0.0005. The last is intentionally set to a low value for the initial experiment since this yields a small number of errors on the link, allowing for clearer observations of the behavior of *cwnd* after a loss event.

In Fig. 4, in addition to the growth of *cwnd* over time, we have plotted the values of *ssthresh* and the $W_{max}$. The link in this case has produced eight (8) errors in packages that contain data. The spikes on *cwnd* that are created after a packet loss are the result of the Fast Recovery algorithm. After the three (3) duplicated ACKs, Fast Recovery inflates the *cwnd* by one package for each additional duplicate ACK. When the TCP acknowledges new data, it deflates the *cwnd* to the value of *ssthesh*, and the algorithm for Congestion Avoidance algorithm kicks in.

In the first congestion epoch, the Congestion Avoidance increases the *cwnd* from *ssthresh* only with the concave profile to $W_{max}$ as a new loss was detected in the same *cwnd* as the loss. The *ssthresh* and $W_{max}$ for the second congestion epoch remain the same but this time the *cwnd* surpasses the current $W_{max}$ and starts slowly to increase until the next packet loss. In the third congestion epoch, we can see the full evolution of *cwnd* from convex to concave region up to the next packet loss. The following package loss is very close in time and the *cwnd* does not reach the current $W_{max}$. This behavior repeats, as observed by Table 1, which encapsulates the time $t$ when packages are lost as well as the value of time when the growth of *cwnd* is expected to change from concave to convex if no further losses appear.

**Table 1.** The first column shows the time that a window reduction has occurred, the second shows the time when $cwnd$ is expected to change profile if no further loss occurs, and the third indicates whether a profile switch actually happened.

| Packet Loss Recorded Time | Switch Expected Time | Profile Switch |
|---|---|---|
| 2.90 | 7.61 | NO |
| 8.72 | 13.42 | YES |
| 16.32 | 21.09 | YES |
| 26.16 | 31.25 | NO |
| 27.70 | 30.70 | NO |
| 30.43 | 34.83 | NO |
| 32.24 | 33.53 | NO |
| 34.80 | 38.59 | NO |

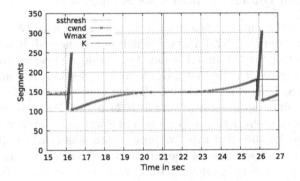

**Fig. 5.** Switch from concave to convex profile, depicted by the green vertical line. (Color figure online)

To further validate the expected profile switch attitude of TCP Cubic, in Fig. 5 the value of $K$ is depicted by zooming into the third congestion epoch of the previous diagram (Fig. 4). Here, we can clearly witness that the alternating concave and convex behavior of $cwnd$ closely follows the theoretical behavior of TCP Cubic as shown in Fig. 5, while $cwnd$ stays almost constant for some time around the $Wmax$.

For the second experimental scenario, as a proof-of-concept, we construct a representative dumbbell topology where two routers are located between four Clients and four Servers at the bottleneck between two endpoints. Figure 6 visualizes the exact topology, whereby our goal is to test the TCP Cubic in a shared link. The links that connect the routers with the Servers and the Clients have a 10 Gbps capacity and no error rate. The default configurations of the routers use drop tail queues with a 10.000 capacity of packets. The bottleneck link between the two routers has a bandwidth of 100 Mbs and a small probability of 0.0005 for error rate.

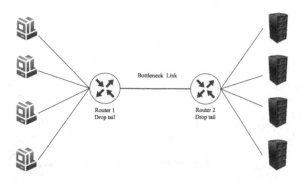

**Fig. 6.** The considered topology for the typical client-server simulation scenarios.

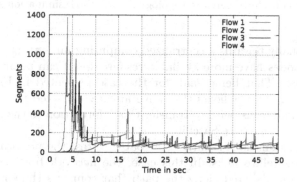

**Fig. 7.** Evolution of *cwnd* over time from 4 flows under the same bottleneck link.

According to Fig. 6, each of the four Clients is connected to its corresponding Server. We investigate the FTP scenario where each Client transfers a big file to the Server and the simulation runs for 50 s. Each connection opens sequentially with a difference of 1 s from the previous one, starting at 1.2 s. The results from this experiment are illustrated in Fig. 7, where it can be observed that for $t > 10$ s the network status has stabilized and all flows have values of *cwnd* close to one another for the remaining duration of the experiment.

## 5.2 Evaluation Under SIoT Scenarios

In this section, the aim is to evaluate the TCP Cubic in SIoT environments and contrast it to the one obtained by TCP NewReno. We begin our investigation by considering a simple SIoT topology, as depicted in Fig. 8, where the Clients and Servers are connected to Gateways. The Gateways, in turn, connect the two components of the network with the remote intervention of the Satellite.

Because opening a TCP connection from an IoT device is expensive in resources, and typical IoT devices, such as low-cost sensors, are hardware-constrained (e.g. due to limited battery) [29], we assume that the IoT devices are connected to sink nodes, which collect the data and then send it deeper into

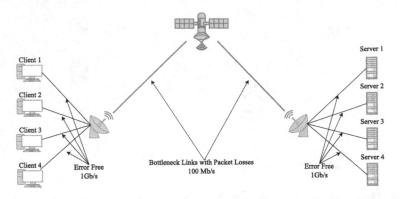

**Fig. 8.** The considered satellite topology for the SIoT simulation scenarios.

the network, usually towards a centralized computing infrastructure, for further analysis. Sink nodes have more available resources and can open and maintain TCP connections. That being said, for the case presented in Fig. 8, the sink nodes are represented as Clients that have already collected the data from the underlying IoT and, thus, wish to transfer this information to the corresponding Servers via the intermediate Satellite.

In the third simulation scenario, the goal is to test the performance of TCP Cubic over the satellite links. In this case, the network bottleneck manifests at the satellite links shared along the path that connects the Clients with the Satellite and the path that connects the Satellite with the Servers, respectively. The links of the Clients and the Servers with their corresponding Gateways are attributed a data rate of 1 Gbps with no error loss while the links connecting the latter with the Satellite have a 100 Mbps data rate with 0.0005 probability for each link to produce an error.

Following, we compare our implementation of TCP Cubic against the TCP NewReno from the INET library (i.e., Fig. 9). TCP NewReno is considered a baseline for satellite communication [3,25], and although today there exist other TCP flavors that are clearly better equipped to handle satellite networks (e.g., consult Sect. 2 for more information), due to TCP NewReno being the only other one that has already been incorporated in the INET library, the authors decided that the particular protocol is the best available alternative to test the performance of TCP Cubic in OMNeT++.

Under this light, we assume an FTP scenario wherein each Client needs to transfer a file size of 15 MiB, and all Clients start the transfer simultaneously (i.e., at 1.2 s). The one-way delay from the Gateway to the Satellite is 100 ms and so the total RTT between each Client and its Server is 400 ms.

To comprehensively visualize and collate the simulation results, the *cwnd* form is separately plotted as a function of time for the TCP Cubic in Fig. 9a and for the TCP NewReno in Fig. 9b. Evidently, TCP NewReno experiences a substantially worse performance relative to the TCP Cubic as all four flows finish significantly later than their corresponding counterparts for the TCP Cubic case.

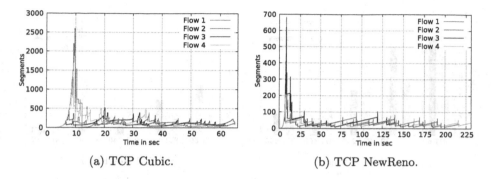

(a) TCP Cubic.                    (b) TCP NewReno.

**Fig. 9.** Comparison of TCP Cubic against TCP NewReno for four flows over the same satellite link.

In fact, two out of its four flows finish after the 200 s time mark, whereas for the TCP Cubic no flow exists that finishes beyond the 70 s. This happens because TCP NewReno reduces the *cwnd* by half each time a package is lost and in the Congestion Avoidance phase it increases the window by $1/cwnd$ for each new ACK, a fact that produces linear growth. The rapid spikes that are observed in Fig. 9b during the beginning are the result of the Fast Recovery algorithm.

Overall, TCP Cubic performs markedly better as all the flows finish much sooner relative to the ones of TCP NewReno. Furthermore, it can be seen that, after 15 s has passed, the network goes into an almost equilibrium state where the flows operate above 150 packages for the whole remainder of the time. It must be noted that, for $t \approx 10$, Flow 1 shows a massive increase in *cwnd*. This is caused by a package loss that appeared much later relative to the other flows and thus the Fast Recovery algorithm receives a large number of duplicate ACKs. Subsequently, around the 12 s time mark, Flow 1 experiences an RTO and, as a result, it reduces the *cwnd* to one package and starts again with the Slow Start algorithm until the new *ssthresh* value is reached, given that no further loss occurs. These observations testify to the ability of TCP Cubic to successfully handle the workload and packet losses in SIoT systems, and better manage the bandwidth allocation among the different flows when compared to TCP NewReno.

To further validate this claim, in the last experimental scenario, given the SIoT topology that was previously presented in Fig. 8, different values on the delay of the satellite links are taken into account, considering a 15 MiB file transfer from each Client to the corresponding Server. Specifically, in this configuration, our aim is to explore the throughput of each Client by enforcing the following RTT values: 60 ms, 120 ms, 240 ms, 400 ms, and 600 ms. Again, the packet loss probability is set to 0.0005 for each satellite link. Figure 10 captures the results of the Clients' averaged throughput, after repeating the experiment for ten independent runs with different seeds for the error rate.

As clearly demonstrated, TCP Cubic (Fig. 10a) has a much higher average throughput than TCP NewReno (Fig. 10b) in all cases. Moreover, for both pro-

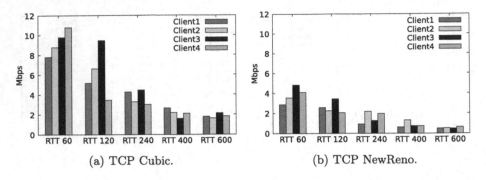

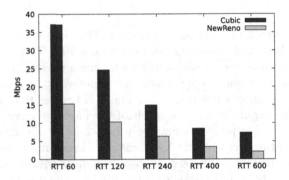

Fig. 10. Simulation results of the average throughput per Client for the TCP Cubic versus the TCP NewReno.

Fig. 11. Average aggregated throughput for TCP Cubic versus TCP NewReno.

tocols, it is observed that the average throughput decreases as the RTT rises. This is to be expected since an increase in the delay also leads to an increase in total transfer time. Of special interest are the cases where the RTT is $\geq 120\,$ms, as these values are more inherent to satellite environments [18]. Still, even under these realistic circumstances, TCP Cubic is observed to have almost double the throughput for most clients, significantly outperforming the TCP NewReno.

To verify this finding, the final plot (i.e., Fig. 11) illustrates the average aggregated throughput of each protocol for all experiments that were executed per RTT value. Clearly, the employment of TCP Cubic results in substantial throughput gains, outperforming the TCP NewReno by a large margin, TCP Cubic performs at least two times the throughput relative to TCP NewReno. Actually, for the worst case where the RTT equates to 600 ms, the TCP Cubic archives almost 7.5 Mbps while the TCP NewReno approximately 2 Mbps. Furthermore, it is observed that as the RTT grows the difference in the average aggregated throughput between the two protocols also grows, a fact that renders TCP Cubic the better overall candidate for dealing with high latency over long network distances such as those found in the SIoT ecosystem.

As a side note, one must keep in mind that TCP NewReno was not specially designed for Long Fat Networks. On the other hand, TCP Cubic is designed specifically for these types of networks and hence it can be seamlessly integrated in satellite communication environments. To this end, we believe that the implementation presented here can become a valuable addition, for practitioners and researchers alike, to the existing arsenal of network simulation tools. Nevertheless, more tests must be carried out before fully assessing its eligibility for SIoT networks, especially in regard to other TCP variants, besides the TCP NewReno, and in combination with more realistic and complex SIoT topologies. We leave the detailed analysis of these matters to future work.

## 6   Conclusions

In this paper, using the INET Framework, the TCP Cubic was developed and presented. To the authors' knowledge, this is the first publicly available implementation of TCP Cubic for the OMNeT++ simulator. Under this scope, a detailed description of the TCP protocol class and functions in the INET was provided along with information about how they are extended to fit the current research needs of TCP Cubic. Simulation results, evaluating its behavior, were in close alignment with the theoretical analysis. A direct comparison of the implemented TCP Cubic against the TCP NewReno was also performed, focusing on SIoT environments and concluding that TCP Cubic is the more suitable candidate with notable augmentations to the overall system performance.

For future work, the authors plan to provide an updated version of TCP Cubic that utilizes for the Slow Start phase the HyStart algorithm [16]. HyStart was not part of the original work on TCP Cubic [17] but since then it has been used in conjunction with TCP Cubic under various networking contexts. Hence, it could prove extremely beneficial to investigate their combination in SIoT systems, as many researchers have already seen promising results in this regard [24]. In parallel, it is believed that the use of the ESTNeT simulator [14], which also embeds the INET Framework, can create more realistic simulations of satellite communications. Thus, its synergy with the presented TCP Cubic implementation is viewed as the next logical step towards shedding light on the more intriguing aspects of the SIoT ecosystem. Furthermore, additional experimentation will be conducted, considering real-world scenarios with a large number of IoT devices, where the scalability of the protocol will be thoroughly tested.

## References

1. Abdelsalam, A., Luglio, M., Patriciello, N., Roseti, C., Zampognaro, F.: TCP wave over Linux: a disruptive alternative to the traditional TCP window approach. Comput. Netw. **184**, 107633 (2021). https://doi.org/10.1016/j.comnet.2020. 107633. https://www.sciencedirect.com/science/article/pii/S1389128620312585

2. Abdelsalam, A., Luglio, M., Roseti, C., Zampognaro, F.: TCP wave resilience to link changes. In: Proceedings of the 13th International Joint Conference on E-Business and Telecommunications, ICETE 2016, pp. 72–79. SCITEPRESS - Science and Technology Publications, LDA, Setubal, PRT (2016). https://doi.org/10.5220/0005966700720079

3. Abdelsalam, A., Roseti, C., Zampognaro, F.: TCP performance for satellite M2M applications over random access links. In: 2018 International Symposium on Networks, Computers and Communications (ISNCC), pp. 1–5 (2018). https://doi.org/10.1109/ISNCC.2018.8531048

4. Akyildiz, I., Morabito, G., Palazzo, S.: TCP-Peach: a new congestion control scheme for satellite IP networks. IEEE/ACM Trans. Network. 9(3), 307–321 (2001). https://doi.org/10.1109/90.929853

5. Akyildiz, I., Zhang, X., Fang, J.: TCP-Peach+: enhancement of TCP-peach for satellite IP networks. IEEE Commun. Lett. 6(7), 303–305 (2002). https://doi.org/10.1109/LCOMM.2002.801317

6. Atzori, L., Iera, A., Morabito, G.: The internet of things: a survey. Comput. Netw. 54(15), 2787–2805 (2010). https://doi.org/10.1016/j.comnet.2010.05.010. https://www.sciencedirect.com/science/article/pii/S1389128610001568

7. Cai, H., Eun, D.Y., Ha, S., Rhee, I., Xu, L.: Stochastic ordering for internet congestion control and its applications. In: IEEE INFOCOM 2007–26th IEEE International Conference on Computer Communications, pp. 910–918 (2007). https://doi.org/10.1109/INFCOM.2007.111

8. Callegari, C., Giordano, S., Pagano, M., Pepe, T.: Behavior analysis of TCP Linux variants. Comput. Netw. 56(1), 462–476 (2012). https://doi.org/10.1016/j.comnet.2011.10.002

9. Cardwell, N., Cheng, Y., Gunn, C.S., Yeganeh, S.H., Jacobson, V.: BBR: congestion-based congestion control. Commun. ACM 60(2), 58–66 (2017). https://doi.org/10.1145/3009824

10. Centenaro, M., Costa, C.E., Granelli, F., Sacchi, C., Vangelista, L.: A survey on technologies, standards and open challenges in satellite IoT. IEEE Commun. Surv. Tutorials 23(3), 1693–1720 (2021). https://doi.org/10.1109/COMST.2021.3078433

11. Claypool, S., Chung, J., Claypool, M.: Comparison of TCP congestion control performance over a satellite network. In: Hohlfeld, O., Lutu, A., Levin, D. (eds.) PAM 2021. LNCS, vol. 12671, pp. 499–512. Springer, Cham (2021). https://doi.org/10.1007/978-3-030-72582-2_29

12. Dai, C.Q., Zhang, M., Li, C., Zhao, J., Chen, Q.: QoE-aware intelligent satellite constellation design in satellite internet of things. IEEE Internet Things J. 8(6), 4855–4867 (2021). https://doi.org/10.1109/JIOT.2020.3030263

13. De Sanctis, M., Cianca, E., Araniti, G., Bisio, I., Prasad, R.: Satellite communications supporting internet of remote things. IEEE Internet Things J. 3(1), 113–123 (2016). https://doi.org/10.1109/JIOT.2015.2487046

14. Freimann, A., Dierkes, M., Petermann, T., Liman, C., Kempf, F., Schilling, K.: ESTNeT: a discrete event simulator for space-terrestrial networks. CEAS Space J. 13, 39–49 (2021). https://doi.org/10.1007/s12567-020-00316-6

15. Fu, J.: TCP cubic memo. https://gist.github.com/fuji246/cffb0e460c14956d7357b57ea6823100. Accessed 13 May 2023

16. Ha, S., Rhee, I.: Taming the elephants: new TCP slow start. Comput. Netw. 55(9), 2092–2110 (2011). https://doi.org/10.1016/j.comnet.2011.01.014

17. Ha, S., Rhee, I., Xu, L.: Cubic: a new TCP-friendly high-speed TCP variant. SIGOPS Oper. Syst. Rev. 42(5), 64–74 (2008). https://doi.org/10.1145/1400097.1400105

18. Kua, J., Loke, S.W., Arora, C., Fernando, N., Ranaweera, C.: Internet of things in space: a review of opportunities and challenges from satellite-aided computing to digitally-enhanced space living. Sensors **21**(23) (2021). https://doi.org/10.3390/s21238117

19. Le, H.D., Pham, A.T.: TCP over satellite-to-unmanned aerial/ground vehicles laser links: Hybla or cubic? In: 2020 IEEE Region 10 Conference (TENCON), pp. 720–725 (2020). https://doi.org/10.1109/TENCON50793.2020.9293761

20. Levasseur, B., Claypool, M., Kinicki, R.: A TCP cubic implementation in NS-3. In: Proceedings of the 2014 Workshop on NS-3, WNS3 2014. Association for Computing Machinery, New York, NY, USA (2014). https://doi.org/10.1145/2630777.2630780

21. Mészáros, Levente, Varga, Andras, Kirsche, Michael: INET Framework. In: Virdis, Antonio, Kirsche, Michael (eds.) Recent Advances in Network Simulation. EICC, pp. 55–106. Springer, Cham (2019). https://doi.org/10.1007/978-3-030-12842-5_2

22. Nguyen, D.C., et al.: 6G internet of things: a comprehensive survey. IEEE Internet Things J. **9**(1), 359–383 (2022). https://doi.org/10.1109/JIOT.2021.3103320

23. Obata, H., Ishida, K., Takeuchi, S., Hanasaki, S.: TCP-Star: TCP congestion control method for satellite internet. IEICE Trans. Commun. **89**(6), 1766–1773 (2006)

24. Peters, B., Zhao, P., Chung, J.W., Claypool, M.: TCP HyStart performance over a satellite network. In: Proceedings of the 0x15 NetDev Conference, Virtual Conference (2021)

25. Pirovano, A., Garcia, F.: A new survey on improving TCP performances over geostationary satellite link. Netw. Commun. Technol. **2**(1), xxx (2013). https://doi.org/10.5539/nct.v2n1p1

26. Postel, J.: Transmission control protocol. Technical report (1981)

27. Rhee, I., Xu, L., Ha, S., Zimmermann, A., Eggert, L., Scheffenegger, R.: CUBIC for fast long-distance networks. RFC 8312, February 2018. https://doi.org/10.17487/RFC8312

28. Roseti, C., Kristiansen, E.: TCP Noordwijk: TCP-based transport optimized for web traffic in satellite networks. In: 26th International Communications Satellite Systems Conference (ICSSC) (2008)

29. Shang, W., Yu, Y., Droms, R., Zhang, L.: Challenges in IoT networking via TCP/IP architecture. NDN Project (2016)

30. Tsipis, A., Papamichail, A., Angelis, I., Koufoudakis, G., Tsoumanis, G., Oikonomou, K.: An alertness-adjustable cloud/fog IoT solution for timely environmental monitoring based on wildfire risk forecasting. Energies **13**(14) (2020). https://doi.org/10.3390/en13143693. https://www.mdpi.com/1996-1073/13/14/3693

31. Varga, A.: Using the OMNeT++ discrete event simulation system in education. IEEE Trans. Educ. **42**(4), 11 (1999). https://doi.org/10.1109/13.804564

32. Varga, A., Hornig, R.: An overview of the OMNeT++ simulation environment. In: ICST (2010). https://doi.org/10.4108/ICST.SIMUTOOLS2008.3027

33. Zhao, P., Peters, B., Chung, J., Claypool, M.: Competing TCP congestion control algorithms over a satellite network. In: 2022 IEEE 19th Annual Consumer Communications Networking Conference (CCNC), pp. 132–138, January 2022. https://doi.org/10.1109/CCNC49033.2022.9700541

# Implementation Framework of a Blockchain Based Infrastructure for Electricity Trading Within a Microgrid

Milan Todorović[1] , Milica Knežević[1(✉)] , Domagoj Ševerdija[2] ,
Slobodan Jelić[3] , and Miodrag J. Mihaljević[1]

[1] Mathematical Institute of the Serbian Academy of Sciences and Arts,
Kneza Mihaila 36, 11000 Belgrade, Serbia
{mtodorovic,mknezevic,miodragm}@mi.sanu.ac.rs
[2] Incepton, Vratnička 23, 31000 Osijek, Croatia
domagoj.severdija@incepton.hr
[3] Faculty of Civil Engineering, University of Belgrade, Bulevar Kralja Aleksandra 73,
11000 Belgrade, Serbia
sjelic@grf.bg.ac.rs

**Abstract.** Smart grid appears as a progression of a traditional electrical grid that ensures sustainable and economically efficient electricity system with enhanced quality, security and safety. The opportunity to produce electricity from renewable energy resources resulted with appearance of new type of participants within the smart grid. In order to provide fair trading environment for these participants significant research activities have been made in order to support the shift from centralized to distributed trading systems. The blockchain technology is recognized as a suitable backbone due to its inherent characteristics of decentralization and distributedness. This paper proposes a novel blockchain-based platform for electricity trading and provides implementation details of its constituting elements. The proposed infrastructure relies on the blockchain with enhanced, energy efficient consensus protocol, and assumes that prosumers of a micro-grid may also act as miners within a mining pool that validates trading transactions. Architecture of the system, employed smart contracts and monitoring of the system operations are described. The paper also points out to an alternative option for the pool mining that provides heavy reduction of the energy consumption in comparison with a traditional Proof-of-Work approach. Finally, a framework for an optimization of the pool manager and pool miners working strategies is given.

**Keywords:** Smart grid · Electricity trading · Blockchain · Consensus protocol · Smart contracts

Supported by the EU H2020 SMART4ALL #3 CTTE "BC4GRID" project.

H. Gao et al. (Eds.): CollaborateCom 2023, LNICST 561, pp. 38–53, 2024.
https://doi.org/10.1007/978-3-031-54521-4_3

# 1   Introduction

The concept of blockchain was introduced fifteen years ago as a basis for a decentralized digital currency Bitcoin [1]. Over the time, blockchain has surpassed the initial application which was exclusively related to cryptocurrencies and finance, and it is seen today as a general-purpose technology. Researchers and developers recognized that many other application domains can utilize the principal blockchain characteristics: decentralization, transparency, immutability and verifiability. One of the key enablers for the widespread adoption and usage of the blockchain technology were smart contracts, which introduced the programmability potential into blockchain. Smart contracts are programs that are stored on blockchain, and their code cannot be altered, similarly to any other blockchain data. They are executed in a decentralized manner by all blockchain nodes. Ethereum was the first, and still most popular, blockchain for smart contracts, with a rich ecosystem of decentralized applications (dApps) and tools for developing, testing, and deploying smart contracts. Some other platforms with smart contract functionality are, for example, Hyperledger Fabric, Solana, Chainlink, Algorand, Tezos, EOS, etc.

A vast amount of research and real-world projects focuses on building blockchain based systems. Blockchain applications include: supply chain management [2,3], electricity sector [4,5], healthcare and medicine [6–8], non-fungible tokens (NFTs) [9], Industry 4.0 [10], e-voting [11], etc. Regarding the electricity sector, a number of research studies as well as industry projects have been investigating the possibilities for integrating blockchain into existing infrastructures through different activities: metering and billing, P2P electricity trading, grid operations and management, renewable energy certificates, electric vehicle charging, etc. Some of the companies involved in the energy sector that initiated the projects based on blockchain are: LO3 Energy (USA) [12], PowerLedger (Australia) [13], TenneT (Netherlands and Germany), SunContract (Slovenia) [14].

This area of research remains highly active and is accompanied by ongoing challenges concerning the utilization of public blockchains to support decentralized electricity trading. Therefore, we propose the development of a decentralized platform based on an energy-efficient public blockchain, which enables secure, trustworthy, and safe decentralized electricity trading. The main contributions of the paper can be summarized as follows:

- A model of a decentralized infrastructure for electricity trading that enables fair participation of prosumers and consumers at the electricity market is proposed. The electricity prices are not dictated by an authority (power grid operator), but they can fluctuate according to supply and demand, and the electricity produced locally can be traded locally within the microgrid.
- The trading platform is blockchain based and it is implemented using smart contracts that provide all the functionalities necessary for user registration and trading activities. The source code of the smart contracts is made publicly available.

- A user-friendly interface that facilitates user interaction with the blockchain is developed. It servers as an entry point for the trading platform and makes calls to the smart contracts intuitive and easy to use. The source code of the trading platform interface is made publicly available.
- The energy-efficiency of the employed blockchain is addressed. In order to solve the problem of high energy consumption, which characterizes certain public blockchains, traditional Proof-of-Work consensus protocol is replaced with the one that allows two types of resources: energy and memory. In addition, since the prevalent mode of blockchain network organization are so call mining pools, the behaviour and certain optimizations regarding utility functions of the pool entities are analyzed.

The remainder of the paper is organized as follows. The model of the proposed infrastructure for blockchain-based energy trading is given in Sect. 2. Section 3 contains implementation details about the blockchain platform and the smart contracts for electricity trading. The developed user interface that facilitates access to the smart contracts and blockchain is described in Sect. 4. Section 5 addresses the energy-efficiency of the blockchain consensus protocol, discusses the roles of the actors in the blockchain network, and analyzes some optimization strategies of the actors. Conclusions are given in Sect. 6.

## 2 Framework for Energy Trading

Smart grid is an advanced transformation of a traditional electrical grid. It is a cyber-physical system that can efficiently integrate the activities of all participants (producers, consumers and prosumers) and ensure sustainable and economically efficient electricity system with low losses, high quality and supply security and safety [15]. Smart grid encompasses advanced technologies in order to monitor and control electricity and data flows. Microgrid is an important part of the smart grid concept. It contains almost all of components of the main grid, but in smaller scale [16]. Microgrids can operate autonomously in island-mode or connected and synchronized with the main grid [17]. The role of microgrids in energy systems become increasingly important. Microgrids support local generation and consumption of energy, thus reducing transmission and distribution losses [18]. In addition, microgrids facilitate the integration of renewable energy sources [19]. Microgrids can also improve security and resilience of the network, and provide ancillary services that facilitate the continuous energy flow in the system.

The natural next step in the evolution of power grids becomes the transition from the centralized model to a decentralized one. The centralized model is not the most fitted to deal with energy management, control and trading among distributed providers, consumers and prosumers. Monopoly of electricity prices that exist in the centralized model goes against the principles of a distributed market. An important role of smart grids is to support prosumers, which are both energy consumers and providers. In the centralized model, prosumers do not have the adequate access to the energy market due to a privileged role of the institutionalized, large-scale providers. The feed-in tariffs and similar incentives often do not apply for selling energy surplus back to the energy grid. This surplus is then usually sold to companies at lower prices and they sell it back at regular prices. Direct energy trading, without intermediaries, brings the potential for energy cost savings. This further promotes local generation of renewable energy. Prosumers can benefit from their investment while profits and value remain within the microgrid and local community [20].

Figure 1 shows a bird-view of the proposed blockchain-based infrastructure for electricity trading within a microgrid.

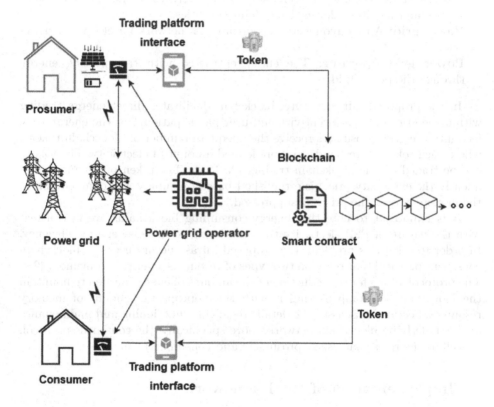

**Fig. 1.** Model for a blockchain-based electricity trading within a microgrid

The main components of the infrastructure are:

- **Consumer:** Users that are consuming the energy delivered through the power grid.
- **Prosumer:** Users that consume the energy and have capabilities to produce it, usually from renewable energy sources. The energy that prosumers generate is usually for their needs, but it can happen that they produce more that they can use, so they can feed the energy to the power grid.

- **Smart meters:** Digital devices that track all energy transfers between the consumers/prosumers and the power grid. The smart meters are registered to the blockchain network so that their owners (consumers/prosumers) can participate in energy trading.
- **Blockchain:** The underlying system for decentralized electricity trading. The blockchain hosts smart contracts that implement the functionalities necessary for smart meter registration, electricity token issuance, and trading. In addition, all trading records are stored in the blockchain in the form of blockchain transactions.
- **Trading platform interface:** GUI that facilitates access to the blockchain and the smart contracts. It enables users to create offers, buy electricity tokens, and monitor relevant blockchain activities.
- **Power grid:** An interconnected cyber-physical network for electricity delivery.
- **Power grid operator:** The entity entrusted with transporting energy through the power grid.

In the proposed infrastructure, blockchain facilitates direct energy trading within the grid and can incentivize end-user participation. For the energy they feed into the grid, prosumers receive the adequate number of blockchain tokens, where each token corresponds to a predefined amount of electricity. The tokens can be traded on the blockchain trading platform. The token price, and consequently the electricity price, is established based on supply and demand. Thus, the monopoly over the prices is suppressed.

It is important to note that energy-consuming blockchains are in contrast with the nature of P2P electricity trading aiming to increase energy efficiency. In order to solve this problem, the proposed infrastructure uses the blockchain consensus protocol that relies on two types of resources, energy and memory [28]. The protocol allows for the reduction of the amount of energy needed to maintain the blockchain by compensating it with the appropriate amount of memory resources. Section 5 discusses the details regarding functioning and maintenance of the underlying blockchain network, more specifically, the consensus protocol, as well as the roles that users (prosumers and consumers) can take.

## 3 Implementation of the Framework

### 3.1 Ethereum Blockchain Platform

Ethereum blockchain [21] was the first blockchain platform to support the creation and utilization of smart contracts, enabling the development of decentralized applications. This novel approach led to Ethereum becoming one of the most popular and enduring blockchain platforms. Ethereum remains an open and permissionless system, welcoming participation from anyone. Nevertheless, it's worth noting that one can also establish a private blockchain based on Ethereum, allowing it to operate in a permissioned manner when needed.

Within the Ethereum platform, each block consists of two main parts: the header and the body [22]. The block's body contains various crucial information regarding the transactions that are in the block. On the other hand, the header of the block contains several essential data fields used to execute the consensus protocol and maintain the security, immutability, and trustworthiness of the blockchain. One of the most noteworthy fields in the header is *ParentHash*, which holds the hash value of the preceding block in the chain. This plays a vital role in ensuring the immutability of the blockchain, as any attempt to modify a block would require modifying all the preceding blocks as well.

The consensus protocol is the primary mechanism that enables blockchain to function without the need for a trusted third party while ensuring the platform's consistency and security. Additionally, the consensus protocol establishes trust among the platform's users. Every miner who publishes a new block must execute the consensus protocol specific to that block. Typically, this protocol involves solving a challenging cryptographic puzzle, with the hash of the newly formed block as an input. Solving the puzzle requires a substantial amount of resources. The most well-known consensus protocol is Proof-of-Work, which relies on computational power as the required resource. However, there are other diverse protocols that utilize different resources such as memory, cryptocurrency, or even computational power for solving real-life problems [23].

In 2022, the official Ethereum platform successfully transitioned to the Proof-of-Stake consensus protocol, which is well-suited for large, established networks [24]. However, the latest implementation of Ethereum, known as *go-ethereum* and developed in the Go language, is designed in a modular manner that allows for the implementation of various new consensus protocols [25].

Another notable feature of the Ethereum platform that renders it adaptable for different applications is its support for smart contracts. These smart contracts represent computer programs executed on the Ethereum platform in a decentralized and distributed manner. They serve as the foundation for implementing decentralized applications based on blockchain systems [26].

## 3.2   Smart Contracts for Electricity Trading

The proposed infrastructure for decentralized electricity trading is based on the Ethereum's smart contract functionality. Through the utilization of the Solidity programming language, we have implemented two distinct smart contracts, which facilitate the realization of the intended decentralized energy platform. These two contracts, namely, *TokenDispenser* and *Trading*[1] are deployed by the Power grid operator.

The *TokenDispenser* contract encompasses functionalities for the prosumer registration within the trading platform. Additionally, it includes a set of methods that are specifically utilized by the prosumers' smart meters. These methods

---

[1] The source can be found at https://github.com/BSolutionsltd/BC4GRID/tree/main/smart-contracts.

are employed when prosumers generate electricity for the grid or receive electricity from it. Upon transmitting electricity to the grid, prosumers are rewarded with ERC20 [27] tokens, which serve as tangible evidence of the quantity of electricity that has been contributed. These ERC20 tokens are subsequently eligible for trading through the *Trading* contract. Furthermore, prosumers also have the option to exchange these tokens for additional electricity from the grid. The *TokenDispenser* contract incorporates the following methods:

– `RegisterSmartMeter`: This function allows registration of smart meters using their respective Ethereum addresses. After a successful registration, users gain access to the trading platform. It is important to emphasize that only the Power grid operator has the authority to register smart meters.
– `UnregisterSmartMeter`: Through this method, users can unregister their smart meters. Once completed, the user's access to the platform is revoked.
– `SendEnergy`: Smart meters associated with users utilize this method when transmitting electricity to the grid. As a result of this transmission, users are rewarded with freshly generated ERC20 tokens, which symbolize the amount of electricity sent.
– `ReceiveEnergy`: Whenever a user seeks to exchange their owned tokens for additional electricity from the grid, this function comes into play. The tokens spent in this exchange process are subsequently removed from circulation.

The *Trading* contract enables users to engage in the buying and selling of ERC20 tokens, that represent electricity units. Users aiming to sell tokens can create offers by specifying the token quantity, price, and offer's expiration time. Existing offers can also be modified. This contract enables users to view active offers, facilitating informed decisions on token purchases. Users are not obligated to purchase the full token quantity from an offer; instead, they can acquire the desired amount. Additionally, the *Trading* contract emits events indicating the creation of new offers, modifications to existing offers, and the conclusion of offers due to expiration. This contract's functionalities provide a mechanism for users to transact tokens representing actual electrical electricity within a decentralized context. The *Trading* contract implements the following methods:

– `CreateEnergyOffer`: Users intending to sell their ERC20 tokens can utilize this method to initiate an offer. This involves specifying the token quantity for sale, the corresponding price, and the offer's deadline. The method executes the transfer of the stipulated token quantity to the Trading smart contract to enable subsequent sales. Additionally, the created offer is recorded within the contract, and the emission of the `OfferCreated` event signifies its initiation.
– `BuyEnergyFromOffer`: This method allows users to purchase a defined quantity of tokens from a specific offer. Users provide the offer's identification, the desired token quantity, and the appropriate amount of the native cryptocurrency designated for payment. The method implements the transfer of the specified token quantity to the buyer and the corresponding cryptocurrency amount to the offer's seller. Furthermore, if tokens are still available for sale within the offer, the `OfferModified` event is triggered. Conversely, if

the offer's token inventory is depleted, the `OfferClosed` event is emitted to signal its completion.

- `ModifyOffer`: This method empowers users to adjust a previously created offer. By providing new values for the token quantity, token price, or offer deadline, users can refine the terms of their offer. This modification triggers an update to the offer, and as a result, the emission of the `OfferModified` event conveys the successful alteration. This functionality enhances user flexibility and responsiveness within the trading process.
- `RetrieveTokens`: This method enables users to reclaim the tokens from their expired offers that have not been sold. This action promotes a streamlined approach to managing unfulfilled offers, ensuring that users can readily reclaim their tokens when a transaction does not occur within the designated timeframe.
- `ListOffers`: This function provides a list of the IDs for all active offers within the system. Users can refer to this list to identify and select offers from which to purchase tokens.
- `GetOfferDetails`: This method retrieves comprehensive information about a specific offer using its ID. Details include the seller's address, the token quantity in the offer, the token price, and the offer's expiration deadline.

# 4   Monitoring of the Energy Trading

Our energy trading monitoring system is designed as a web service that uses the web3.js API to interact with the Ethereum Blockchain with user and administrator portals. This application seamlessly connects to the blockchain and provides access to the smart contract responsible for blockchain transactions and recording transaction data. Variables such as the electricity price are configured in a standard-compliant manner. The web application provides the functionality outlined in Fig. 2 and allows users to both generate and sell electricity (in the role of a producer) and buy and consume tokens (in the role of a consumer).

Smart meter data on electricity consumption and production is collected in a monitoring database used exclusively by the monitoring system to store user input data, while transaction data (smart contracts, tokens, etc.) is stored in a decentralized repository based on the blockchain technology implemented in the Etherium platform. We provide functionalities with two main roles: **administrator** and **prosumer**. The administrator role is used for system configuration, user account management, smart contract monitoring, security, and compliance. Administrators are responsible for configuring user account settings and restrictions, application settings, blockchain integration, and standards. User account management includes creating, modifying, and deleting user accounts, granting and revoking permissions, and security management. Administrators manage the deployment and maintenance of smart contracts for power transactions.

The prosumer role, on the other hand, allows prosumers to access their user profile, producer information, power purchases, surplus power sales, transaction history, and account statistics. The user profile includes personal

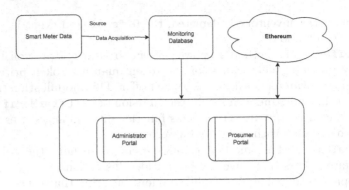

**Fig. 2.** Monitoring System architecture

information, address, and account balance. This balance is divided into two categories: remaining energy in kilowatt hours (kWh) and the corresponding currency. Transactions are processed in kWh and tokens. If the user produces energy, the prosumer role allows access to details about his energy production facilities. For example, the interface can display the number of active solar panels and their daily output. The two main functions of the prosumer role are buying electricity (Fig. 3a) and selling surplus electricity (Fig. 3b). The platform will allow consumers to buy electricity through this application. They can buy electricity from a centralized (government) power source or from specific producers and prosumers on the open market. The platform will display available market offers and allow users to place purchase orders at existing prices or create their own purchase offers. Since users can also be producers of electrical energy, our platform allows them to create offers for all the energy they do not consume and sell it on the open market. Other features of the prosumer role include an overview of the user's transaction history (Fig. 4a) and user statistics (Fig. 4b). This includes information such as daily consumption, daily production (if the user is also a producer), and other relevant account-related data.

## 5   Optional Consensus Protocol and Pool Mining

### 5.1   Summary of the Approach

Recently, an alternative approach to the traditional ones and the related pool mining have been reported and considered in [28–31].

We consider the following pool mining approach reported in [30]. Note that the considered architecture and the employed consensus protocol require two types of resources: energy and memory. The pool mining system consists of two entities: Pool Manager (PM) and pool miners. PM possess computational and memory resources. Computational resources of PM are for PM's evaluations and memory resources are for renting to the pool miners. Memory resources of PM contain certain in advances specified tables. Computational and memory

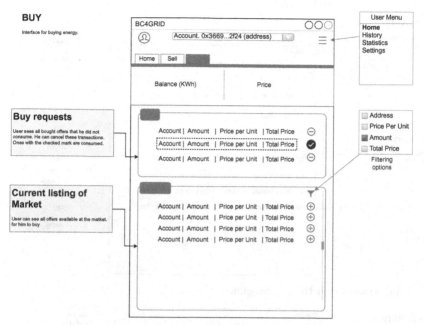

**BUY**

Interface for buying energy.

**Buy requests**

User sees all bought offers that he did not consume. He can cancel these transactions. Ones with the checked mark are consumed.

**Current listing of Market**

User can see all offers available at the market. for him to buy

(a) Buy Mockup: Electricity Purchase

**SELL**

Interface to sell energy.

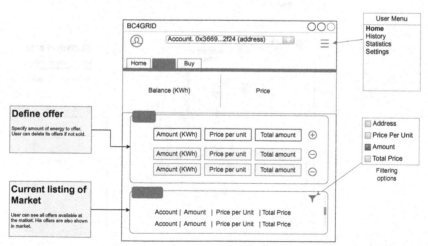

**Define offer**

Specify amount of energy to offer. User can delete its offers if not sold.

**Current listing of Market**

User can see all offers available at the market. His offers are also shown in market.

(b) Sell Mockup: Selling Excess Power

**Fig. 3.** Mockups of the Buy and Sell screens.

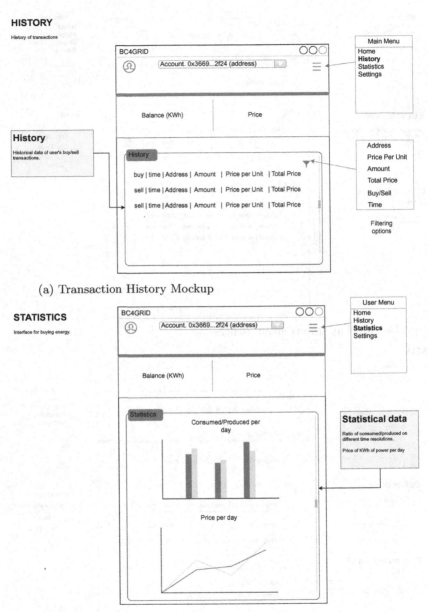

(a) Transaction History Mockup

(b) User Statistics Mockup

**Fig. 4.** Mockups of the Buy and Sell screens.

resources of PM could be considered as PM cloud. PM communicates with the pool miners through the dedicated gate. Main role of the pool miners is to perform certain evaluations required for solving the consensus protocol puzzle and considered pool mining setting assumes that only PM could complete puzzle solving. Accordingly, pool miners require only computational resources but, as the pool mining participants, they also should support PM by renting non overlapping parts memory resources of PM. The design setting assumes that certain miners could have own tables in order to perform malicious activities.

A mining pool is formed and initialized during the registration phase, when the pool manager registers all miners interested in joining and contributing their mining work to the pool. In this phase, each miner declares the size of the subtable he supports, i.e. rents it from the pool manager, and gets informed about the reward for pool mining contribution. The architectural framework is given in Fig. 5.

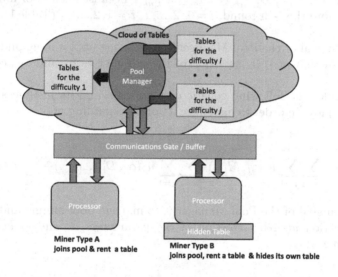

**Fig. 5.** Pool mining architectural framework, [30].

### 5.2 A Framework for the Strategies of the Blockchain Pool Manager and Miners

**An Optimized Strategy of the Pool Manager. Assumption 1.** Before beginning each mining round, the Pool Manager knows:
(i) $a_t$, because it is known when the mining block is given,
(ii) an upper bound on $E_t^{(PM)}$, because it is under control of PM,

**Table 1.** Notation

| | |
|---|---|
| $a_t$ | an award that the Pool Manager receives for inclusion of a block in the $t$-th mining round |
| $D_t^{(i)}$ | number of candidates submitted to the Pool Manager by the $i$-th miner in the $t$-th mining round |
| $M_t^{(i)}$ | the memory rented from the Pool Manager by the miner $i$ in the $t$-th mining round |
| $E_t^{(PM)}$ | energy spent by Pool Manager in the $t$-th mining round |
| $\alpha_t$ | the award rate granted by the Pool Manager in the $t$-th mining round |
| $\beta_t$ | the energy cost rate in the $t$-th mining round |
| $\gamma_t$ | the memory cost rate rented from the Pool Manager by a miner in the $t$-th mining round |
| $I$ | number of miners in the mining pool |
| $T$ | number of the mining rounds |

(iii) the range of $M_t^{(i)}$, $M_{t,min}^{(i)} \leq M_t^{(i)} \leq M_{t,max}^{(i)}$ because each pool miner should declare it before the $t$-th round, $i = 1, 2, ..., I$, $t = 1, 2, ..., T$.

(iv) the range of $D_t^{(i)}$, $D_{t,min}^{(i)} \leq D_t^{(i)} \leq D_{t,max}^{(i)}$ because each pool miner should declare it before the $t$-th round, $i = 1, 2, ..., I$, $t = 1, 2, ..., T$ (Table 1).

The main goal of the Pool Manager is to manage pool mining and maximize its utility function $u(\cdot)$, by selection of the parameters $\alpha_t$ and $\gamma_t$ according to Assumption 1.

We consider the following generic cost function and its instances that Pool Manager employs in order to maximize its profit regarding operation of the pool.

$$u(\cdot) = \sum_{t=1}^{T} a_t + \sum_{i=1}^{I} \sum_{t=1}^{T} u_1(\gamma_t, M_t^{(i)}) - \sum_{i=1}^{I} \sum_{t=1}^{T} u_2(\alpha_t, D_t^{(i)}, M_t^{(i)}) - \sum_{t=1}^{T} u_3(\beta_t, E_t^{(PM)})$$

(1)

The main goal of the Pool Manager is to manage pool mining and maximize its cost function $u(\cdot)$, by selection of the parameters $\alpha_t$ and $\gamma_t$ according to Assumption 1.

## Optimization Scenario

- According to Assumptions 2 and 3, the Pool Manager optimizes $\alpha_t$ and $\gamma_t$ in order to maximize the utility function $u(\cdot)$, before beginning of each mining round $t = 1, 2, ..., T$.
- According to the obtained $\alpha_t$ and $\gamma_t$, each miner $i$, optimizes $M_t^{(i)}$ and $E_t^{(i)}$ to be employed in the $t$-th mining round, $t = 1, 2, ..., T$, $i = 1, 2, ..., I$.

**Table 2.** Additional Notation.

| $E_t^{(i,sell)}$ | the energy a prosumer $i$ sells in the $t$-th mining round |
|---|---|
| $E_t^{(i,purchase)}$ | the energy a prosumer $i$ purchase in the $t$-th mining round |
| $E_t^{(i)}$ | the mining energy employed by the miner $i$ in the $t$-th mining round |
| $c$ | energy spending rate to obtain $D_t^{(i)}$ data employing $E_t^{(i)}$ |

**An Optimized Strategy of the Prosumer.** We consider the following generic cost function of a pool miner and its instantiates.

$$f^{(i)}(\cdot) = \sum_{t=1}^{T} f_1(\beta_t, E_t^{(i,sell)}) - \sum_{t=1}^{T} f_2(\beta_t, E_t^{(i,purchase)}) +$$
$$\sum_{t=1}^{T} f_3(\alpha_t, D_t^{(i)}, M_t^{(i)}) - \sum_{t=1}^{T} f_4(\beta_t, E_t^{(i)}) - \sum_{t=1}^{T} f_5(\gamma_t, M_t^{(i)})$$

(2)

where

$$D_t^{(i)} = cE_t^{(i)} \ , \ t = 1, 2, ..., T .$$

The parameters $c, \alpha_t, \beta_t, \gamma_t$ in the basic consideration can be considered as independent from the variables $E_t^{(i,sell)}$, $E_t^{(i)}, M_t^{(i)}$, $t = 1, 2, ..., T$.

**Optimization Goal.** In the basic setting, the utility function $f^{(i)}$ should be maximized by selection of $E_t^{(i,sell)}$, $E_t^{(i,purchase)}$ $E_t^{(i)}$ and $M_t^{(i)}$ for the given $c, \alpha_t, \beta_t, \gamma_t$, $t = 1, 2, ..., T$ (Table 2).

# 6   Conclusions

This paper presents implementation details of a novel blockchain-based platform for electricity trading. Energy efficiency of the proposed solution is achieved through an advanced blockchain consensus protocol, that allows a trade-off between energy and memory resources necessary for blockchain maintenance. Theoretical analysis of different working strategies for the participants and the corresponding utility functions are given. All the primary functionalities of the trading system, necessary for user registration, electricity token issuance based on the amount of electricity fed into the grid, management of trading offers, etc. have been implemented. Source code of the smart contracts, which provide the aforementioned functionalities, is made publicly available. In addition, access to the trading platform is enabled via user interface developed to assist smooth interaction with the implemented functionalities.

# References

1. Nakamoto, S.: Bitcoin: A Peer-to-Peer Electronic Cash System (2008). https://bitcoin.org/bitcoin.pdf
2. Queiroz, M.M., Telles, R., Bonilla, S.H.: Blockchain and supply chain management integration: a systematic review of the literature. Surg. Endosc. Other Interv. Tech. **25**(2), 241–254 (2020). https://doi.org/10.1108/SCM-03-2018-0143
3. Risso, L.A., Ganga, G.M.D., Godinho Filho, M., de Santa-Eulalia, L.A., Chikhi, T., Mosconi, E.: Present and future perspectives of blockchain in supply chain management: a review of reviews and research agenda. Comput. Ind. Eng., 109195 (2023)
4. Nour, M., Chaves-Ávila, J.P., Sánchez-Miralles, Á.: Review of blockchain potential applications in the electricity sector and challenges for large scale adoption. IEEE Access **10**, 47384–47418 (2022). https://doi.org/10.1109/ACCESS.2022.3171227
5. Uddin, S.S., et al.: Next-generation blockchain enabled smart grid: conceptual framework, key technologies and industry practices review. Energy AI, 100228 (2023)
6. Attaran, M.: Blockchain technology in healthcare: challenges and opportunities. Int. J. Healthcare Manag. **15**(1), 70–83 (2022). https://doi.org/10.1080/20479700.2020.1843887
7. Saeed, H., et al.: Blockchain technology in healthcare: a systematic review. PLoS ONE **17**(4) (2022). https://doi.org/10.1371/journal.pone.0266462
8. Mahajan, H.B.: Integration of healthcare 4.0 and blockchain into secure cloud-based electronic health records systems. Appl. Nanosci. (2022). https://doi.org/10.1007/s13204-021-02164-0
9. Kugler, L.: Non-fungible tokens and the future of art. Commun. ACM **64**(9), 19–20 (2021). https://doi.org/10.1145/3474355
10. Chen, Y., Lu, Y., Bulysheva, L., Kataev, M.Y.: Applications of blockchain in industry 4.0: a review. Inf. Syst. Front. (2022). https://doi.org/10.1007/s10796-022-10248-7
11. Huang, J., He, D., Obaidat, M.S., Vijayakumar, P., Luo, M., Choo, K.K.R.: The application of the blockchain technology in voting systems: a review. ACM Comput. Surv. **54**(3) (2021). https://doi.org/10.1145/3439725
12. Mengelkamp, E., Gärttner, J., Rock, K., Kessler, S., Orsini, L., Weinhardt, C.: Designing microgrid energy markets: a case study: The Brooklyn Microgrid. Appl. Energy **210**, 870–880 (2018)
13. PowerLedger: Whitepaper (2019). https://assets.website-files.com/612e1d86b8aa434030a7da5c/612e1d86b8aa434027a7dd6d_power-ledger-whitepaper.pdf
14. Suncontract: Whitepaper (2017). https://suncontract.org/wp-content/uploads/2020/12/whitepaper.pdf
15. EU Commission Task Force for Smart Grids - Expert Group 1: Functionalities of smart grids and smart meter (2010)
16. Yoldaş, Y., Önen, A., Muyeen, S.M., Vasilakos, A.V., Alan, I.: Enhancing smart grid with microgrids: challenges and opportunities. Renew. Sustain. Energy Rev. **72**, 205–214 (2017). https://doi.org/10.1016/j.rser.2017.01.064
17. Marnay, C., el al.: Microgrid evolution roadmap. In: Proceedings of the 2015 International Symposium on Smart Electric Distribution Systems and Technologies (EDST), pp. 139–44. IEEE (2015)

18. Kamel, R.M., Chaouachi, A., Nagasaka, K.: Carbon emissions reduction and power losses saving besides voltage profiles improvement using microgrids. Low Carbon Econ. **1**(1), 1 (2010)
19. Mihaylov, M., et al.: SCANERGY: a scalable and modular system for energy trading between prosumers. In: Proceedings of the 2015 International Conference on Autonomous Agents and Multiagent Systems, IFAAMAS, pp. 1917–18 (2015)
20. Guoa, Y., Wanb, Z., Cheng, X.: When blockchain meets smart grids: a comprehensive survey. High-Confidence Comput. **2**(2), 100059 (2022)
21. Ethereum Whitepaper. https://ethereum.org/en/whitepaper/. Accessed 20 Sept 2023
22. Wood, G.: Ethereum: a secure decentralised generalised transaction ledger berlin version 2BCDB2D, 25 August 2023. https://ethereum.github.io/yellowpaper/paper.pdf. Accessed 18 Sept 2023
23. Bamakan, S.M.H., Motavali, A., Bondarti, A.B.: A survey of blockchain consensus algorithms performance evaluation criteria. Expert Syst. Appl. **154**, 113385 (2020)
24. Proof-of-Stake (POS). https://ethereum.org/en/developers/docs/consensus-mechanisms/pos/. Accessed 18 Sept 2023
25. go-ethereum: official go implementation of the Ethereum protocol. https://geth.ethereum.org/. Accessed 18 Sept 2023
26. Metcalfe, W.: Ethereum, smart contracts, dApps. In: Yano, M., Dai, C., Masuda, K., Kishimoto, Y. (eds.) Blockchain and Crypto Currency. ELIAP, pp. 77–93. Springer, Singapore (2020). https://doi.org/10.1007/978-981-15-3376-1_5
27. ERC-20 Token Standard. https://ethereum.org/en/developers/docs/standards/tokens/erc-20/. Accessed 19 Sept 2023
28. Mihaljević, M.J.: A blockchain consensus protocol based on dedicated time-memory-data trade-off. IEEE Access **8**, 141258–141268 (2020)
29. Mihaljević, M.J., Wang, L., Xu, S., Todorović, M.: An approach for blockchain pool mining employing the consensus protocol robust against block withholding and selfish mining attacks. Symmetry **14**(8), 1711, 28 (2022)
30. Mihaljević, M.J., Todorović, M., Knežević, M.: An evaluation of power consumption gain and security of flexible green pool mining in public blockchain systems. Symmetry **15**, 924 (2023). https://doi.org/10.3390/sym15040924
31. Mihaljević, M.J., Knežević, M., Urošević, D., Wang, L., Xu, S.: An approach for blockchain and symmetric keys broadcast encryption based access control in IoT. Symmetry **15**, 299 (2023). https://doi.org/10.3390/sym15020299

# Resource Cooperative Scheduling Optimization Considering Security in Edge Mobile Networks

Cheng Fang[1,3], Peng Yang[1,2(✉)] (iD), Meng Yi[1,2] (iD), Miao Du[1,2] (iD), and Bing Li[1,2] (iD)

[1] Key Laboratory of Computer Network and Information Integration, Southeast University, Ministry of Education, Nanjing, China
pengyang@seu.edu.cn
[2] School of Computer Science and Engineering, Southeast University, Nanjing, China
[3] School of Cyber Science and Engineering, Southeast University, Nanjing, China

**Abstract.** With the rapid development of technologies such as the Internet of Things and artificial intelligence, the contradiction between limited user computing resources and real-time, fast, and safe processing of large amounts of data has become an urgent issue. The emergence of edge computing provides IoT applications with a low-latency, high-bandwidth, and high-performance computing service. Due to the complexity and dynamics of the edge computing environment itself, and the limited resources of the terminal, the security issue of resource collaborative scheduling in the edge mobile network has become an important research topic. Different from existing work, this paper proposes an efficient and secure multi-user resource cooperative scheduling model, which comprehensively considers resource allocation, task offloading, QoE requirements, and data security. In the model, ChaCha20 encryption technology is introduced as a security mechanism to prevent data from being maliciously stolen by attackers during the offloading process, and computing speed is used as an indicator to quantify QoE requirements. A resource collaborative scheduling algorithm that integrates security mechanisms and computing acceleration is also proposed to minimize the total cost of optimizing the edge computing system. Finally, the effectiveness and superiority of the model and algorithm are verified by simulation experiments.

**Keywords:** Edge Computing · Edge Mobile Network · Resource Collaborative Scheduling · Security Mechanism · Computing Acceleration

## 1 Introduction

In recent years, with the support of mobile Internet, especially 5G technology, the Internet of Things (IoT) has developed rapidly. Various applications of production and life, i.e., self-driving cars, drone flight, Virtual Reality/Augmented Reality (VR/AR), and mobile healthcare are emerging. The novel scenarios require not only very low and deterministic network latency, but also massive, heterogeneous, and diverse data access. The centralized computing and processing model of traditional cloud computing faces tremendous computational and network pressure and cannot meet the demands of the

Internet of Everything [1]. In this context, the edge computing system becomes an effective solution [2]. In edge computing, to better support high-density, high-bandwidth, and low-latency service scenarios, an effective way is to build a service platform (edge data center) on the network edge close to users, providing storage, computation, and network resources, as well as sinking some critical services to the edge of the access network so as to reduce the loss of bandwidth and latency caused by network transmission and multi-level forwarding [3]. Figure 1 illustrates the edge computing paradigm.

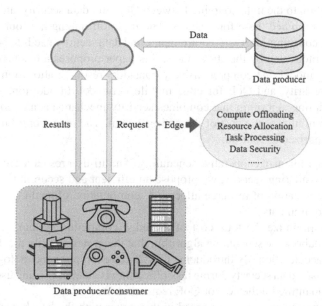

**Fig. 1.** Edge computing paradigm.

In edge computing, static end devices (e.g., sensors in smart homes, cameras in public places), and dynamic end devices (e.g., drones and vehicles) are involved in this environment, which give a challenge for resource management [4]. Suppose resource scheduling does not efficiently utilize dispersed resources. In that case, it can lead to under-utilization of the actual available resources, which in turn leads to as high latency and high energy consumption. In contrast, if an efficient resource scheduling strategy is applied, resources can be efficiently combined to create available and cost-effective pools of computational resources, thus optimizing the resource management problem [5]. Considering the importance of resource scheduling, several studies seek to optimize the weighted sum of latency and energy consumption in edge computing systems and try to find the trade-off replacement relationship between them. However, in practical scenarios, in addition to latency and energy consumption, the resource scheduling process focuses on some factors such as user quality of experience (QoE) and data security. Currently, more and more users start to pay attention to their subjective feelings, and their QoE demand is sensitive, while the requirement of low latency cannot completely cover the QoE demand of users, so this motivates us to focus on QoE in the process of resource scheduling. In addition, QoE requirements are closely related to data security, as attackers can easily insert interference factors into unencrypted task data so as to achieve a good user experience, and wireless interference between mobile users can also inadvertently reduce user QoE metrics due to the shared wireless channels while encrypting task data can ensure data integrity. Therefore, it is necessary to consider the element of data security along with QoE. Currently, although some works [6, 7] have focused on the four factors of latency, energy consumption, QoE, and data security, most of the studies have jointly analyzed two or three of these factors and they have not paid sufficient attention to the tight coupling between QoE and data security, and the studies have not well combined these four factors. The trade-off among the four factors, i.e., latency, energy consumption, QoE requirements, and data security needs to be addressed.

Therefore, motivated by the above facts, this paper proposes a resource collaborative scheduling model that comprehensively considers resource allocation, computing offload, data security, and QoE for edge mobile networks. In addition, we design a resource scheduling algorithm that combines security mechanisms and computational acceleration to minimize the cost of the entire system. The main contributions of this study are summarized as follows:

- To solve the problem of cooperative scheduling of multi-user resources in edge mobile networks considering security, we propose an efficient and secure integrated model for joint optimization of resource allocation, computation offloading, data security, and QoE requirements.
- In order to minimize the total cost of the edge computing system, we propose a resource collaborative scheduling algorithm that integrates security mechanisms and computing acceleration. By introducing ChaCha20 encryption technology as a security mechanism, data security during task offloading is guaranteed, and use computing speed as a quantified indicator for QoE requirements.
- By comparing the algorithm proposed in this paper with the benchmark algorithm, the proposed algorithm is evaluated from multiple perspectives such as energy consumption, latency, security decision, task offload rate, and QoE. Simulation results prove the validity and superiority of the proposed algorithm.

The rest of this paper is organized as follows, with related work given in Sect. 2. Section 3 describes the system integration model of this paper in terms of resource allocation, computation offloading, data security, and QoE. The problem formulation is given in Sect. 4 for the problem to be solved. In Sect. 5, the algorithm design is given in this paper. In Sect. 6, simulation experiments are performed to demonstrate the effectiveness of the proposed model and algorithms. Finally, Sect. 7 concludes the whole paper.

## 2   Related Work

In this section, we first present some related work with different objectives and point out their shortcomings. Then, we give the motivation for the research in this paper.

## 2.1 Latency or Energy Consumption

Guo *et al.* [8] formulated a task offloading and computational resource scheduling problem as an energy consumption minimization problem. They used DVFS [9] technique to directly reduce energy consumption via adjusting the processor frequency. Also, to achieve the goal of low-energy offloading, they proposed a distributed dynamic offloading and computational resource scheduling algorithm. However, they only considered the energy consumption reduction by tuning the processor frequency without considering the QoE requirements of user. Deng *et al.* [10] study the offloading problem in the framework of green and sustainable mobile edge computing in IoT systems. To minimize the overall system response time, they used the Lyapunov technique to decompose the formulation problem into a convex optimization problem, then proposed a dynamic parallel computational offloading and energy management algorithm (DPCOEM). Finally, the near-optimal solution of the algorithm is also implemented [11]. However, the solution complexity of convex optimization problems is often high, and the practicality in realistic scenarios is poor.

## 2.2 Latency or Energy Consumption

Lu *et al.* [12] started their analysis from a simple case and extended it to the complex cases afterward, where they modelled the multi-user resource allocation problem in edge computing and use an approximation algorithm for local search to solve the NP, achieving the goal of minimizing the cost. However, the approximation algorithm they used easily falls into a local optimum and cannot guarantee the performance of the solution. Li *et al.* [13] proposed a game-theoretic scheme to optimize the offloading strategy of joint computing-intensive and bandwidth-intensive resources to minimize the system cost. However, the optimal solution obtained from their proposed scheme may not be the global optimal solution. Meng *et al.* [14] proposed a fault-tolerant dynamic resource scheduling approach using a game-theoretic scheduling mechanism that jointly considers cost and system latency to solve the joint cost-latency problem for mobile edge computing and thus meet the requirement of minimizing the application cost by a user-defined deadline. However, their study of scheduling only under a two-tier architecture instead of a three-tier architecture is less practical. In addition, they ignore the security privacy issues during offloading. The fault tolerance of their scheduling method is greatly reduced and the security risk is elevated when there is a security attack at the edge layer.

## 2.3 QoE

Ning *et al.* [15] studied the intelligent scheduling problem of in-vehicle edge computing, divided the original complex problem into two relatively simple subproblems, and proposed a two-sided matching scheme and a DQN method to schedule vehicle requests meeting the strict QoE requirements of mobile smart vehicles. However, both of the above studies require huge parameters and a long learning time, which makes it difficult to balance the delay, energy consumption, and QoE requirements. In addition, both studies are a black-box process, which poses significant security risks [16]. Guo and Zhang *et al.* [17] studied the energy-efficient computation offloading management schemes for mobile edge computing systems with small cell networks, combining the advantages of both genetic algorithms and particle swarm optimization algorithms is used to design a suboptimal algorithm to solve the computation offloading problem, that is minimizing the energy consumption of all user devices with consideration of QoE.

## 2.4 Data Security

Slađana Jošilo and György Dán [18] studied the secure offloading decision problem of coordinated wireless devices, they prove the existence of pure policy Nash equilibrium by building a game theoretic model of the problem and propose a polynomial complexity algorithm for computational equilibrium to solve the problem. Ibrahim *et al.* [19] studied the computational offloading and resource allocation problem of mobile edge computing and proposed a multi-user offloading model with data security, using AES [20] encryption as the security layer, and integrated security, computation offloading, and resource allocation to determine the optimal computation offloading decision for all mobile users to minimize the time and energy consumption of the whole system. Zhang *et al.* [21] studied the ARM-based big. LITTLE processor architecture in edge environment [22, 23] for the energy-efficient task offloading problem, they presented the task offloading problem as a computational resource scheduling problem and proposed a computational resource scheduling algorithm (MUCRS) to minimize the time and energy costs by finding the pure policy Nash equilibrium point through a game theoretic model. In order to strengthen the security of transmitted data, Xu et al. [24] proposed a computational offloading method called BeCome that supports blockchain, and uses a non-dominated sorting genetic algorithm to generate a balanced resource allocation strategy.

## 2.5 Motivation

From the given analysis of the existing studies although many different types of solutions have been given for different research objectives, most of the research objectives are too low dimensioned and do not jointly consider the additional impact that QoE, for example, some users who are using latency-sensitive applications are very strict in their QoE requirements in addition to high latency requirements. Latency requirements cannot simply be equated with QoE requirements. It is also observed that while a portion of the work has studied the joint optimization of latency, energy consumption and QoE, the security of the data transmission during offloading has not been adequately considered in these research efforts. This can be fatal in some scenarios, as resource scheduling is meaningless if data security risks occur during the process of resource scheduling in edge computing systems. In addition, some work focuses on jointly optimizing the four aspects of latency, energy consumption, QoE requirements, and data security, unfortunately, the solutions provided by these studies do not weigh the above four factors well, some work fails to tightly couple QoE requirements with data security, while some work gives a compromise solution that sacrifices energy consumption for latency and QoE improvements, which is not suitable for resource-constrained devices.

In summary, focusing on these issues mentioned above, the work in this paper aims to consider resource allocation and computational offloading, and focuses on the tight coupling between QoE and data security in order to minimize the overall cost of edge computing systems and seek a tradeoff between the four aspects of latency, energy consumption, QoE, and data security.

## 3  System Model

This section focuses on the system model used in this study. The architecture of the edge computing system is given in Fig. 2. Specifically, the multi-user task offloading in the mobile edge computing system, where $M = \{1, 2,..., N\}$ is defined as a set of mobile users (MUs) connected to a single Macro Base Station (MBS), and the mobile edge server is located in the MBS. Each mobile user device generates various tasks. For easy reference, some of the notations used in this section are summarized in Table 1.

Usually, we can describe any task $T = \{D, c, \alpha, \gamma, \tau\}$. Thus, we can use $T_i = \{D_i, c_i, \alpha_i, \gamma_i, \tau_i\}$ to represent each MU i-generated task. Where $D_i$ denotes the data size of $T_i$ generated by MU i, $c_i$ denotes the processing density (in CPU cycles/bit) of $T_i$, which may vary and can be obtained by the task analyzer [23, 24]. $\alpha_i$ $(0 \leq \alpha_i \leq 1)$ denotes the parallelizable fraction of $T_i$, which is an important parameter to determine the QoE. Unlike many researches that ignore the return process due to the small values of the processed results [17, 25–27], this paper pays attention to the return process of the results because it focuses on the information carried by the returned values of the results. Denote $\gamma_i$ as the ratio of the data size of the returned result to the initial task data size of $T_i$, and $\tau_i$ as the delay constraint of $T_i$. Denote the wireless bandwidth of the end device assigned to task $T_i$ as B. N MUs are in the edge computing environment, which are associated with a single macro base station and an edge server through a wireless channel. The generated task $T_i$ can be processed locally or offloaded to the edge or cloud for processing. The offloading operation is based on different requirements such as energy consumption, latency, cost, and QoE. $\lambda_i$ $(0 \leq \lambda_i \leq 1)$ is denoted as the offloading decision variable of task $T_i$ generated by MU I, representing the ratio of the offloaded data size to the total data size of task $T_i$. If $\lambda_i = 0$, task $T_i$ may be processed locally; if $\lambda_i = 1$, task $T_i$ can be completely offloaded. Otherwise, $\lambda_i D_i$ is offloaded and $(1 - \lambda_i) D_i$ is processed locally.

### 3.1  Local Computing Model

Task processing in local: the number of CPU cores of different MU i is denoted as $n_i$, the processing power (i.e., CPU frequency in cycles/sec) of each core allocated by MU i for local computation is denoted as $f_i^l$, then the power consumption of each core of user MU i for local processing of data is denoted as,

$$p_i^l = \kappa_1 \left(f_i^l\right)^3. \tag{1}$$

where $\kappa_1$ is a coefficient reflecting the relationship between processing power and power consumption on the user of mobile terminal device [28].The local computation time of task $T_i$ generated by MU i: Based on Amdahl's law [29], The local computation time can

**Table 1.** List of symbols in the system model.

| Notation | Description |
|---|---|
| $M$ | Collection of user devices |
| $N$ | Total number of mobile user (MUs) |
| $i$ | Corresponding i-th MU |
| $T_i$ | Tasks generated by MU i |
| $D_i$ | Size of task data generated by MU i |
| $c_i$ | Processing density of $T_i$ |
| $\alpha_i$ | Parallelizable fraction of $T_i$ |
| $\gamma_i$ | The ratio of the data size of the returned result to the initial task data size of $T_i$ |
| $\tau_i$ | Delay constraint of $T_i$ |
| $\lambda_i$ | Offloading decision variables for MU i-generated task $T_i$ |
| $n_i$ | Number of CPU cores for different MU i |
| $f_i^l$ | The processing power of each core allocated by MU i for local computation |
| $r_i$ | Data transfer rate for offloading data from task Ti to the edge over the wireless communication link |
| $P_i$ | The transmission power of the mobile user device MU i |
| $h_i$ | Channel power gain |
| $\omega_0$ | Channel noise power density |
| $m_i$ | Number of cores allocated by the edge server for processing of tasks generated by different MU i |
| $f_i^e$ | Processing power per core of the edge server assigned to MU i |
| $r_{i'}$ | Data transfer rate during result return |
| $P_0$ | The transmission power of the edge server |
| $A_i^l$ | Local computation speed for task $T_i$ |
| $A_i^e$ | Edge computation speed for task $T_i$ |
| $S_i$ | Binary security decision for each MU i |
| $p_i^l$ | Power consumption per core for user MU i for local data processing |
| $t_i^l$ | Local computation time for MU i |
| $E_i^l$ | Local computation power consumption for MU i |
| $p_i^e$ | Power consumption per core for edge processing data |
| $t_i^e$ | Edge server computation time |
| $E_i^e$ | Edge energy consumption |
| $\beta_i$ | Total number of CPUs required for encryption computation tasks on MU |

*(continued)*

**Table 1.** (*continued*)

| Notation | Description |
|---|---|
| $\eta_i$ | Total number of CPUs required for decryption compute tasks on the edge server |
| $t_i^s$ | Total time for MU i to perform compute offload operations with security decisions |
| $E_i^s$ | Total energy consumption executed by MU i during computing offload operations with security decisions |
| $C_i^l$ | The total cost of MU to perform all tasks locally |
| $C_i^s$ | The total cost of performing all tasks on the edge server |
| $w_i^t$ | Weighted parameter for execution time of MU i decisions |
| $w_i^e$ | Weighted parameters of energy consumption for MU i decisions |

**Fig. 2.** Edge computing system.

be composed of the computation time of the serialized part and the computation time of the parallel part, and the computation time of the serialized part can be expressed as,

$$t_i^{ls} = \frac{c_i(1-\alpha_i)(1-\lambda_i)D_i}{f_i^l}. \tag{2}$$

The computation time of the parallel part can be expressed as,

$$t_i^{lp} = \frac{c_i\alpha_i(1-\lambda_i)D_i}{f_i^l n_i}. \tag{3}$$

From the above, it can be calculated that the local computation time of MU i can be expressed as,

$$t_i^l = t_i^{ls} + t_i^{lp} = \frac{c_i(1 - \lambda_i)D_i}{f_i^l}\left(1 - \alpha_i + \frac{\alpha_i}{n_i}\right). \tag{4}$$

Then the locally calculated energy consumption of MU i: the locally calculated energy consumption equation is,

$$E_i^l = p_i^l t_i^{ls} + n_i p_i^l t_i^{lp} = \kappa_1 c_i D_i (1 - \lambda_i)\left(f_i^l\right)^2. \tag{5}$$

## 3.2 Communication Model

Offloading process: data from task $T_i$ is offloaded to the edge via a wireless communication link. The data transfer rate is denoted it by $r_i$. The data transmission rate can be characterized by a wireless transmission model based on Shannon's formula [25]. $P_i$ is the transmission power of the mobile user device MU I, $h_i$ is the channel power gain, $\omega_0$ is denoted as the channel noise power density.

When data is offloaded from the mobile user device to the edge over a specified wireless bandwidth B, the data transfer rate can be expressed as,

$$r_i = B \log_2 1 + \frac{P_i h_i^2}{\omega_0 B}. \tag{6}$$

Transmission delay: Based on the above analysis, the transmission delay for offloading $\lambda_i D_i$ bit data to the edge can be obtained by,

$$t_i^{off} = \frac{\lambda_i D_i}{r_i}. \tag{7}$$

Energy consumption: the energy consumption of the terminal device transmitting the offloaded $\lambda_i D_i$ bit data is expressed as,

$$\begin{aligned} E_i^{off} &= P_i t_i^{off} \\ &= \frac{\lambda_i D_i P_i}{r_i}. \end{aligned} \tag{8}$$

Computation time in edge: $\lambda_i D_i$ bits of data are offloaded to the edge after the edge processes the data. $m_i$ is denoted as the number of cores allocated by the edge server for processing tasks generated by different MU i. $f_i^e$ denotes the processing power (CPU frequency in cycles/sec) of each core of the edge server allocated to MU i. In general, the processing power at edge is much larger than the processing power at the local terminal. Therefore, the following comparison equation holds,

$$f_i^e \gg f_i^l. \tag{9}$$

The power consumption of each core processing data at edge can be expressed as,

$$p_i^e = \kappa_2 \left(f_i^e\right)^3. \tag{10}$$

where $\kappa_2$ is a coefficient reflecting the relationship between edge-side processing power and energy consumption The computation time of the offloaded $\lambda_i D_i$ bit data includes the computation time of the serialized part and the computation time of the parallelizable part. The computation time of the serialized part can be expressed as,

$$t_i^{es} = \frac{c_i \lambda_i (1 - \alpha_i) D_i}{f_i^e}. \tag{11}$$

The computation time of the parallel part can be expressed as,

$$t_i^{ep} = \frac{c_i \lambda_i \alpha_i D_i}{f_i^e m_i}. \tag{12}$$

From the above, it can be calculated that the edge calculation time can be expressed as,

$$t_i^e = t_i^{es} + t_i^{ep} = \frac{c_i \lambda_i D_i}{f_i^e} \left( 1 - \alpha_i + \frac{\alpha_i}{m_i} \right). \tag{13}$$

Energy consumption in edge: the formula for calculating the edge energy consumption of data $\lambda_i D_i$ bits is,

$$E_i^e = p_i^e t_i^{es} + m_i p_i^e t_i^{ep} = \kappa_2 c_i \lambda_i D_i \left( f_i^e \right)^2 \tag{14}$$

Result return: After the task $T_i$ is processed, the result can be returned to the mobile terminal device. $r_i'$ is denoted as the data transfer rate during the result return, and $P_0$ is the transfer power of EN. Similar to the offloaded data transfer rate, $r_i'$ can be expressed formally as,

$$r_i' = B \log_2 1 + \frac{P_0 h_i^2}{\omega_0 B}. \tag{15}$$

Transmission delay of result return: Based on the above analysis, the sending delay of $\gamma_i D_i$ bit result return can be expressed as,

$$t_i^{ret} = \frac{\gamma_i D_i}{r_{i'}}. \tag{16}$$

Energy consumption of result return: the EN energy consumption for transmission of the $\gamma_i D_i$ bits of the processing result to the mobile terminal device is expressed as,

$$E_i^{ret} = P_0 t_i^{ret} = \frac{\gamma_i D_i P_0}{r_{i'}}. \tag{17}$$

### 3.3 QoE Model

QoE requirements are a key consideration for mobile user devices before making task offloading decisions, and computation speed can be used to quantify this requirement.

Note that computation speed refers to the speed improvement ratio of processing tasks at the edge compared to local computing.

If the $(1 - \lambda_i)$ $D_i$ bit data of task $T_i$ is computed locally, a speedup $A_i^l$ is obtained, and this speedup can be expressed as,

$$A_i^l = \frac{1}{(1 - \alpha_i) + \frac{\alpha_i}{n_i}}. \tag{18}$$

Similarly, if the task is processed at the edge server, a speedup $A_i^e$ is obtained, which can be expressed as,

$$A_i^e = \frac{1}{(1 - \alpha_i) + \frac{\alpha_i}{m_i}}. \tag{19}$$

## 3.4 Data Security

Data security: In the case of computation offloading, each MU i can send data about the computation tasks to be processed to the edge server via a wireless communication channel. However, these data are prone to data security issues during transmission. Thus, security decisions need to be introduced to protect computing tasks from data security threats. ChaCha20 encryption is a new cryptography technology adopted by Google [30]. It is powerful and especially on ARM platforms with lean instruction set CPUs. ChaCha20 encryption performs three to four times better than AES in the same configuration of cell phones and it is also more adaptable to mobile environments. Compared to AES, the utilization of ChaCha20 encryption as the securing task data reduces the amount of data generated by encryption and decryption. In turn, improving the user experience, reducing waiting time, and indirectly saving battery life.

Denote $S_i \in \{0, 1\}$ as the binary security decision for each MU i, which is made individually by each MU based on the privacy requirements of the application data. $S_i = 0$ means that the mobile terminal device MU i offloads the computational task using no encryption; and $S_i = 1$ means that the mobile terminal device MU i encrypts the computational task and data using ChaCha20 encryption before transmission to the edge server. The edge server further decrypts the data after receiving the task and data, then executes the computational task and sends the processed result back to MU i.

$\beta_i$ and $\eta_i$ are used to denote the total number of CPU cycles required to encrypt and decrypt the data of the computational tasks at the MU and the edge server, respectively. Thus, considering the application of encryption techniques, the additional overhead in terms of time and energy for remote execution of computational tasks on the edge server can be expressed respectively,

$$t_i^{sec} = t_i^{enc} + t_i^{dec} = S_i \lambda_i \left( \frac{\beta_i}{n_i f_i^l} + \frac{\eta_i}{m_i f_i^e} \right), \tag{20}$$

$$E_i^{sec} = n_i p_i^l t_i^{enc} + m_i p_i^e t_i^{dec} = S_i \lambda_i \left( \kappa_1 \left( f_i^l \right)^2 + \kappa_2 \left( f_i^e \right)^2 \right). \tag{21}$$

Given the previous subsection, the communication process, the computational process, and the security model are considered, the total time and energy consumption of the MU i are executed when a security computational offload operation is applied,

$$t_i^s = t_i^{off} + t_i^e + t_i^{ret} + t_i^{sec}, \tag{22}$$

$$E_i^s = E_i^{off} + E_i^e + E_i^{ret} + E_i^{sec}. \tag{23}$$

Based on Eqs. (4), (5), (22), and (23), the total overhead of performing all tasks locally and remotely on the MU and edge servers in terms of execution time and energy consumption can be calculated as follows,

$$C_i^l = w_i^t t_i^l + w_i^e E_i^l, \tag{24}$$

$$C_i^s = w_i^t t_i^s + w_i^e E_i^s. \tag{25}$$

where $w_i^t$ and $w_i^e \in [0,1]$ are denoted as the weighted parameters of execution time and energy consumption of MU i's decision, respectively. When user i is more concerned about the energy consumption of its device than the latency, $w_i^e = 1$ and $w_i^t = 0$; when MU i is executing a latency-sensitive application, the concern is more about the time than the energy consumption, so $w_i^t = 1$ and $w_i^e = 0$. We set different values of $w_i^e$ and $w_i^t$ for different objectives.

## 4 Problem Formulation

In this paper, the joint model of resource allocation, computation offloading, QoE requirements, and data security is formulated as a joint optimization problem in a system with multiple mobile users and a single-edge server. The objective of this paper is to minimize the cost of the entire system, note that cost is defined as a linear combination of latency and energy consumption, data security is defined as a security decision, and QoE requirements are quantified as computational speedup as a priori judgment condition for offloading decisions. Thus, the problem formulation is,

$$min_{\lambda_i} \left[ \sum_{i=1}^{N} \lambda_i C_i^s + \sum_{i=1}^{N} (1 - \lambda_i) C_i^l \right], \forall i \in N \tag{26}$$

$$\begin{aligned}
\text{s.t} \quad &C1 : \left[ \lambda_i E_i^s + (1 - \lambda_i) E_i^l \right] \leq E_i^l, \\
&C2 : \sum_{i=1}^{N} \lambda_i r_i \leq B, \\
&C3 : \sum_{i=1}^{N} \lambda_i r_i \prime \leq B, \\
&C4 : \sum_{i=1}^{N} \lambda_i m_i^{max} f_i^s \leq F, \\
&C5 : \min\{t_i^l, t_i^s\} \leq \tau_i, \\
&C6 : 0 \leq \lambda_i \leq 1, \\
&C7 : 0 \leq \alpha_i \leq 1, \\
&C8 : f_i^e \gg f_i^l, \\
&C9 : S_i \in \{0, 1\}, \\
&C10 : w_i^t \in [0, 1], \\
&C11 : w_i^e \in [0, 1].
\end{aligned}$$

The objective is to minimize the cost of the whole system. The constraint C1 is to limit the total energy consumption of all MUs. Constraint C1 means that the total energy consumption of remote execution is not higher than the total energy consumption of local execution in the process of computation offloading. Constraints C2 and C3 give the bandwidth limitation of the wireless communication channel. Constraint C4 limits the upper of the processing power in edge server. Constraint C5 limits the total execution time to be less than or equal to the latency constraint, ensuring the deadline requirement for task completion. Constraint C6 ensures that the computation offloading decision ranges between 0 and 1. Constraint C7 guarantees that the parallelizable fraction is between 0 and 1. Constraint C8 indicates that the processing capacity of the edge server is larger than the processing capacity of the local endpoint. Constraint C9 indicates that the security decision is a binary offloading decision. Constraint C10 and constraint C11 indicate that the weighted parameters of execution time and energy consumption of MU i decision are in the interval from 0 to 1, respectively.

It can be observed that the problem in Eq. (26) is a mixed-integer linear programming problem where the objective function and all the associated constraints are linear. Therefore, the optimal value of the offloading decision for each MU can be obtained using the branch-and-bound method [31].

## 5    Algorithm Design

The algorithm designed in this paper integrates computational resources, communication resources, task offloading, user QoE requirements, and security decisions to seek a trade-off between four aspects. As shown in Algorithm 1. The algorithm gives a detailed procedure for optimal task offloading for multiple users in edge computing systems. The time complexity of the algorithm is $O(N)$, and N denotes the total number of mobile users. The inputs to the algorithm are the task quintets of all MUs i, the corresponding kernel processing power of all MUs, and the number of additional cycles required for MU task data encryption, while the output of the algorithm is the set of optimal offloading policies corresponding to each of all MUs, and this set can be used as a policy profile.

The algorithm just starts by initializing the offloading decisions of all MUs by assigning them all a value of 0. After a given time slot t, each MU sends a reconnaissance message to the edge server and along with the number of MU self-generated cores for wireless channel transmission and fast MBS processing, the MBS returns the number of CPU cores $m_i$ assigned to MU i. The small reconnaissance packets are ignored at the wireless channel and MBS The delay and energy consumption of the small reconnaissance packet at the wireless channel and MBS are ignored because of its tiny data volume. After obtaining the kernel information of MBS, MU computes the local computation speedup and the edge computation speedup. Only when the edge computation speedup is greater than the local computation speedup, the task offloading make sense, otherwise, the offloading decision should choose local for processing. After that, the transfer rate corresponding to all MU i offloading tasks and the transfer rate of the returned results from MBS is further calculated. Finally, the edge server is used to determine the optimal offloading decision for each MU i. Specifically, the branch-and-bound method (BAB) is used to find the set of optimal offloading decisions $\lambda^*$ in Eq. (26) under the constraints C1 to C11, so as to minimize the cost of the whole system.

---

**Algorithm 1:** A Cooperative Resource Scheduling Algorithm Integrating Security Mechanism and Computing Acceleration

---

**Input:** $T_i = \{D_i, c_i, \alpha_i, \gamma_i, \tau_i\}, \forall i \in N$; Processing power $f_i^l$ of MU; Number of additional cycles $\beta_i$

**Output:** The set of all MU's respective optimal offloading decisions $\lambda_i, \forall i \in N$

---

1.  Initialization: initialize the offload decision for each MU i, i.e., $\lambda_i = 0, \forall i \in N$
2.  **for** all MU i and a given time slot t **do**
3.      **Transmit** $T_0 = \{1, c_i, 0, \gamma_i, \tau_i\} \cup \{n_i\}$ to MBS
4.      **Return** $m_i$
5.  **end for**
6.  **while** $i \leq N$ **do**
7.      $A_i^l = \dfrac{1}{(1-\alpha_i)+\frac{\alpha_i}{n_i}}$
8.      $A_i^e = \dfrac{1}{(1-\alpha_i)+\frac{\alpha_i}{m_i}}$
9.      **if** $A_i^l \geq A_i^e$ **then**
10.         $\lambda_i = 0$
11.     **else**
12.         $\lambda_i > 0$ && $\lambda_i \leq 1$
13.     **Calculate** $r_i = B \log_2\left(1 + \frac{P_i h_i^2}{\omega_0 B}\right), \forall i \in N$
14.         $\lambda_i = BAB(min_{\lambda_i}\left[\sum_{i=1}^{N}\lambda_i C_i^s + \sum_{i=1}^{N}(1-\lambda_i)C_i^l\right], \forall i \in N)$
15.         $O(\lambda_i) = \{\lambda_1, \lambda_2, ..., \lambda_N\}$
16.         $i = i+1$
17.     **Return** $O(\lambda_i)$
18. **end for**

---

# 6  Experiment

In this section, this paper first introduces the experimental environment and parameter settings, then simulates and analyzes the proposed model and algorithm in term of energy consumption, latency, cost, security decision, task offloading rate, and QoE.

## 6.1  Experimental Environment and Parameter Settings

In this paper, the simulation experiments are done in the EdgeCloudSim simulation tool [32], which runs on a PC equipped with an AMD Ryzen 5 4600H CPU, 3.0 GHz frequency, and 16 GB RAM capacity, and which runs on the Windows 11 Business Editions platform. An edge computing system with 60 MUs is considered, and the number of CPU cores per MU is randomly assigned from the set $\{2, 4, 6, 8\}$, which ensures the randomness of the number of cores in different MU. The corresponding computational capacity of each MU is randomly allocated from the set $\{0.4, 0.5, ..., 1.0\}$ GHz, which can better distinguish the heterogeneous capacity among different MU. The CPU computing power of the edge server is set to 20 GHz. The data size of each

MU-generated task is between 2000 KB and 5000 KB, and the workload of the task ranges from 500 to 1500 (Megacycles). The transmission power of each mobile user device MU i is fixed at 100 mW. The corresponding wireless channel bandwidth is set to 20 MHz, and the corresponding channel gain and channel noise are $10^{-3}$ and $10^{-9}$, respectively. Finally, $w_i^t$ and $w_i^e$ are randomly assigned from the set {0, 0.2, 0.5, 0.8, 1.0} to meet different requirements. In addition, the number of additional CPU cycles required to encrypt and decrypt the transmission data is set to 200 Megacycles. To ensure the rationality of the security decisions, the security decisions are set randomly in the simulation experiments, which means that the security decisions are made by the mobile user devices to decide whether to adopt them or not. In order to reduce the error of the experiment, 50 simulations were performed and the results were summed and averaged after 50 different results were obtained to ensure the rigor of the experiment.

## 6.2  Experimental Results and Analysis

Figure 3 shows the relationship between the task offloading rate of mobile user MUs and the total number of mobile users in both cases, with and without the security decision. It can be observed that when the number of mobile users MUs is between 0 and 40, the task offloading rate of users in both cases with and without security decisions is close to 100%, while when the number of mobile users exceeds 40, the task offloading rate starts to decrease in both cases. The reason is that when the number of mobile users increases, mobile users choose to offload tasks to the edge server, which inevitably causes congestion in the wireless communication channel, and the final result is that the overall task offload rate decreases for everyone.

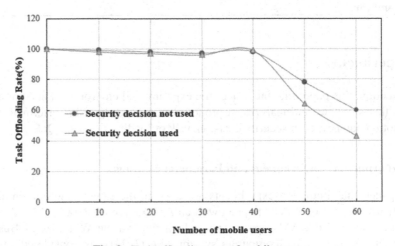

**Fig. 3.**  Task offloading rate of mobile users.

Figure 4 shows the variation of the calculated acceleration value. As the number of users becomes larger, the mutual interference between MUs becomes more frequent due to the shared wireless communication channel. Mutual interference between MUs

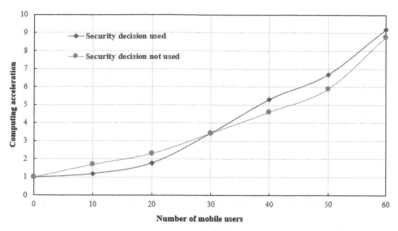

**Fig. 4.** Calculated acceleration values for mobile users.

becomes more frequent, and when the security decision is adopted. An encryption technique can guarantee the data integrity and reduce the mutual interference between MUs in a certain procedure, which in turn improves the value of computational acceleration.

The analysis in terms of task offloading rate and QoE have been given above, and we compares the three aspects of latency, energy consumption, and cost. Figure 5 reflects the relationship between the number of mobile users and energy consumption. From the figure, it can be seen that the proposed model is lower than the literature [33, 34] in terms of energy consumption, regardless of whether the model proposed in this paper uses security decisions or not because the model and algorithm have a good resource scheduling strategy. When the security decision is used, the energy consumption when the security decision is naturally more than the energy consumption when the security decision is not used because both MU and edge server need to operate on additional encryption and decryption, which requires additional energy consumption.

Figure 6 illustrates the relationship between the number of mobile users and the average latency. It can be noted that the curves in the literature [33, 34] become steeper and their average latency grows faster as the number of mobile subscribers increases. This is because the two aforementioned works do not sufficiently focus on the solutions of the trade-off problem, which in turn leads to increasingly steeper curves and longer delays. In contrast, the model proposed in this paper has a flatter growth rate of the curve with or without the security decision. Note that the lowest average latency is observed in the case where no security decision is used because the MU and edge server do not require additional CPU cycles to process the encryption and decryption operations in the case where no security decision.

Finally, the simulation experiments focus on the cost of the whole system, Fig. 7 shows the relationship between the number of MUs and the total cost. It can be seen that the total cost of the proposed model in this paper is slightly higher than the literature [34] when the number of MUs is approximately less than or equal to 20. While when the number of MUs increases further, the proposed model is the lowest and the best among the three comparisons. The fact is that this paper takes into account delay, energy

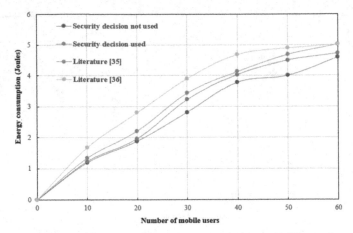

**Fig. 5.** Relationship between energy consumption and MU quantity.

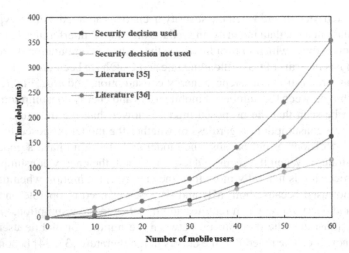

**Fig. 6.** Average latency versus MU quantity.

consumption, QoE, and data security and solves the trade-off problem well. Further, Fig. 8 shows the comparison between the proposed model with and without security decision and literature [33, 34]. Regarding the percentage of total cost savings, the percentage of total cost savings is the largest when the security decision is not adopted, while the percentage of total cost savings after security decision is similar to literature [33], which is due to the efficient algorithm proposed in this paper. The algorithm works well with the security decision to reduce the cost as much as possible while ensuring data security.

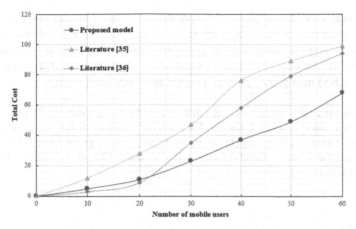

**Fig. 7.** Number of MU versus total cost.

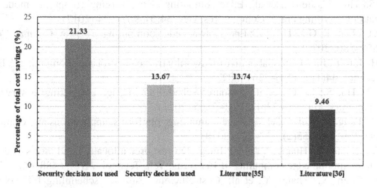

**Fig. 8.** Comparison of total cost savings percentage.

# 7  Conclusion

In this study, for edge mobile networks considering security, this paper proposes an efficient and secure multi-user resource cooperative scheduling model, which comprehensively considers resource allocation, task offloading, QoE requirements and data security, and optimizes The goal is to minimize system overhead. The problem is modeled as a mixed integer linear programming problem. To solve this problem, this paper proposes a resource cooperative scheduling algorithm that integrates security mechanisms and computing speed, and introduces ChaCha20 encryption as a security decision to prevent task data from being maliciously stolen by attackers during the offloading process. At the same time, computing speed is used as an indicator to quantify QoE requirements. In addition, this paper conducts simulation experiments and analyzes on the proposed model in terms of energy consumption, delay, cost, whether to use security decisions, task offload rate, and QoE, and compares the proposed model with benchmark values. Finally, the simulation results show that the proposed model and algorithm are effective.

Future work considers expanding the problem from a multi-user single-edge server scenario to a multi-user multi-edge server or even a multi-user multi-task multi-edge server scenario and considers a novel game-theoretic mechanism as a solution to the above problems. Another direction is to consider the problem of distributed resource scheduling (DRS) in edge computing, which is still very challenging.

**Acknowledgments.** This work was supported in part by the Consulting Project of Chinese Academy of Engineering under Grant 2023-XY-09, the National Natural Science Foundation of China under Grant 62272100, and in part by the Fundamental Research Funds for the Central Universities and the Academy-Locality Cooperation Project of Chinese Academy of Engineering under Grant JS2021ZT05.

# References

1. Wei, S., Hui, S., Jie, C., et al.: Edge computing—an emerging computing model for the internet of everything era. J. Comput. Res. Dev. **54**(5), 907–924 (2017)
2. Jiang, C., Fan, T., Gao, H., et al.: Energy aware edge computing: a survey. Comput. Commun. **151**, 556–580 (2020)
3. Xin, H., Jun, T., Jian, L.: Collaborative trustworthy framework for edge computing. J. Electron. Inf. Technol. **44**(12), 4256–4264 (2022)
4. Luo, Q., Hu, S., Li, C., et al.: Resource scheduling in edge computing: a survey. IEEE Commun. Surv. Tutorials **23**(4), 2131–2165 (2021)
5. Xin, Z., Fang, L., Zhi, C., et al.: Edge computing: platforms, applications and challenges. J. Comput. Res. Dev. **55**(2), 327–337 (2018)
6. He, W., Zhang, Y., Huang, Y., et al.: Integrated resource allocation and task scheduling for full-duplex mobile edge computing. IEEE Trans. Veh. Technol. **71**(6), 6488–6502 (2022)
7. Lu, Y., Chen, X., Zhang, Y., et al.: Cost-efficient resources scheduling for mobile edge computing in ultra-dense networks. IEEE Trans. Netw. Serv. Manage. **19**(3), 3163–3173 (2022)
8. Guo, S., Liu, J., Yang, Y., et al.: Energy-efficient dynamic computation offloading and cooperative task scheduling in mobile cloud computing. IEEE Trans. Mob. Comput. **18**(2), 319–333 (2018)
9. Chandrakasan, A.P., Sheng, S., Brodersen, R.W.: Low-power CMOS digital design. IEICE Trans. Electron. **75**(4), 371–382 (1992)
10. Deng, Y., Chen, Z., Yao, X., et al.: Parallel offloading in green and sustainable mobile edge computing for delay-constrained IoT system. IEEE Trans. Veh. Technol. **68**(12), 12202–12214 (2019)
11. Vaidya, U., Mehta, P.G., Shanbhag, U.V.: Nonlinear stabilization via control Lyapunov measure. IEEE Trans. Autom. Control **55**(6), 1314–1328 (2010)
12. Pasteris, S., Wang, S., Herbster, M., et al.: Service placement with provable guarantees in heterogeneous edge computing systems. In: IEEE INFOCOM 2019-IEEE Conference on Computer Communications, pp. 514–522. IEEE (2019)
13. Li, Q., Zhao, J., Gong, Y.: Cooperative computation offloading and resource allocation for mobile edge computing. In: 2019 IEEE International Conference on Communications Workshops (ICC Workshops), pp. 1–6. IEEE (2019)
14. Meng, S., Li, Q., Wu, T., et al.: A fault-tolerant dynamic scheduling method on hierarchical mobile edge cloud computing. Comput. Intell. **35**(3), 577–598 (2019)

15. Ning, Z., Dong, P., Wang, X., et al.: Deep reinforcement learning for vehicular edge computing: an intelligent offloading system. ACM Trans. Intell. Syst. Technol. (TIST) **10**(6), 1–24 (2019)
16. Zhang, L., Zhou, W., Xia, J., et al.: DQN-based mobile edge computing for smart Internet of vehicle. EURASIP J. Adv. Sig. Process. **2022**(1), 1–16 (2022)
17. Guo, F., Zhang, H., Ji, H., et al.: An efficient computation offloading management scheme in the densely deployed small cell networks with mobile edge computing. IEEE/ACM Trans. Networking **26**(6), 2651–2664 (2018)
18. Jošilo, S., Dán, G.: Computation offloading scheduling for periodic tasks in mobile edge computing. IEEE/ACM Trans. Networking **28**(2), 667–680 (2020)
19. Elgendy, I.A., Zhang, W., Tian, Y.C., et al.: Resource allocation and computation offloading with data security for mobile edge computing. Futur. Gener. Comput. Syst. **100**, 531–541 (2019)
20. Daemen, J., Reijndael, R.V.: The advanced encryption standard. Dr. Dobb's J. Softw. Tools Prof. Programmer **26**(3), 137–139 (2001)
21. Zhang, J., Zheng, R., Zhao, X., et al.: A computational resources scheduling algorithm in edge cloud computing: from the energy efficiency of users' perspective. J. Supercomput., 1–22 (2022)
22. Stepanovic, S., Georgakarakos, G., Holmbacka, S., et al.: An efficient model for quantifying the interaction between structural properties of software and hardware in the ARM big. LITTLE architecture. Concurrency Comput. Pract. Exp. **32**(10), e5230 (2020)
23. Xu, X., Zhang, X., Gao, H., et al.: BeCome: blockchain-enabled computation offloading for IoT in mobile edge computing. IEEE Trans. Industr. Inf. **16**(6), 4187–4195 (2019)
24. Panneerselvam, S., Rinnegan, S.M.: Efficient resource use in heterogeneous architectures. In: Proceedings of the 2016 International Conference on Parallel Architectures and Compilation, pp. 373–386 (2016)
25. Miettinen, A.P., Nurminen, J.K.: Energy efficiency of mobile clients in cloud computing. HotCloud **10**(4–4), 19 (2010)
26. Melendez, S., McGarry, M.P.: Computation offloading decisions for reducing completion time. In: 2017 14th IEEE Annual Consumer Communications & Networking Conference (CCNC), pp. 160–164. IEEE (2017)
27. Wang, C., Liang, C., Yu, F.R., et al.: Computation offloading and resource allocation in wireless cellular networks with mobile edge computing. IEEE Trans. Wireless Commun. **16**(8), 4924–4938 (2017)
28. Mao, Y., Zhang, J., Song, S.H., et al.: Stochastic joint radio and computational resource management for multi-user mobile-edge computing systems. IEEE Trans. Wireless Commun. **16**(9), 5994–6009 (2017)
29. Du, J., Zhao, L., Feng, J., et al.: Computation offloading and resource allocation in mixed fog/cloud computing systems with min-max fairness guarantee. IEEE Trans. Commun. **66**(4), 1594–1608 (2017)
30. Amdahl, G.M.: Validity of the single processor approach to achieving large scale computing capabilities. In: Proceedings of the April 18–20, Spring Joint Computer Conference, pp. 483–485 (1967)
31. Konopiński, M.K.: Shannon diversity index: a call to replace the original Shannon's formula with unbiased estimator in the population genetics studies. PeerJ **8**, e9391 (2020)
32. Nir, Y., Langley, A.: ChaCha20 and Poly1305 for IETF Protocols (2018)
33. Boyd, S., Mattingley, J.: Branch and bound methods. Notes EE364b, Stanford University, 07 (2007, 2006)
34. Sonmez, C., Ozgovde, A., Ersoy, C.: EdgeCloudSim: an environment for performance evaluation of edge computing systems. Trans. Emerg. Telecommun. Technol. **29**(11), e3493 (2018)

35. Elgendy, I.A., Zhang, W.Z., Zeng, Y., et al.: Efficient and security multi-user multi-task computation offloading for mobile-edge computing in mobile IoT networks. IEEE Trans. Netw. Serv. Manage. **17**(4), 2410–2422 (2020)
36. Bibi, A., Majeed, M.F., Ali, S, et al.: Secured optimized resource allocation in mobile edge computing. Mob. Inf. Sys. **2022** (2022)

# Edge Computing and Collaborative Working

# DQN-Based Applications Offloading with Multiple Interdependent Tasks in Mobile Edge Computing

Jiaxue Tu[1], Dongge Zhu[2], Yunni Xia[1(✉)], Yin Li[3], Yong Ma[4], Fan Li[5], and Qinglan Peng[6]

[1] College of Computer Science, Chongqing University, Chongqing, China
xiayunni@hotmail.com
[2] Electric Power Research Institute of State Grid Ningxia Electric Power Co., Ltd., Yinchuan, Ningxia, China
[3] Guangzhou Institute of Software Application Technology, Guangzhou, China
[4] School of Computer and Information Engineering, Jiangxi Normal University, Nanchang, Jiangxi, China
[5] Sichuan University, Chengdu, China
[6] School of Artificial Intelligence, Henan University, Zhengzhou, China

**Abstract.** Recently, Vehicular Edge Computing (VEC) is evolving as a solution for offloading computationally intensive tasks in in-vehicle environments. However, when the number of vehicles and users is large, pure edge resources may be insufficient and limited, most existing work focuses on minimizing system latency by designing some offloading strategies. Therefore, hybrid multilayer edge structures are in dire require of mission deployment strategies that can synthesize cost and mission latency. In this paper, we argue that each application can be decomposed into multiple interdependent subtasks, and that the different subtasks can be deployed separately into different edge layers in a hybrid three-tier edge computing infrastructure for execution. We develop an improved DQN task deployment algorithm based on Lyapunov optimization to jointly optimize the average workflow latency and cost under a long-term cost constraint, and simulation results clearly show that, comparing with the traditional approach, our proposed method effectively reduces the cost consumption by 92.8% while sacrificing only some latency.

**Keywords:** VEC · Computation Offloading · Latency · Lyapunov Optimization · DQN

## 1 Introduction

Mobile Internet computation is rapidly growing, many new services, such as cloud computing and edge computing [1], continue to emerge, AR/VR. Meanwhile vehicles are becoming more and more important in providing computing power and access to the Internet, where mobile vehicles can collect data and

H. Gao et al. (Eds.): CollaborateCom 2023, LNICST 561, pp. 77–92, 2024.
https://doi.org/10.1007/978-3-031-54521-4_5

perform a number of intensive computational tasks to make intelligent decisions [2–4]. However, these compute-intensive applications often result in overloaded and sluggish mobile services because mobile devices typically have less capacity and resources than traditional centralized cloud centers. In this case, the user may have a poorer quality of experience when in-vehicle services are available [5,6], which may even lead to some serious traffic accidents [2,7].

To solve the problem of mismatch between vehicle resource demand and limited resources, the model called mobile cloud computing, has been proposed. Mobile cloud computing combines cloud computing with the mobile environment. In this model, when the local vehicle's resources are overloaded, the vehicle offloads the application to a traditional cloud server over a wireless network [8]. While utilizing remote computing resources on cloud servers can be effective in reducing computational latency, communication latency can increase [9,10].

Mobile Edge Computing (MEC) is coming out to face these challenges. That is, pushing services to the edge of the network. By placing services closer to the vehicle, MEC perfectly complies with the low transmission latency requirements of applications and effectively eases the demand for computing resources in the vehicle [11]. Vehicular Edge Computing (VEC) has received more and more attention in recent years, for VEC growing as an important branch of MEC [12], because it improved cloud computing capabilities to the vehicle. As shown in Fig. 1, in order to provide a high quality of service to the users, lots of cloud services are placed on the units of roadside, which can be achieved by the vehicles through network. In this solution, compute-intensive and latency-sensitive applications can execute on the RSUs.

Recently, extensive research efforts were paid on VEC-based task offloading and scheduling. A dynamic task allocation scheme is be proposed by yang et al. [13], it ensure quality of service. He et al. consider use game theoretic methods to solve task allocation problems and task allocation as a gaming system [14], Chiara Caiazzade et al. [15] studied the LTE nodes' energy consumption in different communication scheme of Request-Response. An efficient predictive combinatorial model to reduce offloading cost is proposed in Zhang et al. [19]. Most of the previous studies have assumed applications composed of independent tasks, and few studies have considered the dependency of task, Zhou et al. [16] obtain a deployment solution, prioritizing applications that meet deadline constraints and tasks that meet dependency constraints. Shabidani et al. [18] considered load balancing under task scheduling in the edge-fog-cloud architecture. By the way, the application of deep learning has become more and more hot, and the research of using deep learning to solve related problems has gradually increased. To achieve the a low latency and energy consumption, Wu et al. [20] uses a deep Q-network based offloading strategy to offload tasks. Zhang et al. [21] proposed the use of a convex optimized DQN model to reduce task latency in mobile edge environments.

Most of the existing work focuses on minimizing system latency by designing some offloading strategies, but these strategies do not consider server pricing. To optimize the balance between system latency and operational cost for multiple on-board applications, it is important to take server pricing into account when designing task scheduling policies.

To address this problem, we incorporate cost constraints into the design of VEC-based time-delay systems and we propose a deep learning method using Lyapunov optimization. And the experimental results show that our proposed scheme is significantly better than the traditional one under the same constraints. Specifically, the proposed algorithm can effectively reduce the system cost by up to 92.8% compared to the traditional scheme, although at the slight expense of the system delay. The major innovations of this work are as follows:

- We develop a DQN-based data offloading algorithm based on Lyapunov optimization and demonstrate that it outperforms both the traditional scheme and the basic DQN algorithm, for minimizing the total delay under a long-term cost constraint.
- We use the improved DQN as the key subroutine to solve the offloading problem and achieve joint optimization under system delay, cost consumption, and long-term cost optimization. Simulation results show that our algorithm maintains a low cost based on a lower level of user latency, although it sacrifices some user delays by deploying a reasonable task offloading policy.

This paper is organized as: in the Sect. 2, we will discuss the VEC based edge-cloud hybrid network architecture and then presents the problem. Section 4 gives the optimization problem solving method based on DQN and Lyapunov optimization algorithm. Numerical analysis is presented in Sect. 5.

## 2   System Model

### 2.1   Network Model

The environment is made up of a three-layer infrastructure, i.e., the cloud layer, the local layer, and the VEC layer. Figure 1 shows the hybrid three-layer architecture for Dependent Aware Vehicle task deployment. The VEC layer comprise $R$ RSUs, each of which are with a location of $[RL_x(j), RL_y(j)]$. The $j^{\text{th}}$ RSU covers a circular area with a radius of $r_j$ and the $j^{\text{th}}$ RSU is equipped with $s_j$ edge servers $(0 < j \leq R)$.

Each vehicle is placed in a different location on a two-dimensional plane as well as on different roads, it's position can be described as $[VL_x(i), VL_y(i)]$. The conditions that need to be met for the rsu $j \in R$ to be accessible to the car $i$ when it is running to a certain location are

$$r_j \geq \sqrt{(RL_x(j) - VL_x(i))^2 + (RL_y(j) - VL_y(i))^2} \tag{1}$$

The number of vehicles is $M$ and the $i^{\text{th}}$ car's speed is $v_i(0 < i \leq M)$. Each vehicle has one application to be executed. Each application consists of interdependent tasks, and the $i^{\text{th}}$ application's size of data is $d_i$.

The vehicles on the different roads can visit the $j^{\text{th}}$ RSU through wireless channel, and every vehicle can access the cloud server at any time from any

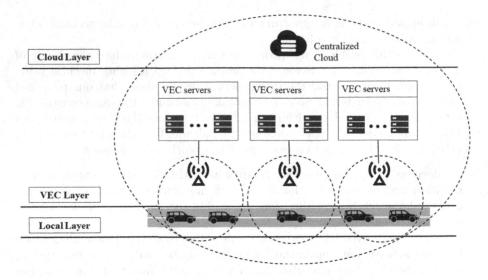

Fig. 1. The system model.

location. We assume centralized cloud has a limited number of servers and infinite resources. Each vehicle can make a choice to place their tasks to the centralized cloud servers or the VEC servers.

## 2.2  Performance Model

This part describes the performance evaluation model of the system. We assume applications are structured rather than monolithic applications, so each task can be pushed to different layers and the structure of each application is defined based on a directed acyclic graph of scientific workflows. The $i^{th}$ application is assumed to be on the $i^{th}$ vehicle, and it contains $K(i)$ tasks, $T_{i,k}$ is denoted as the $k^{th}$ task $(0 < k \leq K(i))$ of the $i^{th}$ application.

We also consider Each computation unit, including centralized cloud, RSU and local computer, has its own cost consumption $p_a$. To minimize the cost of in-vehicle applications and users on edge servers while reducing average task latency, we try to find some of the offloading strategies at a macro level that reduces both the average elapsed time of all applications and the cost consumption of the server. The transfer time of the calculation results is negligible because the data size of an application's calculation results is much smaller than the size of the input data. We denote $MakeSpan_i$ as the total latency of application $A_i$ and $cost_a$ as the total cost of local computing, MEC or centralized cloud. We will describe $cost_a$ in the next section. Time of task $T_{i,k}$ can be apart into two parts in our makespan model, named uplink delay and Application Makespan.

*Uplink Delay.* When task $T_{i,k}$ is chosen to be performed on VEC servers or the centralized cloud, the uplink delay needs to be taken into account due to the distance or limited bandwidth between them.

$$Rate_i^j = BV2E \cdot \log_2(1 + \frac{P_i \cdot g_j^i}{N_0}) \tag{2}$$

$BV2E$ denotes the bandwidth among vehicles and VEC servers, $N_0$ indicates the noise power, and $P_i$ represents transmission power of the vehicle $i$, and $g_j^i$ denotes the bandwidth among vehicle $i$ and RSU $j$.

For VEC computation, the uplink delay of $k^{\text{th}}$ task with data size $d_{i,k}$ of application $A_i$ to VEC servers can be given as

$$t_{i,k}^{uplinkE} = \frac{d_{i,k}}{Rate_i^j} \tag{3}$$

Then, we define $BV2C$ as the bandwidth among vehicles and the remote cloud server. The transmission rate of the remote cloud server and the uplink delay from the vehicle to the centralized cloud server can be expressed as follows:

$$Rate_c^j = BV2C \cdot \log_2(1 + \frac{P_i \cdot g_i^c}{N_0}) \tag{4}$$

$$t_{i,k}^{uplinkC} = \frac{d_{i,k}}{Rate_i^c} \tag{5}$$

*Application Makespan.* The servers that choosed by the vehicle $i^{\text{th}}$ can be described as $Des_i$, $Des_i = \{1, 2, ..., S+2\}$, the number of servers in the choosed RSU is $S$. And 1 represents compute task in local, that is, the task is computed on the vehicle's local system, deploying locally will have very low cost but high latency; $S + 2$ indicates deploy task on the centralized cloud server where it is very fast but also expensive to execute the task; 2 to $S + 1$ means execute it on VEC servers and tasks executed on vehicle edge servers will enjoy some speed over local blocks and will cost less than in the cloud.

A task $T_{i,k}$, it's readiness time is the latest time at which all of its predecessors have been done, then the ready time $RT_{i,k}$ can be be expressed as follows:

$$RT_{i,k} = \max_{T_{i,h} \in pre(T_{i,k})} RFT_{i,h} \tag{6}$$

$T_{i,h} \in pre(T_{i,k})$ means the pre task must be completed before task $T_{i,k}$ is ready and $pre(T_{i,k})$ indicates all parent tasks of the current task $T_{i,k}$. When all the pre tasks have been completed, the present task $T_{i,h}$ is ready to transmit.

Then we denoted $AT_{i,k,s}$ as the earliest time that one of the server $s \in Des_i$ is accessible for task $T_{i,k}$. The starting time of one task is duration between its ready time and the available time of the choosed VEC server. Consequently, the starting time $ST_{i,k,s}$ of task $T_{i,k}$ over server $s$ is:

$$ST_{i,k,s} = \max(RT_{i,k}, AT_{i,k,s}) \tag{7}$$

Only when the task is ready and the server is available, the task can be deployed on the server. Then we denote $ET_{i,k,s}$ as the execution time that task $T_{i,k}$ over server $s$, $s \in Des_i$, $ET_{i,k,s}$ is thus:

$$ET_{i,k,s} = \frac{d_{i,k}}{f_s} \qquad (8)$$

where $d_{i,k}$ is the data size of the task $T_{i,k}$, and $f_s$ means the computation rate of server $s$, $s \in Des_i$.

The finishing time $FT_{i,k,s}$ of task $T_{i,k}$ over server $s$, $s \in Des_i$ are tied to which layer the mission is ultimately deployed to, thus, the finish time can be given as

$$FT_{i,k,s} = \begin{cases} ST_{i,k,s} + ET_{i,k,s}, & if \ s = 1 \\ ST_{i,k,s} + t_{i,k}^{uplinkE} + ET_{i,k,s}, & if \ s \in \{2, ..., S+1\} \\ ST_{i,k,s} + t_{i,k}^{uplinkC} + ET_{i,k,s}, & otherwise \end{cases} \qquad (9)$$

When all the small tasks in the application $A_i$ are deployed, obviously, the final completion time of the terminated tasks in the application is the completion time of the entire application. $t_{i,K}$ denotes terminated task of application $A_i$, and the makespan of application $A_i$ is thus:

$$MakeSpan_i = RFT_{i,K} \qquad (10)$$

And the averaged makespan of all $M$ applications over the vehicles is

$$AveSpan = \frac{1}{i} \cdot \sum_{i=1}^{M} MakeSpan_i \qquad (11)$$

And One of our optimization metrics is the Maximum completion time for all computational tasks MakeSpan

$$MakeSpan = \max_{1 \le i \le M} \max_{1 \le k \le K} \sum_{s=1}^{S+2} (ET_{i,k,s} \cdot x_{i,k,s}) \qquad (12)$$

where $x_{i,k,s}$ represents whether the $k^{th}$ task of the $i^{th}$ application is scheduled on server $s$, $x_{i,k,s} = \{0, 1\}$ represents the task $t_{i,k}$ is scheduled or not.

## 2.3   Cost Model

We will present the cost model of the system in this section. We assume that each computation unit, including centralized cloud, RSU and local computer, has its own cost consumption $p_s$. For the cost reduction purpose, we consider $cost_s$ as the total cost of local severs, MEC servers or centralized cloud, $cost_s(t)$ as the total cost up to time $t$

$$cost_s = \sum_{i=1}^{M} \sum_{k=1}^{K} ET_{i,k,s} \cdot x_{i,k,s} \cdot p_s \qquad (13)$$

where $ET_{i,k,s}$ represents the execution duration of the $k^{\text{th}}$ task of the $i^{\text{th}}$ application on server $s$, $x_{i,k,s} = \{0,1\}$ represent the task $t_{i,k}$ is schedule in server $s$ or not.

$AvgCost$ denotes the average cost of each application, it also represents the average cost of solving each user's application needs.

$$AvgCost = \frac{\sum_{s=1}^{S+2} cost_s}{M} \tag{14}$$

where $ET_{i,k,s}$ represents the execution time that the $k^{\text{th}}$ task of the $i^{\text{th}}$ application applied in server $s$. One prerequisite before achieving our optimization goal is that the Average user cost is not allowed to exceed a threshold, i.e., there is an upper limit to the cost of our design requirement.

Total cost is an important metric for our optimization goal. So we should keep the operating cost of the rented edge servers as low as possible.

$$Cost = \sum_{s=1}^{S+2} cost_s \tag{15}$$

## 3  Problem Formulation

In this paper, we set a total of two optimization metrics. We want the scheduling algorithm to make the maximum completion time of all computational tasks as short as possible, while the operating cost of the rented edge servers is low. The problem is formulated as follows:

$$\min f_1 = \max_{1 \le i \le M} \max_{1 \le k \le K} \sum_{s=1}^{S+2} (ST_{i,k,s} + t_{i,k}^{uplink} + ET_{i,k,s}) \cdot x_{i,k,s} \tag{16}$$

$$\min f_2 = \sum_{i=1}^{M} \sum_{k=1}^{K} \sum_{s=1}^{S+2} ET_{i,k,s} \cdot x_{i,k,s} \cdot p_s \tag{17}$$

s.t.

$$\lim_{T \to \infty} \frac{1}{T} \sum_{t=1}^{T} \sum_{s=1}^{S+2} cost_a(t) \le Q_m \tag{18}$$

$$i \in [1, M], k \in [1, K], s \in [1, S+2], x_{i,k,s} = \{0,1\} \tag{19}$$

$$ST_{i,k,s} \ge 0, t_{i,k}^{uplink} \ge 0, ET_{i,k,s} \ge 0, p_s \ge 0 \tag{20}$$

The constraint (18) is the constraint of the long-term cost for the mobile users, it requires the average user cost not to exceed the limit of $Q_m$. And $ST$ represents start time of task scheduling, $ET$ denotes the time taken by the task to execute on the server, $t_{i,k}^{uplink}$ denotes the different uplink delays, $t_{i,k}^{uplink} = 0$ when the task chooses to be deployed locally. Their corresponding subscripts $i, k, s$ denote scheduling the $k^{\text{th}}$ task of application $i^{\text{th}}$ to server $s$. In this case $x_{i,k,s} = 1$, otherwise $x_{i,k,s} = 0$. $p_s$ stands for the cost per unit required to run the server $s$. Traditional optimization methods are difficult to solve the problem of multi-objective optimization under resource-poor conditions proposed in this paper. Therefore, we propose an optimization algorithm based on DQN and Lyapunov to solve this problem.

# 4   Proposed Algorithm and Analysis

In this section, we will develop an algorithm using the Lyapunov optimization framework and then evaluate the capabilities of the algorithm in terms of minimizing latency and smoothing out cost consumption.

## 4.1   Lyapunov Optimization Algorithm

Solving (16) (17) directly is difficult for the conflicting cost constraints for mobile users and the task offloading decisions are also different in each time slot. Thus, we intend to use Lyapunov optimization to build a cost-insufficient queue that guides the data task offloading strategies to follow the cost constraints.

Due to the stochastic and dynamic identity of the data flow task, it seems difficult to find out the generation of the next time slot task, therefore, we should allocate the existing resources in the current time slot to make sure that the system queue can be stabilized for a long period of time. Then, the queue length $q(t)$ at the beginning of time slot $t$ follows the equation as

$$q(t + 1) = q(t) + \sum_{s=1}^{S+2} cost_s^{new}(t) - \sum_{s=1}^{S+2} cost_s^{finish}(t) \tag{21}$$

where $q(0) = 0$, and $q(t + 1)$ is the queue backlog from the cost constraint in the time slot $t$, which indicating the deviation of the current energy consumption, $cost_s^{(new)}$ represents new unscheduled servers' cost added at time $t$ and $cost_s^{(finish)}$ indicates the cost of the servers that all tasks scheduled are completed and no tasks are scheduled at time $t$.

In order to characterize the total queue length of the system, we denote $q(t)$ is the set of current system load states, and defines the Lyapunov equation as

$$L(t) = \frac{1}{2} \cdot q^2(t) \tag{22}$$

Equation (21) represents the level of queue backlog in the system. Within each time slot, the scheduler gives a decision such that the Lyapunov equation always remains under a bound, then the system is always stable. Therefore, we make the Lyapunov equation always remain in a region with low congestion by reducing the Lyapunov-drift.

$$\Delta(q(t)) = L(t + 1) - L(t) \tag{23}$$

The Lyapunov drift $\Delta(q(t))$ represents the degree of change in the total queue length in the Lyapunov equation after one time slot, The extent of this change depends on the current choice of strategy, and an effective strategy can result in a small change in $\Delta(q(t))$. Therefore, adding queue stability to makespan and cost consumption optimization, that is adding Lyapunov drift to the reward function of DQN, we will explain it in the next section.

## 4.2   DQN-Based Multi-objective and Multi-workflow Offloading

We propose a Deep Reinforcement Learning-based Multi-Objective Multi-Workflow Scheduling (DRLMOMWS) algorithm. Under edge computing, this scheduling algorithm program will be configured to the edge server, when there is a computing task deployed to the edge server, the program will take the working state of the edge server cluster and currently pending tasks, make their information as inputs to the model, and after the algorithmic model, the corresponding scheduling scheme will be obtained. We use DQN as a reinforcement learning algorithm and employed multiple intelligences.

The multi-workflow offloading problem in this paper can be modeled as a Markov decision model. At time slot $t$, the agent first gets an initial state $s_t \in S$ from the environment, after getting the initial state, the agent will get the next action $a_t$ according to the given policy $\pi$. The agent then feeds this action $a_t$ back to the environment, and the environment body executes the action which causing a change in state from $s_t$ to $s_{t+1}$. At the same time, the agent receives $r_t$ as a reward from the ambient body as feedback.

Specifically, we define state space as $S = \{L_i, \alpha\}$, where $L_i = \{location x_i(t), location y_i(t)\}$ denotes the 2D coordinate position of the vehicle where the app that needs to make a decision is currently located, $\alpha = \{\alpha_1(t), \alpha_2(t), ..., \alpha_{S+2}(t)\}$ denotes indicates the current readytime of the local server, MEC server, and cloud server. And the action space is $A = \{\rho_1, \rho_2 ... \rho_n\}$, where $\rho_i$ is the server to which the decision-making app can be deployed, and the vehicle in which the app is located needs to be within the range of the server. Next, the intelligent body selects an action from the discrete set of actions $a_t \in A$ according to its strategy, and then receives a reward given by the environment. We argue that the benefits of the offloading decision problem are related to the latency of the applications in the system as well as the average user cost.

$$R_{makespan} = [\frac{ET_{i,k,s}(a) - (makespan_{new} - makespan_{old})}{ET_{i,k,s}(a)}]^3 \quad (24)$$

$$R_{cost} = [\frac{cost_{worst} - ET_{i,k,s}(a) \cdot p_s}{cost_{worst} - cost_{best}}]^3 + \Delta(q(t)) \quad (25)$$

Than the intelligence tries to obtain the maximized expected discounted return value by $R_t = \sum_{\tau=t}^{\infty} \gamma^{\tau-t} \cdot r_\tau$. Where $\gamma \in [0,1]$ is the discount factor to weigh the importance of future and current returns.

For an intelligent that makes decisions according to a stochastic strategy $\pi$, the state-action pair $(s, a)$ and the value definition of the state are respectively

$$Q^{\pi}(s, a) = E[R_t | s_t = s, a_t = a, \pi] \tag{26}$$

$$V^{\pi}(s) = E_{a-\pi(s)}[Q^{\pi}(s, a)] \tag{27}$$

With a defined strategy $a = \arg\max_{a' \in A} Q^*(s, a')$, The better Q function can be defined as $Q^*(s, a) = \max_{\pi} Q^{\pi}(s, a)$, it can satisfy $V^*(S) = \max_a Q^*(s, a)$. Intuitively, the value function V measures the importance of the ambient body being in a particular state $s$, while the Q function measures the importance of the change in reward value that would result from choosing each possible action while in that state.

The DQN algorithm uses a convolutional neural network to predict Q-values, thus solving the problem of Q-functions that are difficult to compute and store in large-scale problems. In addition to this, DQN introduces an empirical playback pool to store the used data, thus breaking the correlation between the data. During the learning process, the intelligence collects a set of empirical datasets through multiple iterations $D_t = \{e_1, e_2, ...e_t\}$, where $e_t = (s_t, a_t, r_t, s_{t+1})$. When we go to train the Q-network, we randomly use a portion of the sample data from the dataset $D_t$ for training, rather than using the standard time-difference method to obtain the current experience.

The ultimate goal of the algorithm is to learn and select the optimal policy that achieves joint optimization of delay and cost for this model by minimizing the loss function.

$$y_i^{DQN} = R_t + \gamma \cdot \max_{a'} Q(s', a'; \theta^-) \tag{28}$$

$$L_i(\theta_i) = E_{(s,a,r,s')-\mu(D)}[(y_i^{DQN} - Q(s, a; \theta_i))^2] \tag{29}$$

where $\theta$ indicates the weights of target network.

For reinforcement learning algorithms for single intelligences, since there are only unique intelligences in the environment, the decisions made by the intelligences I are able to be executed and reacted to the environment. However, for multi-intelligents environments, there is a possibility that the decisions of multiple intelligences may conflict, therefore, we take measures to deal with situations of conflicting decision-making: maximize the rewards of all intelligences

$$\max_{\pi_s \in \delta(A(s))} \sum_{i \in I} \sum_{a \in A(s)} \pi_s(a) \cdot Q_i(s, a) \tag{30}$$

Since DQN is used as the reinforcement learning algorithm, the training of the model will take a lot of time since it involves a deep neural network, so we use two scheduling programs with the same initial weights of the neural network at the same time, one of them is responsible for training and refining the network model, and the other is only responsible for making decisions. Since there is no need to train the model, the program that makes the decision does not involve the back propagation process, and the computation time is fast enough to satisfy real-time.

Based on the above description, we can summarize in Algorithm 1 the basic flow of our online algorithm for giving Lyapunov-based DQNs.

---
**Algorithm 1** Deep Q Learning algorithm
---
1: Initialize function Q with random weights
2: Initialize memory D with capacity C
3: **for** *episode* $= 1, 2, 3, ...$ **do**
4:     Initialize sequence $s_l = \{x_l\}$
5:     Initialize preprocessed sequenced $\phi = \phi(s_i)$
6:     **for** $t = 1$ to T **do**
7:         With probabilty $\epsilon$ select random action $a_t \in A$
8:         otherwise select $a_t = \max_a Q^*(\phi(s_t), a; \theta$
9:         Execute action $a_t$ in environment and observe reward $r_t$ and state $s_t$
10:         Store transition$(\phi_t, a_t, r_t, \phi_{t+1})$ in D
11:         Sample random minibatch of tansitions $(\phi_t, a_t, r_t, \phi_{t+1})$ from D
12:         Set $y_j = r_j + \gamma \cdot \max_a Q(\phi_{j+1}, a'; \theta)$
13:         Perform a gradient descent step on $(y_j - Q(\phi_t, a_j l\theta)^2)$
14:     **end for**
15: **end for**
---

## 5   Simulation and Discussions

In this section, we will evaluate the performance and nausea due to the Lyapunov optimization-based DQN algorithm introduced in this paper in terms of both the average latency of the in-vehicle application execution and the average cost of the user application.

### 5.1   Simulation Setup

For the simulation experiment, we assume that 5 RSUs are contained in MEC system and each RSU contains 5 VEC servers. One centrailized cloud is contained in environment and this cloud contains two cloud servers. The processing speed of local vehicles fall between $6 \times 10^6$ to $1 \times 10^7$ kB/s and the execution rate of VEC servers are $2.4 \times 10^7$ to $4.7 \times 10^7$ kB/s, the execution rate of cloud server is about 2 times as much as edge servers. The channel bandwidth among vehicles and RSUs is 3.7 MHz, the channel gain $G_n$ among vehicles and RSUs is $20^{-4}$. The transmission power of each vehicle is 120 mW. There are 30 mobile vehicles randomly distributed within the rsu coverage and move with random trajectories and each vehicle is distributed from 1 to 4 m/s. The datasize of tasks are between $2 \times 10^7$ to $5 \times 10^7$ KB. The noise power $N_0$ is $10^{-10}$ mW. Local servers are inexpensive, while cloud servers cost is about 50 times as much as edge servers. The DAG for some of the applications is shown in Fig. 2.

In the simulation, we compare the Lyapunov optimization scheme proposed in this chapter with the original scheme without Lyapunov optimization as well as with three traditional schemes for two aspects of application latency and average user cost under changing unique conditions.

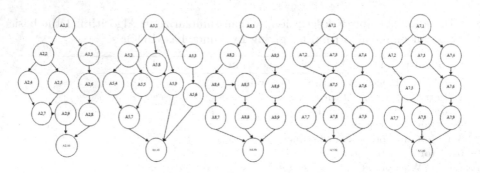

**Fig. 2.** The workflows of 5 vehicles in the experiment.

- Random Selection (RS): Computing the TPQ, the TPQ is the task list that sorted by the last start time of all tasks, select tasks from TPQ, and then deploy tasks $A_{i,k}$ to a random VEC server $r \in Des_i$.
- MAMTS: Computing the TPQ, Select tasks from TPQ, and the TPQ is the task list that sorted by the last start time of all tasks, then system will deploy task $A_{i,k}$ to the server $r \in Des_i$ choosed by MAMTS algorithm [8].
- Greedy Selection (GS): Computing the TPQ, the TPQ is the task list that sorted by the last start time of all tasks, select tasks from TPQ, and then greedily deploy the task to VEC server $r \in Des_i$, because it could provide the task for the least execution time [17].

## 5.2   Performance Comparison

Figure 3 shows the cost consumption per unit time slot of our proposed DQN-based multi-objective multi-intelligence task deployment algorithm before and after using Lyapunov optimization. The results show that Lyapunov-opt further reduces the task latency from the original algorithm while strictly adhering to the long-term energy constraint. Moreover, after Lyapunov-opt, the cost of task execution becomes smoother and more uniformly distributed in a macroscopic sense.

In Fig. 3, we can also see that in the first about one thousand time segments, the energy consumption with Lyapunov optimization will be slightly higher than without Lyapunov optimization, this phenomenon occurs because the Liapunov optimization is to average the overall cost consumption to the various time periods, and try to maintain the balance of the cost queue and slow down the peak of the peak period of the peak period of time, Therefore, in the early stage, the cost of the optimized model is slightly higher than the non-optimized model.

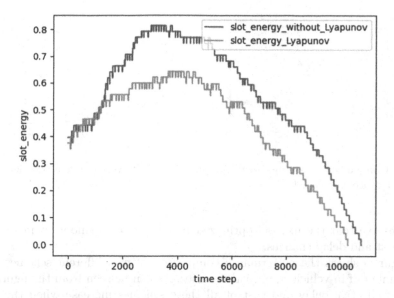

**Fig. 3.** Comparisons of Slot cost with Lyapunov or not.

Figure 4 shows the comparison of the average task latency and average cost consumption of the different approaches at different processing speeds. As can be seen from the figure, although the average latency of our algorithm is almost three times that of the other algorithms, the gap between the latencies gradually decreases as the processing speed of the server increases. On the other hand, the total cost consumption of our method can be reduced by 60% or more compared to other methods. This is because conventional methods do not consider energy consumption, which consumes a significant amount of cost while achieving the minimum average interval latency. In contrast, our scheme employs Lyapunov optimization, which greatly satisfies the cost constraints despite a slight sacrifice in delay performance.

Analyzing Fig. 4 in more detail, we can see from the left sub-figure that since the traditional method does not consider the cost, the change in the average cost consumption will be disorderly, while our method maintains a low cost consumption in the case that the server speed becomes gradually faster; in the right sub-figure we can see that the average task latency of our method decreases gradually with the increase of the server processing speed, the reason that there is a rebound in the middle segment is that our method is considering the joint optimization of latency and cost. The reason that there is a rebound in the middle segment is that our method is a joint optimization considering delay and cost, and combined with the left figure we can see that the cost is decreasing during this period, then the corresponding delay will have a rise. But we can

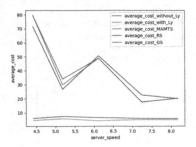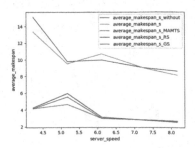

**Fig. 4.** Comparison of average cost of applications and average makespan delay with different processing speed

also observe that the method optimized by Lyapunov is smoother in terms of both cost and delay changes.

Figure 5 shows the performance comparison of five different schemes when the number of in-vehicle applications varies. As can be seen from the figure, the average effective delay and cost of all these schemes increase when the number of applications increases. Compared with the other strategies, our proposed strategy is two to three times higher than the traditional methods in terms of average delay, but the gap between the average delay decreases as the number of edge users increases; also, our proposed strategy increases the average cost very slowly and the average cost consumption is much smaller than the other algorithms.

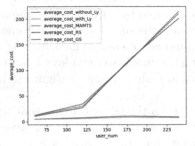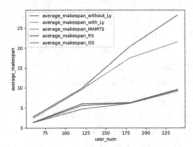

**Fig. 5.** Comparison of average cost of applications and average makespan delay with different number of applications

It can also be seen from Fig. 5 that the increase in edge users implies a high-pressure environment at the edge. Facing high-pressure environments, it can be seen from the left subfigure that our approach consistently keeps the average cost low, although there is a relatively small increase in the average cost. Meanwhile, it can be seen from the right subfigure that the optimized approach using Lyapunov is able to further reduce the average latency and further optimize the task offloading strategy in more high-pressure environments, but in contrast to the traditional scheme, the reason for our higher average latency may be that our proposed scheme focuses on task offloading, while the comparison scheme considers both task scheduling and task offloading.

## 6 Conclusions

In this paper, we propose a DQN algorithm based on Lyapunov optimization that acts mainly on vehicle-mounted applications with interdependent tasks. These tasks can be deployed to different layers in a hybrid three-tier edge computing environment. We assume that each application is represented by a DAG. Our optimization problem is defined as minimizing the average cost of all mobile users and the average latency of all applications subject to long-term cost constraints. We then propose an algorithm based on Lyapunov optimization and DQN with multi-objective multi-intelligentsia for generating task offloading solutions. Simulation results clearly show that our proposed approach outperforms other algorithms in terms of both application latency and combined user cost tradeoffs. For the method proposed in this paper, there are some limitations, for example, this paper only considers task offloading without considering task scheduling, which can lead to some time-sensitive task timeouts. For future improvement, the scheduling of tasks can be considered along with task offloading and the deadline of tasks can be considered as one of the rewards of DQN.

**Acknowledgement.** This work was supported in part by the Key Research and Development Project of Henan Province under Grant No. 231111211900, in part by the Henan Province Science and Technology Project under Grant No. 232102210024.

## References

1. Kumar, S., Bhagat, L., Jin, J.: Multi-neural network based tiled 360° video caching with mobile edge computing. J. Netw. Comput. Appl. **201**, 103342 (2022). https://doi.org/10.1016/j.jnca.2022.103342
2. Hu, X., Wang, J., Zhong, C.: Statistical CSI based design for intelligent reflecting surface assisted MISO systems. Sci. China Inf. Sci. **63**(12) (2020). https://doi.org/10.1007/s11432-020-3033-3
3. Lai, X., Fan, L., Lei, X., Deng, Y., Karagiannidis, G.K., Nallanathan, A.: Secure mobile edge computing networks in the presence of multiple eavesdroppers. IEEE Trans. Commun. **70**(1), 500–513 (2022). https://doi.org/10.1109/TCOMM.2021.3119075
4. Na, Z., et al.: UAV-based wide-area internet of things: an integrated deployment architecture. IEEE Network **35**(5), 122–128 (2021). https://doi.org/10.1109/MNET.001.2100128
5. Quan, W., Cheng, N., Qin, M., Zhang, H., Chan, H.A., Shen, X.: Adaptive transmission control for software defined vehicular networks. IEEE Wirel. Commun. Lett. **8**(3), 653–656 (2019). https://doi.org/10.1109/LWC.2018.2879514
6. Lee, E., Lee, E.K., Gerla, M., Oh, S.Y.: Vehicular cloud networking: architecture and design principles. IEEE Commun. Mag. **52**(2), 148–155 (2014). https://doi.org/10.1109/MCOM.2014.6736756

7. Li, T., Gao, C., Jiang, L., Pedrycz, W., Shen, J.: Publicly verifiable privacy-preserving aggregation and its application in IoT. J. Netw. Comput. Appl. **126**, 39–44 (2019). https://doi.org/10.1016/j.jnca.2018.09.018

8. Liu, Y., et al.: Dependency-aware task scheduling in vehicular edge computing. IEEE Internet Things J. **7**(6), 4961–4971 (2020). https://doi.org/10.1109/JIOT.2020.2972041

9. Lin, W., et al.: A hardware-aware CPU power measurement based on the power-exponent function model for cloud servers. Inf. Sci. **547**, 1045–1065 (2021). https://doi.org/10.1016/j.ins.2020.09.033

10. Hu, L., Yan, H., Li, L., Pan, Z., Liu, X., Zhang, Z.: MHAT: an efficient model-heterogenous aggregation training scheme for federated learning. Inf. Sci. **560**, 493–503 (2021). https://doi.org/10.1016/j.ins.2021.01.046

11. Mao, Y., You, C., Zhang, J., Huang, K., Letaief, K.B.: A survey on mobile edge computing: the communication perspective. IEEE Commun. Surv. Tutorials **19**(4), 2322–2358 (2017). https://doi.org/10.1109/COMST.2017.2745201

12. Hou, X., Li, Y., Chen, M., Wu, D., Jin, D., Chen, S.: Vehicular fog computing: a viewpoint of vehicles as the infrastructures. IEEE Trans. Veh. Technol. **65**(6), 3860–3873 (2016). https://doi.org/10.1109/TVT.2016.2532863

13. Zhou, Z., Liu, P., Chang, Z., Xu, C., Zhang, Y.: Energy-efficient workload offloading and power control in vehicular edge computing, pp. 191–196 (2018). https://doi.org/10.1109/WCNCW.2018.8368975

14. He, Q., et al.: A game-theoretical approach for mitigating edge DDoS attack. IEEE Trans. Dependable Secur. Comput. **19**(4), 2333–2348 (2022). https://doi.org/10.1109/TDSC.2021.3055559

15. Caiazza, C., Giordano, S., Luconi, V., Vecchio, A.: Edge computing vs centralized cloud: impact of communication latency on the energy consumption of LTE terminal nodes. Comput. Commun. **194**, 213–225 (2022). https://doi.org/10.1016/j.comcom.2022.07.026

16. Zhou, Y., et al.: A novel approach to applications deployment with multiple inter-denpendent tasks in a hybrid three-layer vehicular computing environment, pp. 251–256 (2021). https://doi.org/10.1109/SMC52423.2021.9659035

17. Zhao, Z., Liu, S., Zhou, M., Guo, X., Xue, J.: Iterated greedy algorithm for solving a new single machine scheduling problem, pp. 430–435 (2019). https://doi.org/10.1109/ICNSC.2019.8743328

18. Shahidani, F., Ghasemi, A., Haghighat, A.: Task scheduling in edge-fog-cloud architecture: a multi-objective load balancing approach using reinforcement learning algorithm, pp. 1337–1359 (2023). https://doi.org/10.1007/s00607-022-01147-5

19. Zhang, K., Mao, Y., Leng, S., He, Y., Zhang, Y.: Mobile-edge computing for vehicular networks: a promising network paradigm with predictive off-loading. IEEE Veh. Technol. Mag. **12**(2), 36–44 (2017). https://doi.org/10.1109/MVT.2017.2668838

20. Wu, Y., Gao, C.: Intelligent task offloading for vehicular edge computing with imperfect CSI: a deep reinforcement approach **55**, 9 (2022). https://doi.org/10.1016/j.phycom.2022.101867

21. Zhang, L., Xia, J., Gao, C., Zhu, F., Fan, C., Ou, J.: DQN-based mobile edge computing for smart internet of vehicle, 45 (2022). https://doi.org/10.1186/s13634-022-00876-1

# Edge Server Deployment Approach Based on Uniformity and Centrality

Xinghong Jiang[1] , Yong Ma[1]([✉]) , Yunni Xia[2] , Qilin Xie[1] ,
and Wenxin Jian[3]

[1] School of Computer and Information Engineering, Jiangxi Normal University,
Nanchang 330027, China
{jxh,may,qilinxie}@jxnu.edu.cn
[2] School of Computer Science, Chongqing University, Chongqing, China
[3] School of Digital Industry, Jiangxi Normal University, Shangrao 334000, China
jianwenxin@jxnu.edu.cn

**Abstract.** In mobile Internet applications that support edge computing, the deployment scheme of edge servers affects the business operation state. Traditional edge servers are deployed on base stations, which do not fully extend the service range of edge servers, resulting in difficult access to edge services. Therefore, this paper proposes the Edge Server Deployment Approach Based on Uniformity and Centrality (ESDA-UC). ESDA-UC considers intersections as candidate deployment locations for edge servers, taking into account traffic density and road network structure. Connection centrality, between centrality, base station centrality, and traffic density are used as the main factors. The intersection centrality of each intersection is calculated as the selection criteria for the deployment location. To avoid concentrating the coverage of edge servers in developed regions of the city, we allocate the number of edge servers according to regional importance. Finally, the improved greedy algorithm is utilized to generate a deployment plan for edge servers. Experiments show that ESDA-UC has higher base station coverage, vehicle coverage, and vehicle coverage time ratios compared to the baseline method.

**Keywords:** Edge computing · Service scope expansion · Deployment · Intersection centrality

## 1 Introduction

With the development of artificial intelligence, big data, and other information technologies, business needs based on the mobile Internet continue to emerge. Existing mobile terminals have limited computing and storage capacity. In cases of complex demands, it is necessary to transfer task data to the cloud for processing. However, the cloud computing center is far from the terminal. Network latency can adversely affect real-time tasks. Edge computing introduces storage and computing resources to the user end, greatly reducing the task transmission

H. Gao et al. (Eds.): CollaborateCom 2023, LNICST 561, pp. 93–110, 2024.
https://doi.org/10.1007/978-3-031-54521-4_6

delay. It is an effective means to improve the degree of completion of real-time tasks. The Edge Server (ES) is an important component of edge computing.

There are two ways for mobile devices to get edge services. A multi-hop approach is used [1], where the transmission of tasks is realized through the base station. The other is a single-hop approach, where the mobile device establishes a connection channel directly with the edge server. The former involves issues such as task transmission path selection and transmission delay. Therefore, the method of establishing a transmission path between the mobile device and the ES is the best way to obtain edge services. However, the number of edge servers is sparse, and the coverage is limited. It is worth studying how to expand the scope of edge services with a limited number of ESs.

At present, a large number of scholars have conducted research for the deployment approach of edge service. Moyukh Laha used intersection centrality as intersection gain to find the optimal intersection as the deployment location for ES using the Dynamic Programming (DP) algorithm [2]. But it only considered the vehicle service demand. Chen Xiaoran [3] proposed a road side unit(RSU) deployment mechanism based on intersection prioritization and deployment uniformity. It proposes a uniformity scheme, considering that the deployment scheme based on intersection prioritization leads to overlapping coverage of roadside units. But it still only considers the service demand for vehicles. Meanwhile, its uniform deployment scheme may lead to edge servers being deployed in a few regions. Noting that there is a close relationship between base stations and ES, Zengshi Qin et al. proposed an edge server deployment scheme based on through the improved Top-K algorithm by taking into account the distance between base stations and edge servers, the weight proportion of base stations in the base station cluster, and the upper limit problem of the computational task [4]. The scheme takes the base station as the deployment location of the edge server. It cannot expand the scope of edge services with a limited number of edge servers. Therefore, it is a challenge to expand the area and scenarios of edge services simultaneously in complex urban road networks.

In this paper, we investigate the ES placement problem in the edge service expansion problem and propose the Edge Server Deployment Approach Based on Uniformity and Centrality(ESDA-UC). Firstly, the intersection centrality is calculated by using the intersection information and base station information. Then the intersection traffic density is calculated based on the cab trajectory data. The intersection priority is obtained by combining intersection centrality and traffic density. In order to avoid the service capacity to be clustered only in the developed regions of the city, we use the intersection location information to generate multiple regions by k-means++ clustering [5]. The number of edge servers in each region is calculated by combining the intersection priority. An improved greedy algorithm is utilized to select suitable intersections from the regions as deployment locations for edge servers.

The main contributions of this paper include the following four aspects.

(1) This paper proposes the concept of base station centrality. This mines hot intersections in urban road networks from different perspectives of edge service expansion.
(2) First, the K-means++ algorithm is used to divide the region. Then, the number of edge servers is allocated according to the average value of intersection priority in the region. Avoiding the problem of edge servers being deployed only in developed subregions of the city.
(3) Using a improved greedy algorithm to select intersections for deployment from the subregion to avoid overlapping edge service ranges.

The rest of this paper is organized as follows. We first describe the related work in Sect. 2. Then Sect. 3 presents the basic definitions and the framework underlying the approach of this paper. In Sect. 4, we describe each step of our method in detail. In Sect. 5, we show our dataset and experimental results. Finally, in Sect. 6, we conclude our paper.

## 2    Related Work

The foundation of edge nodes placement problem starts with comprehensive research available on similar topics such as base station, and road side unit.

Base station placement problem are addressed in [6]. The literature proposes to solve the model by an improved differential evolutionary algorithm. The algorithm has two sets of variation and restart strategies to adapt to different traffic volumes, which can dynamically adjust the base station deployment strategy according to the traffic volume. Dai et al. [7] trained a predictor of received signal strength without propagation model based on machine learning model. The coverage performance of the base station deployment has been optimized by a multi-objective heuristic approach. Literature [8] proposes a strategy for deploying microbase stations in 5G HetNets to obtain high energy efficiency. It optimizes the objective values and makes trade-offs under different user distribution probabilities to improve the adaptability to different user distribution scenarios.

RSU is a communication node installed inside the infrastructure. Ghosh D [9] addresses this trade-off by incorporating a new scheme called Cross-Impact Analysis System for Optimal RSU Deployment (IIA-ORD). The main goal of IIA-ORD is achieved by modeling the transportation network as a connectivity graph and executing a modified K-shell and TOPSIS-based framework. The literature [10] investigates the delay and roadside unit deployment problem for in-vehicle self-organizing networks in cities. It is demonstrated that the roadside unit deployment problem is an uncertain polynomial time hard problem. A binary differential evolution scheme is proposed to maximize the number of roads covered by deployed roadside units. The literature [11] proposes a geometry-based sparse coverage protocol that aims to consider the geometric properties of the road network, the vehicle movement patterns and resource constraints. Sengathir J et al. [12] proposed Honey Badger Optimization Algorithm based

RSU Deployment (HBOA-RSUD) scheme. A multi-objective fitness function is utilized to improve the VANET network coverage.

In recent years, there have been several studies on edge server placement in urban vehicular networks. The literature [13] describes the edge server configuration problem in a smart city mobile edge computing environment as a multi-objective constrained optimization problem. To achieve this, edge servers are placed at some strategic locations. Laha M et al. [2] jointly considered the structural characteristics of the road network, ranked the candidate sites for edge node placement using complex network-based centrality metrics and vehicle traffic distribution of the network. In the literature [14], a more efficient low-energy placement scheme is proposed to formulate the server deployment problem as a multi-objective optimization problem. Luo F et al. [15] proposed a deep reinforcement learning-based edge server placement algorithm. The edge server placement problem is modeled as a Markov decision process, formalized in state space, action space and reward function, and finally solved using a reinforcement learning algorithm to achieve optimal placement. The literature [16] transforms the edge server deployment problem into a minimum dominating set problem in graph theory, and proposes a greedy-based solution algorithm for edge servers whose capacity can be configured on demand, with the key idea of iteratively selecting the nodes that can connect as many nodes as possible under constraints such as delay, degree, and cluster size.

Using base stations directly as the deployment location of edge servers is not able to expand the scope of edge services with a limited number of edge servers. The deployment approach of RSU roadside units only considers the service demand of vehicles. In order to expand the edge service scope and balance the service demand in different regions, this paper designs and optimizes the edge server deployment approach in a two-dimensional city scenario.

## 3    Preliminaries

We assume that all edge servers have the same communication range. ES can exchange information with vehicles or base stations within the communication range. Dubey B.B. proposed that by using intersections as deployment locations for edge servers, the coverage of edge servers to vehicles will increase by about 15% compared to other locations [3]. The increase in the coverage of edge services results in better coverage continuity for vehicles. Thus, the edge service with better continuity is provided to the vehicles [17]. ES deployed at intersections can also establish connectivity with base stations. In summary, ES deployed at intersections extends the scope and continuity of edge services. Therefore, this paper uses all intersections in the target road network as a set of candidate deployment locations for edge servers. Figure 1 is a schematic diagram of the services provided by ES deployed at the intersection.

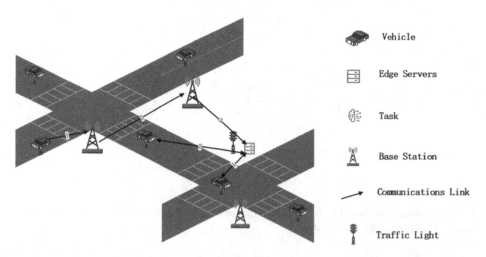

| | Vehicle |
| | Edge Servers |
| | Task |
| | Base Station |
| | Communications Link |
| | Traffic Light |

**Fig. 1.** Schematic diagram of edge services. Car A establishes direct communication links with the ES at both neighboring intersections. Car B establishes an indirect communication link with the ES through the base station.

### 3.1   Road Model

The urban road network is a complex network system consisting of intersections and the road edges between intersections. $G = (V, E, S)$ represents the road network graph with p intersections, in which V and E denote the intersection set $V = \{v_1, v_2, \ldots, v_p\}$ and the edge set $\{e_{ij}\}$ of G. $e_{ij} = (v_i, v_j)$ denotes an edge connecting intersection $v_i$ and $v_j$, and $S \in \{0,1\}^{p \times p}$ is a adjacency matric storing $G'$s topological structure, in which an entry $S_{ij} = 1$ if $e_{ij} \in E$; otherwise, $S_{ij} = 0$. Assume that there are s base stations in the city. The set of base stations is denoted as $B = \{b_1, b_2, \ldots, b_s\}$.

### 3.2   Coverage Model

Mobile devices can establish an indirect connection to the $ES$ through a base station or a direct connection to the ES. Therefore, both the number of base stations within communication range and intersection traffic flow should be considered when selecting ES deployment locations. The ES deployment problem is represented by the coverage model $C\left(C^R, VE, r, m\right)$, where $C^R$ denotes the set of base stations that can be covered by the deployed ES, VE denotes the number of vehicles that can be covered by the deployed ES, r denotes the communication radius of the ES, and m denotes the number of ESs deployed in the road network.

Typically, the coverage scope of an ES is represented by a circle. The location of the center of the circle is the deployment location of the ES. Denoting the set of intersections where ES is deployed by $V^R$, $v_i^R$ denotes that ES is deployed at intersection $v_i$. $C_i^R$ is the set of base stations covered at intersection $v_i$. $VE_i$ is

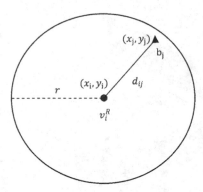

**Fig. 2.** Coverage model. The black origin in the diagram indicates the ES and the black triangle indicates the base station.

the number of vehicles passing through intersection $v_i$. As shown in Fig. 2, base station $b_j$ is located within the ES coverage scope at $v_i^R$. For any base station $b_j$, the way to determine whether it is within the coverage scope at $v_i^R$ and update $C_i^R$ is as follows:

$$C_i^R = \begin{cases} C_i^R \cup \{b_j\}, & d_{ij} \leqslant r \\ C_i^R, & \text{otherwise} \end{cases}$$

Suppose the coordinates of base station $b_j$ are $(x_j, y_j)$. If base station $b_j$ is in ES coverage scope, then $b_j$ is added to the set $C_i^R$. where $d_{ij}$ denotes the distance between $v_i$ and $b_j$, and is calculated using the Euclidean distance $d_{ij} = \sqrt{(x_j - x_i)^2 + (y_j - y_i)^2}$.

The set of base station and vehicle coverage for all ESs deployed is $C^R = \mathrm{U}_{i=1}^m C_i^R$ and $VE = \mathrm{U}_{i=1}^m VE_i$, respectively. The optimization deployment objective in this paper is to cover as many base stations and vehicles as possible for the determined number of ESs.

### 3.3   Framework

The simple framework of the methodology of this paper is shown in Fig. 3. The framework consists of four parts: intersection information collection, hotspot intersection mining, region segmentation and ES deployment location selection. Intersection information collection is the first step of the system model. The collected intersection information includes the latitude and longitude of the intersection, vehicle trajectory data, and the latitude and longitude information of the base station. According to the intersection information, the static centrality and traffic density of the intersection are calculated to get the priority of each intersection. Deploying ES at intersections with high priority can obtain a higher coverage scope. In order to avoid ES is only concentrated in a few subregions, we partition the city. When selecting the deployment location within a region, in order to avoid the overlap of ES coverage we use an improved greedy algorithm to generate the final deployment plan.

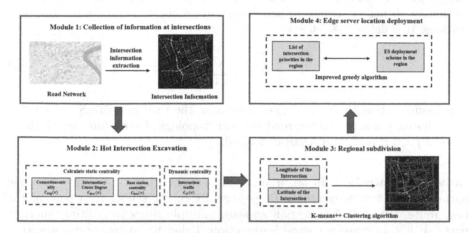

**Fig. 3.** The framework diagram of the methodology in this paper. The framework consists of four parts: Collection of intersection informations, Hotspot intersection Excavation, Regional subdivision and Edge server location deployment.

## 4   Edge Server Deployment Approach Based on Uniformity and Centrality

In this section our approach is discussed in detail. Firstly, the hotspot intersection mining algorithm is introduced. Then the edge server deployment scheme is discussed, which consists of two parts: region partitioning and intersection deployment location selection.

### 4.1   Hot Intersection Excavation

We use centrality [18] to mine urban hotspot intersections. In this section, we discuss four influencing factors for hotspot intersection mining: traffic density, connection centrality, base station centrality, and intermediary centrality.

**Traffic Density:** The traffic density of an intersection refers to the number of vehicles passing through the intersection per unit time. Edge servers are deployed at an intersection with high traffic density, which improves the number and duration of vehicle coverage for the ES. The traffic density of intersection $v_i$ is denoted as $C_{Tf}(v_i)$. The calculation formula is as follows:

$$C_{Tf}(v_i) = \frac{t(v_i)}{Tl} \tag{1}$$

$t(v_i)$ represents the number of vehicles passing through intersection $v_i$ during a fixed period. $Tl$ represents the length of the unit time.

**Degree Centrality:** The degree centrality of an intersection refers to the number of intersections directly connected to it by roads. An intersection with a large degree of connectivity centrality has a higher structural importance. Intersections with higher structural importance are more likely to cover more base stations. It is defined as follows:

$$c_{\deg}(v_i) = \sum_{j=1}^{p} S_{ij} \tag{2}$$

It is assumed that there are $p$ intersections in the road network. $S \in \{0,1\}^{p \times p}$ is a adjacency matric storing road network topological structure, in which an entry $S_{ij} = 1$ if $e_{ij} \in E$; otherwise, $S_{ij} = 0$.

**Between Centrality:** In an urban road network, there are always multiple paths between two destinations. People usually choose the shortest path as the best route. When an intersection appears multiple times in multiple shortest paths, it is considered a central intersection. Using ES at intersections with a high the between centrality improves ES vehicle coverage. It is defined as follows:

$$c_{\mathrm{btw}}(v_i) = \sum_{v_s \neq v_i \neq v_t} \frac{\sigma_{s,t}(v_i)}{\sigma_{s,t}} \tag{3}$$

$\sigma_{s,t}$ represents the number of shortest paths between any two intersections $v_s$ and $v_t$. $\sigma_{s,t}(v_i)$ represents the number of shortest paths between intersections $v_s$ and $v_t$ that pass through intersection $v_i$.

**Base Station Centrality:** In urban environments, telecom departments tend to deploy more base stations for prosperous subregions, so the number of base stations around an urban intersection reflects the prosperity of that intersection [19]. The higher the prosperity of the intersection, the more suitable as an edge server deployment location. The base station centrality of intersection $v_i$ is denoted as $C_{bm}(v_i)$ and is calculated as follows:

$$C_{bm}(v_i) = \frac{m(v_i)}{M} \tag{4}$$

m $(v_i)$ denotes the number of base stations that can be covered by deploying ES at intersection $v_i$, while $M$ denotes the total number of base stations.

Traffic density, connection centrality, between centrality, and base station centrality reflect the importance of the intersection in different dimensions. In order to conveniently measure the importance of the four influencing factors, the four influencing factors are normalized in terms of values. The calculation formula is as follows:

$$X = \frac{x - \min(x)}{\max(x) - \min(x)} \tag{5}$$

where $X$ is the data after normalization, $x$ is the source data, min($x$)is the minimum value in the source data, and max($x$) is the maximum value in the source data.

After normalization of the influence factors, the four influence factors are considered together to calculate the intersection priority.

$$p_{v_i} = wf \times C_{de.g.}(v_i) + wc \times C_{btw}(v_i)$$
$$+wl \times C_{bm}(v_i) + wb \times C_{Tf}(v_i) \tag{6}$$

where $p_{v_i}$ is the intersection priority of urban intersection $v_i$. $wf$, $wc$, $wl$ and $wb$ are the weights of connection centrality, between centrality, base station centrality, and traffic density, respectively, all of which take positive values and $wf + wc + wl + wb = 1$. Parameters are set with reference to the deployment realities and are set by the edge server deployers.

## 4.2   Edge Servers Deployment Rules

There are developed subregions in every city and multiple intersections in this subregion will have higher priority. Selecting intersections for edge servers deployment only from the dimension of intersection centrality will result in edge servers being concentrated in a few subregions. We perform the following steps to improve service coverage and server continuity for edge services. Firstly, the city region is divided into multiple subregion based on the intersection latitude and longitude coordinates. Second, the number of edge servers in the region is obtained based on the mean value of intersection priority in the subregion. Finally, a greedy algorithm is used to select a suitable intersection from the subregion as the deployment location.

**Region Division.** In this paper, K-means++ clustering is performed using the latitude and longitude location information of the intersections to generate multiple clusters of intersections, and the range of the clusters of intersections is treated as an subregion. As shown in Fig. 4, the k-means++ algorithm adds the initial centroid generation scheme to the k-means algorithm. Assume that $s$ city subregions are generated. We finally output the set of intersections under all city subregions K = $\{K_1, K_2, \ldots, K_s\}$.

**ES Allocation Strategy Under Subregion.** In this paper, using the intersection priority, we can calculate the average value of intersection priority between subregions. It is found that due to the large differences in the level of development between urban subregions, the average values of priority among subregions differed significantly. If the number of edge servers is allocated entirely based on the regional intersection priority average value. It will lead to an unbalanced distribution of the number of edge servers. In extreme cases, there will be excess edge service capacity in developed subregions and insufficient or even non-existent edge services capacity in less developed subregions.

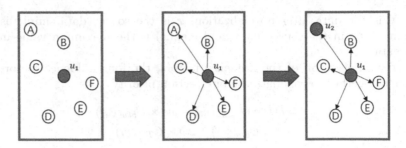

**Fig. 4.** Schematic diagram of center point selection in the diagram, point $u_1$ is the center point. $u_1$ is calculated with the distance from all the remaining points. The point A, which is furthest away, is used as the center point.

In order to improve the utilization rate of edge services. We call a certain percentage of ES, as the number of edge servers that are evenly distributed among all subregions. This part of the ES quantity is called the base number. The ratio of the base number to the total number of ESs is denoted as $\lambda$. The remaining ESs are allocated proportionally. Subregions with higher mean intersection priority are allocated more. The specific steps are as follows.

(1) Calculate the base number of subregions to obtain the number of remaining edge servers that denoted as $n$.
(2) Calculate the average value of intersection priority of each subregion. $a_i$ indicates the average value of intersection priority of the ith subregion. The range of i is $[1, s].s$ denotes the number of urban subregions. $p_j$ indicates the intersection priority of intersection j, and $M$ indicates the number of intersections existing in subregion i. The calculation formula is as follows:

$$a_i = \frac{\sum_{j=1}^{M} p_j}{M} \tag{7}$$

(3) Calculation of the importance of intersection subregion. $A_i$ denotes the importance of intersection subregion i, and the formula is as follows:

$$A_i = \frac{a_i}{\sum_{j=1}^{s} a_j} \tag{8}$$

(4) The number of edge servers added to the base number in the subregion is calculated based on the intersection subregion importance degree. The calculation formula is as follows:

$$n_i = [\text{n} \times A_i + \epsilon] \tag{9}$$

The number of ES added to subregion $i$, which are denoted as $n_i$. Where $[\cdot]$ indicates rounding down. To ensure that ES is not left over, we set $\epsilon$ to 0.5.

**Allocation Strategy of Edge Servers in the Subregion.** The intersections within the subregion are spatially close to each other. When edge server deployment intersections are selected based solely on intersection priority, the resulting service scope may overlap. To avoid this, a greedy algorithm is used in this study to select deployment intersections within the subregion. The specific steps are as follows.

(1) Select an intersection with the highest priority from the intersections in the subregion as the deployment intersection of the edge server.
(2) Remove the deployment intersection and the intersections under its coverage from the region.
(3) Repeat steps (1) (2) until the required number of intersections are identified.

---

**Algorithm 1. ESDA-UC**

---

**Require:** Urban road network: G=(V,E,S), Intersection latitude and longitude information:$(lat, lon)$.
**Ensure:** Abnormal sub-regions sets: $AR_t$
1: Initialize the intersection priority set:$U \leftarrow \varnothing$;
2: Initialize the set of intersections under the city subregion:$K \leftarrow \varnothing$;
3: Initialize the set of intersection means :$A \leftarrow \varnothing$;
4: Initialize a set of deployment intersections for edge servers:$AR \leftarrow \varnothing$;
5: **for** $i = 1$ to $len(V)$ **do**
6:    Calculate $C_{Tf}(v_i), C_{btw}(v_i), C_{Tf}(v_i), C_{bm}(v_i)$;
7:    $p_{v_i} = wf \times C_{deg}(v_i) + wc \times C_{btw}(v_i) + wl \times C_{bm}(v_i) + wb \times C_{Tf}(v_i)$;
8:    $U.\text{append}(p_{v_i})$;
9: **end for**
10: $K = \{K_1, K_2, \ldots, K_s\} \leftarrow$ K-means $+ +(lat, lon)$
11: **for** $i = 1$ to $len(K)$ **do**
12:    $a_i = \frac{\sum_{j=1}^{M} p_{v_j}}{M}$
13:    $A \leftarrow A.\text{add}(a_i)$;
14: **end for**
15: **for** $i = 1$ to $len(A)$ **do**
16:    $A = \frac{a_i}{\sum_{j=1}^{s} a_j}$
17:    $n = \lceil n \times A + \epsilon \rceil$
18:    **for** $t = 1$ to $n$ **do**
19:       $k_{\max} = K_i.\text{selectMax}()$
20:       **if** $distance(k_{\max}) > coverage$ **then**
21:          $AR \leftarrow AR.\text{add}(k_{\max})$;
22:          $K_i \leftarrow K_i.\text{remove}(k_{\max})$;
23:       **end if**
24:    **end for**
25: **end for**
26: **return** AR

---

Algorithm 1 shows how the three main functional modules are organized in the ESDA-UC framework. Lines 5–9 show the steps of hotspot intersection mining. We first calculate degree centrality, between centrality, base station centrality and traffic density for each intersection. Then, the intersection priority is calculated by fusing the centrality metrics. In line 10, the intersection area is divided according to the intersection information. In lines 11–14, we compute the priority metrics to obtain the region based on the intersection priorities in the region. Lines 15–17, we compute the number of ES deployments in the region based on the region prioritization. Lines 18–24, we discover the intersections deployed with ES from the region using the improved greedy algorithm. Line 26, returns the set of deployed intersections for the edge server.

## 5    Experiment

To evaluate the effectiveness of our method, we conduct extensive experiments on real datasets. The experiments are run on a workstation equipped with an Intel i7-12700H CPU and an NVIDIA GeForce RTX 3060 Laptop GPU. The experimental code is all implemented in python. We first perform quantitative analysis on the real dataset. In order to enhance the effectiveness of the scheme, optimization experiments were conducted for the relevant parameters.

### 5.1    Baselines

**Uniform-Based Deployment Approach (UDA):** UAD [20] uses the k-means++ algorithm to cluster the intersections and generate small regions equal to the number of edge servers. Equal number of edge servers are assigned to each small region.

**Edge Server Deployment Approach Based on Based on Degree Centrality (ESDA-DC):** ESDA-DC uses the connectivity centrality of intersections as an evaluation metric. Suitable intersections in urban region are selected as deployment locations for edge servers.

**Edge Server Deployment Approach Based on Based on Between Centrality (ESDA-BC):** ESDA-BC uses the between centrality of intersections as an evaluation metric. Suitable intersections in urban region are selected as deployment locations for edge servers.

**Edge Nodes Placement in 5G Enabled Urban Vehicular Networks: A Centrality-Based Approach(CBA):** The Closeness centrality, Betweenness centrality, and traffic flow of the intersection are taken as the deployment benefits, and the deployment budget is taken as the backpack capacity. The dynamic programming method is used to obtain the deployment scheme [2].

**Edge Server Placement Method Based on Delay and Energy Awareness (ESPE-DE):** An edge server deployment scheme based on improved Top-K algorithm [4].

## 5.2   Real Cities Dataset

In this paper, a rectangular region of 12 km$^2$ between 121°45′27″ ∼ 121°49′ east longitude and 31°21′49″ ∼ 31°24′84″ north latitude in Shanghai is selected as the target region. The region contains 1236 vehicle intersections. Figure 5 shows the electronic map and road network diagram of the target region.

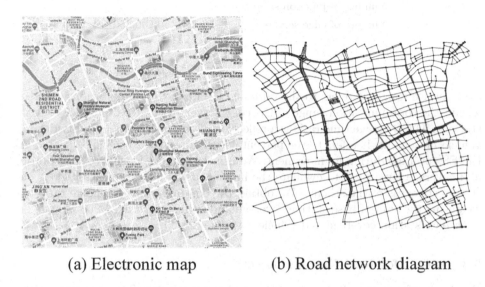

(a) Electronic map                (b) Road network diagram

**Fig. 5.** (a) Electronic maps of the target region. (b) A road map of the target region. The black nodes in the map are intersections. Black lines between nodes indicate roads.

The urban data we collected includes location information for each intersection, centrality data, intersection traffic flow data, and base station location information. To obtain the intersection location information and centrality metrics, we first download the geospatial data through OpenStreetMap and then use the OSMnx package [21] to extract the intersection information and calculate the Between Centrality and Degree Centrality for each intersection. We calculate the base station centrality of each intersection based on the intersection location information and the base station location information. The base station location information in the target region is obtained from the real-edge environment dataset Telecom [22–24], which records the latitude and longitude data of 3,233 base stations within the urban region of Shanghai. We utilized the Shanghai cab trajectory data to calculate the traffic density of each intersection in the month of July 2007. The detailed experimental parameter are shown in Table 1.

We use base station coverage, vehicle coverage, and coverage time ratio as metrics to evaluate the effectiveness of the deployment scheme. Vehicle coverage is a direct reflection of the service scope. It refers to the ratio of the number of vehicles covered within the communication range of the edge server to the total number of vehicles. Base station coverage is an indirect reflection of the

Table 1. Experimental parameter setting

| Parameter | Value |
|---|---|
| Scenario | 12 km$^2$ |
| Number of intersections | 1236 |
| $wf/wc/wl/wb$ | 0.2/0.2/0.3/0.3 |
| Number of junction subregions | 5 |
| Number of edge servers | 50,100,150,200,250 |
| $\lambda$ | 0.4 |

edge service range. It refers to the ratio of the number of base stations covered within the communication range of the edge server to the total number of base stations. The coverage time ratio is a reflection of the coverage continuity during vehicle movement. It refers to the percentage of time that a vehicle is located in the ES coverage during its movement. We use the comprehensive coverage ratio and coverage time ratio to evaluate the impact of the number of subregions on the effectiveness of the scheme. We obtain the comprehensive coverage ratio by weighting the sum of base station coverage and vehicle coverage. The weights of both base station coverage and vehicle coverage are 0.5.

## 5.3   Result for Real Urban Dataset

We first perform quantitative analysis on the real dataset. The communication radius of the edge server is 100 m. The number of edge servers are set as 50, 100, 150, 200 and 250 respectively. The weights of the four influencing factors in the ESDA-UC scheme are set as $wf/wc/wl/wb = 0.2/0.2/0.3/0.3$. The target region is partitioned into 5 sub-regions. The weight of both base station coverage and vehicle coverage in the comprehensive coverage is 0.5. Setting $\lambda = 0.4$ during the experiment.

The experimental results of the methods in this paper and the baseline method are presented in Fig. 6. As the number of ESs increases, all methods improve on every metric. On all the metrics, our method outperforms ESDA-DC and ESDA-BC. This shows that our method is computationally effective for centrality improvement. From the experimental results, our method is not worse than ESPE-DE in terms of base station coverage. Our method outperforms ESPE-DE in terms of vehicle coverage and vehicle coverage time. This proves that the method in this paper is stronger than the base-station-based deployment method in terms of service scenarios and scope. CBA outperforms ESDA-DC and ESDA-BC in each metric. This is due to the fact that CBA integrates the structural characteristics of the road network and the traffic flow characteristics. But the CBA does not overcome the problem of overlapping service scope. Therefore it is weak with our method in all evaluation metrics. In ESDA-DC, ESDA-BC, and CBA, ES is deployed at intersections with high centrality. The probability of obtaining edge service is low when the vehicle leaves the central subregion. This leads to weak edge service coverage continuity. UDA uses a uniform deployment scheme, and vehicle movement characteristics have relatively little impact on coverage continuity. Therefore, UDA outperforms ESDA-DC, ESDA-BC, and CBA in terms of coverage continuity. Our approach considers both region characteristics and intersection centrality. Therefore, it outperforms the baseline approach in coverage continuity.

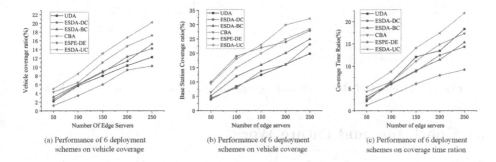

(a) Performance of 6 deployment schemes on vehicle coverage

(b) Performance of 6 deployment schemes on vehicle coverage

(c) Performance of 6 deployment schemes on coverage time ration

**Fig. 6.** The performance of this paper's methodology on each of the evaluation indicators.

## 5.4 Parameter Analysis

This section also verifies the effect of the number of subregions on the comprehensive coverage in the ES number 250 dataset. The experimental results are shown in Fig. 7. From Fig. 7(a), it can be seen that the comprehensive coverage rate shows a significant decrease with the increase in the number of subregions. However, there is a brief rebound in the interval from 15 to 25. As the number of subregions increases, ESs that were originally assigned to hot intersections are assigned to other intersections. This leads to a decrease in the comprehensive coverage rate. The brief recovery of the combined coverage is due to the increase in the number of regions, which elevates the number of ESs at the hotspot intersections. Then the number of regions continues to increase, making the method in this paper similar to the UDA effect. As a result, the comprehensive coverage rate remains stable. From Fig. 7(b), it can be observed that as the number of regions increases, the coverage time first appears to be elevated and then decreases. This is due to the fact that ES is concentrated in developed regions when the number of regions is small. As the number of regions increases, ES is deployed at most of the hotspot subregions. This leads to a decrease in coverage time.

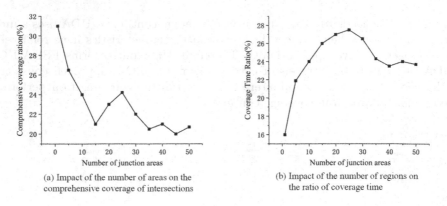

(a) Impact of the number of areas on the comprehensive coverage of intersections

(b) Impact of the number of regions on the ratio of coverage time

**Fig. 7.** The effect of the number of regions on the effectiveness of our method

## 6    Conclusion and Future Work

In this paper, we propose an edge service expansion method based on uniformity and centrality. We find that most intersections in urban environments can realize D2D connectivity with surrounding base stations by collecting base station location information and intersection location information. Based on this finding, in this paper, we take the intersection location as the deployment location of the edge server, and expand the edge service range through the connection between the base station and the edge server. In the specific intersection selection process, we introduce the concept of intersection centrality for discussing the importance degree of intersections. Deploying edge servers only in terms of the importance degree of intersections tends to lead to the concentration of edge coverage in a few regions. Therefore, we first divide the city into sub-regions and allocate the number of edge servers based on the regional importance degree. Finally, the greedy algorithm is utilized to determine the deployment intersections in the entire set of regional intersections.

There exists some extended work in this paper that can be addressed in future work. In this paper, the city is divided into sub-regions in order to avoid concentrating the edge service capacity in the busy subregions of the city. This paper empirically assigns a base number of edge servers to each sub-region, a practice that does not adequately expand the edge service scope. Therefore, in future work, the impact of the value of the base number on the edge service scope needs to be investigated. It should be noted that when mining intersection dynamic centrality in this paper, the intersection dynamic centrality is calculated only from traffic flow due to limited data. However, the dynamic centrality of urban intersections can be mined more deeply by combining the data of intersection pedestrian flow, vehicle flow and urban POI (Point of Interest). Based on the existing data, city managers can fully explore the centrality of intersections to achieve a higher degree of edge service expansion.

**Acknowledgment.** This work was funded by the Jiangxi Normal University Post-graduate Study Abroad Programme Fund. This work was supported by the Jiangxi Provincial Education Department Postgraduate Innovation Fund Project Grant (YC2022-s351).

# References

1. Deng, Y., Chen, Z., Chen, X., et al.: Task offloading in multi-hop relay-aided multi-access edge computing. IEEE Trans. Veh. Technol. **72**(1), 1372–1376 (2022)
2. Laha, M., Kamble, S., Datta, R.: Edge nodes placement in 5G enabled urban vehicular networks: a centrality-based approach. In: 2020 National Conference on Communications (NCC), Kharagpur, India, pp. 1–6 (2020). https://doi.org/10.1109/NCC48643.2020.9056059
3. Chen, X., Tang, X., Chen, W., Chai, M.: Roadside unit deployment mechanism for urban vehicular networks. J. Chin. Comput. Syst. **42**(3), 601–608 (2021)
4. Qin, Z., Xu, F., Xie, Y., et al.: An improved top-K algorithm for edge servers deployment in smart city. Trans. Emerg. Telecommun. Technol. **32**(8), e4249 (2021)
5. Ren, Y.Y., Wang, H., Wang, J.X., et al.: The sub-block demarcation with K-Means++ in each province's interior and establishment analysis of the relative horizontal velocity field model in Mainland China. Chin. J. Geophys. **63**(7), 2516–2533 (2020)
6. Sun, X., Zhang, T., Xu, J., et al.: Energy efficiency-driven mobile base station deployment strategy for shopping malls using modified improved differential evolution algorithm. Appl. Intell. **53**, 1–21 (2022)
7. Dai, L., Zhang, H.: Propagation-model-free base station deployment for mobile net works: integrating machine learning and heuristic methods. IEEE Access **8**, 83375–83386 (2020)
8. Guo, W., Koo, J., Siddiqui, I.F., et al.: QoS-aware energy-efficient MicroBase station deployment for 5G-enabled HetNets. J. King Saud Univ.-Comput. Inf. Sci. **34**(10), 10487–10495 (2022)
9. Ghosh, D., Katehara, H., Rawlley, O., et al.: Artificial intelligence-empowered optimal roadside unit (RSU) deployment mechanism for internet of vehicles (IOV). In: 2022 IEEE 23rd International Symposium on a World of Wireless, Mobile and Multimedia Networks (WoWMoM), pp. 495–500. IEEE (2022)
10. Cheng, H., Fei, X., Boukerche, A., et al.: GeoCover: an efficient sparse coverage protocol for RSU deployment over urban VANETs. Ad Hoc Netw. **24**, 85–102 (2015)
11. Sengathir, J., Deva Priya, M.: Christy Jeba Malar A, et al. Honey Badger Optimization Algorithm-Based RSU Deployment for Improving Network Coverage in VANETs. In: Sharma, D.K., Peng, S.L., Sharma, R., Jeon, G. (eds.) ICMETE 2022, pp. 179–193. Springer, Singapore (2023). https://doi.org/10.1007/978-981-19-9512-5_16
12. Wang, S., Zhao, Y., Xu, J., et al.: Edge server placement in mobile edge computing. J. Parallel Distrib. Comput. **127**, 160–168 (2019)
13. Li, Y., Wang, S.: An energy-aware edge server placement algorithm in mobile edge computing. In: 2018 IEEE International Conference on Edge Computing (EDGE), pp. 66–73. IEEE (2018)
14. Luo, F., Zheng, S., Ding, W., et al.: An edge server placement method based on reinforcement learning. Entropy **24**(3), 317 (2022)

15. Zeng, F., Ren, Y., Deng, X., et al.: Cost-effective edge server placement in wireless metropolitan area networks. Sensors **19**(1), 32 (2018)
16. Dubey, B.B., Chauhan, N., Pant, S.: Effect of position of fixed infrastructure on data dissemination in vanets. Int. J. Res. Rev. Comput. Sci. **2**(2), 482 (2011)
17. Landherr, A., Friedl, B., Heidemann, J.: A critical review of centrality measures in social networks. Wirtschaftsinformatik **52**, 367–382 (2010)
18. Kibiłda, J., Galkin, B., DaSilva, L.A.: Modelling multi-operator base station deployment patterns in cellular networks. IEEE Trans. Mob. Comput. **15**(12), 3087–3099 (2015)
19. Kui, X., Du, H., Xiao, X., Li, Y.: Realistic vehicular mobility trace driven RSU deployment scheme. J. Beijing Univ. Posts Telecom **38**(1), 114–118 (2015)
20. Boeing, G.: OSMnx: new methods for acquiring, constructing, analyzing, and visualizing complex street networks. Comput. Environ. Urban Syst. **65**, 126–139 (2017)
21. Li, Y., Zhou, A., Ma, X., et al.: Profit-aware edge server placement. IEEE Internet Things J. **9**(1), 55–67 (2021)
22. Guo, Y., Wang, S., Zhou, A., et al.: User allocation-aware edge cloud placement in mobile edge computing. Softw. Pract. Exp. **50**(5), 489–502 (2020)
23. Wang, S., Guo, Y., Zhang, N., et al.: Delay-aware microservice coordination in MO bile edge computing: a reinforcement learning approach. IEEE Trans. Mob. Comput. **20**(3), 939–951 (2019)
24. Yang, B., Ma, Y., Ma, Z., et al.: The study on key technology of secure access to the resource pool management. J. Jiangxi Normal Univ. Nat. Sci. Ed. (06), 639–643 (2020). https://doi.org/10.16357/j.cnki.issn1000-5862.2020.06.16

# Budget-Constrained Contention-Aware Workflow Scheduling in a Hybrid Cloud

Qingliang Zhang, Xinyue Shu, and Quanwang Wu[✉]

Chongqing University, Chongqing, China
zql@stu.cqu.edu.cn, wqw@cqu.edu.cn

**Abstract.** Private clouds offer high controllability but lack scalability, while public clouds provide high scalability with limited controllability. The hybrid cloud paradigm combining them can well balance controllability and scalability nowadays. Increasing numbers of workflow applications are being deployed on a hybrid cloud and this paper investigates how to effectively minimize workflow makespan within a user-specified budget. It first establishes a practical communication contention-cognizant workflow scheduling model for hybrid clouds, where a queueing mode is used to handle multiple data contending for the scarce cross-cloud bandwidth resources. A Budget-constrained Contention-aware Workflow Scheduling (BCWS) heuristic is proposed to optimize the workflow makespan within a given budget. It chooses a subset of cloud instances and allocates each task from the workflow to computing resources sequentially with its data communications scheduled as well. In experiments, traditional contention-agnostic scheduling techniques such as GRP-HEFT, PSO, IPPTS etc. are adapted to the considered model before comparison with the proposed method BCWS. Experimental results verify the superiority of BCWS as it can always achieve the best makespan.

**Keywords:** Hybrid Cloud · Communication Contention · Budget Constraint · Workflow Scheduling

## 1 Introduction

As a new computing paradigm, cloud computing provides highly scalable applications, platforms, and hardware services to end-users through the Internet. In particular, private clouds offer high controllability but lack scalability, while public clouds provide high scalability but limited controllability. Hence, the hybrid cloud paradigm that combines the two provides a superior balance of controllability and scalability. In this paradigm, end-users can use public cloud resources based on a "pay-as-you-go" mode, and keep sensitive data in private cloud, thus significantly reducing costs and operational expenses. In a hybrid cloud environment, workflow scheduling faces two challenges: effective scheduling and communication contention.

© ICST Institute for Computer Sciences, Social Informatics and Telecommunications Engineering 2024
Published by Springer Nature Switzerland AG 2024. All Rights Reserved
H. Gao et al. (Eds.): CollaborateCom 2023, LNICST 561, pp. 111–127, 2024.
https://doi.org/10.1007/978-3-031-54521-4_7

First, effective scheduling under budget constraints refers to the rational arrangement and allocation of tasks resources within a computing system to maximize resource utilization. It includes two inseparable segments [1], namely 1) resource provisioning, and 2) task scheduling. In the context of a limited budget, providing appropriate resources to meet task requirements is crucial. This involves intelligently allocating computing resources, necessitating a balance between performance and cost to achieve optimal resource provisioning. Task scheduling focuses on optimizing task sequences and execution times to minimize the makespan. In task scheduling, tasks involving sensitive information should be allocated within private cloud resources to address privacy issues [2, 3]. This comprehensive approach optimizes performance, resource utilization, and budget adherence, fostering stability and efficiency within hybrid cloud environments.

Second, communication contention refers to the situation where multiple data streams compete for limited bandwidth resources. When workflows are deployed in a hybrid cloud, data transfers may take place between public and private clouds or within a single cloud platform. Since there is only one duplex communication channel connecting the private and public platforms, if multiple senders transmit data across the platforms, multiple data may compete for scarce bandwidth resources, which may cause further delays. Although there are also a few studies concentrating workflow scheduling in hybrid clouds [4, 5], none of them tackle the potential data communication contention for workflow scheduling. Thus, communication contention can easily become a bottleneck in executing workflows.

With the above challenges as motivation, this paper establishes a practical scheduling model to capture workflow deployment in hybrid clouds. We introduce an instance provisioning mechanism and a workflow scheduling algorithm, named budget-constraint contention-aware workflow scheduling (BCWS). BCWS contains two stages: (1) Resource Provisioning (RP) and (2) Task and Data Scheduling (TDS). RP focuses on selecting instances that are billed on an hourly basis when making purchase decisions. TDS schedules tasks with incoming data to computing and communication resources sequentially. Moreover, a look-ahead task selection mechanism is designed. The experiments are conducted with realistic workflows, and the results verify the superiority of BCWS.

The remaining part is structured in the following manner. Section 2 reviews the scheduling methods which have been proposed in literature. Section 3 introduces the problem formulation and system model for hybrid cloud, while Our proposed method BCWS is presented in Sect. 4. Further, Sect. 5 gives experimental results and analysis, and Sect. 6 concludes the whole paper and points out future work.

## 2   Related Work

We first review the literature on workflow scheduling under budget constraint and then discuss communication contention in workflow execution.

### 2.1   Budget-Constrained Workflow Scheduling

In [6], the authors introduced two budget-constrained algorithms, namely "Loss" and "Gain," for scheduling Directed Acyclic Graph (DAG) workflows in grid environments.

In [7], Jia Yu et al. proposed a budget-constraint scheduling approach that utilized genetic algorithms to optimize workflow execution time while meeting the budget. In [8], the Budget-constrained Heterogeneous Earliest Finish Time (BHEFT) was proposed, which is an extension of the HEFT algorithm. BHEFT defines a suitable plan by minimizing the makespan so that the user's budget and deadline constraints are met. With the emergence of hybrid clouds, workflow scheduling has embraced the use of hybrid clouds to harness the benefits of both internal and external resources. The scheduling approach can be described as a cost model aimed at minimizing execution time while considering the rental cost of public resources. This is achieved by providing the user with a list of resources available for execution [9]. Regarding the billing of instance usage time, cloud providers offer various billing options, including billing by seconds and billing by hours. Users can select the billing mode that best suits their specific needs. Billing by seconds is ideal for short-duration usage scenarios, as users are charged only for the actual number of seconds used [10]. On the other hand, billing by hours is more suitable for longer-duration usage, with charges being calculated on an hourly basis, rounding up any partial hour to the nearest whole hour [9].

However, many existing budget-constrained workflow methods consider instance billing based on billing by seconds rather than billing by hours. The integral instance hour increases the difficulty for solving the makespan minimization problem. In [11], Xiaotong Wang et al. introduced an evolutionary algorithm based on Particle Swarm Optimization (PSO). This PSO-based approach considers the hourly-based cost model in the context of budget-constrained workflow scheduling. In [12], the authors propose a new algorithm named GRP-HEFT which includes two steps, a new resource provision strategy and assigns tasks based on the HEFT algorithm, achieving very good results.

## 2.2  Communication Contention in Workflow Execution

Communication contention refers to the situation that multiple data communications contend for a specific network resource at the same time. Task duplication in contention-aware scheduling models is studied in [13]. Benoit et al. [14] introduced a bidirectional one-port architectural model to capture endpoint contention. Efficient contention-aware and fault-tolerant scheduling algorithms are then designed. Recently, Özkaya et al. [15] described new list-based scheduling heuristics based on clustering for homogeneous processors, based on a duplex single-port communication model.

To avoid network communication contention, Genez et al. [16] introduced an estimation mechanism to address imprecise information regarding the available inter-cloud link bandwidth and how it affects the estimation of makespan and cost. Son et al. [17] proposed priority-aware resource placement algorithms considering both host and network resources for software-defined networking-enabled clouds, where network flows can be reconfigured dynamically and adapted to network traffics. For data-intensive workflow scheduling in a DC, Wu et al. [18] proposed a practical scheduling model that takes into account communication contention between endpoints in the interfaces connecting servers with a communication network. Efficient contention-aware scheduling algorithms are then designed. Mithila propose latency-based vector scheduling of many-task applications, where communication latency is measured for making decisions on task allocation [19].

# 3   Workflow Scheduling Model in a Hybrid Cloud

In this section, we formally describe the budget-constrained contention-aware workflow scheduling problem in hybrid cloud. We first present the workflow and resource model, and then describe the scheduling model with contention awareness. Finally, we formulate the problem mathematically as a constrained problem.

## 3.1   Workflow and Resource Model

A directed acyclic graph (DAG) can represent a workflow application, DAG $= (N, E, W, D)$, where, (1) $N$ represents a set of tasks which are indivisible individual applications, $N = \{n_1, n_2, ..., n_k\}$. (2) $E$ denotes a set of edges representing precedence dependencies among tasks. A precedence dependence $e_{i,j} \in E$ between tasks $n_i \in N$ and $n_j \in N$ indicates that $n_j$ can start executing only after $n_i$ finishes. (3) $W$: is a weighing vector whose $w_i$ represents the computation load of $n_i \in N$. (4) $D: E \rightarrow R^+$ is a matrix whose entry $d_{i,j}$ indicates data amount to be transferred from $n_i$ to $n_j$. To generalize a workflow with one entry and one exit, two dummy tasks $n_{entry}$ and $n_{exit}$ with zero computational workload are added to its start and end, respectively. $succ(n_i)$ and $pred(n_i)$ denote the set of $n_i$'s immediate successors and immediate predecessors, respectively.

In hybrid cloud, a private cloud provides a limited number of computation resources $R = \{r_1, r_2, ..., r_m\}$, while a public cloud provides an 'infinite' number of resources $U = \{u_1, u_2, ..., u_n\}$. $U$ are used on demand. A hybrid cloud is a set of resources, consisting of resources on the private cloud and resources of the public cloud, which is denoted as $V = R \cup U = \{v_1, v_2, ..., v_l\}$. Based on the computational capacity and price of the resources, we can classify $V$ into different types of resources, which are represented by $P = \{p_1, p_2, ..., p_k\}$.

We use $s_{i,j}$ to indicate the execution time of the $n_i$ on $v_j$ with the type of $p_k$. Cloud providers specify the processing power of different types of the provided instances use a metric names Compute Unit ($CU$) or similar concepts such as mean performance [20]. Hence, we denote the compute unit of $p_k$ by $CU_k$. A higher value of $CU$ potentially results in greater computing capacity. For several scientific standard workflows, the execution time of tasks on Xeon@2.33 GHz CPUs (CU $= 8$) has been published [21]. This principle resembles the commonly applied concept for estimating the task execution duration within scientific workflows, especially in the domain of static workflow scheduling [20, 22]. The CU value is inversely correlated with the task execution time. The task $n_i$ execution time for the instance with $CU = 1$ is the reference execution time of the task, denoted by $ref\_time(w_i)$. Accordingly, the execution time of task $n_i$ on $v_j$ with the type of $p_k$, is

$$s_{i,j} = \frac{ref\_time(w_i)}{CU_k} \tag{1}$$

Furthermore, privacy is a major point of concern for users when executing workflows. Sending all data to a public cloud could pose a potential risk for workflow users. In hybrid clouds, users can keep sensitive tasks, denoted as $S$ ($S \subseteq N$), residing in a private cloud. Remaining tasks (i.e., $O = N\text{-}S$) that do not involve privacy issues can be executed on both $R$ and $U$.

For data transmission, the external network channel connecting the two platforms goes through the Internet, and its corresponding bandwidth resource, denoted as $b_{ext}$. Without losing generality, we assume that the internal bandwidth is the same for each platform, which is denoted as $b_{int}$.

## 3.2 Contention-Aware Scheduling Model

When deploying workflows in a hybrid cloud, data transfers may take place between public and private clouds or within a single cloud platform. Due to only one duplex communication channel connecting the public and private cloud platforms, if multiple senders transfer data across platforms at the same time, multiple data may compete for scarce bandwidth resources. On the contrary, since the computing resources within the cloud platform are well connected to each other based on advanced data center networking technologies (e.g., software defined networking) [17], the influence of network communication contention can be disregarded in comparison to inter-platform bandwidth resources when multiple data communications occur simultaneously within a cloud platform.

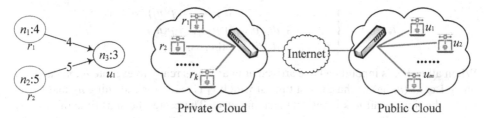

**Fig. 1.** Simple workflow example and data transmission in a hybrid cloud

Figure 1 illustrates a deployment scheme of a workflow on a hybrid cloud. The green lines indicate the internal data links and red lines indicate the external data links. The communication contention occurs in the red lines. Suppose that both tasks $n_1$ and $n_2$ marked in red indicate that they contain sensitive information, and are respectively allocated to resources $r_1$ and $r_2$. Task $n_3$ is allocated to resource $u_1$. In addition, the bandwidth resources of external data channels and speed of private computation resources and are both 1. According to traditional scheduling model [4, 23, 24], the start time of $n_3$ on resource $u_1$ is the maximum value among its predecessors' finish time plus data transfer time, resulting in a start time of 10. However, this scheduling method is not suitable. When $n_1$ and $n_2$ try to send data to $n_3$, communication contention occurs for external data channels.

Specifically, each data communication involved in contention proceeds one after another to avoid contention and the communication order can be determined by policies like FCFS (First Come First Service). For example, in Fig. 1, communication from $n_1$ to $n_3$ proceeds first ahead of that from $n_2$ to $n_3$. In this way, the time for $n_1$ to finish sending data to $n_3$ is 8, that for $n_2$ is 13, so the start time of $n_3$ on $u_1$ is 13.

To address the communication contention, this paper adopts the queuing approach, which means that each data sender is allowed to exclusively occupy the whole bandwidth resource. Suppose that task $n_i$ is scheduled to execute on the cloud platform $p(n_i)$ and between them there is a precedence dependence $e_{i,j}$. When $n_i$ and $n_j$ are deployed in the same cloud ($p(n_i) = p(n_j)$), the data transfer of $e_{i,j}$ can start when task $n_i$ finishes. If $p(n_i) \neq p(n_j)$, the data transfer $e_{i,j}$ can start when task $n_i$ finishes and $b_{ext}$ is ready for transferring $e_{i,j}$. That is, it additionally requires that the external bandwidth resource is not occupied by other data senders. Let $t_\diamond (e_{i,j}, b_{ext})$ be the earliest time when $b_{ext}$ is ready for transferring $e_{i,j}$ and $t_\bullet (n_i)$ be $n_i$'s finish time. The data transfer of $e_{i,j}$ can start at

$$t_0(e_{i,j}) = \begin{cases} t_\bullet(n_i) & \text{if } p(n_i) = p(n_j) \\ \max\{t_\bullet(n_i), t_\diamond(e_{i,j}, b_{ext})\} & \text{otherwise} \end{cases} \quad (2)$$

Queueing mode stipulates that no contention from other senders emerges during the transmission of $e_{i,j}$. If $n_i$ and $n_j$ reside in the same cloud, $b_{int}$ can be used for calculating $e_{i,j}$'s transfer finish time. Otherwise, $b_{ext}$ can be used for calculating $e_{i,j}$'s transfer finish time. In addition, when $n_i$ and $n_j$ are assigned to in the same instance (i.e. $v_l = v_m$), $e_{i,j}$'s transfer time is 0 because the intermediate data can be direct accessed locally. In summary, $e_{i,j}$'s transfer finish time can be obtained via

$$t_\bullet(e_{i,j}) = \begin{cases} t_0(e_{i,j}), & \text{if } p(n_i) = p(n_j), v_l = v_m \\ t_0(e_{i,j}) + d_{i,j}/b_{ext}, & \text{if } p(n_i) \neq p(n_j) \\ t_0(e_{i,j}) + d_{i,j}/b_{int}, & \text{otherwise} \end{cases} \quad (3)$$

When all task $n_i$'s input data have arrived at $v_l$ and $v_l$ is ready to execute $n_i$, $n_i$ can start on $v_l$. Let $t_\diamond (n_i, v_l)$ be the earliest time at which $v_l$ is ready for executing $n_i$, and $t_\triangle (n_i, v_l)$ be the time of all $n_i$'s input data arriving at $v_l$. Therefore, the start time of $n_i$ on $v_l$ can be calculated as

$$\begin{aligned} t_0(n_i, v_l) &= \max\{t_\diamond(n_i, v_l), t_\triangle(n_i, v_l)\} \\ &= \max\{t_\diamond(n_i, v_l), \max_{n_p \in pred(n_i)}\{t_\bullet(e_{p,i})\}\} \end{aligned} \quad (4)$$

The finish time of $n_i$ on $v_l$ can be obtained via

$$t_\bullet(n_i, v_l) = t_0(n_i, v_l) + s_{i,l} \quad (5)$$

The makespan of a workflow refers to the total execution time required for completing all tasks and it can be gained via

$$makespan = \max_{n_i \in N}\{t_\bullet(n_i)\} \quad (6)$$

To ensure the budget constraint for running workflow, the cost($C$) can be obtained via

$$C = \sum_{v_l \in M_v} Pr(p_k) \times \left\lceil \frac{t_\bullet(v_l) - t_0(v_l)}{3600} \right\rceil + \sum_{e_{i,j} \in E, p(n_i) \neq p(n_j)} d_{i,j} \times Pr(b_{ext}) \quad (7)$$

Where $Pr(p_k)$ represents the cost of execution of the $v_l$ with the type $p_k$ for an hour usage. And $t_0(v_l)$ is the the starting time point of instance $v_l$'s execution, while $t_\bullet (v_l)$

is $v_l$'s completion time. We utilize an instance model billed on an hourly basis. As all execution times in our system are specified in seconds, we divide them by 3,600 to determine the hourly cost. $Pr(b_{ext})$ represents the billing of transferring data across clouds. The networking expenses of the intra-cloud are deemed negligible, while the networking expenses of the inter-cloud need to be billed.

## 3.3 Problem Definition

The solution not only includes assigning tasks to time slices of computational resources, but also assigning data transfers to time slices of communication resources. Specifically, the scheduling solution can be represented as a ternary $\{M_N, M_E, M_V\}$, where:

1) $M_N$ includes all task-resource mappings. Each task mapping is a 4-tuple $[n_i, v_l, t_\circ(n_i), t_\bullet(n_i)]$, which indicates that task $n_i$ is deployed on the computation resource $v_l$, during the period from $t_\circ(n_i)$ to $t_\bullet(n_i)$.
2) $M_E$ includes mappings between data transmission and external bandwidth resources $b_{ext}$, and each mapping is a 4-tuple $[e_{i,j}, \mu, t_\circ(e_{i,j}), t_\bullet(e_{i,j})]$, which indicates that if the Boolean variable $\mu$ is true, data communication $e_{i,j}$ occupies the upstream channel of $b_{ext}$ during the time from $t_\circ(e_{i,j})$ to $t_\bullet(e_{i,j})$, and otherwise the downstream channel is busy.
3) $M_V$ represents the public cloud resources used and the start and end times of their operation and each mapping is a 3-tuple $[v_l, t_\circ(v_l), t_\bullet(v_l)]$.

Based on the above analysis, we aim to minimize the makespan when deploying workflows in a hybrid cloud environment without violating the budget $B$ constrain, which can be formulated as the following constrained optimization problem:

$$\min makespan$$
$$s.t. \ C \leq B \tag{8}$$

# 4 Methodology

This section describes a Budget-constrained Contention-aware Workflow Scheduling (BCWS) heuristic. It includes two basic stages. 1) Resource Provisioning (RP) strategy, which is responsible for choosing a subset of instances from all instances in the pool of cloud IaaS resources, and 2) Task and Data Scheduling (TDS), which not only allocates each task from the list to computing resources but allocates inter-platform data communications to $b_{ext}$ explicitly.

## 4.1 Resource Provisioning Strategy

The first stage consists of two steps: 1) selecting the instance type and 2) selecting the corresponding quantity for each type of instance.

| Algorithm 1 Resource Provisioning (RP) |
| --- |
| 1:   Assign all non-dominated instance types of public cloud to the set $I$; |
| 2:   Sort $I$ according to the efficiency rate of the instance types; |
| 3:   **while** $I$ is not empty **do**: |
| 4:       remain Budget($R$)←$B$; |
| 5:       The set of taken instances $Y$ = {}; |
| 6:       **while** $(R >= p^{Cheapest})$ **do**: |
| 7:           pick instance $p_i$ from the $I$; |
| 8:           Take $n = \lfloor R/Pr(p_i) \rfloor$ instances from the type $p_i$ and add them to $Y$; |
| 9:           $R = R - Pr(p_i) \times n$; |
| 10:     **end while**; |
| 11:     $\{M_N, M_E, M_V\} \leftarrow$ run TDS (Algorithm 2) with $Y$ and $R$; |
| 12:     Calculate makespan and cost $C$ of the created assignment $\{M_N, M_E, M_P\}$; |
| 13:     **if** $B$-$C$ can buy more efficient instance type $p_j$ **then**: |
| 14:         add instance from type $p_j$ to $Y$; |
| 15:         $\{M_N, M_E, M_V\} \leftarrow$ rerun TDS with $Y$; |
| 16:     **end if**; |
| 17:     remove the first item from the $I$; |
| 18: **end while**; |
| 19: return the best assignment $\{M_N, M_E, M_V\}$; |

Initially, we begin by examining the list of instance types to identify and eliminating any dominated instance types. An instance type $p_j$ is dominated by instance type $p_i$ if $Pr(p_i) \leq Pr(p_j)$ and $CU_i \geq CU_j$. The remaining non-dominated instances after removing the dominated ones are then appended to a list referred to as $I$. Subsequently, the list is sorted in descending order based on the efficiency rate ($ER$) of each instance type (line 2), which is defined as follows:

$$ER_k = \frac{CU_k}{Pr(p_k)} \tag{9}$$

The workflow scheduling gives priority to instances with a higher efficiency rate (Line 1–2). We prioritize selecting as many instances as possible from the most efficient instance type and include them in the $Y$ (Line 7–8). The remaining budget $R$ (i.e., the available budget is insufficient to acquire any additional most-efficient instances) is used to buy the second most efficient instance. This process continues until the remaining budget is not enough even to take one more of the cheapest instances (Line 6–10). $p^{Cheapest}$ denotes the price of the cheapest instance type.

The generated set of instances $Y$, is given as an input to the TDS algorithm, and the scheduling phase begins (Line 11). The TDS completes the assignment by filling the values of $\{M_N, M_E, M_V\}$. The details of TDS will be explained in Sect. 4.2.

Pay attention to the remaining amount (i.e., Budget $B$ minus total cost $C$). If a more efficient instance (refer to instance types that have been removed from the $I$) can be purchased, execute it again after purchase. Compare the new makespan with the previous one and record the better one (Line 13–16). Next, the most-efficient instance type is removed from $I$, and the algorithm continues to the next iteration with the remaining items in the $I$. The algorithm terminates when the list is empty. Eventually, the best assignment found across all iterations returns the final solution.

## 4.2 Task and Data Scheduling

Constructing an ordered list of tasks by a certain attribute is the basis for executing scheduling algorithms.

Here, a task property for ordering tasks is defined which is specific to the considered model. Before presenting it formally, the concept of outbound communication duration for a task $n_i$, denoted as $\lambda(n_i)$, is first introduced, which represents the sum of all outgoing communication time of $n_i$. Considering sensitive tasks($S$) can only be allocated to the private cloud and it is better to allocate insensitive tasks($O$) to the public cloud for faster processing, it is defined based on tasks' privacy sensitivity as,

$$\lambda(n_i) = \max\left\{ \max_{n_k \in X \cap succ(n_i)} \frac{d_{i,k}}{b_{int}}, \sum_{n_j \in (N-X) \cap succ(n_i)} \frac{d_{i,j}}{b_{ext}} \right\} \tag{10}$$

where, $X$ represent tasks in the workflow with the same privacy sensitivity with $n_i$, that is, if $n_i$ is a sensitive task, $X$ is $S$, and otherwise it is $O$. For a sensitive task, if its successor task is also privacy sensitive, the internal bandwidth $b_{int}$ is used for calculation, and otherwise $b_{ext}$ is used instead.

Based on this design, we define a new heterogeneity and contention-oriented upward rank $\mu$ for task ordering as follows:

$$\mu(n_i) = \lambda(n_i) \times (1 + \frac{\delta^+(n_i)}{\delta^*}) + \max_{n_j \in succ(n_i)} \{\mu(n_j)\} + \bar{s} \tag{11}$$

$\delta^+(n_i)$ represents $n_i$'s out-degree (i.e., the number of $n_i$'s immediate successor tasks), and $\delta^*$ represents the maximum out-degree value of tasks in the given workflow graph. The property $\mu$ of task $n_i$ measures its execution time, its outbound communication duration $\lambda(n_i)$, and the maximum $\mu$ value among its successors. Note that the impact of $\lambda(n_i)$ is additionally enhanced by multiplying the coefficient $1 + \delta^+(n_i)/\delta^*$. This is because a larger $\delta^+(n_i)$ value implies that $n_i$ has more successor tasks, and the finish of $n_i$ can trigger execution of more tasks in parallel. Hence, the normalized $\delta^+(n_i)$ value is introduced to reflect the priority of a task in this regard. $\bar{s}$ represents the average runtime of $n_i$ on virtual machines. $\mu(n_{exit})$ is 0, and by traversing the workflow graph upward from $n_{exit}$, the $\mu$ property of each task can be recursively calculated.

The whole procedure of TDS is shown in Algorithm 2. In this phase, not only tasks are assigned to instance resources, but data transmissions are also allocated to bandwidth resources. At first, prepare the computation resources $\psi$ of private cloud (Line 1). Then, the task list is constructed by sorting tasks in a descending order of $\mu$ values (Line 2). TDS then traverses the tasks in the list in sequence and chooses a computation resource for each task. Additionally, it allocates cross-cloud data communications to external bandwidth resources.

**Algorithm 2 Task and Data Scheduling**

1:    prepare computation resource $\psi$ of private cloud;
2:    sort tasks by a decreasing order of $\mu(n_i)$;
3:    **for** each task $n_i$ in the task list **do**
4:        $best \leftarrow +\infty, T_1 \leftarrow \varnothing, T_2 \leftarrow \varnothing, best^* \leftarrow +\infty, T^*_1 \leftarrow \varnothing, T^*_2 \leftarrow \varnothing$;
5:        prepare *candidates* for $n_i$;
6:        sort $pred(n_i)$ by their finish time increasingly;
7:        calculate and prepay $c(n_i)$;
8:        **for** each $v_l$ in *candidates* **do**
9:            **for** each $n_i$'s predecessor $n_j$ **do**
10:               calculate $t_o(e_{j,i})$ via (2) and $t_\bullet(e_{j,i})$ via (3);
11:               **if** $p(n_j) \neq p(v_l)$ **then**
12:                   tentatively allocate $e_{j,i}$ to $b_{ext}$;
13:               **end if**
14:           **end for**
15:           calculate $t_o(n_i, v_l)$ via (4), $t_\bullet(n_i, v_l)$ via (5) and $t_\Delta(n_i, v_l)$ via (12);
16:           **if** $t_\Delta(n_i, v_l) < best$ **then**
17:               $best \leftarrow t_\Delta(n_i, v_l)$;
18:               $T_1 \leftarrow$ record the above tentative operations;
19:               $T_2 \leftarrow <n_i, v_l, t_o(n_i), t_\bullet(n_i)>$;
20:           **end if**
21:           **if** $t_\Delta(n_i, v_l) < best^*$ and *Adding_Not_Change_the_Cost*$(n_i, v_l)$ **then**
22:               $best^* \leftarrow t_\Delta(n_i, v_l)$;
23:               $T^*_1 \leftarrow$ record the above tentative operations;
24:               $T^*_2 \leftarrow <n_i, v_l, t_o(n_i), t_\bullet(n_i)>$;
25:           **end if**
26:           withdraw the above tentative operations;
27:       **end for**
28:       choose $\{T_1, T_2\}$ or $\{T^*_1, T^*_2\}$ to allocate edges and $n_i$ based on the values of $T_2$ and $T^*_2$;
29:       recovering a portion of the prepaid amount;
30:   **end for**
31:   return the generated schedule $\{M_N, M_E, M_V\}$;

When preparing computation resource *candidates* for $n_i$ (Line 5), only private cloud resources $\psi$ are considered if $n_i$ is a sensitive task or certain parent tasks $n_p$ of the $n_i$ didn't prepay $c(n_p)$ ($c(n_p)$ means that the cost for the $n_p$ outbound communication transmission). Otherwise, both private computation resources $\psi$ and public computation cloud resources $Y$ can be used. For task $n_i$, it sorts $n_i$'s immediate predecessors by their finish time increasingly for data communication allocation (Line 6). Line 7 calculates the cost $c(n_i)$ and makes a prepayment. Prepayment is to consider the worst case, that is, the budget is not enough to use the public cloud resources to execute the $n_i$'s subtasks. The purpose is to have enough transmission budget to transfer data between $n_i$ and its subtasks to the private cloud, thus ensuring that the entire workflow has a feasible solution. It is worth noting that this is divided into three scenarios. 1) $\beta \geq c(n_i)$: directly prepay; 2) $\beta < c(n_i)$ but amount converted from unused instances can prepay the balance: these instances are converted into corresponding amounts and added to $\beta$, and the instances are removed from *candidates* and $Y$; 3) other situations: only the private cloud resources are used as *candidates* (i.e., remove $Y$ from *candidates*).

For each task $n_i$, we keep two sets of parameters, 1) the minimum $t_\Delta(n_i, v_l)$ of the task on all instances, and 2) the minimum $t_\Delta(n_i, v_l)$ of the task on instance that assigning $n_i$ to them does not change the execution cost of the instance.

Next, each candidate $v_l$ of $n_i$ is traversed to search for the best one (Lines 8–27). For each $n_i$'s immediate predecessor $n_j$, TDS checks whether $n_j$ is deployed in a different platform from $v_l$, and if so, the cross-cloud data communication $e_{j,i}$ is tentatively allocated to $b_{ext}$ (Lines 11–13). In fact, if $p(n_j)$ is public and $p(v_l)$ is private, the downstream channel is used and otherwise the upstream one is used.

$t_0(n_i, v_l)$ can be acquired with an insertion-based policy based on data communication allocation (Line 15): $n_i$ is inserted between already scheduled tasks in $v_l$ if the idle time slot between them is enough for executing $n_i$, and otherwise, it is allocated after the last task on $v_l$. Accordingly, $n_i$'s finish time can be obtained. TDS not only considers the finish time of $n_i$, but also the potential cross-cloud data communications from $n_i$. Considering that sensitive tasks can only be allocated to the private cloud and it is better to allocate insensitive ones to the public cloud for faster processing, the potential cross-cloud data transmission time is estimated as,

$$t_\Delta(n_i, v_l) = t_\bullet(n_i, v_l) + \begin{cases} \sum_{n_j \in succ(n_i) \cap O} d_{i,j}/b_{ext}, & \text{if } v_l \in R \\ \sum_{n_j \in succ(n_i) \cap S} d_{i,j}/b_{ext}, & \text{if } v_l \in U \end{cases} \tag{12}$$

Hence, if allocating $n_i$ onto $v_l$ achieves a lower value of $t_\Delta(n_i, v_l)$, the current *best* value is updated to it. Meanwhile, the above temporary data communication allocation operations are recorded as $T_1$, and the task allocation operation $(n_i, v_l, t_0(n_i), t_\bullet(n_i))$ is recorded as $T_2$ (Lines 18–19). In line 21–25, the minimum $t_\Delta(n_i, v_l)$ on the instance for which adding $n_i$ does not change the cost. After that, the tentative operations in this task iteration are all withdrawn.

After the traverse of *candidates* for $n_i$, TDS selects the best one for executing $n_i$ which minimizes $t_\Delta(n_i, v_l)$, we need to make a decision about the scheduling of the task with respect to the value of $T_2$ and $T_2^*$ (Line 28). The case $T_2 = T_2^*$ implies that assigning the task to the instance that yields the minimum $t_\Delta(n_i, v_l)$ of the task does not increase the cost of running the instance. In this case, it easily follows $T_1$ to schedule data communications, and follows $T_2$ to schedule $n_i$. However, when $T_2 \neq T_2^*$, follows $T_1$ and $T_2$ to schedule task and edge could result in a budget violation since RP already used all the budget to take as much as instance that it affords. Indeed, RP assumes that each of the taken instances will run only for maximum one hour. Hence, running an instance for more than one hour can lead to a budget violation. Removing this instance ensures that the algorithm remains within budget constraints. However, assigning the task to this instance increases the running cost (as it needs to operate for an extra hour). To offset this cost increase, another instance of the same type, located in $Y$, is also removed.

Figure 2 provides an illustrative example of this scenario. The earliest finish time of the $n_i$, exceeds a full-hour regardless of the type of instance selected. There is an unused instance with the same type as instance 1, the unused instance 2 is removed, thereby the instance 1 can run for an extra hour. If there is no such an unused instance, TDS follows $T_1^*$ and $T_2^*$ rather than $T_1$ and $T_2$ to schedule related data to avoid budget violation. Follow $T_1^*$ and $T_2^*$ to schedule the task and edges may not be as good as following $T_1$ and $T_2$, but this avoids the risk of a budget violation. The worst scenario is when there are not enough idle instances available in the public cloud. At this point, we can take

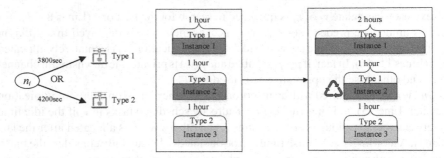

**Fig. 2.** An illustrative example showing the behavior of the TDS when the total execution time of the tasks hosted by an instance exceeds a full hour.

advantage of the almost free running of instances in the private cloud and deploy this task according to $T_1^*$ and $T_2^*$.

Finally, iterating through all incoming edges of $n_i$, if they belong to the same cloud, recovering the prepaid amount associated with those edges (Line 29). The workflow returns the generated schedule after all tasks have been mapped.

## 5  Performance Evaluations

### 5.1  Experimental Settings

We select four different kinds of realistic scientific workflows here: Montage, LIGO, Cybershake and SIPHT. These workflows have different structures and can be divided into I/O intensive workflows and CPU intensive workflows. Specifically, Montage is an astronomy application used to generate custom mosaics of the sky, involving a large number of I/O intensive tasks; The CPU intensive tasks involved in the LIGO workflow, which analyzes data from coalescing compact binary systems to detect gravitational waves; Cybershake is used to describe earthquake hazards and is a data-intensive workflow that requires large resource and memory requirements; SIPHT is used to automate the search for sRNA encoding-genes for bacterial replicons which is primarily a CPU-bound workflow. For each application, Fig. 3 depicts the structure of relatively small workflows.

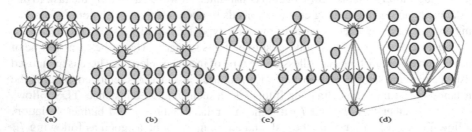

**Fig. 3.** Structure of scientific workflows. (a) Montage. (b) LIGO. (c) Cybershake. (d) SIPHT.

**Table 1.** Characteristics of Cloud Instances Used in Our Experiments

| Type Id | Type | CU | Price ($) | Type Id | Type | CU | Price ($) |
|---------|------|-----|-----------|---------|------|-----|-----------|
| $p_1$ | m1.small | 1.7 | 0.06 | $p_5$ | m3.large | 7.5 | 0.225 |
| $p_2$ | m1.medium | 3.75 | 0.12 | $p_6$ | m1.xlarge | 15 | 0.48 |
| $p_3$ | m3.medium | 3.75 | 0.113 | $p_7$ | m3.xlarge | 15 | 0.45 |
| $p_4$ | m1.large | 7.5 | 0.24 | $p_8$ | m3.2xlarge | 30 | 0.9 |

We choose two sizes for each workflow type: 50, 100 tasks. Moreover, tasks are divided into privacy-sensitive and privacy-insensitive ones: the former can only be deployed in a private cloud, whereas the latter can be deployed to a public or private cloud. We introduce a privacy factor $\beta$ to represent the proportion of privacy-sensitive tasks in a workflow (i.e., $\beta = |S|/|N|$), and $\beta \times |N|$ tasks are randomly selected from the workflow and set to be privacy-sensitive. A larger $\beta$ indicates more private tasks and it is set to 0.1 in default.

For the hybrid cloud platform, the internal bandwidth $b_{int}$ is set to 1Gb/s, while the external one $b_{ext}$ is set to 10Mb/s. As shown in Table 1, the public resources are conducted based on Amazon EC2 instances. The US East General-Purpose instance group with purchase-on-demand option is used. This is the same list of cases used in [12] to run experiment. Computation unit of private resources is 1. The characteristics of the instance types are provided in Table 1. And the number of available private computation resources is 4. Transferring data from the internet into Amazon EC2 is free of charge, so the cost of transferring data from a private cloud to a public cloud over the internet is disregarded. The cost of transferring data from a public cloud to a private cloud is $0.09/GB, with a monthly free quota of 100GB. The default budget is 1$. These parameters remain constant across the following experiments unless otherwise indicated for the purpose of highlighting their effects.

We conduct two sets of sensitivity experiments to evaluate the performance of our algorithms under the cost coefficient $\theta$, the privacy coefficient $\beta$.

First, we vary the cost coefficient $\theta$ to simulate different complexities of budget constraints. A larger $\theta$ represents more instances can be purchased. Second, we vary the privacy coefficient $\beta$ to simulate different privacy heterogeneities in hybrid cloud. A higher value of $\beta$ means that more tasks in the workflow can only be performed in the slower private cloud.

We carefully choose and adapt the following representative scheduling techniques as baselines: (1) GRP-HEFT, a novel resource provisioning mechanism and a workflow scheduling algorithm; (2) PSO [11] an evolutionary computation technique called Particle Swarm Optimization (3) IPPTS [23], an improved predict priority task scheduling method to minimize the scheduling length. According to the experiments in [11], 160 iterations and 100 particles can result in the best makespan. For the parameter setting of PSO, the number of particles is set to 100, and the number of iterations is 160.

**Table 2.** Makespan results for scheduling methods

| DAG | BCWS | GRP-HEFT | PSO | IPPTS |
|---|---|---|---|---|
| Montage 50 | **30.44** | 31.12 | 57.09 | 44.83 |
| Montage 100 | **45.49** | 47.46 | 117.13 | 73.17 |
| LIGO 50 | **866.48** | 876.85 | 1208.41 | 1082.46 |
| LIGO 100 | **912.11** | 955.34 | 1869.41 | 1225.66 |
| Cybershake 50 | **140.00** | 142.05 | 207.17 | 153.56 |
| Cybershake 100 | **194.26** | 196.71 | 332.81 | 206.13 |
| SIPHT 50 | **1074.98** | 1086.28 | 1442.11 | 2036.15 |
| SIPHT 100 | **1167.98** | 1191.29 | 1865.90 | 1645.44 |

## 5.2 Results of Overall Experiments

Table 2 lists the average makespan results for all methods, where the best value for each workflow is highlighted in bold. We can observe that for each workflow case, BCWS achieves the best makespan. For example, the makespan of BCWS for LIGO 100 is 912.11 whereas those of the others are all greater than 950. The performance gap between them becomes larger when the task number in a workflow rises. A crucial aspect is that BCWS takes into account the potential data communication contention while considering the task scheduling to instances.

Figure 4 shows the results obtained by comparing the algorithms under different cost coefficient $\theta$. Here, we vary $\theta$ from 0.5\$ to 4\$ with a step of 0.5\$ for performance evaluation. We have the following observation that the completion time is decreasing as $\theta$ is increasing. This is because a larger value means that more in-stances can be purchased. When there are more instances to choose from, makespan is gradually decreasing. For example, the decrease in the time span is most noticeable when the amount increases from 0.5\$ to 1.0\$. The reason is that 0.5\$ can only purchase a small number of better instances. When the budget exceeds 1\$, there are numerous available instances, and at this point, the downward trend in makespan slows down. Compared to other algorithms, BCWS consistently maintains the best performance.

Figure 5 shows the results obtained by comparing the algorithms under different privacy coefficient $\beta$. Here, we vary $\beta$ from 0.05 to 0.4 with a step of 0.05 for performance evaluation. We can observe that the makespan of each method generally increases as the $\beta$ value rises. This is because more tasks in the workflow can only be executed in slower private resources as the $\beta$ value is higher. Although situations vary for different workflow types, BCWS performs the best among all in each case.

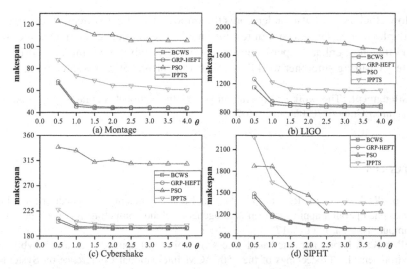

**Fig. 4.** Performance comparison with regards to cost factor $\theta$

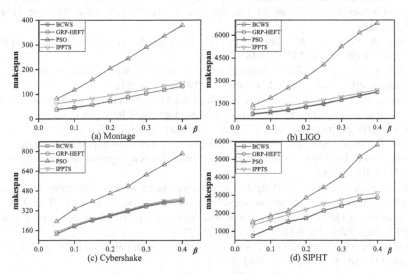

**Fig. 5.** Performance comparison with regards to privacy factor $\beta$

## 6 Conclusion

This paper effectively addresses the intricate challenges of effective scheduling and communication contention in hybrid cloud environments. The practical scheduling model and the Budget-Constraint Contention-Aware Workflow Scheduling (BCWS) algorithm offer robust solutions. Notably, the challenge of billing instances based on hourly rates is skillfully tackled. BCWS intelligently navigates this complexity by seamlessly integrating instance provisioning strategies and queuing mechanisms, optimizing both resource allocation and communication management. This strategic approach not only optimizes workflow efficiency but also underscores the importance of cost-effectiveness in hybrid cloud deployments. The successful resolution of these challenges augments the overall system efficiency, enhances performance, and fosters stability within the hybrid cloud, ultimately ensuring smoother workflow execution across varied resource pools.

**Acknowledgment.** This work is supported in part by the National Natural Science Foundation of China under Grant 61702060 and 61672117.

# References

1. Chen, W., Xie, G., Li, R., Bai, Y., Fan, C., Li, K.: Efficient task scheduling for budget constrained parallel applications on heterogeneous cloud computing systems. Futur. Gener. Comput. Syst. **74**, 1–11 (2017)
2. Miller, G.: A hybrid attribute based access control model applied to data in a hybrid cloud environment. In: Proceedings of the 15th ACM International Conference on Systems and Storage, p. 150 (2022)
3. Azumah, K.K., Maciel, P.R.M., Sørensen, L.T., Kosta, S.: Modeling and simulating a process mining-influenced load-balancer for the hybrid cloud. IEEE Trans. Cloud Comput. **11**, 1999–2010 (2023)
4. Pasdar, A., Lee, Y.C., Almi'ani, K.: Hybrid scheduling for scientific workflows on hybrid clouds. Comput. Netw. **181**, 107438 (2020)
5. Zhu, J., Li, X., Ruiz, R., Xu, X.: Scheduling stochastic multi-stage jobs to elastic hybrid cloud resources. IEEE Trans. Parallel Distrib. Syst. **29**, 1401–1415 (2018)
6. Sakellariou, R., Zhao, H., Tsiakkouri, E., Dikaiakos, M.D.: Scheduling workflows with budget constraints. In: Gorlatch, S., Danelutto, M. (eds.) Integrated Research in GRID Computing, pp. 189–202. Springer, Boston (2007). https://doi.org/10.1007/978-0-387-47658-2_14
7. Yu, J., Buyya, R.: A budget constrained scheduling of workflow applications on utility grids using genetic algorithms. In: 2006 Workshop on Workflows in Support of Large-Scale Science, pp. 1–10. IEEE (2006)
8. Zheng, W., Sakellariou, R.: Budget-deadline constrained workflow planning for admission control in market-oriented environments. In: Vanmechelen, K., Altmann, J., Rana, O.F. (eds.) Economics of Grids, Clouds, Systems, and Services, pp. 105–119. Springer, Heidelberg (2012). https://doi.org/10.1007/978-3-642-28675-9_8
9. Farahabady, M.R.H., Lee, Y.C., Zomaya, A.Y.: Pareto-optimal cloud bursting. IEEE Trans. Parallel Distrib. Syst. **25**, 2670–2682 (2014)
10. Lin, X., Wu, C.Q.: On scientific workflow scheduling in clouds under budget constraint. In: 2013 42nd International Conference on Parallel Processing, pp. 90–99. IEEE (2013)
11. Wang, X., Cao, B., Hou, C., Xiong, L., Fan, J.: Scheduling budget constrained cloud workflows with particle swarm optimization. In: 2015 IEEE Conference on Collaboration and Internet Computing (CIC), pp. 219–226 (2015)
12. Faragardi, H.R., Sedghpour, M.R.S., Fazliahmadi, S., Fahringer, T., Rasouli, N.: GRP-HEFT: a budget-constrained resource provisioning scheme for workflow scheduling in IaaS clouds. IEEE Trans. Parallel Distrib. Syst. **31**, 1239–1254 (2020)
13. Sinnen, O., To, A., Kaur, M.: Contention-aware scheduling with task duplication. J. Parallel Distrib. Comput. **71**, 77–86 (2011)
14. Benoit, A., Hakem, M., Robert, Y.: Contention awareness and fault-tolerant scheduling for precedence constrained tasks in heterogeneous systems. Parallel Comput. **35**, 83–108 (2009)

15. Özkaya, M.Y., Benoit, A., Uçar, B., Herrmann, J., Catalyürek, Ü.V.: A scalable clustering-based task scheduler for homogeneous processors using DAG partitioning. In: 2019 IEEE International Parallel and Distributed Processing Symposium (IPDPS), pp. 155–165 (2019)
16. Genez, T.A., Bittencourt, L.F., da Fonseca, N.L., Madeira, E.R.: Estimation of the available bandwidth in inter-cloud links for task scheduling in hybrid clouds. IEEE Trans. Cloud Comput. **7**, 62–74 (2019)
17. Son, J., Buyya, R.: Priority-aware VM allocation and network bandwidth provisioning in software-defined networking (SDN)-enabled clouds. IEEE Trans. Sustain. Comput. **4**, 17–28 (2018)
18. Wu, Q., Zhou, M., Wen, J.: Endpoint communication contention-aware cloud workflow scheduling. IEEE Trans. Autom. Sci. Eng. **19**, 1137–1150 (2022)
19. Mithila, S.P., Baumgartner, G.: Latency-based Vector Scheduling of Many-task Applications for a Hybrid Cloud. In: 2022 IEEE 15th International Conference on Cloud Computing (CLOUD), pp. 257–262 (2022)
20. Durillo, J.J., Prodan, R.: Multi-objective workflow scheduling in Amazon EC2. Clust. Comput. **17**, 169–189 (2014)
21. Juve, G., Chervenak, A., Deelman, E., Bharathi, S., Mehta, G., Vahi, K.: Characterizing and profiling scientific workflows. Futur. Gener. Comput. Syst. **29**, 682–692 (2013)
22. Chen, Z.G., et al.: Multiobjective cloud workflow scheduling: a multiple populations ant colony system approach. IEEE Trans. Cybern. **49**, 2912–2926 (2019)
23. Djigal, H., Feng, J., Lu, J., Ge, J.: IPPTS: an efficient algorithm for scientific workflow scheduling in heterogeneous computing systems. IEEE Trans. Parallel Distrib. Syst. **32**, 1057–1071 (2021)
24. Lei, J., Wu, Q., Xu, J.: Privacy and security-aware workflow scheduling in a hybrid cloud. Futur. Gener. Comput. Syst. **131**, 269–278 (2022)

# A Dichotomous Repair-Based Load-Balanced Task Allocation Strategy in Cloud-Edge Environment

Zekun Hu, Pengwei Wang$^{(\boxtimes)}$, Peihai Zhao, and Zhaohui Zhang

School of Computer Science and Technology, Donghua University, Shanghai, China
{wangpengwei,peihaizhao,zhzhang}@dhu.edu.cn

**Abstract.** Load balancing is a hot issue in the current cloud-edge environment. However, due to the characteristics of edge computing, load balancing needs to be better integrated with edge devices and edge networks to provide higher performance and reliability. The presence of a large number of overloaded nodes may lead to load imbalance and thus affect the efficiency of nodes. To solve this problem, the key is how to allocate tasks to the appropriate resources. To this end, this work proposes a dichotomous task allocation policy Dichotomous Repair (DREP) to achieve efficient task allocation and overall load balancing of edge nodes in cloud-edge environment. The proposed policy consists of five steps: grouping, adjustment, filtering, greed and repair. The dichotomous policy is adopted to generate the initial allocation scheme according to the number of edge nodes, and then the overloaded and underloaded nodes are repaired by the subsequent two-stage repair policy to maintain the load balance. Finally, through extensive experiments, we evaluate the proposed method and the results show that it outperforms other algorithms in terms of workload balancing.

**Keywords:** Load balancing · Task allocation · Dichotomous · Edge computing · Cloud-edge

## 1 Introduction

Cloud-edge computing is a hot research direction at this stage [1], which is a new architectural model that combines the advantages of cloud computing and edge computing. The cloud center can make up for the lack of computing resources at the edge, while the edge nodes can provide computation and services with lower latency [2]. However, the overall performance may be affected due to improper task allocation in edge computing. Specifically, if the resources requested by a task exceed the remaining resources of a node, the task cannot be assigned to that node, thus affecting the efficiency of subsequent allocations. Neglecting the capacity and workload of nodes can also lead to poor node performance, slow task processing, and unbalanced data center load, and the advantages of cloud-edge computing cannot be realized.

© ICST Institute for Computer Sciences, Social Informatics and Telecommunications Engineering 2024
Published by Springer Nature Switzerland AG 2024. All Rights Reserved
H. Gao et al. (Eds.): CollaborateCom 2023, LNICST 561, pp. 128–148, 2024.
https://doi.org/10.1007/978-3-031-54521-4_8

In order to achieve load balancing in data centers [3], it is crucial to efficiently assign tasks to the appropriate nodes. Therefore, an efficient task allocation strategy is needed to assign user-submitted task requests to the most appropriate nodes to improve node efficiency and reduce user waiting time while maintaining load balancing. However, there is still room for improvement in the current research on load balancing task allocation strategies, mainly focusing on the following aspects. First, the existing scheduling strategies can be further improved in terms of flexibility, so that they can be better adjusted dynamically according to the real-time load situation and resource status. Second, current research focuses mainly on the load situation of nodes, and pays relatively little attention to the unique characteristics and demands of tasks themselves. Such methods may bring some imbalance in resource allocation, thus failing to achieve better load balancing.

In order to better improve the shortcomings of previous work and solve the problem of unbalanced workload of edge nodes, this paper proposes a new task scheduling algorithm DREP, which employs a bisection-based idea to flexibly deal with task allocation and improve the adaptability of the system. By successively bisecting the current task set, a better initial task allocation scheme is obtained, which provides a good basis for subsequent load balancing, and self-healing is performed in combination with the node's capacity and load, which fully utilizes the node's resources and improves the overall efficiency. Specifically the main contributions of this paper are as follows:

- A load balancing algorithm is proposed, which fully considers the processing capacity of nodes as well as the load sizes of different tasks, and achieves a highly consistent load balancing effect by dynamically adjusting the task allocation of each edge node. It is worth emphasizing that this algorithm not only performs well in homogeneous environments, but is also applicable to heterogeneous environments.
- With the consideration of task size and the number of edge nodes, this paper proposes a grouping strategy based on the dichotomous idea to dichotomize the task set appropriately according to the number of edge nodes, thus forming a good initial allocation scheme.
- We propose a two-stage repair strategy to adjust task allocation. By moving suitable tasks from the overloaded nodes to the underloaded nodes, the strategy achieves a highly consistent edge node load rate and effectively improves the overall performance.

The rest of this paper is organized as follows. Section 2 briefly introduces the current work on task allocation methods and load balancing in edge computing and cloud computing environments. Section 3 illustrates the imperfections of current work through an example. Section 4 describes the relevant issues and formalizes them. Section 5 describes in detail the design and implementation process of algorithm. Section 6 presents the experimental results, which demonstrate the effectiveness of proposed algorithm. We conclude the paper in Sect. 7.

## 2  Related Work

This section reviews two aspects related to our research, including task allocation and load balancing in cloud and edge computing.

### 2.1  Task Allocation

Task allocation refers to the assignment of user-submitted task requests to heterogeneous available resources. Appropriate task allocation not only improves resource utilization, but also minimizes makespan by executing the assigned tasks in a shorter period of time. Therefore, more research is needed in area of cloud task scheduling or task allocation in order to efficiently map tasks to available resources and to improve quality of service (QoS) parameters.

In order to focus on the energy consumption problem caused by task allocation in cloud computing, Gai et al. [4] proposed a management model in a heterogeneous cloud environment, which can effectively reduce the energy consumption in mobile cloud systems. Zhou et al. [5] proposed an improved ITSA algorithm to enhance the resource utilization and QoS in cloud environment by binding the size tasks to form task pairs through the gain value of task exchange and then scheduling with greedy policies. However, their approach is limited to scenarios where the task sizes do not differ much. Panda et al. [6] introduced a multi-cloud environment to break the limited resources of a single cloud during peak demand, and proposed an improved Min-Min algorithm and Max-Min algorithm, which is divided into three phases: matching, allocation and scheduling. Ali et al. [7] divided the tasks into five categories, each with similar properties, and based on the execution time of tasks, the ones with shorter execution time are scheduled first. Scheduling is divided into two steps, first determining the category of a task and then identifying a task in that category. Er-raji and BenaNaoufal [8] proposed a multi-parameter-based global task scheduling strategy for the priority task scheduling problem in distributed data centers in cloud computing. Zhang and Zhou [9] proposed a two-stage scheduling method based on a two-stage scheduling approach in order to improve the scheduling performance and efficiency of cloud. In the first stage, a Bayesian classifier is used to classify tasks with historical scheduling data to create a certain number of virtual machines to save time, and in the second stage, a dynamic scheduling algorithm is used to match with specific virtual machines.

With the development of technology, edge computing is integrated into people's life as a new technology. In order to get low latency and efficient services, users can assign tasks to nearby edge nodes.

Therefore how to assign task scheduling to edge nodes becomes an important issue. Su et al. [10] proposed an improved NSGA-II algorithm to solve the task scheduling of edge computing, using a dynamic adaptive strategy to adjust the crossover rate and mutation rate to improve the population search efficiency, which improves the search efficiency while maintaining the population diversity and finally obtains a set of optimal solution sets. Shen [11] proposed a hierarchical task scheduling strategy for the latency cost problem, with an edge node layer for processing simple tasks and dividing them into three priority levels and a frog server layer for processing complex tasks and returning accurate computation results. To make full use of the limited computational resources, Yang and Poellabauer [12] prioritized tasks based on attributes such as task CPU and combine reinforcement learning for task scheduling, but the proposed scheme is based on too many good assumptions and constrained to a practical system.

## 2.2   Load Balancing

The goal of load balancing is to ensure that the state of each host in cloud computing or edge computing is balanced to achieve high availability of computing platform as a whole. While making full use of computing resources, it ensures that each host can achieve optimal business performance and work efficiency.

Load balancing in the cloud refers to the distribution of load to the active components associated with the processing tasks. Ruan et al. [13] proposed a strategy to calculate the optimal work utilization of hosts, dividing hosts into different blocks according to different PPRs, and keeping each host in the optimal block through VM allocation and migration framework to achieve the best balance between host utilization and energy consumption, However, because of the energy consumption constraint, there is still a large variation in load between hosts. In [14–17], the problem of consolidation of virtual machines is investigated for consolidating overloaded or underloaded hosts through virtual machine placement and migration strategies so as to keep the workload of hosts in an appropriate range. Zhou et al. [18] solved the problem of reducing high energy consumption in cloud data centers with minimal service level agreement (SLA) violations by proposing two new adaptive energy-aware algorithms for overloaded and underloaded vm's and considering their application types. In another paper [5], Zhou proposed a task-based load balancing problem for cloud environments by swapping the gain values and binding the one with the smallest gain value and the one with the largest gain value to form a task pair for the purpose of load balancing, but it is not applicable to scenarios with large differences in task loads.

Although edge computing makes up for the shortcomings of cloud computing, however, edge nodes are usually heterogeneous and have relatively weak computing power. How to fully utilize the resources of edge nodes, reasonably allocate tasks, and achieve load balancing in edge computing is also a problem. Dong et al. [19] proposed a deployment policy HEELS based on the analysis of heuristic task clustering method and firefly swarm optimization algorithm, so as to solve the long-term load balancing problem of edge computing federated cloud as a whole. Li et al. [20] combined greedy algorithm with genetic algorithm to minimize the number of edge servers while ensuring load balancing among edge servers and QoS requirements of users. Li et al. [21] classified edge nodes into three categories based on their attributes: light, normal, and heavy, and intermediated nodes assign new tasks to light nodes to achieve load balancing. Dong et al. [22] studied the load balancing problem of federated cloud-edge data centers and proposed a task deployment strategy JCETD based on pruning algorithm and deep reinforcement learning in order to achieve efficient deployment and overall load balancing of cloud-edge tasks.

Task scheduling has been considered for load balancing, both in cloud and edge environments. However, due to the complexity and diversity of scheduling, load balancing algorithms may not be flexible enough to effectively deal with complex task scheduling problems or even resource scarcity. In addition, most of the current research focuses on making servers host the same number of tasks or minimizing the number of servers to achieve load balancing without considering task size, node capacity, and resource availability, which leads to significant differences in server load and cannot achieve an approximate consistency.

## 3    Motivation Example

In this section we use an example to compare the differences between the algorithms. The scenario is to process several input tasks ti which are assumed to have no sequential relationship and are not dependent on each other, and task allocation is operated by the proxy server, including the calculation of total number of resources for the tasks.

We use Table 1 to map the resource requirements for each task. Here we consider CPU resources and memory resources, and both are weighted to get the total requested resources. For example, task 1 requires 100 CPU resources and 92 memory resources, for a total of 96 resources.

**Table 1.** Resource requirements for each task in motivation example.

| Task | $t_1$ | $t_2$ | $t_3$ | $t_4$ | $t_5$ | $t_6$ | $t_7$ | $t_8$ | $t_9$ | $t_{10}$ |
|---|---|---|---|---|---|---|---|---|---|---|
| CPU | 100 | 10 | 20 | 30 | 42 | 90 | 1 | 6 | 55 | 76 |
| Memory | 92 | 26 | 46 | 32 | 88 | 106 | 1 | 36 | 113 | 108 |
| Total requested resources | 96 | 18 | 33 | 31 | 65 | 98 | 1 | 21 | 84 | 92 |

**Table 2.** Computing resources for edge nodes.

| Edge Nodes | $e_1$ | $e_2$ | $e_3$ |
|---|---|---|---|
| CPU | 120 | 200 | 250 |
| Memory | 140 | 200 | 350 |
| Total Resources | 130 | 200 | 300 |

The tasks need to be processed at the edge nodes, and there are three edge nodes. Different edge nodes have different computational resource capabilities. We use Table 2 to represent the computational resources of each edge node, and the resource requirements for each task on each node should not exceed the amount of resources that can be provided by that node. For edge node $e_1$, it has a total CPU resource of 120 units and a total memory resource of 140 units.

In cloud and edge computing environments, greed is a simple and effective approach. In this example, we obtained a task allocation scheme by greedy policy as $\{t_3, t_7, t_8\}$, $\{t_2, t_4, t_5\}$, $\{t_1, t_9\}$ with the load factor of edge nodes as 42.31%, 57%, and 60% with a standard deviation of 0.077. In addition, we also tried an improved ITSA [5] algorithm by combining task binding to form task pairs for allocation scheduling, resulting in allocation schemes of $\{t_6, t_7\}$, $\{t_1, t_2\}$, $\{t_4, t_8, t_9, t_{10}\}$ with load ratios of 76.15%, 57% and 76% for edge nodes, respectively, with a standard deviation of 0.0899.

The existing task allocation schemes do not consider the capacity and load of the nodes, resulting in unsatisfactory load balancing. In contrast, a better allocation scheme $\{t_6\}$, $\{t_1, t_3\}$, $\{t_2, t_4, t_5, t_7, t_8, t_9\}$ can result in edge nodes with load ratios of 70%, 64.5%, and 73.3% with a standard deviation of only 0.036. A small value of standard deviation indicates a more balanced load distribution across edge nodes. This means that under this distribution scheme, the difference in the load carried by each edge node is very small and the load is more evenly distributed among the nodes. Therefore, the purpose of this paper is to propose an algorithm to generate a better task allocation scheme that results in better load balancing. The details of algorithm will be given in the subsequent sections.

## 4    Concept and Proposed Model

We will define the system model and some key definitions in this section.

### 4.1    Models and Definitions

In cloud-edge environment, the task allocation problem can be briefly described as follows: the agent server collects $n$ independent computational tasks and allocates them to a joint data center composed of $m$ edge nodes and 1 cloud, considering both heterogeneous and homogeneous environments of nodes, and solves the load balancing problem of edge nodes through high-quality allocation schemes and policies.

**Definition 1.** In cloud-edge environment, the agent server collects $n$ task requests which form a set $T = \{t_1, t_2, \ldots, t_i \ldots, t_n\}$, where $t_i$ denotes the $i$-th task. Assume that the $n$ tasks are independent of each other and have no priority or time restrictions, and each task is represented by $t_i(R_i^{cpu}, R_i^{mem})$, where $R_i^{cpu}$ denotes the CPU resources required by the task and $R_i^{mem}$ denotes the memory resources required by the task.

**Definition 2.** In cloud-edge environment, assume that there are $m$ edge nodes. Define the edge node set $E = \{e_1, e_2, \ldots, e_j \ldots, e_m\}$, where $e_j$ denotes the $j$-th edge node. Assume that the capacity of edge node is denoted by $e_j(S_j^{cpu}, S_j^{mem})$, where $S_j^{cpu}$ denotes the CPU capacity of edge node $j$ and $S_j^{mem}$ denotes the memory capacity of edge node $j$.

**Definition 3.** In order to distribute the task sets collected by the agent server to the federated data center at cloud-edge, it is necessary to ensure that the resources available at the edge nodes can accommodate the current task sets. The total resources of edge node are expressed as:

$$Q_j = \alpha S_j^{cpu} + \beta S_j^{mem} \tag{1}$$

$$\alpha + \beta = 1 \tag{2}$$

The amount of used resources of edge node $j$ is expressed as follows:

$$L_j = \sum_{i=1}^{k} R_i^j \tag{3}$$

$$R_i^j = \alpha R_i^{cpu} + \beta R_i^{mem} \tag{4}$$

where $R_i^j$ denotes the total requested resources for the $i$-th task on the $j$-th edge node, $k$ denotes the number of tasks assigned to that edge node. We refer to [22] for evaluating CPU and memory, $\alpha$ is the weight of CPU, and $\beta$ is the weight of memory. In this paper we consider that the task's CPU and memory requirements are considered equally important, and thus $\alpha$ and $\beta$ are equal.

**Definition 4.** Load balancing refers to the balanced degree of load distribution on each node, and this paper uses the standard deviation of resource load ratio of edge nodes to express the degree of load balancing, where the resource load ratio of edge node $j$ is expressed as:

$$G_j = \frac{L_j}{Q_j} \tag{5}$$

The resource load ratio of each edge node can be calculated by (1) (2)(3) (4) (5), and then the load balancing degree of edge data center can be calculated by using the standard deviation formula.

$$W = \sqrt{\frac{1}{m} \sum_{j=1}^{m} (G_j - \frac{1}{m} \sum_{j=1}^{m} G_j)^2} \tag{6}$$

The problem of this paper can be formalized:

$$min \sqrt{\frac{1}{m} \sum_{j=1}^{m} (G_j - \frac{1}{m} \sum_{j=1}^{m} G_j)^2}$$

$$s.t. C1 \quad \sum_{i=1}^{k} R_i^{cpu} \leq S_j^{cpu} \quad \forall j \in m$$

$$C2 \quad \sum_{i=1}^{k} R_i^{mem} \leq S_j^{mem} \quad \forall j \in m \tag{7}$$

In summary, the ultimate goal of this paper is to achieve load balancing in the edge data center under the condition that the resource constraints of each edge node are satisfied. That is, to make W as small as possible.

## 4.2  Problem Statement

In cloud-edge environments, task requests need to be assigned to different edge nodes and cloud center for processing. However, when the amount of resources required for a task request exceeds the remaining resources of a certain node, it will lead to an overload problem and reduce the computational and operational capacity of that data center, thus failing to achieve the desired load balancing. Therefore, when facing large-scale task requests and limited computing resources in edge computing centers, different task allocation schemes and resource allocation strategies will produce different computing efficiency and load balancing states. Optimizing task allocation schemes is an important means to achieve high-quality computing services and load balancing. Therefore, this paper designs a high-quality task allocation scheme to solve the problem of load imbalance of edge nodes.

## 5  Load Balancing DREP Algorithm

### 5.1  System Architecture Design

In our model, the process of task assignment is mainly grouping, adjustment, filtering, greed and repair in five parts, and Fig. 1 shows the operation flow of our proposed model. Different from other algorithms, our algorithm can take into account both homogeneous and heterogeneous environments.

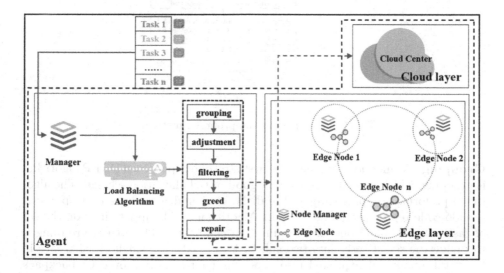

Fig. 1. The framework of DREP.

## 5.2   Algorithm Implementation

**Overall Process.** Figure 2 depicts a flow of our algorithm as a whole, covering five key steps. First, we group the tasks based on the number of edge nodes, and then reconcile the groups with each other to avoid getting trapped in a local optimal solution. Then, we filter out some sets of tasks that do not meet the constraints and assign them to suitable edge nodes in a greedy manner. Finally, the capacity and load of edge nodes are combined to repair so that the load ratio of each node is close to the mean value. The purpose of the grouping is to get a good initial distribution scheme. An adjustment mechanism is introduced to avoid falling into a local optimum among the groups. Then for the tasks that cannot be carried in the nodes need to be eliminated and greedily assigned to other nodes that can carry them. Finally, in order to achieve load balancing, the load rate of each edge node is approximated to be the same using a repair strategy.

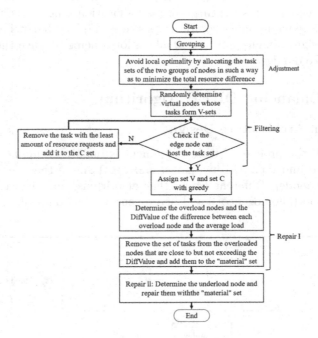

**Fig. 2.** Flow chart of the proposed method.

**Grouping.** As mentioned earlier, the first step of our proposed DREP algorithm is grouping, which is used to generate a good initial allocation scheme. The algorithm performs grouping through the dichotomous idea, and the corresponding pseudo-code representation is given in Algorithm 1. The inputs include the set of tasks, initial conditions, and termination conditions. The goal of grouping is to divide the set of tasks into two sub-task sets with the smallest difference in the total amount of requested resources, similar to the improved 01 backpack problem, in which we analogize tasks to items, but we care only about the weight of the items, not their value, so the core of the problem is how to choose the items so that the weight of the backpack is closest to half of the total item weight. This is a classical dynamic programming problem. The core mechanism of the algorithm is that for each task, if the remaining capacity of the backpack is less than the weight of the current item, it can only be chosen not to put it in. Conversely, it can be considered to put in, choosing the larger of these cases according to the properties of dynamic programming. Where $dp[i][j]$ means the maximum gain that can be obtained for the first $i$ items with capacity $j$.

---

**Algorithm 1:** Group

---

**Input**: $Task, EndNum, Num$
**Output**: $Taskassignment$

1 **if** $Task.size == 1$ or $EndNum == Num$ **then**
2     $Result$.append($Task$)
3     **return**
4 **end**
5 **for** $i = 0$ to $Task.size$ **do**
6     $Sum+ = Task[i]_{Load}$
7 **end**
8 Initialize the parameter $dp$
9 **for** $i = 1$ to $Task.size + 1$ **do**
10     **for** $j = 1$ to $Sum/2 + 1$ **do**
11        **if** $j >= Task[i-1]_{Load}$ **then**
12           $dp[i][j] = max(dp[i-1][j], dp[i-1][j - Task[i-1]_{Load}]+$
13           $Task[i-1]_{Load})$
14        **else**
15           $dp[i][j] = dp[i-1][j]$
16        **end**
17     **end**
18 **end**
19 The set of $Task$ can be divided into $Task1$ and $Task2$ according to the $dp$
20 $Num = Num + 1$
21 Group ($Task1, Num, StartNum$)
22 Group ($Task2, Num, StartNum$)

---

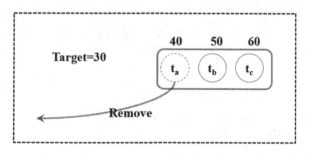

**Fig. 3.** Example for remove.

**Repair.** In order to keep the load ratio of each edge node close to the mean, we propose a two-stage repair algorithm. The first phase quickly reduces the load to near-average by eliminating some tasks from the overloaded nodes; the eliminated task set and other tasks that do not get assigned become the second phase "materials" that is then assigned to the underloaded nodes. The repair idea is to eliminate or select the most suitable task set from a set in order to bring the node to the desired load ratio. The most suitable task set is the one for which the total amount of requested resources should converge to, but not exceed the target value. Here, the problem is likewise analogous to the 01 backpack problem, with the difference that the weight of the backpack no longer converges to half of the total item weight, but to the target value TargetValue. We give the pseudo-code representation in Algorithm 2. The input of the algorithm consists of task set Task of the overloaded node and the target value TargetValue, and the output is the "materials" task set RepairTaskSet core. The difference with Algorithm 1 is that there may be no tasks on the overloaded node that converge to and do not exceed the target value, as shown in the Fig. 3, In this case, the task that requests the least amount of resources is eliminated by default to ensure that the load on the overloaded node can be reduced.

Suppose there are $n$ edge nodes and $m$ tasks. First determine the number of bisections, our approach is to find a power of 2 closest to the number of nodes n, expressed as $n + x = 2^a$, where $x$ serves to keep $n$ near the smallest power of 2, so the number of bisections is $a$, so $a = \log(n+x)$. In each bisection operation, a dynamic planning operation is performed to minimize the difference between the resources of the two groups of tasks divided, with the outer layer traversing the tasks sequentially, and the inner loop determining inside by constantly changing the capacity (from 1 to $s/2$) whether the minimization of the difference can be produced, which is performed a total of $m * \frac{s}{2}$ times, thus the total time complexity is $O(\log(n + x)ms)$. Similarly, we can calculate the time complexity of the other steps, and overall the time complexity of DREP is $O(n^2)$.

---

**Algorithm 2:** Pick_Tasks

Input: $Task, TargetValue$
Output: $RepairTaskSet$

1 **for** $i = 1$ *to* $Task.size + 1$ **do**
2     **for** $j = 1$ *to* $TargetValue + 1$ **do**
3         **if** $j >= Task[i]_{Load}$ **then**
4            | $dp[i][j] = max(dp[i-1][j], dp[i-1][j - Task[i]_{Load}] + Task[i]_{Load})$
5         **else**
6            | $dp[i][j] = dp[i-1][j]$
7         **end**
8     **end**
9 **end**
10 $SetT$ stores the set of tasks that match the $TargetValue$
11 **if** $SetT.size \; != 0$ **then**
12     | $RepairTaskSet = RepairTaskSet + SetT$
13 **else**
14     Find the task $T$ with the lowest load value
15     $RepairTaskSet.add(T)$
16 **end**
17 **return** $RepairTaskSet$

## 5.3  Running Example

In this section we will use a concrete example to illustrate our algorithmic ideas.

First, we group the task set according to the number of edge nodes. To determine the number of dichotomies, we use the method of finding the smallest power of 2 that can contain the number of edge nodes and perform $x$ dichotomies. For example, our example has three edge nodes, so $x$ equals 2. That is, the task set is divided into four groups, each group corresponding to one edge node assignment scheme, as shown in Fig. 4, as follows: $\{t_2,t_4,t_{10}\},\{t_1,t_3\},\{t_5,t_9\},\{t_6,t_7,t_8\}$. The extra set we assume is assigned to virtual nodes, which will be processed in the later filtering steps.

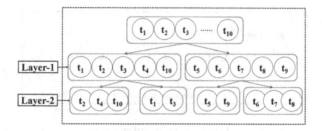

**Fig. 4.** Step 1: grouping.

In the second step, we take the adjustment step to avoid local optima in the process of generating sub-task sets. Specifically, a set of tasks in a frontier node is combined with a set of tasks in a trailing edge node, and the set of tasks within the two groups is redistributed to obtain an allocation that minimizes the difference in total resource requirements, as shown in the Fig. 5, In this example, the reconciled results change from $\{t_2,t_4,t_{10}\},\{t_1,t_3\},\{t_5,t_9\},\{t_6,t_7,t_8\}$ to $\{t_4,t_6,t_7\},\{t_1,t_3\},\{t_5,t_9\},\{t_2,t_8,t_{10}\}$.

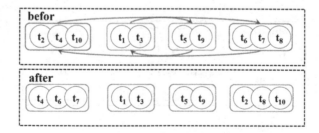

**Fig. 5.** Step 2: adjustment.

Next, we need to filter out the set of tasks that cannot satisfy the resource constraints and solve the set of tasks on the virtual nodes. For the virtual nodes, we directly select them using a random strategy, assuming that edge node 4 is a virtual node. Then, we check each edge node in turn for the presence of insufficient resources, where the amount of resources that the node can provide is less than the amount of resources required by the task. If it exists, we sort the set of tasks on the edge nodes in ascending order of the total requested resources and then eliminate the tasks one by one until all resource constraints are satisfied. As shown in Fig. 6. In this example, only edge node 1 cannot satisfy the constraint, and the set of tasks belonging to it is sorted into $t_7$, $t_4$,$t_6$ in ascending order, and $t_7$ is eliminated to satisfy the constraint. After filtering, we get the task set as $\{t_4,t_6\}$,$\{t_1,t_3\}$,$\{t_5,t_9\}$, The remaining $\{t_2,t_7,t_8,t_{10}\}$ are considered as the set of tasks to be assigned.

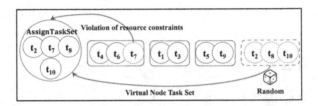

**Fig. 6.** Step 3: filtering.

Then what we expect is to achieve a load-rate balance, not to carry the same amount of resources, so edge nodes with more capacity should carry more tasks. Therefore, we use a greedy strategy to sequentially assign the set of tasks generated by filtering to the edge node with the lowest current load factor subject to the resource constraints. In this example, the current load rates of edge nodes are 99.23%, 64.5%, and 49.7%, so the first element $t_2$ in the set of tasks generated by filtering is added to the edge node 3 with the lowest current load rate, and then the load rate is updated and the process is cycled. The results after greedy are $\{t_4,t_6\}$,$\{t_1,t_3\}$,$\{t_2,t_5,t_7,t_8,t_9\}$. As shown in Fig. 7.

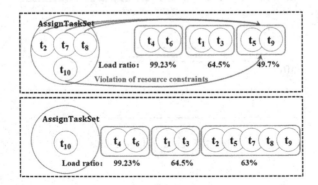

**Fig. 7.** Step 4: greed.

Finally, we combined the capacity of edge nodes and the current task allocation to achieve load balancing through a two-phase repair strategy. As shown in
Fig. 8. In the first stage, we fix overloaded nodes (nodes above the mean value)
and remove part of task set based on the difference between the load ratio of the
nodes and the mean value, so that their total requested resources converge to but
are not higher than the difference. If such a combination does not exist, the task
with the smallest total requested resources is removed by default. In this example, only the load ratio of edge node 1 exceeds the mean value, and the task with
the smallest total requested resources $t_4$ is removed by default. In the second
stage, we repair the nodes below the mean value, and the "materials" for repair
comes from the set of tasks removed in the first stage and the remaining set of
tasks to be allocated in the greedy step ($\{t_4, t_{10}\}$). The difference in resources is
calculated based on the mean value, and some tasks from the set of "materials"
that are close to but not higher than the target resources are added to the node.
For the second edge node, the node needs only 22.16 resources to reach the mean
value, but there are no tasks in the task set that satisfy the condition, so the
node gives up the repair. The third edge node requires 37.73 resources to reach
around the mean value, and we find a task $t_4$ in the task set that satisfies the
condition and assign it to this node. With such a repair strategy, we successfully
keep the load ratio of each edge node at or near the mean value and achieve the
purpose of load balancing.

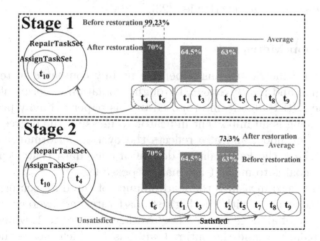

**Fig. 8.** Step 5: repair.

With our optimization scheme, the final set of tasks $\{t_6\}$, $\{t_1, t_3\}$,
$\{t_2, t_4, t_5, t_7, t_8, t_9\}$ are assigned to edge nodes and task$t_{10}$ is assigned to the cloud
respectively. The reduction in load balancing degree is 56.6% compared to ran-
dom policy, 53.2% compared to greedy policy, and 59.96% compared to ITSA
algorithm. Therefore, our scheme has smaller standard deviation and more balanced load.

# 6  Performance Evaluation and Analysis

In this section, we mainly evaluate the performance of the DREP algorithm and verify the effectiveness of the algorithm. We have selected four policy-generated schemes, namely greedy, random, ITSA and DVMC, for experimental comparison with the DREP algorithm proposed in this paper, and then most graphically display the final simulation results.

Greedy policy: Assign tasks to the edge node with the lowest current load factor each time until no compute resources are available. After that, the remaining tasks are assigned to the cloud center.

Random policy: Each task in the task set is randomly assigned in the edge node until there are no available compute resources. After that, the remaining tasks are assigned to the cloud center.

ITSA: Considering both small and large tasks, for each task in the task set, the task with the lowest load value and the task with the highest load value are bound together to form a task pair, and the task pair is assigned to the edge node with the lowest load ratio [5].

DVMC: The task loads are sequentially assigned to edge nodes after sorting them in decreasing order. Through overload detection, the overloaded nodes are adjusted and the task with the highest load value is preferred for removal from the overloaded node. If the node is still overloaded after one migration, the task with the next highest load value is selected for removal. This process is repeated until the node is no longer overloaded [23].

## 6.1  Evaluation Metrics

The experimental metrics in this paper are mainly compared in terms of load balancing degree and max/average. Through simulation experiments, the effectiveness of the DREP algorithm proposed in this paper is finally proved.

Load balancing is an important indicator to measure the degree of load balance of each edge node, and also reflects the overall performance of the data center. From Eq. 6, the load balance degree of edge data center can be calculated, and the goal is to make it as small as possible.

Max/average also measures the load balance of the data center, where max refers to the edge node with the highest load rate and average refers to the average load rate of all edge nodes. Max/average is closer to 1, which means the load is more balanced, and the optimal value is 1, which means the load rates of all edge nodes are the same.

We constructed two experimental environments, using setting 1 to simulate a homogeneous environment and setting 2 to simulate a heterogeneous environment. And Table 3 shows the parameter settings for our experiments.

**Table 3.** Parameterization of the experiment

| Variable Name | Parameter | Parameter Value |
|---|---|---|
| task | $R_i^{cpu}$ $(m)$ | [1, 1000] |
|  | $R_i^{mem}$ $(MB)$ | [1, 1000] |
| edge | $S_j^{cpu}$ $(m)$ | [5000, 50000] |
|  | $S_j^{mem}$ $(MB)$ | [5000, 30000] |

- Setting 1: 500 tasks with 10 edge nodes of the same capability.
- Setting 2: 500 tasks with 15 edge nodes of all different capabilities.

## 6.2  Heterogeneous Environments

Under setting 2, we compared the load balancing degree of the five algorithms, and the load rate of each edge node of the five algorithms is shown in Fig. 9. The more balanced the load, the smoother the line, and the line of the DREP algorithm tends to be straight, so the overall performance of the DREP algorithm is the best. Greedy algorithm performs well in load balancing but it has low overall load factor. This is because it will assign the tasks that do not fulfill the requirements of the nodes to the cloud for processing, without considering other edge nodes.

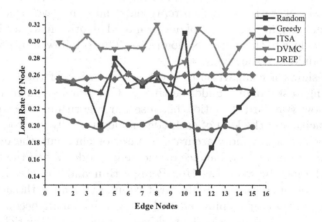

**Fig. 9.** Comparison on load rate.

In order to compare the advantages and disadvantages among the algorithms more clearly, we calculated the standard deviation of the five algorithms, as shown in Fig. 10. By comparing with the other four algorithms, the standard deviation of the load rate of each node of the DREP algorithm proposed in this paper is the smallest only 0.0032, because the DREP algorithm can assign the tasks to the most suitable edge nodes according to their sizes, keeping their load ratios on similar levels.

Because there is a random strategy in our proposed algorithm, so we conducted 10 times more comparisons with the current suboptimal greedy algorithm. The results are shown in Fig. 11, as can be seen from the figure, the standard deviations of our proposed algorithms all stay around 0.004, which are lower than the results of the greedy strategy.

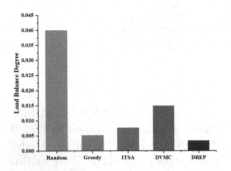

**Fig. 10.** Compare on load balancing under setting 2.

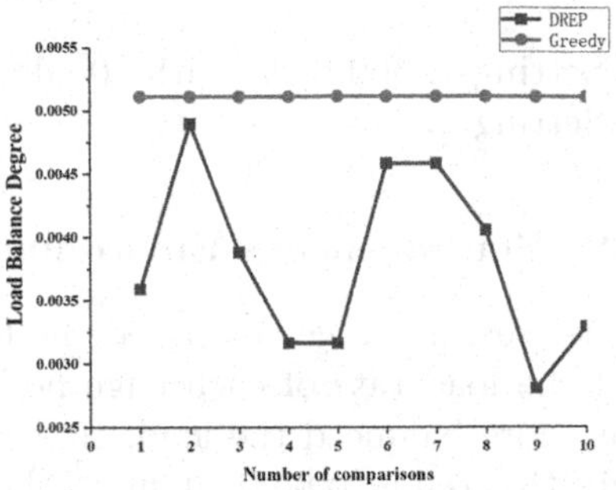

**Fig. 11.** Comparison of DREP and Greedy Strategies.

Figure 12 represents the comparison of max/average for the five algorithms. The most ideal case ratio is 1, which represents the same load ratio for all edge nodes. And the max/average value of our proposed algorithm is only 1.013, which is already very close to the most ideal load case. This is followed by greedy, ITSA, DVMC and random, respectively.

Figure 13 shows a comparison of the load balancing of the five algorithms with increasing task volume under setting 2. Our proposed algorithm always maintains a low standard deviation because our algorithm takes into account both the capacity and the load of each edge node in a fully heterogeneous environment, which makes it more accurate to filter or eliminate the most suitable task set to maintain the load balance of each edge node. When the task volume is 100–300, the gap between the DREP algorithm and the greedy and ITSA algorithms is not obvious, but as the task volume increases, the advantages of the DREP algorithm keep coming out and the load balancing becomes more and more effective. This is because as the task volume increases, the richer the set of "materials" in the repair phase becomes, so the possibility of load-rate balancing at each edge node becomes greater.

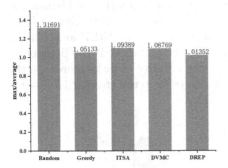

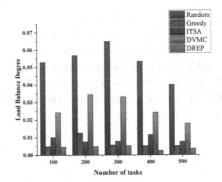

**Fig. 12.** Comparison on max/average under setting 2.

**Fig. 13.** Comparison of load balancing degree under setting 2.

### 6.3 Homogeneous Environment

We also verified the effectiveness of the DREP algorithm in a homogeneous environment, where we compared the five algorithms in terms of both the degree of load balancing and max/average under setting 1. Figure 14 shows that in terms of load balancing degree, the standard deviation of the DREP algorithm is only 0.0005, which is 68.65% lower than the next best greedy algorithm; Fig. 15 shows that in terms of max/average, the result of the DREP algorithm is only 1.005, which is very close to the ideal case.

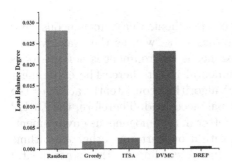

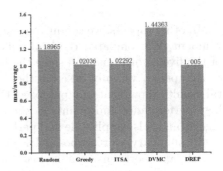

**Fig. 14.** Comparison on load balancing degree under setting 1.

**Fig. 15.** Comparison on max/average under setting 1.

In setting 1, we compare the load balancing performance of five algorithms with different number of tasks, as shown in Fig. 16. When the number of tasks is 100, the four algorithms perform similarly except for the random algorithm, where the ITSA algorithm has the best load balancing effect and the DREP algorithm has the second best effect. The reason for this situation is that when the number of tasks is small and the requested resources do not differ much, the load of a single task on a node does not have a great impact on the load balancing. Therefore, the greedy algorithm maintains load balancing by assigning tasks to the node with the lowest current load rate. In this case, the DREP algorithm is unable to repair the load ratio of each edge node because there is too little or no "materials" for the repair phase. However, as the number of tasks increases, the DREP algorithm has the advantage of being able to keep the standard deviation around 0.0004.

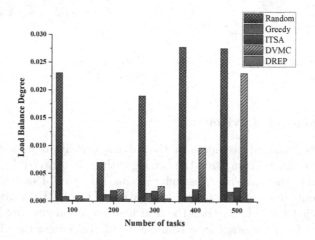

**Fig. 16.** Comparison on load balancing degree under setting 1.

In other aspects, we conducted the same experiments in a homogeneous environment. We compared the load balancing degree as well as the Max/average of the five algorithms, and since the homogeneous environment is not the focus of this paper, we only describe the experimental results here. The experimental results show that our proposed DREP algorithm consistently achieves the best performance and maintains the most balanced load. Therefore, the DREP algorithm is also applicable and performs better in a homogeneous environment.

In summary, our proposed DREP algorithm outperforms other algorithms overall and performs well in load balancing. According to the experimental results, our method is more suitable for scenarios with a larger number of tasks, because each edge node can have more choices in the repair phase and can better keep the load ratio around the mean by picking the most suitable task set according to its own load.

## 7    Conclusion

In this paper, we propose a task allocation strategy DREP based on the idea of dichotomous repair, which aims to achieve load balancing among edge nodes and improve the quality of service. Specifically, a dichotomous strategy is used to generate a good initial allocation scheme based on the number of edge nodes, and then a two-stage repair strategy is proposed for overloaded and underloaded nodes to adjust the load ratio of edge nodes to a relatively approximate level. By comparing the experimental results of the other four allocation algorithms, the DREP algorithm shows better performance and can balance the load among the nodes well and improve the quality of service. In order to further improve the performance and load balancing of cloud-edge computing, we plan to analyze and study from the perspective of distributed multi-cloud and edge. Under the premise of providing high-quality services to users, we will reasonably schedule tasks to multi-cloud and edge to maximize the benefits of data centers and users.

**Acknowledgements.** Pengwei Wang is the corresponding author. This work was partially supported by the National Natural Science Foundation of China (NSFC) under Grant 61602109, DHU Distinguished Young Professor Program under Grant LZB2019003, Shanghai Science and Technology Innovation Action Plan under Grant 22511100700, Fundamental Research Funds for the Central Universities.

# References

1. Shi, W., Cao, J., Zhang, Q., et al.: Edge computing: vision and challenges. IEEE Internet Things J. **3**(5), 637–646 (2016)
2. Zhu, T., Shi, T., Li, J., et al.: Task scheduling in deadline-aware mobile edge computing systems. IEEE Internet Things J. **6**(3), 4854–4866 (2018)
3. Chen, W., Liu, B., Huang, H., et al.: When UAV swarm meets edge-cloud computing. The QoS perspective. IEEE Network **33**(2), 36–43 (2019)
4. Gai, K., Qiu, M., Zhao, H.: Energy-aware task assignment for mobile cyber-enabled applications in heterogeneous cloud computing. J. Parallel Distrib. Comput. **111**, 126–135 (2018)
5. Zhou, Z., Wang, H., Shao, H., et al.: A high-performance scheduling algorithm using greedy strategy toward quality of service in the cloud environments. Peer Peer Netw. Appl. **13**, 2214–2223 (2020)
6. Panda, S.K., Gupta, I., Jana, P.K.: Task scheduling algorithms for multi-cloud systems: allocation-aware approach. Inf. Syst. Front. **21**, 241–259 (2019)
7. Ali, H.G.E.D.H., Saroit, I.A., Kotb, A.M.: Grouped tasks scheduling algorithm based on QoS in cloud computing network. Egypt. Inform. J **18**(1), 11–19 (2017)
8. Er-raji, N., Benabbou, F.: Priority task scheduling strategy for heterogeneous multi-datacenters in cloud computing. Int. J. Adv. Comput. Sci. Appl. **8**(2) (2017)
9. Zhang, P., Zhou, M.: Dynamic cloud task scheduling based on a two-stage strategy. IEEE Trans. Autom. Sci. Eng. **15**(2), 772–783 (2017)
10. Su, C., Gang, Y., Jin, C.: Genetic algorithm based edge computing scheduling strategy. In: 2021 4th International Conference on Data Science and Information Technology, Shanghai, China (2021)
11. Shen, X.: A hierarchical task scheduling strategy in mobile edge computing. Internet Technol. Lett. **4**(5), e224 (2021)
12. Yang, J., Poellabauer, C.: SATSS: a self-adaptive task scheduling scheme for mobile edge computing. In: 2021 International Conference on Computer Communications and Networks (ICCCN), Athens, Greece, pp. 1–9 (2021)

13. Ruan, X., Chen, H., Tian, Y., et al.: Virtual machine allocation and migration based on performance-to-power ratio in energy-efficient clouds. Future Gener. Comput. Syst. **100**, 380–394 (2019)
14. Wang, H., Tianfield, H.: Energy-aware dynamic virtual machine consolidation for cloud datacenters. IEEE Access **6**, 15259–15273 (2018)
15. Zahedi Fard, S.Y., Ahmadi, M.R., Adabi, S.: A dynamic VM consolidation technique for QoS and energy consumption in cloud environment. J. Supercomput. **73**(10), 4347–4368 (2017)
16. Saadi, Y., El Kafhali, S.: Energy-efficient strategy for virtual machine consolidation in cloud environment. Soft Comput. **24**(19), 14845–14859 (2020)
17. Liang, B., Dong, X., Wang, Y., Zhang, X.: Memory-aware resource management algorithm for low-energy cloud data centers. Future Gener. Comput. Syst. **113**, 329–342 (2020)
18. Zhou, Z., Abawajy, J., Chowdhury, M., et al.: Minimizing SLA violation and power consumption in Cloud data centers using adaptive energy-aware algorithms. Future Gener. Comput. Syst. **86**, 836–850 (2018)
19. Dong, Y., Xu, G., Ding, Y., et al.: A 'joint-me' task deployment strategy for load balancing in edge computing. IEEE Access **7**, 99658–99669 (2019)
20. Li, X., Zeng, F., Fang, G., et al.: Load balancing edge server placement method with QoS requirements in wireless metropolitan area networks. IET Commun. **14**(21), 3907–3916 (2020)
21. Li, G., Yao, Y., Wu, J., et al.: A new load balancing strategy by task allocation in edge computing based on intermediary nodes. EURASIP J. Wirel. Commun. Netw. **2020**(1), 1–10 (2020)
22. Dong, Y., Xu, G., Zhang, M., et al.: A high-efficient joint 'cloud-edge' aware strategy for task deployment and load balancing. IEEE Access **9**, 12791–12802 (2021)
23. Sissodia, R., Rauthan, M.S., Barthwal, V.: A multi-objective adaptive upper threshold approach for overloaded host detection in cloud computing. Int. J. Cloud Appl. Comput. (IJCAC) **12**(1), 1–14 (2022)

# DPIM: Dynamic Pricing Incentive Mechanism for Mobile Crowd Sensing

Weiwei Xing[ID], Xinwei Yao[✉][ID], and Chufeng Qi[ID]

College of Computer Science and Technology, Zhejiang University of Technology, Hangzhou, Zhejiang, China
{xingweiwei,xwyao,qichufeng}@zjut.edu.cn

**Abstract.** As an emerging paradigm for collecting sensory data, Mobile Crowd Sensing (MCS) technology has found widespread application. The successful application of MCS technology relies not only on the active participation of participants but also on the continuous demand for sensing task from data requestors. However, existing researchers predominantly focus on designing participant incentive mechanisms to attract participant to engage in the sensing activities, while the incentive mechanisms for data requestors are rarely addressed. To address the gap, we conceptualize the interactions between data requestors and participants as a queueing process. Building upon utility theory, we propose Dynamic Pricing Incentive Mechanism (DPIM) that dynamically offers optimal incentive guidance to the sensing platform. Moreover, we devise two distinct utility optimization modes for data requestors: one for maximizing their utility and the other for achieving utility equilibrium. These modes are tailored to meet the distinct utility requirement of the sensing platform and data requestors. Through simulations and theoretical analysis, we demonstrate that DPIM effectively provides incentives for the sensing platform across different utility modes.

**Keywords:** Mobile Crowd Sensing (MCS) · Queueing theory · Utility theory · Incentive mechanism · Utility equilibrium mode

## 1 Introduction

With the rapid development of advanced technologies, such as artificial intelligence, humans require a large amount of data to make informed decisions. However, driven by the demand for sensory data, traditional Internet of Things (IoT) technology has exhibited deficiencies in sensing coverage, real-time performance, data types, and so on [1]. Fortunately, diverse intelligent mobile devices embedded with powerful sensors are becoming increasingly popular, such as smartphones, smart bracelets, and drones. Additionally, these devices are equipped with multiple powerful sensors, such as global position system receivers, cameras, and microphones, which can be used as the sensing units [2]. Consequently, Mobile Crowd Sensing (MCS) emerges as an appealing paradigm that empowers human to collaboratively monitor a diverse range of human activities and

H. Gao et al. (Eds.): CollaborateCom 2023, LNICST 561, pp. 149–164, 2024.
https://doi.org/10.1007/978-3-031-54521-4_9

environment [3]. Leveraging the improved context of human awareness, MCS boasts numerous advantages, including flexible and cost-effective deployment, multi-source heterogeneity of sensory data, wide coverage, and high scalability [4]. Presently, MCS technology has found successfully applications in various fields, including smart agriculture [5,6], environmental monitoring [7,8], traffic monitoring [9,10] etc.

The successful application of MCS technology cannot be achieved without incentive mechanisms for both data requestors and participants. To attract data requestors to publish more sensing tasks in MCS system and stimulate participant to engage in the sensing activities, it is crucial to design incentive mechanisms that reduce data requestor payment for releasing the sensing tasks while increasing participant rewards for implementing and uploading sensory data. Nowadays, numerous incentive mechanisms have been studied and can be categorized into entertainment points incentive mechanism, monetary incentive mechanism, and trust and reputation incentive mechanism. Among these, the monetary incentive mechanism is assumed to be the most direct and effective one [11].

One of the most popular monetary incentive mechanisms is based on the auction model. Wang et al. designed the participant incentive mechanism based on reverse auction, in which sensing platform selects participants according to task budget and participant bids [12]. Wang et al. proposed a double auction scheme with personalized privacy incentive, in which participants provide their bids that involves both participant resource consumption and privacy cost [13]. Ng et al. introduced an all-pay auction to attract the edge devices to participate in the coded computation tasks, wherein all edge devices submit their bids, and the cloud server maximize its utility by determining rewards for the winners [14]. It can be observed that the incentive mechanisms [12–14] solely consider the participant incentive within constraints like data requestor budgets, sensory data quality requirements, while the incentives for data requestors are not addressed.

Additionally, some incentive mechanisms are based on the two-sides MCS system, wherein data requestors directly provide rewards to participants. Gao et al. formulated the interactions between data requestors and participants as a two-stage Stackelberg differential game model, considering the average behavior of participants to solve the dynamic sensing task pricing problem [15]. Liu et al. adopted a model-free reinforcement learning based pricing approach to optimize pricing policy to achieve the lower payments and robustness requirement across varying quality levels [16]. Han et al. proposed a novel ex-ante posted pricing mechanism to jointly determine an appropriate posted price and a set of candidate participants, aiming to minimize the total expected cost of paying the participants [17]. It is evident that the incentive mechanisms [15–17] provide participant rewards and are constrained by the sensing tasks budget from data requestors, while not addressing the incentive requirements of data requestors.

Some studies also leverage utility theory to design incentive mechanisms. Ma et al. proposed transforming the dual objectives of minimizing the payment and maximizing the task coverage ratio into a comprehensive utility function for joint optimization [18]. Yucel *et al.* addressed the task assignment problem, aiming to simultaneously maximize the system utility and participants satisfaction [19]. Liu *et al.* introduced the concepts of capital deposit and intertemporal choice from behavioral economics, devising an addiction incentive mechanism that influences the participant utility and demand function [20]. Sarker *et al.* developed a workload allocation policy that strikes a reasonable tradeoff between participant utility and sensing platform profit [21]. Obviously, the incentive mechanisms mentioned above primarily consider sensing platform utility or participant utility, while utility requirements from data requestors have not received sufficient attention in the researches [18–21].

It is undeniable that the successful application of MCS technology is inseparable from the continuous demand for sensory data by data requestors. Without such demands, sensing activities would not have occurred, and the widespread application of MCS technology would not have been possible. Therefore, it is crucial to design a reasonable incentive mechanism to encourage data requestor to publish sensory data demands, referred to as the sensing task in MCS system. To the best of our knowledge, this work represents the first research endeavor that seeks to address the data requestor incentive issue in MCS by leveraging queueing theory and utility theory. The main contributions of the paper can be summarized as follows:

- Abstract MCS system as a queuing system, and model the utilities of data requestors, participants, and the sensing platform based on utility theory.
- Propose the Dynamic Pricing Incentive Mechanism (DPIM) that provides incentive guidance for the sensing platform, with the existence of a feasible optimal incentive solution being proved.
- Introduce the data requestor utility maximization mode and data requestor utility equilibrium mode to cater to the distinct utility requirements of the sensing platform and data requestors.
- Conduct simulations and analysis to demonstrate the effectiveness of the proposed incentive mechanism.

The remainder of this paper is organized as follows. In Sect. 2, we present the system model and problem formulation. Then, in Sect. 3 we introduce the design of proposed incentive mechanism. Section 4 carries on the experimental results and related analysis and the conclusion is given in Sect. 5.

## 2   Preliminary and Problem Formulation

In the MCS system, sensing activities are initiated by data requestors and proceed only when data requestors accept the sensing task pricing offered by the sensing platform. Consequently, if the pricing surpasses the expectations of data requestors, they may decline to publish the sensing tasks, causing an immediate halt in sensing activities. As a result, designing an effective incentive mechanism to encourage data requestors to publish sensing tasks in the MCS system holds immense significance.

## 2.1    Model Introduction

The MCS system under study comprises a sensing platform, data requestors, and participants. The interactions between data requestors and participants can be conceptualized as a continuous-time queueing process with $t \geq 0$. This process monitors the number of data requestors and participants within the system. We assume that the arrival process for data requestors and participants respectively follows Poisson distribution with rates $\lambda$ and $\mu$. New participants join the queue at a rate of $\mu^a$, while participants already in the system exit the MCS system with a probability $q_e \geq 0$. The queueing process for data requestors and participants is depicted in Fig. 1.

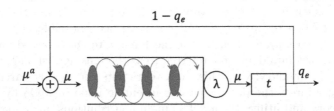

**Fig. 1.** Data requestor and participant queueing process

For data requestor, we assume that their expected pricing for a sensing task is independent of the distribution $F_U$, where $U$ signifies the expected pricing for publishing a sensing task. If the pricing $P > 0$ offered by the sensing platform is lower than the data requestor's expected pricing, that is, $U \geq P$, the sensing task will be published. If not, data requestor will forego publishing the sensing task.

For participant, we assume that the expected reward for a sensing task is independent of the distribution $F_W$, where $W$ represents the participant's expected reward for accepting sensing task. If the reward $p > 0$ provided by sensing platform exceeds the participant expected reward, that is, $p \geq W$, the participant will accept the sensing task. Otherwise, the participant will decline it. Additionally, participants can decide whether to remain in MCS system after completing a sensing task.

For sensing platform, to achieve the optimal incentive, we propose DPIM in which sensing platform dynamically offers reward $p$ to participants and provides pricing $q_c p$ to data requestors, with $q_c$ being the pricing coefficient. Consequently, the revenue of sensing platform becomes $(q_c - 1)p$. Considering that the sensing platform also has profit requirements, therefore, $q_c - 1 \geq 0$.

For ease of reference, Table 1 presents a compilation of the major variables utilized in the paper.

**Table 1.** Parameter setting for simulation.

| Variables | Descriptions |
|---|---|
| $p$ | Participant reward |
| $P$ | Data requestor pricing |
| $q_c$ | Data requestor pricing coefficient |
| $\lambda_0$ | Data requestor initial arrival rate |
| $\lambda_r$ | Data requestor real arrival rate |
| $\hat{\lambda}$ | Data requestor effective arrival rate |
| $\mu^a$ | New participant arrival rate |
| $\mu_0$ | Participant initial arrival rate |
| $\mu_r$ | Participant real arrival rate |
| $q_e$ | Participant departure rate |
| $F_U$ | Data requestor expected pricing distribution |
| $F_W$ | Participant expected reward distribution |
| $U$ | Data requestor expected pricing |
| $W$ | Participant expected reward |
| $u_r$ | Data requestor utility |
| $u_p$ | Sensing platform utility |
| $u_w$ | Participant utility |
| $T_c$ | Sensing platform cost for sensing activity |
| $P_W$ | Participant cost for executing sensing tasks |

## 2.2 Utility Model Definition

Since the number of completed sensing tasks in a steady-state condition is determined by the successful matching rate between data requestors and participants, the effective data requestor arrival rate can be denoted as $\hat{\lambda}$, Therefore, the utilities of the data requestor, participant, and sensing platform can be formulated as follows.

The data requestor's utility is the difference between the value of sensory data and the payment made to the sensing platform. Thus, the data requestor utility model $u_r$ can be formulated as follows:

$$u_r = \hat{\lambda}\frac{1}{\bar{F}_U(q_c p)} \int_{q_c p}^{\infty} (U - q_c p) f_U(U) dU \tag{1}$$

The participant's utility is the difference between the reward provided by sensing platform and the actual cost incurred by the participant while performing the sensing tasks. Hence, the participant utility model $u_w$ can be represented as follows:

$$u_w = \hat{\lambda}\left[\frac{1}{F_W(p)} \int_0^p (p - W) f_W(W) dW - P_W\right] \tag{2}$$

Among it, $P_W$ represents the actual cost paid by participant for collecting the sensory data.

The sensing platform's utility is the difference between the expense paid by data requestor, the operation loss of the sensing platform, and the participant reward. Thus, the sensing platform utility model $u_p$ can be represented as follows:

$$u_p = \hat{\lambda}\big[(q_c - 1)p - T_c\big] \tag{3}$$

Among it, $T_c$ signifies the operational loss incurred by the sensing platform in managing the sensing activities.

Based on the utility models described above, we propose DPIM which provides the optimal data requestor pricing $q_c p$ and participant reward $p$ to achieve different utility requirements under various utility modes.

## 3    Design of DPIM

The data requestor initial arrival process signifies the potential sensing task requests within the MCS system, and we assume it follows Poisson distribution with rate $\lambda_0$. Consequently, the data requestor real arrival rate $\lambda_r$, which reflects the effective rate of released sensing tasks, can be expressed as follows [22]:

$$\lambda_r = \lambda_0 \bar{F}_U(q_c p) = \lambda_0 \big[1 - F_U(q_c p)\big] \tag{4}$$

Assuming the participant initial arrival process to the available-participants queue follows a Poisson distribution with rate $\mu_0$, and when the queueing process is in a steady-state, we obtain,

$$\mu^a = \mu_r q_e = \mu_0 F_W(p) \tag{5}$$

Among it, $\mu_r$ indicates the rate of participants who accept the sensing tasks.

With the MCS system parameters remaining constant, it is evident that $p$ and $q_c$ are the only two variables in the equations. In the MCS system, since the successful matching amount between data requestors and participants in steady-state is determined by the real arrival rate of data requestors or participants, the real and effective data requestor arrival rate $\hat{\lambda}(q_c, q)$ can be redefined as follows:

$$\hat{\lambda}(q_c, q) = \min\left\{\lambda_0 \bar{F}_U(q_c p), \frac{\mu_0}{q_e} F_W(p)\right\} \tag{6}$$

The existing incentive mechanisms typically aim to maximize sensing platform utility. However, the sensing platform utility maximization mode solely considers the utility requirement of the sensing platform, disregarding the utility requirement of the data requestor. Thus, we introduce the data requestor maximization mode and data requestor utility equilibrium mode.

## 3.1   Data Requestor Utility Maximization Mode

Based on the definition of data requestor utility model, data requestor utility maximization mode under DPIM can be formulated as follows:

$$\max \ u_r = \hat{\lambda}(q_c, p) \left[ \frac{1}{\bar{F}_U(q_c p)} \int_{q_c p}^{\infty} (U - q_c p) f_U(U) dU \right]$$

$$s.t. \ (q_c - 1)p - T_c \geq 0$$

$$\frac{1}{F_W(p)} \int_0^p (p - W) f_W(W) dW - P_W \geq 0 \qquad (7)$$

$$\hat{\lambda}(q_c, p) = \min \left\{ \lambda_0 \bar{F}_U(q_c p), \frac{\mu_0}{q_e} F_W(p) \right\}$$

Model (7) is employed to determine the optimal incentive for data requestors and participants under DPIM. If a solution for the model does not exist, it loses its role in providing incentive guidance. Therefore, proving the existence of an optimal incentive is necessary.

**Theorem 1.** *Given* $(\lambda_0, \mu_0) \in R_+^2$, $q_c \in [1, M_1]$, $p \in [M_2, M_3]$, *and continuous distribution* $F_U, F_W$, *where* $M_1$, $M_2$ *and* $M_3$ *are all finite real value, the optimal participant reward* $p$ *and pricing coefficient* $q_c$ *that maximize data requestor utility must exist.*

*Proof.* The proof process can be divided into two steps. First, define a closed interval, and then prove that the model is continuous on the closed interval, thereby demonstrating the existence of a feasible solution for the model within the closed interval.

**Step 1:** Since the participant reward $p$ and pricing coefficient $q_c$ are the only two variables in the model, and considering $q_c \in [1, M_1]$ and $p \in [M_2, M_3]$, it is evident that the model exists within the closed interval.

**Step 2:** Prove the continuity of model (7). By the definition of continuity, let the function $y = f(x)$ be defined in the neighborhood of any point $x_0$ in the model interval. If $\lim_{\Delta x \to 0} \Delta y = \lim_{\Delta x \to 0} [f(x_0 + \Delta x) - f(x_0)] = 0$, then $y = f(x)$ is continuous at point $x_0$, indicating the model's continuity within the interval. Let $q_{c1}$ and $p_1$ be any points in the domain, and assume their increment are respectively $\Delta q_{c1}$ and $\Delta p_1$. Therefore,

$$\lim_{\substack{\Delta q_{c1}\to 0 \\ \Delta p_1 \to 0}} \Delta y = \lim_{\substack{\Delta q_{c1}\to 0 \\ \Delta p_1 \to 0}} \left[ f(q_{c1}+\Delta q_{c1}, p_1+\Delta p_1) - f(q_{c1}, p_1) \right]$$

$$= \lim_{\substack{\Delta q_{c1}\to 0 \\ \Delta p_1 \to 0}} \left( min\left\{ \lambda_0 \bar{F}_U(q_{c1}+\Delta q_{c1})(p_1+\Delta p_1), \frac{\mu_0}{q_e} F_W(p_1+\Delta p_1) \right\} \right.$$

$$\left\{ \frac{1}{\bar{F}_U\left((q_{c1}+\Delta q_{c1})(p_1+\Delta p_1)\right)} \int_{(q_{c1}+\Delta q_{c1})(p_1+\Delta p_1)}^{\infty} (U-(q_{c1}+\Delta q_{c1}) \right.$$

$$(p_1+\Delta p_1)) f_U(U)dU + \frac{1}{F_W(p_1+\Delta p_1)} \int_0^{p_1+\Delta p_1} (p_1+\Delta p_1-W)f_W(W)dW$$

$$\left. -P_W + [(q_{c1}+\Delta q_{c1}-1)(p_1+\Delta p_1)-T_c] \right\} - min\left\{ \lambda_0 \bar{F}_U(q_{c1}p_1), \frac{\mu_0}{q_e}F_W(p_1) \right\}$$

$$\left\{ \frac{1}{\bar{F}_U(q_{c1}p_1)} \int_{q_{c1}p_1}^{\infty} (U-q_{c1}p_1)f_U(U)dU + \frac{1}{F_W(p_1)} \int_0^{p_1} (p_1-W)f_W(W)dW \right.$$

$$\left. \left. -P_W + [(q_{c1}-1)p_1 - T_c] \right\} \right)$$

Since $1 \le q_c \le M_1$, $M_2 \le p \le M_3$, and both $F_U$ and $F_W$ are continuous distributions, we have $\bar{F}_U(q_c p) \ge 0$ and $F_W(p) \ge 0$. Therefore, $\lim_{\substack{\Delta q_{c1}\to 0 \\ \Delta p_1 \to 0}} \Delta y = 0$.

It can be concluded that model (7) is continuous within the closed interval, confirming the existence of a feasible solution. In other words, the model must have a solution within the defined domain to maximize data requestor utility.

## 3.2   Sensing Platform Utility Maximization Mode

As per the definition of the sensing platform utility model, the sensing platform utility maximization mode under DPIM can be expressed as follows:

$$\max \ u_p = \hat{\lambda}(q_c, p) \left[ (q_c - 1)p - T_c \right]$$
$$s.t. (q_c - 1)p - T_c \ge 0$$
$$\frac{1}{F_W(p)} \int_0^p (p-W)f_W(W)dW - P_W \ge 0 \qquad (8)$$
$$\hat{\lambda}(q_c, p) = \min \left\{ \lambda_0 \bar{F}_U(q_c p), \frac{\mu_0}{q_e} F_W(p) \right\}$$

Model (8) is utilized to determine the optimal incentive under DPIM. If a solution of the model does not exist, then it loses its function of providing incentive guidance for the sensing platform. Therefore, it is imperative to prove the existence of the optimal incentive under sensing platform utility maximization mode. Since the proof process is akin to Theorem 1, we will not reiterate it here.

## 3.3   Data Requestor Utility Equilibrium Mode

The data requestor utility equilibrium mode pertains to the utility equilibrium between the sensing platform and data requestors. This equilibrium can be expressed as follows:

$$u_p - u_r = 0 \qquad (9)$$

Substituting equations (1) and (3) into equation (9), we obtain,

$$\frac{1}{\bar{F}_U(q_c p)} \int_{q_c p}^{\infty} (U - q_c p) f_U(U) dU - \left[ (q_c - 1)p - T_c \right] = 0 \tag{10}$$

Taking Eq. (10) as the additional nonlinear equality constraint for model (8), the data requestor utility equilibrium model can be formulated as follows:

$$\begin{aligned}
\max\ u_p &= \hat{\lambda}(q_c, p)[(q_c - 1)p - T_c] \\
s.t.(q_c - 1)&p - T_c \geq 0 \\
\frac{1}{F_W(p)} &\int_0^p (p - W) f_W(W) dW - P_W \geq 0 \\
\hat{\lambda}(q_c, p) &= \min \left\{ \lambda_0 \bar{F}_U(q_c p), \frac{\mu_0}{q_e} F_W(p) \right\} \\
\frac{1}{\bar{F}_U(q_c p)} &\int_{q_c p}^{\infty} (U - q_c p) f_U(U) dU - \left[ (q_c - 1)p - T_c \right] = 0
\end{aligned} \tag{11}$$

Model (11) is employed to determine the optimal incentives for data requestors and participants under DPIM. It is imperative to prove the existence of the optimal incentive solution. Based on the proof of the existence of feasible solutions for the sensing platform utility maximization mode, it can be deduced that a feasible solution must exist for the data requestor utility equilibrium mode as well. Thus, we will not repeat the proof process.

## 4   Experiments

To demonstrate the effectiveness and performance of DPIM, simulations and analysis are carried out under various utility modes.

### 4.1   Parameter Setting

Simulations involve altering fundamental parameters of the MCS system, such as the data requestor and participant initial arrival rates, data requestor expected

**Table 2.** Parameter setting for simulation.

| Simulation parameters | Value | Unit |
|---|---|---|
| Data requestor initial arrival rate | 5000 | |
| Participant initial arrival rate | 1000 | |
| Participant leave rate | 0.8 | |
| Data requestor expected pricing | $N(50, 10)$ | RMB |
| Participant expected reward | $N(35, 5)$ | RMB |
| Participant cost | 5 | RMB |
| Sensing platform cost | 0.15 | |

pricing, and participant expected reward, while keeping other parameters constant. The performance of the proposed incentive mechanism, data requestor utility, and sensing platform utility are thoroughly analyzed. The initial parameter setting for the simulations are presented in Table 2. For clarity, we abbreviate the term 'sensing platform utility maximum mode' as 'PUM', 'data requestor utility equilibrium mode' as 'DRUE', and 'data requestor utility maximum mode' as 'DRUM'.

## 4.2   Simulation and Analysis

**Impact of Data Requestor Initial Arrival Rate.** The participation of data requestor in sensing activities directly influences the sensing task demand within MCS system, thereby significantly impacting the incentive mechanism. In the simulation, the data requestor initial arrival rate is varied between 1000 and 6000. The simulation results are depicted in Figs. 2 and 3.

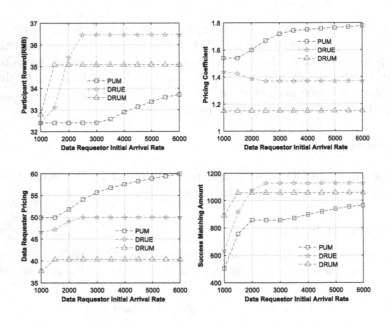

**Fig. 2.** Data requestor initial arrival rate impacts on incentives

In Fig. 2, the increase of data requestor initial arrival rate corresponds to an upward trend in participant reward, data requestor pricing and successful matching amount under each utility mode. Given the constant participant initial arrival rate, once the number of sensing tasks surpasses the maximum participant supply, the augmentation of participant reward no longer bring more participants, leading to a stabilization of the incentive. In practice, as participant

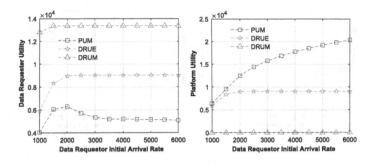

**Fig. 3.** Data requestor initial arrival rate impacts on utilities

reward increases, it is highly likely that more participants will engage in sensing activities, causing participant supply to expand and the successful matching count to increase.

Figure 3 illustrates the influence of the data requestor initial arrival rate on the utilities of both the sensing platform and data requestors. Evidently, as the data requestor initial rate remains low, both data requestor and sensing platform utilities rise. It can be deduced from the incentive analysis that with a substantial increase in the data requestor initial rate, both the incentive and successful matching count stabilize. Consequently, the utilities of the sensing platform and data requestor also stabilize.

**Impact of Participant Initial Arrival Rate.** The participation of participants in sensing activities directly affects the participant supply within the MCS system, which also exerts a significant influence on the incentive mechanism. In the simulation, the participant initial arrival rate is varied between 200 and 6200. The simulation results are shown as Figs. 4 and 5.

In Fig. 4, it can be observed that with an increase in the participant initial arrival rate, the participant reward, pricing coefficient, and data requestor pricing display a downward trend, while the count of successfully matched sensing tasks exhibits an upward trend. Given the fixed data requestor initial arrival rate, when the number of participants exceeds the maximum sensing task demand, the reduction in data requestor pricing does not result in more sensing tasks being performed. Consequently, the incentive eventually stabilizes. In practice, as data requestor pricing decreases, it is certain that more sensing tasks will be released, leading to an increase in the successful matching count of sensing tasks.

Figure 5 illustrates the impact of the participant initial arrival rate on the utilities of both the sensing platform and data requestors. Clearly, when the data requestor initial rate is low, both data requestor and sensing platform utilities increase. As revealed by the incentive mechanism analysis, when the data requestor initial rate becomes sufficiently high, the utilities of both data requestors and the sensing platform stabilize.

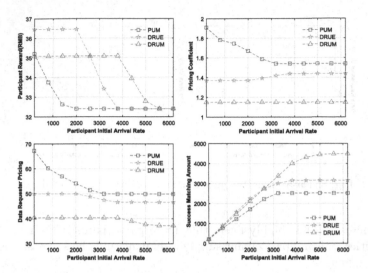

**Fig. 4.** Participant initial arrival rate impacts on incentives

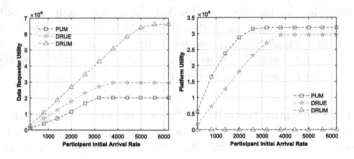

**Fig. 5.** Participant initial arrival rate impacts on utilities

**Impact of Data Requestor Expected Pricing.** The data requestor expected pricing is a significant factor influencing the incentive mechanism. In the simulation, the data requestor expected pricing is adjusted between 50 and 100. The simulation results are presented in Figs. 6 and 7.

In Fig. 6, it can be observed that an increase in the data requestor expected pricing leads to an upward trend in both participant reward and the pricing coefficient. This trend arises from the fact that higher data requestor expected pricing stimulates more sensing task demands within the MCS system. Consequently, the sensing platform enhances the participant reward to attract more participants to meet the heightened sensing task demands. Simultaneously, the platform mitigates the increased sensing task demand by elevating data requestor pricing.

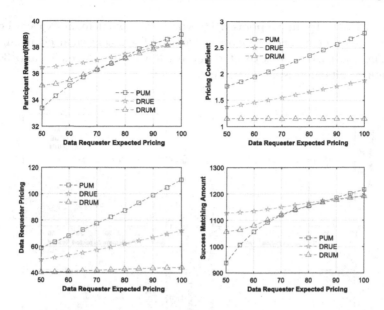

**Fig. 6.** Data requestor expected pricing impacts on incentives

Figure 7 reveals that an increase in data requestor expected pricing results in an upward trend for both the sensing platform and data requestor utilities. In the context of the sensing platform utility maximization mode, an increase in data requestor expected pricing has limited impact on data requestor utility. Conversely, within the data requestor utility equilibrium mode, the rise in data requestor expected pricing minimally affects sensing platform utility.

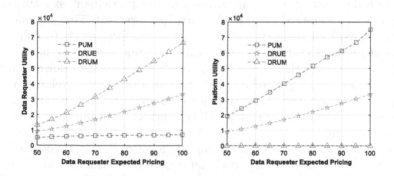

**Fig. 7.** Data requestor expected pricing impacts on utilities

**Impact of Participant Expected Reward.** The participant expected reward constitutes another significant factor influencing the incentive mechanism. In the simulation, the participant expected reward is varied between 10 and 30. The simulation results are displayed in Figs. 8 and 9.

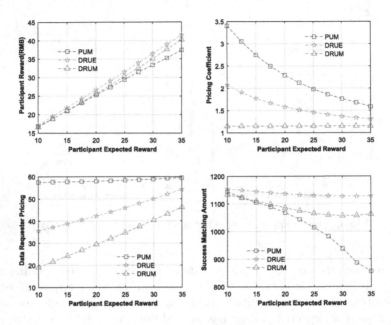

**Fig. 8.** Participant expected reward impacts on incentive mechanism

Figure 8 demonstrates that an increase in the participant expected reward corresponds to an upward trend in the participant reward. This alignment with intuition stems from the fact that the sensing platform needs to enhance the participant reward to attract more participants. Simultaneously, data requestor pricing increases, even though the pricing coefficient exhibits a downward trend. The count of successfully matched tasks exhibits a negative correlation with the participant expected reward. According to economic theory, the rise in participant expected reward unavoidably reduces both the sensing task demand and the participant supply.

Figure 9 illustrates that both sensing platform and data requestor utilities decline with an increase in the participant expected reward. This result is anticipated from the analysis of the incentive mechanism. Furthermore, within the sensing platform utility maximization mode, the increase in participant expected reward has a minimal impact on data requestor utility. In contrast, under the data requestor utility equilibrium mode, the increase in participant expected reward has a slight impact on sensing platform utility.

Furthermore, it is evident that both the pricing coefficient and data requestor pricing are consistently the lowest under the data requestor utility equilibrium

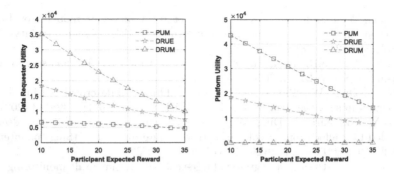

**Fig. 9.** Participant expected reward impacts on utilities

mode, and the highest under the sensing platform utility maximization mode. Moreover, the data requestor utility mode consistently maximizes data requestor utility, while the sensing platform utility mode maximizes the sensing platform. To achieve a balance between data requestor and sensing platform utilities, the sensing platform can dynamically adjust the incentive based on different utility modes and real-time parameters of the MCS system, such as data requestor expected pricing, and the participant and data requestor arrival rates.

## 5   Conclusion

In this paper, to design the incentive mechanism for data requestors, we first abstract the interaction between data requestors and participants in sensing activities as a queueing process and introduce DPIM based on utility theory. Then, to satisfy the data requestor's utility requirements, we have designed both the data requestor utility maximization mode and the data requestor utility equilibrium mode, each accompanied by a proof of the existence of a feasible solution. Finally, simulation results demonstrate that the sensing platform can effectively manage the demand for sensing tasks and the supply of participants through the incentive mechanism. Moreover, the utility of both data requestors and the sensing platform can be satisfied in their respective utility modes.

**Acknowledgments.** This research was supported by "Leading Goose" R&D Program of Zhejiang under Grant No. 2023C03154, and "Pioneer" R&D Program of Zhejiang under Grant No. 2023C01029.

## References

1. Perez, A.J., Zeadally, S.: Secure and privacy-preserving crowdsensing using smart contracts: issues and solutions. Comput. Sci. Rev. **43**, 100450 (2022)
2. Middya, A.I., Dey, P., Roy, S.: IoT-based crowdsensing for smart environments. In: Internet of Things for Smart Environments, pp. 33–58 (2022)

3. Capponi, A., Fiandrino, C., Kantarci, B., et al.: A survey on mobile crowdsensing systems: challenges, solutions, and opportunities. IEEE Commun. Surv. Tutor. **21**(3), 2419–2465 (2019)
4. Wu, Y., Zeng, J.R., Peng, H., et al.: Survey on incentive mechanisms for crowd sensing. J. Softw. **27**(8), 2025–2047 (2016)
5. Sun, Y., Ding, W., Shu, L., et al.: On enabling mobile crowd sensing for data collection in smart agriculture: a vision. IEEE Syst. J. **16**(1), 132–143 (2021)
6. Sun, Y., Nurellari, E., Ding, W., et al.: A partition-based mobile-crowdsensing-enabled task allocation for solar insecticidal lamp internet of things maintenance. IEEE Internet Things J. **9**(20), 20547–20560 (2022)
7. Fascista, A.: Toward integrated large-scale environmental monitoring using WSN/UAV/crowdsensing: a review of applications, signal processing, and future perspectives. Sensors **22**(5), 1824 (2022)
8. Shang, L., Zhang, Y., Ye, Q., et al.: Smartwatersens: a crowdsensing-based approach to groundwater contamination estimation. In: IEEE International Conference on Smart Computing (SMARTCOMP), pp. 48–55 (2022)
9. Jiang, Z., Zhu, H., Zhou, B., et al.: CrowdPatrol: a mobile crowdsensing framework for traffic violation hotspot patrolling. IEEE Trans. Mob. Comput. (2021)
10. Plašilová, A., Procházka, J.: Crowdsensing technologies for optimizing passenger flows in public transport. In: 1st International Conference on Advanced Innovations in Smart Cities (ICAISC), pp. 1–6 (2023)
11. She, R.: Survey on incentive strategies for mobile crowdsensing system. In: IEEE 11th International Conference on Software Engineering and Service Science (ICSESS), pp. 511–514. IEEE (2020)
12. Wang, K., Chen, Z., Zhang, L., Liu, J., Li, B.: Incentive mechanism for improving task completion quality in mobile crowdsensing. Electronics **12**(4), 1037 (2023)
13. Wang, J., Liu, H., Dong, X., et al.: Personalized location privacy trading in double auction for mobile crowdsensing. IEEE Internet Things J. **10**(10), 8971–8983 (2022)
14. Ng, J.S., Lim, W.Y.B., Garg, S., et al.: Collaborative coded computation offloading: an all-pay auction approach. In: ICC 2021-IEEE International Conference on Communications, pp. 1–6 (2021)
15. Gao, H.: Mean-field-game-based dynamic task pricing in mobile crowdsensing. IEEE Internet Things J. **9**(18), 18098–18112 (2022)
16. Liu, Y., Liu, F., Wu, H.T., et al.: PriDPM: privacy-preserving dynamic pricing mechanism for robust crowdsensing. Comput. Netw. **183**, 107582 (2020)
17. Han, K., Huang, H., Luo, J.: Quality-aware pricing for mobile crowdsensing. IEEE/ACM Trans. Networking **26**(4), 1728–1741 (2018)
18. Ma, G., Chen, H., Huang, Y., et al.: Utility-based heterogeneous user recruitment of multi-task in mobile crowdsensing. IEEE Internet Things J. (2023)
19. Yucel, F., Bulut, E.: User satisfaction aware maximum utility task assignment in mobile crowdsensing. Comput. Netw. **172**, 107156 (2020)
20. Liu, J., Huang, S., Li, D., Wen, S., Liu, H.: Addictive incentive mechanism in crowdsensing from the perspective of behavioral economics. IEEE Trans. Parallel Distrib. Syst. **33**(5), 1109–1127 (2021)
21. Sarker, S., Razzaque, M.A., Hassan, M.M., et al.: Optimal selection of crowdsourcing workers balancing their utilities and platform profit. IEEE Internet Things J. **6**(5), 8602–8614 (2019)
22. Banerjee, S., Riquelme, C., Johari, R.: Pricing in ride-share platforms: a queueing-theoretic approach. Available at SSRN 2568258 (2015)

# Blockchain Applications

# Efficient and Revocable Anonymous Account Guarantee System Based on Blockchain

Weiyou Liang[1], Yujue Wang[2], Yong Ding[1,4], Hai Liang[1(✉)], Changsong Yang[1], and Huiyong Wang[3]

[1] Guangxi Key Laboratory of Cryptography and Information Security, School of Computer Science and Information Security, Guilin University of Electronic Technology, Guilin, China
lianghai@guet.edu.cn
[2] Hangzhou Innovation Institute of Beihang University, Hangzhou, China
[3] School of Mathematics and Computing Science, GuilinUniversity of Electronic Technology, Guilin, China
[4] Institute of Cyberspace Technology, HKCT Institute for Higher Education, Hong Kong SAR, China

**Abstract.** The fast expansion of information technology and public concern for personal privacy and security have raised expectations for the authentication process. Although existing anonymous authentication schemes can achieve anonymous authentication and accountability, they all require users to apply for certificates from the authorization authority, resulting in a significant certificate storage overhead for the authority. Additionally, they have not implemented certificate revocation for anonymous users, which allows malicious users to potentially engage in malicious behavior. Therefore, this paper proposes an efficient and revocable anonymous account guarantee system based on blockchain (ERAAS). The system implements a guarantor mechanism where anonymous users can authenticate their identities through the guarantees provided by guarantors without the need to apply for certificates, reducing the storage overhead of certificates. Furthermore, the system utilizes cryptographic accumulators to enable fast revocation of accounts, preventing malicious users from engaging in further malicious behavior. Moreover, in this system, the certificate authority (CA) can enhance the system's ability to handle concurrent requests by allocating group keys to the registration authority (RA), authorizing them to register guarantors and sign guarantees. Security analysis indicates that the proposed scheme enjoys anonymity, traceability, and revocability and can resist forgery attacks. The experimental comparison demonstrates its practicality.

**Keywords:** Authentication · Anonymity · Revocable · Supervision · Blockchain

H. Gao et al. (Eds.): CollaborateCom 2023, LNICST 561, pp. 167–186, 2024.
https://doi.org/10.1007/978-3-031-54521-4_10

# 1    Introduction

With the fast growth of information technology, more and more individuals are used to working, buying, and socializing online. The Internet, like anything else, has both advantages and disadvantages. On one hand, its emergence has brought convenience to people's lives, such as online signing of multi-party electronic contracts [27], online chatting, and more, effectively removing geographical limitations for humanity. However, its popularity is accompanied by security worries [12]. One of them is the illegal access of malevolent users to valuable data or services. In applications like smart grids, if data becomes accessible to malicious actors, it can lead to issues such as user privacy breaches [4]. In order to lessen the likelihood of these security events, researchers have performed a significant amount of work on identity authentication systems. Identity identification technology research is still a prominent topic today.

In the online world, authentication is essential for safeguarding personal and other sensitive data from unauthorized access by third parties, preventing users from participating in improper online behavior, and ensuring that a computer is not hacked or infected with a harmful virus [28]. The most prevalent identity authentication tool in the realm of identity authentication technology is the digital certificate. It is a cryptographic system that functions as the Internet's passport. After the verifier has the digital certificate offered by the presenter, using the public key and private key information it possesses, it may then determine whether the communication originated from a particular individual [13]. Of course, digital certificates have a relatively large privacy leakage problem because the presenter needs to expose all her attributes when presenting the certificate. This may not seem important, but it is. Wherever you least expect it, a breach of your personal information might occur. According to the Identity Theft Resource Center, the number of hacked records holding sensitive personally identifiable information (PII) is growing. PII is any information that may be used to identify or track a person [19]. Hence, we require a novel authentication mechanism capable of both confirming identity like digital certificates and concealing individual identities.

Consequently, the researchers came up with the concept of anonymous authentication. It is possible for a user who is required to verify herself to do so without disclosing her identity. This makes it possible to limit access while still protecting the privacy of the user. For applications like blockchain, which prioritize privacy protection, anonymous authentication plays a significant role in ensuring security [24]. Currently, anonymous authentication techniques may be loosely categorized as schemes based on public key cryptosystems, schemes of cryptosystems based on identity, schemes based on pseudonyms, and mixed schemes [17]. IBM's identity mixer scheme, which allows users to selectively present their own identity attributes, is one of the most prominent anonymous authentication schemes. Other people cannot determine her specific identity even if they see the certificate she presents, and they cannot link the anonymous certificates she presented multiple times [3].

Even though an anonymous authentication method, such as the identity mixer technique, may accomplish identity authentication and safeguard user identity privacy, it will be susceptible to anonymity abuse owing to the absence of a supervisor. Therefore, we must employ regulators to uncover and penalize bad behavior by anonymous users [25]. Liang et al. [14,15] suggested a double-layer structure for CA supervision that assures the efficiency of supervision and certificate issuing. During the authentication process, users can undergo anonymous authentication without disclosing their full identity attributes. When a user behaves maliciously, the CA may identify an anonymous user by utilizing the supervisory private key. However, like this kind of scheme, the user must register with the CA and apply for a certificate to accomplish anonymous authentication. In this situation, CA's storage overhead is high. Cheng et al. [5] presented a technique that may conduct anonymous authentication, monitor, and decrease certificate storage. There may be two main issues with this scheme in real-world applications. In the original method, there is just one CA. Thus, when a significant number of guarantee requests are sent in a short period of time, the CA's processing efficiency becomes problematic. Also, the previous strategy merely oversaw the guarantor but did not account for the deactivation of the harmful anonymous account, so it may request services again.

## 1.1  Our Contributions

This paper proposes an ERAAS system based on blockchain that not only achieves anonymous authentication but also incorporates accountability and revocation mechanisms. The system aims to prevent the misuse of anonymity and the possibility of malicious users engaging in subsequent illegal activities. The specific contributions of this system are outlined below.

1. The ERAAS system implements anonymous and controllable authentication, allowing legitimate users to authenticate without revealing personal information. For malicious behavior by anonymous users, trusted authorities can trace the guarantor's real identity through evidence chains, preventing abuse. Security and usability are confirmed through analysis and experiments.
2. In ERAAS, guarantors can use their polynomial to generate account guarantees, allowing users to authenticate without authority-issued certificates, reducing storage overhead for the authority.
3. The ERAAS system implements a revocation mechanism to prevent malicious users from reusing their accounts for authentication after removal from the accumulator, effectively deterring future malicious activities. This mechanism offers fast revocation and consistent additional authentication time, independent of the number of revocations, making it a fixed overhead cost.
4. The ERAAS system also proposes to authorize RAs using group signature technology so that RAs can issue guarantee certificates for guarantors and sign for anonymous account guarantees, thus improving the system's ability to handle concurrent requests.

## 1.2   Related Works

Over the course of the last several decades, user authentication systems have grown more widespread in the activities that we participate in a daily basis. Their major objective is to effectively stop unauthorized users from accessing sensitive data and services [22]. The digital certificate, which associates a user's identifying information with a specific collection of data, is the identity authentication technique that is used the most often nowadays. In 1988, ITU-T established the standard for digital certificates and released the first version of X.509 [9]. After that, digital certificates became a key method of identity identification, and the standard for them was established by ITU-T. Even up to the present day, there are still a significant number of researchers working at X.509. Zulfiqar et al. [29] evaluated the revocation processes used by the highest-ranking websites. Their data indicates that the adoption of the online certificate status protocol (OCSP) has been much slower than increases in public key strength and sequence number randomization. However, the use of OCSP facilitates the rapid validation of X.509 certificates and the rejection of expired certificates. Saleem et al. [20] proposed a framework named ProofChain. It is a decentralized public key infrastructure (PKI) solution that was introduced by Saleem et al. and is built on the blockchain. It facilitates complete trust across decentralized CA groups. Although a digital certificate such as X.509 may accomplish identity verification, because it requires the presenter to demonstrate her identity attributes, the identity privacy of the user is compromised in this instance. Therefore, individuals need a new authentication technique that can both authenticate their identities and secure their privacy.

In order to protect user privacy and complete identity authentication at the same time, researchers have conducted a lot of research. Gao et al. [6] proposed a proxy mobile IPv6-based anonymous authentication mechanism for vehicular ad hoc networks (VANETs). The method is equipped with pseudonyms, identity-based password procedures, and a number of crucial authentication protocols that protect the anonymity of users. Liu et al. [16] designed an anonymous authentication technique that does not need tamper-resistant devices using lattice-based encryption. For anonymous vehicle authentication, this technique may produce a fictitious identifier for each vehicle. In addition, the technique is capable of preventing channel-testing assaults. Wang, Xu and Gu [21] suggested an enhanced authentication technique based on the cryptography of elliptic curves. Their approach can withstand offline password guessing attacks, desynchronization assaults, and session key disclosure attacks, while also achieving anonymous user authentication to safeguard user privacy.

Banerjee et al. [2] introduced an anonymous authentication technique that enables users to connect across insecure communication channels while protecting critical information. This strategy provides demonstrable security. It is more secure and resilient compared to prior methods. Han et al. [7] proposed an anonymous authentication scheme for VANETs based on fog computing, which can protect the privacy of vehicles. This scheme designs a pseudonym update and tracking approach that is based on fog computing. This strategy has the potential to minimize the amount of time it takes to authenticate valid cars, which in turn will increase overall efficiency. At the same time, the system makes use of self-authentication, which lessens the burden of communication placed on the center and enhances the efficiency of the authentication process.

Although anonymous authentication can protect the privacy of users, complete anonymous authentication will lead to the abuse of anonymity, so regulators need to carry out supervision. Based on the rotating group signature scheme of elliptic curve cryptography, Mehmood et al. [17] proposed an anonymous authentication scheme for healthcare applications based on intelligent clouds. When using an untrusted authentication server, this approach may ensure the user's anonymity and avoid eavesdropping. In addition, it offers a tool for tracking to prevent anonymous misuse. Jegadeesan et al. [10] proposed a safe and efficient privacy-preserving anonymous authentication scheme, which anonymously verifies users with less computational cost. At the same time, it can also disclose the actual identity of the misbehaving doctor at a very low computational cost, avoiding the situation where the doctor's anonymity is abused. Jiang, Ge and Shen [11] proposed a method for anonymous authentication based on the group signature scheme, which enables anonymous authentication of automobiles with adjacent vehicles or roadside infrastructures. With the private key, the authority can trace an anonymous user's real identity during harmful incidents.

Arasan et al. [1] developed a computationally efficient and more secure anonymous authentication technique for cloud users, which may enable anonymous mutual authentication between cloud users and cloud servers, safeguarding the privacy of users and servers. The scheme's suggested condition-tracking method may guarantee that a trustworthy third party can remove the cloud user's or service provider's access to the cloud environment in the event of harmful activity. Zhang et al. [26] suggested an anonymous authentication scheme for batch verification based on elliptic curves, which may significantly increase the authentication efficiency of the system since it enables batch verification. At the same time, the implementation of anonymous authentication that it provided may help secure users' personal information. Naturally, in the event that anonymous users engage in malevolent behavior, illegal cars may also be traced in order to provide conditional privacy protection. Cheng et al. [5] proposed an anonymous account guarantee scheme based on polynomials. This method guarantees the legitimacy of anonymous accounts. A legitimate user can guarantee multiple anonymous accounts, which can reduce the storage overhead of trusted centers to store certificates.

## 2   System Model and Security Requirements

### 2.1   System Model

As shown in Fig. 1, an ERAAS system consists of six types of entities.

- CA: It is a trusted participant in the entire system, responsible for issuing certificates to RA, enabling RA to have the authority to issue certificates to

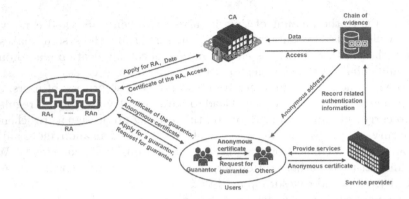

**Fig. 1.** The ERAAS system model.

guarantors and sign guarantees for ordinary users. At the same time, when there is a dispute between a service provider and a malicious user, CA can trace the real identity of the guarantor and revoke the malicious account.

- RA: It is an organization recognized by CA that can issue certificates to guarantors and sign guarantees for users. Its main responsibility is to issue certificates to guarantors and sign guarantees for ordinary users, and it can also trace the real identity of the guarantor.
- Guarantor: A user who has qualified guarantee status and possesses a certificate issued by the RA. The guarantor can use their credentials to guarantee the anonymous accounts of both themselves and other ordinary users.
- Others: They are ordinary users without guaranteed capability. Before undergoing anonymous identity authentication, they need to find a guarantor to guarantee their own anonymous account.
- Service provider: A trusted service provider who has access to the system. After successfully verifying the anonymous identity presented by the user, the service provider provides services to the user and broadcasts the corresponding record to the entire network, generating a corresponding block to record relevant information. Otherwise, the service provider will refuse to provide services to the user.
- Chain of evidence: The evidence chain leverages blockchain's tamper-evident properties for evidence preservation. Service providers broadcast user-specific service details, anonymous certificates, and related information to the network, storing them on the blockchain. In case of disputes needing arbitration, the CA traces the guarantor's true identity via certificates on the chain.

After the establishment of the ERAAS system, the CA confirms the highest degree of the polynomial and the maximum value of the coefficient, generates a tracking key and a group public key, and initializes the value of the accumulator. Then, during the authorization stage, RA applies for registration with CA, and CA assigns group member private keys to RA. CA sends the private keys of the group members and the accumulator through a secure channel to RA.

Following verification of RA's identity during the guarantor registration stage, the guarantor applies for registration with RA using the real identity and an identity tag *pse*. The RA receives the registration request from the guarantor and verifies their real identity. If passed, RA assigns the guarantor a unique polynomial and stores the actual identity information along with the polynomial.

A user who requires an anonymous account guarantee finds a guarantor to offer a guarantee at the guarantee application stage. Based on the user's private address, the guarantor figures out the guarantee value and sends it to RA to be checked and signed. The anonymous identity can be used for authentication once it has been guaranteed by the guarantor and signed by the RA.

During the service request stage, the user only needs to provide the service provider with their anonymous account and the guarantor's signature. After verification, the service provider provides the service. The service provider records the user's anonymized address, signature, and obtained services on the blockchain once the service is concluded.

During the supervision stage, the service provider provides the CA with the record's block hash value, and the CA uses its tracking key to locate the RA. Then, RA investigates the guarantor's real identity. In addition, the CA can revoke the pernicious account's address to prevent it from engaging in malicious activities in the future.

## 2.2  Security Requirements

A secure ERAAS system should satisfy the following requirements.

- Anonymity: Without access to the identity information of the guarantor, an adversary cannot guess the true identity of the guarantor of the certificate presented by an honest user during anonymous authentication.
- Traceability: An adversary can't collude with the RA for an untraceable signature or recover the guarantor's polynomial from an anonymous account's guarantee value, preventing them from forging a valid anonymous certificate.
- Revocability: After an anonymous account exhibits malicious behavior, the CA should be able to revoke the account to ensure that the malicious account cannot pass identity authentication again.
- Anti-forgery attack: Without access to the private key of RA and the polynomial of the guarantor, an adversary cannot forge a valid certificate.

## 3  ERAAS Construction

This paper designs an ERAAS system based on blockchain. The process of the whole system is as follows.

### 3.1  System Setup (Setup)

The CA selects a large prime number $p$, and confirms the format of polynomial functions, such as equation (1), where the highest power of the polynomial function is $n \in Z_p$, and polynomial coefficients are $a_0, \cdots a_n \in Z_p$. Assuming a polynomial function represents a guarantor, the number of guarantors they can represent is shown in the Table 1.

$$f(x) = a_n x^n + a_{(n-1)} x^{n-1} + \cdots + a_1 x + a_0 \qquad (1)$$

**Table 1.** The number of guarantors

|            | $n = 3$ | $n = 4$ | $n = 5$ | $n = 6$ |
|------------|---------|---------|---------|---------|
| $a = 2^5$  | $2^{15}$ | $2^{20}$ | $2^{25}$ | $2^{30}$ |
| $a = 2^{10}$ | $2^{30}$ | $2^{40}$ | $2^{50}$ | $2^{60}$ |
| $a = 2^{15}$ | $2^{45}$ | $2^{60}$ | $2^{75}$ | $2^{80}$ |

Thus, the system does not need to use large coefficients or high power polynomial functions to distinguish all guarantors. Then it chooses two bilinear cyclic groups $G_1 = \langle g_1 \rangle$, $G_2 = \langle g_2 \rangle$, satisfying bilinear pairing $e : G_1 \times G_2 \rightarrow G_T$. CA randomly selects $g_3 \in G_1$ and a collision-resistant hash function $H : \{0,1\}^* \rightarrow Z_p$. Finally, it outputs parameters $Para(f(x), n, G_1, G_1, G_T, e, g_1, g_2, g_3, g_4, g_5, p, H)$.

### 3.2 Generate Key (Genkey)

The CA randomly selects $d, s, t \in Z_p^*$, and $D = g_1^d$, $S = g_2^s$, and $T = g_1^t$. Thus, the CA gets the secret group key $GSK = (d, s, t)$, and the public group key $GPK = (D, S, T)$. Besides, it randomly selects $z, v \in Z_p^*$ and computes $L = g_3^l$, $Acc_0 = g_2^v$. Then, it outputs the public key $PK(D, S, T, L, v, (g_3^l, g_3^{l^2}, \cdots, g_3^{l^q}))$.

### 3.3 RA Registration (RReg)

If the $RA_i$ wants to get the power to register for the guarantor and the ability to issue a certificate, it needs to use its physical identity to register with the CA, then the $RA_i$ will get a private key. The specific process of the registration described is as follows.

1. The CA randomly selects an element $x_i \in Z_p^*$ and calculates

$$R_i = g_1^{(d-x_i)(s*x_i)^{-1}} \qquad (2)$$

   Since $R_i = g_1^{r_i}$, we know $x_i + r_i * s * x_i = d$.
2. The CA checks whether $x_i$ is different from the previous ones. If not, the CA will repeat the previous step.
3. The private key $RSK_i$ of the registration center is $x_i$. The CA stores the corresponding identity information and $R_i^{x_i}$.

CA sends $x_i$ and $l$ to the $RA_i$ through a secure connection.

## 3.4   Guarantor Registration (GReg)

It is not necessary for all users to complete the phase. The guarantor must be aware that once she guarantees her own or another person's account, she will be responsible for the actions of the anonymous account. Therefore, the guarantor should not guarantee an unknown person's anonymous account.

During the first step of the guarantor registration procedure, the guarantor will send a message $m_r$ to $RA_i$ through a secure channel to verify its identity. When the $RA_i$ receives a message $m_r$ from a new guarantor, it will sign the message $m_r$ with its group's private key so that the guarantor can authenticate its legal identity. The specific signature process is described as follows.

1. The $RA_i$ randomly selects $k_a \in Z_p^*$ and calculates auxiliary values as follows.

$$A_1 = g_1^{k_a} \tag{3}$$
$$A_2 = R_i^{x_i} \cdot T^{k_a} \tag{4}$$
$$Q_1 = e(T, S)^{k_a} \tag{5}$$

2. The $RA_i$ calculates the challenge value as follows.

$$C_{au} = H(m_r, A_1, A_2, Q_1) \tag{6}$$

3. Then $RA_i$ calculates $w_a = k_a * C_{au} + x_i$. It outputs the signature as follows.

$$Sig := (A_1, A_2, C_{au}, w_a) \tag{7}$$

Once the guarantor has $RA_i$'s signature, she will perform identity verification utilizing the group public keys and information $m_r$. The following are the specific steps that make up the verification process.

1. The guarantor calculates the auxiliary value $\tilde{Q}_1$ as follows.

$$\tilde{Q}_1 = \frac{e(A_2, S) \cdot e(g_1, g_2)^{w_a}}{e(A_1^{C_{au}} \cdot D, g_2)} \tag{8}$$

2. The guarantor calculates the challenge value.

$$C'_{au} = H(m_r, A_1, A_2, \tilde{Q}_1) \tag{9}$$

3. Finally, the guarantor checks whether $C'_{au} = C_{au}$ holds. If true, the guarantor accepts $Sig$ and registers with the $RA_i$. Otherwise, she rejects $Sig$.

After the guarantor accepts the signature, she registers with the $RA_i$. To differentiate herself from the other users, the guarantor is expected to choose a unique pseudonym $pse$ and generate an $ID$ to serve as verification of her identity. After that, she selects a polynomial function $f()$ at random, making sure that it is compliant with the format for polynomials that was established during the setup phase. This function necessitates the use of the highest possible power, denoted by $n$, as well as a finite field, which is denoted by the prime element $p$.

Then, she sends $RA_i$ a registration request *regreq* across a secure connection, and the request will include the following information.

$$regreq := (pse, ID, f())  \tag{10}$$

When the $RA_i$ receives a registration request from a new guarantor, it is required to check certain components of the request. First, it is necessary for $RA_i$ to verify the guarantor's actual identity through $ID$. Second, the $RA_i$ has to make sure that the guarantor has not already received certificates on the blockchain network while using the same pseudonym *pse*. After that, the $RA_i$ verifies that the guarantor's request contains a polynomial function in the correct format. In the fourth step, the $RA_i$ is responsible for ensuring that the polynomial function $f()$ inside the blockchain network is unique. At last, the $RA_i$ will upload the guarantor's registration request to the blockchain. After the preceding steps, the $RA_i$ provides the guarantor with a registration response. In the event that any of the above steps are unsuccessful, the guarantor's registration will be invalid, she will be informed of her failure, she has to redo the guarantor registration phase with a new pseudonym or new polynomial function due to $RA_i$'s reply. Otherwise, she will receive a registration success reply, she is permitted to use the pseudonym *pse* and polynomial function $f()$ in future transactions.

### 3.5    Account Guarantee (AGua)

Before executing anonymous identity guarantee phase, the guarantor must be recognized, however, that if the number of accounts the guarantor has insured is equal to or more than the utmost power of the polynomial function, the guarantor faces the possibility of polynomial leaking. The greater the number of accounts guaranteed, the greater the dangers.

To guarantee an account with address *add*, the guarantor must first choose a random number $salt \in Z_n$, and then she generates a guaranty key $(xgk, ygk)$ for the anonymous account as follows.

$$xgk = H(pse, f(), add, salt)  \tag{11}$$
$$ygk = f(xgk)  \tag{12}$$

Subsequently, the guarantor transmits the following information *acguareq* through a secure connection to $RA_i$ as an anonymous account guarantee request *acguareq*.

$$acguareq := (pse, add, xgk, ygk)  \tag{13}$$

When the $RA_i$ accepts the request *acguareq*, she will verify it with the following steps. $RA_i$ obtains the polynomial function $f()'$ from the blockchain with the same pseudonym *pse*. Then she calculates $xgk$ and $ygk$ in the same way for each conceivable salt value (from 0 to $n$) to see if there would be any salt value that satisfies the result in *acguareq*. In the event that the request is legitimate, the $RA_i$ will sign the guarantee as follows.

1. The $RA_i$ randomly selects $k_g \in Z_p^*$ and calculates auxiliary values as follows.

$$A_3 = g_1^{k_g} \tag{14}$$

$$A_4 = R_i^{x_i} \cdot T^{k_g} \tag{15}$$

$$Q_2 = e(T, S)^{k_g} \tag{16}$$

2. The $RA_i$ calculates the challenge value $C_{gu}$.

$$m_g = H(add, xgk, ygk) \tag{17}$$

$$C_{gu} = H(m_g, A_3, A_4, Q_2) \tag{18}$$

3. The $RA_i$ sets the address $add$'s witness $W_i = Acc_{old}$ and issues new accumulator's value $Acc_{new}$ as follows.

$$Acc_{new} = Acc_{old}^{l+H(add)} \tag{19}$$

4. Then the $RA_i$ calculates $w_g = k_g * C_{gu} + x_i$. She outputs the certificate $Cert$ as follows.

$$Cert := (pse, add, xgk, ygk, A_3, A_4, C_{au}, w_g, W_i, Acc_{new}) \tag{20}$$

Besides, it broadcasts a join message $m_{join}$ as follows.

$$m_{join} := (state = join, value = H(add), Acc_{join} = Acc_{old}) \tag{21}$$

When the guarantor receives the certificate $Cert$ from the $RA_i$ through a secure connection, she verifies it as the following steps.

1. Firstly, she determines if the account has been joined.

$$e(g_3, Acc_{new}) = e(L \cdot g_3^{H(add)}, W_i) \tag{22}$$

If the equation is hold, the address $ass$ is valid and further verification is performed. Otherwise, the certificate $Cert$ is invalid.

2. Secondly, she should calculate the auxiliary value $\tilde{Q}_2$ as follows.

$$\tilde{Q}_2 = \frac{e\,(A_4, S) \cdot e(g_1, g_2)^{w_g}}{e(A_3^{C_{gu}} \cdot D, g_2)} \tag{23}$$

3. The guarantor calculates the challenge value $C'_{gu}$ as follows.

$$m_g = H(add, xgk, ygk) \tag{24}$$

$$C'_{gu} = H(m_g, A_3, A_4, \tilde{Q}_2) \tag{25}$$

4. Finally, the guarantor checks whether $C'_{gu} = C_{gu}$ holds. If true, the guarantor will accept $Cert$ and send it to the owner of the anonymous account. Otherwise, she will reject it.

When other users obtain the message $m_{join}$, they first check the state to make sure that it is a registration message. Then they update their own membership witness according to the $value$ and $Acc_{join}$. They compute their new witness $W_{new}$ as follows.

$$W_{new} = W_i^{(value-H(add))} \cdot Acc_{join} \tag{26}$$

## 3.6  Show Certificate (SCert)

If the user would like to seek the service of the service provider anonymously, she must provide the guarantee $ACert$ she received from the guarantor, which is shown as follows.

$$ACert := (add, xgk, ygk, A_3, A_4, C_{au}, w_g, W_i) \tag{27}$$

## 3.7  Verify Certificate(VCert)

When the service provider receives the guarantee $ACert$, she will verify its validity. If the verification is passed, she will provide the service to the user and record the corresponding records on the chain, otherwise, she will refuse to provide the service. The specific process of verification is as follows.

1. First, she determines if the account has been revoked. Then she does the following step.

$$e(g_3, Acc_{new}) = e(L \cdot g_3^{H(add)}, W_i) \tag{28}$$

   If the equation holds, the address $add$ is valid and further verification is performed. Otherwise, the authentication fails.
2. The guarantor calculates the challenge value $C'_{gu}$ as follows.

$$m_g = H(add, xgk, ygk) \tag{29}$$
$$C'_{gu} = H(m_g, A_3, A_4, \tilde{Q}_2) \tag{30}$$

3. Finally, the service provider checks whether $C'_{gu} = C_{gu}$ holds.

If true, the service provider accepts $ACert$, providing services and uploading relevant information to the blockchain. Otherwise, she rejects it.

## 3.8  Supervision (Sup)

When there is a dispute between the service provider and the anonymous user, the service provider provides CA with the block hash of the anonymous certificate presented by the anonymous user. When the CA gets the certificate $ACert$, it will do the following steps.

1. Firstly, it must check the validity of the certificate $ACert$. If the certificate is invalid, then it aborts and outputs $\perp$. Otherwise, it continues.
2. It needs to revoke the user's right to get services, it computes $Acc_{new}$ as follows and issues it.

$$Acc_{new} = Acc_{old}^{1/(H(add)+l)} \tag{31}$$

   She broadcasts a remove message $m_{leave}$.

$$m_{leave} := (state = revoke, value = H(add), Acc_{leave} = Acc_{new}) \tag{32}$$

3. The CA has a list of polynomial functions $PFList$, it needs to find the suspect polynomial functions according to $xgk$ and $ygk$, listing a polynomial functions list $Sus\_PFList$.

$$0, 1 \longleftarrow ygk = f(xgk), f() \in PFList \tag{33}$$

4. Then, based on $Sus\_PFList$, CA checks whether the account guarantee keys are generated from a specific user as follows.

$$0, 1 \longleftarrow xgk = H(pse, f(), add, salt)$$
$$0 \leqslant salt \leqslant n, (pse, f()) \in Sus\_PFList \tag{34}$$

If a hash result matches $xgk$, the specific user is a cheater. CA will broadcast it to prevent others from being cheated again.

When others obtain the message $m_{leave}$, they first check the state to make sure that it is revocation message. Then they update their own membership witness $W_{new}$ according to the $value$ and $Acc_{leave}$ as follows.

$$W_{new} = (W_i / Acc_{leave})^{1/(value - H(add))} \tag{35}$$

## 4    Analysis

### 4.1    Security Analysis

**Theorem 1.** *Without the tracking key and the information of the guarantors, no one can obtain the true identity of the guarantor.*

*Proof.* In the ERAAS system, when users present their certificates, they need to present the guarantee values $xgk$ and $ygk$ generated by the guarantors and also need to present the signature generated by RA, indicating that their certificate is authorized by RA. At the same time, users also need to present their witness value $W_i$ to prove that they are legitimate and not revoked users. According to [5], when the number of guarantors does not exceed the highest degree of polynomial function, the attacker cannot obtain the polynomial of the guarantor, i.e., the attacker cannot obtain the information of the guarantor through the guarantee values $xgk$ and $ygk$, which realizes the anonymity of the guarantor.

RA uses the group signature technology in [8] for signing users' certificates. According to [8], when the CA is trusted, i.e., when the tracking key is not leaked, solving for the value $A_4/A_3^t$ is infeasible, which means that RA cannot be found through the anonymous certificates, ensuring the anonymity of RA and guarantors. The dynamic accumulator [18] used in the ERAAS system does not leak any information about the anonymous account or any information related to the guarantor, ensuring the anonymity of the guarantor. Therefore, the ERAAS system supports the anonymity of guarantors.

**Theorem 2.** *By using the tracing key and the stored information of the guarantors, the real identity of the corresponding guarantor can be traced.*

*Proof.* In the ERAAS system, when a user presents an anonymous certificate, they need to provide the guarantee values $xgk$ and $ygk$, and the user needs to show the signature generated by RA for the guarantee to prove that their guarantee is authorized and valid. The user also needs to provide their witness value $W_i$ to prove that their anonymous account is valid. According to [5], if the number of accounts guaranteed by a guarantor does not exceed the highest degree of a polynomial, the adversary cannot recover the polynomial of the guarantor, ensuring the non-forgeability of the guarantor's polynomial.

RA uses group signature technology in [8] to sign the user's guarantee, and according to Theorem 3 in [8], if the ECDL hypothesis holds in a bilinear group, the group signature is traceable. According to [18], the ERAAS system can ensure that the adversary cannot forge the witness value of a revoked user and pass the verification, nor can they forge the witness value of an unauthorized user and pass the verification.

In summary, CA can trace RAs through anonymous certificates. With the guarantee values $xgk$ and $ygk$ on the anonymous certificate and the information of the guarantors stored by the RA, the unique guarantee polynomial can be identified, and therefore, the CA can trace the real identity of the guarantor. Therefore, the ERAAS system satisfies the traceability property.

**Theorem 3.** *Without the private key of the RA, a malicious account address cannot be re-certified after being removed from the accumulator.*

*Proof.* In the ERAAS system, when users present anonymous certificates, they need to provide their accumulator witness value $W_i$ to the service provider. According to [18], in the absence of the registration authority's private key, if a user's account in the ERAAS system has been removed from the accumulator, the user cannot re-add the account address to the accumulator, and the witness value $W_i$ provided by the user cannot satisfy $e(g_3, Acc_{new}) = e(L \cdot g_3^{H(add)}, W_i)$, making it impossible to complete the authentication. Therefore, once a malicious account address is removed from the accumulator, users will not be able to use that account address for identity authentication again. Thus, the ERAAS system designed in this paper satisfies revocability.

**Theorem 4.** *Without the private key of the RA and the polynomials, an attacker cannot forge a valid certificate.*

*Proof.* When a user provides an anonymous certificate in the ERAAS system, they are required to supply the guarantee values $xgk$ and $ygk$ as well as the signature produced by RA for the guarantee to demonstrate that their guarantee is legitimate. To demonstrate the legitimacy of anonymous account, the user must additionally supply their witness value $W_i$. According to [5], if the number of accounts it guarantees does not exceed the polynomial's highest degree, the adversary cannot retrieve the guarantor's polynomial, ensuring the non-forgeability of the guarantor's polynomial. Similarly, when issuing a certificate, RA's key is used to sign the certificate, and it is known from [8] that an adversary cannot forge a valid signature. It is also known from [18] that if the adversary does not have the key, they cannot add an account address to the accumulator and cannot prove the validity of an anonymous account. In summary, without the private key of the RA and the polynomials, adversaries cannot forge polynomials, nor can they forge the RA's signature as the signature of an anonymous certificate, and they cannot add a malicious account address to the accumulator. Therefore, the system proposed in this paper can resist forgery attacks.

## 4.2  Theoretical Analysis

This section will compare the Identity Mixer scheme [3], the supervised anonymous authentication scheme [23], the anonymous account guarantee scheme [5], and the ERAAS system in terms of functionality. Table 2 summarizes the similarities and differences in functionality between the Identity Mixer scheme [3], the supervised anonymous authentication scheme [23], the anonymous account guarantee scheme [5], and the ERAAS system. In terms of functionality, all of these schemes achieve anonymous authentication. However, the Identity Mixer scheme [3] is completely anonymous, so in case of disputes, it is impossible to trace the person who presented the anonymous certificate. To address this issue, the supervised anonymous authentication scheme [23], the anonymous account guarantee scheme [5], and the ERAAS system introduce regulators to achieve the ability to track the real identity of the malicious users. In order to reduce the storage overhead of certificates, the anonymous account guarantee scheme [5] and the ERAAS system provide guarantee functions, which means that users who only need to be authenticated can find a guarantor to guarantee their anonymous accounts instead of registering with the organization using their real identities. At the same time, the system proposes a revocability function to prevent malicious accounts from performing multiple malicious activities.

Table 2. Functionality comparison

| Scheme | Authentication | Anonymous | Supervision | Guaranteeable | Revocable |
|---|---|---|---|---|---|
| Camenisch et al. [3] | ✓ | ✓ | ✗ | ✗ | ✗ |
| Wang et al. [23] | ✓ | ✓ | ✓ | ✗ | ✗ |
| Cheng et al. [5] | ✓ | ✓ | ✓ | ✓ | ✗ |
| ERAAS | ✓ | ✓ | ✓ | ✓ | ✓ |

## 4.3  Experimental Analysis

We evaluate the performance of ERAAS through experimental analysis. We use the jpbc library and commons-codec-1.7 library in Java to simulate the system and the anonymous account guarantee scheme [5] on a platform with Microsoft Windows 10 operating system, Intel(R) Core(TM) i5-7700 @3.6GHz. The elliptic curve used is of type A ($y^2 = x^3 + x$), with a prime number $q$ of 171 bits.

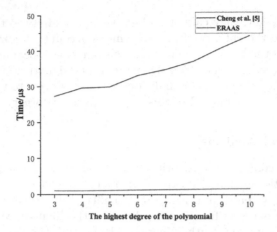

**Fig. 2.** Comparison of average concurrent processing times in GReg.

During the registration of a guarantor, the RA randomly generates a unique polynomial for each guarantor. However, the time required to randomly generate a polynomial is related to the number of coefficients in the polynomial. According to the data in Fig. 2, we can see that in the GReg phase, the higher the degree of the polynomial, the more coefficients the center needs to generate randomly, so the time to generate the guarantor polynomial will also increase. When fifty guarantors simultaneously send registration requests, Cheng et al.'s scheme [5] only has one center, so only one request can be processed at a time, and other guarantors have to wait, resulting in a high average processing delay. In contrast, the ERAAS system can have multiple RAs processing requests, which can effectively reduce the processing delay for concurrent requests. Therefore, when the highest degree of the polynomial is equal, the processing delay for concurrent registration requests in Cheng et al.'s scheme [5] is greater than that in the ERAAS system. By setting up multiple RAs properly, the system can effectively reduce the registration delay for guarantors.

In the ERAAS system, the AGua phase mainly consists of three stages, including the time for guarantee computation by the guarantors, the time for the RA to sign the guarantee value, and the time for the user to verify the guarantee signature. Since the signature and verification times are fixed, the overall time of the AGua phase mainly depends on the time taken by the guarantors to compute the guarantee value. The computation time of the guarantee value increases with the increase in the highest degree and the maximum coefficient of the polynomial. As shown in Fig. 3, when the highest degree of the polynomial is equal, the larger the maximum coefficient of the polynomial, the longer the time required for AGua. With the same maximum coefficient in the polynomial, higher polynomial degrees result in increased AGua phase time. To reduce AGua phase overhead and enhance guarantee efficiency in ERAAS, lower maximum values for polynomial coefficients and degree should be chosen.

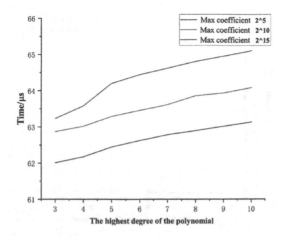

**Fig. 3.** Processing time in AGua of the ERAAS system.

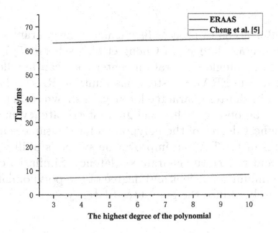

**Fig. 4.** Processing time in AGua for a single request.

In the AGua phase, if only considering the case of processing a single guarantee request, the efficiency comparison between Cheng et al.'s scheme [5] and the ERAAS system is shown in Fig. 4. As shown in Fig. 4, the time cost of the guarantee increases with the highest degree of the polynomial. When the highest degree of the polynomial generated by the guarantor is the same, Cheng et al.'s scheme [5] has a higher efficiency in processing guarantees than the ERAAS system. This is because the ERAAS system adopts a group signature scheme for guarantee signature generation, and the center needs to add the guaranteed account to the accumulator. While Cheng et al.'s scheme [5] adopts a more efficient ECDSA signature scheme, in the case of processing a single guarantee request, the guarantee efficiency of Cheng et al.'s scheme [5] is higher.

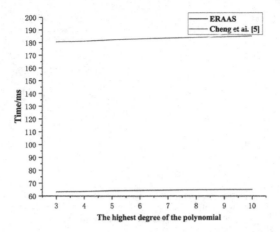

**Fig. 5.** The average AGua time for concurrent requests.

When the center needs to process fifty concurrent guarantee requests in the AGua phase, the average latency in Cheng et al.'s scheme [5] is longer because the scheme only has a single registration center that can handle one request at a time. In contrast, the ERAAS system has multiple RAs to handle guarantee requests, resulting in shorter guarantee latency, as shown in Fig. 5. Furthermore, from Fig. 5, it can be observed that the guaranteed latency increases with the increase in the highest degree of the polynomial for the same scheme. Therefore, reasonable settings of the RA can improve the system's ability to process concurrent requests and reduce the guaranteed latency. Similarly, choosing smaller values for the maximum coefficient and degree of the polynomial in the ERAAS system can effectively reduce the guaranteed latency.

## 5  Conclusion

This paper proposed an ERAAS system where blockchain was employed to ensure the non-repudiation of evidence. In the ERAAS system, a user who only needs identity authentication can request a guarantor to provide an anonymous account guaranty for her without the need to apply for a certificate with her real identity, thus reducing the storage cost of certificates. At the same time, the system sets up multiple RAs, and in the case of concurrency, the average latency for users to obtain a guaranty is reduced. In order to prevent malicious accounts from repeating malicious behavior, the ERAAS system also provides a revocation mechanism. Accounts that have engaged in malicious behavior will be revoked and cannot be authenticated again. The security analysis indicated that the proposed ERAAS system satisfies anonymity, traceability and revocability and can resist forgery attacks. The comparison with existing solutions demonstrated that the proposed ERAAS system improves the efficiency of the RA in processing concurrent requests and has good practicality.

**Acknowledgements.** This article is supported in part by the National Key R&D Program of China under project 2020YFB1006003, the Guangxi Natural Science Foundation under grant 2023GXNSFAA026236, the National Natural Science Foundation of China under projects 62162017, 62172119 and 61962012, the Zhejiang Provincial Natural Science Foundation of China under Grant No. LZ23F020012, the Guangdong Key R&D Program under project 2020B0101090002, and the special fund of the High-level Innovation Team and Outstanding Scholar Program for universities of Guangxi.

# References

1. Arasan, A., Sadaiyandi, R., Al-Turjman, F., Rajasekaran, A.S., Selvi Karuppuswamy, K.: Computationally efficient and secure anonymous authentication scheme for cloud users. Personal Ubiquit. Comput. 1–11 (2021). https://doi.org/10.1007/s00779-021-01566-9
2. Banerjee, S., Odelu, V., Das, A.K., Chattopadhyay, S., Park, Y.: An efficient, anonymous and robust authentication scheme for smart home environments. Sensors **20**(4), 1215 (2020)
3. Camenisch, J., et al.: Specification of the identity mixer cryptographic library. IBM Research-Zurich, pp. 1–48 (2010)
4. Cao, Y.N., Wang, Y., Ding, Y., Guo, Z., Wu, Q., Liang, H.: Blockchain-empowered security and privacy protection technologies for smart grid. Comput. Stand. Interfaces **85**, 103708 (2022)
5. Cheng, L., Liu, J., Jin, Y., Li, Y., Wang, W.: Account guarantee scheme: making anonymous accounts supervised in blockchain. ACM Trans. Internet Technol. (TOIT) **21**(1), 1–19 (2021)
6. Gao, T., Deng, X., Guo, N., Wang, X.: An anonymous authentication scheme based on pmipv6 for VANETs. IEEE Access **6**, 14686–14698 (2018)
7. Han, M., Liu, S., Ma, S., Wan, A.: Anonymous-authentication scheme based on fog computing for VANET. PLoS ONE **15**(2), e0228319 (2020)
8. Ho, T.H., Yen, L.H., Tseng, C.C.: Simple-yet-efficient construction and revocation of group signatures. Int. J. Found. Comput. Sci. **26**(5), 611–624 (2015)
9. I'Anson, C., Mitchell, C.: Security defects in CCITT recommendation x. 509: the directory authentication framework. ACM SIGCOMM Comput. Commun. Rev. **20**(2), 30–34 (1990)
10. Jegadeesan, S., Azees, M., Babu, N.R., Subramaniam, U., Almakhles, J.D.: EPAW: efficient privacy preserving anonymous mutual authentication scheme for wireless body area networks (WBANS). IEEE Access **8**, 48576–48586 (2020)
11. Jiang, Y., Ge, S., Shen, X.: AAAS: an anonymous authentication scheme based on group signature in VANETs. IEEE Access **8**, 98986–98998 (2020)
12. Khan, N., Zhang, J., Jan, S.U.: A robust and privacy-preserving anonymous user authentication scheme for public cloud server. Secur. Commun. Netw. 2022 (2022)
13. Lal, N.A., Prasad, S., Farik, M.: A review of authentication methods. Int. J. Sci. Technol. Res. **5**, 246–249 (2016)
14. Liang, W., Wang, Y., Ding, Y., Zheng, H., Liang, H., Wang, H.: An efficient anonymous authentication and supervision system based on blockchain. In: 2022 7th IEEE International Conference on Data Science in Cyberspace (DSC), pp. 306–313. IEEE (2022)
15. Liang, W., Wang, Y., Ding, Y., Zheng, H., Liang, H., Wang, H.: An efficient blockchain-based anonymous authentication and supervision system. Peer-to-Peer Networking and Applications, pp. 1–20 (2023)

16. Liu, H., Sun, Y., Xu, Y., Xu, R., Wei, Z.: A secure lattice-based anonymous authentication scheme for VANETs. J. Chin. Inst. Eng. **42**(1), 66–73 (2019)
17. Mehmood, A., Natgunanathan, I., Xiang, Y., Poston, H., Zhang, Y.: Anonymous authentication scheme for smart cloud based healthcare applications. IEEE access **6**, 33552–33567 (2018)
18. Nguyen, L.: Accumulators from Bilinear Pairings and Applications. In: Menezes, A. (ed.) CT-RSA 2005. LNCS, vol. 3376, pp. 275–292. Springer, Heidelberg (2005). https://doi.org/10.1007/978-3-540-30574-3_19
19. Rana, R., Zaeem, R.N., Barber, K.S.: An assessment of blockchain identity solutions: Minimizing risk and liability of authentication. In: 2019 IEEE/WIC/ACM International Conference on Web Intelligence (WI), pp. 26–33. IEEE (2019)
20. Saleem, T., et al.: ProofChain: an x. 509-compatible blockchain-based PKI framework with decentralized trust. Comput. Netw. **213**, 109069 (2022)
21. Wang, F., Xu, G., Gu, L.: A secure and efficient ECC-based anonymous authentication protocol. Secur. Commun. Netw. 2019 (2019)
22. Wang, X., Yan, Z., Zhang, R., Zhang, P.: Attacks and defenses in user authentication systems: a survey. J. Netw. Comput. Appl. **188**, 103080 (2021)
23. Wang, Z., Fan, J., Cheng, L., An, H.Z., Zheng, H.B., Niu, J.X.: Supervised anonymous authentication scheme. J. Softw. **6**, 1705–1720 (2019)
24. Wen, B., Wang, Y., Ding, Y., Zheng, H., Qin, B., Yang, C.: Security and privacy protection technologies in securing blockchain applications. Inf. Sci. **645**, 119322 (2023)
25. Zhang, L., Li, H., Li, Y., Yu, Y., Au, M.H., Wang, B.: An efficient linkable group signature for payer tracing in anonymous cryptocurrencies. Futur. Gener. Comput. Syst. **101**, 29–38 (2019)
26. Zhang, M., Zhou, J., Zhang, G., Zou, M., Chen, M.: EC-BAAS: elliptic curve-based batch anonymous authentication scheme for internet of vehicles. J. Syst. Architect. **117**, 102161 (2021)
27. Zhang, T., Wang, Y., Ding, Y., Wu, Q., Liang, H., Wang, H.: Multi-party electronic contract signing protocol based on blockchain. IEICE Trans. Inf. Syst. **105**(2), 264–271 (2022)
28. Zimmermann, V., Gerber, N.: The password is dead, long live the password-a laboratory study on user perceptions of authentication schemes. Int. J. Hum Comput. Stud. **133**, 26–44 (2020)
29. Zulfiqar, M., Janjua, M.U., Hassan, M., Ahmad, T., Saleem, T., Stokes, J.W.: Tracking adoption of revocation and cryptographic features in x. 509 certificates. Int. J. Inf. Secur. **21**(3), 653–668 (2022)

# Computing Resource Allocation for Hybrid Applications of Blockchain and Mobile Edge Computing

Yuqi Fan[1(✉)], Jun Zhang[1], Xu Ding[2], Zhifeng Jin[1], and Lei Shi[1]

[1] School of Computer Science and Information Engineering, Anhui Province Key Laboratory of Industry Safety and Emergency Technology, Hefei University of Technology, Hefei 230601, Anhui, China
{yuqi.fan,zhang-jun,2019170960,shilei}@hfut.edu.cn
[2] Institute of Industry and Equipment Technology, Hefei University of Technology, Hefei 230009, Anhui, China
dingxu@hfut.edu.cn

**Abstract.** In mobile edge computing (MEC), each user chooses and then offloads the task to an edge server, whereas data security is a concern in MEC due to the lack of trust between users and edge servers. Blockchain is introduced to provide a reliable environment for MEC. In blockchain-based MEC, edge servers are used as the nodes in both MEC and blockchain. After processing the users' tasks, the edge servers upload the results and other task-related information to the blockchain. The edge servers simultaneously execute two kind of tasks, i.e., the tasks offloaded by the users and the blockchain tasks. Therefore, the user offloading decision affects the processing latency of MEC tasks, and there is a trade-off between the resource allocation for MEC and blockchain tasks. However, most existing studies optimize the resource allocation for blockchain and MEC individually, which leads to the suboptimal performance of blockchain-based MEC. In this paper, we study the problem of user offloading decision and the computing resource allocation of edge servers for MEC and blockchain tasks, with the objective to minimize the total processing delay of MEC and blockchain tasks. We propose an algorithm for joint computing resource allocation for MEC and blockchain (JMB). Theoretical analysis proves that JMB is a 3.16-approximation algorithm. Simulation results show that JMB can effectively reduce the delay in blockchain-based MEC.

**Keywords:** Edge computing · Blockchain · Computing offloading · Resource allocation

This work is partially supported by Major Science and Technology Projects in Anhui Province of China (202003a05020009) and National Natural Science Foundation of China (62002097).

H. Gao et al. (Eds.): CollaborateCom 2023, LNICST 561, pp. 187–206, 2024.
https://doi.org/10.1007/978-3-031-54521-4_11

# 1  Introduction

With the rapid development of computation-intensive mobile applications such as voice control, face recognition, interactive games, etc., it is difficult for users with limited resources to obtain satisfactory user experience [17]. In order to improve the quality of service (QoS) of users, mobile edge computing (MEC) rises rapidly.

Data security is a concern in MEC due to the lack of trust between users and edge servers [9], since the edge servers and the network environments are not fully trusted in MEC. The data may belong to multiple owners, and the data stored in the edge servers may be modified or misused by unauthorized users [22]. As a promising solution for data security protection, blockchain is able to provide a reliable environment for MEC [10], since blockchain has the characteristics of decentralization, immutability, traceability, transparency, etc.

A blockchain-based MEC system consists of two subsystems, i.e., MEC and blockchain, as shown in Fig. 1. In the MEC subsystem, each user offloads the computation-intensive task to an edge server through wireless communication, and the edge server executes the MEC tasks offloaded by the users. A large number of tasks offloaded to an edge server result in long task execution time. A large amount of computing resources on an edge server lead to short task execution time. Therefore, a user needs to choose an appropriate edge server for offloading the task. In the blockchain subsystem, the edge server uploads the results and other task-related information to the blockchain. The edge servers treat the records uploaded from the MEC as transactions, which are verified and packaged into a block [14]. When the entire blockchain network reaches consensus, the new block is added to the blockchain.

In blockchain-based MEC, edge servers are used as the nodes in both MEC and blockchain, executing MEC tasks and blockchain tasks simultaneously. The execution of both kinds of tasks consumes computing resources, and hence the rational allocation of edge server computing resources is necessary to reduce the task processing latency of blockchain-based MEC. The problem of computing resource allocation in MEC [1,3,6,12] or blockchain [2,8,11,16,19] has been studied previously. However, the existing methods optimize the resource allocation for blockchain and MEC individually. That is, the resource allocation for one subsystem assumes that it exclusively occupies the computing resources of each edge server, which leads to the imbalance between blockchain and MEC. On the one hand, when the MEC occupies excessive computing resources, the execution of MEC tasks on the edge servers is fast. However, the blockchain shares few computing resources, rendering slow block generation, which results in the high latency and low throughput of the entire blockchain-based MEC. On the other hand, when the blockchain uses too many computing resources, the delay of MEC task execution increases, which leads to the slow generation of data to be packaged into the blocks. Accordingly, the generation of blocks becomes slow and the throughput of the whole blockchain-based MEC system is low. In both of the above two cases, the system throughput decreases, which will lead to the degradation of QoS of mobile users.

It is obvious that there is a trade-off between the resource allocation for MEC and blockchain tasks. Therefore, random resource allocation will lead to the suboptimal performance of blockchain-based MEC. In this paper, we study the user offloading decision and the computing resource allocation of edge servers for both MEC and blockchain tasks to effectively reduce the total latency in blockchain-based MEC. The main contributions of this paper are as follows:

1. In blockchain-based MEC, we formulate the problem of user offloading decision and the computing resource allocation of edge servers for MEC and blockchain tasks, with the aim to minimize the total processing delay of both MEC and blockchain tasks.
2. We propose an algorithm for joint computing resource allocation for MEC and blockchain (JMB), which consists of 5 steps. First, JMB relaxes the problem constraints to obtain the relaxed problem. Second, JMB solves the relaxed problem and obtains the fractional optimal solution. Third, JMB modifies the fractional optimal solution to obtain the feasible fractional solution. Fourth, JMB performs the clustering operation on the users and the edge servers according to the feasible fractional solution to form multiple initial clusters. Finally, JMB maps the users to the edge servers in each initial cluster and obtains the feasible integer solution satisfying the relaxed constraints. Theoretical analysis proves that JMB is a 3.16-approximation algorithm.
3. We conduct experiments through simulations, and the experimental results show that JMB can effectively reduce the delay in blockchain-based MEC.

The rest of this paper is organized as follows. Section 2 introduces the related work. The system model is formulated and analyzed in Sect. 3. Section 4 presents in detail the proposed algorithm and analyzes the algorithm theoretically. The experiments are given in Sect. 5, and Sect. 6 concludes the paper.

## 2  Related Work

In a blockchain-based MEC system, edge servers need to execute both MEC and blockchain tasks, and both kinds of tasks consume computing resources. Therefore, it is crucial to allocate the computing resources of edge servers reasonably to reduce the total system delay.

In terms of computing resource allocation for MEC, Rahma et al. [1] proposed a blockchain-based distributed MEC framework to support low-latency, secure and anonymous data communication in on-demand data sharing scenarios. Liu et al. [12] proposed an adaptive block size based framework, which considers two offloading modes, namely offloading to a server or a nearby device, and formulated the issues of resource allocation, scheduling of offloading, and adaptive block size as an optimization problem. Cui et al. [3] proposed a blockchain based containerized edge computing platform for Internet of Vehicles. The platform was integrated with blockchain to improve the security of the network. A heuristic container scheduling algorithm was developed to schedule computing tasks to appropriate edge servers to reduce the computing latency. He et al. [7]

proposed a blockchain based framework for edge computing resource allocation in Internet of Things (IoT). The framework specifies the step-by-step process of a single transaction between IoT endpoints and edge servers. Furthermore, the work designed a smart contract in a private blockchain network that utilizes a machine learning algorithm, Asynchronous Advantage Actor-Critic (A3C), to allocate edge computing resources. Fan et al. [6] formulated a Stackelberg game with the cloud/edge computing service provider (CESP) as the leader and users as the followers for cloud/edge computing resource management. They also modeled the resource allocation and pricing at the CESP as a mixed-integer programming problem (MIP) with the objective to optimize the CESP's revenue and proposed an iterative greedy-and-search based resource allocation and pricing algorithm.

In terms of resource allocation for blockchain, Kang et al. [9] proposed a reputation-based data sharing scheme in the vehicle edge network, which introduced consortium blockchain and smart contracts to achieve secure data storage and prevent unauthorized data sharing. Liu et al. [11] modeled the joint optimization problem of mining task offloading and cryptographic hash caching for blocks, and proposed an alternating direction method of multipliers for the problem. Sharma et al. [16] proposed a new blockchain-based distributed mobility management scheme to meet the distributed security requirements of fog networks. Jiao et al. constructed an auction-based market model to determine the computing offloading strategy for miners and the allocation of computing resources to edge servers [8]. Xiao et al. [19] proposed a blockchain edge network trust mechanism and an edge server computing resource allocation algorithm based on reinforcement learning. Chang et al. [2] proposed an edge computing based blockchain incentive mechanism for miners to purchase edge server computing resources, and established a two-stage Stackelberg game between miners and edge servers.

In a blockchain-based MEC system, the execution of both MEC and blockchain tasks require computing resources. The random user offloading decision and the arbitrary resource allocation for MEC and blockchain will lead to a large system processing delay. Therefore, it is crucial to allocate computing resources of edge servers reasonably. However, most of the current research optimizes the resource allocation for blockchain and MEC individually, and little literature jointly considers the optimization of blockchain and MEC, which results in the suboptimal performance of blockchain-based MEC. In this paper, we study the problem of the user offloading decision and the computing resource allocation of edge servers for both MEC and blockchain tasks to effectively reduce the total latency in blockchain-based MEC.

## 3    Problem Definition

### 3.1    System Model of MEC and Blockchain Task Execution

In a blockchain-based MEC system, there are multiple users (IoT devices, sensors, wearables, etc.) and multiple edge servers. Each user needs to run a computation-intensive task. The user chooses and then offloads the task to an edge server. The edge servers process the tasks offloaded by the users and simultaneously act as blockchain nodes communicating in a P2P manner [4] to form a blockchain. After executing the task offloaded by the user, the edge server treats the task execution result and other task-related information as a "transaction" to be recorded in the blockchain [14]. Multiple transactions are packaged into a block, and the edge server broadcasts the generated block to all the blockchain nodes which verify the received block. We generally call block generation and

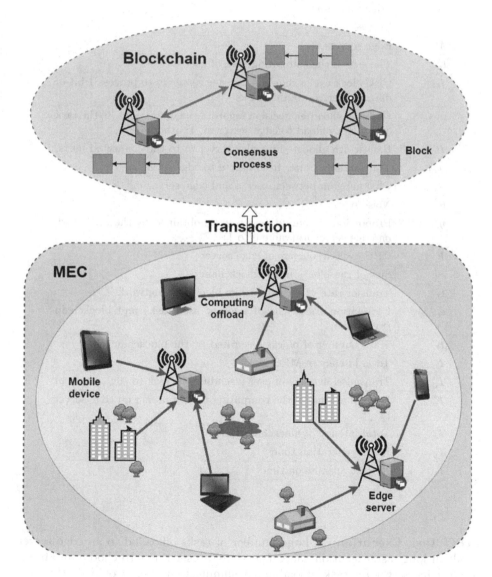

**Fig. 1.** System model.

consensus as blockchain tasks. Therefore, each edge server needs to complete two kinds of tasks: the offloaded tasks from the users in the MEC and the blockchain tasks, as shown in Fig. 1. The symbols used in this paper are shown in Table 1.

**Table 1.** Table of symbols and notations

| Notation | Definition |
|----------|------------|
| $u$ | User $u$ |
| $m$ | Edge servers $m$ |
| $U$ | User set |
| $M$ | Edge servers set |
| $l_u$ | The size of the computing task of user $u$ |
| $f_m$ | CPU clock cycles required by edge server $m$ to process 1 bit of data in user computing tasks |
| $x_{u,m}$ | User $u$'s offloading decision regarding edge server $m$ (0: the task of $u$ is not offload to edge server $m$, 1: otherwise) |
| $B_m$ | Bandwidth allocated by edge server $m$ to the connected users |
| $p_{u,m}$ | Transmission power from user $u$ to edge server $m$ |
| $g_{u,m}$ | Channel gain between user $u$ and edge server $m$ |
| $\theta^2$ | Noise power |
| $y_m$ | Proportion of computing resources obtained by the MEC task on edge server $m$ (value 0 to 1) |
| $F$ | CPU cycle frequency of edge server |
| $S_b$ | Size of the blocks in the blockchain |
| $C$ | Transfer rate of the link in the blockchain network |
| $\omega$ | Correlation coefficient of sizes of user tasks and blockchain transactions |
| $K$ | Total number of blocks generated by the blockchain |
| $T_{u,m}$ | Total latency of MEC tasks |
| $T_{u,m}^t$ | Transmission delay of user $u$ sending the task to edge server $m$ |
| $T_{u,m}^c$ | Execution time of the computing task of user $u$ on edge server $m$ |
| $T_k$ | Total latency of blockchain tasks |
| $T_g$ | Block generation time |
| $T_t$ | Block transmission time |

**MEC Task Execution.** A large number of tasks offloaded to an edge server result in long task execution time. Therefore, a user needs to choose an appropriate edge server for task offloading. Assuming that user $u$ offloads the task with size $l_u$ to server $m$, the task execution delay is calculated as

$$T_{u,m} = x_{u,m}(T^t_{u,m} + T^c_{u,m}) \tag{1}$$

where $T^t_{u,m}$ represents the transmission delay of user $u$ sending data to edge server $m$, and $T^c_{u,m}$ denotes the execution time of the task offloaded by user $u$ to edge server $m$.

We use $p_{u,m}$ to denote the transmission power from user $u$ to edge server $m$, and use $g_{u,m}$ to represent the channel gain between user $u$ and edge server $m$. The transmission rate from user $u$ to edge server $m$ is calculated by (2) [20]:

$$r_{u,m} = B_m \log_2(1 + \tfrac{p_{u,m}g_{u,m}}{\theta^2}) \tag{2}$$

where $B_m$ is the network bandwidth between edge server $m$ and user $u$, and $\theta^2$ is the noise power. The transmission delay of user $u$ sending data to edge server $m$ is:

$$T^t_{u,m} = \tfrac{l_u}{r_{u,m}} \tag{3}$$

A large amount of computing resources on an edge server lead to short task execution time. The execution time of the offloaded task by user $u$ on edge server $m$ is calculated as [20]:

$$T^c_{u,m} = \tfrac{l_u f_m}{y_m F} \tag{4}$$

where $F$ is the CPU cycle frequency of the edge server, $f_m$ is the CPU clock cycles required by edge server $m$ to process 1 bit of data in the tasks, and $y_m$ is the proportion of computing resources allocated to the MEC tasks on edge server $m$. A large $y_m$ leads to fast MEC task processing.

**Blockchain Task Execution.** The total delay of data processing in the blockchain includes the delay of block generation and block transmission, which is as follows:

$$T_k = T_g + T_t \tag{5}$$

where $T_g$ is the time required for the blockchain to generate a new block and $T_t$ is the block transmission time during the consensus process.

The time for the blockchain to generate a new block is calculated as:

$$T_g = \tfrac{1}{K} \sum_{m \in M} \sum_{u \in U} \tfrac{x_{u,m} l_u f_m \omega}{(1-y_m)F} \tag{6}$$

where $\omega$ is the correlation coefficient between the MEC tasks and the blockchain tasks. More tasks offloaded to an edge server leads to larger MEC task processing latency and more blockchain transactions. A large $y_m$ results in slow blockchain task processing, although it can reduce the MEC task running time.

In the blockchain, we assume that the time of data transmission during consensus is:

$$T_t = \frac{S_b}{C} \tag{7}$$

where $S_b$ is the size of a block, and $C$ denotes the data transmission rate on the link between the edge servers.

## 3.2 Problem Model

Each edge server in the system is not only an entity that runs tasks in the MEC, but also a node in the blockchain. There is a trade-off between the resource allocation for MEC and blockchain tasks, and the user offloading decision also affects the processing latency of MEC tasks. In this paper, we minimize the total processing delay of offloaded tasks in the MEC and blockchain tasks by deciding the offloading choices of computing tasks for users and the allocation of computing resource of edge servers for MEC and blockchain tasks. That is, our objective is to

$$\min_{x_{u,m}, y_m} \left( \sum_{m \in M} \sum_{u \in U} T_{u,m} + \sum_{k \in K} T_k \right)$$

$$s.t.$$

$$\text{(C1)}: \sum_{m \in M} x_{u,m} = 1, \forall u \in U \tag{8}$$

$$\text{(C2)}: x_{u,m} \in \{0,1\}, \forall u \in U, m \in M$$

$$\text{(C3)}: 0 < y_m < 1, \forall m \in M$$

Constraint (C1) requires that the computing task of each user is offloaded to one and only one edge server. Constraint (C2) dictates the mapping relationship between user $u$ and edge server $m$, where 1 means that the task of user $u$ is offloaded to edge server $m$ and 0 otherwise. Constraint (C3) demands that the proportion of computing resource of each edge server allocated for MEC is in the range of (0, 1).

## 4    Algorithm for Joint Computing Resource Allocation for MEC and Blockchain

It is known that the problem of user offloading decision and computing resource allocation of edge servers in MEC is $NP$-hard. The problem in this paper needs to consider the resource allocation for both MEC and blockchain. Therefore, the problem in this paper is also $NP$-hard.

In this section, we propose JMB for the problem of user offloading decision and the computing resource allocation of edge servers for MEC and blockchain tasks. JMB consists of 5 steps. First, JMB relaxes the problem constraints to obtain the relaxed problem. Second, JMB solves the relaxed problem and obtains the fractional optimal solution. Third, JMB modifies the fractional optimal solution to obtain the feasible fractional solution. Fourth, JMB performs the clustering operation on the users and the edge servers according to the feasible fractional solution to form multiple initial clusters. Finally, JMB maps the users to the edge servers in each initial cluster and obtains the feasible integer solution satisfying the relaxed constraints.

## 4.1 User's Offloading Decision and Edge Server's Computing Resource Allocation Algorithm

We take (1) and (5) into (8), and rewrite the problem model (8) as (9).

$$\min_{x_{u,m},y_m} \sum_{m \in M} \sum_{u \in U} \left( \frac{l_u x_{u,m}}{r_{u,m}} + \frac{l_u f_m x_{u,m}}{y_m F} + \frac{l_u f_m \omega x_{u,m}}{(1 - y_m) F} \right) + K \frac{S_b}{C}$$

s.t.

$$(C1): \sum_{m \in M} x_{u,m} = 1, \forall u \in U \tag{9}$$

$$(C2): x_{u,m} \in \{0,1\}, \forall u \in U, m \in M$$

$$(C3): 0 < y_m < 1, \forall m \in M$$

The objective function (9) includes both integer variables $x_{u,m}$ and continuous variables $y_m$. Therefore, the problem is a mixed integer nonlinear programming problem, which is difficult to solve. We introduce a new variable $z_m$, and let

$$z_m = \frac{\sum_{u \in U} x_{u,m} l_u}{y_m} + \frac{\sum_{u \in U} x_{u,m} l_u \omega}{1 - y_m}, \forall u \in U, \forall m \in M \tag{10}$$

The problem defined by (9) can then be transformed into:

$$\min_{x_{u,m},z_m} \sum_{m \in M} \sum_{u \in U} \frac{l_u x_{u,m}}{r_{u,m}} + \sum_{m \in M} \frac{f_m z_m}{F} + K \frac{S_b}{C}$$

s.t.

$$(C1): \sum_{m \in M} x_{u,m} = 1, \forall u \in U \tag{11}$$

$$(C2): x_{u,m} \in \{0,1\}, \forall u \in U, m \in M$$

We obtain $z_m = 0$, if and only if $\sum_{u \in U} x_{u,m} l_u = 0$. We can get $\sum_{u \in U} x_{u,m} l_u > 0$ and $\sum_{u \in U} x_{u,m} l_u \omega > 0$ because $x_{u,m} \in \{0,1\}$, $\omega \in (0,1]$ and $l_u > 0$ ($\forall u \in U, m \in M$), when $\sum_{u \in U} x_{u,m} l_u \neq 0$. We can obtain $z_m \geq (\sqrt{\omega} + 1)^2 \sum_{u \in U} x_{u,m} l_u$ because $0 < y_m < 1, \forall m \in M$, and $\omega \in (0,1]$. Without loss of generality, let $\omega = 1$ and we can obtain $z_m \geq 4 \sum_{u \in U} x_{u,m} l_u$.

Taking the value range of $z_m$ into (11), and we can obtain the mixed-integer linear programming problem defined as (12).

$$\min_{x_{u,m},z_m} \left( \sum_{m \in M} \sum_{u \in U} d_{u,m} x_{u,m} + \sum_{m \in M} a_m z_m + e \right)$$

s.t.

$$\text{(C1):} \sum_{m \in M} x_{u,m} = 1, \forall u \in U \tag{12}$$

$$\text{(C2):} 4 \sum_{u \in U} x_{u,m} l_u \leq z_m$$

$$\text{(C3):} x_{u,m} \in \{0,1\}, \forall u \in U, m \in M$$

$$\text{(C4):} z_m \geq 0, \forall m \in M$$

where $a_m = \frac{f_m}{F}$, $d_{u,m} = \frac{l_u}{r_{u,m}}$ and $e = K \frac{S_b}{C}$.

We relax the integer variable $x_{u,m}$ to obtain the linear programming problem (13).

$$\min_{x_{u,m},z_m} \left( \sum_{m \in M} \sum_{u \in U} d_{u,m} x_{u,m} + \sum_{m \in M} a_m z_m + e \right)$$

s.t.

$$\text{(C1):} \sum_{m=1}^{M} x_{u,m} = 1, \forall u \in U \tag{13}$$

$$\text{(C2):} 4 \sum_{u \in U} x_{u,m} l_u \leq z_m$$

$$\text{(C3):} x_{u,m} \geq 0, z_m \geq 0, \forall u \in U, m \in M$$

Given a feasible fractional solution $(x, z)$ to the linear programming problem (13) and a parameter $\alpha \in (0,1)$, we define $d_u(\alpha)$ for any user $u$ as follows: Consider the ordering $\pi$ such that $d_{\pi(1)u} \leq d_{\pi(2)u} \leq \cdots \leq d_{\pi(M)u}$, $d_u(\alpha) := d_{\pi(m^*)u}$, where $m^* := \min\{m : \sum_{i=1}^{m} x_{\pi(i)u} \geq \alpha\}$. If edge server $m$ and user $u$ satisfy $0 < x_{u,m} < 1$ in the fractional solution $(x, z)$, edge server $m$ is fractionally connected to user $u$.

The edge servers are sorted in the non-ascending order of the distance to user $u$, and $\pi(i^*)$ is the first edge server satisfying $\sum_{i=1}^{m} x_{\pi(i)u} > \alpha$.

We denote $F_{u'}$ as the edge server fractionally connected with user $u'$, and $G_{u'}$ (including $u'$) as the set of users fractionally connected with the edge server in $F_{u'}$.

Algorithm 1 shows the process of JMB. First, JMB solves the relaxed problem (Lines 1–2). JMB randomly chooses $\alpha$ which is uniformly distributed in $(\beta, 1)$, and solves the linear programming problem (11) (such as the simplex method) to obtain the optimal solution $(x^*, z^*)$. Second, JMB modifies the fractional optimal solution (Lines 3–16). For each user $u$, JMB computes $d_u(\alpha)$, where $d_u(\alpha) := d_{\pi(m*)u}$ and $m* := \min\{m : \sum_{i=1}^{m} x_{\pi(i)u} \geq \alpha\}$, and then computes $\beta_u^\alpha$ for

**Algorithm 1. JMB**

---

**Input:** Parameter $\beta \in (0,1)$.
**Output:** Integer feasible solution $(\hat{x}, \hat{z})$.
1: Randomly choose $\alpha$ that follows a uniform distribution on $(\beta, 1)$;
2: Solve problem (13) to obtain $(x^*, z^*)$;
3: **for** $u \in U$ **do**
4:     Calculate $d_u(\alpha)$;
5: **end for**
6: **for** $u \in U$ **do**
7:     Compute $\beta_u^\alpha := \sum\limits_{i=1}^{m^*} x^*_{\pi(i)u} \geq \alpha$;
8:     **for** $m \in M$ **do**
9:         **if** $d_{u,m} \leq d_u(\alpha)$ **then**
10:             $\bar{x}_{u,m} := \frac{x^*_{u,m}}{\beta_u^\alpha}$;
11:         **else**
12:             $\bar{x}_{u,m} := 0$;
13:         **end if**
14:     **end for**
15: **end for**
16: $\bar{z}_m := z^*_m$;
17: **for** $u \in U$ **do**
18:     $F_u := \{m \in M : \bar{x}_{u,m} > 0\}$;
19: **end for**
20: $U' := \varnothing$;
21: **while** $U \neq \varnothing$ **do**
22:     $u' := \arg\min\{d_u(\alpha)\}$, where $u'$ is the cluster center;
23:     $U' := U' \cup \{u'\}$;
24:     $G_{u'} := \{u \in U : F_u \cap F_{u'} \neq \varnothing\}$;
25:     $U := U \backslash G_{u'}$;
26: **end while**
27: **for** $u' \in U'$ **do**
28:     **for** $u \in G_{u'}$ **do**
29:         Connect $u$ to the nearest edge server, and the corresponding integer feasible solution is denoted as $(\hat{x}, \hat{z})$;
30:     **end for**
31: **end for**
32: **return** $(\hat{x}, \hat{z})$.

---

each user $u$ based on $\beta_u^\alpha := \sum\limits_{i=1}^{m^*} x^*_{\pi(i)u} \geq \alpha$. JMB modifies the fractional optimal solution $(x^*, z^*)$ by comparing $d_{u,m}$ and $d_u(\alpha)$, and obtains the corresponding feasible fractional solution $(\bar{x}, \bar{z})$. Third, JMB forms the initial clusters (Lines 17–26). For each user $u$, JMB computes the set $F_u$ of edge servers fractionally connected with $u$. In the unassigned user set $U$, JMB selects user $u'$ with the smallest $d_u(\alpha)$ as the cluster center. JMB works out the set $G_{u'}$ of users fractionally connected with the edge server in $F_{u'}$, and removes the users in set $G_{u'}$ from $U$. We call $(\{u'\}, F_{u'}, G_{u'})$ the initial cluster centered on $u'$. The process of the third stage is repeated until $U$ is empty (each node is put into an initial cluster). Finally, JMB maps the users to the edge servers (Lines 27–31). For each cluster, JMB connects the users in each initial cluster to the nearest edge server in the cluster to obtain a feasible integer solution that satisfies the relaxed constraints.

## 4.2   Algorithm Analysis

Based on the feasible solution obtained by Algorithm 1, we denote the total computing latency of edge servers as $Z$ ($Z = \sum\limits_{m \in M} a_m \hat{z}_m$) and the total network delay caused by task offloading as $X$ ($X = \sum\limits_{m \in M} \sum\limits_{u \in U} d_{u,m} x_{u,m}$).

**Lemma 1.** *In the computing resource allocation scheme obtained by Algorithm 1, the total computing latency of edge servers satisfies:*

$$Z \le \frac{1}{\alpha} \sum_{m \in M} a_m z_m^* \tag{14}$$

*Proof.* From Algorithm 1, it can be concluded that $\{F_{u'}\}_{u' \in U'}$ is mutually disjoint. Each edge server exists independently, and $(\bar{x}, \bar{z})$ is feasible. Therefore,

$$
\begin{aligned}
Z &= \sum_{u' \in U'} a_m \le \sum_{u' \in U'} \sum_{m \in F_{u'}} a_m \bar{x}_{u',m} < \sum_{u' \in U'} \sum_{m \in F_{u'}} a_m \bar{z}_m \\
&< \frac{1}{\alpha} \sum_{u' \in U'} \sum_{m \in F_{u'}} a_m z_m^* \le \frac{1}{\alpha} \sum_{m \in M} a_m z_m^*
\end{aligned}
\tag{15}
$$

The lemma is proven.

It can be seen from Algorithm 1 that the number of edge servers is always no less than the number of clusters, and each cluster has users offloading the computing tasks to the edge servers. The number of edge servers in a cluster is no less than 1, and always less than the number of users.

**Lemma 2.** $d_u(\alpha) \le \dfrac{1}{1-\alpha} \sum\limits_{m \in M} d_{u,m} x_{u,m}^*.$

*Proof.* From the definition of $d_u(\alpha)$, we obtain:

$$\sum_{i=m^*}^{M} x_{\pi(i)u}^* \ge 1 - \alpha \tag{16}$$

Therefore,

$$
\begin{aligned}
d_u(\alpha) &\le \frac{1}{1-\alpha} \sum_{i=m^*}^{M} d_{\pi(i)u} x_{\pi(i)u}^* \le \frac{1}{1-\alpha} \sum_{i=1}^{M} d_{\pi(i)u} x_{\pi(i)u}^* \\
&= \frac{1}{1-\alpha} \sum_{m \in M} d_{u,m} x_{u,m}^*
\end{aligned}
\tag{17}
$$

The lemma is proven.

**Lemma 3.** *In the computing resource allocation scheme obtained by Algorithm 1, the total network delay caused by task offloading satisfies*

$$X \le \frac{3}{1-\alpha} \sum_{m \in M} \sum_{u \in U} d_{u,m} x_{u,m}^* \tag{18}$$

*Proof.* For any user $u \in U$, we consider the following two cases.

(1) Case 1: $u \in U'$. We connect $u$ to the edge server with the least network delay, and hence the network delay incurred by the task offloading decision of $u$ does not exceed $d_u(\alpha)$.

(2) Case 2: $u \notin U'$. It can be obtained from Step 4 of Algorithm 1 that there exists $u \in U'$, $\tilde{m} \in N_{u'} \cap N_u$ and $u \in G_{u'}$. We connect $u$ to $m'$. According to the triangle inequality and Lemma 2, we can know that the network delay incurred by the task offloading decision of $u$, i.e., $d_{m',u}$, satisfies

$$d_{m',u} \le d_{m',u'} + d_{\tilde{m},u'} + d_{\tilde{m},u} \le 2d_{u'}(\alpha) + d_u(\alpha) \le 3d_u(\alpha)$$
$$\le \frac{3}{1-\alpha} \sum_{m \in M} d_{u,m} x_{u,m}^* \tag{19}$$

The lemma is proven from the above two cases. $\qquad\blacksquare$

From Lemma 1 and Lemma 3, we can derive:

$$Z + X + e \le \frac{1}{\alpha} \sum_{m \in M} a_m z_m^* + e + \frac{3}{1-\alpha} \sum_{m \in M} \sum_{u \in U} d_{u,m} x_{u,m}^* \tag{20}$$

**Lemma 4.** *For any user $u$, we have*

$$\int_0^1 d_u(\alpha) d\alpha = \sum_{m=1}^M d_{u,m} x_{u,m}^* \tag{21}$$

*Proof.* Without loss of generality, we assume $d_{u,1} \le d_{u,2} \le \dots \le d_{u,M}$, and let $m_1 < m_2 < \dots < m_i$ be all the edge servers satisfying the condition of $x_{u,m}^* > 0$. Let $x_{u,m_0}^* = 0$, and then function $d_u(\alpha)$ is a step function.

$$d_u(\alpha) = d_{u,m_k}, \alpha \in \left(\sum_{s=0}^{k-1} x_{u,m_s}^*, \sum_{s=1}^k x_{u,m_s}^*\right], k = 1, \dots, i \tag{22}$$

We verify (22) through the following two value ranges of $\alpha$.

First, we assume that the value of $\alpha$ satisfies $\alpha \in (0, x_{u,m_1}^*]$. According to the definitions $d_u(\alpha) := d_{\pi(m*)u}$ and $m* := \min\{m : \sum_{i=1}^m x_{\pi(i)u} \ge \alpha\}$ of $d_u(\alpha)$, we know $m_1 = \min\{m : \sum_{i=1}^m x_{\pi(i)u} \ge \alpha\}$. Therefore, the value of $d_u(\alpha)$ is $d_{u,m_1}$ and the value of $k$ is 1, satisfying (22).

Second, we assume that the value of $\alpha$ satisfies $\alpha \in (x^*_{u,m_1}, x^*_{u,m_1} + x^*_{u,m_2}]$. According to the definitions of $d_u(\alpha)$, we know $m_2 = \min\{m : \sum\limits_{i=1}^{m} x_{\pi(i)u} \geq \alpha\}$. Therefore, the value of $d_u(\alpha)$ is $d_{u,m_2}$ and the value of $k$ is 2, satisfying (22).

The analysis of the other values of $\alpha$ within $(0,1)$ is similar to that above, and we omit the analysis.

According to the geometric meaning of definite integral, we derive

$$\int_0^1 d_u(\alpha)d\alpha = \sum_{k=1}^{i} d_{u,m_k} x^*_{u,m_k} = \sum_{m=1}^{M} d_{u,m} x^*_{u,m} \tag{23}$$

The lemma is proven.

**Theorem 1.** *Let $\beta = e^{-3}$, and the expected delay of the feasible solution obtained by Algorithm 1 does not exceed 3.16 times the optimal solution to the problem defined as (12).*

*Proof.* For a given $\alpha$ from Lemma 1 and Lemma 3, we know that the delay of the solution obtained by Algorithm 1 dose not exceed $\frac{1}{\alpha} \sum\limits_{m \in M} a_m z^*_m + 3 \sum\limits_{u \in U} d_u(\alpha)$.

Therefore, the expectation of the delay of the solution obtained by Algorithm 1 does not exceed

$$E[\frac{1}{\alpha} \sum_{m \in M} a_m z^*_m + 3 \sum_{u \in U} d_u(\alpha)]$$

$$= E[\frac{1}{\alpha}] \sum_{m \in M} a_m z^*_m + 3 \sum_{u \in U} E[d_u(\alpha)]$$

$$= \int_\beta^1 \frac{1}{1-\beta} \frac{1}{\alpha} d\alpha \sum_{m \in M} a_m z^*_m + 3 \sum_{u \in U} (\int_\beta^1 \frac{1}{1-\beta} d_u(\alpha)d\alpha)$$

$$\leq \frac{\ln(1/\beta)}{1-\beta} \sum_{m \in M} a_m z^*_m + \frac{3}{1-\beta} \sum_{u \in U} \int_0^1 d_u(\alpha)d\alpha \tag{24}$$

$$= \frac{\ln(1/\beta)}{1-\beta} \sum_{m \in M} a_m z^*_m + \frac{3}{1-\beta} \sum_{u \in U} \sum_{m \in M} d_{u,m} x^*_{u,m}$$

$$\leq \max\{\frac{\ln(1/\beta)}{1-\beta}, \frac{3}{1-\beta}\}(\sum_{m \in M} a_m z^*_m + \sum_{u \in U} \sum_{m \in M} d_{u,m} x^*_{u,m})$$

When $\beta = e^{-3}$, we have

$$\frac{\ln(1/\beta)}{1-\beta} = \frac{3}{1-\beta} = \frac{3}{1-e^{-3}} \leq 3.16 \tag{25}$$

For any user $u$, $d_u(\alpha)$ is a step function. By examining the function values at all segment points, $\alpha$ can be chosen such that $\frac{1}{\alpha} \sum\limits_{m \in M} a_m z^*_m + 3 \sum\limits_{u \in U} d_u(\alpha)$ reaches the minimum value, and we obtain

$$\frac{1}{\alpha} \sum_{m \in M} a_m z_m^* + 3 \sum_{u \in U} d_u(\alpha)$$

$$\leq E[\frac{1}{\alpha} \sum_{m \in M} a_m z_m^* + 3 \sum_{u \in U} d_u(\alpha)] \leq 3.16 (\sum_{m \in M} a_m z_m^* + \sum_{m \in M} \sum_{u \in U} d_{u,m} x_{u,m}^*)$$

$$(26)$$

The theorem is proven.

**Theorem 2.** *Algorithm 1 is a 3.16-approximation algorithm for the problem of user offloading decision and the computing resource allocation of edge servers for MEC and blockchain tasks.*

*Proof.* According to the feasible integer solution $(\hat{x}, \hat{z})$ obtained by Algorithm 1, the values of all $x_{u,m}$ and $z_m$ can be known. We can calculate the value of $y_m$ by taking $z_m$ into (10). In the interval $(0, 1)$, one $z_m$ value may correspond to two $y_m$ values at the same time. If and only if $y_m$ has two values in the interval $(0, 1)$, without loss of generality, we choose to take the larger number of the two, since taking either of the two corresponding values of $y_m$ has no influence on the feasible solution $(\hat{x}, \hat{z})$. Therefore, we can obtain the feasible solution to the problem defined as (8). That is, Algorithm 1 is a 3.16-Approximate algorithm for the problem of user offloading decision and the computing resource allocation of edge servers for MEC and blockchain tasks.

The theorem is proven.

## 5  Performance Evaluation

### 5.1  Experimental Setup

In the experiments, we consider a blockchain-based MEC system, which includes 40 users and 5 edge servers. The parameters of the system are shown in Table 2. We evaluate the performance of JMB by using the following 2 benchmark algorithms: FMB and RMB.

(1) FMB [18]: The edge servers allocate computing resources to MEC and blockchain tasks at a fixed ratio, i.e., (0.7:0.3), and FMB uses the users' offloading decision obtained by JMB.
(2) RMB [20]: Each user randomly selects an edge server to offload the task and the edge servers allocate computing resources in the same way as JMB.

### 5.2  Total Processing Latency of MEC and Blockchain Tasks

Figure 2 shows the impact of different numbers of users on the total system latency caused by each algorithm, when the number of users varies from 20 to 100. It can be observed that the total delay incurred by JMB, FMB and RMB

**Table 2.** Table of simulation parameters

| Simulation Parameters | Ranges |
|---|---|
| Bandwidth $B_m$ | 179 KHz - 180 KHz [5] |
| Computing task size $l_u$ | 200 KB-1000 KB [13] |
| Noise power $\theta^2$ | −174 dBm/Hz [15] |
| The transmission rate of the link in the blockchain network $C$ | $15 * 10^6$ bit/s [15] |
| The number of CPU cycles required for 1 bit $f_m$ | 995 cycle/bit - 1000 cycle/bit [13] |
| Block size, $S_b$ | 8 MB [13] |
| The CPU cycle frequency of edge server, $F$ | 16 GHz [21] |

increases with the increase of the number of users. More computing tasks need to be run with more users. Therefore, each edge server needs to execute more computing tasks, resulting in an increase in the total system latency.

In Fig. 2, both FMB and RMB incur a higher total latency than JMB at a given number of users. The total system latency obtained by JMB is approximately 92% of that by FMB and 93% of that by RMB. As the number of users increases, the number of computing tasks each edge server needs to process increases. RMB uses a random policy to make the user offloading decisions, and does not make a reasonable offloading decision based on the network latency between the users and the edge servers. Each edge server in FMB does not allocate the computing resources appropriately based on the processing capability of the edge servers and the task sizes. Therefore, as the number of computing tasks in the system increases, JMB can always execute more tasks in a given amount of time. Figure 3 shows the impact of the number of edge servers on the total latency in blockchain-based MEC, where the number of edge servers increases from 3 to 7. The results show the total latency of JMB and FMB decreases as the number of edge servers increases. The total computing power within the system

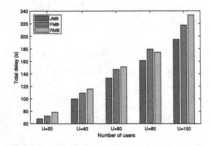

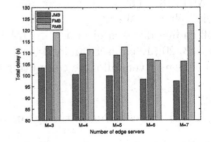

**Fig. 2.** The impact of the number of users on the total latency.

**Fig. 3.** The impact of the number of edge servers on total latency.

increases with the increasing number of the edge servers, and hence the system can execute more user tasks. Therefore, the total latency of the system decreases as the number of edge servers increases. However, as the number of edge servers continues to increase, the total latency decreases slowly, since the users have a limited resource requirement from the edge servers. Therefore, the reduce in the total latency is not significant with the continuous increase of the number of edge servers. RMB randomly selects the edge servers for the users, and the computing tasks are not necessarily offloaded to the newly added edge servers with the increasing number of edge servers. Therefore, the total system latency of RMB does not always decrease as the number of edge servers increases.

In Fig. 3, JMB always obtains the lowest total system delay. In addition, the total latency of JMB is about 9% and 8% lower than that of RMB and FMB, respectively. As the number of edge servers increases, the number of task offloading options available to the users in the system increases. Compared with the other two algorithms, JMB can offload the tasks to the edge servers that are appropriate for the whole system according to the users' tasks and network latency. For each edge server, a reasonable proportion of computing resources is allocated to the MEC and the blockchain tasks, respectively, according to the processing rate of the edge servers and the task sizes. Therefore, JMB can make better use of the edge servers than FMB and RMB. As a result, JMB obtains the lowest total system latency. Figure 4 shows the impact of users' computational tasks on the total latency incurred by each algorithm. It can be seen that the total delay of the three algorithms increases with the increase of users' computing task sizes. The edge servers need more time to process the users' tasks, when the sizes of users' tasks increase. As a result, the total latency also increases.

Figure 4 shows that the delay incurred by algorithm JMB is always less than that by FMB and RMB. The total latency of JMB is less than that of FMB by 5.0%, 7.1%, 8.3%, 9.1%, and 9.6%, and less than that of RMB by 8.0%, 11.5%, 16.4%, 17.2%, and 14.5%, when the task size is 200KB, 400KB, 600KB, 800KB, and 1000KB, respectively. JMB takes into account the sizes of users' tasks and the transmission rate between edge servers, when selecting edge servers for users to offload computing tasks. Therefore, with the increase of users' computing task sizes, JMB significantly reduces the transmission delay of the system compared with RMB. JMB allocates computing resources according to the sizes of the users' tasks processed by edge servers tasks. Compared with FMB, JMB allocates the computing resources more reasonably and efficiently.

Figure 5 shows the impact of the number of clock cycles that the edge server takes to process 1 bit of data ($f_m$) on the total latency of the blockchain-based MEC system. Figure 5 shows that the total delay of each algorithm increases with the increase of the number of clock cycles that the edge servers process 1 bit data. $f_m$ affects the speed of task processing. A small value of $f_m$ means that the edge server will spend less CPU cycles on processing users' and blockchain tasks. Therefore, the total latency obtained by each algorithm increases with the increase of the number of clock cycles of the edge servers processing 1 bit data.

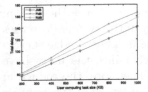 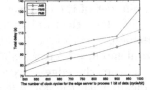 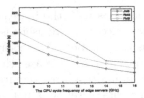

**Fig. 4.** The impact of user computing task size on total latency.

**Fig. 5.** The impact of the number of clock cycles that the edge server processes 1 bit data on the total delay.

**Fig. 6.** The impact of CPU cycle frequency on the total system latency.

As can be seen from Fig. 5, the total system delay of JMB is lower than that of FMB and RMB. When $f_m$ is 900 and 1000, the total system latency of JMB is respectively 8.0% and 8.5% lower than that of FMB. When $f_m$ is 800 and 1000, JMB's total system latency is respectively 12.8% and 15.8% lower than RMB's. JMB makes the user offload decision based on $f_m$ and the transmission rate of sending the user's task to the edge server. For each user, JMB arranges the most reasonable edge servers for task offloading, reducing the total delay of task transmission and task processing in the system. Therefore, the performance of RMB is inferior to that of JMB. In addition, JMB adjusts the computing resource allocation ratio based on $f_m$. As a result, JMB's total system latency is lower than FMB's.

Figure 6 illustrates the impact of the edge server's CPU cycle frequency on the total system delay. Obviously, the total latency of each algorithm decreases with the increase of the edge server CPU cycle frequency. The higher the CPU cycle frequency, the stronger the computing power of the edge server, and the faster the processing of MEC and blockchain tasks. As a result, the latency of each algorithm decreases as the CPU cycle frequency increases. Therefore, the total latency of each algorithm decreases with the increase of the edge server CPU cycle frequency.

Figure 6 demonstrates that the total system latency of JMB is always lower than that of FMB and RMB. JMB achieves lower total system latency than FMB by up to 10%. The total system latency of JMB is better than that of RMB by up to 30%. JMB optimizes users' offloading decisions and dynamically adjusts the computing resource allocation for the MEC and the blockchain tasks based on the processing rate of the edge servers and the transmission delay between the users and the edge servers. Therefore, JMB can reduce the network delay and processing latency of users' tasks in the blockchain-based MEC system, which makes JMB achieve better performance than RMB and FMB.

## 6   Conclusions

In this paper, we studied the problem of user offloading decision and the computing resource allocation of edge servers for MEC and blockchain tasks, with the objective to minimize the total processing delay of MEC and blockchain tasks in blockchain-based MEC. We proposed an algorithm for joint computing resource allocation for MEC and blockchain (JMB) which consists of 5 steps. First, JMB relaxes the problem constraints to obtain the relaxed problem. Second, JMB solves the relaxed problem and obtains the fractional optimal solution. Third, JMB modifies the fractional optimal solution to obtain the feasible fractional solution. Fourth, JMB performs the clustering operation on the users and the edge servers according to the feasible fractional solution to form multiple initial clusters. Finally, JMB maps the users to the edge servers in each initial cluster and obtains the feasible integer solution satisfying the relaxed constraints. Theoretical analysis proved that JMB is a 3.16-approximation algorithm. The simulation results demonstrated that JMB could achieve the favorable balance between the MEC and the blockchain task processing. JMB obtains superior performance in terms of total system latency under different parameters of the number of users, the sizes of user tasks, the number of clock cycles that the edge server processes 1 bit data, the number of edge servers, and the CPU cycle frequency of edge servers.

# References

1. Rahman, M.A., et al.: Blockchain-based mobile edge computing framework for secure therapy applications. IEEE Access **6**, 72469–72478 (2018)
2. Chang, Z., Guo, W., Guo, X., Zhou, Z., Ristaniemi, T.: Incentive mechanism for edge-computing-based blockchain. IEEE Trans. Industr. Inf. **16**(11), 7105–7114 (2020)
3. Cui, L., et al.: A blockchain-based containerized edge computing platform for the Internet of vehicles. IEEE Internet Things J. **8**(4), 2395–2408 (2020)
4. Demers, A.J., et al.: Epidemic algorithms for replicated database maintenance. In: Proceedings of the Sixth Annual ACM Symposium on Principles of Distributed Computing, pp. 1–12. ACM, Vancouver, British Columbia, Canada, August 1987
5. Du, J., Zhao, L., Chu, X., Yu, F.R., Feng, J., I, C.L.: Enabling low-latency applications in LTE-A based mixed fog/cloud computing systems. IEEE Trans. Veh. Technolo. 68(2), 1757–1771 (2018)
6. Fan, Y., Wang, L., Wu, W., Du, D.: Cloud/edge computing resource allocation and pricing for mobile blockchain: an iterative greedy and search approach. IEEE Trans. Comput. Soc. Syst. **8**(2), 1–13 (2021)
7. He, Y., Wang, Y., Qiu, C., Qiuzhen Lin, Li, J., Ming, Z.: Blockchain-based edge computing resource allocation in IoT: a deep reinforcement learning approach. IEEE Internet Things J. **8**(4), 2226–2237 (2020)
8. Jiao, Y., Wang, P., Niyato, D., Suankaewmanee, K.: Auction mechanisms in cloud/fog computing resource allocation for public blockchain networks. IEEE Trans. Parallel Distrib. Syst. **30**(9), 1975–1989 (2019)
9. Kang, J., et al.: Blockchain for secure and efficient data sharing in vehicular edge computing and networks. IEEE Internet Things J. **6**(3), 4660–4670 (2018)
10. Li, Z., Kang, J., Yu, R., Ye, D., Deng, Q., Zhang, Y.: Consortium blockchain for secure energy trading in industrial Internet of Things. IEEE Trans. Indus. Inform. **14**(8), 3690–3700 (2017)

11. Liu, M., Yu, F.R., Teng, Y., Leung, V.C.M., Song, M.: Computation offloading and content caching in wireless blockchain networks with mobile edge computing. IEEE Trans. Veh. Technol. **67**(11), 11008–11021 (2018)
12. Mengting Liu, Yu, F.R., Teng, Y., Leung, V.C.M., Song, M.: Distributed resource allocation in blockchain-based video streaming systems with mobile edge computing. IEEE Trans. Wirel. Commun. **18**(1), 695–708 (2018)
13. Liu, M., Yu, F.R., Teng, Y., Leung, V.C.M., Song, M.: Performance optimization for blockchain-enabled industrial Internet of things (IIoT) systems: a deep reinforcement learning approach. IEEE Trans. Indus. Inform. **15**(6), 3559–3570 (2019)
14. Ma, Z., Wang, X., Jain, D.K., Khan, H., Gao, H., Wang, Z.: A blockchain-based trusted data management scheme in edge computing. IEEE Trans. Indus. Inf. **16**(3), 2013–2021 (2020)
15. Mao, Y., Zhang, J., Song, S., Letaief, K.B.: Stochastic joint radio and computational resource management for multi-user mobile-edge computing systems. IEEE Trans. Wirel. Commun. **16**(9), 5994–6009 (2017)
16. Sharma, V., You, I., Palmieri, F., Jayakody, D.N.K., Li, J.: Secure and energy-efficient handover in fog networks using blockchain-based DMM. IEEE Commun. Mag. **56**(5), 22–31 (2018)
17. Suankaewmanee, K., et al.: Performance analysis and application of mobile blockchain. In: 2018 International Conference on Computing. Networking and Communications, ICNC, pp. 642–646. IEEE Computer Society, Maui, HI, USA, March 2018
18. Tang, Q., Fei, Z., Zheng, J., Li, B., Guo, L., Wang, J.: Secure aerial computing: convergence of mobile edge computing and blockchain for UAV networks. IEEE Trans. Veh. Technol. **71**(11), 12073–12087 (2022)
19. Xiao, L., Ding, Y., Jiang, D., Huang, J., Wang, D., Li, J., Vincent Poor, H.: A reinforcement learning and blockchain-based trust mechanism for edge networks. IEEE Trans. Commun. **68**(9), 5460–5470 (2020)
20. Xu, S., et al.: Deep reinforcement learning assisted edge-terminal collaborative offloading algorithm of blockchain computing tasks for energy Internet. Int. J. Elect. Power Energy Syst. **131**, 107022 (2021)
21. Xu, Y., Zhang, H., Ji, H., Yang, L., Li, X., Leung, V.C.M.: Transaction throughput optimization for integrated blockchain and MEC system in IoT. IEEE Trans. Wirel. Commun. **21**(2), 1022–1036 (2021)
22. Yu, W., et al.: A survey on the edge computing for the Internet of Things. IEEE Access **6**, 6900–6919 (2018)

# Blockchain-Based EMR Enhancement: Introducing PMI-Chain for Improved Medical Data Security and Privacy

Bo Cui$^{(\boxtimes)}$ , Tianyu Mei, and Xu Liu

Inner Mongolia University, Inner Mongolia Key Laboratory of Wireless Networking and Mobile Computing, Hohhot 010021, China
cscb@imu.edu.cn

**Abstract.** We have created a solution called PMI-Chain to address the challenges faced by Electronic Medical Records (EMR) management systems. These challenges include data security, patient privacy, and access regulation, which are becoming increasingly complex. PMI-Chain is a blockchain-based system that aims to tackle these issues. Traditional EMR systems rely on centralized medical data storage, exposing them to risks such as cyberattacks and data breaches and reducing patient autonomy over their medical records. PMI-Chain is a secure and confidential data-sharing platform for patients, medical institutions, and insurance companies. It uses token-based smart contracts and dual ElGamal homomorphic encryption to protect vast amounts of medical data while allowing for reliable sharing among institutions. Patients have control over their encrypted medical records, and an advanced encryption scheme keeps their information private during insurance claim processing. PMI-Chain has undergone security analysis and testing, showcasing its robust security features and exceptional stability. Additionally, compared to other available solutions, it boasts a 44% and 67% reduction in encryption and decryption time overhead.

**Keywords:** Blockchain · EMR · Access control · Homomorphic cryptosystem

## 1 Introduction

In this rapidly advancing information technology age, Electronic Medical Record (EMR) management systems [1] have become essential components of contemporary medical institutions. These systems are essential as they integrate diverse patient data elements such as diagnostic imaging, detailed clinical narratives, expert assessments, and familial genetic patterns [2]. It is important to note that electronic medical records are not only accessible to doctors but also to external entities like insurance companies. This can cause data security, patient privacy, and access regulation issues. As medical institutions adopt these technologies,

© ICST Institute for Computer Sciences, Social Informatics and Telecommunications Engineering 2024
Published by Springer Nature Switzerland AG 2024. All Rights Reserved
H. Gao et al. (Eds.): CollaborateCom 2023, LNICST 561, pp. 207–224, 2024.
https://doi.org/10.1007/978-3-031-54521-4_12

they face challenges that intersect with technological innovation, privacy, and compliance with regulations.

EMR systems have a central medical data storage that can be vulnerable to cyberattacks and data breaches, posing significant risks. One major concern is that patients do not have control over their medical records, which are stored in different EMR systems used by various medical institutions. This fragmentation hinders patients' direct access to and controls over their records. Additionally, patient privacy concerns frequently inhibit data sharing and interoperability between medical entities [3]. This obstruction of data flow can cause diagnostic redundancy when patients switch medical institutions, leading to an inefficient allocation of medical resources [4]. Moreover, EMR system administrators within these institutions can directly manipulate medical data, potentially facilitating fraudulent acts like insurance fraud, leading to financial losses. In addition, there is a risk of patient privacy being breached when insurance companies and other non-medical entities handle claims and review medical records. These challenges emphasize the importance of thoroughly assessing current EMR systems and developing innovative solutions that balance data accessibility, security, and patient privacy.

Numerous medical data management systems today strive to overcome previously mentioned challenges. However, despite their efforts, they often fail to meet the rigorous demands of reliability, security, and traceability crucial to medical data systems. The innovative evolution of blockchain technology emerges as a fitting solution to these issues. Blockchain's verifiability, decentralization, and immutability features [5] closely align with the pressing need for secure storage of individual health records. In a regulated blockchain system, the distributed ledger, maintained by multiple organizations, ensures medical data protection within the chain, facilitating sharing across different medical institutions. In the blockchain, every transaction within a block is given a unique timestamp and added to the chain in a way that cannot be altered. This ensures that medical data is valid and authentic, making blockchain a promising addition to EMR technology [6]. However, blockchain's inherent transparency poses concerns for the security of private data on the chain. Therefore, applying blockchain technology in the medical sector requires a careful equilibrium between data security and privacy.

Our paper presents PMI-Chain, a secure and confidential data-sharing platform for patients, medical institutions, and insurers. With PMI-Chain, we ensure fine-grained access control through token-based blockchain smart contracts. Patients can use tokens to retrieve their encrypted medical records from the smart contracts, which are encrypted using Elliptic Curve Cryptography (ECC) and symmetric keys. Patients can authenticate their records by matching the hash values stored within the blockchain network. Additionally, we integrate dual ElGamal homomorphic encryption technology with the blockchain smart contract to encrypt claim materials and amounts, enabling non-plaintext verification of health insurance claims. Another noteworthy contribution of PMI-Chain is its ability to facilitate secure data sharing between healthcare institutions, further enhancing patient care. This paper's main contributions include:

- The proposed platform is a secure and trustworthy medical information service that integrates patients, medical institutions, and insurance agencies. It is based on blockchain technology and smart contracts, ensuring medical data's authenticity. This interactive system offers a collaborative environment for studying medical-patient insurance.
- We propose a smart contract access control system that uses tokens to control access to encrypted medical data. This system allows for fine-grained control of patient information updates and improves the speed and efficiency of the access policy process. This system can securely store and share medical data between institutions.
- Our secure request system uses advanced homomorphic cryptography and improved ElGamal cryptography. This enables insurers to settle medical claims encrypted, ensuring patient privacy is protected from potential privacy violations.
- We have conducted a security analysis of PMI-Chain and found that it meets various security standards. It can also handle threats like illegal collaborations between doctors and clouds. Our tests have shown that PMI-Chain has a 44% lower encryption and a 67% lower decryption time overhead, and more stable performance than existing methods.

The rest of this paper is organized as follows. We introduce the related work in Sects. 2. We present the PMI-Chain in detail in Sect. 3. The correctness, security, privacy and efficiency analysis are described in Sect. 4. Finally, we conclude this paper in Sect. 5.

## 2   Related Work

The digital transformation of healthcare has significantly impacted the way medical resources are allocated. Electronic Medical Records (EMR), celebrated for their instantaneous data exchange, seamless integration into healthcare workflows, and intuitive interfaces, have seen a remarkable evolution in recent years [7,8]. In their work, Li et al. [7] highlighted the semi-trusted cloud computing environments equipped with multi-level permissions. These environments seek to mitigate the risk of unauthorized access, managing an array of user role attributes via multiple permissions. The transition from conventional data centers to cloud servers, facilitated by cost-effective and secure cloud storage, has given rise to a cloud-augmented EMR architecture. This transition propels a significant surge in work efficiency. However, the involvement of third-party cloud providers may pose threats to the privacy, confidentiality, and integrity of the data. Moreover, the inherent security risks associated with cloud computing environments can lead to potential data loss. With the continuous advancement of blockchain technology, an increasing amount of research is being dedicated to its feasible application within EMR systems.

Azaria et al. [3] introduced MedRec, a prototype for distributed medical information sharing on the Ethereum platform utilizing blockchain smart contracts.

This system kept chain data in a third-party database and relied on identity verification mechanisms to ensure the accuracy and integrity of outsourced EMR. However, it could not safeguard the security of the third-party database, nor prevent unethical practices like encouraging cloud servers to alter EMR data. Cao et al. [9] proposed a solution to such issues with a secure, cloud-assisted EMR. This strategy employed an Ethereum-based blockchain to protect outsourced medical data, thereby reducing the likelihood of third-party manipulation or corruption, but it resulted in patients losing control and ownership of their medical data. Attempting to address this, Saini et al. [10] developed a distributed dynamic access control mechanism using smart contracts, empowering patients with ownership and secure sharing of their sensitive health records. However, this solution did not support inter-institutional EMR sharing. To mitigate these limitations, Fengqi et al. [2] proposed a method incorporating semi-strategy hiding and partial ciphertext CP-ABE for dynamic permission changes (SHDPCPC-CP-ABE). This strategy allowed fine-grained access control for encrypted medical data, facilitating safe exchange of health information among medical entities.

Privacy of medical data is a major concern in the healthcare industry. As blockchain technology is applied to the medical field, a balance must be struck between data security and data privacy. Research on privacy protection for blockchain-based EMR is generally divided into encryption-based and access control-based privacy protection. In the former, Benil et al. [11] devised an enhanced Elliptic Curve Cryptography (ECC) digital signature algorithm, employing Message Authentication Codes to encrypt medical data stored in the cloud for confidentiality. However, in data-sharing scenarios such as big data analysis in healthcare and insurance claim settlements, data availability must be ensured. Ding et al. [12] constructed Derepo, a private data safe storage and sharing model based on blockchain and homomorphic encryption technology, achieving privacy protection and data computability through the introduction of homomorphic encryption. On the other hand, access control-based privacy protection is exemplified by Zhang et al. [13] who proposed a blockchain-based fine-grained access control and permission revocation data sharing scheme, BDSS. It facilitated data sharing between medical institutions via fine-grained access control technology and safeguarded patient privacy through a permission revocation mechanism. However, in scenarios involving uncertain data sharers, it's impossible to predetermine access control policies. Dewangan et al. [14] proposed a data collection method based on the medical Internet of Things, generating unique tokens for users through their biometric features and random keys. This token-based design pattern enables secure access control to medical data without needing to determine data sharers in advance.

The analyses presented above underscore that data security and privacy protection remain crucial research topics for blockchain-based EMR systems. Despite various proposals, a comprehensive and secure medical data management system that accomplishes dynamic access control and privacy protection is yet to be realized. Most current systems do not fully address the data security and privacy breach issues that may arise during the three-way interactions among hospitals, patients, and insurance companies.

## 3   The Proposed PMI-Chain

### 3.1   Overview

In this section, we elaborate on the construction of PMI-Chain, which is built upon token-based smart contracts for access control and an improved version of ElGamal encryption. As depicted in Fig. 1, PMI-Chain comprises five entities: patients, hospitals, doctors, the blockchain, and smart contracts.

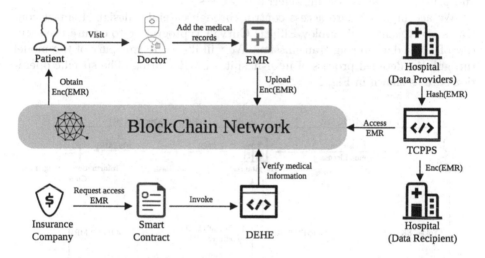

**Fig. 1.** The architecture of the PMI-Chain.

The PMI-Chain framework provides secure EMR management through a sequence of well-defined steps. Medical institutions generate and upload EMR to the blockchain for secure storage, based on patient authorization. Upon completing a diagnosis, physicians trigger a smart contract, which executes specific encryption processes, subsequently uploading the ciphertext to the blockchain. Patients then decrypt to access their updated medical records. When sharing information between medical institutions, hash medical data are exchanged via the blockchain. Patients possess exclusive Token tokens and ECC key pairs. The recipient retrieves the data using the Token and verifies it through a smart contract. Finally, patients use their private key to decrypt the data, ensuring secure retrieval. Insurance companies retrieve the EMR ciphertext via hash indices provided by medical institutions and validate these using claim verification smart contracts. Upon successful validation, a reimbursement calculation smart contract computes the claim amount. With this system, insurance claim processing can be accomplished through a homomorphic encryption system without accessing the plaintext of the medical records, thereby ensuring both operational efficiency and patient privacy.

## 3.2  Token-Based Access Control for Blockchain Smart Contracts

In the core research of secure medical data sharing, we have constructed a token-based blockchain smart contract access control privacy protection scheme (TBSC-ACPPS). This scheme integrates the concept of tokens from the Cap-BAC model, and uses smart contracts to manage EMR retrieval as well as token generation and distribution. Its aim is to enhance platform efficiency, reduce human errors, thereby providing an efficient strategy for medical data sharing and privacy protection during referral processes.

We accomplish secure access control through carefully designed smart contracts and tokens, and employ Elliptic Curve Cryptography to ensure the security of EMR data during transmission. We will illustrate this part of the model through the detailed process of inter-hospital EMR sharing. The specific operations are as shown in Fig. 2.

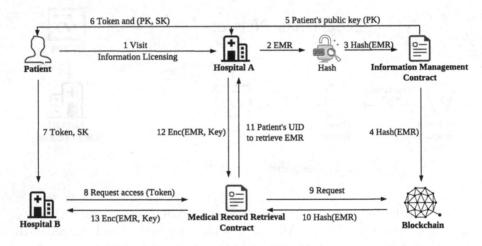

**Fig. 2.** Token-based access control for blockchain smart contracts.

Upon the conclusion of a patient's visit, the attending physician generates an EMR. This EMR undergoes a hash computation and is securely uploaded to the blockchain, with the smart contract producing a corresponding blockchain hash index. Simultaneously, a unique, patient-specific token and a cryptographic key pair are generated, with the public key sent directly to the initial hospital. In scenarios where the patient is referred to a different hospital, the incoming physician can retrieve the patient's EMR directly from the blockchain using this unique token. The smart contract verifies the patient's identity, accesses the blockchain-stored EMR hash with the token, and securely encrypts the EMR before transmission. If the EMR hashes align, the smart contract dispatches both the EMR cipher and key cipher to the new physician. The patient, with the private key, decrypts the data to access the EMR in plain text. A pivotal feature of our TBSC-ACPPS is the robust token-based access control module. This module, encompassing token generation, transfer, verification, and updating, significantly enhances the system's security, optimizes resource utilization, and assures the trustworthy sharing of EMRs, alongside comprehensive patient privacy protection.

**Smart Contract Design:** There are three smart contracts in TBSC-ACPPS, which are information management contract, medical record retrieval contract and token update contract.

*A. Information Management Contract.* The patient's EMR need to be stored as evidence in the blockchain. To speed up the process of uploading information and optimize storage space, the TBSC-ACPPS only uploads the SHA-256 hash value of the medical record information (*patient_EMRHash*) to the blockchain for storage.

$$patient\_EMRHash = SHA-256(patient\_EMR) \tag{1}$$

After the contract uploads *patient_EMRHash* to the blockchain network and obtains the hash index, it generates an ECC key pair $(PK, SK)$ and a unique Token for the patient, which is used for retrieving medical records.

The ECC key pair is generated by selecting a point $G$ on the elliptic curve $E$ as the generator and assuming the order of $G$ to be $n$, where $n$ is a prime number. Finally, a private key $k(k < n)$ is chosen to generate the public key $Q = kG$. The Token is the patient's exclusive Token, which includes the patient's unique identity (*patient_UId*), the on-chain hash value (*blockChain_hash*), the hospital's blockchain address (*hos_address*), and a timestamp (*time*), as demonstrated below:

$$Token = \{patient\_UId, blockChain\_hash, hos\_address, time\} \tag{2}$$

In the end, the contract sends the Token and the key pair $(PK, SK)$ to the patient, and also sends the public key $PK$ to the hospital. This allows for the encrypted transmission of subsequent medical records, ensuring the privacy of the patient during the transmission process.

*B. Medical Record Retrieval Contract.* When a patient seeks treatment in another hospital, there is a need to retrieve the medical records from the previous hospital. The patient gives the Token to the doctor who uses it through the smart contract to access the patient's medical history. Initially, the contract verifies the operator's permissions and the Token. If successful, the contract retrieves the medical record hash (*blockChain_EMRHash*) via the on-chain hash value index (*blockChain_hash*) in the Token and sends the patient identity marker (*patient_UId*) from the Token to the hospital using the hospital blockchain address (*hos_address*). The hospital then locates the original patient medical record via *patient_UId*, calculates the SHA-256 hash of the record, encrypts the original record using symmetric encryption, encrypts the symmetric key (*Key*) using the patient's public key (*PK*), and sends the medical record's hash value (*hos_EMRHash*), the encrypted medical record (*Enc(EMR)*), and the encrypted key (*Enc(Key)*) to the smart contract. Lastly, the contract compares the *blockChain_EMRHash* and *hos_EMRHash* from the blockchain. If they match, it proves that the medical record hasn't been tampered with, and the doctor receives the (*Enc(EMR)*) and (*Enc(Key)*) for the patient to decrypt using their private key (*SK*).

In the smart contract for retrieving medical records, the original (*patient_EMR*) is encrypted first using symmetric encryption to get *Enc(EMR)*:

$$Enc(EMR) = E(Key, patient\_EMR) \tag{3}$$

And the key is encrypted as follows:

$$\begin{aligned} Enc(Key) &= (Cipher1, Cipher2) \\ Cipher1 &= Key + rQ \\ Cipher2 &= rG \end{aligned} \tag{4}$$

where r is a random number ($r < n$, $n$ is the order of $G$), $Q$ is the patient's public *key*, and *Cipher1* and *Cipher2* are two ciphertexts. Subsequently, the patient uses their ECC private key (*SK*) to decrypt, obtaining the *patient_EMR*:

$$Cipher1 - k \times Cipher2 = Key + rQ - krG = Key + rkG - krG = Key \tag{5}$$

$$patient\_EMR = D(Key, Enc(EMR)) \tag{6}$$

where $k$ is the patient's private key (*SK*).

*C. Token Update Contract.* When a patient's Token expires, the patient can request the Token Update Contract to refresh their Token. Initially, the smart contract verifies whether the patient possesses the requisite authority to request the token, then proceeds to update the token, which includes refreshing the timestamp.

### 3.3 Privacy Protection via Dual ElGamal Encryption in Blockchain Smart Contracts

In insurance claim scenarios, fraudulent medical claims often occur due to the difficulty in verifying the authenticity of reimbursement data provided by patients. Furthermore, processing medical insurance claims requires accessing patients' reimbursement data for proof of claim, which risks leaking the patient's private information. To address these issues, we propose a dual ElGamal homomorphic encryption privacy protection scheme based on blockchain smart contracts (DEHE-BSC). Leveraging the tamper-proof and traceable nature of the blockchain provides secure evidence storage for reimbursement data, while smart contracts enable data to be recorded on-chain and facilitate claim data verification. The improved ElGamal homomorphic encryption technology is adopted to carry out medical insurance claims in ciphertext form, thereby safeguarding patient privacy.

We will describe a specific claims process to provide a detailed explanation of security claims. The specific steps are shown in Fig. 3.

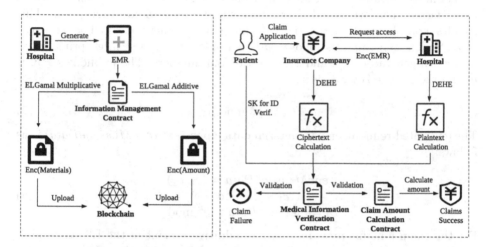

**Fig. 3.** Dual ElGamal homomorphic encryption privacy protection scheme based on blockchain smart contracts.

After the medical visit, the hospital generates the patient's EMR and activates the on-chain smart contract. This contract splits the EMR data and uses ElGamal homomorphic encryption to encrypt the minimal dataset required for insurance claims, along with the claim amount. These two encrypted pieces of data are then uploaded to the blockchain for secure storage. When a patient files a claim, the insurance company extracts the encrypted EMR data from the blockchain using the ciphertext hash value and executes a specific computation. The hospital performs the same operation on the corresponding plain-text EMR in its database. Both parties send their results to the claim verification smart contract, and the patient provides the decryption key. The contract automatically decrypts the insurance company's encrypted result and compares it with the hospital's plain-text result. If the results match, the claims smart contract retrieves the encrypted claim amount from the blockchain, performs the necessary computations, and finalizes the claim. If the results do not match, it indicates potential malicious tampering with the EMR data, and the insurance company may refuse the claim.

**Smart Contract Design:** The core content architecture of DEHE-BSC, which mainly includes the attestation of medical information verification, claim auxiliary verification, and claim amount calculation.

A. *Medical Information Verification Contract.* During the insurance claim process, insurance companies need to verify the authenticity of user data (*message*), as well as the accuracy of claim amounts. Considering the size and differing purposes of the data, to improve operational efficiency, the Medical Information Verification Contract splits the message into reimbursement data (*messageData*) and treatment cost (*messageCost*), each encrypted using different homomorphic encryption techniques.

For messageData, the ElGamal multiplication homomorphic technique, which offers faster encryption and decryption speeds, is used for encryption. This enables non-plaintext verification of the reimbursement data. The key pair $(PK, SK)$ is generated as follows: $p$ is a randomly selected large prime number, $g$ is a generator of $p$, and $x$, $k$ are random numbers. The public key $PK$ is $y$, and the private key $SK$ is $x$.

$$y = g^x \bmod p \tag{7}$$

The encrypted reimbursement material data ciphertext (*encMessageData*) is as follows:

$$encMessageData = (c_1, c_2)$$
$$c_1 = g^k \bmod p \tag{8}$$
$$c_2 = messageData \times y^k \bmod p$$

For the claim amount *messageCost*, an additive variant of the ElGamal addition homomorphic encryption algorithm is used for encryption. This allows for non-plaintext computation of claim amounts. The encrypted treatment cost (*encMessageCost*) is as follows:

$$encMessageCost = (c_1, c_2)$$
$$c_1 = g^k \bmod p \tag{9}$$
$$c_2 = a^{messageCost} \times y^k \bmod p$$

where $a$ is a constant chosen at random.

B. *Claim Auxiliary Verification Contract.* After a patient initiates an insurance claim with the insurance organization, the insurance company must apply to the medical institution for the hash index to access the encrypted medical record on the chain: $encMessageData_1, encMessageData_2, encMessageData_3$ ... $encMessageData_n$. The multiplication result of the ciphertext data of multiple entries for this patient, encMessageDatamult, is obtained for verification.

$$encMessageData_{mult} = encMessageData_1 \times \cdots \times encMessageData_n \tag{10}$$

The hospital performs the same calculation on the patient's corresponding plaintext data of materials, obtaining the multiplication result of all the plaintext data of the materials, $messageData_{mult}$.

$$messageData_{mult} = messageData_1 \times messageData_2 \cdots messageData_n \tag{11}$$

The Claim Auxiliary Verification Contract performs consistency verification on the encrypted calculation results provided by the insurance organization and the hospital using the *Key* provided by the patient. If the verification passes, it indicates that there has been no data tampering, and the claim proceeds; otherwise, the claim is terminated.

*C. Claim Amount Calculation Contract.* After the consistency verification by the Claim Auxiliary Verification Contract, it implies that there are no malicious activities such as data tampering. Then, the Claim Amount Calculation Contract performs homomorphic calculations on the ciphertext of the claim amount and decryption operations on the calculation results. First, it fetches several ciphertexts of the claim amounts for this patient from the blockchain: $encMessageCost_1$, $encMessageCost_2$, $encMessageCost_3$...$encMessageCost_n$. Then, the contract calculates the multiple ciphertext data of this patient, obtaining the summation result of all treatment cost ciphertexts, $encMessageCost_{add}$.

$$encMessageCost_{add} = encMessageCost_1 + \cdots + encMessageCost_n \quad (12)$$

Next, the treatment cost ciphertext result, $encMessageCost_{add}$, is decrypted.

$$encMessageCost_{add} = (c_1, c_2)$$

$$a^{messageCost_{add}} = \frac{c_2}{c_1{}^x} = \frac{a^{messageCost_{add}} y^k}{g^{kx}} = \frac{a^{messageCost_{add}} g^{xk}}{g^{xk}} \bmod p \quad (13)$$

$$cost = messageCost_{add} = \log_a a^{messageCost_{add}}$$

The *cost* is the plaintext of the real treatment costs of the patient, which has been verified for security and claim amount.

**DEHE:** Within the DEHE-BSC framework, the data receiver processes ciphertext encrypted using Dual ElGamal Homomorphic Encryption (DEHE), performing computations and decryption verification on the results. DEHE is built upon the ElGamal public-key cryptosystem and carries out multiplicative homomorphic encryption on the minimum EMR data set, leveraging its efficient encryption and decryption to verify reimbursement data swiftly. In parallel, DEHE employs an additive variant of the ElGamal encryption to encrypt the reimbursement amount, using its homomorphic properties for claims calculation. The security of DEHE stems from the complexity of the discrete logarithm problem in finite fields, which ensures the safety of the ciphertext. The specific process of the DEHE algorithm is illustrated in Algorithm 1.

The DEHE algorithm encompasses functions for key generation, encryption, decryption, and homomorphic computation. Its inputs can be plaintext, ciphertext, or computational data, and its outputs are key pairs, ciphertext, plaintext, or computational results. During key generation, the ElGamal algorithm generates a key pair for the patient. The encryption process divides plaintext data into reimbursement data and treatment costs, which are then encrypted using ElGamal multiplicative homomorphism and its additive variant, respectively. The decryption process utilizes the patient's private key to decrypt the ciphertext.

---

**Algorithm 1:** DEHE Algorithm

---

**Input**  : *plainText* or *cipherText* or *message*
**Output**: *Key* or *encPlainText* or *decCipherText* or *calculationResult*

1  **Function** *genKey()*:
    // Key Generation Function.
2    $SK \leftarrow x$ ;
3    $PK \leftarrow g^x \bmod p$ ;
4    $Key \leftarrow SK + PK$;
5    **return** *Key* // Return the key pair;
6  **Function** *encryption(plainText)*:
    // Dual ElGamal Homomorphic Encryption Function.
7    $encPlainTextData \leftarrow Enc(plainText.data)$;
8    $encPlainTextCost \leftarrow Enc(plainText.cost)$;
9    $encPlainText \leftarrow encPlainTextData + \mathrm{str}(encPlainTextCost)$;
10   **return** *encPlainText* // Return the ciphertext;
11 **Function** *decryption(cipherText)*:
    // Decryption Function.
12   $decCipherText \leftarrow Dec(cipherText, SK)$ // Decrypt using the private key;
13   **return** *decCipherText* // Return the plaintext;
14 **Function** *homomorphicCalculation(message)*:
    // Homomorphic Calculation Function.
15   **if** *message.type* $==$ *data* **then**
      // ElGamal multiplication homomorphic calculation.
16     calculationResult $\leftarrow$ multElGamal(message) ;
17   **else if** *message.type* $==$ *cost* **then**
      // ElGamal addition homomorphic calculation.
18     calculationResult $\leftarrow$ addElGamal(message) ;
19   **end**
20   **return** *calculationResult* ;

---

The homomorphic computation function performs corresponding computations based on the data type.

## 4    Analysis

### 4.1    Correctness Analysis

**Theorem 1.** *Definition of Correctness Concern: Upon the insurance institution transmitting the computational outcome* $Enc(M_1)$ *to the smart contract, the contract is capable of invoking the patient's decryption key 'Key' to decipher it. The decrypted result is then juxtaposed with the unencrypted computational outcome* $M_2$ *from the hospital's end to validate the congruence of both datasets* $M_1$ *and* $M_2$. *This juxtaposition ascertains whether the data has undergone any unauthorized modifications.*

*Proof.* Let us presume the patient's unencrypted data to be $m_1, m_2$. Consequently, the ciphertexts calculated by the insurance institution will be $Enc(m_1)$ and $Enc(m_2)$. Given that ElGamal exhibits multiplicative homomorphism, it would employ the rules of multiplication, thereby yielding:

$$Enc\,(M_1) = Enc\,(m_1) \times Enc\,(m_2) \tag{14}$$

Given the circumstances,

$$
\begin{aligned}
Enc\,(M_1) &= Enc\,(m_1) \times Enc\,(m_2) \\
&= \left(g^{k_1}, m_1 y^{k_1}\right) \times \left(g^{k_2}, m_2 y^{k_2}\right) \\
&= \left(g^{k_1+k_2}, m_1 m_2 y^{k_1+k_2}\right) \\
&= Enc\,(m_1 m_2)
\end{aligned}
\tag{15}
$$

Therefore, post-decryption of $Enc(M_1)$ using the decryption $Key$, we obtain M1, the value of which is equivalent to $m_1 m_2$. Since $M_2$ employs identical multiplication operations, the resultant value of $M_2$ is also $m_1 m_2$. Thus, when $M_1$ equals $M_2$, it can be inferred that the patient data has remained untampered.

## 4.2   Security Analysis

**Theorem 2.** *Definition of Security Concern: An insurer should not be able to infer any information about $m_1, m_2, ...m_n$ using $Enc(m_1), Enc(m_2), ...Enc(m_n)$.*

*Proof.* The well-established ElGamal encryption scheme's security relies on the inherent difficulty of the Discrete Logarithm Problem in finite fields, and the insurer can only access the patient's ciphertext.

Suppose the insurer obtains encrypted data $Enc(m_1), Enc(m_2), ...Enc(m_n)$ and is privy to the public key $y$, a large prime number $p$, and the generator $g$. Given that the patient's private key $x$ is kept secure, the insurer would have to reverse compute the value of $x$ from the equation below to obtain the plaintext $m_1, m_2, ...m_n$:

$$y = g^x \bmod p \tag{16}$$

This computation belongs to the Discrete Logarithm Problem, a notoriously hard problem that consists of determining the value of $x$ when a large prime number $p$, its corresponding generator $g$, and a value $y$ are given. The difficulty of computing $x$ increases exponentially with the size of $p$.

Therefore, when the value of p is sufficiently large, it can be asserted that this scheme is secure, implying that the insurer cannot decipher the patient's plaintext $m$ using the ciphertext $Enc(m)$.

## 4.3   Privacy Analysis

Patient medical records are not directly stored on the blockchain. Instead, we use a double ElGamal encryption algorithm to encrypt these records and store them within medical institutions, while the blockchain only saves the associated hash values. This approach significantly reduces the possibility of patient medical data leakage. Even if the blockchain is maliciously attacked, patient privacy cannot be compromised. In addition, we proposed a token-based access control strategy that achieves fine-grained access control and deep privacy protection. Only users with the corresponding tokens can retrieve the encrypted medical records through smart contracts and finally decrypt the patient's medical records using the user's private key.

In the insurance claims process, insurance companies can only receive the ciphertext of patient medical information, and under a secure encryption scheme, this ciphertext is undecipherable. Through the consistency verification mechanism of DEHE, insurance companies can only obtain the calculation result and cannot access specific patient medical records, thereby ensuring the privacy of patient-sensitive data during interactions with third parties.

### 4.4 Efficiency Analysis and Comparison

We set up a local Ethereum blockchain network using the Geth client and constructed a set of smart contracts deployed on the channel. The DPPChain platform was implemented on a PC equipped with an Intel Core CPU i7-10875H and a GeForce RTX 2070 GPU. For privacy protection, we implemented Dual ElGamal Homomorphic Encryption using Java. For interaction between the system and blockchain data, we used Ethereum's official web3j to handle the interchange process between Ethereum and the application layer. Next, we will delve into the each part of the PMI-Chain system and discuss its efficiency.

**Efficiency of DEHE-BSC:** In this section, we tested the encryption and decryption performance of the DEHE-BSC scheme executed by PMI-Chain during the insurance claim process, and compared it with the methods proposed in two related papers. Wenyu et al. [15] first introduced a privacy protection mechanism for insurance claims into the medical information platform, implementing the claims process using basic homomorphic encryption, which we refer to as HE-Chain. The EHRChain system proposed in [2] is a medical information processing platform with superior overall performance. It uses an improved homomorphic encryption technique, effectively reducing the computational load during encryption and decryption processes, thereby enhancing the model's efficiency.

*Performance Testing of Encryption.* As shown in Fig. 4a and Fig. 5a, compared to HE-Chain and EHRChain, the encryption strategy adopted by PMI-Chain increases the encryption speed by 44% and 12% respectively, and its performance is more stable. This is mainly because PMI-Chain uses an improved ElGamal encryption algorithm, whose encryption process mainly involves exponential and modular exponentiation operations with fewer number theory operations involved. These operations are relatively fast in computation, and they can be accelerated by using efficient algorithms such as fast power algorithm. On the other hand, the encryption process of the Paillier algorithm used in HE-Chain

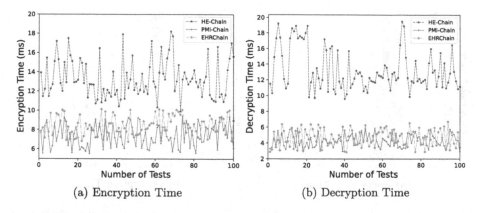

**Fig. 4.** Comparison of the time to perform 100 encryption and decryption tests for HE-Chain, PMI-Chain and EHRChain.

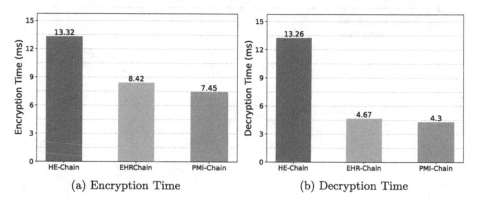

**Fig. 5.** Compare the average time of 100 encryption and decryption tests performed by HE-Chain, PMI-Chain and EHRChain.

involves multiplication and modulus operations of large numbers, as well as some complex number theory operations. These operations are relatively slower, and as the length of the key increases, the computation time will increase as well. Although EHRChain has improved the basic Paillier algorithm, its key generation process still involves more complex number theory calculations, including the generation of large primes and some complex number theory operations, which could make key generation more time-consuming. On the contrary, in the PMI-Chain, the key generation process usually only involves steps such as selecting a prime number and generating random numbers, making it more efficient.

*Performance Testing of Decryption.* As shown in Fig. 4b and Fig. 5b, in terms of decryption time, the performance of PMI-Chain has increased by 67% and 8% respectively compared to HE-Chain and EHRChain. Similar to the encryption process, this is because the operations such as exponentiation and modular exponentiation involved in the decryption process of DEHE can be accelerated

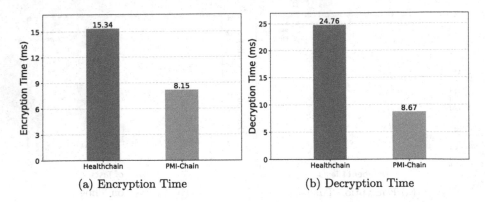

(a) Encryption Time          (b) Decryption Time

**Fig. 6.** Compare the average time of 100 encryption and decryption tests performed by Healthchain and PMI-Chain.

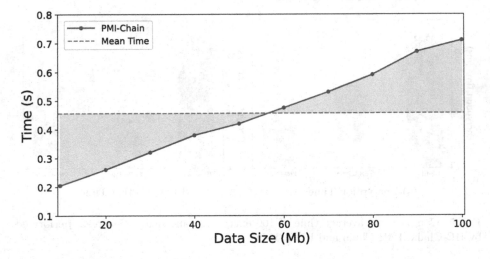

**Fig. 7.** Time of token generation under different data sizes

by efficient algorithms. In contrast, the decryption process based on the Paillier algorithm involves multiplication and modulus operations of large numbers, and its decryption operations are more complex, requiring more number theory computations, thereby resulting in a relatively longer decryption time.

**Efficiency of TBSC-ACPPS:** In this section, we test the encryption, decryption, and token generation performance of the TBSC-ACPPS scheme implemented by PMI-Chain during the process of medical institutions data sharing. We compare it with Healthchain [16]. Healthchain has designed a system that ensures privacy protection of medical data, thereby realizing reliable data sharing between medical institutions.

*Performance Testing of Encryption:* We conducted 100 encryption tests on the aforementioned schemes, taking the average of the results as the final data, as shown in Fig. 6a. The results show that the encryption processing time for Healthchain is 15.34 ms, while our PMI-Chain only takes 8.15 ms. It is evident that PMI-Chain offers the best encryption performance with the least time consumption.

*Performance Testing of Decryption:* As shown in Fig. 6b, the decryption test results indicate that the decryption processing time for Healthchain is 24.76 ms, and our PMI-Chain only takes 8.67 ms. This once again proves that PMI-Chain outperforms the other schemes in terms of decryption performance. This can be attributed to the lower computational complexity of PMI-Chain compared to Healthchain. Healthchain's medical record encryption scheme is more complex than PMI-Chain, resulting in a longer encryption time. It employs more complex number-theoretical computations compared to the point operations on the elliptic curve used by PMI-Chain, leading to a longer decryption time.

*Time Consumption for Token Generation:* Besides encryption and decryption activities, the speed at which tokens are generated plays a vital role in determining the overall system performance. Within the TBSC-ACPPS system, each patient token principally includes elements such as the User ID ($UId$), an on-chain hash value ($hash$), the address of the hospital's blockchain ($address$), and a timestamp ($time$).

We conducted a series of tests on the speed of token generation using medical record samples of varying sizes, ranging from 10 MB to 100 MB. As depicted in Fig. 7, the TBSC-ACPPS system effectively confines the token generation time to under one second. Even when the size of the medical record data in the test is 100MB, the time required to generate a token remains impressively low, at just 0.716 s.

## 5   Conclusions

In conclusion, this paper has presented the PMI-Chain, an innovative system that employs token-based smart contracts and dual ElGamal homomorphic encryption to establish a secure, confidential, and fine-grained access control-enabled data sharing platform for patients, medical institutions, and insurance companies. The platform addresses significant challenges inherent in traditional EMR systems, such as the risk of data breaches, limited patient autonomy over medical records, fragmented and inefficient allocation of medical resources, and potential violations of patient privacy. Our analysis demonstrates that the PMI-Chain provides a significant performance improvement over existing methods, with lower encryption and decryption time overhead and more stable performance.

**Acknowledgements.** This work is supported by the National Natural Science Foundation of China (61962042) and Science and Technology Program of Inner Mongolia Autonomous Region (2020GG0188), and Natural Science Foundation of Inner Mongolia (2022MS06020), and the Central Government Guides Local Science and Technology

Development Fund (2022ZY0064), and the University Youth Science and Technology Talent Development Project (Innovation Group Development Plan) of Inner Mongolia A. R. of China (Grant No. NMGIRT2318).

# References

1. Hillestad, R., et al.: Can electronic medical record systems transform health care? Potential health benefits, savings, and costs. Health Aff. **24**(5), 1103–1117 (2005)
2. Li, F., Liu, K., Zhang, L., Huang, S., Wu, Q.: EHRchain: a blockchain-based EHR system using attribute-based and homomorphic cryptosystem. IEEE Trans. Serv. Comput. **15**(5), 2755–2765 (2021)
3. Azaria, A., Ekblaw, A., Vieira, T., Lippman, A.: MedRec: using blockchain for medical data access and permission management. In: 2016 2nd International Conference on Open and Big Data (OBD), pp. 25–30. IEEE (2016)
4. Zhu, W.: Research on theoretica framework on excessive medica treatment and hierarchica medical system based on the perspective of supply side. Chinese Health Econ. **37**(3), 8–10 (2018)
5. Nakamoto, S.: Bitcoin: A peer-to-peer electronic cash system. Decentralized business review (2008)
6. Stafford, T.F., Treiblmaier, H.: Characteristics of a blockchain ecosystem for secure and sharable electronic medical records. IEEE Trans. Eng. Manage. **67**(4), 1340–1362 (2020)
7. Li, M., Yu, S., Zheng, Y., Ren, K., Lou, W.: Scalable and secure sharing of personal health records in cloud computing using attribute-based encryption. IEEE Trans. Parallel Distrib. Syst. **24**(1), 131–143 (2012)
8. Xhafa, F., Feng, J., Zhang, Y., Chen, X., Li, J.: Privacy-aware attribute-based PHR sharing with user accountability in cloud computing. J. Supercomput. **71**, 1607–1619 (2015)
9. Cao, S., Zhang, G., Liu, P., Zhang, X., Neri, F.: Cloud-assisted secure eHealth systems for tamper-proofing EHR via blockchain. Inf. Sci. **485**, 427–440 (2019)
10. Saini, A., Zhu, Q., Singh, N., Xiang, Y., Gao, L., Zhang, Y.: A smart-contract-based access control framework for cloud smart healthcare system. IEEE Internet Things J. **8**(7), 5914–5925 (2020)
11. Benil, T., Jasper, J.: Cloud based security on outsourcing using blockchain in e-health systems. Comput. Netw. **178**, 107344 (2020)
12. Ding, Y., Sato, H.: Derepo: a distributed privacy-preserving data repository with decentralized access control for smart health. In: 2020 7th IEEE International Conference on Cyber Security and Cloud Computing (CSCloud)/2020 6th IEEE International Conference on Edge Computing and Scalable Cloud (EdgeCom), pp. 29–35. IEEE (2020)
13. Zhang, L., et al.: BDSS: blockchain-based data sharing scheme with fine-grained access control and permission revocation in medical environment. KSII Trans. Internet Inf. Syst. **16**(5), 1634–1652 (2022)
14. Dewangan, N.K., Chandrakar, P.: Patient-centric token-based healthcare blockchain implementation using secure internet of medical things. IEEE Trans. Comput. Soc. Syst. **10**, 3109–3119 (2022)
15. Xu, W., Wu, L., Yan, Y.: Privacy-preserving scheme of electronic health records based on blockchain and homomorphic encryption. J. Comput. Res. Dev. **55**(10), 2233–2243 (2018)
16. Wang, B., Li, Z.: Healthchain: a privacy protection system for medical data based on blockchain. Future Internet **13**(10), 247 (2021)

# BGET: A Blockchain-Based Grouping-EigenTrust Reputation Management Approach for P2P Networks

Yang Peng[1]([✉])(iD), Jie Huang[1,2](iD), Sirui Zhou[1], Zixuan Ju[1], Xiaowen Wang[1](iD), and Peihao Li[1](iD)

[1] School of Cyber Science and Engineering, Southeast University, NanJing 211189, Jiangsu, China
{seu_py,jhuang,220224873,220224737,xiaowenwang,lipeihao}@seu.edu.cn
[2] Science and Technology on Communication Networks Laboratory, Shijiazhuang 050000, Hebei, China
http://www.springer.com/gp/computer-science/lncs

**Abstract.** Trust, as an effective way to reduce complexity and risks of systems, is experiencing various challenges in distinguishing reliable partners of distribution environment like Peer to Peer (P2P) networks. As one of the most known and successful reputation management systems, the EigenTrust reputation management system has been widely used. However, this kind of system uses centralized reputation calculation strategy, which relies heavily on the mechanisms of global ranking and pre-trusted peers. It causes high-reputation peers to center around pre-trusted peers and uncontrolled spread of inauthentic downloads, as a consequence, other low-reputation peers will be marginalized despite potentially they could be honest. To deal with these problems, we put forward a blockchain-based grouping-EigenTrust (BGET) reputation management approach. BGET uses grouping-ET algorithm to manage reputations of different peers, which utilizes uniform grouping strategy and intragroup random walk strategy to divide peers into different groups to guarantee the uniform distribution of high reputation peers and limit the spread of inauthentic downloads. Moreover, BGET provides reliable verification services based on blockchain, which can improve the credibility and quality of transactions. Through simulations, we proved that BGET has good extensibility and robustness. BGET can effectively maintain higher success rate of tasks even there are many malicious peers in the network.

**Keywords:** P2P Networks · Reputation Management · EigenTrust · Blockchain

## 1 Introduction

P2P networks are designed to improve network resilience, in which members are peer to peer and no longer subject to or subordinate to each other. Up to today,

H. Gao et al. (Eds.): CollaborateCom 2023, LNICST 561, pp. 225–242, 2024.
https://doi.org/10.1007/978-3-031-54521-4_13

P2P networks are used for a wide range of applications, from resources sharing [17] and social networking [11,13] to Internet of Things [19,20], electricity trading [27] and governance [8]. They offer advantages over traditional networks, including increased resilience, transparency, and security. However, how to effectively measure trust relationships among unacquainted peers in these networks is a longstanding challenge.

To ensure the security of P2P networks, a reliable reputation system is essential, which can identify peers who are honest and reputable, while also detect those who are deceitful, malicious, or self-serving. Reputation is a global perception of an entity's behavior based on the trust that other entities have established [18]. Therefore, many reputation systems have been suggested, such as Eigen-Trust (ET) [7], PeerTrust [24] and PowerTrust [29], etc. However, these systems need to rank the reputation values of their members to distinguish honest peers from malicious ones. This will lead to some fatal problems that peers in the system will naturally cluster around the peers with high reputation and the effects of low ones will be marginalized. Even ET, one of the most popular and used reputation system, can't get away with these.

ET was first proposed for P2P file-downloading systems to help peers acquire resources from trusted peers [7], which is achieved by calculating a global reputation value, consists of a local trust value determined by peer's previous behavior and a propagation-based recommendation trust value, for each peer and sorting them. ET has two essential mechanisms, a group of pre-trusted peers and global ranking, which are utilized to help peers choose who to interact with. Obviously, the pre-trusted peers have more opportunities to earn high reputations, since they have higher initial reputation values to make them trustworthy. However, this also prompts other peers, who expect to gain high reputation, to gather around and connected with them. In this condition, the pre-trusted peers could become a wonderful medium to spread inauthentic downloads. If they accept downloads from malicious peers accidentally, they will help spread these inauthentic files to the entire network more efficiently, since there are many peers connected to them. Additionally, feedback and evaluation in ET come from the subjective level of the service requester, which is very beneficial for malicious peers to engage in fraudulent activities. Because honest peers always tell the truth, while malicious ones can intentionally lower their ratings for services provided by honest peers, in order to lower their reputation rankings (i.e. bad-mouthing attack [6]). Although ET performance well in many scenes, it causes peers to converge around the pre-trusted peers and high-ranking peers, and the peers that are 'far away' from the them will be ranked very low despite potentially being honest [4]. To sum up, the primary limitation of ET is the aggregation problem caused by pre-trusted peers and global ranking.

*Contributions:* we propose the BGET approach for P2P networks to maintain the uniform distribution of high reputation peers and provide a fair collaborative environment for peers, where there is no longer the concentration of high-reputation peers and the marginalization of low-reputation peers. Among the main contributions of this paper are:

- We characterize the negative implications of ET: pre-trusted peers and global ranking, as shown in Sect. 3. Peers that are pre-trusted have higher reputation values and are easier to accumulate reputation values, which also make them more likely to cause uncontrolled spread of inauthentic downloads. If pre-trusted peers receive inauthentic downloads carelessly, then the inauthentic downloads will be spread to the whole network faster. In the long run, the whole network will control by minority peers with high reputation and the influence of low reputation peers on the entire network will decrease and eventually be marginalized. To tackle these problems we propose the blockchain-based grouping-EigenTrust (BGET) reputation management approach for P2P networks.
- To avoid the aggregation of high-reputation peers and limit the spread of inauthentic downloads among pre-trusted peers, we put a uniform grouping strategy into ET, and propose the grouping-ET algorithm to manage the reputation of peers. The grouping-ET algorithm utilizes uniform grouping strategy to divide peers in the network to a uniform state and uses intragroup random strategy to suggest peers select interactive objects that from the same group as themselves in a random way. By doing so, we can provide a more fair trading condition for honest peers by limiting the opportunities of malicious ones to manipulate transactions.
- The transitivity of recommendation trust is a critical process of reputation convergence, and is also a good opportunity for malicious peers to manipulate. To guarantee the reliability of recommendation trust, we introduce blockchain technology into BGET to provide verification services, which can verify the identity and evidences of trust of both parties involved in the transactions.
- We design a series of simulations to test the credibility and performance of BGET. The results show that BGET can achieve better transaction success rates than original ET, and also exhibit better robustness in the face of attacks.

The rest of the paper is organized as follows: Sect. 2 summarizes previous works on reputation management system, especially on ET and blockchain based methods. Section 3 analyzes ET algorithm and its limitations. Section 4 describes our BGET approach to address the problems in exiting reputation management systems. The evaluation process and result discussion are presented in Sect. 5. Finally, a conclusion with a summary is provided in Sect. 6.

## 2   Related Work

Reputation management methods are designed to collect and analyze data about the reputation of individuals, organizations, and products on various online platforms [5]. Reputation management methods are not only widely used in P2P networks, but also widely used in various scenarios such as social networks [28], internet of things [9], internet of vehicles [23], and so on. With the deepening of the research, many reputation systems have been put forward. Aberer and Despotovic [1] presented a reputation-based trust management approach, which can be implemented in P2P environment and scales well for very large numbers of participants. In [21], Credence, an innovative reputation system based on objects, is introduced as a solution to evaluate the credibility of online content and combat content pollution by securely collecting and managing endorsements from trustworthy peers. For distribution environment, Xue et al. [25] design a robust and distributing reputation system, DHTrust, which is modeled by DHT (Distributed Hash Table) trust overlay network (DHTON). Can and Bhargava [3] propose a Self-ORganizing Trust model (SORT) that aims to decrease malicious activity in a P2P system by establishing trust relations among peers in their proximity.

ET Algorithm is a famous trust-based reputation management approach, which uses the principle of eigenvector centrality to compute the trustworthiness of each peer. With the further research on ET, many variants and extensions have been proposed to address specific challenges and limitations of the original ET algorithm. Kurdi et al. in [12] propose a HonestPeer algorithm to dynamically select the most reputable peers based on the quality of the shared files, instead of relying solely on a static group of pre-trusted peers. AlhussainK et al. [2] introduce the EERP approach to track, identify and isolate malicious peers by analyzing the logs of peer interactions. Besides, many scholars have studied personalizing ET, and propose a series of methods. Chiluka et al. [4] introduce a reputation system called PETS (Personalized ET using Social network), Lin et al. [15] propose the Personalized ET reputation system, Li et al. [14] propose PersonalTrust pre-trust reputation management model. These researches have studied the pre-trusted mechanism of ET and found some ways to choose the pre-trusted peer based on their own tastes, and can detect various types of malicious behaviors that were not detected by the original ET algorithm. Although these methods are more flexible than ET, the aggregation problem caused by pre-trusted peers still exist. Moreover, many of them overlook the global ranking mechanism, which can also lead to similar problems.

In recent years, blockchain is widely used in internet of things (IoT) to manage the trust relationship of members. Yang et al. [26] propose a decentralized trust system for vehicular networks. Wu and Liang [22] utilize the mobile edge nodes to calculate the trustworthiness of sensor nodes and put forward the blockchain-based trust management mechanism (BBTM) approach. Kouicem et al. [10] design a hierarchical and scalable blockchain-based trust management protocol, which achieve the mobility support in decentralized IoT systems. In order to comprehensively study the development status of blockchain-based trust management systems (BC-TMSs), Liu et al. [16] conduct a serious survey on the current state of the arts, in which introduces the recent advances, open issues, and future research directions toward realizing reliable and sound BC-TMSs for IoT. The decentralized, tamper resistance, and traceable features of blockchain are very suitable for the reputation management requirements in P2P networks, which can overcome identity impersonation and fraud issues between entities that are unfamiliar.

# 3    Analysis of ET

## 3.1    Algorithmic Overview

Considering a file-downloading scene in P2P networks, there are $m$ peers, including a pre-trusted group, $P$, which is known to be trustworthy. The initial reputation of pre-trusted peers is setting to $\frac{1}{|P|}$.

Assuming there is a peer $i$, who downloaded files from peer $j$. Then, there will be a local trust value, $S_{ij}$, to represent the total number of authentic downloads from peer $i$ to peer $j$. To avoid malicious peers giving other malicious peers arbitrarily high local trust values, $S_{ij}$ should be normalized as $c_{ij} = \frac{\max(s_{ij},0)}{\sum_j \max(s_{ij},0)}$, representing how much peer $i$ trust peer $j$ based on their historical transaction records. This formula ensures that all values of $c_{ij}$ are between 0 and 1. Up to this point, peer $i$ have completed the trust evaluation of peer $j$.

To expand its knowledge, peer $i$ need to study the viewpoints of other peers in the network. A feasible approach is to access knowledge from its neighbors and the neighbors of its neighbors. Then, peer $i$ will get a aggregation reputation vector:

$$\vec{t_i} = (C^\top)^n \vec{c_i} \tag{1}$$

after n iterations.

In real applications, there will be a group of malicious peers who know each other, and they will give each other high trust values, but give all others low trust values. This issue is addressed by taking

$$\vec{t}^{(k+1)} = (1-\alpha)C^\top \vec{t}^{(k)} + \alpha \vec{p} \tag{2}$$

where $\alpha$ is a constant less than 1.

## 3.2    Security Analysis

ET has two typical aspects: pre-trusted peers and global ranking, which make it is different from other trust management methods. On the contrary, these two mechanisms also bring performance limitations to it.

The pre-trusted mechanism is designed to avoid the manipulation of malicious peers. Firstly, when there are malicious individuals in the networks, the convergence rate of $t = (C^\top)^n \widetilde{p}$ is faster than $t = (C^\top)^n \widetilde{e}$, where $\widetilde{e}$ represents the previous trust value. Secondly, when there are slothful individuals, which means they don't trust anyone and don't download files from anyone they couldn't trust, then we could define $c_{ij} = p_j$. In other word, if peer $i$ couldn't trust anyone, then $i$ could choose the ones that are pre-trusted. Finally, when there are many malicious peers want to manipulate the process of reputation evaluation, the pre-trusted peers can relieve this situation. ET suggests every peer to choose the pre-trusted peers with a certain probability $\alpha$, as shown in Eq. (2). However, the peers close to the pre-trusted ones are more likely to be selected by other peers. So, they can earn more reputation than the peers who are far away from the pre-trusted ones. Chiluka et al. [4] have proved this observation in their researches. They found the peers closer to the pre-trusted ones have higher reputation rankings, while those farther away will be marginalized. Furthermore, if a pre-trusted peer downloads an inauthentic file from a malicious peer carelessly, the wandering mechanism would allow the file to be easily accepted by other peers, leading to a chain of inauthentic downloads [12]. As a consequence, we think the pre-trusted mechanism of ET will lead to the aggregation problem of high-reputation peers, which deviates from the original intention of decentralized design in P2P networks and also lead to uncontrolled spread of inauthentic downloads.

Global ranking is an intuitive way to reflect the trust level of peers in a community. In principle, the higher the ranking, the more trustworthy the peer is. However, this open approach also provides more opportunities for malicious peers to take advantage of. When there are many malicious individuals in the networks, they will improve their reputation by providing authentic downloads to high-reputation ones, while providing inauthentic downloads to low-reputation ones. Besides, they can give high scores to other malicious peers who collude with them, and give honest peers low scores to weaken their influence on the network. In the long run, the negative impact will spread throughout the entire network.

Although the pre-trusted peers and global ranking mechanisms bring the ET good performance to distinguish honest peers from malicious ones and maintain a stable reputation network when there are few malicious peers, the performance will be poor when the number of malicious peers in the network is large. So, how to mitigate these adverse impacts is crucial for improving the performance of such reputation management methods.

## 4    BGET Approach

BGET is designed as a distributed reputation management approach for P2P networks, in which all peers can effectively distinguish trusted ones from non-trusted ones, choose reliable ones to interact with and resist the manipulation of malicious peers, as shown in Fig. 1.

The cores of BGET consist of three critical points: 1) distinguish trusted peers from non-trusted ones, 2) prevent peers from aggregating around high-reputation peers and 3) provide verifiable reputation management services. The first point is a basic require for reputation management methods and the existing ones all can basically meet this requirement to a certain extent. The ET method is one of the most popular and successful methods. It combines local trust and recommendation trust, which makes it more accurate in the evaluation of reputations of peers. The second one and the third one are the two key facets of BGET approach. As we stated earlier, the mechanism of global ranking and pre-trusted peers will cause the aggregation problem, so we design a group strategy

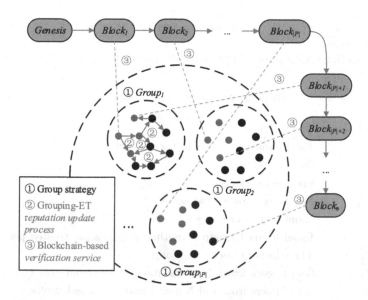

**Fig. 1.** BGET approach. The red points represent the pre-trusted peers and the blue points represent the peers with high reputation values, while the black ones represent the peers with low reputation values. $|P|$ is the number of pre-trusted peers and $n$ is the number of peers in the network.

to maintain the balance of reputation in the network. The peers in the network will be divided into different group according to the number of pre-trusted peers and the scale of network. By doing this, we can evenly distribute the pre-trusted peers to the network and avoid the aggregation of high-reputation peers. Besides, the slothful peers can only choose to trust the pre-trusted peer in the same group as them. Finally, to decrease the success rate and quality of interact, the non-trusted peers always provide forged data and records to confuse the trusted ones. To go along with this, the blockchain-based reputation verification services are provided in BGET to deal with the problem of fake. With the help of blockchain's tamper resistance and traceability features, BGET can achieve automated periodic verification services, which also adds a supplement safeguard to the non-trusted peer detection process.

The BGET approach mainly includes three processes: 1) using uniform grouping strategy to divide peers to different groups, which can avoid all high-reputation peers gathering together, 2) using grouping-ET reputation updating algorithm to calculate peers' reputation values to ensure dynamic and safe updates of peers' reputations, and 3) providing blockchain-based verification services to detect suspicious behaviors in transactions, such as forged transaction records, etc.

As mentioned above, BGET not only has the advantages of ET, but also achieves uniform distribution of high-reputation peers in the network and provides reliable verification services to ensure the credibility of peers' reputations updating.

The notations used in our approach are shown in Table 1

Table 1. Notations and descriptions.

| Notation | Description |
|---|---|
| $m$ | Total number of peers in the network |
| $i, j$ | Peers in the network |
| $P$ | Pre-trusted group |
| $|P|$ | Number of pre-trusted peers |
| $N$ | Number of peer groups |
| $l_i$ | Label to mark group $i$ whether include a pre-trusted peer |
| $N_i$ | The number of peers in group $i$ |
| $A_i$ | Set of peers which have downloaded files from peer $i$ |
| $B_i$ | Set of peers from which peer $i$ have downloaded files |
| $\alpha$ | The probability of pre-trust being selected in ET |
| $s_{ij}$ | Total number of authentic downloads from peer $i$ to peer $j$ |
| $c_{ij}$ | Normalized value of $s_{ij}$ |
| $C$ | Matrix of $c_{ij}$ |
| $n$ | Number of iterations |
| $t_i$ | Trust value of peer $i$ |
| $[t]$ | Matrix of $t_i$ |
| $N_{ver}$ | the number of transactions that need to be verified |
| $Tx_{peer}$ | represents the total number of peer's transaction records |

## 4.1   Grouping-ET Reputation Updating Algorithm

The reputation calculate algorithm used in BGET approach is an enhanced version of ET, grouping-ET, which combines the uniform grouping strategy and intragroup random walk strategy. In detail, the algorithm process is shown in algorithm 1.

**System Initialization.** 1) Before the system starts, the parameters, including $m$, $P$, $N$, $l_i$, $A_i$ and $B_i$, will be initialized firstly. $P$ represents a pre-trusted peers group, where only pre-trusted peers are present, and $|P|$ is its size. $m$ is the total number of peers in the network, $N$ is the number of groups after the peers is divided, $l_i$ is a label to mark group $i$ whether include a pre-trusted peer, which is 1 if yes and 0 if no. 2) considering the scene of peer $j$ downloads files from peer $i$, then, there will generate two sets: $A_i$ and $B_i$. $A_i$ represents the set of peers which have downloaded files from peer $i$ and $B_i$ represents the set of peers from which peer $i$ have downloaded files. The initial values of $A_i$ and $B_i$ are null.

---

**Algorithm 1:** Grouping-ET Algorithm.

**Input:** Number of peers - $m$; Pre-trusted peers group - $P$; Number of peer groups - $N$; Label to mark group $i$ whether include a pre-trusted peer - $l_i$; Error parameter - $\epsilon$; Set of peers which have downloaded files from peer $i$ - $A_i$; Set of peers from which peer $i$ have downloaded files - $B_i$.

**Output:** Matrix of global reputations of all peers - $[t]$.

1  **for** $x = 1$ to $N$ **do**
2      $y = Random(N)$ ;
3      **if** $peer_x \in P$ **then**
4          **if** $l_y = 0$ **then**
5              $Group_y \leftarrow peer_x$;
6              $l_y = 1$;
7          **else**
8              $y = Random(N)$ ;
9      **else**
10         $Group_y \leftarrow peer_x$;
11 $peer\ j$ choose peer $i$ from $Group_j$ to download files;
12 **foreach** $Group_i$ **do**
13     **foreach** $peer\ i$ **do**
14         Query all peers $j \in A_i$ & $j \in Group_j$;
15         **repeat**
16             $t_i^{(k+1)} = \alpha(c_{1i}t_1^{(k)} + c_{2i}t_2^{(k)} + \cdots + c_{mi}t_m^{(k)}) + \alpha p_i$;
17             Send $c_{ij}t_i^{(k+1)}$ to all peers j $\in B_i$;
18             Compute $\delta = \left| t_i^{(k+1)} - t_i^{(k)} \right|$;
19             Wait for all peers $j \in A_i$ & $j \in Group_j$ to return $c_{ji}t_j^{(k+1)}$;
20         **until** $\delta < \epsilon$;
21 **return** $[t]$.

---

**Uniform Grouping Strategy.** The goal of this strategy is to keep the balance of global reputations of different groups and avoid the aggregation of high-reputation peers. The number of groups, $N$, is a decisive parameter in the process of grouping. It's worth noting that there are three possible values of $N$: $N < |P|$, $N = |P|$ and $N > |P|$, and we analyze the effects of different values of $P$ through the comparative experiment in Sect. 5.4. According to the result, we set $N = |P|$, which can achieve an optimal balance between the groups. Therefore, the peers in the network will be divided to $N$ groups and each group only has one pre-trusted peers. As shown in the line 1 to 10 of algorithm 1, each pre-trusted peer will be distributed to a different group with the help of label $l_i$. If group $y$ has included a pre-trusted peer, then $l_y = 1$ and peer $x$ will be distributed to another group with $l_y = 0$. By doing so, the high-reputation peers are no longer clustered together at a single center, but are scattered across different groups.

**Intragroup Random Walk Strategy.** In original ET, peer $j$ will utilize a random walk way to select a objective peers from the whole network to downloads files. In specific, peer $j$ will select a pre-trusted peer with a probability of $\alpha$ and other peers in the network with a probability of $1 - \alpha$. However, this way will lead to two serious problems: 1) it is a highly uncertain task to choose the value of parameter $\alpha$, which will cause a significant impact on the probability distribution and 2) if pre-trusted peers accidentally accepted inauthentic files, they will spread them to the whole network faster, since they have more opportunities to be selected. Unlike original ET, our Grouping-ET algorithm utilize intragroup random walk strategy to achieve this goal, which suggest peers to select objective peers from their own group with a random way, as shown in line 11 of algorithm 1 and Fig. 1. In Fig. 1, every circle presents a group and points represent peers in the network. Compare to global random walk strategy of original ET algorithm, our intragroup random walk strategy limits the scope of peers' activities, which can effectively limit malicious peers collaborate with other malicious peers in other groups. In this way, we not only eliminate the influence of parameter $\alpha$, but also stop the spread of inauthentic files and improve the effectiveness of reputation updating. Next, peer $j$ selected a peer $i$ in this way and downloaded some files from peer $i$. Then, peer $j$ will be added into set $A_i$. In the same way, peer $i$ will also maintain a set $B_i$ that it have downloaded files from.

**Reputation Updating.** As shown algorithm 1, except for no longer using the original parameter $\alpha$ in ET, the other processes of reputation updating is roughly the same as ET. As demonstrated in intragroup random walk strategy, to eliminate the uncertainty of parameter $\alpha$, we redefine $\alpha$ to a random parameter and let $\alpha = \frac{1}{N_i}$, where $N_i$ represents the number of peers in group $i$. Then, the updating process is shown in line 12 to 20 of algorithm 1. For every transaction, the reputation updating process will be invoked to update the reputation of both parties involved in the transaction. It is worthy noting that, since the improvement of uniform grouping strategy and intragroup random walk strategy, our method has lower complexity than original ET algorithm, which is discussed in Sect. 5.1.

**Blockchain-Based Verification Services.** As stated in uniform grouping strategy and intragroup random walk strategy, transactions are limited in peers' own groups. There is no doubt about that honest peers will adhere strictly to these regulations, but malicious peers may take risks. These regulations can only limit the behaviors of honest ones, the malicious ones have no reason to comply. Therefore, it is necessary to develop rules that can fairly limit the behaviors of all members. In view of this, the blockchain-based verification services will be an effective way to ensure the correctness and effectiveness of transactions. By consulting the non-manipulable historical transaction records stored in blocks, BGET can discover different violations such as falsification of data or transaction records and so on.

## 4.2    Blockchain-Based Verification Services

Another key point of BGET is to provide verification services, which can prevent dishonest peers from engaging in fraudulent behaviors. To achieve this, BGET designs several verification services based on blockchain for reputation updating, the process is shown in Fig. 2.

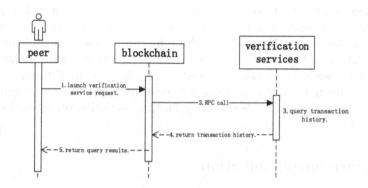

**Fig. 2.** Verification services based on blockchain.

For P2P environment, there are a large number of peers and frequent transactions. To verify every transaction is not a reasonable way as it will result in a significant waste of time and computing resources. Therefore, in BGET, the verification service is set to activate once every 100 times transactions. The detail verification polices are as follows:

- For peers who have no abnormal transactions, in order to ensure the efficiency of the system, high-reputation peers of each group can be exempted from verification. For those who have abnormal transactions or low-reputation values, they need to follow the latter policies.
- For new members, they only have a handful of historical transactions and just need to verify a small number of transactions at random.
- For slothful peers, who are honest but rarely engage in transactions, also need to verify a small number of transactions at random.
- For most of normal peers, the number of transactions that need to be verified is: $N_{ver} = (1 - t_{peer})Tx_{peer}$, $t_{peer}$ represents the reputation value of the peer and $Tx_{peer}$ represents the total number of peer's transaction records. In order not to affect efficiency, there is no need to verify all records every time, but only to verify the most recent records, since the earlier records have already been verified. Here, $Tx_{peer} = 100$ which means that only $N_{val}$ out of the last 100 records need to be verified each time.
- Penalties. If a peer is found to provided inauthentic resources to other peers, it could be a malicious peer or just a victim who accept inauthentic resources from others. In this situation, the peers will be deducted twice the points

that should be earned for this transaction to reduce the likelihood of it being selected next time. If a peer is found to have forged its transaction records to improve its rating in the past, it must be a malicious node. Then, the reputation of this peer will be clear to zero.

According to the polices of BGET, peers must choose the peers in the same group with them to interact with. If the verification services find a peer has transaction records that completed with peers in other groups, the peer will be recognized as malicious peer and these downloads will also be marked as inauthentic downloads. Besides, blockchain has the characteristic of traceability. When inauthentic files are found, the source can be traced and the inauthentic files can be cleaned up as much as possible. With the help of these verification services, all members in the network will have a more fair environment, where peers can trade with each other securely and the updating of reputation also be more credibly.

## 5    Performance Evaluation

In this section, we analyse the time complexity of BGET and simulate several scenes to study its behaviors. Besides, we compare the performance of BGET to a simple P2P network where no reputation management system is implemented, original ET [7] and HonestPeer [12], a popular variant of ET.

### 5.1    Algorithm Complexity and Convergence Overhead

According to algorithm 1, the complexity of BGET is mainly dependent on the calculation of $t_i^{(k+1)}$ in formula (2) and the convergence overhead. Unlike the original ET algorithm which needs to be iterated over the whole network, BGET is sampler. In original ET algorithm, although $C^{\top}$ in formula (1) is sparse, since most of $c_{ij}$ have a value of 0, it still needs to traverse all peers in the network every loop. However, BGET approach only needs to converge within the group where the peers belong to, greatly reducing the convergence time. Moreover, the convergence overhead is also affected by impact of number of loop. Same as above, the number of iterations required within each group is also smaller than ET. Hence, the algorithm complexity and convergence overhead of BGET are superior to the original ET algorithm.

### 5.2    Simulation Setup

Our evaluation is based on the simulation execution with many simulation cycles. In every simulation cycle, we build a simulation network with different number of peers, include honest peers and malicious peers, (as demonstrated in Table 2). Honest peers always provide authentic downloads, while malicious peers always provide inauthentic downloads. Every peer has two status: query and standby. In query status, peer $i$ will issue a request and wait for responses. Other peers in standby status receive the request and return acknowledgments to indicate that they can provide the service. The query peers will choose a service provider $j$ based on BGET approach from the set of hits. Then peer $i$ gives a score of 0 to 1 based on the quality of the downloaded files. At the end of each simulation cycle, the global reputation values of all peers in the network will be calculated according to our BGET algorithm. These results will be utilized in the upcoming simulation cycles for the next selection of service provider.

All simulations are carried on an Ubuntu 22.04.2 LTS (GNU/Linux 5.15.0-71-generic x86_64) laptop with one 16 core CPU. The software tools we used is PyCharm 2020.1, we simulate all the peers and blockchain in it to evaluate the performance of BGET.

It is noting that although the experimental scenario is set to file-downloading, the BGET approach can be adapted to various transaction scenario, such as e-commerce, file sharing, social networks, and so on.

**Table 2.** Configuration of the simulation parameters.

| Parameter | Value |
|---|---|
| $m$ | 500-3500 (step=500) |
| $|P|$ | 5/10/15 |
| $N$ | 5/10/15 |
| % Proportion of malicious peers | 10%-100% (step=10%) |
| # Simulation cycles | 25 |
| # Runs for each experiment | 5 |

### 5.3   Evaluation Criteria

In file-sharing scene, a commonly used evaluation criteria is the rate of inauthentic downloads, which reflects the whole health of the network in decreasing the frequency of downloads of fraudulent files. The smaller the rate of inauthentic downloads, the better the system performance. The rate of inauthentic downloads is defined as:

$$\text{Rate of inauthentic downloads} = \frac{\#\text{downloads of fraudulent files}}{\#\text{downloads done by all peers}} \quad (3)$$

### 5.4   Results and Analysis

In our BGET approach, the number of the pre-trusted peers, $|P|$, is an important parameter of uniform grouping strategy. There are three situations: (i) $N < |P|$, the number of pre-trusted peer divided into each peer group will be unbalanced and greater than 1. (ii) $N = |P|$, the distribution of pre-trusted peers is balance and all groups have the same number of pre-trusted peers, all of which are 1. (iii)

$N > |P|$, some groups will not contain pre-trusted peers, which will cause them to lose an advantage in competition. To evaluate the impact of these settings on the system performance, we fix the value of $N$ to 10, number of peer to 1000, and conduct comparative experiments based on different values of $|P|$ and proportion of malicious peers. The result is shown in Fig. 3.

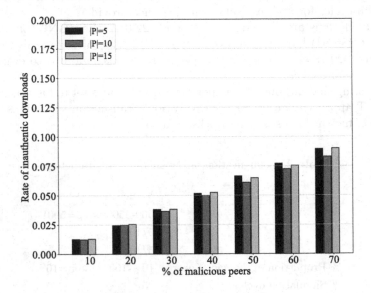

**Fig. 3.** The effect of $|P|$ on BGET approach. $per\_num = 1000$.

In Fig. 3, when the proportion of malicious peers is less than 30%, the rates of inauthentic downloads in the system of these three conditions are almost the same. As the malicious peers proportion increases, the gap of the inauthentic downloads rates also chases up. To be specific, when $N = |P|$, the inauthentic rate is minimum, and it is slightly better when $N < |P|$ than when $N > |P|$. Hence, setting $N = |P|$ is more conducive to the security assurance of the system, especially when the proportion of malicious peers is larger. In the upcoming experiments, the values of $N$ and $|P|$ both are set to 10 to maintain the balance of uniform grouping.

Then, to evaluate the performance of BGET approach under different threat environments, we consecutively conduct different simulation experiments based on the different configuration parameters, as shown in Table 1. The results are shown in Fig. 4.

Figure 4 illustrates the variation trends of inauthentic downloads rates for different methods under different situations that with different number of peers. Only the simple method experiences a spike when the total number is increased from 500 to 1000, and continue to maintain a growth state. Other than that, other methods all remain a stable state, that is, these methods are insensitive

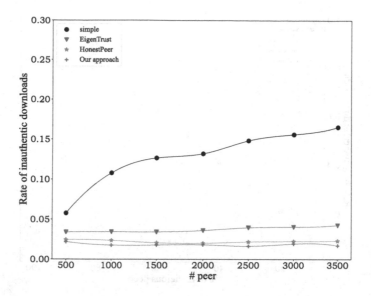

**Fig. 4.** The effect of peers number to different methods.

to the expansibility of network. So, BGET fairly meets the needs of large scale distributed system.

Finally, to evaluate the impact of different malicious rates on the effectiveness of our BGET approach, we simulate different scenarios with different malicious rates. The result is shown in Fig. 5.

Figure 5 shows the reactions of different methods when the proportion of malicious peers increases. The ET and HonestPeer methods have similar growth curve, and the HonestPeer is superior to ET. When the proportion of malicious peers exceeds 65%, both of them have an inauthentic download rates over 60%, which is higher than the simple method. It indicates that the performance of these methods will be awful when most peers in the network are malicious peers. As you can imagine, the user experience in this case will be terrible. By comparison, the inauthentic downloads rate of our BGET approach grows steadily with a fixed and small growth rate and only shows slight reaction to the increase of malicious peers when the rate below 80%, and the inauthentic download rate can be stabilized at around 10%. However, after the malicious rate exceeds 80%, the rate of inauthentic downloads of BGET also experience a dramatic increase. That is to say, the malicious rate of 80% is the limit value at which our method can maintain acceptable performance, which is far better than ET and HonestPeer. Of course, this is a reasonable phenomenon. When almost all members in a network are malicious, even the best method cannot achieve ideal performance. It's worth noting that even if there are no malicious peers in the network, inauthentic downloads still account for almost 5% - this accounts for mistakes users make when creating and sharing a file, e.g., by providing the wrong meta-data or creating and sharing an unreadable file [7].

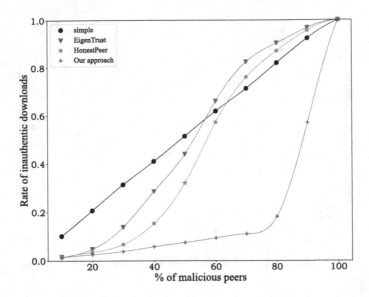

**Fig. 5.** The effect of proportion of malicious peers to different methods. $peer\_num =$ 1000.

On the whole, our BGET approach has good scalability when the scale of network increases and responds well to different size of peers and malicious rates. BGET can maintain a low inauthentic downloads rate when the malicious rate is lower than 80%. Compare to methods such as ET and HonestPeer, BGET exhibit strong robustness when facing harsh environments with a large number of malicious peers.

## 6 Conclusion

In this paper, we expounded why peers will gather around the pre-trusted peers and high-reputation peers, and this aggregation will drive the network towards centralization, which is contrary to the original intention of P2P networks. Besides, the pre-trust mechanism will lead to uncontrolled spread of inauthentic downloads. To address these problems, we proposed a BGET reputation management approach for P2P networks. In BGET, we utilized uniform grouping strategy to prevent the aggregation of high-reputation peers, put forward a grouping-GT reputation updating algorithm and design some reliable verification services based on blockchain to avoid the fraud of malicious peers. Finally, we employed several simulations to evaluate the effectiveness of BGET. The results showed that BGET not only exhibits strong scalability for the increasing number of peers, but also strong robustness for the increasing proportion of malicious peers. For the success rate of downloading authentic files, BGET can keep the rate of inauthentic downloading at around 10% when the malicious rate below 80%, which is far better than ET and HonestPeer.

In future work, we will focus on evaluation parameters and different malicious attacks to improve the robustness of our approach, and study the schemes that we could integrate our approach into the consensus process of some mature blockchain networks, such as Hyperledger, EOS and so on.

# References

1. Aberer, K., Despotovic, Z.: Managing trust in a peer-2-peer information system. In: Proceedings of the 2001 ACM CIKM International Conference on Information and Knowledge Management, Atlanta, Georgia, USA, November 5-10, 2001, pp. 310–317. ACM (2001). https://doi.org/10.1145/502585.502638
2. Alhussain, A., Kurdi, H.A.: EERP: an enhanced Eigentrust algorithm for reputation management in peer-to-peer networks. Procedia Comput. Sci. **141**, 490–495 (2018). https://doi.org/10.1016/j.procs.2018.10.137
3. Can, A.B., Bhargava, B.K.: SORT: a self-organizing trust model for peer-to-peer systems. IEEE Trans. Dependable Secur. Comput. **10**(1), 14–27 (2013). https://doi.org/10.1109/TDSC.2012.74
4. Chiluka, N., Andrade, N., Gkorou, D., Pouwelse, J.A.: Personalizing Eigentrust in the face of communities and centrality attack. In: IEEE 26th International Conference on Advanced Information Networking and Applications, AINA, 2012 , Fukuoka, Japan, March 26-29, 2012, pp. 503–510. IEEE Computer Society (2012). https://doi.org/10.1109/AINA.2012.48
5. Govindaraj, R., Priya, G., Chowdhury, S., Kim, D., Tran, D., Le, A.: A review on various applications of reputation based trust management. Int. J. Interact. Mob. Technol. **15**(10), 87 (2021). https://doi.org/10.3991/ijim.v15i10.21645
6. Jøsang, A., Golbeck, J.: Challenges for robust trust and reputation systems. In: 5th International Workshop on Security and Trust Management (STM 2009) (2009)
7. Kamvar, S.D., Schlosser, M.T., Garcia-Molina, H.: The Eigentrust algorithm for reputation management in P2P networks. In: Proceedings of the Twelfth International World Wide Web Conference, WWW 2003, Budapest, Hungary, May 20-24, 2003, pp. 640–651. ACM (2003). https://doi.org/10.1145/775152.775242
8. Karjalainen, R.: Governance in decentralized networks (2020). https://doi.org/10.2139/ssrn.3551099
9. Khan, Z.A., Abbasi, U.: SORT: A self-organizing trust model for peer-to-peer systems. Electronics **9**(3), 415 (2020). https://doi.org/10.3390/electronics9030415
10. Kouicem, D.E., Imine, Y., Bouabdallah, A., Lakhlef, H.: Decentralized blockchain-based trust management protocol for the internet of things. IEEE Trans. Dependable Secur. Comput. **19**(2), 1292–1306 (2022). https://doi.org/10.1109/TDSC.2020.3003232
11. Kremenova, I., Gajdos, M.: Decentralized networks: the future internet. Mob. Netw. Appl. **24**, 2016–2023 (2019). https://doi.org/10.1007/s11036-018-01211-5
12. Kurdi, H.A.: HonestPeer: an enhanced Eigentrust algorithm for reputation management in P2P systems. J. King Saud Univ. Comput. Inf. Sci. **27**(3), 315–322 (2015). https://doi.org/10.1016/j.jksuci.2014.10.002
13. Lee, J., Becker, K.: Organizational usage of social media for corporate reputation management. J. Asian Financ. Econ. Bus. **6**(1), 231–240 (2020). https://doi.org/10.13106/jafeb.2019.vol6.no1.231

14. Li, M., Guan, Q., Jin, X., Guo, C., Tan, X., Gao, Y.: Personalized pre-trust reputation management in social P2P network. In: 2016 International Conference on Computing, Networking and Communications, ICNC 2016, Kauai, HI, USA, February 15-18, 2016. pp. 1–5. IEEE Computer Society (2016). https://doi.org/10.1109/ICCNC.2016.7440695

15. Lin, Y.J., Yang, H.W., Yang, C.C., Lin, W.: A traceable and fair transaction mechanism for digital rights management on P2P networks. J. Internet Technol. **14**(7), 1043–1051 (2013). https://doi.org/10.6138/JIT.2013.14.7.04

16. Liu, Y., Wang, J., Yan, Z., Wan, Z., Jäntti, R.: A survey on blockchain-based trust management for internet of things. IEEE Internet Things J. **10**(7), 5898–5922 (2023). https://doi.org/10.1109/JIOT.2023.3237893

17. Lu, K., Wang, J., Li, M.: An Eigentrust dynamic evolutionary model in P2P file-sharing systems. Peer-to-Peer Netw. Appl. **9**, 599–612 (2016). https://doi.org/10.1007/s12083-015-0416-1

18. Resnick, P., Kuwabara, K., Zeckhauser, R., Friedman, E.: Reputation systems. Commun. ACM **43**(12), 45–48 (2000). https://doi.org/10.1145/355112.355122

19. Su, S., Tian, Z., Liang, S., Li, S., Du, S., Guizani, N.: A reputation management scheme for efficient malicious vehicle identification over 5G networks. IEEE Wirel. Commun. **27**(3), 46–52 (2020). https://doi.org/10.1109/MWC.001.1900456

20. Tian, Z., Gao, X., Su, S., Qiu, J., Du, X., Guizani, M.: Evaluating reputation management schemes of internet of vehicles based on evolutionary game theory. IEEE Trans. Veh. Technol. **68**(6), 5971–5980 (2019). https://doi.org/10.1109/TVT.2019.2910217

21. Walsh, K., Sirer, E.G.: Fighting peer-to-peer SPAM and decoys with object reputation. In: Proceedings of the 2005 ACM SIGCOMM Workshop on Economics of Peer-to-Peer Systems, P2PECON 2005, Philadelphia, Pennsylvania, USA, August 22, 2005, pp. 138–143. ACM (2005). https://doi.org/10.1145/1080192.1080204

22. Wu, X., Liang, J.: A blockchain-based trust management method for internet of things. Pervasive Mob. Comput. **72**, 101330 (2021). https://doi.org/10.1016/j.pmcj.2021.101330

23. Xiao, Y., Liu, Y.: BayesTrust and Vehiclerank: constructing an implicit web of trust in VANET. IEEE Trans. Veh. Technol. **68**(3), 2850–2864 (2019). https://doi.org/10.1109/TVT.2019.2894056

24. Xiong, L., Liu, L.: Peertrust: supporting reputation-based trust for peer-to-peer electronic communities. IEEE Trans. Knowl. Data Eng. **16**(7), 843–857 (2004). https://doi.org/10.1109/TKDE.2004.1318566

25. Xue, W., Liu, Y., Li, K., Chi, Z., Min, G., Qu, W.: DHTrust: a robust and distributed reputation system for trusted peer-to-peer networks. Concurr. Comput. Pract. Exp. **24**(10), 1037–1051 (2012). https://doi.org/10.1002/cpe.1749

26. Yang, Z., Yang, K., Lei, L., Zheng, K., Leung, V.C.M.: Blockchain-based decentralized trust management in vehicular networks. IEEE Internet Things J. **6**(2), 1495–1505 (2019). https://doi.org/10.1109/JIOT.2018.2836144

27. Liu, Y., Wu, L., Li, J.: Peer-to-peer (p2p) electricity trading in distribution systems of the future. Elect. J. **32**(4), 2–6 (2019). https://doi.org/10.1016/j.tej.2019.03.002

28. Yu, B., Singh, M.P.: A social mechanism of reputation management in electronic communities. In: Klusch, M., Kerschberg, L. (eds.) CIA 2000. LNCS (LNAI), vol. 1860, pp. 154–165. Springer, Heidelberg (2000). https://doi.org/10.1007/978-3-540-45012-2_15

29. Zhou, R., Hwang, K.: PowerTrust: a robust and scalable reputation system for trusted peer-to-peer computing. IEEE Trans. Parallel Distrib. Syst. **18**(4), 460–473 (2007). https://doi.org/10.1109/TPDS.2007.1021

# Privacy-Preserving Blockchain Supervision with Responsibility Tracking

Baodong Wen[1], Yujue Wang[2], Yong Ding[1,3(✉)], Haibin Zheng[2,4], Hai Liang[1],
Changsong Yang[1], and Jinyuan Liu[2]

[1] Guangxi Key Laboratory of Cryptography and Information Security,
School of Computer Science and Information Security,
Guilin University of Electronic Technology, Guilin, China
`stone_dingy@126.com`
[2] Hangzhou Innovation Institute of Beihang University, Hangzhou, China
[3] Institute of Cyberspace Technology, HKCT Institute for Higher Education,
Hong Kong SAR, China
[4] WeBank Institute of Financial Technology, Shenzhen University, Shenzhen, China

**Abstract.** Blockchain technology is a strategic technology to support
the development of digital economy, which helps to promote data sharing, improve the efficiency of communication and build a trusted system. With the continuous development of blockchain technology, security
problems caused by lack of regulation are also frequent. Also, the supervision process needs to check the data information on the blockchain,
which may lead to the disclosure of users' privacy information. To solve
the above problems, this paper proposes a privacy protection blockchain
supervision scheme (PBS) that supports ciphertext supervision and malicious user tracking. The PBS supports the supervision of ciphertext data
on the blockchain, meaning that regulators do not need to decrypt it and
can perform supervision without plaintext. This ensures that the private
data of users on the blockchain would not be compromised in the process
of supervision. Moreover, the scheme supports the tracking of the sender
of the offending information. Theoretical analysis and comparison show
that the proposed PBS can effectively ensure the privacy of user data on
blockchain, and experimental analysis demonstrates the practicability of
the scheme.

**Keywords:** blockchain supervision · equality test · privacy
protection · malicious user tracking

## 1 Introduction

Blockchain integrates distributed storage, peer-to-peer network, consensus mechanism, cryptography and other technologies, making on-chain data open, trans-
parent, non-tamperable, and traceable. Blockchain has created a new collaboration model that does not rely on a third party to establish trust in an untrusted
environment, and has carried out extensive explorations in many fields such as

© ICST Institute for Computer Sciences, Social Informatics and Telecommunications Engineering 2024
Published by Springer Nature Switzerland AG 2024. All Rights Reserved
H. Gao et al. (Eds.): CollaborateCom 2023, LNICST 561, pp. 243–262, 2024.
https://doi.org/10.1007/978-3-031-54521-4_14

finance [3], unmanned aerial vehicle [2], copyright [17] and supply chain [6]. Thus, blockchain builds a brand new value transfer network, which is the key supporting technology for building the next-generation Internet trusted infrastructure.

The difficulty of tampering with blockchain data makes it difficult to modify and delete the data on the blockchain through traditional methods, which increases the difficulty of supervising harmful information on the chain and poses new challenges for information management [20]. At present, there is still a lack of effective supervision methods in the blockchain system. When attackers threaten the security of the system and illegal users use the blockchain to commit illegal acts, the system cannot hold the attackers and illegal users accountable. Therefore, once harmful information such as violence, terrorism and pornography is written into the blockchain, it can not only spread rapidly using its synchronization mechanism, but also difficult to modify and delete these information.

The openness and transparency of blockchain system data is the basis for building a decentralized trust ecosystem, but it also brings serious challenges to the privacy protection of blockchain systems [7]. The open source sharing protocol in the blockchain enables data to be recorded and stored synchronously at all user sides. For attackers, data copies can be obtained in more locations, and useful information such as blockchain applications, users, and network structures can be analyzed. Encrypting the data on the chain is a way to achieve privacy protection [16]. However, in the supervision system, it is difficult for the regulator to effectively review the ciphertext when supervising the data in the blockchain.

Li et al. [5] proposed a two-layer adaptive blockchain supervision model to solve the problems of difficult supervision and poor privacy in the production of off-site modular housing. In this model, the first layer is the user's private side chain, and the second layer is mainly used for communication and transactions between users. The model allows each participant to access the status and records of the entire process, while protecting the privacy of material suppliers, manufacturers and contractors. Wen et al. [15] proposed a blockchain regulatory framework using attribute-based encryption and a dual-chain model. In this architecture, the regulator first obtains plaintext data from the business chain for the first round of supervision. After the supervision is completed, it is encrypted with attribute-based encryption and sent to the regulatory party. The authorized regulatory party can decrypt the ciphertext and conduct the second round of supervision. However, the above scheme cannot supervise the ciphertext data in the blockchain, that is, the regulator must review the plaintext when supervising. Data senders often do not want regulators to obtain their own private information, thus there is a lack of a mechanism to supervise ciphertext in the current blockchain supervision system.

## 1.1  Our Contributions

In order to solve the problem that it is difficult to supervise the ciphertext data when monitoring the blockchain, this paper proposes a blockchain supervision scheme that supports the equality test of ciphertext. The scheme uses the ciphertext equality test technology to compare the encrypted keywords of user data and the keywords that central regulatory want to supervise. When the two keywords are the same, the supervision scheme compares the ciphertext of the keywords and outputs the result that the keywords are equal. In order to avoid the problem that a single regulator has a single point of failure, this paper sets up two regulators to perform joint supervision. The central regulatory authorizes two local regulators, and after authorization, the regulators conduct non-interactive supervision, which reduces the efficiency problems caused by interaction. In order to track the illegal users and prevent regulators from forging keywords and abusing tokens, signcryption is used to track accountability. Central regulatory regularly supervise the supervision records, and when they find that there is illegal supervision or improper supervision, they will be held accountable in time.

## 1.2 Related Works

In terms of blockchain regulation, Marian [8] suggested using unique identifiers to identify users, giving up the anonymity protection provided by the Bitcoin system. This can improve the detection probability of suspicious users, so as to investigate and sanction traders who use the Bitcoin system to conduct illegal and criminal activities. Yong et al. [20] proposed a vaccine regulatory traceability system that combines machine learning with blockchain. The system uses smart contracts to record vaccines, and can also track information about violating vaccines. In order to supervise vaccine production, Peng et al. [9] designed a two-layer blockchain to record and manage production data. The two-layer blockchain stores private information and public information respectively, thus realizing the privacy protection of production information.

Privacy in blockchain is also one of the key research directions. Bünz et al. [1] proposed a distributed payment mechanism for smart contracts, in which account balances are encrypted and cryptographic proofs are used to secure transactions between users. This mechanism is compatible with other smart contract platforms such as Ethereum. Rahulamathavan et al. [10] constructed an IoT application-level privacy protection architecture through attribute-based encryption. This architecture guarantees the confidentiality of data and devices in blockchain-based IoT systems. Zhang et al. [21] proposed a privacy predictor protocol, which extends the data security function of HTTP/TLS protocol to ensure the privacy and non-tampering of data transmission from various private data sources.

Ciphertext equality test allows testing the equivalence of ciphertexts without decrypting them [13]. Depending on the number of servers used for the comparison, it can be classified into single-server model and dual-server model. Under the single-server model, Yang et al. [19] proposed a public key encryption scheme that supports ciphertext equivalence comparison, which can ensure that the tester can detect whether two ciphertexts encrypted by different public keys are equal without decrypting the ciphertext. To address the issue of the lack of ciphertext equivalence comparison in signature and encryption protocols among multiple systems, Xiong et al. [18] proposed a heterogeneous signcryption scheme for wireless body area network. The scheme aims to meet requirements such as data authenticity, privacy protection, and security, and achieves efficient implementation of the signcryption scheme by addressing critical issues such as key management and certificate management. In order to ensure the secure sharing of data between remote servers, Wang et al. [14] proposed a proxy re-encryption scheme that supports the equivalence comparison of ciphertexts. This scheme supports users to join the group dynamically, and also supports the distinction and proof of encrypted data.

In the single-server model, the ciphertext equivalence comparison process can be performed by a single server. Although this simplifies the system's workflow, it may also be vulnerable to offline keyword guessing attacks, whereby the server constructs keyword ciphertext multiple times and performs equivalence tests using authorization tokens. If the comparison succeeds, it means that the server has successfully guessed the keyword, which violates the principle of not allowing the server to know the keyword and poses a certain security risk. The dual-server model can effectively prevent offline keyword guessing attacks by having two servers collaborate with each other to perform the equivalence comparison process, thereby improving the security and robustness of the system. Tang [11] proposed a ciphertext equivalence comparison scheme that supports user authorization and dual-server interaction. In this scheme, only one authorization instruction is required to allow any authorized party to perform ciphertext equivalence test. In order to protect the privacy of data in cloud servers and resist keyword guessing attacks, Zhao et al. [22] proposed a dual-server authorized ciphertext equivalence test scheme, in which user data is stored in the main server to reduce local storage.

### 1.3  Organization

The remainder of this paper is organized as follows. Section 2 describes the system model and requirements. A description of our PBS scheme is presented in Sect. 3. In Sect. 4, the security and performance of our PBS scheme are evaluated and compared. Section 5 concludes the paper.

## 2  System Model and Requirements

### 2.1  System Model

As shown in Fig. 1, a PBS system consists of three types of entities, namely, central regulatory ($CR$), local regulatory ($LR$) and users.

- $CR$: $CR$ is responsible for registering users and $LR$. At the same time, $CR$ can grant regulatory authority to $LR$. If $LR$ violates the supervision rules, $CR$ will track the $LR$.
- $LR$: $LR$ is responsible for supervising the ciphertexts of keywords uploaded by user. When $LR$ discovers that there are illegal keywords in user data, $LR$ reports the illegal information to CR.

- User: User uploads data ciphertext to the blockchain. The data ciphertext consists of two parts, the business content ciphertext and the keyword ciphertext. Keywords are used to summarize key parts of the business content.

In the PBS system, users upload the ciphertext of transaction content and keywords to the blockchain. $LR$ must obtain $CR$'s authorization before performing supervision. During the supervision process, two authorized $LR$s will conduct joint supervision. When illegal data is found, $LR$ will send a violation report to $CR$, and $CR$ will be responsible for tracking the illegal users. At the same time, $CR$ will supervise the $LR$'s supervision records, and if there is any violation of supervision, $LR$ will be tracked.

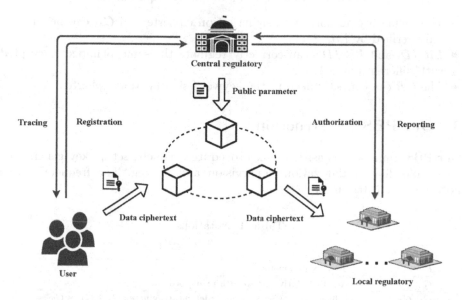

**Fig. 1.** System model of PBS.

## 2.2   System Requirements

A secure PBS system has to satisfy the following requirements.

- Privacy protection: Encryption should be used to ensure the privacy of user transaction data and keywords. At the same time, the keywords set by the user should allow the authorized regulator to supervise the ciphertext.
- Resistance of offline keyword guessing attack: When supervising the data uploaded by users, the regulators should be jointly supervised, that is, two regulators should jointly perform the supervision in one supervision process. This can avoid the problem of excessive concentration of regulatory power. In addition, the system should be resistant to offline keyword guessing attacks when two regulators are not colluding.

- Authenticity verification: In the PBS system, malicious users may pretend to be others to upload illegal data. Also, malicious regulators may query keywords that are not within the scope of their own supervision. To defend against this attack, it is necessary to verify the origin of data uploaded by users and keywords regulated by regulators.
- Access control: The system should ensure the access control of the data content on the blockchain, and prohibit unauthorized users from operating the data content, that is, the transaction content uploaded by users is only allowed to be viewed by authorized users, and the keyword ciphertext is only allowed to be supervised by authorized regulators.

A correct PBS system has to satisfy the following requirements.

- The regulatory authorization signcryption ciphertext of $CR$ can be successfully verified by $LR$.
- $LR\ ID_l$ and $LR\ ID_{l'}$ can correctly regulate the same plaintext encrypted with different public keys.
- The $CR$ can correctly decrypt the keyword signcryption ciphertext.

## 3    Our PBS Construction

Our PBS framework consists of six procedures, namely, setup, key generation, data uploading, authorization, supervision and tracing. The frequently used notations are listed in Table 1.

**Table 1.** Notations

| Notations | Descriptions |
|---|---|
| $l$ | Security parameter |
| $G$ | A multiplicative group with prime order $q$ |
| $G_1, G_2, G_T$ | Bilinear groups with prime order $p$ satisfying $e : G_1 \times G_2 \rightarrow G_T$ |
| $g_1, g_2$ | Generators $G_1$ and $G_2$ respectively |
| $H_1, H_2, H_3, H_4$ | Cryptographic hash functions |
| $sk_u = (x_u, y_u)$ | Private key of user $ID_u$ |
| $pk_u = (X_u, Y_u)$ | Public key of user $ID_u$ |
| $Tr_u$ | Transactions sent by user $ID_u$ |
| $K_u$ | Keywords of user $ID_u$ data |
| $\sigma_u$ | Keyword signcryption ciphertext of user $ID_u$ transaction $Tr_u$ |
| $\sigma_c$ | User $ID_u$ keyword $K_u$ signcryption ciphertext |
| $T_c, T_c'$ | Authorized supervision tokens for $LR\ ID_l$ and $LR\ ID_{l'}$ respectively |
| $K_c$ | Keywords that CR want to supervise |
| $\rho_l^*, \rho_l'^*$ | Equality test parameter |
| $\omega_l'$ | Supervision records |
| $J$ | Supervision result |
| $t$ | Timestamp |

## 3.1   Setup

Given the security parameter $l \in Z^+$, $CR$ chooses a multiplicative group $G$ with prime order $q$, where $g$ is a generator of group $G$. Next, $CR$ chooses a bilinear map $e : G_1 \times G_2 \to G_T$, where $G_1$ and $G_2$ are multiplicative groups of prime order $p$, and they have $g_1$ and $g_2$ as their generators respectively.

$CR$ selects four collision-resistant hash functions $H_1 : \{0,1\}^* \to Z_q$, $H_2 : \{0,1\}^* \to \{0,1\}^k$, $H_3 : \{0,1\}^* \to G_1$ and $H_4 : \{0,1\}^* \to Z_p$, where $k$ is a polynomial in $l$. Finally, $CR$ publishes $(l, q, p, g, g_1, g_2, e, G, G_1, G_2, G_T, H_1, H_2, H_3, H_4)$ as the public parameters of the system. $CR$ chooses a secure ciphertext-policy attribute-based encryption scheme $F$ and sends it to the blockchain.

## 3.2   Key Generation

User $ID_u$ chooses $x_u \in_R Z_q, y_u \in_R Z_p$, and calculates

$$X_u = g^{x_u}$$

$$Y_u = g_1^{y_u}$$

Finally, user $ID_u$ outputs the public-private key pair $(pk_u, sk_u)$, where $pk_u = (X_u, Y_u)$ and $sk_u = (x_u, y_u)$. Note that $CR$ and $LR$ can respectively generate their public-private key pairs $(pk_c, sk_c)$ and $(pk_l, sk_l)$ in the similar way.

## 3.3   Data Uploading

The user $ID_u$ uses attribute-based encryption $F$ to encrypt the transaction data in transaction $Tr_u$ and upload it to the blockchain. For the keyword $K_u \in \{0,1\}^k$ of the transaction $Tr_u$, user $ID_u$ chooses $\alpha_u, \varphi_u \in_R Z_q, \beta_u \in_R Z_p$ and calculates the keyword signcryption ciphertext $\sigma_u = (c_{1,u}, c_{2,u}, c_{3,u}, c_{4,u}, U_u, v_u)$ as follows

$$c_{1,u} = g^{\alpha_u}$$

$$c_{2,u} = g_1^{\beta_u}$$

$$c_{3,u} = H_2(X_c^{\alpha_u}) \oplus K_u$$

$$c_{4,u} = Y_c^{\beta_u} \cdot H_3(K_u)$$

$$I_u = g^{\varphi_u}$$

$$U_u = H_1(I_u \| c_{1,u} \| c_{2,u} \| c_{3,u} \| c_{4,u})$$

$$v_u = U_u x_u + \varphi_u \quad \mod q$$

Finally, user $ID_u$ sends the keyword signcryption ciphertext $\sigma_u = (c_{1,u}, c_{2,u}, c_{3,u}, c_{4,u}, U_u, v_u)$ to blockchain.

## 3.4    Authorization

The $CR$ completes the authorization by sending the authorization signcryption to $LR\ ID_l$ and $LR\ ID_{l'}$. $CR$ chooses $\eta, \lambda, \gamma \in_R Z_p$, $\varphi_T \in_R Z_q$, and calculates

$$T_{1,c} = g_2^{\gamma}$$

$$T_{2,c} = g_2^{y_c\gamma - \eta H_4(X_l)}$$

$$T_{3,c} = g_2^{\lambda H_4(X_{l'})}$$

$$T_c = (T_{1,c}, T_{2,c}, T_{3,c})$$

$$I_T = g^{\varphi_T}$$

$$U_T = H_1(I_T \| T_c)$$

$$v_T = U_T x_c + \varphi_T \mod q$$

Finally, $CR$ sends the authorization signcryption ciphertext $\sigma_T = (T_c, U_T, v_T)$ to $LR\ ID_l$. After receiving the ciphertext $\sigma_T$, $LR\ ID_l$ verifies the following equation.

$$H_1(g^{v_T} \cdot X_c^{-U_T} \| T_c) \overset{?}{=} U_T \tag{1}$$

If Eq. (1) holds, it shows that $\sigma_T$ is sent by $CR$, which can effectively prevent illegal entities from pretending to be authorized by $CR$.

Also, $CR$ chooses $\varphi_{T'} \in_R Z_q$ and calculates

$$T'_{1,c} = g_2^{\gamma}$$

$$T'_{2,c} = g_2^{y_c\gamma - \lambda H_4(X_{l'})}$$

$$T'_{3,c} = g_2^{\eta H_4(X_l)}$$

$$T'_c = (T'_{1,c}, T'_{2,c}, T'_{3,c})$$

$$I'_T = g^{\varphi'_T}$$

$$U'_T = H_1(I'_T \| T'_c)$$

$$v'_T = U'_T x_c + \varphi'_T \mod q$$

Finally, $CR$ sends the authorization signcryption ciphertext $\sigma'_T = (T'_c, U'_T, v'_T)$ to $LR\ ID_{l'}$. After receiving the ciphertext $\sigma'_T$, $LR\ ID_{l'}$ verifies the following equation.

$$H_1(g^{v'_T} \cdot X_c^{-U'_T} \| T'_c) \overset{?}{=} U'_T \tag{2}$$

If Eq. (2) holds, it implies that $\sigma_T$ is sent by $CR$, which can effectively prevent illegal entities from pretending to be authorized by $CR$.

## 3.5  Supervision

**Distribute Ciphertext to Be Compared.** When $CR$ wants to check whether the transaction keywords uploaded by users contain the keyword $K_c$ through $LR$ $ID_l$ and $LR\ ID_{l'}$, $CR$ chooses $\alpha_c, \varphi_c \in_R Z_q^*, \beta_c \in_R Z_p^*$, and calculates regulatory keyword signcryption ciphertext $\sigma_c = (c_{1,c}, c_{2,c}, c_{3,c}, c_{4,c}, U_c, v_c)$ as follows

$$c_{1,c} = g^{\alpha_c}$$

$$c_{2,c} = g_1^{\beta_c}$$

$$c_{3,c} = H_2(X_c^{\alpha_c}) \oplus K_c$$

$$c_{4,c} = Y_c^{\beta_c} \cdot H_3(K_c)$$

$$I_c = g^{\varphi_c}$$

$$U_c = H_1(I_c \| c_{1,c} \| c_{2,c} \| c_{3,c} \| c_{4,c})$$

$$v_c = U_c x_c + \varphi_c \mod q$$

Finally, $CR$ sends regulatory keyword signcryption ciphertext $\sigma_c = (c_{1,c}, c_{2,c}, c_{3,c}, c_{4,c}, U_c, v_c)$ to $LR\ ID_l$ and $LR\ ID_{l'}$.

After receiving the ciphertext $\sigma_c$, the $LR\ ID_l$ uses the following steps to verify the authenticity.

$$H_1(g^{v_c} \cdot X_c^{-U_c} \| c_{1,c} \| c_{2,c} \| c_{3,c} \| c_{4,c}) \overset{?}{=} U_c \tag{3}$$

If Eq. (3) is satisfied, it implies that $\sigma_c$ comes from the $CR$, so as to prevent illegal entities from impersonating the $CR$ to illegally distribute regulatory keywords.

**Joint Supervision.** When the user $ID_u$ publishes the transaction $Tr_u$ to the blockchain, the $LR\ ID_l$ obtains the keyword signcryption ciphertext $\sigma_u$ uploaded by the user $ID_u$ and verifies the following equation.

$$H_1(g^{v_u} \cdot X_u^{-U_u}\|c_{1,u}\|c_{2,u}\|c_{3,u}\|c_{4,u}) \overset{?}{=} U_u \tag{4}$$

If the verification is successful, it indicates that the data source is legal. $LR\ ID_l$ adds records $r = (ID_u, X_u, \sigma_u, ID_l)$ to table $a$ of regulatory records,

$$\rho_l = \frac{e(c_{4,u}, g_2^\gamma)}{e(c_{2,u}, g_2^{y_c\gamma - \eta H_4(X_l)})}$$

$$\mu_l = e(c_{2,c}, g_2^{\lambda H_4(X_{l'})})$$

and sends $\rho_l$, $\mu_l$ and $c_{2,u}$ to $LR\ ID_{l'}$.

$LR\ ID_{l'}$ computes

$$\rho_l' = \frac{e(c_{4,c}, g_2^\gamma)}{e(c_{2,c}, g_2^{y_c\gamma - \lambda H_4(X_{l'})})}$$

$$\rho_l^* = \frac{\rho_l}{e(c_{2,u}, g_2^{\eta H_4(X_l)})} \tag{5}$$

$$\rho_l'^* = \frac{\rho_l'}{\mu_l} \tag{6}$$

$LR\ ID_{l'}$ compares $\rho_l^*$ with $\rho_l'^*$. If $\rho_l^* = \rho_l'^*$, $K_c$ is contained in the ciphertext $c_u$ of the user's keyword.

$LR\ ID_{l'}$ adds supervision record $\omega_l'$ to regulatory records table $b$ and uploads it to the blockchain.

$$\omega_{l'} = (ID_\omega\|ID_l\|ID_{l'}\|\sigma_c\|\sigma_u\|J\|t)$$

where $ID_\omega$ is the identity of $\omega_l'$, $J$ is the supervision result and $t$ is timestamp.

### 3.6   Tracing

If an illegal keyword is found in $\sigma_c$, the $LR\ ID_l$ will be matched with $\sigma_u$ in the regulatory record $\omega_l'$ and $\sigma_u$ in the record $r$ in table $a$ of the regulatory record. Then $LR\ ID_l$ will report the records $\omega_l'$ and $r$ to $CR$. $CR$ uses the $ID_u$ in $r$ to trace the user who sent the unauthorized data. After successful tracing, $CR$ will handle the violator according to its own regulatory rules.

$CR$ reviews the regulatory records generated by $LR$ at any time. $CR$ first checks whether it can decrypt the ciphertext $\sigma_u$ using Eq. (7). If it cannot, it means that the user did not use the public key of the $CR$ when uploading the ciphertext. $CR$ queries Table 1 of $LR\ ID_l$ to find the user $ID_u$ by searching for $\sigma_u$ and then traces the user. $CR$ uses Eq. (8) to decrypt the ciphertext $\sigma_c$ in the regulatory record.

$$\hat{K}_u = c_{3,u} \oplus H_2(c_{1,u}^{x_c}) \tag{7}$$

$$\hat{K}_c = c_{3,c} \oplus H_2(c_{1,c}^{x_c}) \tag{8}$$

If the decryption is successful, the $CR$ checks whether the $LR$ $ID_l$ and $LR$ $ID_{l'}$ search for keywords that are not within the scope of their search. Also, $CR$ checks whether the supervision results are correct. If there is non-compliance by $LR$ $ID_l$ and $LR$ $ID_{l'}$, the $CR$ conducts identification tracking according to supervision records.

**Theorem 1.** *The above proposed PBS construction is correct.*

*Proof.* For the correctness of verification by $LR$ $ID_l$ on signcryption ciphertexts $\sigma_T$ from $CR$, the Eq. (1) holds as follows

$$
\begin{aligned}
H_1(g^{v_T} \cdot X_c^{-U_T} \| T_c) &= H_1(g^{v_T} \cdot g^{x_c \cdot (-U_T)} \| T_c) \\
&= H_1(g^{U_T x_c + \varphi_T} \cdot g^{x_c \cdot (-U_T)} \| T_c) \\
&= H_1(g^{\varphi_T} \| T_c) \\
&= H_1(I_T \| T_c)
\end{aligned}
$$

Therefore, the token sent by $CR$ can be correctly verified.

For the correctness of ciphertext supervision, the Eq. (5) and Eq. (6) holds as follows

$$
\begin{aligned}
\rho_l^* &= \frac{\rho_l}{e(c_{2,u}, g_2^{\eta H_4(X_l)})} \\
&= \frac{e(c_{4,u}, g_2^{\gamma})}{e(c_{2,u}, g_2^{y_c \gamma - \eta H_4(X_l)}) \cdot e(c_{2,u}, g_2^{\eta H_4(X_l)})} \\
&= \frac{e(Y_c^{\beta_u} \cdot H_3(K_u), g_2^{\gamma})}{e(g_1^{\beta_u}, g_2^{y_c \gamma - \eta H_4(X_l)}) \cdot e(g_1^{\beta_u}, g_2^{\eta H_4(X_l)})} \\
&= \frac{e(g_1^{y_c \cdot \beta_u} \cdot H_3(K_u), g_2^{\gamma})}{e(g_1^{\beta_u}, g_2^{y_c \gamma - \eta H_4(X_l)}) \cdot e(g_1^{\beta_u}, g_2^{\eta H_4(X_l)})} \\
&= \frac{e(g_1^{y_c \cdot \beta_u}, g_2^{\gamma}) \cdot e(H_3(K_u), g_2^{\gamma})}{e(g_1^{\beta_u}, g_2^{y_c \gamma - \eta H_4(X_l)}) \cdot e(g_1^{\beta_u}, g_2^{\eta H_4(X_l)})} \\
&= \frac{e(g_1^{y_c \cdot \beta_u}, g_2^{\gamma}) \cdot e(H_3(K_u), g_2^{\gamma})}{e(g_1^{\beta_u}, g_2^{y_c \gamma}) \cdot e(g_1^{\beta_u}, g_2^{-\eta H_4(X_l)}) \cdot e(g_1^{\beta_u}, g_2^{\eta H_4(X_l)})} \\
&= e(H_3(K_u), g_2^{\gamma})
\end{aligned}
$$

$$\rho_l'^* = \frac{\rho_l'}{\mu_l}$$

$$= \frac{\rho_l'}{e(c_{2,c}, g_2^{\lambda H_4(X_{l'})})}$$

$$= \frac{e(c_{4,c}, g_2^{\gamma})}{e(c_{2,c}, g_2^{y_c\gamma - \lambda H_4(X_{l'})}) \cdot e(c_{2,c}, g_2^{\lambda H_4(X_{l'})})}$$

$$= \frac{e(Y_c^{\beta_c} \cdot H_3(K_c), g_2^{\gamma})}{e(g_1^{\beta_c}, g_2^{y_c\gamma - \lambda H_4(X_{l'})}) \cdot e(g_1^{\beta_c}, g_2^{\lambda H_4(X_{l'})})}$$

$$= \frac{e(g_1^{y_c \cdot \beta_c} \cdot H_3(K_c), g_2^{\gamma})}{e(g_1^{\beta_c}, g_2^{y_c\gamma - \lambda H_4(X_{l'})}) \cdot e(g_1^{\beta_c}, g_2^{\lambda H_4(X_{l'})})}$$

$$= \frac{e(g_1^{y_c \cdot \beta_c}, g_2^{\gamma}) \cdot e(H_3(K_c), g_2^{\gamma})}{e(g_1^{\beta_c}, g_2^{y_c\gamma - \lambda H_4(X_{l'})}) \cdot e(g_1^{\beta_c}, g_2^{\lambda H_4(X_{l'})})}$$

$$= \frac{e(g_1^{y_c \cdot \beta_l}, g_2^{\gamma}) \cdot e(H_3(K_c), g_2^{\gamma})}{e(g_1^{\beta_c}, g_2^{-\lambda H_4(X_{l'})}) \cdot e(g_1^{\beta_c}, g_2^{y_c\gamma}) \cdot e(g_1^{\beta_c}, g_2^{\lambda H_4(X_{l'})})}$$

$$= e(H_3(K_c), g_2^{\gamma})$$

Therefore, if $K_l$ and $K_u$ are equal, then $\rho_l^*$ and $\rho_l'^*$ are also equal.

For the correctness of the $CR$'s decryption of the keyword signcryption ciphertext, the Eq. (7) holds as follows

$$\hat{K}_u = c_{3,u} \oplus H_2(c_{1,u}^{x_c})$$
$$= H_2(X_c^{\alpha_u}) \oplus K_u \oplus H_2(g^{\alpha_u \cdot x_c})$$
$$= H_2(g^{x_c \cdot \alpha_u}) \oplus K_u \oplus H_2(g^{\alpha_u \cdot x_c})$$
$$= K_u$$

Therefore, $CR$ can correctly decrypt ciphertext to get keyword.

## 4   Analysis

### 4.1   Security Analysis

**Theorem 2.** *The PBS scheme proposed in this paper supports privacy protection of user data.*

*Proof.* When the sender wants to upload data to the blockchain, they will process the data information using ciphertext-policy attribute-based encryption. In addition, for the convenience of regulation, the sender also needs to summarize the keywords of the data to be uploaded. For these keywords, the sender uses encryption algorithms based on equality test techniques to encrypt them. When generating the keyword signcryption ciphertext $\sigma_u = (c_{1,u}, c_{2,u}, c_{3,u}, c_{4,u}, U_u, v_u)$, the generation process of element $c_{1,u}, c_{2,u}, c_{3,u}, c_{4,u}$ are similar to the algorithm for generating ciphertext in the scheme [11]. The difference is that in the scheme [11], $c_{3,u}$ is concatenated with a random number, and there is an additional ciphertext element $c_{5,u}$. Under the CDH and DDH assumptions, according to Theorem 3 in the scheme [11], the PBS scheme has indistinguishability under chosen ciphertext attack. In addition, $LR$ has no right to decrypt the keyword signcryption ciphertext during regulation, thus the PBS scheme realizes the privacy protection of user data.

**Theorem 3.** *The PBS scheme proposed in this paper is resistant to offline keyword guessing attacks.*

*Proof.* When $CR$ wants to regulate user data, it authorizes $LR\ ID_l$ and $LR\ ID_{l'}$ to carry out the specific regulatory process through token. $LR\ ID_l$ generates intermediate parameters from the token and keyword signcryption ciphertext and sends them to $LR\ ID_{l'}$. $LR\ ID_{l'}$ uses the intermediate parameters, token, and keyword signcryption ciphertext to perform ciphertext equality test and outputs the comparison result. According to scheme [11], the regulatory process is jointly executed by two local regulatory agencies. Under the premise that the two local regulatory agencies do not collude, it can prevent a single local regulatory agency from forging keyword signature ciphertext. Therefore, when the two $LR$s do not collude, the PBS scheme can resist offline keyword guessing attacks.

**Theorem 4.** *The PBS scheme proposed in this paper supports the verification of the authenticity of data sources.*

*Proof.* When data sender sends keyword data, they use signcryption technology to process keywords. If regulators discover illegal data, they use the signature of the data sender for positioning and tracking of the violator. To prevent $LR$ from forging authorization tokens and keyword signature ciphertexts, the signcryption technology is also used by the $CR$ when sending tokens and distributing keyword signcryption ciphertexts for regulation, ensuring the authenticity verification of the data source.

**Theorem 5.** *The proposed PBS scheme supports data access control.*

*Proof.* The data sender uses ciphertext-policy attribute-based encryption to process the plaintext data and embeds the user data access policy when encrypting the plaintext data. Only authorized users whose attribute set matches the access policy can successfully decrypt the ciphertext to obtain plaintext data when accessing the data. Therefore, only authorized users are allowed to view plaintext data, achieving data access control. In addition, during the supervision period, only $LR$ authorized by $CR$ is allowed to carry out supervision. According to Theorem 4 in [11], under the CDH and DBDH assumptions, the $CR$ can distribute authorizations, i.e., determine the $LR$s that have the authority to regulate. The authorization information can be verified during regulation to prevent unauthorized access. Therefore, the PBS scheme supports data access control.

## 4.2    Theoretical Analysis

This section compares the schemes of Wang et al. [12], Yong et al. [20] and Peng et al. [9] with our PBS scheme. As shown in Table 2, Wang et al.'s scheme [12], Peng et al.'s scheme [9] and our scheme support privacy protection while supervising. Our PBS scheme supports the supervision of data ciphertext on the blockchain, that is, the regulator can complete the supervision without decrypting the ciphertext, which further enhances the privacy of user data. In addition, the scheme of Yong et al. [20] and our scheme support the tracing of malicious users.

**Table 2.** Functional comparison

| Scheme | Privacy protection | Ciphertext supervision | User tracking | Advantage |
|---|---|---|---|---|
| Wang et al. [12] | $\checkmark$ | $\diagdown$ | $\diagdown$ | Improve the safety and consensus efficiency of rice supply chain supervision |
| Yong et al. [20] | $\diagdown$ | $\diagdown$ | $\checkmark$ | Support the intelligent supervision of vaccine expiration and fraudulent data |
| Peng et al. [9] | $\checkmark$ | $\diagdown$ | $\diagdown$ | High supervision efficiency and low memory overhead |
| PBS | $\checkmark$ | $\checkmark$ | $\checkmark$ | Support non-interactive ciphertext supervision |

We compare the computational complexity of Tang's scheme [11], Huang et al.'s scheme [4], and the PBS scheme. Table 3 lists the theoretical calculation time of the three schemes in key generation, encryption, authorization, ciphertext equality test, and decryption phases, respectively, where $T_{exp}$ represents the time for an exponentiation, $T_{PA}$ represents the time for a bilinear pairing, and $T_H$ represents the time for a hash.

In the key generation phase, Tang's scheme [11], Huang et al.'s scheme [4], and the PBS scheme have the same complexity, requiring two exponentiation operations. In the encryption stage, Tang's scheme [11] and Huang et al.'s scheme [4] both use four exponentiation operations. The PBS scheme requires an additional exponentiation operation to sign the data for regulation, but this ensures the authenticity of the data source. In the authorization stage, Tang's scheme [11] and Huang et al.'s scheme [4] require five exponentiation operations. PBS scheme needs four exponentiation operations. Huang et al.'s scheme [4] requires two hash operations, while the PBS scheme requires three hash operation. In the ciphertext equality test stage, Tang's scheme [11] uses six bilinear pairing operations, Huang et al.'s scheme [4] uses six exponentiation operations, two bilinear pairing operations, and three hash operations. The PBS scheme requires six bilinear pairing operations in the ciphertext equality test stage, which takes longer due to the need for two $LRs$ to jointly execute regulation. Tang's scheme [11] and Huang et al.'s scheme [4] both require two exponentiation operations and four exponentiation operations, respectively, in the decryption stage, while the PBS scheme only requires one exponentiation operation.

**Table 3.** Theoretical comparison

| Scheme | Key generation | Encryption | Authorization | Ciphertext equality test | Decryption |
|---|---|---|---|---|---|
| Tang [11] | $2T_{exp}$ | $4T_{exp} + 3T_H$ | $5T_{exp}$ | $6T_{PA}$ | $2T_{exp} + 2T_H$ |
| Huang et al. [4] | $2T_{exp}$ | $4T_{exp} + 2T_H$ | $5T_{exp} + 2T_H$ | $6T_{exp} + 2T_{PA} + 3T_H$ | $4T_{exp} + 2T_H$ |
| PBS | $2T_{exp}$ | $5T_{exp} + 3T_H$ | $4T_{exp} + 3T_H$ | $6T_{PA}$ | $T_{exp}$ |

### 4.3 Experimental Analysis

The PBS scheme was implemented using the Java and Solidity programming languages on a Windows 10 operating system with an Intel(R) Core(TM) i5-7500 CPU @ 3.40 GHz and 16 GB of RAM. The PBS scheme used FISCO BCOS 2.0 as the underlying framework for the consortium blockchain. The Type A pairing was used with a prime order $q$ of 256-bits, and the element size of $G$ was 512-bits. A prime order $p$ of 170-bits was used for the multiplicative group.

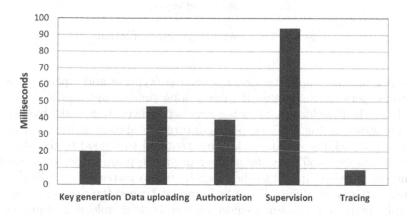

**Fig. 2.** Time cost of each phase.

Figure 2 shows the time costs of the PBS scheme in the key generation, data uploading, authorization, supervision, and tracing phases. As can be seen from the figure, it takes about 20 ms to generate a public-private key pair for a single user, and about 47 ms to upload keywords, which requires 5 exponential calculations. It takes about 39 ms to authorize a single supervisor. In the supervision phase, there are two steps: setting supervision keywords and joint supervision. Because the setting supervision keywords phase requires 5 exponential calculations, and joint supervision requires 6 bilinear pairing operations, the time cost is relatively large, taking about 94 ms in total. It takes about 9 ms to trace a user.

As shown in Fig. 3, in the keyword encryption stage of PBS scheme, the time required for encryption is counted when the number of keywords increases from 1 to 10. As the number of keywords gradually increases, the required time also increases. When the number of keywords is 10, the required time is approximately 463.14 ms. Thus, it can be seen from Fig. 3 that the time required for encryption keys is proportional to the number of keywords.

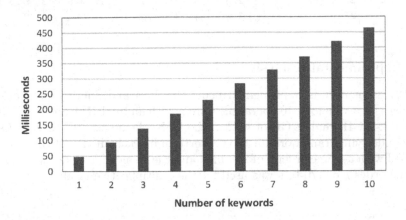

**Fig. 3.** Time cost of keyword encryption.

During the data upload stage, keyword encryption and ciphertext upload need to be performed. Because it takes a long time to upload the data to the blockchain, the time for uploading the keyword signcryption to the blockchain is listed separately in Fig. 4. The experimental results show that when the number of signcryption ciphertexts is 1, the time required to upload to the blockchain is approximately 0.465 s. As the number of signcryption ciphertexts increases, the time required to upload to the blockchain also increases accordingly. From the observation of the figure, it can be found that when the number of signcryption ciphertexts is 5, the time required for ciphertext upload is approximately 0.491 s. When the number of signcryption ciphertexts is 10, the time required for ciphertext upload is approximately 0.525 s. When the number of signcryption ciphertexts changes from 1 to 10, the time spent uploading to the blockchain increases by approximately 0.06 s. As the number of signcryption ciphertexts increases exponentially, the upload time does not increase exponentially, but shows a linear growth trend.

Figures 5 and 6 show the status information of the signcryption ciphertext uploaded to the blockchain. Figure 5 displays the transaction information on the blockchain, including block hash, block height, contract address, transaction hash and timestamp. The block hash and block height describe the block in which the current transaction is located, while the transaction hash represents the hash value of a transaction in the block, which serves as a unique index for easy retrieval. The required information can be quickly retrieved from the blockchain by using the hash. Figure 6 shows the transaction receipt after it is uploaded to the blockchain, including block hash, gas used, block number and transaction hash. The block hash, block number, and transaction hash in the

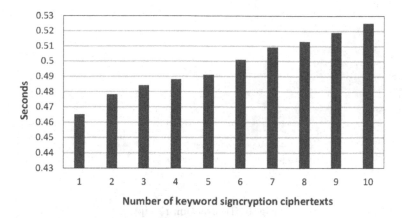

**Fig. 4.** Time cost of uploading keyword signcryption ciphertext to blockchain.

transaction receipt correspond to the block hash, block height, and transaction hash in the transaction information. The purpose of this correspondence is to better protect and track transaction information. When users or regulatory agencies want to query a transaction, they can quickly locate it by using the block hash, block height, and transaction hash. The gas used represents the amount of gas required to publish this transaction. The more operations required for upload or operation, the more gas is consumed.

| Transaction Hash | Block Height | Create Time |
|---|---|---|
| 0x3261a979fe3b3f3f0ed8407f67cffed19dc2f4850a3ad9450976df389000o4e9 | 1156 | 2023-02-26 09:46:45 |

Transaction Info | Transaction Receipt

| | |
|---|---|
| Block Hash: | 0xacb1f35a77b530579Sb837429996549a4a8f3a863c5aebb43d7730d4e13d696e |
| Block Height: | 1156 |
| Gas: | 30000000 |
| From: | 0x83309d045a19c44dc3722d15a6abd472f95866ac |
| To: | 0x0a68f060b46e0d8f969383d260c34105ea13a9dd |
| nonceRaw: | |
| Hash: | 0x3261a979fe3b3f3f0ed8407f67cffed19dc2f4850a3ad9450976df389000o4e9 |
| Timestamp: | 2023-02-26 9:46:45 |
| Input: | |

Decode

**Fig. 5.** Transaction information.

| Transaction Hash | Block Height | Create Time |
|---|---|---|
| 0x3261a979fe3b3f3f0ed8407f67cffed19dc2f4850a3ad9450976df389000c4e9 | 1156 | 2023-02-26 09:46:46 |

Transaction Info    Transaction Receipt

output:
blockHash:        0xacb1f35a77b5305795b837429996549a4a8f3a083c5aebb43d7730d4e13d698e
gasUsed:          377258
blockNumber:      1156
contractAddress:  0x0000000000000000000000000000000000000000
from:             0x83309d045a19c44dc3722d15a6abd472f95866ac
transactionIndex: 0x0
to:               0x0a68f060b46e0d8f69383d260c34105ea13a9dd
logsBloom:        0x0000000000000000000000000000000000000000000000000000000000000000000000000000000000000000000000000000000000000000000000000000000000
                  0000000000000000000000000000000000000000000000000000000000000000000000000000000000000000000000000000000000000000000000000000000000
                  0000000000000000000000000000000000000000000000000000000000000000000000000000000000000000000000000000000000000000000000000000000000
                  0000000000000000000000000000000000000000000000000000
transactionHash:  0x3261a979fe3b3f3f0ed8407f67cffed19dc2f4850a3ad9450976df389000c4e9
status:           0x0
logs:             []

**Fig. 6.** Transaction receipt.

## 5    Conclusion

With the rapid development of the digital economy, the crucial role of blockchain as a trust network and trust machine is constantly expanding. However, the data storage structure of blockchain determines that it is difficult to tamper with blockchain data, which also objectively increases the risk of harmful information on the blockchain, as well as the privacy protection of sensitive data. In order to effectively regulate data on blockchain, this paper proposes a blockchain supervision scheme that supports privacy protection, ciphertext supervision and user tracking. The scheme uses ciphertext equality test technology to realize ciphertext supervision on blockchain. This can further protect the privacy of user data. The effectiveness of the scheme is proved by security analysis and experiment analysis.

**Acknowledgments.** This article is supported in part by the National Key R&D Program of China under project 2022YFB2702901, the Guangxi Natural Science Foundation under grant 2019GXNSFGA245004, the National Natural Science Foundation of China under projects 62162017 and 62172119, Zhejiang Provincial Natural Science Foundation of China under Grant No. LZ23F020012, the Guangdong Key R&D Program under project 2020B0101090002, the Swift Fund Fintech Funding, the special fund of the High-level Innovation Team and Outstanding Scholar Program for universities of Guangxi, and the Innovation Project of GUET Graduate Education 2022YCXS084.

## References

1. Bünz, B., Agrawal, S., Zamani, M., Boneh, D.: Zether: towards privacy in a smart contract world. In: Bonneau, J., Heninger, N. (eds.) FC 2020. LNCS, vol. 12059, pp. 423–443. Springer, Cham (2020). https://doi.org/10.1007/978-3-030-51280-4_23
2. Da, L., Liang, H., Ding, Y., Wang, Y., Yang, C., Wang, H.: Blockchain-based data acquisition with privacy protection in UAV cluster network. CMES-Comput. Model. Eng. Sci. **137**(1), 879–902 (2023)

3. Gorkhali, A., Chowdhury, R.: Blockchain and the evolving financial market: a literature review. J. Ind. Integr. Manage. **7**(01), 47–81 (2022)
4. Huang, K., Tso, R., Chen, Y.C., Rahman, S.M.M., Almogren, A., Alamri, A.: PKE-AET: public key encryption with authorized equality test. Comput. J. **58**(10), 2686–2697 (2015)
5. Li, X., Wu, L., Zhao, R., Lu, W., Xue, F.: Two-layer adaptive blockchain-based supervision model for off-site modular housing production. Comput. Ind. **128**, 103437 (2021)
6. Liu, J., Zhang, H., Zhen, L.: Blockchain technology in maritime supply chains: applications, architecture and challenges. Int. J. Prod. Res. **61**(11), 3547–3563 (2023)
7. Ma, Y., Sun, Y., Lei, Y., Qin, N., Lu, J.: A survey of blockchain technology on security, privacy, and trust in crowdsourcing services. World Wide Web **23**(1), 393–419 (2020)
8. Marian, O.: A conceptual framework for the regulation of cryptocurrencies. U. Chi. L. Rev. Dialogue **82**, 53 (2015)
9. Peng, S., et al.: An efficient double-layer blockchain method for vaccine production supervision. IEEE Trans. Nanobiosci. **19**(3), 579–587 (2020)
10. Rahulamathavan, Y., Phan, R.C.W., Rajarajan, M., Misra, S., Kondoz, A.: Privacy-preserving blockchain based IoT ecosystem using attribute-based encryption. In: 2017 IEEE International Conference on Advanced Networks and Telecommunications Systems (ANTS), pp. 1–6. IEEE (2017)
11. Tang, Q.: Public key encryption schemes supporting equality test with authorisation of different granularity. Int. J. Appl. Cryptogr. **2**(4), 304–321 (2012)
12. Wang, J., et al.: Blockchain-based information supervision model for rice supply chains. Comput. Intell. Neurosci. **2022** (2022). Article ID 2914571
13. Wang, Y., Pang, H., Deng, R.H., Ding, Y., Wu, Q., Qin, B.: Securing messaging services through efficient signcryption with designated equality test. Inf. Sci. **490**, 146–165 (2019)
14. Wang, Y., et al.: Secure server-aided data sharing clique with attestation. Inf. Sci. **522**, 80–98 (2020)
15. Wen, B., Wang, Y., Ding, Y., Zheng, H., Liang, H., Wang, H.: A privacy-preserving blockchain supervision framework in the multiparty setting. Wirel. Commun. Mob. Comput. **2021** (2021). Article ID 5236579
16. Wen, B., Wang, Y., Ding, Y., Zheng, H., Qin, B., Yang, C.: Security and privacy protection technologies in securing blockchain applications. Inf. Sci. **645**, 119322 (2023)
17. Xiao, X., Zhang, Y., Zhu, Y., Hu, P., Cao, X.: Fingerchain: copyrighted multi-owner media sharing by introducing asymmetric fingerprinting into blockchain. IEEE Trans. Netw. Serv. Manage. **20**, 2869–2885 (2023)
18. Xiong, H., Hou, Y., Huang, X., Zhao, Y., Chen, C.M.: Heterogeneous signcryption scheme from IBC to PKI with equality test for WBANs. IEEE Syst. J. **16**(2), 2391–2400 (2021)
19. Yang, G., Tan, C.H., Huang, Q., Wong, D.S.: Probabilistic public key encryption with equality test. In: Pieprzyk, J. (ed.) CT-RSA 2010. LNCS, vol. 5985, pp. 119–131. Springer, Heidelberg (2010). https://doi.org/10.1007/978-3-642-11925-5_9
20. Yong, B., Shen, J., Liu, X., Li, F., Chen, H., Zhou, Q.: An intelligent blockchain-based system for safe vaccine supply and supervision. Int. J. Inf. Manage. **52**, 102024 (2020)

21. Zhang, F., Maram, D., Malvai, H., Goldfeder, S., Juels, A.: DECO: liberating web data using decentralized oracles for TLS. In: Proceedings of the 2020 ACM SIGSAC Conference on Computer and Communications Security, pp. 1919–1938 (2020)
22. Zhao, M., Ding, Y., Tang, S., Liang, H., Wang, H.: Public key encryption with authorized equality test on outsourced ciphertexts for cloud-assisted IoT in dual server model. Wirel. Commun. Mob. Comput. **2022** (2022). Article ID 4462134

# Code Search and Completion

# JARAD: An Approach for Java API Mention Recognition and Disambiguation in Stack Overflow

Qingmi Liang, Yi Jin, Qi Xie, Li Kuang$^{(\boxtimes)}$, and Yu Sheng

School of Computer Science, Central South University, Changsha 410018, China
{qmliang,8209200329,8209190322,kuangli,shengyu}@csu.edu.cn

**Abstract.** Invoking APIs is a common way to improve the efficiency of software development. Developers often discuss various problems encountered or share the experience of using the API in communities, like Stack Overflow and GitHub. To avoid the duplicate discussion of issues and support downstream tasks such as API recommendation and API Mining, it is necessary to recognize APIs mentioned in these communities and link them to the fully qualified name. This work is often referred to as the task of API mention recognition and disambiguation in informal texts, which is the main focus of our paper. We start from Java posts in Stack Overflow and analyze the proportion of the posts that involve discussion on API (API Post for short), with short names or fully qualified names, and the characteristics of API Post. We also extract the APIs associated with more than 30,000 posts in Stack Overflow, and automatically establish $< post, APIs >$ pairs to construct the dataset JAPD. Finally, we propose a novel approach JARAD to infer the associated APIs in a post. In our approach, we first use BiLSTM and CRF to fuse context information in text and code snippets to obtain a set of associated API candidates. The candidate API is then scored by the frequency of the API type appearing in the post to infer API's fully qualified name. Our evaluation experiments demonstrate that JARAD achieves 71.58%, 76.84% and 74.12% on Precision, Recall and F1 respectively.

**Keywords:** Java API · Mention Recognition · API Disambiguation · Research Analysis · Dataset · Stack Overflow

## 1 Introduction

Invoking the Application Programming Interface (API) is an effective means for developers to reuse code. The official API documentation is an effective means to guide developers to call APIs correctly. However, due to the limited information and scattered knowledge in the official documentation, developers have to discuss various problems that they encountered in the process of calling APIs in the communities, like Stack Overflow and GitHub. They always refer to APIs in discussions by their simple names and aliases, which makes it more difficult for

H. Gao et al. (Eds.): CollaborateCom 2023, LNICST 561, pp. 265–283, 2024.
https://doi.org/10.1007/978-3-031-54521-4_15

developers to search API-related knowledge in the communities. It not only leads to knowledge waste but also brings difficulties to some downstream tasks such as API recommendation [15, 16, 33] and API Mining [15, 16, 18, 19].

To know exactly which APIs are referred to in the discussion, extensive research was performed to recognize APIs mentioned in discussions, and infer APIs' fully qualified names. In the early days, researchers used rule-based methods [3, 17]. For example, Christoph Treude [3] solved the API mention recognition task by summarizing regular expression rules after observing a large number of sentences. Later, some methods based on machine learning [1, 2, 10, 13, 14] also became popular in this field. ARCLIN [2] recognizes API mentions of text fragments in posts based on neural networks, and infers the fully qualified name of the associated API using the similarity comparison.

However, existing methods for API mention recognition and disambiguation field still suffer from the following deficiencies: (1) There is no research to analyze the proportion of developers' discussions about APIs and what characteristics exist in these discussions, resulting in a lack of clear understanding of this work; (2) There is no available, sufficient, and general dataset to support the research. Researchers have to annotate the dataset manually [2, 5], which undoubtedly brings tedious and repetitive work to researchers; (3) Some existing research methods have certain limitations: some methods [2, 10] only exploit the information of the text fragment, ignoring code snippets in the discussion. However the discussants will also attach relevant codes, which are also an effective basis to help reason about the exact API. Some methods are only aimed to a few specific libraries [1, 2, 5], rather than general-purpose development languages.

To solve the above dilemmas, this paper conducts a series of researches about the posts in Stack Overflow. First, we filtered out posts not related to Java, investigated the proportion of API Post (the posts that involve discussions on API, API Post for short) in Java posts and with fully qualified names, and analyzed related features for API Post. Next, we automatically labeled more than 30,000 entries based on the APIs' fully qualified names and their links in the official Java API documentation. We automatically pointed out the fully qualified names of the APIs involved in the posts establishing $< post, APIs >$ pairs and constructed a general dataset JAPD (Java API Post Dataset). Finally, we proposed an approach called JARAD to decompose the task into Java API Recognition And Disambiguation. We first used Bidirectional Long Short-Term Memory (BiLSTM) and Conditional Random Fields (CRF) fusing contextual information to identify API mentions in text and code snippets, and initially obtained the set of API candidates. We then scored the candidate APIs using the frequency of the API type in the post and obtain the fully qualified names of the APIs associated with the post.

To verify the effectiveness of our method, we evaluated JARAD on the proposed JAPD. We tested the effect of two components of JARAD, i.e. API mention recognition and disambiguation. And JARAD achieved a Precision of 71.58%, Recall of 76.84%, and F1 measure of 74.12%. Overall, the main contributions of this paper are as follows:

1. To our best knowledge, we are the first to conduct a research analysis on Java API Post in Stack Overflow. We observe the relevant characteristics of API Post, which provides a basis to construct the dataset and propose the JARAD.
2. We provide a usable dataset called JAPD for the field of API mention recognition and disambiguation. We used a text-based approach and labeled 35,825 records automatically. This effectively relieves the pressure on researchers to label data manually.
3. We propose a novel approach called JARAD to automatically infer the fully qualified names of Java APIs involved in a post, taking into account both text and code snippets in the discussion. JARAD performs better on Recall than the state-of-the-art model ARCLIN based on the Python dataset.

The data related to JARAD is available at link[1]. The rest of the paper is organized as follows. The Sect. 2 is the research analysis of this paper. Section 3 presents our dataset for API recognition and disambiguation in Stack overflow for Java. Section 4 and 5 present our approach and results, respectively, and discuss the strengths and weaknesses of this paper. Section 6 introduces the related work. Finally, we concluded the paper in Sect. 7.

## 2   Research Analysis

### 2.1   Research Problem

To study the API recognition and disambiguation tasks of code and text in Stack Overflow posts more clearly, we conduct research on posts with the following questions:

1. What is the percentage of API Post out of all Java-related posts?
2. In API Post, what is the percentage of APIs that appear with their full name?
3. What are the key features for associating API in the API Post?

Investigating the first two questions helps us understand the need for research in this field. The results of the third problem help us propose the better approach called JARAD to solve API recognition and disambiguation tasks. It should be noted that we define Java API Post as the post with Java API provided by the official Java JDK or a third-party dependent package, but not user-defined method. Furthermore, we define API Fully Qualified Name Post as the post with API appearing in the form of a fully qualified name.

### 2.2   Research Observation

The data for the research in this paper comes from the official dataset provided by Stack Overflow[2]. The data update time is March 7, 2022 and the total number

---

[1] https://anonymous.4open.science/r/JARAD-EDAE.
[2] https://archive.org/details/stackexchange.

of posts reaches 55,513,870. We first observed the tag search results[3] with 'Java' as the search keyword, and took 11 tags as the investigation targets: $< java >$, $< java - 8 >$, $< javadoc >$, $< java - stream >$, $< java.util.scanner >$, $< java - io >$, $< java - time >$, $< java.util.concurrent >$, $< java - 2d >$, $< javax.imageio >$, and $< java - threads >$. The total number of posts related to these tags is 1,879,900. Their proportions are shown in the 'Proportion' column of Table 1. It is not practical to check these posts manually. Therefore, we adopt the statistical sampling [20] and obtained the posts to be investigated. In order to ensure a certain degree of confidence in the error range of the estimated accuracy, we set the number of samples to 384 based on previous research experience [21,22]. However, due to the large proportion of posts with $< Java >$ tags, we set the sampling quantity, as shown in the 'Sampling Quantity' column of Table 1 to control the number of posts for each tag within a reasonable range.

**Table 1.** Related data of empirical study.

| Tags | PostNum | Proportion | Sampling Quantity | API Post Quantity | API Fully Qualified Name Post |
|---|---|---|---|---|---|
| java | 1830876 | 97.39% | 104 | 63 | 10 |
| java-8 | 22108 | 1.18% | 100 | 84 | 11 |
| javadoc | 2835 | 0.15% | 100 | 14 | 4 |
| java-stream | 10354 | 0.55% | 10 | 9 | 0 |
| java.util.scanner | 6134 | 0.33% | 10 | 10 | 7 |
| java-io | 1696 | 0.09% | 10 | 10 | 5 |
| java-time | 1513 | 0.08% | 10 | 6 | 2 |
| java.util.concurrent | 1328 | 0.07% | 10 | 8 | 5 |
| java-2d | 1071 | 0.06% | 10 | 9 | 0 |
| javax.imageio | 1054 | 0.06% | 10 | 10 | 2 |
| java-threads | 931 | 0.05% | 10 | 10 | 2 |
| Total | 1879900 | 1 | 384 | 233 | 48 |

To add credibility to the survey, we used majority voting to answer the three questions above for each post. Two researchers investigated the posts and answered the questions above. Their observations are carried out independently without interfering with each other. They both have more than three years of Java development experience. If they have different or uncertain answers to a question, the third researcher who has more than five years of Java development experience is asked to answer the question.

## 2.3   Research Result

We use the statistic Cohen's Kappa to evaluate the results. If Cohen's Kappa greater than 0.8, there is firm agreement between the results of the two individuals. In our research, Cohen's Kappa of our two researchers achieved 0.91.

---

[3] https://stackoverflow.com/tags.

Through the investigation of posts by three researchers, we came to the following conclusions.

**API Post Make up 61% of all Java Post.** There are 233 API Post of 384 Java Post. The proportion of the API Post tagged with $< Java >$ or $< Javadoc >$ is the lowest among the 11 tags we selected. The proportion of API Post tagged with $< java - stream >$, $< java.util.scanner >$, $< java - io >$, $< java-time >$, $< java.util.concurrent >$, $< java-2d >$, $< javax.imageio >$, and $< java-threads >$ achieve 90%. It is not difficult to find that these tags with high proportion are package names related to the Java development language. Figure 1 shows two examples of an API Post and a non-API Post. As shown in Fig. 1(b), it cannot be inferred that the post is discussing the API even if the class tag 'japplet' of Java exists in the post. In other words, the tag can be used as an enhanced condition for judging whether there is an API mention, but it cannot be used as a sufficient condition for API Post or to filter API Post.

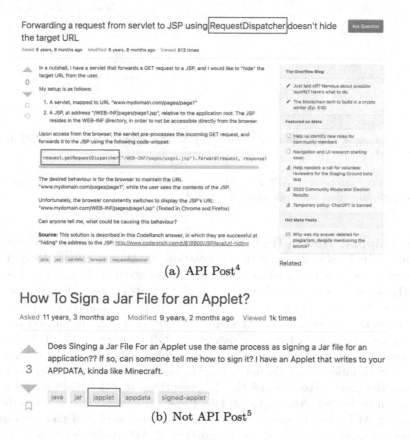

(a) API Post[4]

(b) Not API Post[5]

**Fig. 1.** Two examples of an API Post and a non-API Post (https://stackoverflow.com/questions/36255963, https://stackoverflow.com/questions/7191411)

**In API Post, the proportion of APIs Appearing as Full Names is 21%.**
The API in the API Fully Qualified Name Post does not necessarily appear
directly in the form of the fully qualified name Package.Class.Method. As long
as the text or code in the discussion can indicate that it belongs to the package
and class of the called API. Similarly, if this condition is not met, the API is
considered to appear in the form of a short name, as shown in Fig. 2(b). We
found that among the 233 API posts, the API in 185 API posts appeared in
the form of a short name, accounting for 79%. In other words, the exact APIs
are unknown in 79% of API Post. This is a waste of API knowledge and adds
certain degree of difficulty to the research work of API Mining. It also shows the
necessity for informal text API mention recognition and disambiguation work.

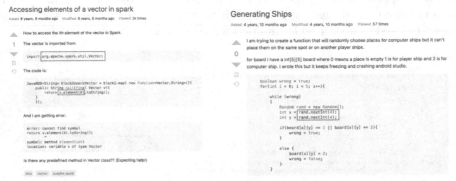

(a) An example of full name API in
API Post[6]

(b) An example of short name API in API
Post[7]

**Fig. 2.** Two examples of API Post (https://stackoverflow.com/questions/23778787,
https://stackoverflow.com/questions/48596384)

**Code Snippets Have a Higher Percentage of API Mentions than Text
Snippets in Posts.** Through the observation, we mainly divide the API mentions in posts into the following four types as shown in Fig. 3: (1) The post
directly discusses the API (shown in Fig. 3(a)). In this case, API mentions may
appear in three places in a post: the title, text in the body, and code in the body.
(2) API is mentioned in the text snippet of the post. The discussion does not
directly mention the API, but will relate the API in other details. (3) There are
API mentions in code snippets of the post, which is similar to the second case.
(4) Other situations that do not belong to the above three, such as API mentions in the image. We counted the API mentions of 233 API Post and results
are shown in Table 2. Among the 233 API Post, the proportion of posts directly
discussing API-related issues is 15.38%, the proportion of API mentions in text
snippets is only 17.31%, and the proportion of API mentions in code reaches
66.92%. The probability of an API mention appearing in a picture is extremely
low. It should be noted that the reason why the 'Total' in Table 2 is greater than
233 is that some posts have API mentions in both text and code.

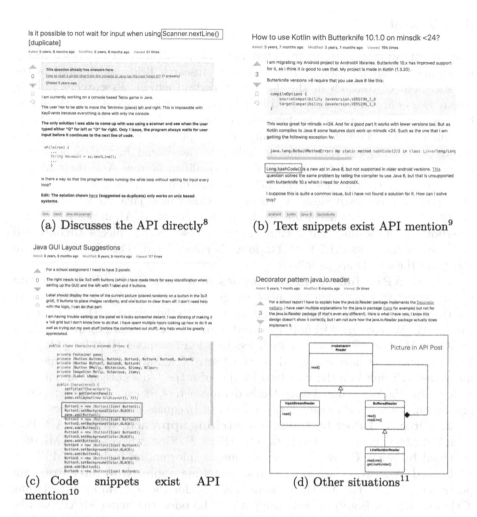

(a) Discusses the API directly[8]

(b) Text snippets exist API mention[9]

(c) Code snippets exist API mention[10]

(d) Other situations[11]

**Fig. 3.** Examples of API mentions in posts (https://stackoverflow.com/questions/44072821, https://stackoverflow.com/questions/55689197, https://stackoverflow.com/questions/21753769, https://stackoverflow.com/questions/46994892)

**Table 2.** API Mention statistics of API Posts

| API Mention | Quantity | Proportion |
|---|---|---|
| Ask related question | 40 | 15.38% |
| Text | 45 | 17.31% |
| Code | 174 | 66.92% |
| Other | 1 | 0.39% |
| Total | 260 | 1.0 |

## 3    Dataset

The lack of available datasets is a non-negligible problem in API mention recognition and disambiguation in informal texts research field, which hinders the advancement of research in this field to a certain extent. Researches [2,5] in recent years have to rely on manual labeling to construct the dataset. With millions of posts, this approach is obviously not realistic. So it is an inevitable trend to construct the dataset automatically. This paper first obtains fully qualified names of all APIs and their links according to the official Java JDK documentation[4], which is called ANAL (APIs' fully qualified Names And their Links). It is unrealistic to study all APIs and some user-defined APIs usually lack generality and representativeness. We chose the widely used java official API. Then we filter irrelevant data according to the appearance of ANAL in posts on Stack Overflow. After cleaning and optimizing the dataset, 35,825 pieces are obtained and the JAPD (Java API Post Dataset) is constructed. The specific steps to construct the JAPD are as follows:

**1. Get APIs' fully qualified names and their links.** To ensure data accuracy and increase persuasiveness, we get ANAL and unify the format. We use the requests and the BeautifulSoup library in Python to parse HTML and get the ANAL. We convert API fully qualified name to the standard format of Package.Class.Method (Parameter), such as: java.io.File.equals (java.lang.Object). The parameter is also expressed in the form of a fully qualified name. We unify the API link into the standard format of https://docs.oracle.com/javase/8/docs/api/Package/Class.html#Method-Parameter-, such as: https://docs.oracle.com/javase/8/docs/api/java/io/File.html#equals-java.lang.Object-.

**2. Filter API Post by the text-matching approach.** We filter API Post from 1,838,095 posts related to 11 tags (see Sect. 2). First, we parse the XML data provided by Stack Overflow to extract major information including Id, Title, Body, and Tags. Next, we use the text-matching approach to filter irrelevant posts according to the ANAL. If there is ANAL for the text snippets(including Title and text in Body) or code snippets in the post, the matched API will be regarded as the associated API of the post. Then we get the $< post, APIs >$ pairs. This approach effectively guarantees the accuracy. When matching the fully qualified name, we ignore the parameter matching because the form of the parameter in the post is diverse as shown in Fig. 4(a). Finally, we delete duplicate pairs, and initially obtained 110,171 $< post, APIs >$ pairs.

---

[4] https://docs.oracle.com/javase/8/docs/api/.

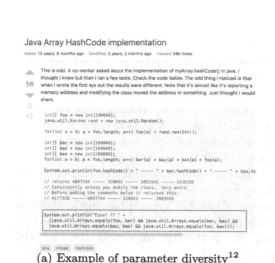

(a) Example of parameter diversity[12]    (b) Example of stack error message[13]

**Fig. 4.** Two examples of posts (https://stackoverflow.com/questions/744735, https://stackoverflow.com/questions/59726805)

**3. Data optimization.** To improve the usability and accuracy of the dataset, we clean and optimize the dataset. The posts with large error message contain the fully qualified names of multiple APIs, but they do not belong to the API Post associating with 6 APIs as shown in Fig. 4(b). We find that API *java.lang.reflect.Method.invoke* and API *java.lang.Thread.run* will appear in such posts with high probability. Besides, posts related to no more than three APIs accounted for 83.05% of all posts. Based on the above observations, We select the larger proportion and more representative posts, and filter following types of posts to optimize the dataset: (1) the posts related to API *java.lang.reflect.Method.invoke* or API *java.lang.Thread.run*. (2) the posts related to more than 3 APIs. We unify the APIs in $< post, APIs >$ pairs into the format of *Package.Class.Method*. When using APIs' links for text matching, the purpose of retaining parameters is to ensure data accuracy as much as possible.

**The JAPD:** After data acquisition and optimization, we obtained the JAPD containing 35,825 $< post, APIs >$ pairs, and 34,160 pairs (95.35%) of the posts with code snippets. The JAPD is associated with 2704 Java APIs. There are 2008 APIs of which simple name are associated with more than one fully qualified name. In other word, 74% of the data is necessary for disambiguation. To make it easier for everyone to reuse the JAPD, we also provide the following data: APIs contained in all packages; the simple names associated with all fully qualified names.

# 4  Approach

## 4.1  Overview

To solve API recognition and disambiguation tasks, we propose a novel approach JARAD to infer the associated APIs in a post. Figure 5 is the architecture of the JARAD (**J**ava **A**PI **R**ecognition **A**nd **D**isambiguation), which mainly includes the following steps: (1) For each post, we perform data processing and parse out its text snippets and code snippets. The 'Title' of the post is treated as text. (2) Next, we train API mention recognition models for text and code respectively, obtain API mentions, and get candidate API set based on the prepared Java API set. If an API is a post-related API, it should be mentioned in the text snippets, the code snippets, or both. (3) Finally, we parse the post content again. The candidate API is scored by the frequency of the API type appearing in the post to infer API's fully qualified name. We perform API disambiguation based on the scores of candidate APIs. We will detail the two important steps of API recognition and API disambiguation in the JARAD.

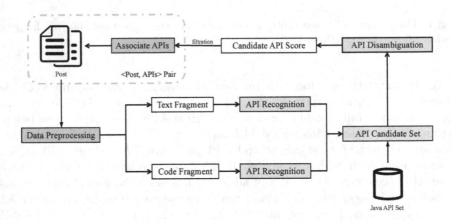

**Fig. 5.** The architecture of JARAD

## 4.2  API Mention Recognition

API mention recognition is implemented as the sequence labeling task. The model is shown in Fig. 6. We utilize Bi-directional Long Short-Term Memory (BiLSTM) and conditional random field (CRF) fusing context information to annotate API mentions in text and code. We first divide the text and code snippets into independent tokens, namely $\{T_1, T_2, T_3, ..., T_{n-1}, T_n\}$. Tokens in both text and code snippets are pre-labeled for training. 'B' and 'O' in the Fig. 6 represent API mentions and non-API mentions respectively. These tokens will be parsed forward and reverse by BiLSTM to solve the problem of long sentence dependence. To more comprehensively integrate context information, we obtain the features of each Token, namely $\{F_1, F_2, F_3, ..., F_{n-1}, F_n\}$. As the output of BiLSTM layer, these features will be the input of the CRF layer. The CRF layer learns the constraint relationship of fragments and predicts the label of each Token through maximum likelihood estimation according to the idea that "the score of the real path is the highest among all the paths".

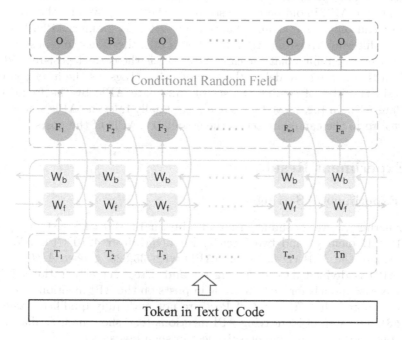

**Fig. 6.** API Mention Recognition Model Diagram

## 4.3  API Disambiguation

Aiming at the task of API disambiguation in informal texts in Stack overflow, Kien Luong et al. [13] proposed the DATYS+. It disambiguates Java API mentions via type scope when given API mentions. DATYS+ takes as input a Stack Overflow thread, API mentions and Java libraries, and outputs a set of APIs and their scores. DATYS+ first extracts the API candidate set from the Java library and API mentions. These candidate APIs are scored according to the frequency of the candidate API type (class or interface) appearing in different scopes of the Stack Overflow thread. DATYS+ considers four mention scopes: (1) Mention Scope, which covers the mention itself; (2) Text Scope, which covers text content, including mentions; (3) Code Scope, which covers code snippets. (4) Code Comments Scope, which covers code comments snippets. DATYS+ then rank the APIs based on the scores of the candidate APIs. Finally, the first candidate API with a score more than 0 is selected as the associated API in this thread.

The API disambiguation method in this paper is improved on the basis of DATYS+. We leverage the frequency of the API type appearing in the above four mention scopes from API Post to score the API mention candidates set. However the DATYS+ filters irrelevant APIs through the 'Tags' in the post. That is, when the prefix of a API does not appear in the 'Tags', DATYS+ filters this candidate API. In our empirical study (see Sect. 2.3), we find that the 'Tags' of a post can only serve as an enhancement factor for linking APIs, but not a reason for filtering irrelevant APIs. In other words, the 'Tags' in a post can only enhance the probability that the candidate API is the correct post-related API. Based on this finding, we delete the step of using 'Tags' as the filter condition. We retain the idea of scoring the set of candidate APIs by the frequency of candidate APIs in the above four scopes. We finally take the APIs whose scores are not zero in the candidate set as the associated APIs of the posts.

## 5   Experiment Result

### 5.1   Experimental Settings

The experiments were conducted on an Ubuntu 18.04.5 LTS system equipped with 128GB memory and two Intel(R) Xeon(R) Silver 4210 CPUs. We train and evaluate the JARAD based on JAPD with 35,825 $< post, APIs >$ pairs. The JAPD is divided into a training set and a test set at a ratio of 5:1. We train separate models for text and code in posts on the API mention recognition task. It is noted that 79% of API Post are not with fully qualified names (see Sect. 2.3). The step of identifying API mentions (e.g. short names, aliases, etc.) allows our method to remain effectiveness in such posts.

### 5.2   Metrics

We use the unified evaluation metrics of sequence labeling tasks to evaluate the JARAD: Precision, Recall, and F1 measure. Precision represents the proportion of the correct APIs that the model predicts. Recall measures the number of APIs correctly inferred in the test set. F1 measure takes both Precision and Recall into account for evaluation. Their formulas are as follows:

$$Precision = \frac{True\ Positive}{True\ Positive + False\ Positive} \tag{1}$$

$$Recall = \frac{True\ Positive}{True\ Positive + False\ Negative} \tag{2}$$

$$F1 = \frac{2 * Precision * Recall}{Precision + Recall} \tag{3}$$

## 5.3    Experimental Results

We first evaluate the effects of the two main components of the JARAD. Due to the discrepancy between text and code on Stack Overflow, we train two API mention recognition models for text and code respectively. We also evaluate the effectiveness of the API disambiguation method which refers to the ability to link the correct API' fully qualified name given the correct API mentions. As shown in Table 3, our API mention recognition model achieves a Precision of 92.08% on code snippets, and our API disambiguation model achieves a Recall of 93.99%.

**Table 3.** Component evaluation results of the JARAD

| Component | Precision | Recall | F1 |
| --- | --- | --- | --- |
| API Recognition for Text | 46.99% | 69.77% | 56.18% |
| API Recognition for Code | 92.08% | 84.24% | 87.98% |
| API Disambiguation | 78.88% | 93.99% | 85.78% |

The overall performance is shown in Table 4. As suggested in the paper [2], our model favors Recall than Precision. So we try to tune model parameters with better Recall. Our JARAD has achieved a Precision of 71.58%, Recall of 76.84%, and F1 measure of 74.12%. In terms of Recall, our method outperforms ARCLIN [2] which achieves a Recall of 73.53%. Compared with ARCLIN as a SOTA model in the field of API mention recognition and disambiguation in informal texts, our method has the following two advantages: (1) ARCLIN works only on the text in the post while our method considers both text and code information; (2) ARCLIN aims at the APIs in the five libraries of Python while our method targets a wider range of dataset, expanding to all APIs in the Java JDK (see Sect. 5.4).

**Table 4.** Evaluation results of the JARAD

| Approach | Precision | Recall | F1 |
| --- | --- | --- | --- |
| APIReal [1] | 78.7% | 60.4% | 68.3% |
| ARCLIN [2] | 78.26% | 73.53% | 75.82% |
| JARAD | 71.58% | **76.84%** | 74.12% |

## 5.4    Discussion

This section first compares the previous methods with the JARAD, highlights the advantages of JARAD, and then discusses the shortcomings of JARAD.

**1. JARAD works on both text snippets and code snippets in posts.** As we have observed empirically, 66.92% of API Post on Stack Overflow are mentioned in code snippets. Among the 35,825 pieces of data in our JAPD dataset, 34,160 pieces contain code snippets, accounting for 95% of the total. These phenomena emphasize to a certain extent that code snippets cannot be ignored in identifying API tasks on Stack Overflow. However, some studies [2, 10] in recent years only considered text snippets. As a SOTA research based on the Python dataset, ARCLIN [2] discards the code snippets during data processing. Although the study [10] is also oriented to the Java dataset, it only considers the sentences in the post and ignores the code snippets.

**2. JARAD aims at a wider range of dataset.** Compared with some studies [1, 2, 5, 10, 12, 13], our method targets the Java language and is applicable to a wider range of dataset containing all Java APIs, rather than targeting a few specific libraries. Due to the popularity of the two development languages Python and Java, researchers are more inclined to use the dataset about them. The data of ARCLIN [2] is based on five libraries of Python: Pytorch, Pandas, Tensorflow, Numpy, and Matplotlib. Their experiments also show that the accuracy of the generalization ability on Matplotlib is only 26.6% on average when using the other four libraries as the training set. Research [10] is based on Java APIs, but their dataset is only based on APIs' links. However, only 804 of our 110,171 unfiltered data are obtained through APIs' links. So we infer the certain extent that the amount of their research data is insufficient, and the number of APIs involved is also inadequate.

**3. The structure of JARAD is simpler, and the training time of an epoch is shorter.** The average time spent by the model inferring the API associated with a post is only 600 ms. Due to the different characteristics of text and code, we train API mention recognition models for them respectively (see Sect. 4.2). We find that it takes only 7 min for the text model to train one epoch and 28 min for the code model. This is the result of our training with CPU. Previous studies used the Bert fine-tuning model but did not elaborate on the training time of the model. To compare the training time of the Bert fine-tuning model with our model, we add the Bert component before the BiLSTM layer of the API mention recognition model in JARAD. We find that it takes 18 min for the text model to train one epoch, and takes one and a half hours for the code model, which is significantly longer than the training time of our JARAD model.

**Threats to Validity:** The JARAD proposed in this paper experiments on the JAPD. We extract the Java API Post to construct the JAPD. The API Post is associated with the API in the official Java JDK documentation. But the API recognition model we proposed cannot distinguish the source of the API. As shown in Fig. 7, when we use the API recognition model trained based on the text snippets in the post to infer the API mentions associated with the text snippets, the model incorrectly recognizes 'drawloop()' as an API mention. But in fact, this is a user-defined method (shown in the code snippet in the post). We infer that both the name 'drawloop' and the brackets of the method are the reasons for the false positives in our API mention recognition model. And 'e.drawloop()' is not recognized as an API mention because our model recognizes that the prefix 'e' of the method is not a valid package or class name. It is undeniable that our model has room for improvement.

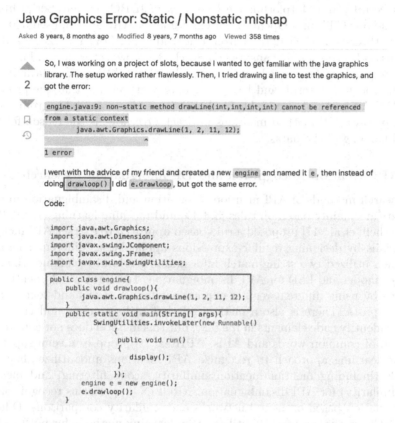

**Fig. 7.** An example of a customed (https://stackoverflow.com/questions/22889139)

Another fact is that the improvement of the JARAD model is not significant enough. Compared with ARCLIN [2], our model is not outstanding in terms of numerical results, which may be the reason for the simpler model structure. But our model has a clear and concise structure, which is easy to understand and explain. We reduce the training cost and get the final model quickly.

## 6   Related Work

### 6.1   API Recognition and Disambiguation Dataset

Datasets are the basis for researchers to train and test models. However, the lack of available and sufficient dataset forces researchers in the field of API recognition and disambiguation in informal texts to use manual labeling methods to construct [2,5,12,13]. Although ARCLIN [2] eliminates the manual labeling step when training the model, it still have to manually label the fully qualified name of the API during testing. Study [5] manually flagged API mentions(600 per lib) in 3600 Stack Overflow posts for six libraries (three Python libraries: Pandas, NumPy and Matplotlib; one Java library: JDBC, one JavaScript library: React, and one C library: OpenGL) for experiments. ARSeek [13] used 380 Stack Overflow threads as their dataset from the study [12]. DATYS [12] regards the questions and corresponding answers on Stack Overflow as threads and manually marks 380 pieces of data, which are associated with the APIs of four Java libraries (Guava, Mockito, AssertJ, and Fastjson). It is worth noting that the proposers of the DATYS method also highlighted that 'there is no available ground truth dataset of Java API method mentions in Stack Overflow' is the reason for their manual labeling of the dataset.

## 6.2   API Mention Recognition and Disambiguation Research

The research methods of API mention recognition and disambiguation in informal texts are mainly based on rules [3,4,17] and machine learning [1,2,9,10,12, 13]. Bacchelli et al. [17] proposed a rule-based approach to extract API mentions from emails by designing regular expressions applicable to different languages. They then utilized two string-match information retrieval techniques (i.e., vector space model and LSI) for API disambiguation. Treude et al. [3] identify API mentions by using different regular expressions for questions and text in Stack Overflow posts. There is also a method [4] that utilizes compound camel-case terms to identify code elements in the text, but this method does not consider the confusion of common words and APIs. APIReal [1] proposes a semi-supervised machine learning approach to recognize API mentions and utilizes heuristics methods (including mention-mention similarity, scope filtering, and mention-entry similarity) for API disambiguation. ARCLIN [2] performs recognition and disambiguation based on neural networks and similarity comparisons. Different from ARCLIN, the method [10] utilizes deep learning methods for both recognition and disambiguation. Because the API mention recognition and disambiguation research in informal texts can be subdivided into two steps, some research will study a certain step independently. For example, the methods of DATYS [12] and ARSeek [13] assume known API mentions and determine the fully qualified names of the mentioned APIs by studying the text and code snippets in the discussion, which is API disambiguation research [1,17,23–28]. API mention recognition and disambiguation Research can support downstream tasks such as API recommendation [15,16,33], API Mining [11,15,16,18,19], API misuse detection [34,35], and API resource retrieval [29–32,36].

## 7   Conclusion and Future Work

Stack Overflow is one of the most popular communities for spontaneous discussions among developers. Browsing past related posts on the community and launching a new post to ask for help are common means for them to solve problems on API invoking. Reasoning about the APIs discussed in previous posts can help them search and filter the massive existing posts to quickly find related APIs or similar problems. This inference task can also help downstream tasks such as API Recommendation and API Mining. This paper conducts an empirical survey of posts on Stack Overflow to study the characteristics of APIs in discussions. Then, according to the APIs' fully qualified names and links in the API official documentation, the dataset of more than 30,000 $< post, APIs >$ pairs is automatically constructed based on the method of text matching. Finally, the approach JARAD is proposed to solve the tasks of API mention recognition and disambiguation linking. Compared with previous methods, the structure of the JARAD used in this paper is simpler and JARAD has a good performance on Recall. In the future, we can extend the research in several aspects. We will improve our method of obtaining the dataset, expand the types of development language, and obtain more general API recognition and disambiguation datasets in informal texts. We will also improve API recognition and disambiguation methods to adapt to more general data.

**Acknowledgements.** This work was supported in part by the High Performance Computing Center of Central South University.

# References

1. Ye, D., Bao, L., Xing, Z., et al.: APIReal: an API recognition and linking approach for online developer forums. Empir. Softw. Eng. **23**, 3129–3160 (2018)
2. Huo, Y., Su, Y., Zhang, H., et al.: ARCLIN: automated API mention resolution for unformatted texts. In: Proceedings of the 44th International Conference on Software Engineering, pp. 138–149 (2022)
3. Treude, C., Robillard, M.P.: Augmenting API documentation with insights from stack overflow. In: Proceedings of the 38th International Conference on Software Engineering, pp. 392–403 (2016)
4. Rigby, P.C., Robillard, M.P.: Discovering essential code elements in informal documentation. In: 2013 35th International Conference on Software Engineering (ICSE), pp. 832–841. IEEE (2013)
5. Ma, S., Xing, Z., Chen, C., et al.: Easy-to-deploy API extraction by multi-level feature embedding and transfer learning. IEEE Trans. Software Eng. **47**(10), 2296–2311 (2019)
6. Ye, D., Xing, Z., Foo, C.Y., et al.: Learning to extract API mentions from informal natural language discussions. In: 2016 IEEE International Conference on Software Maintenance and Evolution (ICSME), pp. 389–399. IEEE (2016)
7. Ge, C., Liu, X., Chen, L., et al.: Make it easy: an effective end-to-end entity alignment framework. In: Proceedings of the 44th International ACM SIGIR Conference on Research and Development in Information Retrieval, pp. 777–786 (2021)
8. Ye, D., Xing, Z., Foo, C.Y., et al.: Software-specific named entity recognition in software engineering social content. In: 2016 IEEE 23rd International Conference on Software Analysis, Evolution, and Reengineering (SANER), vol. 1, pp. 90–101. IEEE (2016)

9. Chen, C., Xing, Z., Wang, X.: Unsupervised software-specific morphological forms inference from informal discussions. In: 2017 IEEE/ACM 39th International Conference on Software Engineering (ICSE), pp. 450–461. IEEE (2017)

10. Yin, H., Zheng, Y., Sun, Y., et al.: An API learning service for inexperienced developers based on API knowledge graph. In: 2021 IEEE International Conference on Web Services (ICWS), pp. 251–261. IEEE (2021)

11. Baltes, S., Treude, C., Diehl, S.: SOTorrent: studying the origin, evolution, and usage of stack overflow code snippets. In: 2019 IEEE/ACM 16th International Conference on Mining Software Repositories (MSR), pp. 191–194. IEEE (2019)

12. Luong, K., Thung, F., Lo, D.: Disambiguating mentions of API methods in stack overflow via type scoping. In: 2021 IEEE International Conference on Software Maintenance and Evolution (ICSME), pp. 679–683. IEEE (2021)

13. Luong, K., Hadi, M., Thung, F., et al.: ARSeek: identifying API resource using code and discussion on stack overflow. In: Proceedings of the 30th IEEE/ACM International Conference on Program Comprehension, pp. 331–342 (2022)

14. Luong, K., Thung, F., Lo, D.: ARSearch: searching for API related resources from stack overflow and GitHub. In: Proceedings of the ACM/IEEE 44th International Conference on Software Engineering: Companion Proceedings, pp. 11–15 (2022)

15. Huang, Q., Xia, X., Xing, Z., et al.: API method recommendation without worrying about the task-API knowledge gap. In: Proceedings of the 33rd ACM/IEEE International Conference on Automated Software Engineering, pp. 293–304 (2018)

16. Rahman, M.M., Roy, C.K., Lo, D.: RACK: automatic API recommendation using crowdsourced knowledge. In: 2016 IEEE 23rd International Conference on Software Analysis, Evolution, and Reengineering (SANER), vol. 1, pp. 349–359. IEEE (2016)

17. Bacchelli, A., Lanza, M., Robbes, R.: Linking e-mails and source code artifacts. In: Proceedings of the 32nd ACM/IEEE International Conference on Software Engineering, vol. 1, pp. 375–384 (2010)

18. Liu, M., Peng, X., Marcus, A., et al.: API-related developer information needs in stack overflow. IEEE Trans. Software Eng. 48(11), 4485–4500 (2021)

19. Velázquez-Rodríguez, C., Constantinou, E., De Roover, C.: Uncovering library features from API usage on Stack Overflow. In: 2022 IEEE International Conference on Software Analysis, Evolution and Reengineering (SANER), pp. 207–217. IEEE (2022)

20. Singh, R., Mangat, N.S.: Elements of Survey Sampling. Springer, Dordrecht (2013). https://doi.org/10.1007/978-94-017-1404-4

21. Li, H., Li, S., Sun, J., et al.: Improving API caveats accessibility by mining API caveats knowledge graph. In: 2018 IEEE International Conference on Software Maintenance and Evolution (ICSME), pp. 183–193. IEEE (2018)

22. Wang, C., Peng, X., Liu, M., et al.: A learning-based approach for automatic construction of domain glossary from source code and documentation. In: Proceedings of the 2019 27th ACM Joint Meeting on European Software Engineering Conference and Symposium on the Foundations of Software Engineering, pp. 97–108 (2019)

23. Antoniol, G., Canfora, G., Casazza, G., et al.: Recovering traceability links between code and documentation. IEEE Trans. Software Eng. 28(10), 970–983 (2002)

24. Dagenais, B., Robillard, M.P.: Recovering traceability links between an API and its learning resources. In: 2012 34th International Conference on Software Engineering (ICSE), pp. 47–57. IEEE (2012)

25. Marcus, A., Maletic, J.I.: Recovering documentation-to-source-code traceability links using latent semantic indexing. In: 25th International Conference on Software Engineering, 2003. Proceedings, pp. 125–135. IEEE (2003)

26. Phan, H., Nguyen, H.A., Tran, N.M., et al.: Statistical learning of API fully quali-
    fied names in code snippets of online forums. In: Proceedings of the 40th Interna-
    tional Conference on Software Engineering, pp. 632–642 (2018)
27. Saifullah, C.M.K., Asaduzzaman, M., Roy, C.K.: Learning from examples to find
    fully qualified names of API elements in code snippets. In: 2019 34th IEEE/ACM
    International Conference on Automated Software Engineering (ASE), pp. 243–254.
    IEEE (2019)
28. Subramanian, S., Inozemtseva, L., Holmes, R.: Live API documentation. In: Pro-
    ceedings of the 36th International Conference on Software Engineering, pp. 643–652
    (2014)
29. Nguyen, T., Tran, N., Phan, H., et al.: Complementing global and local contexts
    in representing API descriptions to improve API retrieval tasks. In: Proceedings of
    the 2018 26th ACM Joint Meeting on European Software Engineering Conference
    and Symposium on the Foundations of Software Engineering, pp. 551–562 (2018)
30. Ye, X., Shen, H., Ma, X., et al.: From word embeddings to document similarities
    for improved information retrieval in software engineering. In: Proceedings of the
    38th International Conference on Software Engineering, pp. 404–415 (2016)
31. Rój, M.: Exploiting user knowledge during retrieval of semantically annotated API
    operations. In: Proceedings of the Fourth Workshop on Exploiting Semantic Anno-
    tations in Information Retrieval, pp. 21–22 (2011)
32. Zhou, Y., Wang, C., Yan, X., et al.: Automatic detection and repair recommenda-
    tion of directive defects in Java API documentation. IEEE Trans. Software Eng.
    **46**(9), 1004–1023 (2018)
33. Xie, W., Peng, X., Liu, M., et al.: API method recommendation via explicit match-
    ing of functionality verb phrases. In: Proceedings of the 28th ACM Joint Meeting
    on European Software Engineering Conference and Symposium on the Foundations
    of Software Engineering, pp. 1015–1026 (2020)
34. Ren, X., Sun, J., Xing, Z., et al.: Demystify official API usage directives with crowd-
    sourced API misuse scenarios, erroneous code examples and patches. In: Proceed-
    ings of the ACM/IEEE 42nd International Conference on Software Engineering,
    pp. 925–936 (2020)
35. Ren, X., Ye, X., Xing, Z., et al.: API-misuse detection driven by fine-grained API-
    constraint knowledge graph. In: Proceedings of the 35th IEEE/ACM International
    Conference on Automated Software Engineering, pp. 461–472 (2020)
36. Li, J., Sun, A., Xing, Z., et al.: API caveat explorer–surfacing negative usages from
    practice: an API-oriented interactive exploratory search system for programmers.
    In: The 41st International ACM SIGIR Conference on Research & Development
    in Information Retrieval, pp. 1293–1296 (2018)

# Enrich Code Search Query Semantics with Raw Descriptions

Xiangzheng Liu[1,2], Jianxun Liu[1,2(✉)], Haize Hu[1,2], and Yi Liu[1,2]

[1] School of Computer Science and Engineering, Hunan University of Science and Technology, Xiangtan, Hunan, China
ljx0934@mail.hnust.edu.cn
[2] Hunan Provincial Key Laboratory for Services Computing and Novel Software Technology, Hunan University of Science and Technology, Xiangtan, Hunan, China

**Abstract.** Code search can recommend relevant source code according to the development intention (query statement) of the demander, thereby improving the efficiency of software development. In the research of deep code search model, code description is used to replace query sentences for training. However, the heterogeneity existing between the query statement and the code description will seriously affect the accuracy of the code search model. In order to make up for the shortcomings of code search, this paper proposes a sentence-integrated query expansion method—SIQE. Unlike previous query expansion methods that focus on word-level expansion, SIQE uses the entire code description fragment as the source of query expansion. And by learning the mapping relationship between the query statement and the code description, the heterogeneity problem between them is compensated. In order to verify the effect of the proposed model in code search tasks, the article conducts code search experiments and analyzes on two languages: python and java. Experimental results show that, compared with the baseline model, SIQE has higher code search results. Therefore, the SIQE model can effectively improve the search effect of query statements, improve the accuracy of code search, and further improve the development of software engineering.

**Keywords:** Code search · Query expansion · Software engineering · Deep learning

## 1 Introduction

In the software development process, a significant part of the work involves writing functional code fragments that are repeatedly written and used in various development projects. Code search technology helps search for functional code fragments based on their code function descriptions. In the early days of code search, information retrieval methods (IR) based on keyword rule matching were used to search for relevant code fragments. Such as [13, 16, 20, 22, 25]. However, these methods heavily rely on the repetition of words between the code and the

© ICST Institute for Computer Sciences, Social Informatics and Telecommunications Engineering 2024
Published by Springer Nature Switzerland AG 2024. All Rights Reserved
H. Gao et al. (Eds.): CollaborateCom 2023, LNICST 561, pp. 284–302, 2024.
https://doi.org/10.1007/978-3-031-54521-4_16

query, leading to search bias when different words are used to represent the same query. In recent years, deep learning (DL) has been applied in code search, such as [2,3,6,15,33]. These DL-based methods jointly embeds code fragments and code descriptions into a high-dimensional vector space. Since obtaining natural language queries is not always feasible, code descriptions are used instead. The similarity between vectors is used to represent the matching degree of code fragments and code descriptions. These methods can learn the semantic relationships between code fragments and code descriptions, enabling the identification of semantically similar words.

```
How can I merge two dictionaries in Python?

"For dictionaries x and y,their Shallowly
combined dictionary z takes values from y,
replacing those from x."

   def merge two dicts(x,y):
      z=x.copy()
      z.update(y)
      return z
```

Fig. 1. A example of qurey-description-code

Although deep learning-based code search takes into account the semantic relationship between code fragments and code descriptions, there are still gaps between the query statement and the code description in practical applications. As shown in Fig. 1, there are two main issues: First, the query statement, such as "How can I merge two dictionaries in Python" is generally shorter than the code description, which may not fully express the queryer's intention. Second, a large number of code descriptions use domain-specific terms that may differ from the queryer's expression. For example, "merge" and "combine" may have similar meanings in the domain but are expressed differently in the query statement. These gaps lead to heterogeneity between the query and description, which can significantly reduce the performance of the original model. To address this issue, researchers have explored various query expansion methods [10,17,19,24,28,30]. For instance: Work [19] used WordNet (a synonym database) to enrich the query statement with keywords from the query. Work [28] used WordSim, a synonym prediction library trained on code search datasets, to reduce the impact of noise in WordNet and expand queries. Work [24] crawled the question-and-answer prediction library on Stack Overflow, extracted meaningful word pairs from it, and automatically expanded the query. Work [30] used reinforcement learning to reconstruct the query statement, where the performance of code search was used as the reward of the reconstruction model. The reconstructed query was then used to perform the search task. By expanding the query statement, these methods aim to bridge the gap between the query and description and improve the accuracy of query results.

These query expansion methods mentioned above can to some extent enrich the semantic information of the query and improve the accuracy of the search. However, there are still some issues that need to be addressed. Firstly, irrelevant word noise may be added in the process of enriching the query. Secondly, the current query expansion methods mainly focus on the expansion of words, without considering the differences in sentence expression between the code describer and the queryer. To tackle these issues, we propose a new approach called Sentence-Integrated Query Expansion (SIQE), which aims to enrich the query sentence and improve its accuracy in code search.

SIQE comprises two main components: the Description Search Model (DS) and the Ensemble Search (ES). The DS model is trained to find the k most semantically relevant code description fragments given an input query statement. The ES component integrates the sentence information from these k description fragments with the original query, and sends the expanded query to the Code Search Model (CS) for improved search accuracy. To reduce the impact of noise, we weight the extended sentence based on its similarity score with the original sentence. Since there is currently no publicly available dataset containing query, code description, and code snippets, we crawled a dataset from Stack Overflow to demonstrate the effectiveness of our approach in experiments. The dataset is extracted from the 22,546 most active Java tag questions and 19,276 most active Python tag questions on Stack Overflow, and it includes query, a code description, and code snippet triplet dataset.

This article makes the following contributions:

- We have prepared a dataset of triples, including query, code description, and code snippet. We used this dataset to verify the gap between searching using query statements and code descriptions.
- We propose the Sentence Integrated Query Expansion method (SIQE). We are the first to recognize the importance of sentence patterns in query expansion, and we add sentence pattern information to the query to improve its accuracy. To reduce the noise impact of expanding useless words, we propose a method of integrating the expanded sentences with weights according to the similarity score between the expanded sentences and the original sentence, thereby improving the accuracy of the search.
- We have conducted extensive experiments on different languages and different code search models, demonstrating the advantages of our method (SIQE). Furthermore, we have made our code and dataset publicly available.

The article is structured as follows: Sect. 2 introduces our method. Section 3 describes our dataset, experimental evaluation indicators, and experimental construction. Section 4 presents the comparative results of the experiments and the conclusions drawn. Section 5 introduces related work. Section 6 summarizes the paper, discusses the limitations of our method, and outlines future prospects.

## 2    Methodology

The overall structure of Sentence Integrated Query Expansion (SIQE) is illustrated in Fig. 3, and it consists of three main components: 1. Code Search Model (CS) 2. Description Search Model (DS) 3. Ensemble Search (ES) First, the CS and DS are trained separately using the code-description data and query-description data, respectively. In the ES stage, when a new query statement is presented, the DS provides k code description fragments with the most similar semantics. These k fragments are used to extend the original query sentence structure and are embedded into a vector through CS along with the original query. To reduce the noise impact of expanding useless words, each of the k vectors is assigned a weight, which is the similarity score between the vector and the original query vector. Finally, the k + 1 vectors are integrated using the parallelogram law of vector spaces to obtain the final query vector, which is used to search for the most similar code fragment in the code space.

### 2.1    Code Search (CS)

The purpose of the Code Search Model (CS) is to develop a suitable method for embedding natural language and code into vectors. Since this work focuses on query expansion, we utilize the existing code search models DeepCS and UNIF [1,6]. These CS models typically consist of two embedding network parts, which are typically composed of Long Short-Term Memory (LSTM) or Convolutional Neural Networks (CNN). The first network embeds the code description (d), and the second network embeds the code (c). The matching degree of the (d, c) pair is determined by calculating the cosine similarity of the two vectors. After calculating the cosine similarity with all codes in the database, the code with the highest similarity score is selected as the search result.

The goal of the CS is to maximize the cosine similarity between the correct code and the original query during training, while minimizing the cosine similarity between the incorrect code and the original query. Specifically, for each sample $(d, c+, c-)$ where d is the code description, $c+$ is the correct code fragment, and $c-$ is the incorrect code fragment randomly selected from the code database, the loss function can be defined as formula 1.

$$L(\theta)_{CS} = \sum_{(D,C+,C-)} max(0, \varepsilon - sim(d, c+) + sim(d, c-)) \qquad (1)$$

where $\theta$ represents the parameters of the code search model, d is the code description vector, $c+$ is the vector of the correct code fragment after embedding, $c-$ is the vector of the incorrect code fragment after embedding, $\varepsilon$ is a hyperparameter that adjusts the minimum tolerance range of the model for the difference between the cosine similarity scores of d and $c+$ and $c-$. This parameter determines whether a sample needs to be added to the overall loss function based on whether the difference between the similarity score calculated by the model for $c+$ and the similarity score calculated by $c-$ is greater than $\varepsilon$. The *sim* function calculates the cosine similarity between two vectors. The goal of the CS is to maximize the cosine similarity between the correct code and the original query during training and minimize the cosine similarity between the wrong code and the original query.

## 2.2 Desc Search (DS)

The Description Search Model (DS) aims to find the k code description fragments that are semantically similar to a given natural language query in the code description database. These k code descriptions are then used to expand the sentences and semantics of the original query. This approach enriches the semantics of the original query and also considers the differences in expression between the code description writing method and the natural language query writing method.

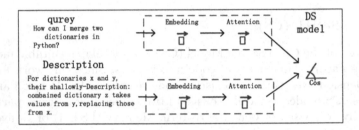

**Fig. 2.** DS model structure

**DS Model.** The Description Search Model (DS) is similar to the Code Search Model (CS) in that it consists of two neural network models that encode natural language inputs and calculate similarity scores. In the case of DS, the goal is to identify the k code description fragments that are most semantically similar to a given natural language query. The DS model is shown in Fig. 2. Since both the query and code description belong to natural language, the attention mechanism is used to build the embedding network. The attention mechanism [29] is a popular structure in the field of natural language processing that has been shown to be effective for various tasks, such as machine translation and text classification.

**Train DS Model.** The purpose of DS training is to maximize the cosine similarity between the query and the correct code description, while minimizing the cosine similarity between the query and a wrong code description randomly selected from the code description database. The DS model uses the gradient descent method to obtain the optimal network parameters. Specifically, for each sample $(q, d^+, d^-)$, where $q$ is a natural language query, $d^+$ is a correct code description fragment, and $d^-$ is a wrong code description fragment randomly selected from the code database, the loss function can be defined as formula 2.

$$L(\theta)_{DS} = \sum_{(Q,D+,D-)} max(0, \varepsilon - sim(q, d+) + sim(q, d-)) \tag{2}$$

where $\theta$ represents the parameters of the DS model, $sim(q, d, \theta)$ is the cosine similarity between the query $q$ and the code description $d$ after being embedded by the DS model, and $\varepsilon$ is a margin hyperparameter that controls the minimum difference between the similarity score of the correct and wrong code description. The loss function aims to make the similarity score between the query and the correct code description higher than that of the wrong code description by at least $\varepsilon$.

## 2.3 Ensemble Search

The purpose of Ensemble Search (ES) is to further reduce the impact of noise and enhance the accuracy of queries based on the extended k-code description fragments of the DS model. Specifically, given a natural language query $q$ and k code description fragments $(d_1, d_2, ..., d_k)$, ES generates the final query expansion vector $q^*$ using the formula 3.

$$q^* = q + \sum_{i=1}^{k} d_i \cdot score_{d_i}, \tag{3}$$

where $q$, $d_1$, and $d_k$ are the vectors embedded by the code search model (CS), and $score_{d_k}$ is the cosine similarity score between $d_k$ and $q$. ES reduces the noise impact of useless information in descriptions by adding cosine similarity weights. The final query expansion vector $q^*$ is obtained by fusing the vectors using the parallelogram rule, and it is used to search for code fragments in the code database using the formula 4.

$$score(c, q) = sim(\underbrace{ES(\overbrace{d_1, \cdots, d_k}^{DS(q)}, q)}_{q^*}, c) \tag{4}$$

where $sim$ represents the similarity between the query and code fragment, and $ES(DS(q), q)$ represents the final query vector $q^*$ obtained using the $k$ vectors recommended by DS.

# 3  Experimental Setup

## 3.1  Dataset

**CodeSearchNetDataset (CSND).** CSND [11] is a large code search corpus collected from the GitHub website and is the most commonly used database in

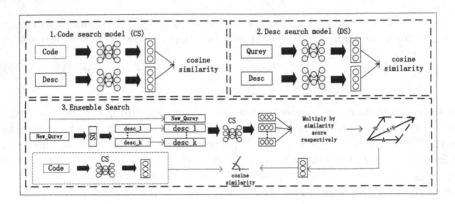

**Fig. 3.** SIQE framework

the field of code search, covering six languages: Go, Java, JavaScript, Python, Php, and Ruby. Each sample in the CSND corpus consists of source code and code description. To preprocess the Python and Java datasets in the corpus, we segment camel case text or text composed of underscores into words and convert them to lowercase. We then count the word frequencies and retain only the 10,000 words with the highest frequency of occurrence as the vocabulary. The corpus information in the preprocessed dataset is shown in Table 1. We train a Code Search model using the CSND dataset.

Although CSND is a large and widely used code search standard dataset, natural language queries are also essential for query expansion. Unfortunately, CSND does not include natural language queries, and currently, there is no open-source dataset that includes queries, code descriptions, and code snippets. To address this gap, we have collected such a dataset by crawling StackOverflow. StackOverflow is a community where software developers from around the world discuss problems and solutions. For each problem description raised by a software developer, other developers provide answers, often including code snippets, and explanations that combine the code snippets with the question. We use these explanations as the code description corpus and the code snippets as the code corpus.

For example, if a software developer raises a question "How do I merge two dictionaries in a single expression?", we use it as a natural language query corpus and then extract the comment "For dictionaries x and y, their shallowly-merged dictionary z takes values from y, replacing those from x." as a description of the code snippet. We also extract the code from the comment: "def merge_two_dicts(x, y): z = x.copy() z.update(y)". Finally, we obtain a data sample containing natural language queries, code descriptions, and code snippets, as shown in Fig. 1.

Since not every question contains code snippets, and comments often contain a lot of useless information, we took the following steps to improve the quality of the collected data:

- We filter out questions starting with keywords such as "what," which mainly include some discussion questions, such as "What are metaclasses in Python?"
- We only collect answers that the questioner has accepted and extract code descriptions and code snippets from them. If the question has no accepted answers, we discard it. If there is no code snippet in the answer or there is no commenting text, we also discard the question.

We extract data from the Python and Java directories in StackOverflow according to the above rules, then undergo the same preprocessing as CSND, and finally obtain our dataset. The dataset information is shown in Table 1.At the same time, we counted the token length of the query, description, and code after processing in the dataset, as shown in Fig. 4. It can be seen that the token length of the query is much less than that of the description. We trained Description Search (DS) model using the collected dataset. The results of the DS training are shown in the Table 2.

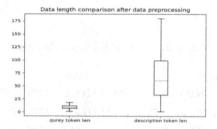

**Fig. 4.** Data length comparison after data preprocessing

**Table 1.** CodeSearchNet dataset compared to collected datasets

| Dataset | | train_set | test_set | avg_code_ token_len | avg_desc_ token_len | avg_qurey_ token_len |
|---|---|---|---|---|---|---|
| CodeSearchNet | java | 450941 | 26717 | 162.41 | 38.83 | – |
| | python | 409230 | 22104 | 167.51 | 54.21 | – |
| Ours | java | 21546 | 1000 | 88.9 | 72.56 | 9.67 |
| | python | 18276 | 1000 | 98.69 | 63.88 | 9.34 |

## 3.2 Evaluation Metric

We use two evaluation metrics to assess the performance of our code search model: *Recall@k* and Mean Reciprocal Rank (*MRR*). These metrics are defined as follows:

- *Recall@k* measures the proportion of correct code fragments among the top k code fragments retrieved by the model. It is calculated as shown in formula 5, where $Q$ represents a sample in the test set, and $I$ is the indicator function that returns 1 when the correct code fragment is among the top k retrieved fragments, and 0 otherwise. We report *Recall@k* values for $k = 1$, 5, and 10.

$$Recall@k = \frac{1}{|Q|} \sum_{i=1}^{|Q|} I(Q_i <= k) \tag{5}$$

- MRR calculates the mean reciprocal rank of the correct code fragment across the entire test set. It is computed as shown in formula 6, where $Q$ represents a sample in the test set, and $Rank(Q_i)$ represents the rank of the correct code fragment returned by the model in the entire test set.

$$MRR = \frac{1}{|Q|} \sum_{i=1}^{|Q|} Rank(Q_i) \tag{6}$$

**Table 2.** DS Search Model Results

|  | Python | | | | Java | | | |
|---|---|---|---|---|---|---|---|---|
|  | R@1 | R@5 | R@10 | MRR | R@1 | R@5 | R@10 | MRR |
| Valid | 0.414 | 0.646 | 0.727 | 0.542 | 0.510 | 0.734 | 0.877 | 0.525 |
| Test | 0.331 | 0.597 | 0.698 | 0.50 | 0.331 | 0.597 | 0.698 | 0.438 |

### 3.3 Baselines

As a query expansion component for code search, SIQE can be used with any code search model. We primarily evaluated our method using two popular code search models: 1. DeepCS [6] is an LSTM-based (Long Short-Term Memory Neural Network) model that embeds text data and uses max-pooling to produce the final output. In addition to considering the text of the code, DeepCS also incorporates method names and API sequence information. Since the API information in the data cannot be extracted, the article modifies the DeepCS model to only incorporate method names in the code vector representation. 2. UNIF [1] is a lightweight code search model. For the query statement, the average pooling is directly used as the embedding vector after the Embedding operation, and the code is embedded through the attention mechanism. UNIF has very high performance and accuracy in the field of code search.

To demonstrate the effectiveness of our query expansion method, we compared it against two popular query expansion methods:

1. The WordNet [19] extension method, which uses the WordNet thesaurus to expand the query by adding synonyms of the query keywords. 2. The frequent itemsets (FP) expansion method, which first identifies frequent itemsets

in the code descriptions by computing their support, and then expands the query keywords using words corresponding to the frequent itemsets. We used the FP-growth algorithm [21] to identify frequent itemsets.

### 3.4 Implementation Details

To begin with, we tokenize the corpus in the dataset based on camel case and underscores. We then select the top 10,000 words from the corpus based on their frequency of occurrence, and encode the corpus according to this vocabulary. Any words that are not in the vocabulary are discarded. Finally, we divide the encoded data into training and test sets. For training the Description Search (DS) model, we use the code description and natural language query parts of the training data. For training the Code Search (CS) model, we use the code descriptions and code fragments of the training data. For each training sample, we add a corresponding negative sample for description search. After training the DS and CS models, we use the DS model to search for relevant code descriptions in the entire test set (excluding correct code description fragments) for a new query, and use this information as query expansion data. We integrate this with the query using the ES method and pass it to the CS model to return the ranking of code fragments. We evaluate the performance of the model using two metrics: Recall@k and MRR. Recall@k measures the proportion of correct code fragments among the first k code fragments returned by the code search model. MRR calculates the reciprocal of the rank of the fragments returned by the code search model in the entire test set. We compared our query expansion method with two popular query expansion methods: WordNet extension and frequent itemset-based expansion. We use the FPgrowth algorithm to construct frequent itemsets. We trained the DS model for 200 epochs with a learning rate of $1e-3$ and a learning rate decay ratio of 0.5. The settings of the CS model are consistent with the original text. All experiments were run on a server with 4 Nvidia 3080TI GPUs and a total memory of 64G. The total training time was 40 h.

## 4 Results

In our previous experimental setup, we compared the impact of using natural language queries and code descriptions as inputs to the code search (CS) model. Next, we evaluated the effectiveness of our Deep Semantics (DS) model by comparing the results obtained using the code descriptions recommended by the DS model and those obtained using randomly selected code descriptions as query expansion. To demonstrate the superiority of our Sentence Integrated Query Expansion (SIQE) method, we compared it with the WordNet query expansion method and the FP query expansion method. Finally, we analyzed the effect of the parameters on the performance of the SIQE model.

### 4.1 Preliminary Experiments

We conducted an experiment to compare the performance of the code search (CS) model using query and code description as inputs. Specifically, we trained two CS models, DeepCS and UNIF, and then tested the models using query and code description. The results, presented in Table 3, show that for both Java and Python, the performance of the CS models is significantly better when using code description as input compared to using query as input for both DeepCS and UNIF models.

**Table 3.** The impact of Description and Query on the model

| Model | Evaluation Set | Python | | | | Java | | | |
|---|---|---|---|---|---|---|---|---|---|
| | | R@1 | R@5 | R@10 | MRR | R@1 | R@5 | R@10 | MRR |
| DeepCS | Description | 0.204 | 0.424 | 0.533 | **0.31** | 0.244 | 0.535 | 0.721 | **0.375** |
| | Qurey | 0.058 | 0.16 | 0.251 | **0.122** | 0.056 | 0.163 | 0.262 | **0.124** |
| UNIF | Description | 0.340 | 0.538 | 0.632 | **0.439** | 0.365 | 0.595 | 0.684 | **0.470** |
| | Qurey | 0.151 | 0.353 | 0.451 | **0.250** | 0.176 | 0.360 | 0.477 | **0.269** |

## 4.2 Main Comparison Results

We conducted several experiments to evaluate the effectiveness of our Sentence Integrated Query Expansion (SIQE) method for code search. First, we compared the performance of the DeepCS and UNIF models using the original query and the query after applying the SIQE method on the Java and Python datasets. Second, we analyzed the impact of using the DS model in the SIQE method by comparing the results obtained using k code description fragments recommended by the DS model and k code description fragments selected randomly. To demonstrate the impact of the similarity score in the SIQE method on the accuracy of code search, we compared the performance of the CS before and after adding the similarity score. Finally, we compared our SIQE method with the current popular query expansion methods, WordNet and FP, and demonstrated the superiority of the SIQE method. Table 4 presents the results of our experiments. In this table, "Query" refers to using a raw query to search for code, "WordNet" refers to searching for code using WordNet-extended queries, "FP" indicates searching for code using the query after FP expansion, "SIQE" stands for searching for code using the SIQE extended query, "SIQE_n" represents searching for code using a query after SIQE expansion that does not use similarity score weighting, and "SIQE_r" represents searching for code using a query after SIQE expansion of descriptions that are not recommended by the DS module but picked randomly. Our experiments led to four main conclusions, which can be inferred from the results presented in Table 4.

**Conclusion 1: Results Show that Using the SIQE Extension Method Significantly Improves the Accuracy of Code Search Compared to Using the Original Query.** It can be seen from the Table 4 that compared with the original query, the SIQE extension method greatly improves the accuracy of the CS. Specifically, the MRR value on the Python dataset increased by 82.7% and 34.3% for the DeepCS and UNIF models, respectively. The R@1, R@5, and R@10 metrics also improved by 70.7%, 85%, 61.8%, 55.6%, 18.6%, and 29.9%. Similarly, on the Java dataset, the MRR value increased by 86.2% and 33.4% for the DeepCS and UNIF models, respectively, and the R@1, R@5, and R@10 metrics all improved by over 40%, with the maximum increase for R@1 being over 70.9%. These results demonstrate that the SIQE extension method can enhance query semantics and significantly improve the accuracy of code search by utilizing recommended code descriptions.

**Table 4.** Performance comparison of different extension models to code search models

| Method | Python | | | | Java | | | |
|---|---|---|---|---|---|---|---|---|
| DeepCS | | | | | | | | |
| | **R@1** | **R@5** | **R@10** | **MRR** | **R@1** | **R@5** | **R@10** | **MRR** |
| Qurey | 0.058 | 0.16 | 0.251 | 0.122 | 0.056 | 0.163 | 0.262 | 0.124 |
| WordNet | 0.076 | 0.214 | 0.392 | 0.144 18.0%↑ | 0.096 | 0.234 | 0.412 | 0.154 24.1%↑ |
| FP | 0.056 | 0.204 | 0.290 | 0.142 16.3%↑ | 0.066 | **0.304** | 0.310 | 0.162 30.6%↑ |
| SIQE | **0.141** | **0.297** | **0.400** | **0.223 82.7%↑** | **0.161** | 0.296 | **0.421** | **0.231 86.2%↑** |
| SIQE_n | 0.131 | 0.265 | 0.387 | 0.210 72.1%↑ | 0.105 | 0.287 | 0.354 | 0.198 59.6%↑ |
| SIQE_r | 0.025 | 0.081 | 0.141 | 0.066 45.9%↓ | 0.031 | 0.121 | 0.165 | 0.084 35.4%↓ |
| UNIF | | | | | | | | |
| | **R@1** | **R@5** | **R@10** | **MRR** | **R@1** | **R@5** | **R@10** | **MRR** |
| Qurey | 0.151 | 0.353 | 0.451 | 0.250 | 0.176 | 0.360 | 0.477 | 0.269 |
| WordNet | 0.171 | 0.374 | 0.459 | 0.268 7%↑ | 0.206 | 0.404 | 0.509 | 0.275 3%↑ |
| FP | 0.191 | 0.386 | 0.480 | 0.285 13.9%↑ | 0.216 | 0.392 | 0.520 | 0.291 8.9%↑ |
| SIQE | **0.236** | **0.419** | **0.587** | **0.336 34.3%↑** | **0.298** | **0.501** | **0.611** | **0.357 33.4%↑** |
| SIQE_n | 0.171 | 0.357 | 0.494 | 0.298 18.8%↑ | 0.179 | 0.402 | 0.472 | 0.274 1.8%↑ |
| SIQE_r | 0.091 | 0.257 | 0.394 | 0.206 17.6%↓ | 0.140 | 0.332 | 0.419 | 0.205 23.7%↓ |

**Conclusion 2: The DS Model in SIQE Plays a Key Role in Query Expansion.** According to Qurey, SIQE, SIQE in the Table 4, We can observe that the SIQE extension method enhances the mrr and Recall values compared to 'Qurey'. Nonetheless, the SIQE extension method without the DS model leads to a decrease in the performance of CS. For instance, the mrr value on the python dataset in the DeepCS model drops from 0.122 to 0.066. This implies that only code descriptions that have semantic similarity with the original query will positively impact the performance, whereas randomly selected non-similar code descriptions will negatively affect the performance. Therefore, this confirms that the DS model is crucial in the SIQE method.

**Conclusion 3: Adding Similarity Score to SIQE as an Extended Weight Enhances the Performance of Code Search Models.** It can be observed that both SIQE and SIQE_N significantly improve the CS compared to the original query. However, the improvement of SIQE is more significant compared to SIQE_N. For instance, on the Java dataset, the UNIF model increases from 0.274 to 0.357. This indicates that adding similarity weight reduces the impact of noise in the query expansion process and plays a role in feature filtering to some extent, thereby further enhancing the performance of the code search model.

**Conclusion 4: The SIQE Extension Method is Superior to the Popular WordNet and FP Methods.** In Table 4, the results for the SIQE, WordNet, and FP data indicate that the SIQE extension method performs better than the WordNet and FP methods. Compared to the current popular WordNet extension method, which is based on thesaurus extension, the SIQE method shows more promising results. For example, the WordNet method improved the DeepCS model by 18.0% on the Python dataset, while the FP method improved the model by 16.3%. In contrast, the SIQE method improved the performance of the code search model from 0.122 to 0.223, an increase of 82.7%. This suggests that the SIQE method, which is based on similar sentence meaning, can more effectively enrich the query semantics and improve the performance of code search.

### 4.3  Parameter Analysis

Since the k code description fragments recommended by the DS model in the SIQE extension method directly affect the representation of the final query vector, the different sources of the code description fragments searched by the DS model will cause the recommended k code description fragments to vary, thus affecting the representation of the final query vector. Therefore, we analyzed the performance variation of the SIQE extension method for different values of k and different sources of DS model searched code description fragments.

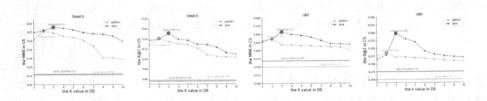

**Fig. 5.** Influence of different k values on code search model

To compare the impact of different k values on the code search model, we compared the MRR and Recall@1 values of the DeepCS and UNIF models in the Java and Python datasets when k varied from 1 to 10. The results are presented in Fig. 5. The graph shows an inverted U shape. For both the DeepCS and UNIF models, the best results were obtained when k was 2 or 3. This is reasonable since, when k is too small, the effect of the DeepCS model cannot be fully leveraged, while when k is too large, more noise data will be generated due

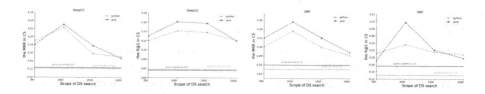

**Fig. 6.** Influence of DS search scope on code search model

to the limitations of the DeepCS model and the data source, which will reduce the ability of the code search model.

To compare the impact of different sources of DS model search code description fragments on the code search model, we selected four search ranges of 500, 1000, 1500, and 2000, and compared the performance of the CS model (with k set to the optimal value). The results are shown in Fig. 6. It can be seen that the best performance was achieved when the search range was about 1000 samples. This is reasonable since, when the search range is too large or too small, the performance of the DS model cannot be fully utilized. Only when the search range is around 1000 samples, which is close to the size of the DS test set, can the DS model search for more appropriate description fragments.

### 4.4   Example Study

Table 5 presents the results of applying different extension models to the original query "How to remove repeated elements from ArrayList?". The FP extension methods tend to find words that frequently co-occur with the keywords in the original query as the extension results, such as "repeated" and "difference", "ArrayList" and "interface", but their extension effect is very limited. The WordNet extension method extends the keywords according to the Word-Net thesaurus, such as "remove" and "get rid of", "repeat" and "duplicate", etc. This greatly enriches the semantics, but also introduces a lot of noise. On the other hand, the SIQE method, by following the recommended Desc1, Desc2, Desc3, and Desc4, greatly enriches the semantics while reducing the noise, and extends the original query with sentence meaning information from the code description, thereby improving the performance of the code search model.

Table 6 shows a negative effect of applying SIQE to the query "go to next page". The correct code ranking in the code search model using the original query is 5, while the ranking after SIQE extension is more than 10. It can be seen that for some queries that are too short, the SIQE method cannot always guarantee a positive effect on the code search model. This may be due to the simplicity of our DS model, which cannot always search for the description statements that are beneficial to the code search model, or due to the insufficient size of the query-description database we collected. We plan to optimize our DS model and expand the query-description database in future work.

**Table 5.** Example1

| Qurey | remove repeated elements from ArrayList? |
|---|---|
| FP | so remove difference repeated elements from ArrayList interface list |
| WordNet | remove take get rid of repeat duplicate recur elements component nent<br>constituent array raiment range list tilt name |
| Desc1 | remove the elements in descending order first index 5 then 3 then 1<br>remove the elements from the list without undesirable side effects |
| Desc2 | use an iterator then it next ( ) give the next item in the array and remove ( )<br>will remove the last value of next ( ) for without giving an exception if keep looping |
| Desc3 | prints the only thing is that re missing from the last matches iterating over all possible substrings and call matches ( regex ) on each substring |
| Desc4 | create a linked hash set from the list contain each element only once and in the same order<br>as the list then create a new list from this |
| Description | remove repeated elements to add the contents to a Set (which will not allow duplicates)<br>and then add the Set back to the ArrayList |
| Code | public void remove_repeated(ArrayList yourList){Set<String> set = new HashSet<>(yourList); yourList.clear(); yourList.addAll(set); } |

**Table 6.** Example2

| Qurey | go to next page |
|---|---|
| Desc1 | use a thread pool to download files in parallel |
| Desc2 | retrieve the next item from the iterator by calling its next ( ) method if default is given |
| Desc3 | use the urllib module to download individual ls |
| Desc4 | Return a column of the given page number. |
| Description | Callback to go to the next tab . Called by the accel key . |
| Code | def accel_next ( self , * args ) :<br>if self.get_notebook().get_current_page()+1==self.get_notebook().get_n_pages () :<br>self.get_notebook().set_current_page (0)<br>else : self . get_notebook ( ). next_page ( ) return True |

# 5  Related Word

## 5.1  Code Search

Today, code search is becoming increasingly important in helping developers find suitable code snippets based on their queries. Code search can significantly improve the efficiency of development and reduce the workload of developers. Early code search methods relied heavily on information retrieval techniques, which primarily used keyword matching. For example, Work [22] combined code keyword matching and PageRank for code search, while Work [9] improved the performance of code search by querying the attributes of keywords. In recent years, researchers have focused on code search methods based on deep learning. These methods use neural networks to jointly embed the query and the code into a high-dimensional vector space and use the cosine similarity between vectors to determine the semantic similarity between the query and the code. For instance, Work [6] proposed the DeepCS model, which uses a bidirectional LSTM network for code search. Work [1] proposed a lightweight attention model called UNIF. Work [27] proposed the CARLCS-CNN code search model based on joint attention representation learning. Work [32] proposed TabCS, an attention-based two-stage code search model. Work [18] proposed GraphSearchNet, which is based on the graph neural network.

## 5.2  Code Representation

Code characterization is an upstream task whose purpose is to learn the semantics of a program by obtaining feature information from the code and using it to represent the code for downstream tasks such as clone detection, defect detection, and code summarization [8,12,14,23,31,34]. For instance, the work by [11] separates the code into tokens and inputs it into a neural network. Meanwhile, [34] builds a code representation model based on the abstract syntax tree while taking into account the upper and lower structure information of the code. With the development of pre-training models such as BERT [4] and language models [26], code search models based on pre-training models have also been proposed. For example, [5] proposed CodeBERT, which is based on the BERT pre-training model. Additionally, [7] proposed GraphCodeBERT, which is based on the graph structure.

# 6  Summary

In this paper, we propose a query extension model called SIQE that is based on the structure of code description statements. SIQE is designed to enrich queries by recommending code descriptions with similar semantics, and to assign weight to each recommended code description to reduce the impact of noise. In the SIQE method, we first propose a query-based code description search model called DS. DS can effectively recommend multiple code descriptions that benefit the code search model, based on the user's input query, to enhance the query semantics. We also crawled the query-description-code corpus from Stack Overflow and validated that the SIQE method outperforms the baseline method through experiments. In future work, we plan to optimize the structure of the DS model and query-description database to further enrich the query semantics and improve the accuracy of code search.

**Acknowledgement.** This work is supported by the National Natural Science Foundation of China [Grant No. 61872139] and the Research Project of Hunan Provincial Education Department [Grant No. 22C0600].

# References

1. Cambronero, J., Li, H., Kim, S., Sen, K., Chandra, S.: When deep learning met code search. In: Proceedings of the 2019 27th ACM Joint Meeting on European Software Engineering Conference and Symposium on the Foundations of Software Engineering, pp. 964–974 (2019)
2. Chen, Q., Zhou, M.: A neural framework for retrieval and summarization of source code. In: Proceedings of the 33rd ACM/IEEE International Conference on Automated Software Engineering, pp. 826–831 (2018)
3. Cheng, Y., Kuang, L.: CSRS: code search with relevance matching and semantic matching. In: Proceedings of the 30th IEEE/ACM International Conference on Program Comprehension, pp. 533–542 (2022)
4. Devlin, J., Chang, M.-W., Lee, K., Toutanova, K.: BERT: pre-training of deep bidirectional transformers for language understanding. arXiv preprint arXiv:1810.04805 (2018)
5. Feng, Z., et al.: CodeBERT: a pre-trained model for programming and natural languages. arXiv preprint arXiv:2002.08155 (2020)
6. Gu, X., Zhang, H., Kim, S.: Deep code search. In: Proceedings of the 40th International Conference on Software Engineering, pp. 933–944 (2018)
7. Guo, D., et al.: GraphCodeBERT: pre-training code representations with data flow. arXiv preprint arXiv:2009.08366 (2020)
8. Haiduc, S., Aponte, J., Marcus, A.: Supporting program comprehension with source code summarization. In: Proceedings of the 32nd ACM/IEEE International Conference on Software Engineering, vol. 2, pp. 223–226 (2010)
9. Haiduc, S., Bavota, G., Marcus, A., Oliveto, R., De Lucia, A., Menzies, T.: Automatic query reformulations for text retrieval in software engineering. In: 2013 35th International Conference on Software Engineering (ICSE), pp. 842–851. IEEE (2013)
10. Huang, Q., Yang, Y., Cheng, M.: Deep learning the semantics of change sequences for query expansion, vol. 49, pp. 1600–1617. Wiley Online Library (2019)
11. Husain, H., Wu, H.-H., Gazit, T., Allamanis, M., Brockschmidt, M.: CodeSearchNet challenge: evaluating the state of semantic code search. arXiv preprint arXiv:1909.09436 (2019)
12. Kamiya, T., Kusumoto, S., Inoue, K.: CCFinder: a multilinguistic token-based code clone detection system for large scale source code. IEEE Trans. Softw. Eng. **28**(7), 654–670 (2002)

13. Le, T.-D.B., Wang, S., Lo, D.: Multi-abstraction concern localization. In: 2013 IEEE International Conference on Software Maintenance, pp. 364–367. IEEE (2013)
14. LeClair, A., Haque, S., Wu, L., McMillan, C.: Improved code summarization via a graph neural network. In: Proceedings of the 28th International Conference on Program Comprehension, pp. 184–195 (2020)
15. Ling, C., Lin, Z., Zou, Y., Xie, B.: Adaptive deep code search. In: Proceedings of the 28th International Conference on Program Comprehension, pp. 48–59 (2020)
16. Linstead, E., Bajracharya, S., Ngo, T., Rigor, P., Lopes, C., Baldi, P.: Sourcerer: mining and searching internet-scale software repositories. Data Min. Knowl. Disc. **18**(2), 300–336 (2009)
17. Liu, J., Kim, S., Murali, V., Chaudhuri, S., Chandra, S.: Neural query expansion for code search. In: Proceedings of the 3rd ACM SIGPLAN International Workshop on Machine Learning and Programming Languages, pp. 29–37 (2019)
18. Liu, S., Xie, X., Siow, J., Ma, L., Meng, G., Liu, Y.: GraphSearchNet: enhancing GNNs via capturing global dependencies for semantic code search. IEEE Trans. Software Eng. **49**, 2839–2855 (2023)
19. Lu, M., Sun, X., Wang, S., Lo, D., Duan, Y.: Query expansion via wordnet for effective code search. In: 2015 IEEE 22nd International Conference on Software Analysis, Evolution, and Reengineering (SANER), pp. 545–549. IEEE (2015)
20. Lv, F., Zhang, H., Lou, J., Wang, S., Zhang, D., Zhao, J.: CodeHow: effective code search based on API understanding and extended boolean model (E). In: 2015 30th IEEE/ACM International Conference on Automated Software Engineering (ASE), pp. 260–270. IEEE (2015)
21. McCardle, P., Cooper, J.A., Houle, G.R., Karp, N., Paul-Brown, D.: Emergent and early literacy: current status and research directions-introduction. Learn. Disabil. Res. Pract. **16**(4), 183–185 (2001)
22. McMillan, C., Grechanik, M., Poshyvanyk, D., Xie, Q., Fu, C.: Portfolio: finding relevant functions and their usage. In: Proceedings of the 33rd International Conference on Software Engineering, pp. 111–120 (2011)
23. Nguyen, A.T., Nguyen, T.T., Al-Kofahi, J., Nguyen, H.V., Nguyen, T.N.: A topic-based approach for narrowing the search space of buggy files from a bug report. In: 2011 26th IEEE/ACM International Conference on Automated Software Engineering (ASE 2011), pp. 263–272. IEEE (2011)
24. Nie, L., Jiang, H., Ren, Z., Sun, Z., Li, X.: Query expansion based on crowd knowledge for code search. IEEE Trans. Serv. Comput. **9**(5), 771–783 (2016)
25. Poshyvanyk, D., Petrenko, M., Marcus, A., Xie, X., Liu, D.: Source code exploration with google. In: 2006 22nd IEEE International Conference on Software Maintenance, pp. 334–338. IEEE (2006)
26. Radford, A., et al.: Language models are unsupervised multitask learners. OpenAI Blog **1**(8), 9 (2019)
27. Shuai, J., Xu, L., Liu, C., Yan, M., Xia, X., Lei, Y.: Improving code search with co-attentive representation learning. In: Proceedings of the 28th International Conference on Program Comprehension, pp. 196–207 (2020)
28. Tian, Y., Lo, D., Lawall, J.: Automated construction of a software-specific word similarity database. In: 2014 Software Evolution Week-IEEE Conference on Software Maintenance, Reengineering, and Reverse Engineering (CSMR-WCRE), pp. 44–53. IEEE (2014)
29. Vaswani, A., et al.: Attention is all you need. In: Advances in Neural Information Processing Systems, vol. 30 (2017)

30. Wang, C., et al.: Enriching query semantics for code search with reinforcement learning. Neural Netw. **145**, 22–32 (2022)
31. Wang, W., Li, G., Shen, S., Xia, X., Jin, Z.: Modular tree network for source code representation learning. ACM Trans. Softw. Eng. Methodol. (TOSEM) **29**(4), 1–23 (2020)
32. Xu, L., et al.: Two-stage attention-based model for code search with textual and structural features. In: 2021 IEEE International Conference on Software Analysis, Evolution and Reengineering (SANER), pp. 342–353. IEEE (2021)
33. Yao, Z., Peddamail, J.R., Sun, H.: CoaCor: code annotation for code retrieval with reinforcement learning. In: The World Wide Web Conference, pp. 2203–2214 (2019)
34. Zhang, J., Wang, X., Zhang, H., Sun, H., Wang, K., Liu, X.: A novel neural source code representation based on abstract syntax tree. In: 2019 IEEE/ACM 41st International Conference on Software Engineering (ICSE), pp. 783–794. IEEE (2019)

# A Code Completion Approach Combining Pointer Network and Transformer-XL Network

Xiangping Zhang[1,2], Jianxun Liu[1,2]([✉]), Teng Long[1,2], and Haize Hu[1,2]

[1] School of Computer Science and Engineering, Hunan University of Science and Technology, Xiangtan 411100, Hunan, China
952259775@qq.com
[2] Hunan Key Lab. for Services Computing and Novel Software Technology, Hunan University of Science and Technology, Xiangtan 411100, Hunan, China

**Abstract.** Code completion is an integral component of modern integrated development environments, as it not only facilitates the software development process but also enhances the quality of software products. By leveraging large-scale codes to learn the probability distribution among code token units, deep learning methods have demonstrated significant improvements in the accuracy of token unit recommendations. However, the effectiveness of code completion with deep learning techniques is hindered by information loss. To alleviate the above problem, we proposed a code language model which combines the pointer network and Transformer-XL network to overcome the limitations of existing approaches in code completion. The proposed model takes as input the original code fragment and its corresponding abstract syntax tree and leverages the Transformer-XL model as the basis model for capturing long-term dependencies. Furthermore, we integrate a pointer network as a local component to predict the out-of-vocabulary words. The proposed method is evaluated on real PY150 and JS150 datasets. The comparative experimental results demonstrate the effectiveness of our model in improving the accuracy of the code completion task at the token unit level.

**Keywords:** Code Completion · Transformer-XL · Pointer Network · Out-of-Vocabulary

## 1 Introduction

The rapid advancement of information technology has increased the complexity of demands placed on software products, resulting in a rise in the difficulty and workload of software development. To address this challenge, improving the quality and efficiency of software development has become a top priority for software engineering researchers. One of the techniques that researchers have been leveraging to enhance the software development environment is code completion technology. This technique is a crucial component of integrated development environments, which predicts class names, method names, and keywords

H. Gao et al. (Eds.): CollaborateCom 2023, LNICST 561, pp. 303–322, 2024.
https://doi.org/10.1007/978-3-031-54521-4_17

in real time, providing developers with multiple options to choose from as they write code. By minimizing spelling errors and enhancing software development efficiency, code completion has become an essential tool in the contemporary software development process [1].

The current research on code completion can be broadly divided into two categories. The first category uses static type information and heuristic rules to predict the token units, such as variable names and method names. However, this approach often overlooks the contextual semantic information of the code, which can lead to inaccurate predictions [2–5]. The second category relies on existing code samples and the semantics of the preceding text to predict the possible token units at the current moment [6–12]. Those works leverage the semantic information of the code to provide more precise and relevant suggestions to developers. Overall, the current research on code completion is aimed at improving the accuracy and efficiency of the software development process by leveraging various techniques, including static type information, semantic information, and heuristic rules. These techniques play a crucial role in the development of modern software products and are constantly evolving to meet the ever-increasing demands of the software engineering industry.

The recent advancement in deep learning techniques has led to a surge of interest in applying these methods to code completion task. By leveraging large-scale codes to learn the probability distribution among code token units, deep learning methods have demonstrated significant improvements in the accuracy of token unit recommendations. However, the important thing to address when using deep learning techniques for code completion task is how to reduce the impact of information loss on the effectiveness of code modeling. The *first* type of information loss in code completion involves the loss of original source code information, which has two aspects. One of the common practices is truncating the source code that exceeds a certain length to be used as input data in deep learning models. However, truncation can result in the loss of valuable information, particularly in dealing with long text data like source code. Table 1 provides statistical information for the two most common datasets used in code completion research. For instance, the PY150 dataset has an average code length of 710.67, and at least 25% of the code fragments in this dataset contain more than 715 words. The JS150 dataset has an average code length of 1739.57, and at least 25% of the code fragments in this dataset contain more than 734 words. Additionally, when converting code into corresponding abstract syntax trees, the number of token units obtained on average is 70% higher than the number of token units in the original codes [13]. Therefore, while deep learning methods have shown potential in improving code completion accuracy, the input length limitation can pose a challenge in handling long text data like source code. The other is the Out-of-Vocabulary (OoV) problem, which arises due to various reasons. Such as, developers often name variables based on their personal preferences during code writing [14]. These variable names tend to occur less frequently than normal token symbols in the entire code corpus, which often results in them being eliminated during code language modeling. As a result, incomplete or inaccurate code suggestions can arise during code completion. To address these issues, researchers are exploring various techniques such as attention mechanisms, memory networks, and pointer networks that can improve the handling of OoV words in code completion. The *second* type of information loss is caused by the limitations of the neural network model itself. It is widely acknowledged that existing neural network language models have limitations when it comes to modeling long text data. In particular, deep learning-based code modeling approaches that use recurrent neural networks (RNNs) tend to suffer from the problem of forgetting information obtained early in the sequence as the number of time steps increases. For instance, if a variable is defined at the beginning of the source code but used at the end of it, the connection between the variable and its usage may be lost, resulting in less effective code language models and poorer performance in code completion tasks.

In this study, we proposed a code language model which combines the pointer network and Transformer-XL network (PTLM) to overcome the limitations of existing approaches in code completion. Our model takes as input the original code fragment and its corresponding abstract syntax tree (AST) and leverages the Transformer-XL model as the basis for capturing long-term dependencies. Furthermore, we integrate a pointer network as a local component to predict out-of-vocabulary words, which often pose challenges in code completion. Our proposed method is evaluated on real PY150 and JS150 datasets, and the comparative experimental results demonstrate the effectiveness of our model in improving the accuracy of the code completion task at the token unit level. The main contributions of this paper can be summarized as the following three points.

- This paper presents experimental results that demonstrate the effectiveness of PTLM in improving code node value prediction and node type prediction tasks. Specifically, the results show that PTLM outperforms several state-of-the-art models on both the PY150 and JS150 datasets.
- This paper presents a novel approach to OoV token prediction using a pointer network, which allows for direct copying of token units from the original input data. Our method ensures information integrity, which in turn enhances the accuracy of code node value prediction.
- This paper investigates the influence of memory unit length on the performance of Transformer-XL model for code completion task. The experimental results reveal that the ideal length of memory units varies depending on the dataset, and selecting the appropriate length can substantially enhance the accuracy of predictions.

The remainder of this paper is organized as follows: Sect. 2 introduces the related works. Section 3 elaborates the proposed approach. Section 4 introduces the dataset and the experimental settings. Section 5 presents the experimental results. Section 6 concludes the paper.

## 2    Related Works

### 2.1    Neural Network-Based Code Completion

Hindle et al. [15] proposed the naturalness of source code that statistical methods could be used to model regular and predictable natural languages.

Tu et al. [16] built on [15] by suggesting that token units in programs have some repetition at a local scale, and that language models often learn only the global laws of the code and ignore the local features in the program. Hou et al. [17] developed an Eclipse plug-in called CACHECA, which combines the Eclipse default completion results with the cache-based $N$-gram model [18], and found that the performance of the combinatorial approach improved by 1/3 relative to the default plug-in, confirming the effectiveness of local repetition laws for code completion. Vinyals et al. [19] proposed pointer networks, which were initially used to solve combinatorial optimization problems as a variant of neural machine translation models. Pointer networks can be used to efficiently replicate words that need to be reused from input code fragments. Programming languages have local repetition laws, and researchers have considered adding pointer network mechanisms to language models to accurately predict locally recurring words. Bhoopchand et al. [20] proposed a streamlined pointer network that primarily addresses the problem of custom identifier prediction. Li et al. [21] proposed pointer mixture network which combines attention mechanism and pointer network for code completion. The model uses the abstract syntax tree sequence as model input and uses two components and a selector to decide whether to predict the next word in the global word list using the global RNN component or to copy a token from the input code fragment using the pointer network. The model improves the code completion accuracy to some extent, but the input of the model is only the AST sequence, which is an abstract generalization of the source code, and many detailed symbols in the original code fragment are not fully reflected in the AST, e.g., punctuation, operators, etc. This makes the token information in the program incomplete, which in turn affects the accuracy of code completion.

The core idea of code language model to accomplish the code completion task is to estimate the probability of the next occurrence of the token unit symbol in the sequence according to the existing code sequence [22]. For a sequence of code fragment $S = [w_1, ..., w_n]$, the probability of its occurrence is shown as Eq. 1:

$$P_\theta(S) = P_\theta(w_1) \prod_{t=2}^{n} P_\theta(w_t | w_{t-1}, \ldots, w_1) \tag{1}$$

where $w_t$ denotes the $t$-th token in the sequences of code fragments $S$ and $\theta$ denotes all parameters included in this model.

Thus, the purpose of the code completion task at the token level is to find the token $w_{t+1}$ that maximizes Eq. 1 based on the existing sequence of incomplete code fragments $S$. This process can be described by Eq. 2.

$$\underset{w_{t+1}}{argmax}\, P_\theta(w_1, \ldots, w_t, w_{t+1}) \tag{2}$$

In the traditional approach to code completion, recurrent neural networks are commonly used for feature extraction of tokens in the code. The obtained hidden state vector $h_t$ is then used to calculate the probability of occurrence of the token at the current time step $t$. As shown in Eq. 3.

$$P_\theta\left(w_t = \tau \mid w_{t-1}, \ldots, w_1\right) = \frac{\exp\left(v_\tau^T h_t + b_\tau\right)}{\sum_{\tau'} \exp\left(v_{\tau'}^T h_t + b_{\tau'}\right)} \tag{3}$$

where $w_t$ denotes the $t$-th token predicted in the code fragment sequence $S$. $h_t$ denotes the hidden state vector generated by the recurrent neural network at time step $t$. $v_\tau$ denotes the representation vector corresponding to the token $\tau$ in the lexicon. $b_\tau$ denotes the bias parameter. This approach has limitations in modeling long-term dependencies in the code, as RNNs tend to forget information obtained earlier in the sequence as the number of time steps increases. Additionally, this approach may not effectively handle the Out-of-Vocabulary problem, as it relies on the pre-defined vocabulary set.

Thus most of the existing work can also be considered as using different feature extraction methods to obtain the hidden states that the code sequence has at different time steps for the prediction of the token that appear at the next time step. The hidden states generated in this process need to contain information about the codes that appear in the previous time steps to be able to better predict the possible token units that will appear in the next time step.

## 2.2 Transformer Model

In recent years, deep learning techniques have been widely used for modeling text sequence data. Recurrent neural networks, particularly Long short-term memory (LSTM) and Gate Recurrent Unit (GRU), were among the most popular model architectures used for this purpose. However, they are limited in their ability to model long dependencies in text sequence data. To address this issue, Vaswani et al. proposed the Transformer neural network model, which uses a self-attentive mechanism to process text sequence data in parallel. Compared to recurrent neural networks, the Transformer model has shown better experimental results and lower resource consumption on a variety of natural language processing tasks [23].

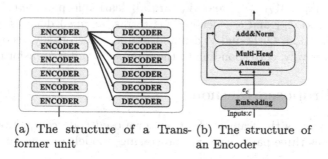

(a) The structure of a Trans-      (b) The structure of
former unit                              an Encoder

**Fig. 1.** The structure of Transformer Unit.

A Transformer unit is illustrated in Fig. 1(a). It includes six encoders and six decoders. The encoder contains two layers, a multi-headed attention layer and a feed-forward neural network layer, respectively. As shown in Fig. 1(b), for a encoder, the input code data $c$ is first converted into the corresponding vector $e_c$ after passing through the embedding layer, after which $e_c$ is fed into a single Transformer. $e_c$ passes through the multi-headed attention layer, and the knowledge contained in the data is extracted from multiple perspectives using a self-attentive mechanism in this layer [24]. The network structure of a single encoder can be represented by the Eq. 4–Eq. 7.

$$e_c = embedding(c) \tag{4}$$

$$z = self\_Attention\_Mechanism\,(e_c) \tag{5}$$

$$n = AddNorm\,(z, e_c) \tag{6}$$

$$o = FFD(n) \tag{7}$$

where $c$ denotes a sequence of code fragments. $embedding$ operation denotes converting each token unit in the code sequence $c$ into its respective corresponding word vector $e_c$. $self\_Attention\_Mechanism$ denotes obtaining the attention score of each element in the code sequence $c$. $AddNorm$ denotes summing the input data and using the layer normalization operation. $FDD$ denotes a simple feed-forward neural network layer. Equation 8–Eq. 13 represent the specific construction methods for the above three operations.

$$AddNorm\,(z, e_c) = layer\_norm(z) + e_c \tag{8}$$

$$FFD\,(x_l) = W_{l,2} \times GELU\,(W_{l,1} \times x_l + b_{l,1}) + b_{l,2} \tag{9}$$

$$self\_Attention\_Mechanism\,(x_l) = W_O \times softmax\left(Q \times \frac{K^T}{\sqrt{d_k}}\right) \times V \tag{10}$$

$$Q = W_Q \times x_l \tag{11}$$

$$K = W_K \times x_l \tag{12}$$

$$V = W_V \times x_l \tag{13}$$

where $W_{l,1}$, $W_{l,2}$, $W_Q$, $W_K$ and $W_V$ are all learnable parameters during the training process. $b_{l,1}$ and $b_{l,2}$ denote bias terms. $gelu(-)$ denotes use the $gelu$ activation function. $Q$, $K$ and $V$ denote the query vector, key vector and value vector, respectively, corresponding to the input data after transforming them.

## 3   The Proposed Method

Figure 2 illustrates the framework of our proposed code completion approach, which contains three parts: code pre-processing, model training, and code completion.

This paper approaches the problem of code completion by dividing the code into two distinct parts. The first part involves processing the source code by utilizing *jieba* library[1] to extract token symbol-level code information. The second

[1] https://pypi.org/project/jieba/.

part involves converting the code into its corresponding abstract syntax tree, and extracting the value and type information of each node by traversing the abstract syntax tree.

During the model training phase, a novel code language model is proposed that combines the Transformer-XL model and the pointer network model to address the issue of modeling long codes. By leveraging the Transformer-XL model's ability to handle long sequence data, high-quality code feature information is obtained. Additionally, the pointer network's capability to select words directly from the context vector as prediction results is utilized to mitigate the impact of the out-of-vocabulary problem in the source code.

Finally, for the code completion part, we adopt the same pre-processing method to handle the code fragments to be completed. After the pre-processing, the code fragments are fed into the trained code language model for prediction, thereby achieving the code completion task.

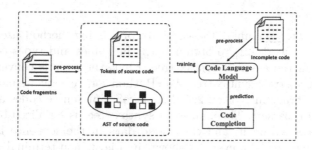

**Fig. 2.** The framework of code completion

### 3.1 Code Pre-processing

In previous research on code completion, model effectiveness was validated by predicting the values and types of nodes in the corresponding abstract syntax tree corresponding of the source code. However, the AST is an abstract representation of code information that overlooks some details of symbols in the original code fragment, such as punctuation and operators. This may result in incomplete semantic information in the program, leading to reduced accuracy in code completion. To overcome this limitation, our paper considers the raw text information of the code as input for the code completion model.

This paper employs the word separation function provided by the *jieba* library to pre-process the original text of the code. This function segments the text primarily based on spaces and also distinguishes punctuation from regular words. Figure 3 showcases how a Python code fragment can be divided into 24 token symbols, which denoted as $w^d$ in this paper, following the use of the word separation program in the *jieba* library.

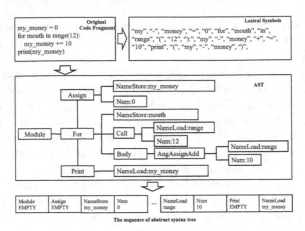

**Fig. 3.** An example of pre-processing python code fragment

In this paper, we employ the code pre-processing method used in existing code completion work [21] to obtain both the values and types corresponding to the nodes in the abstract syntax tree. First, the code is converted into the corresponding abstract syntax tree. The Python source code are parsed by using the standard library in Python 2.7. The JavaScript source codes are parsed by using the Acorn parser[2]. Then, abstract syntax trees is serialized by performing depth-first traversal on it, and each node data in the sequence is denoted as $w_i^a = [type_i, value_i]$. However, as shown in Fig. 3, non-terminal nodes in the abstract syntax tree do not have corresponding values. Therefore, when the abstract syntax tree is traversed depth-first, a *Empty* symbol is added to these nodes to unify the input data of the subsequent neural network. For example, the Module is transformed into *Module:Empty*.

## 3.2   Transformer-XL Based Code Language Model

The proposed code language model based on Transformer-XL is structured as shown in Fig. 4. Following code pre-processing, the transformed code data is first converted into vector format before being fed into the neural network for feature extraction. As stated earlier, this study utilizes the token symbols $w^d$ and node symbols $w_i^a$ in the abstract syntax tree. To convert these symbols into corresponding word vector representations, we employ embedding techniques from the PyTorch framework, as demonstrated in Eq. 14–16.

$$e_i^s = embedding\,(w_i^s) \tag{14}$$

$$e_i^{type} = embedding\,(type_i) \tag{15}$$

$$e_i^{value} = embedding\,(value_i) \tag{16}$$

---

[2] https://github.com/acornjs/acorn.

where $e_i^s$, $e_i^{type}$, $e_i^{value}$ denote the vector representation corresponding to the $i$-th token symbol $w^d$, the $i$-th node type symbol and the $i$-th node value symbol in the original text of the code, respectively.

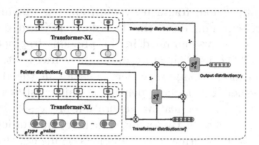

**Fig. 4.** The structure of the proposed model

This paper utilizes the Transformer-XL neural network model to effectively model the three aforementioned features. The fundamental characteristic of the Transformer-XL network is its segment-level recursive mechanism that establishes connections between various segments via a memory module [24]. The segment-level recursive mechanism in the Transformer-XL neural network enables the modeling of long-range dependencies in the text. Furthermore, this mechanism facilitates information interaction between different fragments and helps to address the fragmentation problem arising from contextual segmentation [24]. As shown in Fig. 5, in the Transformer-XL model, two consecutive fragments $s_\tau = [e_{\tau,1}, ..., e_{\tau,L}]$ and $s_{\tau+1} = [e_{\tau+1,1}, ..., e_{\tau+1,L}]$ of length $L$ are set. The Transformer introduced in the previous section is actually a stack of multiple encoders and decoders, so $h_\tau^n \in R^{L \times d}$ is used to denote the implied state corresponding to the $\tau$-th consecutive fragment $s_\tau$ in the $n$-th layer, and $d$ denotes the length of the implied state. Then, the implied state corresponding to the $\tau + 1$-st consecutive fragment $s_{\tau+1}$ in the $n$-th layer can be obtained from Eq. 17–Eq. 21 as follows.

$$\widetilde{h}_{\tau+1}^{n-1} = \left[ SG\left( h_\tau^{n-1} \right) : h_{\tau+1}^{n-1} \right] \tag{17}$$

$$q_{\tau+1}^n = h_{\tau+1}^{n-1} W_q^T \tag{18}$$

$$k_{\tau+1}^n = \widetilde{h}_{\tau+1}^{n-1} W_k^T \tag{19}$$

$$v_{\tau+1}^n = \widetilde{h}_{\tau+1}^{n-1} W_v^T \tag{20}$$

$$h_{\tau+1}^n = Transformer\_Layer\left( q_{\tau+1}^n, k_{\tau+1}^n, v_{\tau+1}^n \right) \tag{21}$$

where the ":" notation indicates that the two vectors are concatenated. $SG(-)$ indicates that the gradient is not back-passed and the implied state from the previous moment is used directly. $q$, $k$, $v$ indicate the query vector, key vector and value vector generated from the implied state, respectively.

While the original Transformer model processed long sequential data by dividing the text into segments, it discarded the linkage information between each segment by simply slicing the long text into shorter segments and modeling the sequence. In contrast, the Transformer-XL model records the implicit state information of previous fragments by introducing a memory unit of length $d_{mem}$. When processing new data, the Transformer-XL model caches and utilizes all the implicit vectors obtained in the previous fragments to participate in the generation of the implicit state of the new fragment. This enables the Transformer-XL to model long-range dependencies in the data. As shown in Fig. 5, the Transformer-XL model appends the implied states generated by the fragments $[e_5^s, e_6^s, e_7^s, e_8^s]$ to the feature generation process of the new code fragments $[e_9^s, e_{10}^s, e_{11}^s, e_{12}^s]$ as well. By setting a memory unit of length $d_{mem} = 4$ to record the implicit state information of previous segments, the Transformer-XL model can solve the long-distance dependence problem. It should be noted that the implicit information of the memory cell is not subject to gradient calculation, i.e., the $SG(-)$ operation in Eq. 17. For more details on the construction of the memory cell, readers may refer to the literature [24].

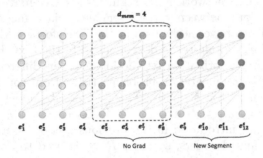

**Fig. 5.** The diagram of the segment in Transformer-XL

In this study, we first employ the Transformer-XL neural network to model the original text information of the code. As depicted in the upper portion of Fig. 4, the preprocessed raw text information is input into the Transformer-XL neural network. Subsequently, Transformer-XL generates the corresponding implicit state $h_{\tau+1}^s$ for this data, as demonstrated in Eq. 22.

$$h_t^s = Transformer\_XL\left(e^s\right) \tag{22}$$

To obtain the complete node information, we combine the vector information corresponding to the node type and node value data obtained from the abstract syntax tree. This is achieved through stitching the two types of data together, resulting in the complete node information represented as $e^{node}$, which is expressed in Eq. 23.

$$e^{node} = \left[e^{type} : e^{value}\right] \tag{23}$$

where the length corresponding to $e^{node}$ is the sum of $e^{type}$ and $e^{value}$.

The Transformer-XL model is utilized for feature extraction of the complete node information $e^{node}$, which is fed into the network as shown in Eq. 24.

$$h_t^n = Transformer\_XL\left(e^{node}\right) \tag{24}$$

where $h_t^n$ denotes the implied state output by $e^{node}$ after the last layer of Transformer-XL model.

In this study, we adopt the pointer mixture neural network architecture and utilize an extra cache space $M_t$ to compute the context vector $c_t$, as described below.

$$A_t = V^T \tanh\left(W^m M_t + \left(W^h h^n\right) 1_L^T\right) \tag{25}$$

$$l_t = softmax\left(A_t\right) \tag{26}$$

$$c_t = M_t l_t^T \tag{27}$$

The context vector $c_t$, the parent vector $p_t$ and $h_t^{node}$ are stitched together to obtain the Transformer-XL token distribution based vector $w_t$, as shown in Eq. 28–Eq. 29.

$$G_t = \tanh\left(W^g \left[c_t : p_t : h_t^{node}\right]\right) \tag{28}$$

$$w_t^n = softmax\left(W^v G_t + b^v\right) \tag{29}$$

In the original pointer mixture network, a selector $S_t^a$ is first set for choosing whether to select features from the global or local pointer component for the current moment vocabulary prediction, as shown in Eq. 30.

$$S_t^a = \sigma\left(W^s \left[h_t^n : c_t\right] + b^s\right) \tag{30}$$

In this paper, an additional global selector $S_t^g$ is set on top of this method, which serves to enable the model to select the appropriate words from the code raw text information and the code abstract syntax tree information as the prediction result. $s_t^g$ is calculated as follows.

$$S_t^g = \sigma\left(W^g \left[S_t^a w_t : (1 - S_t^a) l_t : h_t^s\right] + b^g\right) \tag{31}$$

where $h_t^s$ is the implicit state corresponding to the code text. $w^g$ is the matrix of learnable parameters in the global selector.

The final layer of the PTLM model outputs the probability distribution $y_t$ for the token prediction at moment $t$.

$$y_t = \left[S_t^g S_t^a w_t : S_t^g (1 - S_t^a) l_t : (1 - S_t^g) h_t^s\right] \tag{32}$$

## 4    Experiments and Settings

### 4.1    Experimental Data

**Table 1.** The statistics of two datasets used in this work

| Dataset | JavaScript | PY150 |
|---|---|---|
| Code Number | 150000 | 150000 |
| Word Number | 229476577 | 106601060 |
| Average Words | 1739.57 | 710.67 |
| Lower Quartile | 89 | 99 |
| Median Number | 251 | 317 |
| Upper Quartile | 734 | 715 |
| Node Types | 95 | 330 |
| Node Number | $2.6 \times 10^6$ | $3.4 \times 10^6$ |

In this study, two benchmark datasets are utilized, namely the JavaScript dataset (JS150)[3] and the Python dataset (PY150)[4]. The two datasets are publicly available and used in previous work [21]. Each dataset consists of 150,000 original code files, accompanied by their corresponding abstract syntax tree data. Both datasets contain 150,000 program files which are stored in their corresponding AST formats, with the first 100,000 used for training and the remaining 50,000 used for testing [21]. The JavaScript dataset contains 44 original node types, while the Python dataset has 181 node types. We following work [21] and consider 95 and 330 node types for JavaScript and Python, respectively. Table 1 presents the essential statistical details of the datasets used in this study.

In the training process of our proposed method, we use specific parameter settings. The initial learning rate is set to 0.00001 and the learning rate decay value is set to 0.6. We conduct 10 training rounds, and each group of experiments is repeated three times, and the average of the three results is presented as the final outcome. All experiments are performed on a server running Ubuntu 16.04, equipped with two Nvidia RTX2080Ti graphics cards, each with 11 GB of video memory.

### 4.2    Evaluation

To assess the effectiveness of the proposed method, we adopt the code completion metric accuracy used in prior work [21]. Accuracy refers to the ratio of correctly

---

[3] https://www.sri.inf.ethz.ch/js150.
[4] https://www.sri.inf.ethz.ch/py150.

predicted completion results to the total number of completion operations. It is calculated using the following formula.

$$Accuracy = \frac{P_{True}}{P_{Total}} \tag{33}$$

where $P_{True}$ indicates the number of correctly predicted token units and $P_{Total}$ indicates the number of all predicted token units.

### 4.3   Baseline Methods

To analyze the effectiveness of the proposed model in this paper for the code completion task, we selected the most effective existing methods for code completion and conducted experimental comparisons. A brief description of these methods is provided below.

- LSTM [25]. The input of each LSTM neural unit comprises two parts, namely the implicit state of the previous neural unit output and the combined information of node types and values present in the nodes of the abstract syntax tree. Once the feature extraction is completed for the entire sequence, the final implied state output is fed into the feed-forward neural network and the softmax layer for predicting the token unit.
- ParentLSTM [21]. This approach generates a fixed-size context vector within a window by leveraging attention scores from previous and current implicit state computations. The model then uses a concatenated vector consisting of the current node's implicit state, the context vector, and the parent node's implicit state as input to the prediction layer.
- Pointer Mixture Network (PMN) [21]. This method extends the ParentLSTM approach by incorporating two components, namely a global RNN and a local pointer, selected by a selector to predict the next token unit from either the global vocabulary or the local context.
- Transformer [26]. To improve computational efficiency and handle longer sequences of text, this method replaces the LSTM neural network with a Transformer neural network. The Transformer network is better suited to model long sequences of text and has superior computational efficiency.
- Transformer-XL [27]. This method utilizes the Transformer-XL neural network for modeling on sequences of abstract grammar trees, as well as for predicting node-to-root paths, which leverages the structural information inherent in the abstract grammar tree. In the implementation, all task weights are set to 0.5.
- CCMC [22]. This method leverages the Transformer-XL model to perform code completion on the PY150 dataset, utilizing a combination of memory and replication mechanisms to enable accurate predictions of out-of-vocabulary words.
- PTLM. The proposed model. This model divides the code into two components, namely the code text information and the code abstract syntax tree information. To tackle the issue of long dependencies in the code, the

Transformer-XL model is integrated into the model to capture the sequential features of both code components. Moreover, to handle the OoV text, which is commonly observed in code analysis tasks, the model is augmented with a pointer neural network that enables it to predict OoV token units.

### 4.4   Research Questions

We conducted a series of experiments to assess the efficacy of the approach proposed in this paper, with a focus on addressing the following research questions.

Research Question 1: What is the effectiveness of the proposed methods in this paper for the code completion task?

To answer this problem, we selected several existing code completion methods that have shown strong performance and utilized the same dataset employed by these methods for comparative evaluation of experimental results.

Research Question 2: The effect of different code structures on the experimental effect of code completion.

In the proposed method, we divided the code into two distinct parts: the code's original text and its corresponding abstract syntax tree. Here we want to examine the impact of these three distinct code structures on the efficacy of the code completion task.

Research question 3: The effect of the length of memory cells in Transformer-XL on the code completion task.

To examine the impact of memory cell length on code completion task, we will experiment with varying memory cell lengths in the Transformer-XL model. The length of the memory cell is essential for the model to retain implicit states in sequence data. This research question aims to explore how different memory cell lengths influence the model's performance on the code completion task.

## 5   Experimental Results and Analysis

### 5.1   Research Question 1

In this paper we selected six baseline methods to perform experiments on the PY150 and JS150 datasets for prediction of node values and node types in the code completion task, respectively. In the experiments we set the optimizer of all the comparison methods to Adam optimizer and the number of implicit units of the LSTM model to 128 and the learning rate to 0.001. For the PTLM model proposed in this paper, we set its extra cache space length to 100 and the number of layers of the Transformer-XL neural network to two layers.

The first is a comparison experiment on the PY150 dataset. The global vocabulary size of the abstract grammar tree nodes in the dataset is 1000, 10,000 and 50,000, where PY_1K, PY_10K and PY_50K represent the global vocabulary size corresponding to the values of the nodes in the dataset, respectively. The main reason for this phenomenon is that it is difficult for the model to construct information about token units that do not appear in the vocabulary, and a larger vocabulary will contain more token units related to node values, and the model can learn the features of these token units and make predictions, thus improving the accuracy of the code completion task. Also according to Table 2, we have the following observations and analyses.

1. Methods based on LSTM models, such as LSTM, Attentional LSTM, and Pointer Mixture Network, achieve lower accuracy on node-type prediction tasks than those based on Transformer models. The reason for this phenomenon is that the length of the sequences obtained after converting the code into an abstract syntax tree increases significantly, and the LSTM-like models are less capable of modeling such long sequences than the Transformer-like models, so they are less effective in the type prediction task.
2. Attentional LSTM model is compared with LSTM model, because Attentional LSTM introduces the attention to the code structure information, i.e., the new vector formed by splicing the implicit state of the current node, the context vector and the implicit state of the node's parent node as the input of the prediction layer. Therefore, Attentional LSTM can achieve better prediction results than the native LSTM model.
3. The Pointer Mixture Network (PMN) model can achieve better results than the LSTM and Attentional LSTM models because it introduces a hybrid pointer mechanism to predict the next token unit from the global word list or local context information by setting a selector, which makes it possible to achieve the prediction of OoV token units. When the vocabulary size is 1000, the Pointer Mixture Network model has a significant improvement over the LSTM and Attentional LSTM models in the node value prediction task. This also shows the effectiveness of the Pointer Network in this model.

The PTLM model achieves better results than other methods for the node type prediction and node value prediction tasks. The PTLM achieves significantly better results than the Pointer Mixture Network, Transformer and Transformer-XL models for the node value prediction task because the PTLM model setting up a global selector, a local selector, and obtaining feature information from different data sources.

**Table 2.** The comparison with different methods on Python dataset

| Model | PY_1K | | PY_10K | | PY_50K | |
|---|---|---|---|---|---|---|
| | type | value | type | value | type | value |
| LSTM | 71.6 | 63.6 | 73.2 | 66.3 | 74.7 | 67.3 |
| Attentional LSTM | 73.2 | 64.9 | 75.5 | 68.4 | 77.8 | 69.8 |
| PMN | 75.2 | 66.6 | 77.8 | 68.9 | 78.4 | 70.1 |
| Transformer | 76.6 | 64.4 | 78.4 | 66.5 | 78.9 | 68.0 |
| Transformer-XL | 77.4 | 65.1 | 79.1 | 67.2 | 80.4 | 69.1 |
| CCMC | 78.0 | 65.0 | 79.3 | 69.6 | 81.4 | 70.2 |
| PTLM | 78.5 | 68.9 | 79.9 | 71.8 | 82.0 | 73.0 |

Also in this paper, experiments are conducted on the JavaScript dataset to compare the effectiveness of different methods on the code completion task. Where JS_1K, JS_10K, and JS_50K denote the global vocabulary size corresponding to the values of the abstract syntax tree nodes in the JS150 dataset of 1000, 10000, and 50000, respectively, the experimental results are shown in Table 3. It can be seen that on this dataset, the better the results achieved by the model on the node value prediction task as the size of the vocabulary table increases because it allows the model to capture more semantic information of the source code.

**Table 3.** The comparison with different methods on JavaScript dataset

| Model | JS_1K | | JS_10K | | JS_50K | |
|---|---|---|---|---|---|---|
| | type | value | type | value | type | value |
| LSTM | 77.2 | 69.9 | 82.6 | 75.8 | 84.9 | 78.6 |
| Attentional LSTM | 79.7 | 71.7 | 85.0 | 78.1 | 86.1 | 80.6 |
| PMN | 81.8 | 74.2 | 85.8 | 78.9 | 86.6 | 81.0 |
| Transformer | 83.1 | 74.4 | 84.7 | 79.9 | 85.8 | 80.2 |
| Transformer-XL | 82.2 | 75.2 | 85.8 | 80.8 | 86.2 | 81.5 |
| PTLM | 84.6 | 75.9 | 87.9 | 81.7 | 88.9 | 83.8 |

## 5.2  Research Question 2

As mentioned in the previous section, in this work we divide the code into two parts: the original code text and the abstract syntax tree of the code. For the original text of the code, we use a simple word division technique to divide it, and feed the divided token into the proposed code language modeling model for feature extraction. For the abstract syntax tree of the source code, we divide the node information into two parts, which are node type and node value. This section will introduce the influence of these three parts of the code on the experimental effect. The experiments are conducted on the PY150 and JS150 datasets, and the effects of the code completion task on the different datasets are obtained by removing these three structures and their combinations in the PTLM model.

In Table 4 and Table 5, "-source" denotes the model obtained by removing the original code text from the PTLM model. "-source, -type" indicates the removal of the original code text data and the node type data in the abstract syntax tree from the PTLM model, and the rest of the model structure can be followed in the same way. For the case of node type removal, we do not perform the task of node type prediction, so it is indicated by "-" in the results presentation. For the part of original code and node value removal, we do not perform the prediction of node values, and similarly, it is indicated by " -" to indicate the results. From Table 4 and Table 5, we observe the following phenomena.

**Table 4.** The comparison with different structure of model on Python dataset

| Model | PY_1K | | PY_10K | | PY_50K | |
|---|---|---|---|---|---|---|
| | type | value | type | value | type | value |
| PTLM | 78.5 | 68.9 | 78.9 | 71.8 | 80.8 | 73.0 |
| -source | 76.4 | 65.1 | 77.1 | 67.2 | 79.4 | 69.1 |
| -type | – | 64.9 | – | 65.7 | – | 66.2 |
| -value | 73.2 | 62.6 | 75.5 | 68.4 | 77.8 | 69.8 |
| -source, -type | – | 60.9 | – | 63.6 | – | 64.9 |
| -source, -value | 71.5 | – | 72.4 | – | 74.4 | – |
| -type, -value | – | 55.9 | – | 56.6 | – | 58.9 |

**Table 5.** The comparison with different structure of model on JS150 dataset

| Model | JS_1K | | JS_10K | | JS_50K | |
|---|---|---|---|---|---|---|
| | type | value | type | value | type | value |
| PTLM | 84.6 | 75.9 | 87.9 | 81.7 | 88.9 | 83.8 |
| -source | 79.3 | 68.1 | 80.2 | 69.8 | 82.7 | 72.0 |
| -type | – | 66.5 | – | 66.9 | – | 68.1 |
| -value | 73.8 | 64.9 | 75.0 | 65.1 | 76.0 | 66.8 |
| -source, -type | – | 60.9 | – | 63.6 | – | 64.9 |
| -source, -value | 69.3 | – | 72.4 | – | 74.1 | – |
| -type, -value | – | 60.9 | – | 63.6 | – | 64.9 |

1. when the PTLM model removes the raw text information of source code (i.e., the "-source" structure result), the effect of the model decreases, especially the prediction accuracy for node values decreases more than the prediction accuracy for node types. This phenomenon suggests that code-source text information can provide information that is not contained in the node values in the abstract syntax tree, and that using code-source text information as model input can improve the effectiveness of the code completion task.

2. When the node type (-type) is removed from the input data, the model is unable to predict the node values. Moreover, comparing the model structures of "-source, -type" and "-source", we can see that the model's effectiveness in the node-value prediction task decreases significantly when the node type is removed. The reason for this phenomenon is that the pairwise correlation between node type and node value splicing can assist the model in predicting node values, e.g., when the node type is known, the prediction range of the corresponding node value is also reduced, thus improving the prediction accuracy.

3. As can be seen in Table 4 and Table 5, the combined structure of the three data types in the code works better for the node type prediction and node

value prediction tasks than the combined case of the other structures. This inspires the need for a comprehensive evaluation of the different features of the code in order to improve the effectiveness of the code analysis task.

## 5.3   Research Question 3

The parameter examined in this section is the effect of the memory cell length $d_{mem}$ in the Transformer-XL model on the experimental effect. The memory cell lengths of all Transformer-XL modules in the PTLM model are set to 50, 100, 150, 200, 250 and 300, and the rest of the parameters are kept consistent for the experiments. The experimental results are shown in Fig. 6.

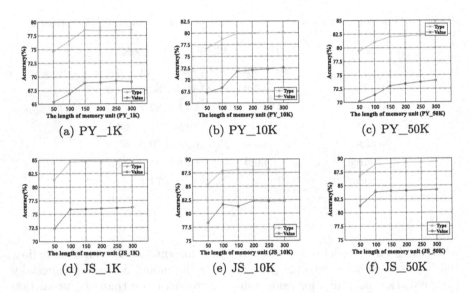

**Fig. 6.** The effect of different length of memory unit

From Fig. 6(a)–Figure 6(f), it can be seen that the performance of the model starts to stabilize at the memory cell length of 150 when the dataset is the PY150 dataset. In contrast, for the JS150 dataset, the performance of the model starts to stabilize at a memory cell length of 100. A reasonable explanation for this phenomenon is that the different distribution of code lengths in the two datasets makes the length of information to be cached by Transformer-XL different. As shown in Table 1, the upper quartile in the PY150 dataset (715) is larger than the upper quartile in the JS150 dataset (734). This indicates that there are some longer length data in the PY150 dataset, and therefore a larger memory cell space needs to be set for the whole PY150 dataset. This experiment shows that setting the memory cell parameters in Transformer-XL needs to be set according to the statistical information of the specific dataset.

During the experiment, we found that the memory consumption of the graphics card increased with the increase of memory cells, so we set the memory cell size to 150 for the PY150 dataset and 100 for the JS150 dataset in the subsequent experiments.

## 6   Conclusions

In this work, we have proposed a code language model that combines the pointer network and the Transformer-XL network to overcome the information loss problem of existing code completion approaches. The proposed model takes as input the original code fragment and its corresponding abstract syntax tree, and uses the Transformer-XL model as the base model for capturing long-term dependencies. The proposed method is evaluated on real PY150 and JS150 datasets. The comparative experimental results demonstrate the effectiveness of our model in improving the accuracy of the code completion task at the token unit level. In the next work, we will explore the complementary effects of the Transformer-XL model at the code API level.

**Acknowledgements.** This work was supported by the National Natural Science Foundation of China (61872139).

## References

1. Izadi, M., Gismondi, R., Gousios, G.: CodeFill: multi-token code completion by jointly learning from structure and naming sequences. In: Proceedings of the 44th International Conference on Software Engineering, pp. 401–412 (2022)
2. Yang, Y., Xiang, C.: Improve language modelling for code completion by tree language model with tree encoding of context (S), pp. 675–777 (2019)
3. Fang, L., Huang, Z., Zhou, Y., Chen., T.: Adaptive code completion with meta-learning. In: Proceedings of the 12th Asia-Pacific Symposium on Internetware, pp. 116–125 (2020)
4. Popov, A., Orekhov, D., Litvinov, D.: Time-efficient code completion model for the R programming language. In: Proceedings of the 1st Workshop on Natural Language Processing for Programming (NLP4Prog 2021), pp. 34–39 (2021)
5. Kyaw, H.H.S., Funabiki, N., Kuribayashi, M.: An implementation of offline answering function for code completion problem in PLAS. In: 2021 IEEE 3rd Global Conference on Life Sciences and Technologies (LifeTech), pp. 162–165 (2021)
6. Raychev, V., Vechev, M., Yahav, E.: Code completion with statistical language models. In: Proceedings of the 35th ACM SIGPLAN Conference on Programming Language Design and Implementation, pp. 419–428 (2014)
7. Robbes, R., Lanza, M.: How program history can improve code completion. In: 2008 23rd IEEE/ACM International Conference on Automated Software Engineering, pp. 317–326 (2008)
8. Proksch, S., Lerch, J., Mezini, M.: Intelligent code completion with bayesian networks. ACM Trans. Softw. Eng. Methodol. **25**(1), 1–31 (2015)
9. Lee, Y.Y., Harwell, S., Khurshid, S.: Temporal code completion and navigation. In: 2013 35th International Conference on Software Engineering (ICSE), pp. 1181–1184 (2013)

10. Nguyen, A.T., Nguyen, H.A., Nguyen, T.T.: GraPacc: a graph-based pattern-oriented, context-sensitive code completion tool. In: 2012 34th International Conference on Software Engineering, pp. 1407–1410 (2012)

11. Omori, T., Kuwabara, H., Maruyama, K.: A study on repetitiveness of code completion operations. In: 2012 28th IEEE International Conference on Software Maintenance (ICSM), pp. 584–587 (2012)

12. Zhang, X., Liu, J., Shi, M.: A parallel deep learning-based code clone detection model. J. Parallel Distrib. Comput. **181**, 104747 (2023)

13. Guo, D., Lu, S., Duan, N.: UnixCoder: unified cross-modal pre-training for code representation. arXiv preprint arXiv:2203.03850 (2022)

14. Shi, J., Yang, Z., He, J., Xu, B., Lo, D.: Can identifier splitting improve open-vocabulary language model of code? In: 2022 IEEE International Conference on Software Analysis, Evolution and Reengineering (SANER), pp. 1134–1138 (2022)

15. Hindle, A., Barr, E.T., Gabel, M.: On the naturalness of software. Commun. ACM **59**(5), 122–131 (2016)

16. Tu, Z., Su, Z., Devanbu, P.: On the localness of software. In: Proceedings of the 22nd ACM SIGSOFT International Symposium on Foundations of Software Engineering, pp. 269–280 (2014)

17. Franks, C., Tu, Z., Devanbu, P.: CACHECA: a cache language model based code suggestion tool. In: 2015 IEEE/ACM 37th IEEE International Conference on Software Engineering, vol. 2, pp. 705–708 (2015)

18. Henkel, J., Lahiri, S.K., Liblit, B.: Code vectors: understanding programs through embedded abstracted symbolic traces. In: Proceedings of the 2018 26th ACM Joint Meeting on European Software Engineering Conference and Symposium on the Foundations of Software Engineering, pp. 163–174 (2018)

19. Vinyals, O., Fortunato, M., Jaitly, N.: Pointer networks. In: Advances in Neural Information Processing Systems, vol. 28 (2015)

20. Bhoopchand, A., Rocktäschel, T., Barr, E.: Learning python code suggestion with a sparse pointer network. arXiv preprint arXiv:1611.08307 (2016)

21. Li, J., Wang, Y., Lyu, M.R.: Code completion with neural attention and pointer networks. arXiv preprint arXiv:1711.09573 (2017)

22. Yang, H., Kuang, L.: CCMC: code completion with a memory mechanism and a copy mechanism. In: Evaluation and Assessment in Software Engineering, pp. 129–138 (2021)

23. Tay, Y., Dehghani, M., Bahri, D., Metzler, D.: Efficient transformers: a survey. ACM Comput. Surv. **55**(6), 1–28 (2022)

24. Dowdell, T., Zhang, H.: Language modelling for source code with transformer-XL. arXiv preprint arXiv:2007.15813 (2020)

25. Liu, C., Wang, X., Shin, R., Gonzalez, J.E., Song, D.: Neural code completion (2016)

26. Kim, S., Zhao, J., Tian, Y., Chandra, S.: Code prediction by feeding trees to transformers. In: 2021 IEEE/ACM 43rd International Conference on Software Engineering (ICSE), pp. 150–162 (2021)

27. Liu, F., Li, G., Wei, B., Xia, X., Fu, Z., Jin, Z.: A self-attentional neural architecture for code completion with multi-task learning. In: Proceedings of the 28th International Conference on Program Comprehension, pp. 37–47 (2020)

# A Code Search Method Incorporating Code Annotations

Qi Li[1,2], Jianxun Liu[1,2(✉)], and Xiangping Zhang[1,2]

[1] School of Computer Science and Engineering, Hunan University of Science and Technology, Xiangtan 411201, Hunan, China
37323474@qq.com

[2] Hunan Key Lab for Services Computing and Novel Software Technology, Hunan University of Science and Technology, Xiangtan 411201, Hunan, China

**Abstract.** Code search is a technique for users to retrieve code snippets from the Code base using natural language, which is dedicated to retrieve the target code accurately and quickly to improve the efficiency of software development. The deep learning based code search technique greatly improves the accuracy of search by learning the relationship between code and query statements. Since it relies on the extracted code features, acquiring more code features is the key to quickly improve the search performance. However, most of the previous works have not taken code annotations into consideration. In this paper, we take code annotations as code features and apply them to code search, which is named ICA-CS (Code Search that Incorporates Code Annotations). In the method, firstly, the code features are embedded to get the corresponding vector representation. It is then processed by bidirectional LSTM (Long Short-Term Memory) network or multi-head attention respectively, followed by features fusion. And finally, the model is trained by joint embedding and using the minimised ranking loss function. As the experimental results show, on the evaluation metric MRR (mean reciprocal rank) compared to the state-of-the-art models DeepCS, SAN-CS, CARLCS-CNN and SelfAtt, the proposed model improves 48.96%, 17.11%, 41.01% and 13.07%, respectively.

**Keywords:** Code search · Code features · Code annotations · Bidirectional LSTM · Multi-head attention

## 1 Introduction

Code search has received a lot of attention in recent years [1–5]. The goal of code search is to perform natural language queries from large code corpora to retrieve code snippets that meet developers' needs [6]. Studies have shown that developers spend an average of 19% of their total development time searching for code online [7], and code search plays an important role in the software development process, helping to improve developer productivity and shorten product development cycles [7, 8].

H. Gao et al. (Eds.): CollaborateCom 2023, LNICST 561, pp. 323–342, 2024.
https://doi.org/10.1007/978-3-031-54521-4_18

Nowadays, there are more and more code resources available. On the popular platform GitHub alone, there will be 413 million open source contributions in 2022 [9]. It follows that most of the code written by developers has already been written by others [10, 11] and that this code is easily accessible on open source platforms. However, developing accurate code search engines faces considerable challenges [10, 12, 13]. Developers often have difficulties in finding satisfactory code in a short period of time, which may affect the development progress of the project. Therefore, how to find the target code efficiently and quickly becomes a major challenge. For this reason, researchers have been trying to explore various code search methods to help developers.

Early code search methods were mainly based on information retrieval (IR) techniques, especially keyword matching mechanisms. For example, Lv et al. proposed CodeHow [14], which combines text similarity and API matching through an extended Boolean model. McMillan et al. proposed the Portfolio [15], which returns a series of functions through keyword matching and the PageRank algorithm [16].Lu et al. used WordNet [17] to expand the synonyms of a query and perform keyword matching of method names. However, these approaches only treat codes and queries as plain text and do not fully utilize the structural or semantic information in the source code, which leads to unsatisfactory code search [1, 18, 19].

To address the above problems, researchers have started to widely apply deep learning techniques in code retrieval tasks to learn deeper semantic information between the query statements and the source code [6]. DeepCS [20] proposed by Gu et al. is one of the pioneers, which is a model that applies deep learning techniques to code search for the first time. DeepCS utilizes recurrent neural network (RNN) and multilayer perceptron (MLP) to represent code snippets and queries as feature vectors, and trained the model by computing the similarity function of code and query statements with a minimized ranking loss function. The results of the study showed that the deep learning approach achieved better performance in code search. Subsequently, many research works followed the framework of DeepCS, focusing on exploring in mining more code features. Shuai et al. proposed a model CARLCS-CNN [4], which utilizes convolutional neural networks (CNNs) and the joint attention mechanism to learn the correlation between code and query. Cambronero et al. proposed a simple model UNIF [2], which utilizes an attention layer for code and query embedding. To mine more code features, Wan et al. proposed MMAN [5], which combines multiple semantic information of code, including source code token sequences, Abstract Syntax Trees (ASTs), and Control Flow Graphs (CFGs). Zeng et al. proposed deGraphCS [1], which proposes data flow and control flow from intermediate representations of code. Liu et al. proposed GraphSearchNet [21] to represent codes and queries using a unified graph structure. These works start from the properties of the code itself and focus on exploring more features of the code to improve the accuracy of the search. However, none of these works considered the impact of code annotations information on the code retrieval task, which may have a significant impact on the accuracy of the search.

Code annotations describe the main functions of the source code through natural language forms and can help developers to understand the code quickly [22]. High-quality code annotations improve the readability and comprehensibility of the code and play an important role in the development and maintenance of the program [23], thus it is an integral part of the code. In the code snippet shown in Fig. 1 and the process of extracting code features, DeepCS extracts method names, application programming interface (API) sequences, and code token sequences from the code [20], and even though it extracts relatively comprehensive information, for code annotations information is not fully captured. These annotations contain a lot of useful information, such as descriptions of parameters, explanations of return values, handling of exceptions, and version information. In addition, users also enter information related to these aspects, such as restrictions on input or return values, when performing code searches [24]. Therefore, code annotations also contain important information that can be helpful for code search tasks.

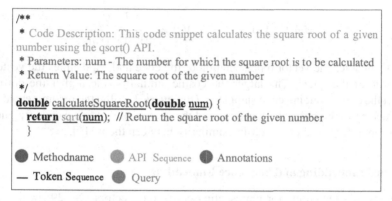

**Fig. 1.** Example of code features extracted

Mainstream code search models have made significant progress in exploring more features, however, code annotations are rarely addressed in existing research and are not explored in depth. For example, literature [25] simply incorporates code annotations into token sequences. Currently, there are fewer works that investigate code annotations in depth in the direction of code search. To address this point, we introduce code annotations into code search and proposes a new model called ICA-CS. Specifically, ICA-CS extracts four features from code: method names, API sequences, code annotations, and code token sequences, and it learns the relationship between code and query statements by using a bidirectional LSTM to process method names and query statements, and a multi-head attention mechanism to process API sequences, code annotations, and code token sequences. The results show that introducing code annotations into code search with deep exploration can significantly improve the performance of code search models.

The contributions of this paper are as follows:

1. We propose the model ICA-CS, which fuses method names, API sequences, code annotations and code token sequences to extract more code features information and significantly improve the accuracy of code search.
2. In this paper, code annotations are introduced into code search as one of the features of code for the first time, and are validated using three models (DeepCS, SAN-CS, and the proposed model ICA-CS). The experiments demonstrate that the search performance of all models is improved after the introduction of code annotations.

## 2 Technical Background

### 2.1 Joint Embedding

Joint embedding is a technique for jointly embedding heterogeneous data into a unified vector space [26], aiming to bring semantically similar concepts of two modalities close to each other in the vector space [27].

Since codes and queries are heterogeneous [20], correlations between them are difficult to detect directly. Therefore, after completing the representation of codes and queries, we jointly embed them. Specifically, the joint embedding is realized by calculating the cosine similarity between code vectors $V_c$ and query vectors $V_q$.

$$sim(V_c, V_q) = cos(V_c, V_q) = \frac{V_c^T \cdot V_q}{||V_c|| \cdot ||V_q||} \tag{1}$$

where $V_c$ denotes the vector representation of the code and $V_q$ denotes the vector representation of the query. The larger the cosine similarity, the higher the correlation between the corresponding code snippet and the query. Finally, the recommendation list is obtained by ranking the query vectors and the vectors of candidate code fragments in descending order based on the cosine similarity between them [19].

### 2.2 Word Embedding and Sequence Embedding

Embedding is a technique for representing entities as vectors [28, 29], which can be used to transform various entities, such as words, utterances, books, etc., into dense vector representations of fixed length so that machines can understand and process them [30]. Among them, word embedding is a typical embedding technique [28, 29], which represents words as fixed-length vectors such that semantically similar words are close together and semantically dissimilar words are farther apart in the vector space [20]. Word embeddings are usually implemented using models such as continuous bag-of-words (CBOW) or Skip-Gram [29], which are trained using a text corpus by building a neural network to capture the relationship between a word and its context [30].

Sequence embedding treats a sentence as a bag of words, and then embeds the words one by one, and finally integrates them into a tensor to represent the embedding vector of the whole sequence. In the process of sequence embedding, since each word is independent of each other, the contextual logical relationship is still preserved after the sequence embedding is completed.

### 2.3 Bidirectional LSTM

LSTM is an RNN architecture designed to solve the gradient vanishing and gradient explosion problems in traditional RNNs [31]. Bidirectional LSTM consists of forward LSTM and backward LSTM. Taking "open an xml file" as an example, the vectors of each word are obtained after sequence embedding, and then these vectors are fed into the forward LSTM and the backward LSTM for computation to obtain their outputs respectively. Finally, the vectors obtained from the forward LSTM and the backward

LSTM are concatenated to obtain the final output vectors. The ability of the bidirectional LSTM to utilize both the previous and subsequent information in the sequence makes it more effective in dealing with code features sequence data, which greatly improves the accuracy of the search.

### 2.4  Multi-head Attention

Multi-head Attention is the key idea in Transformer [32], which is widely used in the field of natural language processing (NLP). An attention function can be described as mapping a query and a set of key-value pairs to an output, where the query, keys, values, and output are vectors. In practice, a set of queries are computed simultaneously using the scaled dot product attention [32] function, which packs them into a matrix $Q$. The keys and values are also packed together into matrices $K$ and $V$. The output matrix is computed as follows:

$$Attention(Q, K, V) = SoftMax(\frac{QK^T}{\sqrt{d_k}})V \qquad (2)$$

where $d_k$ is the dimension length and $Q$, $K$ and $V$ represent the query, key and value matrices.

To further improve the expressiveness of self-attention, the query, keys and values are projected h times with different linear projections and then the projections are concatenated to obtain the final output, a computational process known as multi-head attention [21, 32]:

$$MultiHead(Q, K, V) = Concat(head_1, \ldots, head_h)W^O$$

$$\text{where head}_i = Attention(QW_i^Q, KW_i^K, VW_i^V) \qquad (3)$$

where the projections are parameter matrices $W_i^Q \in R^{d_{model} \times d_k}$, $W_i^K \in R^{d_{model} \times d_k}$, $W_i^V \in R^{d_{model} \times d_v}$ and $W^O \in R^{hd_v \times d_{model}}$, h is the number of heads.

On the basis of multi-attention, in order to better extract the values of the feature vectors, we employ an average pooling strategy to extract the key information. Average pooling is a feature extraction method that performs an averaging operation on each feature dimension in the input data to obtain a single value representing the feature. Similar to the average pooling strategy is the maximum pooling strategy, but it is not used, on the one hand due to the fact that it only focuses on the highest feature values, which may ignore some important features [19]. On the other hand based on the experimental results, it is found that the average pooling strategy can obtain better performance.

## 3  The Proposed Model

Figure 2 illustrates the general framework of the proposed model, which is divided into three main parts: model representation, feature extraction, and model training. In the model characterization, the extracted codes and queries are transformed into vector representations using embedding techniques to characterize the features information in the form of vectors. The code includes four features information: method name, API sequence, code annotations and code token sequence. The feature extraction part mainly extracts the feature vectors after the model characterization. For method name and query, the feature information is extracted by using bidirectional LSTM network, while for API sequence, code annotations and code token sequence, the feature information is extracted by using multi-attention and average pooling strategies. After the feature extraction is completed, the four features information of the code is sent to the fusion layer for features fusion, and the vector representation of the code is obtained by representing the code segments with the fused features. The model training part utilizes the obtained vector representations of the code and the query, calculates the similarity between them through the cosine similarity function, and ranks them. Then, the model is trained using a minimized ranking loss function to optimize the performance of the model. Through the collaboration of these three parts, the proposed model ICA-CS is able to perform code search more accurately, thus improving the efficiency and accuracy of code retrieval.

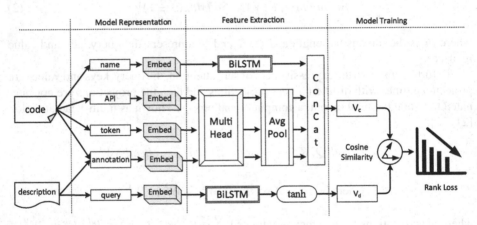

**Fig. 2.** The framework of the proposed method.

### 3.1 Code Representation

Code characterization is mainly divided into the following four aspects: method name, API sequence, code annotations and code token sequence. Specifically, the four features information are first characterized as vectors after embedding, then feature extraction is performed by the corresponding model, and finally the four extracted feature vectors are sent to the fusion layer for feature fusion to obtain the final vector representation, i.e., code vector. The following is the detailed operation of the code characterization part.

**Method Name.** The method name is a brief summary of the function of the whole code, has strong contextual logic and is usually short in length. The bidirectional LSTM network is adopted for feature extraction, using the output of the last time step therein to represent the entire information of a sentence. Suppose a method name is denoted as

$S_m = [m_1, m_2, ..., m_n]$, which after passing through the embedding layer is denoted as $E_m = [em_1, em_2, ..., em_n]$, and is then fed into a bidirectional LSTM network, which outputs its hidden vectors to represent the method names $V_m$. The whole process can be represented as:

$$V_m = BiLSTM(Embed(S_m)) \tag{4}$$

**API Sequences.** In code, API sequences usually consist of multiple API calls, which are usually long in length [30]. Although there is a logical relationship between some related APIs, most of them may not have direct correlation with each other, and their semantic information may not be fully captured using bi-directional LSTM networks, so multi-head attention is used to extract the information of API sequences. Suppose an API sequence $S_a = [a_1, a_2, ..., a_n]$, after the embedding layer is denoted as $E_a = [em_1, em_2, ..., em_n]$, which is then fed into the multi-head attention to get $M_a$, followed by average pooling to obtain the final vector representation of the API sequence $V_a$. The whole process can be represented as:

$$M_a = AvgPool(MultiHead(Embed(S_a))) \tag{5}$$

**Code Annotations.** The information in code annotations includes many, such as the description of parameters, the explanation of return values, the handling of exceptions and the description of specific code, etc. In order to fully utilize the various information in code annotations, we adopt the multi-head attention mechanism to extract the features of code annotations. Let a code annotations $S_o = [o_1, o_2, ..., o_n]$, which is represented as $E_o = [eo_1, eo_2, ..., eo_n]$, which is subsequently fed into the multi-head attention to get $M_o$, after average pooling to get the final vector representation of the code annotations $V_o$. The whole process can be represented as:

$$M_o = AvgPool(MultiHead(Embed(S_o))) \tag{6}$$

**Code Token Sequences.** For the code token sequences, which are a collection of all words in code, there is usually no strict order relationship, so it is a reasonable choice to use multi-head attention to extract the information. Let the code token sequence as $S_t = [t_1, t_2, ..., t_n]$, denoted as $E_t = [et_1, et_2, ..., et_n]$, which is subsequently fed into the multi-head attention to obtain $M_t$, and after average pooling, the final vector representation of the code token sequence $V_t$ is finally obtained. The whole process can be expressed as:

$$M_t = AvgPool(MultiHead(Embed(S_t))) \tag{7}$$

**Code Features Fusion.** According to the above operation, the vector representation of the four features of the code has been obtained, and now it is ready to fuse these features to get the final code vector representation. We do not use simple summation for fusion, but chooses concatenation, the concatenation operation can connect the information between each feature in an orderly manner, preserving the independent information of each feature. Subsequently, a linear transformation is performed on the concatenated vector, and finally the activation function $tanh()$ is used to obtain the final code vector $V_c$. The whole process can be expressed as:

$$V_c = tanh(Linear(Concat(V_m, V_a, V_o, V_t))) \tag{8}$$

## 3.2 Query Representation

The query statement usually contains the code function or problem description that the user wants to find, and has a strong contextual logical relationship, it is a good choice to use a bidirectional LSTM network to extract the information of the query statement. A query statement $S_q = [q_1, q_2, ..., q_n]$, which is represented as $E_q = [eq_1, eq_2, ..., eq_n]$ after the embedding layer, is then fed into a bidirectional LSTM network, which outputs its hidden vector and finally uses an activation function $tanh()$ to obtain the final query vector $V_q$. The whole process can be represented as:

$$V_q = tanh(BiLSTM(Embed(S_q)))$$ (9)

## 3.3 Model Training

Through the above steps, the code vector $V_c$ and the vector representation of the corresponding query $V_q$ can be obtained, and in order to measure the match between the code vector and the query vector, the cosine similarity is used to measure the similarity between them. Specifically, in the training phase, in order for the model to learn the correct code-query matching relationship, the ternary $< c, d+, d- >$ is used for training, where c denotes the code snippet, $d+$ denotes the query statement that matches with code c, and d- denotes the irrelevant query statement. The goal of training is to make the similarity of $< c, d+ >$ as high as possible, i.e., to bring the matching code and query vectors closer together, and to minimize the similarity of $< c, d- >$, i.e., to keep the irrelevant code and query vectors as far away as possible [20]. To achieve this goal, the model is trained by minimizing the ranking loss function [33, 34], which is represented as follows:

$$L(\theta) = \sum_{c \in C d+, d- \in D} max(0, \beta - sim(c, d^+) + sim(c, d^-))$$ (10)

where $\theta$ represents the parameters of the model, C denotes the code portion of the dataset, D denotes the query statement portion of the dataset, and $sim()$ denotes the function that calculates the similarity between the code and the code descriptions, and we use the cosine similarity function. $\beta$ is a constant and is set to 0.35 in the experiment.

**Optimizer.** In order to optimize the training process of the model, the AdamW optimizer is used and the learning rate is varied linearly. This adjustment can effectively avoid the instability of the model in the early stage of training and help accelerate the convergence speed of the model. Specifically, the linear variation of the learning rate is carried out during the training process according to the following equation:

$$Lr = Or \cdot Cr \, where Cr = \begin{cases} 1.0/current & , current < warmup \\ 1.0 & , current \geq warmup \end{cases}$$ (11)

where $Lr$ represents the current learning rate, $Or$ represents the set learning rate, the value is 1e–4. $Cr$ represents the change rate, the current training times $current$ is less than the set number of times $warmup$, $Cr$ is the inverse of the number of training times, the current training times $current$ is greater than or equal to the set number of times $warmup$, $Cr$ value is 1.0. In this experiment, $warmup = epoch * 0.05$, $epoch$ represents the number of times the model needs to be trained.

# 4 Experiments Setup

## 4.1 Dataset

**Date Cleaning:** Data cleaning is an important step in data processing to ensure data quality and consistency. We use the original dataset disclosed by degraphCS [1]. It should be noted that we use its original dataset rather than the dataset used in the paper, which is cleaned according to the following cleaning rules.

- Remove duplicate code snippets;
- Remove code snippets without code descriptions;
- Remove code snippets that are less than 3 lines long;
- Remove code snippets where the number of words in the query statement is less than 3;
- Remove code snippets with non-English code descriptions;
- Remove code snippets that have too high a percentage of single characters in query statements

Finally, 43,363 pieces of data were obtained through data cleaning, which were divided into 39,363 training sets and 4,000 test sets. When conducting the test, we use one correct candidate and 3,999 interference items to test the model, i.e., the model will retrieve all the code resources of the codebase, so that the test method can more realistically reflect the effect of the model in the actual application.

**Word Split Rules:** split the words from the feature information in the code and convert them to lowercase form so that the machine can understand and process them better. Two splitting rules are used to handle different forms of words: the camel case and the special character rule. The camel case splits words based on case, for example, "readXmlFiles" is split into "read", "xml" and "files". And the special character rule splits according to the specific character "_". For example, "read_xml_files" is split into "read", "xml" and "files". By using these splitting rules, the machine can embed different forms of words into the common vector space and understand the same semantics expressed by these words. This can help improve the model's ability to understand and express code features information, thus improving the accuracy and performance of code search.

## 4.2 Evaluation of Indicators

In order to evaluate the effectiveness of the proposed model ICA-CS, three common evaluation metrics are used, which are $SuccessRate@k$, $MRR$ and $NDCG@k$.

$SuccessRate@k$ is used to measure whether the correct result is included in the top k recommended results, i.e., whether the user requirement item is successfully recommended to the user, as defined below:

$$SuccessRate@k = \frac{1}{|Q|}\sum_{q=1}^{|Q|}\delta(Rank_q) \tag{12}$$

where $|Q|$ is the number of samples, which can be interpreted as the number of user's requirement items. $Rank_q$ is the position of the result of the $q_{th}$ query in the list of items recommended by the model, and $\delta()$ is used to express whether the correct result of the $q_{th}$ query is included in the list of k results recommended by the model, and its value is 1 if it is in; otherwise, it is 0. The k in *SuccessRate@k* are taken to be 1, 5, and 10, and the higher their scores are, indicating that more users' demanded items have been successfully recommended to the users.

*MRR* (mean reciprocal rank) is the average of the inverse rank of a set of queries Q in the top k ranked results, *MRR* measures the position of the user's demand in the top k recommended results and is computed as follows:

$$MRR = \frac{1}{|Q|} \sum_{q=1}^{|Q|} \frac{1}{Rank_q} \tag{13}$$

where $|Q|$ is the number of samples, which can be interpreted as the number of user's input queries. $Rank_q$ is the position of the result of the $q_{th}$ query in the list of items recommended by the model. The higher *MRR* score indicates, the better performance of the model search.

*NDCG@k* (normalized discounted cumulative gain at k) is a metric used to evaluate the accuracy of the sorted results. Recommender systems usually return a list of results to the user, and since there may be many results and the user will only view the first part, *NDCG@k* is used to measure the accuracy of the first k recommendations in the sorted results. It is the division of *DCG* (discounted cumulative gain) and *IDCG* (ideal discounted cumulative gain), where *DCG*, *IDCG* and *NDCG* are calculated as follows:

$$DCG@k = \sum_{i=1}^{k} \frac{2^{rel_i} - 1}{log_2(i+1)} \qquad IDCG@k = \sum_{i=1}^{k} \frac{2^{rel_i^{ideal}} - 1}{log_2(1+i)}$$

$$NDCG@k = \frac{1}{|Q|} \sum_{q=1}^{|Q|} \frac{DCG@k}{IDCG@k} \tag{14}$$

where $|Q|$ is the number of samples, $rel_i$ is the relevance of the $i_{th}$ item in the recommendation ranking results, $rel_i^{ideal}$ denotes that it is the relevance of the $i_{th}$ item in the ideal ranking results, and $k$ denotes the maximum value that can be given to the query, and the value is taken to be 10, for the purpose of this experiment. A code search model with high *NDCG@k* scores implies that it not only has a high overall search quality, but also ranks the results that the user needs in the top position.

For the above evaluation metrics, larger values represent higher search accuracy and better model performance. In order to demonstrate the performance of the model more intuitively, we use the following formula for the evaluation of model performance improvement:

$$improvement = \frac{P_{new} - P_{old}}{P_{old}} \tag{15}$$

$P_{new}$ is the performance of the improved model, and $P_{old}$ is the performance of the original model. The larger the value of *improvement*, the greater the improvement in model performance.

### 4.3 Baseline Models

- **DeepCS:** DeepCS [20] applies deep learning to code search for the first time, capturing semantic information of code from method names, API sequences, and code token sequences, etc., representing the source code and query statements using uniform vectors and computing the similarity.
- **SAN-CS:** SAN-CS [30] is a code search model based on self-attention networks, which utilizes self-attention networks to perform joint representation of code snippets and their descriptions separately.
- **CARLCS-CNN:** CARLCS-CNN [4] uses a co-attention mechanism to learn the correlation matrix between embedded codes and queries and jointly participate in their semantic relations.
- **SelfAtt:** SelfAtt is one of the four baseline models used by CodeSearchNet [25] and is the best performing model, which uses the BERT [35] encoder to encode the code and the query, and then computes a similarity score between the code and query representations.

### 4.4 Experimental Parameters

First, the data set is organized by setting the batch size to 64, and constructing separate vocabularies for each code features (method name, API sequence, code annotations, code token sequence) and query statement, and storing the 10,000 most frequent words in the data set in their respective vocabularies. In each batch, code features and query statements are padded to reach the maximum length using a special marker "PAD", which is set to 0. In addition, all features in the dataset are split into sequences according to the specified splitting rules and converted to lower case, e.g. and converted to lowercase, for example, "open_xml_files" will be split into "open xml files" sequence, "readTxtFiles" will be split into "read txt files". Next, we use the AdamW optimizer to update the model parameters, set the initial learning rate to 1e-4, and adopt a variable learning rate for warm-up, with a warm-up ratio of 0.05. The number of training times is set to 300, and the gradient trimming threshold is set to 5 in order to prevent the gradient from exploding. The word embedding size is set to 1024, the dimension of the bidirectional LSTM network is set to 512, and a multi-head attention mechanism with 4 attention heads is also used. To minimize the possibility of overfitting, the dropout is set to 0.1. All experiments are run experimentally on a server with Ubuntu 18.04.5 operating system using dual 2080ti GPUs.

## 5 Experimental Results

In this section, in order to evaluate the performance of the proposed model in terms of code search, the following questions are posed for investigation:

- **Question 1:** How is the performance of the proposed model compared to some state-of-the-art models? In addition, can code annotations be used as code features and how much does it improve the accuracy of code search?

- **Question 2:** Is the bidirectional LSTM network used in the model better than other recurrent neural networks? Does the multi-head attention mechanism perform better compared to other attention mechanisms? Is the average pooling strategy better than the maximum pooling strategy?
- **Question 3:** Which of the four features (method names, API sequences, code annotations, and code token sequences) is used in the model and which one contributes the most?
- **Question 4:** How much do different parameters affect the model?

Question 1 explores the performance of the model ICA-CS proposed in this paper and the effect of code annotations on code search; Question 2 discusses the effectiveness of the neural network model used in ICA-CS; Question 3 explores the contribution of individual features; and Question 4 discusses the effect of the model's parameters on the search performance.

### 5.1 Question 1: Model Performance and the Extent to Which Code Annotations Improve the Performance of Code Searching

Table 1 demonstrates the performance evaluation results of the model proposed and the comparison model on the test samples of the dataset, and it can be clearly seen that the proposed model significantly outperforms the comparison model in all evaluation metrics. Compared with the comparison model DeepCS, the proposed model improves 73.65%, 36.92% and 25.99% on SuccessRate@1, 5 and 10, and 48.96% and 43.08% on MRR and NDCG@10, respectively. Compared to the comparison model SAN-CS, the proposed model improves 24.56%, 11.49% and 9.52% on SuccessRate@1, 5 and 10, and 17.11% and 15.23% on MRR and NDCG@10, respectively. Compared with the comparison model CARLCS-CNN, the proposed model improves 61.45%, 29.69% and 20.6% on SuccessRate@1, 5 and 10, and 41.01% and 35.97% on MRR and NDCG@10, respectively. Compared to the comparison model SelfAtt, the proposed model improves 18.74%, 8.63% and 7.01% on SuccessRate@1, 5 and 10, and 13.07% and 11.52% on MRR and NDCG@10, respectively.

The combined results show that the proposed model significantly outperforms all the compared models in code search. The ICA-CS model synthesizes a variety of features to achieve better performance in code search, and also adopts a more appropriate mechanism for extracting information for different features, and thus is able to achieve significant performance improvement.

In order to verify whether code annotations can be used as a feature of the code, code annotations are added to DeepCS, SAN-CS and ICA-CS models and the performance is evaluated. The results are shown in Table 1, where the performance of all models is significantly improved after adding code annotations. Adding code annotations to DeepCS improves 18.13%, 10.7%, and 6.7% at SuccessRate@1, 5, and 10, and 11.94% and 10.54% at MRR and NDCG@10, respectively. Similarly, adding code annotations to SAN-CS improves 10.42%, 5.78% and 4.27% on SuccessRate@1, 5 and 10, and 7.68% and 6.81% on MRR and NDCG@10, respectively. Whereas, in the proposed model, the addition of code comments equally improves the performance by 18.64%, 7.66% and 6.09% on SuccessRate@1, 5 and 10, and 12.09% and 10.48% on MRR and NDCG@10, respectively.

**Table 1.** Experimental results of the proposed model and the comparison models

| Model | SR@1 | SR@5 | SR@10 | MRR | NDCG@10 |
|---|---|---|---|---|---|
| DeepCS | 0.2383 | 0.4393 | 0.5298 | 0.3368 | 0.3749 |
| SAN-CS | 0.3322 | 0.5395 | 0.6095 | 0.4284 | 0.4655 |
| CARLCS-CNN | 0.2563 | 0.4638 | 0.5535 | 0.3558 | 0.3945 |
| SelfAtt | 0.3485 | 0.5537 | 0.6238 | 0.4437 | 0.4810 |
| ICA-CS | **0.4138** | **0.6015** | **0.6675** | **0.5017** | **0.5364** |
| DeepCS | 0.2383 | 0.4393 | 0.5298 | 0.3368 | 0.3749 |
| | **0.2815** | **0.4863** | **0.5653** | **0.3770** | **0.4144** |
| SAN-CS | 0.3322 | 0.5395 | 0.6095 | 0.4284 | 0.4655 |
| | **0.3668** | **0.5707** | **0.6355** | **0.4613** | **0.4972** |
| ICA-CS | 0.3488 | 0.5587 | 0.6292 | 0.4476 | 0.4855 |
| | **0.4138** | **0.6015** | **0.6675** | **0.5017** | **0.5364** |

In summary, code annotations can be an important feature of code and can significantly improve the accuracy of code search. In particular, for SuccessRate@1, the performance improvement brought by the addition of code annotations is most obvious, which indicates that code annotations play a key role in accurately matching the relationship between code and query.

## 5.2   Question 2: Performance of Individual Components Used in the Model

In order to study the advantages of bidirectional LSTM, RNN, Bidirectional RNN (BiRNN) and LSTM networks are chosen as a comparison and the results are shown in Table 2. The following conclusions can be drawn, (1) LSTM networks perform significantly better than RNN networks. This is because LSTM networks have memory cells compared to traditional RNN networks, which can effectively solve the long-term dependency problem, enabling the model to achieve better performance when dealing with long sequences. (2) The performance of using bi-directional neural networks is better than unidirectional neural networks. By studying the principle of LSTM network, it can be found that LSTM network prefers to learn the information at the end of the sentence and ignores the more distant head information. In concise code, the head information is not less important than the tail information, so using the inverse LSTM in a bidirectional LSTM network can preserve the head information and combine it with the tail information of the forward LSTM, thus comprehensively capturing the contextual logical relationships in the code features, and thus improving the accuracy of the code search.

In order to verify the advantages of the multi-attention mechanism, this experiment uses self-attention, attention mechanism, summation mechanism and averaging mechanism as a comparative experiment. Self-attention utilizes the self-attention network to learn the different weights of the node vectors while attention utilizes the attention

**Table 2.** Performance of the proposed model using various neural network models

| Model | SR@1 | SR@5 | SR@10 | MRR | NDCG@10 |
|---|---|---|---|---|---|
| RNN | 0.1128 | 0.2678 | 0.3565 | 0.1865 | 0.2209 |
| BiRNN | 0.1763 | 0.3590 | 0.4468 | 0.2674 | 0.3007 |
| LSTM | 0.2795 | 0.4778 | 0.5573 | 0.3733 | 0.4100 |
| ICA-CS | **0.4138** | **0.6015** | **0.6675** | **0.5017** | **0.5364** |
| self-attention | 0.3455 | 0.5575 | 0.6290 | 0.4427 | 0.4812 |
| attention | 0.3065 | 0.5083 | 0.5935 | 0.4038 | 0.4418 |
| average | 0.2667 | 0.4743 | 0.5555 | 0.3653 | 0.4030 |
| sum | 0.2137 | 0.4160 | 0.5065 | 0.3109 | 0.3485 |
| ICA-CS | **0.4138** | **0.6015** | **0.6675** | **0.5017** | **0.5364** |
| Max Pooling | 0.2988 | 0.5020 | 0.5750 | 0.3947 | 0.4308 |
| ICA-CS | **0.4138** | **0.6015** | **0.6675** | **0.5017** | **0.5364** |

network to learn the different weights of the node vectors. Average averages the vectors across all the nodes, and sum sums the vectors of all nodes.

All these mechanisms aim to extract more critical features information. As can be seen from Table 2, the multi-head attention mechanism achieves the best performance on all evaluation metrics, and also the attention mechanism outperforms the sum and average mechanisms. We argue that, firstly, the attention mechanism can focus more on important information, thus ignoring unimportant information; secondly, the use of the multi-head attention mechanism can extract the critical information of the code features more effectively, thus improving the accuracy of the model.

The maximum pooling operation is compared with the average pooling operation used in ICA-CS, and the results are shown in Table 2. The results show that the average pooling operation is more suitable for ICA-CS, and the maximum pooling operation selects the most prominent features information, but this may not be able to represent all the features information completely. In contrast, the average pooling operation can fuse more features information and express the overall features more accurately, which improves the search performance. Therefore, the average pooling operation is a more effective strategy.

## 5.3 Question 3: Ablation Experiments

In this experiment, four features of the code (method names, API sequences, code annotations, and code token sequences) are experimented with separate deletions to validate the contribution of each feature to the performance of the model. As can be seen in Table 3, method name has the greatest impact on search performance, followed by code token sequence, followed by code annotations, while API has the least impact on code search. We speculate that this is because the method name best visualizes the specific function of the code, and therefore has the most significant impact on code search performance. Whereas not every piece of code involves an API sequence, therefore API has less impact on code search performance.

**Table 3.** Results of ablation experiments

| Model | SR@1 | SR@5 | SR@10 | MRR | NDCG@10 |
|---|---|---|---|---|---|
| -w/o methodname | 0.2375 | 0.4253 | 0.5028 | 0.3277 | 0.3618 |
| -w/o api | 0.4012 | 0.5847 | 0.6455 | 0.4863 | 0.5189 |
| -w/o annotations | 0.3488 | 0.5587 | 0.6292 | 0.4476 | 0.4855 |
| -w/o token | 0.2988 | 0.5038 | 0.5890 | 0.3962 | 0.4353 |
| ICA-CS | **0.4138** | **0.6015** | **0.6675** | **0.5017** | **0.5364** |

### 5.4 Question 4: Sensitivity Experiments

Sensitivity experiments are conducted in various aspects such as number of heads, annotations length, learning rate, dimension size, batch size, and $\beta$-value, respectively. As can be seen in Fig. 3, the model is insensitive to the number of heads and code annotations length, and its performance is relatively stable and fluctuates little. For dimension and batch size, the model is slightly sensitive and the search performance improves slowly as the dimension increases. It is interesting to note that the ICA-CS model is very sensitive to the learning rate and the $\beta$-value, and there are significant peaks in these two hyperparameters. Specifically, the model obtains the best results when the learning rate is set to 1e-4, while the model achieves the best search performance when the $\beta$ value is set to 0.35. This suggests that choosing appropriate values when adjusting the learning rate and $\beta$-value of the model can significantly improve the performance of the model.

## 6  Related Work

### 6.1  Code Search

Code search has been a popular field since the development of software engineering. Early works were mainly based on Information Retrieval (IR) techniques and Natural Language Processing (NLP) techniques, focusing on textual features of source code. For example, Lu et al. used some synonyms generated from WordNet to extend the query to improve the query to improve the hit rate [17]. McMillan et al. proposed.

Portfolio [15], which first computes the pairwise similarity between a query and a set of functions, and then uses a propagation activation algorithm to propagate the similarity scores through a pre-computed call graph. Linstead et al. proposed a code retrieval tool based on the Lucene implementation of the code search tool Sourcerer [36], which combines the textual content of a program with structural information to extract fine-grained structural information from the source code. Lv et al. proposed CodeHow [14], a

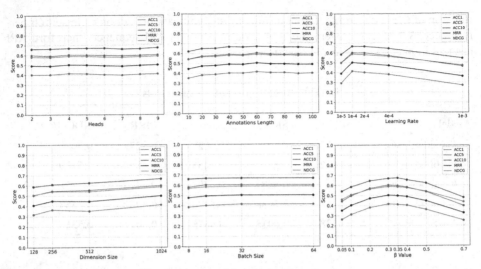

**Fig. 3.** Results of Sensitivity Experiments

code search tool that combines extended Boolean models with API matching. Although these works were able to produce some accurate results, code search engines based on IR techniques mainly focus on syntactic features and lack attention to semantic features, so the semantic gap between code and query is not well addressed.

With the development of deep learning technology, more and more works have started to apply deep learning to code search. For example, DeepCS [20] introduced by Gu et al. extracts method names, API sequences, and code token sequences as code features, and embeds these features information and queries into a shared space in order to retrieve code snippets through query vectors. Shuai et al. proposed a convolutional neural network (CNN)-based code search model CARLCS-CNN [4], which computes the common attention representation of code queries to improve the performance of code search. Cambronero et al. proposed a simple model UNIF [2] that extends NCS by joint deep learning to design two embedding networks to further tune the code and query embeddings. Husain et al. released the CodeSearchNet [25] challenge, which collects and makes public a dataset that explores some basic encoders for code search. Wan et al. proposed MMAN [5], which utilizes data from multiple modalities (code token sequences, ASTs, and CFGs) to better represent code with good results. Zeng et al. proposed DEGraphCS [1], which integrates code tokens, data flow, and control flow into variable-based graphs, which allows for a more accurate representation of the semantics of the code.

Overall, with the application and development of deep learning techniques, significant progress has been made in the field of code search, and researchers continue to explore new models and methods to improve the accuracy and efficiency of code search.

## 6.2 Attention Mechanism

Attention mechanism is a technique that simulates the human reading and listening process, which allows the model to learn to pay attention to key parts of the data, and is widely used in NLP and image description generation, and many experimental results have shown that attention mechanism has excellent performance in learning semantics [37–39]. In the field of code search, Cambronero et al. proposed UNIF [2] using unsupervised techniques and attention mechanisms with good results. Ueda et al. proposed a request estimation method using LSTM and four attention mechanisms to represent sentences from multiple perspectives and obtained excellent results [40].

On the basis of attention, Vaswani et al. proposed a self-attention mechanism, as well as a Transformer model based entirely on a self-attention network [32], which achieved significant success in a variety of NLP tasks, thus leading to a trend of using self-attention in the field of Artificial Intelligence. Zhang et al. proposed a self-attentive generative adversarial network which can generate features by using all the feature location cues to generate details [41]. Fang et al. introduced SANCS [30], which introduced self-attention to code search with remarkable success. Liu et al. proposed GraphSearchNet [21], which employs a bi-directional GGNN to capture the local structural information and employs multi-attention global dependencies.

Meanwhile, researchers also proposed a joint attention mechanism for learning interactive semantic information from two input data. Zhang et al. proposed a new joint attention-based network to capture the correlation between aspects and contexts, and the results showed good performance [42]. Xu et al. introduced TabCS [43] in the field of code search applying the traditional attention mechanism to extract the semantics of codes and queries, and applying a joint attention mechanism to address the semantic gap between codes and queries.

These studies demonstrate the important role of attention mechanisms in code search and provide powerful tools and methods to improve the accuracy and efficiency of code search.

# 7 Conclusion and Future Work

In this paper, a model named ICA-CS is proposed for code search task. The model introduces code annotations as additional features of the code in addition to considering method names, API sequences and code token sequences. For feature extraction, the ICA-CS model employs a bidirectional LSTM and a multi-head attention mechanism to obtain a more comprehensive and accurate representation of the code. In addition, the model maps code vectors and query vectors to a common vector space using joint embedding for code search. The experimental results show that compared to the state-of-the-art models DeepCS, SAN-CS, CARLCS-CNN, and SelfAtt, the proposed model ICA-CS achieves a significant improvement in the evaluation metrics MRR, which are 48.96%, 17.11%, 41.01% and 13.07%, respectively.

Future work will continue to extend the experiments of ICA-CS model on different language datasets to verify its effectiveness on different code styles and semantics. Meanwhile, considering the rich structural information embedded in code annotations, further research directions will involve the introduction of graph neural network techniques to better handle the code search task and improve the performance of the model on structural information such as code annotations. These explorations will further enhance the performance and efficiency in the field of code search.

# References

1. Zeng, C., et al.: deGraphCS: embedding variable-based flow graph for neural code search. ACM Trans. Softw. Eng. Methodol. **32**, 34 (2023)
2. Cambronero, J., Li, H., Kim, S., Sen, K., Chandra, S.: When deep learning met code search. In: Proceedings of the 2019 27th ACM Joint Meeting on European Software Engineering Conference and Symposium on the Foundations of Software Engineering, pp. 964–974 (2019)
3. Chen, Q., Zhou, M.: A neural framework for retrieval and summarization of source code. In: Proceedings of the 33rd ACM/IEEE International Conference on Automated Software Engineering, pp. 826–831 , numpages = 6 Association for Computing Machinery (2018)
4. Shuai, J., et al.: Improving code search with co-attentive representation learning. In: Proceedings of the 28th International Conference on Program Comprehension, pp. 196–207 (2020)
5. Wan, Y., et al.: Multi-modal attention network learning for semantic source code retrieval. In: 2019 34th IEEE/ACM International Conference on Automated Software Engineering (ASE), pp. 13–25 IEEE (2019)
6. Ling, X., et al.: Deep graph matching and searching for semantic code retrieval. ACM Trans. Knowl. Discov. Data **15**, 88 (2021)
7. Brandt, J., Guo, P.J., Lewenstein, J., Dontcheva, M., Klemmer, S.R.: Two studies of opportunistic programming: interleaving web foraging, learning, and writing code. In: Proceedings of the SIGCHI Conference on Human Factors in Computing Systems 1589–1598 Association for Computing Machinery, Boston, MA, USA (2009)
8. Robillard, M.P.: What makes APIs hard to learn? Answers from developers. IEEE Softw. **26**, 27–34 (2009)
9. GitHub. The 2022 State of the Octoverse. https://octoverse.github.com/. Accessed 15 Mar 2023
10. Rahman, M.M. et al.: Evaluating how developers use general-purpose web-search for code retrieval. In: Proceedings of the 15th International Conference on Mining Software Repositories, pp. 465–475. Association for Computing Machinery, Gothenburg, Sweden (2018)
11. Grazia, L.D., Pradel, M.: Code search: a survey of techniques for finding code. ACM Comput. Surv. **55**, 220 (2023)
12. Furnas, G.W., Landauer, T.K., Gomez, L.M., Dumais, S.T.: The vocabulary problem in human-system communication. Commun. ACM **30**, 964–971 (1987)
13. Kevic, K., Fritz, T.: Automatic search term identification for change tasks. In: Companion Proceedings of the 36th International Conference on Software Engineering 468–471. Association for Computing Machinery, Hyderabad, India (2014)
14. Lv, F., et al.: CodeHow: effective code search based on API understanding and extended boolean model (E). In: 2015 30th IEEE/ACM International Conference on Automated Software Engineering (ASE), pp. 260–270 (2015)
15. McMillan, C., Grechanik, M., Poshyvanyk, D., Xie, Q., Fu, C.: Portfolio: finding relevant functions and their usage. In: Proceedings of the 33rd International Conference on Software Engineering, pp. 111–120. Association for Computing Machinery, Waikiki, Honolulu, HI, USA (2011)

16. Langville, A.N., Meyer, C.D.: Google's PageRank and Beyond: The Science of Search Engine Rankings. Princeton University Press, Princeton (2006)
17. Meili, L., Sun, X., Wang, S., Lo, D., Yucong, D.: Query expansion via WordNet for effective code search. In: 2015 IEEE 22nd International Conference on Software Analysis, Evolution, and Reengineering (SANER), pp. 545–549 (2015)
18. Hu, F., et al.: Revisiting code search in a two-stage paradigm. In: Proceedings of the Sixteenth ACM International Conference on Web Search and Data Mining 994–1002 Association for Computing Machinery, Singapore, Singapore (2023)
19. Deng, Z., et al.: Fine-grained co-attentive representation learning for semantic code search. In: 2022 IEEE International Conference on Software Analysis, Evolution and Reengineering (SANER), pp. 396–407 (2022)
20. Gu, X., Zhang, H., Kim, S.: Deep code search. In: Proceedings of the 40th International Conference on Software Engineering, pp. 933–944 (2018)
21. Liu, S., et al.: GraphSearchNet: Enhancing GNNs via capturing global dependency for semantic code search. IEEE Trans. Softw. Eng. **49**, 1–16 (2023)
22. Sridhara, G., Hill, E., Muppaneni, D., Pollock, L., Vijay-Shanker, K.: Towards automatically generating summary comments for Java methods. In: Proceedings of the 25th IEEE/ACM International Conference on Automated Software Engineering, pp. 43–52. Association for Computing Machinery, Antwerp, Belgium (2010)
23. Chen, X., Yu, C., Yang, G., et al.: Bash code comment generation method based on dual information retrieval. J. Softw. **34**(03), 1310–1329 (2023)
24. Song, Q.W.: Research on Code Search Technology Based on Features of Code and Comment. Southeast University, Nanjing (2020)
25. Husain, H., Wu, H.-H., Gazit, T., Allamanis, M., Brockschmidt, M.: CodeSearchNet Challenge: Evaluating the State of Semantic Code Search. arXiv:1909.09436 (2019)
26. Xu, R., Xiong, C., Chen, W. & Corso, J.J. Jointly modeling deep video and compositional text to bridge vision and language in a unified framework. In: Proceedings of the Twenty-Ninth AAAI Conference on Artificial Intelligence, pp. 2346–2352 AAAI Press, Austin, Texas (2015)
27. Karpathy, A., Fei-Fei, L.: Deep visual-semantic alignments for generating image descriptions. In: 2015 IEEE Conference on Computer Vision and Pattern Recognition (CVPR), pp. 3128–3137 (2015)
28. Mikolov, T., Sutskever, I., Chen, K., Corrado, G., Dean, J.: Distributed representations of words and phrases and their compositionality. In: Proceedings of the 26th International Conference on Neural Information Processing Systems, vol. 2, pp. 3111–3119. Curran Associates Inc., Lake Tahoe, Nevada (2013)
29. Mikolov, T., Chen, K., Corrado, G., Dean, J.: Efficient estimation of word representations in vector space. arXiv preprint arXiv:1301.3781 (2013)
30. Fang, S., Tan, Y.-S., Zhang, T., Liu, Y.: Self-attention networks for code search. Inf. Softw. Technol. **134**, 106542 (2021)
31. Sak, H., Senior, A., Beaufays, F.: Long short-term memory based recurrent neural network architectures for large vocabulary speech recognition. arXiv:1402.1128 (2014)
32. Vaswani, A., et al.: Attention is all you need. In: Proceedings of the 31st International Conference on Neural Information Processing Systems, pp. 6000–6010. Curran Associates Inc., Long Beach, California, USA (2017)
33. Collobert, R., et al.: Natural language processing (Almost) from Scratch. J. Mach. Learn. Res. **12**, 2493–2537 (2011)
34. Frome, A., et al.: DeViSE: a deep visual-semantic embedding model. In: Proceedings of the 26th International Conference on Neural Information Processing Systems, vol. 2, pp. 2121–2129 Curran Associates Inc., Lake Tahoe, Nevada (2013)

35. Devlin, J., Chang, M.-W., Lee, K., Toutanova, K.: BERT: pre-training of deep bidirectional transformers for language understanding. arXiv:1810.04805 (2018)
36. Linstead, E., et al.: Sourcerer: mining and searching internet-scale software repositories. Data Min. Knowl. Disc. **18**, 300–336 (2009)
37. Liu, M., Yin, H.: Cross attention network for semantic segmentation. In: 2019 IEEE International Conference on Image Processing (ICIP), pp. 2434–2438 (2019)
38. Bai, X.: Text classification based on LSTM and attention. In: 2018 Thirteenth International Conference on Digital Information Management (ICDIM), pp. 29–32 (2018)
39. Yadav, S., Rai, A.: Frequency and temporal convolutional attention for text-independent speaker recognition. In: ICASSP 2020–2020 IEEE International Conference on Acoustics, Speech and Signal Processing (ICASSP), pp. 6794–6798 (2020)
40. Ueda, T., Okada, M., Mori, N., Hashimoto, K.: A method to estimate request sentences using LSTM with self-attention mechanism. In: 2019 8th International Congress on Advanced Applied Informatics (IIAI-AAI), pp. 7–10 (2019)
41. Zhang, H., Goodfellow, I., Metaxas, D., Odena, A.: Self-attention generative adversarial networks. arXiv:1805.08318 (2018)
42. Zhang, P., Zhu, H., Xiong, T., Yang, Y.: Co-attention network and low-rank bilinear pooling for aspect based sentiment analysis. In: ICASSP 2019 - 2019 IEEE International Conference on Acoustics, Speech and Signal Processing (ICASSP), pp. 6725–6729 (2019)
43. Xu, L., et al.: Two-stage attention-based model for code search with textual and structural features. In: 2021 IEEE International Conference on Software Analysis, Evolution and Reengineering (SANER), pp. 342–353 (2021)

# CUTE: A Collaborative Fusion Representation-Based Fine-Tuning and Retrieval Framework for Code Search

Qihong Song[1,2], Jianxun Liu[1,2(✉)], and Haize Hu[1,2]

[1] School of Computer Science and Engineering, Hunan University of Science and Technology, Xiangtan, China
904500672@qq.com
[2] Key Laboratory of Knowledge Processing and Networked Manufacturing, Hunan University of Science and Technology, Xiangtan, Hunan, China

**Abstract.** Code search aims at searching semantically related code snippets from the large-scale database based on a given natural descriptive query. Fine-tuning pre-trained models for code search tasks has recently emerged as a new trend. However, most studies fine-tune models merely using metric learning, overlooking the beneficial effect of the collaborative relationship between code and query. In this paper, we introduce an effective fine-tuning and retrieval framework called CUTE. In the fine-tuning component, we propose a Collaborative Fusion Representation (CFR) consisting of three stages: pre-representation, collaborative representation, and residual fusion. CFR enhances the representation of code and query, considering token-level collaborative features between code and query. Furthermore, we apply augmentation techniques to generate vector-level hard negative samples for training, which further improves the ability of the pre-trained model to distinguish and represent features during fine-tuning. In the retrieval component, we introduce a two-stage retrieval architecture that includes pre-retrieval and refined ranking, significantly reducing time and computational resource consumption. We evaluate CUTE with three advanced pre-trained models on CodeSearchNet consisting of six programming languages. Extensive experiments demonstrate the fine-tuning effectiveness and retrieval efficiency of CUTE.

**Keywords:** Code search · Collaborative fusion representation · Fine tuning · Hard negative sample · Data augmentation

## 1 Introduction

With the development of the open-source community, code search and reuse are becoming essential for improving coding efficiency. Giving a descriptive natural language query, how to accurately retrieve semantically relevant code snippets (positive samples) from others (negative samples) in large repositories has become a crucial challenge [1]. In early studies, code search models mainly

H. Gao et al. (Eds.): CollaborateCom 2023, LNICST 561, pp. 343–362, 2024.
https://doi.org/10.1007/978-3-031-54521-4_19

employed the Information Retrieval (IR) technique [2–4], based on superficial textual similarity, which was limited by the vast gap. The gap refers to code and query from different forms in grammar and expression [5], but we need to find code and query pairs that express the same semantics. With the development of Deep Learning (DL), Metric Learning (ML) [6] used in DL models can align code and query features in a high-dimensional vector space [7–9], reducing linguistic disparities and facilitating similarity calculation, because ML aims at shrinking the vector distance of positive pairs while enlarging the distance of negative pairs. As illustrated in Fig. 1, after the process of ML, the relevant code and query vectors are aggregated together, while the unrelated vectors are pushed apart. Recently, pre-trained models related to programming languages have been proposed, demonstrating excellent performance on code search tasks [10–12]. Pre-trained models are large DL models pre-trained on multiple pre-training tasks, such as masked language modeling, replaced token detection, etc., on large-scale datasets to learn universal features and patterns about programming and natural language. The pre-trained models can then be fine-tuned toward specific code search tasks. However, most existing research has focused on the pre-training phase, simply fine-tuned models through supervised ML in the fine-tuning phase for code search task, especially regarding the representation approach and the composition of training samples [13,14].

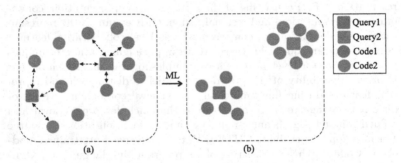

**Fig. 1.** (a) Vector distribution of code and query. (b) Vector distribution after ML.

For the representation approach, current studies [11–13] generally treat the pre-training model as an encoder to obtain the final representation of code and query. These vectors are directly used to calculate similarity for ML, ignoring the potential benefits of the token-level mapping relationships (collaborative features) between code and query. Hard negative samples are those negative samples similar to positive ones in vector space but should be far apart. Those samples can help guide the model to correct its mistakes more quickly and enhance the representational ability [15–17]. However, model training is performed using mini-batch data that consists of multiple code-query pairs in most code search studies [18,19], where each query has only one relevant code snippet as a positive sample. The remaining code samples within the mini-batch are considered as negative samples, and they are randomly sampled. Therefore, the mini-batch typically does not contain or contain only a small number of corresponding hard negative samples. Most of these negative samples are easily distinguished from positive samples in vector space, becoming the model performance bottleneck [20].

In this work, we propose CUTE, a collaborative fusion representation-based fine-tuning and retrieval framework, which aims to provide a new paradigm for high-performance fine-tuning and efficient retrieval for code search. Performance improvement is mainly achieved via two key factors of the fine-tuning component: CFR and hard negative sample augmentation. ①There are token-level associations between code-query pairs. For example, as a code-query pair shown in Fig. 2, the token in the query like "contents" has a solid semantic association with the tokens like "file" and "input" in code. Inspired by the co-attention mechanism [21–23], we propose CFR to enhance the representative ability, which consists of three parts: pre-representation (PR), collaborative representation (CR), and residual fusion (RF). The PR stage first represents the code and query as original vectors. The CR stage captures the token-level collaborative features between the original vectors of code and query. The RF stage builds a residual structure [24] to fuse the collaborative vectors and original vectors, alleviating the information lost and benefiting the integrity and accuracy of the representations. ②Inspired by Generative Adversarial Networks (GAN) [25], we employ vector-level augmentation techniques to generate hard negative samples similar to the labeled positive samples for training, which can significantly increase the matching difficulty of code-query pairs. It is worth mentioning that vector-based augmentation does not require modifying the raw data but only involves augmentation based on the vector, which avoids the consumption of time and computational resources.

```
// Read the contents of the file by line
public static void ReadFile(String filePath)
{
        FileReader inputFile = new FileReader(filePath);
        BufferedReader bufferReader = new BufferedReader(inputFile);
        String line;
        while ((line = bufferReader.readLine()) != null){
                System.out.println(line);
        }
        bufferReader.close();
}
```

Fig. 2. An example of a code-query pair.

To provide high-performance code search services, CUTE requires capturing the token-level collaborative features between a given query and all code snippets in the code repository, which results in longer search time. To improve efficiency, we introduce a two-stage retrieval architecture for the retrieval component of CUTE. In the pre-retrieval stage, we conducted pre-representation to the whole codebase in advance. We thus only need to pre-represent the given query and then select the top-$k$ candidate snippets by computing cosine distance. In the refined ranking stage, we conduct CR and RF to the candidate code vectors and query from the previous stage to get the final vectors with collaborative features. Finally, we rerank the obtained top-$k$ candidate codes based on the final vector and return the re-fined results to the user.

The key contributions of this work can be summarized as follows:

- We propose CUTE, a fine-tuning and retrieval framework for code search, which can be directly applied to fine-tune any pre-trained language model, ensuring both retrieval performance and efficiency.
- For the fine-tuning component, we propose a three-stage representation method CFR, where the collaborative representation stage captures the token-level collaborative features between code and query. Unlike previous studies, we adopt vector-level data augmentation techniques to generate hard negative for better fine-tuning performance.
- For the retrieval component, a two-stage retrieval architecture is proposed, including pre-retrieval and refined ranking, which optimizes the retrieval process and improves the retrieval efficiency.
- We conduct extensive experiments on dataset CodeSearchNet for six programming languages with three advanced pre-training models. The results demonstrate the structural rationality and superior performance of the proposed CUTE.

## 2   Related Work

### 2.1   Deep Learning Models for Code Search

Deep learning models can represent code and query into vector space and compare the similarity of aligned feature vectors. Gu et al. [7] combined DL with code search for the first time and proposed the DeepCS, which embeds code and query respectively by two LSTMs and learns the semantic relationship among them. Based on DeepCS, researchers have built models based on DL technologies such as CNN, GNN, and self-attention mechanisms [9,18,26]. Regarding the processing of model inputs, some researchers have transformed code into different forms of Abstract Syntax Tree (AST) sequences for syntactic representation [27,28]. In addition, some models also use transfer learning, meta-learning, and other techniques to increase the model's generalizability for different databases [29,30].

Pretrained models are large DL models trained on large datasets using unsupervised learning techniques to learn statistical and structural features of the input data, which can be fine-tuned for specific downstream tasks. Recently, transformer-based code pretraining models have made significant progress in tasks such as code search, code clone detection, and code completion, etc. They are pre-trained from different perspectives. CodeBERT, CodeT5, and RoBERTa (code) are pretrained by multiple tasks based on code semantic understanding [11,31]. To enhance the awareness of code structure features, GraphCodeBERT, StructCoder, and UniXcoder [10,12,32] introduce inputs and pretraining tasks related to data flow and AST.

In the fine-tuning for the code search task, ML merely directly obtains the final representation by the pre-trained model, with weaknesses in fine-tuning for the code search task. We thus propose a general fine-tuning and retrieval framework for code search, CUTE, with a better representation approach and sampling strategy.

## 2.2  Collaborative Attention Mechanism

The attention mechanism [21–23] is widely used in Computer Vision (CV) and Natural Language Processing (NLP), allowing deep learning models to focus on critical parts of the data. Since most models' inputs contain multimodal information, researchers have proposed a collaborative attention mechanism to capture the mapping association among them. This mechanism mainly uses attention mechanism to explore the essential parts of the interaction association between multiple inputs. For example, Ma et al. [33] proposed a multi-step co-attention model for multi-label classification, specifically using the collaborative attention mechanism to analyze the connection between the original text and the leading label, which filter out the error accumulation problem caused by the error prediction. Zhang et al. [34] proposed a network based on the collaborative mechanism to capture the aspect information and surrounding contexts to assign the correct polarity to a given sentence. Shuang et al. [35] applied the mechanism to a CNN model to capture the input connection and improve the code representation ability.

Inspired by the mechanism, we incorporate collaborative representation into the CFR component of CUTE to capture the token-level collaborative features between code and query, which serves as a crucial part for achieving high-performance code search.

## 3  Methodology

### 3.1  Overall Architecture

The overall architecture of CUTE is shown in Fig. 3, which contains two components: fine-tuning and retrieval component. In the fine-tuning component, we first use vector-level data augmentation techniques to generate hard negative samples to enlarge the mini-batch. We then propose a three-stage CFR method to represent code and query. Specifically, the PR captures the features of code and query, and the CR captures the token-level collaborative features between code and query, and finally, the RF integrates all features to obtain complete representation vectors. In this component, the encoder (the pre-trained model) is fine-tuned using metric learning based on the representations obtained from CFR.

In the retrieval stage, we propose a two-stage retrieval architecture consisting of pre-retrieval and refined ranking. We compute the cosine similarity between the representations of code snippets in the codebase (conducted PR in advance) and the pre-representation vector of the given query. The top-$k$ most similar code snippets are selected as the pre-retrieval results. In the refined ranking stage, we perform CR and RF on the candidate code list obtained from pre-retrieval and the given query statement to obtain more accurate representation vectors. The $k$ candidate codes are rearranged based on vector distances to obtain the final recommended code list. This approach balances effectiveness and efficiency, enabling high-speed and high-performance code search.

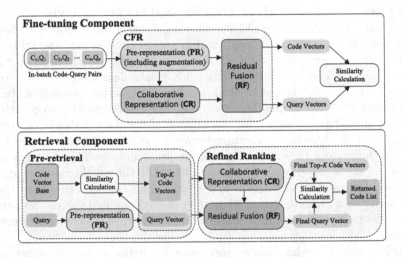

**Fig. 3.** Overall architecture of CUTE.

## 3.2   Fine-Tuning Component

In this section, we present the details of the fine-tuning component, including how to generate hard negative samples to enlarge mini-batch, CFR, and how to fine-tune the model using ML.

**Generate In-Batch Hard Negative Samples.** For a given query, code snippets related to it are called positive samples, and code snippets unrelated to it are called negative samples. Among the negative samples, there exist special samples which are close to the anchor sample but should be far away. Specifically, they are similar to the anchor sample vector but have different semantics.

The samples are defined as hard negative samples. They can help guide a model to correct its mistakes more quickly and effectively during training. However, most existing code search models have not paid enough attention to the samples. Specifically, most existing studies treat other samples in the mini-batch as negative samples during model training. These samples are randomly sampled from the training set (only with a few or no hard negative samples), which resulted in them being easily distinguishable and thus cannot fully optimize the model.

Inspired by GAN, we employ vector-level augmentation techniques to generate hard negative samples for the in-batch samples to enhance the fine-tuning performance. At the vector-level, data augmentation is achieved by perturbing the given code vector, we generate hard negative samples that are similar to the original samples by employing linear interpolation. Linear interpolation mainly uses the features of another sample to augment the given sample, and the method is calculated as Eq. 1.

$$V_i^{'} = \lambda V_i + (1 - \lambda)V_j \tag{1}$$

where $V_i$ is the given sample vector, $V_j$ is randomly sampled from other samples. $\lambda$ is the interpolation coefficient sampled from a uniform distribution $U(\alpha, \beta)$, and $\alpha$, $\beta$ are mutable parameters near 1.0.

**Collaborative Fusion Representation (CFR).** Our proposed CFR consists of three stages: pre-representation (PR), collaborative representation (CR), and residual fusion (RF). The details are shown in Fig. 4.

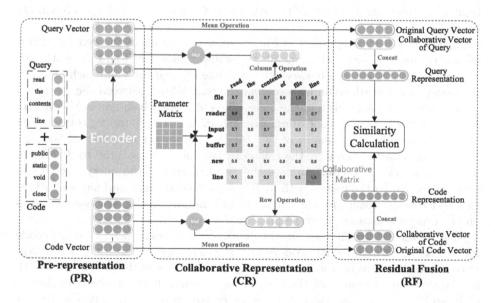

**Fig. 4.** The architecture of three-stages CFR.

*Pre-representation (PR).* PR is used to embed semantic features of code and query respectively into a fixed-length dense vector. In detail, given a code and a query of length $m$ and $n$, we tokenize them into two sequences $S_C = \{C_1, C_2, ..., C_m\}$ and $S_Q = \{Q_1, Q_2, ..., Q_n\}$, then feed them into a encoder to capture the semantic features respectively. Since the encoder embeds each token as the same representation dimension $d$, we obtain the final representations $O_C \in \mathbb{R}^{d \times m}$ and $O_Q \in \mathbb{R}^{d \times n}$ by passing the tokenized sequences $S_C$ and $S_Q$ through the encoder, respectively, which are calculated as Eq. 2 and Eq. 3.

$$O_C = PR(S_C) \tag{2}$$

$$O_Q = PR(S_Q) \tag{3}$$

*Collaborative Representation (CR).* After PR, we obtain the collaborative vectors by conducting row & column operations on the matrix $I$. The matrix is computed by multiplying the two original vectors $O_C$ and $O_Q$ of code and query as Eq. 4.

$$I = tanh(O_C^T U O_Q) \tag{4}$$

where the parameter matrix $U \in \mathbb{R}^{d \times d}$ is introduced to construct collaborative matrix, which continuously be optimized during the training. We use the hyperbolic tangent function to normalize the collaborative value between code and query. The normalization is to facilitate the subsequent calculation.

The collaborative matrix represents the strength of the association between each token of code and query. Since the matrix $I$ is obtained by multiplying the feature vectors of code and query from the PR stage, so each element $I_{ij}$ of $I$ represents the matching level of the $i$th token $C_i$ in code and the $j$th token $Q_j$ in query.

Specifically, the middle part of Fig. 4 shows the details of the generated collaborative matrix $I$ from the code-query example shown in Fig. 1. The $i$th row represents the match level between the $i$th token in the code and each token in the query, and the $j$th column represents the match level between the $j$th token in the query and each token in the code. The color of each square in the matrix represents the mapping association strength of the corresponding tokens. The higher the association strength of two tokens, the darker the color of the corresponding square. Therefore, the collaborative matrix is essential to determine whether the code's function satisfies the requirements of the query. We should primarily consider the tokens with high association strength and pay less attention to irrelevant tokens for the similarity calculation. In this way, we can focus on the crucial semantics for code-query matching.

To obtain the weight that should be assigned to each token in query/code for matching with the whole code/query segment, we perform a series of row & column operations on the collaborative matrix. Since each element in the $i$th row of the matrix represents the association strength between the $i$th token in code and each token in query, the vector consisted of the matrix $I$'s $i$th row thus shows the strength of the association between the $i$th token in code and the corresponding whole query segment. We conduct the max-pooling operation on the rows of the matrix as Eq. 5. Specially, we take the maximum value of the $i$th row vector as the strength of the $i$th token in code matched with the whole given query. Similarly, for the column vectors of the matrix, we do the same operation as Eq. 6 to get the strength of the $j$th token in query.

$$d_i^C = maxpooling(I_{i,1}, I_{i,2}, \dots, I_{i,n}) \tag{5}$$

$$d_j^Q = maxpooling(I_{1,j}, I_{2,j}, \dots, I_{m,j}) \tag{6}$$

where $d_i^C$ denotes the association strength value of the $i$th token in the code, and $d_j^Q$ denotes the strength value of the $j$th token in the query. Therefore, the strength values of the code and query's tokens can be expressed as follows:

$$d^C = [d_1^C, d_2^C, \dots, d_m^C] \tag{7}$$

$$d^Q = [d_1^Q, d_2^Q, \dots, d_n^Q] \tag{8}$$

To unify the scale, we use the *softmax* function to normalize $d_i^C$ and $d_i^Q$ to $w_i^C$ and $w_i^Q$ as Eq. 9 and Eq. 10. They denote the matching weight of each token in the code and query.

$$w_i^C = \frac{exp(d_i^C)}{\sum_{k=1}^{m} exp(d_k^C)} \tag{9}$$

$$w_i^Q = \frac{exp(d_i^Q)}{\sum_{k=1}^{n} exp(d_k^Q)} \tag{10}$$

The final token-level weight vectors $W^C \in \mathbb{R}^m$ and $W^Q \in \mathbb{R}^n$ for code and query are shown in Eq. 11 and Eq. 12.

$$W^C = [w_1^C, w_2^C, \dots, w_m^C] \tag{11}$$

$$W^Q = [w_1^Q, w_2^Q, \dots, w_n^Q] \tag{12}$$

Based on the weight vectors of the code and query obtained from the collaborative matrix, we combine the original vectors $O_C$ and $O_Q$ obtained from the PR stage with corresponding weights $W^C$ and $W^Q$ by dot product operations as Eq. 13 and Eq. 14. Finally, we obtain the collaborative vectors $V_C$ and $V_Q$ of the code and query, which highlight the token-level crucial collaborative features.

$$V_C = O_C W^C \tag{13}$$

$$V_Q = O_Q W^Q \tag{14}$$

*Residual Fusion (RF).* The original vectors are semantic features of code and query from the PR stage. Collaborative vectors are obtained by adding token-level collaborative features to the original vectors of code and query. The obtained collaborative vectors will lose some original features in the CFR operation flow. In order to alleviate the information lost during the CFR processes, we treat the collaborative vectors generated in the previous stage as semantic residuals. Then, we fuse original vectors $O_C$ and $O_Q$, which contain relatively complete semantic information, with the semantic residuals $V_C$ and $V_Q$ to generate the final representation vectors $C$ and $Q$ of code and query as Eq. 15 and Eq. 16. In this way, it not only alleviates the representation loss but also makes the model easier to train by the residual structure. The final generated representations and not only highlight the crucial semantic information by the CFR, but also maximize the integrity of the semantic features.

$$C = V_C \oplus O_C \tag{15}$$

$$Q = V_Q \oplus O_Q \tag{16}$$

**Whole Fine-Tuning Process.** The fine-tuning process of our proposed CUTE is shown in the fine-tuning component of Fig. 3. Randomly sampled code-query pairs form a mini-batch, they can be represented by CFR, and we can compute the similarity of the obtained vectors to get the matching code snippets. The optimization of the entire fine-tuning process follows ML, aiming to minimize the distance between relevant code and query vectors while maximizing the distance between irrelevant code and query vectors.

In the CFR, we first perform PR on the samples within the mini-batch, generating the original code and query vectors. Next, we apply vector-level augmentation techniques to perturb the original vectors, generating $M$ hard negative samples for each original sample. By augmenting the mini-batch with hard negative samples, we can enhance the efficiency and effectiveness of fine-tuning. Subsequently, we perform CR on the pre-represented and augmented sample vectors. This process incorporates token-level collaborative features between code and query, facilitating the matching between relevant code and query pairs. Finally, we construct a residual structure to fuse the original and collaborative vectors, generating the final representation vectors of code and query.

In a mini-batch with the size of $B$, there exists a unique code positive sample vector $C_r$ that is semantically related to a given query vector $Q_r$. Since each sample is augmented to generate $M$ corresponding hard negative samples, the mini-batch size becomes $(M+1)B$, with the remaining $MB+B-1$ code snippets vectors $C_s$ being negative samples semantically unrelated to $Q_r$. Given a query, ML aims to minimize the distance between the query and its positive sample while maximizing the distance between the query and its negative samples. The ML loss value of the query $Q_r$ in a mini-batch can be calculated as equation Eq. 17, where the dot product is used to calculate similarity. The total loss value is the average of each query loss value.

$$L_r = -log \frac{exp(Q_r \cdot C_r)}{exp(Q_r \cdot C_r) + \sum_{s=1, s \neq r}^{B(M+1)} exp(Q_r \cdot C_s)} \tag{17}$$

## 3.3   Retrieval Component

The two-stage retrieval architecture of our proposed CUTE is shown in the retrieval component of Fig. 3, which includes pre-retrieval and refined ranking.

In the refined ranking stage, we obtained the top-$k$ most relevant code snippets from the previous stage. Then we perform CR and RF on these pre-representation vectors, which yields representation vectors that consider the collaborative features of given query and candidate code snippets. Next, we rearrange the code snippets and return the final results. Specifically, we have the $K$ candidate original code vectors and the original given query vector from the pre-retrieval stage. We capture the token-level collaborative features between the candidate code snippets and the query by employing CR. We then fuse these features with the original features obtained from previous stage using RF, resulting in the final vectors for candidate code and query. Finally, we rearrange the code snippets from the pre-retrieval stage and provide the user with the final retrieval results.

# 4   Experimental Evaluation

In order to investigate the structural rationality and the performance of CUTE on code search, several experiments are conducted to answer the following research questions:

- **RQ1:** How effective is the fine-tuning effectiveness of CUTE in code search task, compared with traditional fine-tuning method?
- **RQ2:** How do the different components of CUTE affect the retrieval efficiency and effectiveness?
- **RQ3:** How to better implement CFR in practice to capture collaborative features between code and query?
- **RQ4:** How to choose the optimal parameters for augmentation to ensure high performance of CUTE?

## 4.1   Experimental Setup

**Dataset.** In this work, we use large-scale dataset CodeSearchNet [31] to evaluate the effectiveness of the proposed CUTE. The dataset contains six different programming language. We removed low-quality data from the dataset following the method of Guo et al. [12], and we extracted some code snippets from the entire dataset used to construct a search codebase for validation and testing. The details of the preprocessed dataset are shown in Table 1.

**Table 1.** Details about the preprocessed CodeSearchNet corpus.

| Language | Training | Validation | Test | Search Codebase |
|---|---|---|---|---|
| Python | 251,820 | 13,914 | 14,918 | 43,827 |
| PHP | 241,241 | 12,982 | 14,014 | 52,660 |
| Go | 167,288 | 7,325 | 8,122 | 28,120 |
| cre Java | 164,923 | 5,183 | 10,955 | 40,347 |
| JS | 58,025 | 3,885 | 3,291 | 13,981 |
| Ruby | 24,927 | 1,400 | 1,261 | 4,360 |

**Evaluation Metrics.** To evaluate the effectiveness of CUTE, we utilize the most widely used mean reciprocal rank (MRR) for code search [7]. It measures the ranking of the target code in the returned code list, and only cares about the ranking of the most relevant code. The higher the MRR value, the higher the first hit code is ranked. It can be calculated as follows:

$$MRR = \frac{1}{|N|} \sum_{j=1}^{|N|} \frac{1}{Rank_j} \qquad (18)$$

where $N$ represents the number of query in the validation/test set, $Rank_j$ denotes the ranking position of the most relevant code in the returned list for the $j$th query.

**Pre-trained Models.** This work fine-tunes the three advanced pre-trained models related to programming language. The details are presented as follows.

*RoBERTa (Code)* [31] is a transformer architecture-based pre-trained model, an improved version of Bert [36]. It is pre-trained on the CodeSearchNet corpus with masked language modeling (MLM) task.

*CodeBERT* [11] is a bimodal pre-trained model for programming language and natural language. It is pre-trained with two tasks: MLM and replaced token detection.

*GraphCodeBERT* [12] is a pre-trained model that incorporates code structure information, and it is pre-trained with three tasks: MLM, code structure edges prediction, and alignment representations of source code and code structure.

**Implementation Details.** All experiments were conducted in a Linux environment using Nvidia GTX 3090 24GB. We employed a traditional fine-tuning approach as our baseline method. This method directly computes the ML loss by leveraging the code and query vectors encoded by the pre-trained model. During training, we input the model with all training data as code-query pairs. We set the augmentation count $M$ to 5 for each code in a mini-batch, the interpolation coefficient $\lambda$ is 0.85, the number of training epochs to 10, the batch size to 32, and the learning rate values for RoBERTa(Code), CodeBERT, and GraphCode-BERT are 1e–5, 1e–5, and 2e–5. During validation/test, we randomly sample 1000 query statements from the validation/test set, search the codebase in the dataset for relevant code snippets, and return the top 100 code snippets for pre-retrieval stage. After refined ranking stage, we return the top 20 code snippets to evaluate the value of MRR.

## 4.2   RQ1: The effectiveness of CUTE

In this section, we evaluate the performance of pre-trained models fine-tuned with both traditional methods and the proposed CUTE in code search tasks. The traditional approach typically represents queries and candidate code snippets as vectors using pre-trained models, then adjusting the distances between vectors through ML for fine-tuning. In contrast, our proposed CUTE considers the collaborative features between code and query. It captures and represents more complete semantic features using a three-stage CFR. Finally, the pre-trained model is also fine-tuned by ML. We select three advanced pre-trained models for programming languages, RoBERTa(Code), CodeBERT, and GraphCodeBERT. We compare the performance of the traditional fine-tuning method with the proposed CUTE on code search tasks across six programming languages, using MRR as the evaluation metric. The results are presented in Table 2.

**Table 2.** Effectiveness of CUTE compared with the traditional fine-tuning method.

| Model | | Ruby | Python | Java | PHP | Go | JS | Average |
|---|---|---|---|---|---|---|---|---|
| RoBERTa(Code) | traditional | 0.625 | 0.620 | 0.654 | 0.588 | 0.865 | 0.575 | 0.655 |
| | CUTE | **0.645** | **0.656** | **0.682** | **0.615** | **0.879** | 0.591 | **0.678↑3.5%** |
| CodeBERT | traditional | 0.633 | 0.642 | 0.674 | 0.619 | 0.878 | 0.595 | 0.674 |
| | CUTE | **0.683** | **0.671** | **0.695** | **0.635** | **0.885** | **0.634** | **0.701↑4.0%** |
| GraphCodeBERT | traditional | 0.709 | 0.690 | 0.689 | 0.648 | 0.896 | 0.637 | 0.712 |
| | CUTE | **0.736** | **0.715** | **0.705** | **0.685** | **0.905** | **0.654** | **0.733↑2.9%** |

The results indicate that, compared to traditional fine-tuning method, the proposed CUTE fine-tuning approach leads to performance improvements of 3.5%, 4.0%, and 2.9% for the three pre-trained models, RoBERTa(Code), Code-BERT, and Graph-CodeBERT, respectively. The results demonstrate the superiority of CUTE in fine-tuning models and further highlight the positive impact of collaborative features between query and code matching.

## 4.3   RQ2: Ablation experiments

We construct ablation experiments to verify the structural rationality of CUTE's fine-tuning and retrieval components.

**Ablation Experiment for CUTE's Fine-Tuning Component.** For the fine-tuning component, we remove the residual fusion (RF), collaborative representation (CR), and the generated negative samples (Hard), respectively, to get the code search performance of three pre-trained models after fine-tuning. The results are shown in Table 3. It is worth noting that if the CR is removed, the RF will also be eliminated. Therefore, in practice, removing the CR means removing both the CR and the RF (CR+RF).

**Table 3.** The ablation experiment results of CUTE's fine-tuning component.

| Model | | Ruby | Python | Java | PHP | Go | JS | Average |
|---|---|---|---|---|---|---|---|---|
| RoBERTa(Code) | CUTE | **0.645** | **0.656** | **0.682** | **0.615** | **0.879** | **0.591** | **0.678** |
| | -Hard | 0.637 | 0.649 | 0.675 | 0.609 | 0.875 | 0.588 | 0.672↓0.9% |
| | -RF | 0.631 | 0.636 | 0.669 | 0.601 | 0.873 | 0.584 | 0.666↓1.8% |
| | -CR-RF | 0.628 | 0.635 | 0.660 | 0.598 | 0.869 | 0.585 | 0.663↓2.2% |
| CodeBERT | CUTE | **0.683** | **0.671** | **0.695** | **0.635** | **0.885** | **0.634** | **0.701** |
| | -Hard | 0.675 | 0.664 | 0.691 | 0.629 | 0.881 | 0.625 | 0.694↓1.0% |
| | -RF | 0.667 | 0.661 | 0.685 | 0.627 | 0.881 | 0.623 | 0.691↓1.4% |
| | -CR-RF | 0.652 | 0.654 | 0.681 | 0.625 | 0.880 | 0.615 | 0.685↓2.3% |
| GraphCodeBERT | CUTE | **0.736** | **0.715** | **0.705** | **0.685** | **0.905** | **0.654** | **0.733** |
| | -Hard | 0.725 | 0.711 | 0.699 | 0.675 | 0.904 | 0.651 | 0.728↓0.7% |
| | -RF | 0.722 | 0.702 | 0.698 | 0.669 | 0.900 | 0.645 | 0.723↓1.4% |
| | -CR-RF | 0.719 | 0.698 | 0.690 | 0.659 | 0.899 | 0.642 | 0.718↓2.0% |

Table 3 shows that removing the RF, CR (RF+CR), and Hard, respectively, all decrease the MRR of the three pre-trained models. The results indicate that each part of CUTE's fine-tuning component plays a crucial role, confirming that the fine-tuning architecture is reasonable.

After removing the generated hard negative samples, the performance of fine-tuned model RoBERTa(Code), CodeBERT, and GraphCodeBERT decreased by 0.9%, 1.0%, and 0.7%, respectively. The results indicate that the generated hard negative samples benefit model optimization during training. After removing the RF, the code search performance of the fine-tuned models decreased by 1.8%, 1.4%, and 1.4%, respectively. The changes indicate that RF compensates for the loss of semantic features of the original code and query vectors during the network propagation process, generating code and query representations with relatively complete semantic features. After removing RF+CR, the fine-tuned models' performance decreased by 2.2%, 2.3%, and 2.0%, respectively. Furthermore, the performance decrease was even greater compared to when only RF was removed under the same conditions. The results show that the token-level collaborative feature captured by CR is beneficial for matching code and query.

**Ablation Experiment for CUTE's Retrieval Component.** We pre-represent the code snippets in the codebase in advance, avoiding the time-consuming of the PR stage during user retrieval. However, performing CR and RF operations on all code snippets and the given query would significantly increase the search time because the CR and RF operations in CFR require operating on the given query original vector and all candidate code original vectors. To balance search effectiveness and efficiency, the retrieval component of our proposed CUTE framework adopts a two-stage retrieval architecture consisting of pre-retrieval and refined ranking.

We compare the retrieval performance and time by removing the pre-retrieval (PRR) and refined ranking (PR) stages separately. Where the retrieval time is the total elapsed time in milliseconds for recommending relevant code for 1000 query statements. Since the retrieval time is only affected by the retrieval operations and not the language type of the retrieved code base, we thus only use the Java sub-dataset of CodeSearchNet for our experiments, and the results are shown in Table 4.

**Table 4.** The ablation results of CUTE's retrieval component.

| Model | RoBERTa(Code) | | | CodeBERT | | | GraphCodeBERT | | |
|---|---|---|---|---|---|---|---|---|---|
| | CUTE | RR | PRR | CUTE | RR | PRR | CUTE | RR | PRR |
| Time (ms) | **7249** | 5178 | 8802 | **6802** | 5233 | 9053 | **7275** | 5389 | 9055 |
| | | ↓28.6% | ↑21.4% | | ↓23.1% | ↑33.1% | | ↓25.9% | ↑24.5% |
| MRR | **0.682** | 0.660 | 0.686 | **0.695** | 0.681 | 0.699 | **0.705** | 0.690 | 0.707 |
| | | ↓3.2% | ↑0.6% | | ↓2.0% | ↑0.6% | | ↓2.1% | ↑0.3% |

The results demonstrate that our proposed two-stage retrieval architecture significantly reduces retrieval time while maintaining relative high performance in code search. Specifically, when we eliminate the RR and conduct retrieval using original vectors of code and query after PR, the retrieval time for the three models decreases by an average of 25.9%. However, due to the lack of collaborative features between the code and the query, the performance drops by an average of 2.4%. It is not cost-effective to trade such a high-performance loss for retrieval efficiency. When we eliminate PRR (calculating the collaborative features between the given code and all candidate code snippets), the average retrieval performance of the three models improves by 0.5%, and the average retrieval time increases by 26.3%. Trading retrieval time for a slight performance improvement is also inappropriate. Through the above analysis, we can conclude the superiority of the two-stage retrieval architecture of the proposed CUTE.

### 4.4   RQ3: The implementation of CFR

In CFR, the CR stage involves a series of row & column operations on the collaborative matrix to obtain collaborative vectors. The RF stage combines the original vectors after PR stage with the collaborative vectors. In this section, we aim to experimentally determine the most appropriate implementation approach for them.

**The Implementation of Collaborative Representation (CR).** From the above mentioned, CR stage conducts a series of row & column operations on the collaborative matrix to generate the weight scores representing the association strength between code and query, where the matching strength of each token in code/query with the whole query/code is obtained by pooling operations. In this section, we compare the effects of the max-pooling operation (Max) and the average-pooling operation (Avg) of CUTE on the code search performance.

**Table 5.** Performance of different pooling operations.

| Laguage | RoBERTa(Code) | | CodeBERT | | GraphCodeBERT | |
|---|---|---|---|---|---|---|
| | Avg | Max | Avg | Max | Avg | Max |
| Ruby | 0.639 | **0.645** | 0.677 | **0.683** | **0.737** | 0.736 |
| Python | 0.654 | **0.656** | 0.668 | **0.671** | 0.708 | **0.715** |
| Java | **0.683** | 0.682 | 0.685 | **0.695** | 0.702 | **0.705** |
| PHP | 0.614 | **0.615** | **0.635** | **0.635** | 0.683 | **0.685** |
| Go | 0.866 | **0.879** | 0.880 | **0.885** | 0.901 | **0.905** |
| JS | **0.593** | 0.591 | 0.629 | **0.634** | 0.649 | **0.654** |
| Average | 0.675 | **0.678** | 0.696 | **0.701** | 0.730 | **0.733** |

In Table 5, we can find that the max-pooling outperforms the average-pooling operation. Before the pooling operation, a particular code/query token has matching scores with each token in the query/code, we need to get the matching score of this token and the whole query/code through a pooling operation. The difference between choosing max-pooling and average-pooling is to choose the highest or the average of matching scores as the weight to measure the association strength. The results in Table 5 show that the highest score is more suitable to be the weight. We conjecture that max-pooling works best because the highest score indicates the highest level of association, which is the most appropriate indicator for semantic association strength.

**The Implementation of Residual Fusion (RF).** In CFR, the RF stage involves the fusion operation between the original and collaborative vectors. The fusion operation can be performed using concatenation (Con), add (Add), or average (Avg). Table 6 presents the impact of these three operations on code search performance.

The results in Table 6 demonstrate that the concatenation operation yields the best average performance across six programming languages and three pre-trained models. The add and average operations exhibit similar performance,

**Table 6.** Performance of different fusion operations.

| Language | RoBERTa(Code) | | | CodeBERT | | | GraphCodeBERT | | |
|---|---|---|---|---|---|---|---|---|---|
| | Avg | Add | Con | Avg | Add | Con | Avg | Add | Con |
| Ruby | 0.642 | 0.641 | **0.645** | 0.680 | **0.684** | 0.683 | 0.731 | 0.734 | **0.736** |
| Python | 0.650 | 0.651 | **0.656** | 0.670 | 0.669 | **0.671** | 0.714 | 0.713 | **0.715** |
| Java | **0.682** | 0.681 | **0.682** | 0.693 | 0.693 | **0.695** | **0.708** | 0.707 | 0.705 |
| PHP | **0.616** | 0.615 | 0.615 | 0.632 | 0.631 | **0.635** | 0.677 | 0.680 | **0.685** |
| Go | 0.877 | **0.881** | 0.879 | 0.882 | 0.884 | **0.885** | 0.903 | 0.904 | **0.905** |
| JS | 0.588 | 0.590 | **0.591** | 0.628 | 0.631 | **0.634** | 0.651 | 0.650 | **0.654** |
| Average | 0.676 | 0.677 | **0.678** | 0.698 | 0.699 | **0.701** | 0.731 | 0.731 | **0.733** |

lower than the concatenation operation. Based on the results, we adopt the concatenation operation as the specific implementation for CFR.

## 4.5   RQ4: Determining the Optimal Parameters for Augmentation

The augmentation operation has two parameters: interpolation coefficient $\lambda$ and augmentaion count $M$. In this section, we aim to experimentally determine the optimal parameters of CUTE. We conduct experiments using the Java dataset of CodeSearchNet.

**Determine the Interpolation Coefficient.** Since the larger the value of $\lambda$, the more similar the hard negative samples generated by linear interpolation will be to the original samples, we take a value of $\lambda$ as 0.7, 0.75, 0.8, 0.85, 0.9, 0.95 to determine the optimal parameter values. The experimental results are shown in Table 7.

**Table 7.** The performance of CUTE with different interpolation coefficient.

| $\lambda$ | RoBERTa(Code) | CodeBERT | GraphCodeBERT |
|---|---|---|---|
| 0.75 | 0.676 | 0.693 | 0.699 |
| 0.8 | 0.680 | **0.695** | 0.701 |
| 0.85 | **0.682** | **0.695** | 0.705 |
| 0.9 | 0.681 | 0.692 | **0.706** |
| 0.95 | 0.673 | 0.691 | 0.697 |

The results indicate that when $\lambda$ is set to 0.85, the generated hard negative samples are most beneficial for fine-tuning the pre-trained models. Specifically, when $\lambda$ is less than 0.85, the generated hard negative samples have limited similarity to the original samples, resulting in a suboptimal utilization of hard negative samples for model optimization. On the other hand, when $\lambda$ is greater than 0.85, the fine-tuning performance gradually declines. We speculate that this is due to the excessively high similarity between the generated hard negative samples and the original samples, making it challenging for the model to distinguish features and reducing its feature extraction capability.

**Determine the Augmentaion Count.** To enhance the fine-tuning effect of CUTE, we augmented each code in the mini-batch $M$ times using vector-level data augmentation techniques. These generated hard negative samples were then included in the mini-batch for training. We experimented with different values of $M$ to determine the optimal value, the results are presented in Table 8.

**Table 8.** The performance of CUTE with different augmentaion count.

| $M$ | RoBERTa(Code) | CodeBERT | GraphCodeBERT |
|---|---|---|---|
| 3 | 0.677 | 0.692 | 0.700 |
| 5 | 0.682 | 0.695 | 0.705 |
| 10 | **0.683** | 0.695 | **0.706** |
| 15 | **0.683** | **0.696** | **0.706** |

The results demonstrate that the higher the augmentation count $M$, the better the fine-tuning performance. By analyzing the results in Table 8, we observe that the fine-tuning performance improvement becomes increasingly slow and even stagnates when $M$ exceeds 5. Additionally, more hard negative samples would increase the resource consumption during training. Therefore, we determine $M$ as 5 to generate hard negative samples to balance effectiveness and efficiency.

## 5   Conclusions

In this paper, we propose CUTE, a collaborative fusion representation-based fine-tuning and retrieval framework for code search tasks. Specifically, we introduce a three-stage collaborative fusion representation method in the fine-tuning component, which captures the token-level collaborative features between code and query, significantly improving representation accuracy. Moreover, we also utilize vector-level augmentation techniques to generate hard negative samples, further enhancing the fine-tuning effect. In the retrieval component, we propose a two-stage retrieval architecture, including pre-retrieval and refined ranking, ensuring retrieval quality while greatly reducing retrieval time. We conducted extensive experiments on CodeSearchNet comprising six programming languages with three pre-trained models, determining the specific implementation and optimal parameters for CUTE. Experiment validation results demonstrate the proposed CUTE's superior fine-tuning and retrieval capabilities. For future work, we plan to delve deeper into the collaborative features between code and query, aiming to achieve higher performance code search.

# References

1. Liu, C., Xia, X., Lo, D., Gao, C., Yang, X., Grundy, J.: Opportunities and challenges in code search tools. ACM Comput. Surv. (CSUR) **54**(9), 1–40 (2021)
2. Linstead, E., Rigor, P., Bajracharya, S., Lopes, C., Baldi, P.: Mining internet-scale software repositories. In: Advances in Neural Information Processing Systems, vol. 20 (2007)
3. Lu, M., Sun, X., Wang, S., Lo, D., Duan, Y.: Query expansion via wordnet for effective code search. In: 2015 IEEE 22nd International Conference on Software Analysis, Evolution, and Reengineering (SANER), pp. 545–549. IEEE (2015)
4. Lv, F., Zhang, H., Lou, J.G., Wang, S., Zhang, D., Zhao, J.: Codehow: effective code search based on api understanding and extended boolean model (e). In: 2015 30th IEEE/ACM International Conference on Automated Software Engineering (ASE), pp. 260–270. IEEE (2015)
5. Biggerstaff, T.J., Mitbander, B.G., Webster, D.E.: Program understanding and the concept assignment problem. Commun. ACM **37**(5), 72–82 (1994)
6. Bellet, A., Habrard, A., Sebban, M.: A survey on metric learning for feature vectors and structured data. arXiv preprint arXiv:1306.6709 (2013)
7. Gu, X., Zhang, H., Kim, S.: Deep code search. In: Proceedings of the 40th International Conference on Software Engineering, pp. 933–944 (2018)
8. Cambronero, J., Li, H., Kim, S., Sen, K., Chandra, S.: When deep learning met code search. In: Proceedings of the 2019 27th ACM Joint Meeting on European Software Engineering Conference and Symposium on the Foundations of Software Engineering, pp. 964–974 (2019)
9. Fang, S., Tan, Y.S., Zhang, T., Liu, Y.: Self-attention networks for code search. Inf. Softw. Technol. **134**, 106542 (2021)
10. Guo, D., Lu, S., Duan, N., Wang, Y., Zhou, M., Yin, J.: Unixcoder: unified cross-modal pre-training for code representation. arXiv preprint arXiv:2203.03850 (2022)
11. Feng, Z., et al.: Codebert: a pre-trained model for programming and natural languages. arXiv preprint arXiv:2002.08155 (2020)
12. Guo, D., et al.: Graphcodebert: pre-training code representations with data flow. arXiv preprint arXiv:2009.08366 (2020)
13. Liu, S., Wu, B., Xie, X., Meng, G., Liu, Y.: Contrabert: enhancing code pre-trained models via contrastive learning. arXiv preprint arXiv:2301.09072 (2023)
14. Niu, C., Li, C., Luo, B., Ng, V.: Deep learning meets software engineering: a survey on pre-trained models of source code. arXiv preprint arXiv:2205.11739 (2022)
15. Ge, W.: Deep metric learning with hierarchical triplet loss. In: Proceedings of the European Conference on Computer Vision (ECCV), pp. 269–285 (2018)
16. Robinson, J., Chuang, C.Y., Sra, S., Jegelka, S.: Contrastive learning with hard negative samples. arXiv preprint arXiv:2010.04592 (2020)
17. Harwood, B., Kumar BG, V., Carneiro, G., Reid, I., Drummond, T.: Smart mining for deep metric learning. In: Proceedings of the IEEE International Conference on Computer Vision, pp. 2821–2829 (2017)

18. Ling, X., et al.: Deep graph matching and searching for semantic code retrieval. ACM Trans. Knowl. Disc. Data (TKDD) **15**(5), 1–21 (2021)
19. Wang, X., et al.: Syncobert: syntax-guided multi-modal contrastive pre-training for code representation. arXiv preprint arXiv:2108.04556 (2021)
20. Suh, Y., Han, B., Kim, W., Lee, K.M.: Stochastic class-based hard example mining for deep metric learning. In: Proceedings of the IEEE/CVF Conference on Computer Vision and Pattern Recognition, pp. 7251–7259 (2019)
21. Yu, Z., Yu, J., Xiang, C., Fan, J., Tao, D.: Beyond bilinear: Generalized multimodal factorized high-order pooling for visual question answering. IEEE Trans. Neural Netw. Learn. Syst. **29**(12), 5947–5959 (2018)
22. Li, L., Dong, R., Chen, L.: Context-aware co-attention neural network for service recommendations. In: 2019 IEEE 35th International Conference on Data Engineering Workshops (ICDEW), pp. 201–208. IEEE (2019)
23. Li, B., Sun, Z., Li, Q., Wu, Y., Hu, A.: Group-wise deep object co-segmentation with co-attention recurrent neural network. In: Proceedings of the IEEE/CVF International Conference on Computer Vision, pp. 8519–8528 (2019)
24. He, K., Zhang, X., Ren, S., Sun, J.: Deep residual learning for image recognition. In: Proceedings of the IEEE Conference on Computer Vision and Pattern Recognition, pp. 770–778 (2016)
25. Goodfellow, I., et al.: Generative adversarial networks. Commun. ACM **63**(11), 139–144 (2020)
26. Wang, H., Zhang, J., Xia, Y., Bian, J., Zhang, C., Liu, T.Y.: Cosea: convolutional code search with layer-wise attention. arXiv preprint arXiv:2010.09520 (2020)
27. Gu, J., Chen, Z., Monperrus, M.: Multimodal representation for neural code search. In: 2021 IEEE International Conference on Software Maintenance and Evolution (ICSME), pp. 483–494. IEEE (2021)
28. Zhang, J., Wang, X., Zhang, H., Sun, H., Wang, K., Liu, X.: A novel neural source code representation based on abstract syntax tree. In: 2019 IEEE/ACM 41st International Conference on Software Engineering (ICSE), pp. 783–794. IEEE (2019)
29. Ling, C., Lin, Z., Zou, Y., Xie, B.: Adaptive deep code search. In: Proceedings of the 28th International Conference on Program Comprehension, pp. 48–59 (2020)
30. Chai, Y., Zhang, H., Shen, B., Gu, X.: Cross-domain deep code search with meta learning. In: Proceedings of the 44th International Conference on Software Engineering, pp. 487–498 (2022)
31. Husain, H., Wu, H.H., Gazit, T., Allamanis, M., Brockschmidt, M.: Codesearchnet challenge: evaluating the state of semantic code search. arXiv preprint arXiv:1909.09436 (2019)
32. Tipirneni, S., Zhu, M., Reddy, C.K.: Structcoder: structure-aware transformer for code generation. arXiv preprint arXiv:2206.05239 (2022)
33. Ma, H., Li, Y., Ji, X., Han, J., Li, Z.: Mscoa: multi-step co-attention model for multi-label classification. IEEE Access **7**, 109635–109645 (2019)
34. Zhang, P., Zhu, H., Xiong, T., Yang, Y.: Co-attention network and low-rank bilinear pooling for aspect based sentiment analysis. In: ICASSP 2019–2019 IEEE International Conference on Acoustics, Speech and Signal Processing (ICASSP), pp. 6725–6729. IEEE (2019)
35. Shuai, J., Xu, L., Liu, C., Yan, M., Xia, X., Lei, Y.: Improving code search with co-attentive representation learning. In: Proceedings of the 28th International Conference on Program Comprehension, pp. 196–207 (2020)
36. Devlin, J., Chang, M.W., Lee, K., Toutanova, K.: Bert: Pre-training of deep bidirectional transformers for language understanding. arXiv preprint arXiv:1810.04805 (2018)

# Edge Computing Scheduling and Offloading

# Roadside IRS Assisted Task Offloading in Vehicular Edge Computing Network

Yibin Xie[1,2], Lei Shi[1,2](✉) ⓘD, Zhehao Li[1,2] ⓘD, Xu Ding[1,2], and Feng Liu[1,2]

[1] School of Computer Science and Information Engineering, Hefei University of Technology, Hefei 230009, China
shilei@hfut.edu.cn
[2] Engineering Research Center of Safety Critical Industrial Measurement and Control Technology, Ministry of Education, Hefei 230009, China

**Abstract.** Vehicular edge computing (VEC) has been recognized as a promising technique to process delay-sensitive vehicular applications. Nevertheless, in order to accommodate the rapid growth in the number of connected vehicles, it's inevitable that there will be an increasing deployment of conventional infrastructure with limited communication ranges. This could potentially lead to escalating costs and impede the full realization of the VEC system. In this paper, a roadside intelligent reflecting surface (IRS) assisted VEC network is introduced, where the IRS is deployed outside the coverage of roadside units (RSUs) to extend the service range. Furthermore, the maximum total number of successful offloading tasks problem within the scheduling time problem is formulated, encompassing the optimization of offloading decisions, computation resource allocation and phase shift of IRS. To tackle the formulated challenging problem, we first decouple the original problem into two subproblems. Then, a heuristic algorithm is proposed, where a many-to-one matching algorithm is proposed to joint optimize offloading decision and the computation resource, and an iterative algorithm is utilized to optimize the phase shift coefficients of IRS. The simulation results validate the effectiveness of the proposed algorithm in comparison to other schemes, and the IRS can effectively maintain network performance even when there are intervals in RSU coverage areas.

**Keywords:** Intelligent Reflecting Surface · Vehicular Edge Computing · Task Offloading · Resource Allocation

## 1 Introduction

In recent years, with the rapid trend towards intelligence, more vehicular applications such as autonomous driving, traffic prediction and other on-board services are emerging [1,2]. Since most of these applications are with massive data and

This work is supported by major science and technology projects in Anhui Province, NO. 202003a05020009.

H. Gao et al. (Eds.): CollaborateCom 2023, LNICST 561, pp. 365–384, 2024.
https://doi.org/10.1007/978-3-031-54521-4_20

low latency requirements, the computational burden is becoming crazy for vehicles. To cope with the problem, mobile edge computing (MEC) framework has been proposed in vehicular networks, which further inspires the vehicular edge computing (VEC) paradigm [3,4]. The VEC framework allows vehicle to offload and execute their latency-sensitive tasks to the nearby edge servers through vehicle-to-infrastructure (V2I) and vehicle-to-vehicle (V2V) or other forms of wireless links, which not only significantly utilizes the computational resources but also improves the quality of service [5–7].

In general, to reap the benefits from VEC, it is crucial to deploy a dedicated access point known as a roadside unit (RSU) in close proximity to users' locations. The RSU can not only exchange information between vehicles and road infrastructure but also enhances vehicular services by integrating edge servers to provide computational support [8]. However, due to the limited communication range of RSU, it is inevitable to deploy a large number of RSUs for fulfilling the service demand from massive connected vehicles [9]. This leads to a subsequent cost concern, covering infrastructure expenses and operating overhead [10]. Moreover, under the fifth-generation (5G) communication background, RSUs employing sophisticated communication techniques tend to incur a lot more energy consumption [11]. Additionally, the rapid growth in the number of connected vehicle users further amplifies this energy burden. Hence, it is necessary to guarantee the communication quality of vehicular networks with low overhead.

Fortunately, owing to the recent progress in programmable meta-materials, a revolutionized technique has emerged, known as the intelligent reflecting surface (IRS), alternatively referred to as the reconfigurable intelligent surface [12]. The IRS is typically composed of a large array of passive reflecting elements, with full control over the phase shift and amplitude of each element [13]. The key function of IRS is to reconfigure wireless channel. More precisely, it can establish a virtual line-of-sight (LoS) link between transceivers to improve communication quality and signal coverage [14]. Since the reflecting elements of IRS are passive, low-cost and easy to deploy, it can enhance the energy and spectral efficiency of wireless networks under little additional cost [15,16]. These benefits have motivated researchers to incorporate IRS into conventional wireless networks, which leads to the emergence of many novel high performance systems, such as IRS-assisted MEC networks and vehicular networks [17,18].

Considering the IRS-assisted MEC scenario, most studies care about the overall offloading capacity and the total energy consumption. The authors in [19] considered an IRS-aided multiuser MEC scenario and propose two algorithms to solve the total energy consumption minimization problem. When combining IRS and other 5G communication technique, Li *et, al.* [20] analyzed sum energy consumption in an IRS-aided multi user MEC system, where users using non-orotology multi access (NOMA). Simulation results show that the proposed RIS-MEC with NOMA scheme can dramatically decrease the sum energy consumption compared to TDMA based methods. Mao *et, al.* [21] proposed an IRS-assisted secure MEC network frame, where eavesdroppers is considered.

Aiming to max-min computation efficiency among all devices, they proposed an iterative algorithm. Simulation results show the proposed method outperforms the conventional scheme without the aid of IRS. The authors in [22] also investigated the secure offloading problem in IRS-assisted MEC network and presented a block coordinate descent algorithm to minimize the total latency. Considering multi base stations scenario, Wang *et, al.* [23] proposed an IRS-assisted edge heterogeneous network, which includes a macro base station and multiple small base station. By introducing a two-timescale mechanism to optimize user association, offloading decision as well as computation resource and phase shift, the long-term energy consumption is minimized.

In terms of the IRS-assisted vehicular networks, existing work mainly focus on deploying IRS for communication link performance improvement. The authors in [24] tried to deploy IRS in a hybrid OMA/NOMA-enabled access environment. By jointly optimizing the transmit power allocation, the IRS's phase shift, and the vehicle active beamforming vector, the total system sum rate is proven to be maximized. Chen *et, al.* in [25] analyzed resource allocation for IRS aided vehicular communications under slowly large-scale fading channel. To maximize V2I link capacity, an alternating optimization algorithm has been proposed. Numerical results demonstrate that the IRS can effectively improve the quality of vehicular communications. For moving vehicular networks, Jiang *et, al.* [26] proposed a novel paradigm coined intelligent reflecting vehicle surface (IRVS) that embeds a massive number of reflection elements on vehicles' surfaces. Simulation results revealed that the IRVS can substantially improve the capacity of moving vehicular networks. The authors in [27] also studied IRS aided mobile vehicles scenario and presented an efficient two-stage transmission protocol for reaping the high IRS passive beamforming gain with low channel training overhead. Simulation results indicate that the proposed method can efficiently achieve the full IRS beamforming gain in the high-mobility communication scenario.

From the perspective of the aforementioned studies, the advantages of IRS are undoubtedly striking. However, the inquiry into whether IRS can meet the requirements of vehicles while being positioned outside the coverage of RSU has not been comprehensively investigated. If the IRS can effectively extend the service range of a RSU, it will have the potential to significantly reduce the costs associated with deploying additional RSUs, particularly in the face of a increasing number of connected vehicles. Motivated by these considerations, we aim to deploy the IRS beyond the coverage of RSU to further explore its ability on expanding service range of VEC network. The main contribution of this article are summarized as follows:

– We propose a roadside IRS-assisted VEC network model, where the IRS is deployed between two RSUs but beyond the coverage of either. An optimization problem is formulated to maximize the number of successful offloading tasks during the scheduling time by jointly optimizing the offloading decision, computation resource allocation and the IRS phase shift coefficients.
– To tackle this challenging problem, we design a heuristic algorithm to first decompose the original problem into two subproblems. Subsequently, the

offloading decision and computation resource allocation are first optimized by solving the first subproblem. Next, the phase shift of IRS is optimized via solving the second subproblem.
- Simulation results show that the proposed algorithm can effectively improve the number of successful offloading compared to other schemes. Besides, the proposed algorithm is able to maintain the network performance even the interval existing between the two RSUs.

The rest of this paper is organized as follows: In Sect. 2, we give the mathematical model of the roadside IRS assisted VEC network and give the corresponding problem formation. In Sect. 3, we design a heuristic algorithm to get a feasible solution. In Sect. 4, we illustrate the simulation results and corresponding analysis. In the final section, we summarize this article.

## 2    System Model and Problem Formation

In this section, we will give the system model and the problem formation. Consider an intelligent reflecting surface (IRS) assisted vehicular edge computing scenario as shown in Fig. 1, where two single antenna RSUs are deployed with certain distance interval on the side of a unidirectional road with two traffic streams. Suppose each RSU is equipped with a MEC server, so that it can provide proper computing services for vehicle users. We further assume that the coverage radius of both RSUs is smaller than the interval between them, which means when a vehicle is on the road, it may not be covered by any RSUs. So we decide to arrange a IRS to extend the service range of RSU. Suppose the IRS is arranged in the middle of these two RSUs, and it has $N$ reflecting elements which can be controlled by the IRS controller. In the scheduling progress, vehicles would offload their computation tasks to MEC severs through the direct vehicle–RSU links or indirect vehicle–IRS–RSU links. Our main objective is to optimize the total number of successful offloading tasks in the whole scheduling progress. In the following, we will first illustrate the channel model and the offloading model, then give the overall problem model.

### 2.1    Channel Model

For one vehicle's task, the task completion time includes the uplink transmission time and the execution time. Without loss of generality, we divide the whole schedule time $T$ equally into multiple identical time slots $t(t \in T)$, where $T$ is the set of time slots. Suppose all channels associated with the mobile vehicles follow block fading, i.e., channels would remain approximately constant during each time slot/block but may vary over different slots/blocks due to the high mobility of vehicles. In addition, we also assume that the channel state information (CSI) of all channels involved is perfectly known by RSUs.

Denote $\mathcal{K}$ as the set of two RSUs, and denote $\mathcal{M}_t$ as the set of vehicles to be served in each slot. For vehicles in the coverage of any RSU, they could

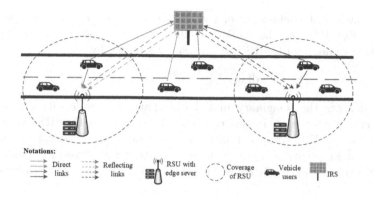

**Fig. 1.** Overview of the model.

upload their tasks through vehicle–RSU links and vehicle–IRS–RSU links, while for vehicles beyond the coverage of RSUs, they could only upload their tasks via vehicle–IRS–RSU links. Thus, the direct channel from vehicle $m(m \in \mathcal{M}_t)$ to the RSU $k(k \in \mathcal{K})$ in time slot $t$ is denoted as $h_{m,k}(t)$, the channel from vehicle $m$ to the IRS and from IRS to RSU $k$ in time slot $t$ are denoted as $\mathbf{h}_m(t) \in \mathbb{C}^{N \times 1}$ and $\mathbf{g}_k^H(t) \in \mathbb{C}^{1 \times N}$, respectively.

Among the three channels described above, the channel $h_{m,k}(t)$ obeys Rayleigh fading and can be expressed as

$$h_{m,k}(t) = \sqrt{\rho(d_{m,k}(t))^{-\lambda}}\ \widetilde{h}_{m,k}(t), \tag{1}$$

where $\rho$ represents the path loss at the reference distance $d_0$, and $\lambda$ is the corresponding path loss exponent of vehicle $m$ to RSU $k$ [28]. Furthermore, $d_{m,k}(t)$ represents the distance between vehicle $m$ and RSU $k$, while $\widetilde{h}_{m,k}(t)$ represents a random scattering component that follows a complex Gaussian distribution with a mean of zero and a variance of one.

Suppose the channel $\mathbf{h}_m(t)$ between IRS and vehicles as well as the channel $\mathbf{g}_k^H(t)$ between RSU and IRS both follow the Rician fading, so $\mathbf{h}_m(t)$ can be modeled as

$$\mathbf{h}_m(t) = \sqrt{\gamma_m(t)}\left(\sqrt{\frac{\xi_m}{1 + \xi_m}}\bar{\mathbf{h}}_m(t) + \sqrt{\frac{1}{1 + \xi_m}}\widetilde{\mathbf{h}}_m(t)\right), \tag{2}$$

where the vector $\bar{\mathbf{h}}_m(t) \in \mathbb{C}^{N \times 1}$ and vector $\widetilde{\mathbf{h}}_m(t) \in \mathbb{C}^{N \times 1}$ are the line-of-sight (LoS) component and non-line-of-sight (NLoS) component, respectively. To be specific, $\bar{\mathbf{h}}_m(t)$ consists of array response, while $\widetilde{\mathbf{h}}_m(t)$ consists of independent elements that follow $\mathcal{CN}(0, 1)$. Besides, $\xi_m$ is the Rician fading factor, which is the ratio of power between the LoS path and the scattered paths, and $\gamma_m(t)$ represents the path loss component from vehicle $m$ to the IRS. It is worth to note that the specific expression of $\mathbf{g}_k(t)$ is similar to (2), which is omitted here due to the limitation of paper length.

The phase shift coefficients of the IRS in time slot $t$ is defined as $\boldsymbol{\theta}(t) = \{\theta_1(t), \ldots, \theta_N(t)\}^T$, and the available value for each phase shift is $[0, 2\pi]$. Then, the reflection matrix of the IRS in time slot $t$ is given by

$$\boldsymbol{\Theta}(t) = \text{diag}(e^{j\theta_1(t)}, e^{j\theta_2(t)}, \cdots, e^{j\theta_N(t)}), \tag{3}$$

where $j$ denotes the imaginary unit. Note that, the amplitudes of all reflecting elements are set to 1. In practice, the phase shifts of the IRS are normally adjusted by the IRS controller using a finite number of discrete values [25]. However, for simplicity of analysis, we assume that the phase shifts can be continuously varied, and we disregard any delays in the adjustment of phase shifts.

## 2.2   Offloading Model

Suppose that in each time slot, each vehicle may generate one computation task that should be executed on the RSU, and these tasks are delay-sensitive, which means the execution deadline should not greater than the time slot length $\tau$. To determine whether a vehicle is transmitting during slot $t$ and to identify the preferred RSU for offloading, we introduce a binary variable $\alpha$ as

$$\alpha_{m,k}(t) = \begin{cases} 1, & \text{if vehicle } m \text{ will offload its task to} \\ & \text{RSU } k \text{ at slot } t; \\ 0, & \text{otherwise.} \end{cases} \tag{4}$$

Furthermore, to indicate whether vehicle $m$ is in the coverage of RSU $k$, we define a binary variable $x_{m,k}(t)$ as

$$x_{m,k}(t) = \begin{cases} 1, & \text{if vehicle } m \text{ is in the coverage of} \\ & \text{RSU } k \text{ at slot } t; \\ 0, & \text{otherwise.} \end{cases} \tag{5}$$

Assume that vehicles offloading their tasks to the same RSU employ Non-Orthogonal Multiple Access (NOMA) for transmission, which means that they will share the same frequency for communication. In contrast, vehicles offload their tasks to other RSUs will use different frequencies for transmission. This indicates that vehicles with different offloading destinations will not encounter any transmission interference. Thus, we could obtain the uplink signal-plus-interference-noise-ratio (SINR) of vehicle $m$ to RSU $k$ as follows,

$$\Gamma_{m,k}(t) = \frac{p_m \left| \mathbf{g}_k^H(t)\boldsymbol{\Theta}(t)\mathbf{h}_m(t) + h_{m,k}(t)x_{m,k}(t) \right|^2 \alpha_{m,k}(t)}{\sum\limits_{\substack{m' \in \mathcal{M}_t \\ \pi_{m'} < \pi_m}} p_{m'} \left| \mathbf{g}_k^H(t)\boldsymbol{\Theta}(t)\mathbf{h}_{m'}(t) + h_{m',k}(t)x_{m',k}(t) \right|^2 \alpha_{m',k}(t) + \sigma^2}, \tag{6}$$

$p_m$ represents the transmit power of vehicle $m$, and $\sigma^2$ denotes the additive white Gaussian noise (AWGN) power. Besides, $\pi_m$ denotes the successive interference cancellation (SIC) decoding order of signal of vehicle $m$, and $\pi_{m'} < \pi_m$ means the signal of vehicle-$m'$ will be decoded after vehicle $m$'s signal.

In this way, the transmit rate from vehicle $m$ to RSU $k$ in slot $t$ can be expressed as

$$R_{m,k}(t) = Blog_2(1 + \Gamma_{m,k}(t)), \tag{7}$$

where $B$ is the uplink bandwidth, $s_m$ represents the task bits from vehicle $m$ that need to be offloaded to the RSU. Therefore, the corresponding transmission delay $T_m^{trans}(t)$ is

$$T_m^{trans}(t) = \frac{s_m(t)}{\sum\limits_{k \in \mathcal{K}} R_{m,k}(t)}. \tag{8}$$

We suppose that the two RSUs have different computation capacities but can both implement parallel computing for independent user computations. Therefore, the computation time $T_m^{com}(t)$ to execute vehicle $m$'s task can be expressed as

$$T_m^{com}(t) = \frac{Cs_m(t)}{\sum\limits_{k \in \mathcal{K}} f_{m,k}(t)\, \alpha_{m,k}(t)}, \tag{9}$$

where $C$ is the number of CPU-cycles needed by executing tasks per bit, and $f_{m,k}(t)$ is the computation resource allocated for executing tasks of vehicle $m$.

Since the size of the computation results are typically small compared to the original tasks, the latency for downloading can be effectively disregarded [29]. Then, the total time delay of completing vehicle $m$'s task is denoted as

$$T_m^{total}(t) = T_m^{trans}(t) + T_m^{com}(t). \tag{10}$$

## 2.3  Problem Formation

To better evaluate whether the task been has been proceed, we define the following variable $\mu_m^{total}$:

$$\mu_m(t) = \begin{cases} 1, & \text{if } T_m^{total}(t) \le D_m; \\ 0, & \text{otherwise}, \end{cases} \tag{11}$$

where $D_m$ denotes the maximum tolerable execution delay of task $s_m$. Then, the total number of task been executed successfully during the time period $T$ is:

$$\mu^{total} = \sum_{t \in T} \sum_{m \in \mathcal{M}_t} \mu_m(t). \tag{12}$$

The main objective of this work is to maximize $\mu^{total}$ by jointly optimizing the phase shift coefficients (i.e., $\boldsymbol{\theta} = \{\boldsymbol{\theta}(0), \cdots, \boldsymbol{\theta}(t), \cdots\}$), the offloading decision variables (i.e., $\boldsymbol{\alpha} = \{\boldsymbol{\alpha}(0), \cdots, \boldsymbol{\alpha}(t), \cdots\}$), and the computation resource allocation variables (i.e., $\boldsymbol{f} = \{\boldsymbol{f}(0), \cdots, \boldsymbol{f}(t), \cdots\}$). Thus, we have the optimization problem as follows.

$$\mathcal{P}1: \max_{\alpha,\theta,f} \mu^{total} \tag{13}$$

$$s.t. \quad (1)-(12),$$
$$C1: \sum_{k\in\mathcal{K}} \alpha_{m,k}(t) \leq 1, \ \forall m \in \mathcal{M}_t, \ \forall t \in \mathcal{T},$$
$$C2: \ 0 \leq \theta_i(t) \leq 2\pi, \ \forall i \in \{1,\cdots,N\}, \ \forall t \in \mathcal{T},$$
$$C3: \ \Gamma_{m,k}(t) > \beta\alpha_{m,k}(t), \ \forall m \in \mathcal{M}_t, \ \forall k \in \mathcal{K}, \ \forall t \in \mathcal{T},$$
$$C4: \sum_{m\in\mathcal{M}_t} f_{m,k}(t) \leq F_k, \ \forall k \in \mathcal{K}, \ \forall t \in \mathcal{T},$$
$$C5: \ 0 \leq f_{m,k}(t) \leq F_k, \ \forall k \in \mathcal{K}, \ \forall m \in \mathcal{M}_t, \ \forall t \in \mathcal{T}.$$

In (13), constraint $C1$ guarantees that each vehicle's task can only be transmitted to one RSU, while constraint $C2$ restricts the phase shift coefficient for each reflecting elements on IRS. Then, constraint $C3$ gives threshold $\beta$ of SINR, which makes sure each vehicle could upload their tasks to RSU. Next, constraint $C4$ and $C5$ together ensure proper allocation of computation resource. Specifically, constraint $C4$ ensures that the overall allocated computation resource should not exceed RSU's computation capacity $F_k(k \in \mathcal{K})$, while constraint $C5$ guarantees the allocated resource for each vehicle's task.

According to (6), (7), (8), (9), the binary variables $\alpha$ and the continuous variables $\theta$ and $f$ are deeply coupled with each other. Therefore, problem $\mathcal{P}1$ is a mix-integer non-convex problem, which is NP-hard and challenging to solve. In the following, we will propose a heuristic algorithm to solve this problem.

## 3   The Proposed Solution

In this section, we will introduce a two-stage heuristic algorithm to tackle the problem $\mathcal{P}1$. To begin with, it is important to notice that the variables $\alpha(t)$, $\theta(t)$, $f(t)$ in each time slot is independent. Therefore, to get the maximum value of $\mu^{total}$, we only need to maximize $\sum_{m\in\mathcal{M}_t} \mu_m(t)$ in each time slot. In this way, we can obtain the following optimization problem in each time slot:

$$\mathcal{P}2: \max_{\alpha(t),\theta(t),f(t)} \sum_{m\in\mathcal{M}_t} \mu_m(t) \tag{14}$$

$$s.t. \quad (1)-(11),$$
$$C1-C5.$$

Problem $\mathcal{P}2$ has the same feature as problem $\mathcal{P}1$, which is non-convex and hard to solve. Therefore, we first divide the problem $\mathcal{P}2$ into two subproblems: 1) the optimization problem $\mathcal{P}3$ of offloading decision $\alpha(t)$ and computation resource allocation $f(t)$; 2) the optimization problem $\mathcal{P}4$ of phase shift coefficients $\theta(t)$. To solve problem $\mathcal{P}2$, we propose a many-to-one matching method under fixed phase shift vector $\theta(t)$. For solving $\mathcal{P}3$, we propose a iterative phase shift optimization method by fixing the variable $\alpha(t)$ and $f(t)$. The proposed optimization algorithm for IRS assisted VEC network is summarized in Algorithm 1. In the following, we will discuss in detail.

---

**Algorithm 1.** The Overall Algorithm

---
**Input:** $\mathcal{M}_t$ : The set of vehicles in slot $t$, $\mathcal{K}$ : The set of RSUs, $\mathcal{T}$: The set of time
   slots.
**Output:** $\alpha^*, f^*, \theta^*$.
1: **for** $t \in \mathcal{T}$ **do**
2:    Initialize phase shift coefficients $\theta^0(t)$.
3:    Obtain offloading decision $\alpha^*(t)$ and resource allocation $f^*(t)$ based on $\theta^0(t)$
      via **Algorithm 2**.
4:    Find feasible phase shift $\theta^*(t)$ based on $\alpha^*(t)$ and $f^*(t)$ via **Algorithm 3**.
5:    Compute $\mu_m^*(t)$ according to $\alpha^*(t)$, $f^*(t)$, $\theta^*(t)$.
6:    Let $\mu^*(t) = \sum\limits_{m \in \mathcal{M}_t} \mu_m^*(t)$.
7: **end for**

---

## 3.1  Optimization of Offloading Decisions and Computation Resource Allocation

When fixing the IRS phase shift coefficients $\theta(t)$, problem $\mathcal{P}2$ can be reduced as

$$\mathcal{P}3: \quad \max_{\alpha(t),\, f(t)} \sum_{m \in \mathcal{M}_t} \mu_m(t), \tag{15}$$

$$s.t. \quad (1) - (11),$$
$$C1, C3, C4, C5.$$

Note that, the problem $\mathcal{P}3$ remains non-convex and hard to be solved directly. However, according to (11) the value of $\mu_m(t)$ is related to the total offloading latency $T_m^{total}(t)$ of each vehicle. If each $T_m^{total}(t)$ keeps a relatively small value, the number of successful offloading tasks will increase. In this way, problem $\mathcal{P}3$ can be further transferred as

$$\tilde{\mathcal{P}}3: \quad \min_{\alpha(t),\, f(t)} \sum_{m \in \mathcal{M}_t} T_m^{total}(t), \tag{16}$$

$$s.t. \quad (1) - (11),$$
$$C1, C3, C4, C5.$$

Now, we focus on finding the optimal $\alpha(t)$ and $f(t)$ to minimize computation time for each vehicle. However, according to (6), (7), (8), (9), it is evident to find variable $\alpha(t)$ and $f(t)$ are deeply coupled, which makes problem $\tilde{\mathcal{P}}3$ is still computationally hard to cope with.

According to constraint $C1$, we know that each vehicle can only select one RSU as its offloading destination, while a RSU can be assigned to multiple vehicles. Therefore, we decide to utilize the many-to-one matching in each time slot for getting the optimal $\alpha(t)$ and $f(t)$.

**Definition 1.** Suppose $\eta$ is a many-to-one matching function that joins vehicle set $\mathcal{M}_t$ and RSU set $\mathcal{K}$. The function $\eta$ should satisfy the following conditions:

1. $|\eta(m)| = 1$ for every vehicle $m \in \mathcal{M}_t$;

2. $|\eta(k)| \leq |\mathcal{M}_t|$ for every RSU $k \in \mathcal{K}$;
3. $m \in \eta(k)$ if and only if $k = \eta(m)$.

In fact, the matching $\eta$ can represent the offloading decision $\boldsymbol{\alpha}(t)$ in the considered scenario. Then, based on **Definition 1.**, we define $U_m(\eta)$ and $U_k(\eta)$ as the utility function for $m$ on $\eta$ and the utility function for $k$ on $\eta$. The two utility functions actually reveal the matching effect. We have

$$U_m(\eta) = -T_m^\eta, \tag{17}$$

where $T_m^\eta$ is the total executing latency of vehicle $m$ as shown in (10) under the matching $\eta$. Besides, $U_k(\eta)$ is expressed as

$$U_k(\eta) = - \max_{m \in \mathcal{M}_t} \{T_m^\eta\}. \tag{18}$$

The above utility functions (17) and (18) show both vehicles and RSUs care about more than their own matching. So, traditional pairwise stable matching may not exist in such condition [30]. To obtain the desire stable matching, we further leverage the concept of two-sided swap stability on the following definitions.

**Definition 2.** Define $\eta_m^{m'} = \{\eta \setminus \{(m,k),(m',k')\}\} \cup \{(m,k'),(m',k)\}$ as a swap matching, where $\eta(m) = k$, $\eta(m') = k'$, and $k \neq k'$.

Normally, a swap matching allows vehicle $m$ and vehicle $m'$ to swap their corresponding matched RSUs with each other, while remaining the matchings between other vehicles and RSUs stable. However, when $k' = 0$, the swap matching will be modified as $\eta_m^0 = \{\eta \setminus (m,k)\} \cup \{(m,k')\}$, where $\eta(m) = k$ and $k \neq k'$. This means that for vehicle $m$, the originally matched RSU $k$ is now changed to $k'$.

**Definition 3.** Given a matching function $\eta$ and a pair of vehicles $(m, m')$, if there exists $\eta(m) = k$ and $\eta(m') = k'$, and satisfies:

1. $\forall z \in \{m, m', k, k'\}, U_z(\eta_m^{m'}) \geq U_z(\eta)$;
2. $\exists z \in \{m, m', k, k'\}, U_z(\eta_m^{m'}) \geq U_z(\eta)$;

then we call $(m, m')$ as a swap-blocking pairs in matching $\eta$.

**Definition 4.** A matching is reckoned to be two-sided exchange stable if and only if there is no swap-blocking pairs exists in $\eta$.

Definition 4 is a criterion that evaluates whether the current matching is stable and guarantees the convergence of many-to-one matching method.

Nevertheless, to proceed the many-to-one steps, we need to tackle the computation resource allocation problem. After obtaining any matching during the whole many-to-one matching process, the computation resource allocation problem $\mathcal{P}3.1$ can be expressed as follows:

$$\mathcal{P}3.1: \quad \min_{f(t)} \sum_{m \in \mathcal{M}_t} T_m^{com}(t), \tag{19}$$

$$s.t. \quad (9), C4, C5.$$

---

**Algorithm 2.** The ODRA Algorithm

---

**Input:** $\mathcal{M}_t$ : The set of vehicles in slot $t$, $\mathcal{K}$ : The set of RSUs, $\boldsymbol{\theta}^0(t)$: The initial set of phase shift coefficients.

**Output:** $\boldsymbol{\alpha}^*(t)$, $\boldsymbol{f}^*(t)$.

1: Initialize a matching $\eta$ on $\mathcal{M}_t \cup \mathcal{K}$.
2: Initialize computation resource allocation $\boldsymbol{f}(t)$ based on initial matching $\eta$.
3: **repeat**
4:     $\exists m \in \mathcal{M}_t$, $\eta(m) = k$.
5:     Vehicle $m$ choose another RSU $k'$ and re-solve problem $\tilde{\mathcal{P}}3.1$ to obtain $\boldsymbol{f}'(t)$.
6:     Compute corresponding SINR $\Gamma_{m,k'}(t)$ according to (6).
7:     **if** vehicle $m$ satisfies $U_m(\eta_m^0) \geq U_m(\eta)$ and $\Gamma_{m,k'}(t) \geq \beta$ **then**
8:         **if** $U_k(\eta_m^0) \geq U_k(\eta)$ or $U_{k'}(\eta_m^0) \geq U_{k'}(\eta)$ **then**
9:             Update matching: $\eta \leftarrow \eta_m^0$.
10:             Update resource allocation: $\boldsymbol{f}(t) = \boldsymbol{f}'(t)$.
11:         **else**
12:             Do not update $\eta$.
13:             The computation resource allocation $\boldsymbol{f}(t)$ remains.
14:         **end if**
15:     **end if**
16:     $\exists m, m' \in \mathcal{M}_t$, and $m \neq m'$, $\eta(m) = k$, $\eta(m') = k'$.
17:     Vehicle $m$ and vehicle $m'$ swapping matched RSUs and re-solve problem $\tilde{\mathcal{P}}3.1$ to obtain $\boldsymbol{f}'(t)$.
18:     Compute corresponding SINR $\Gamma_{m,k'}(t)$ and $\Gamma_{m',k}(t)$ according to (6).
19:     **if** vehicle $m$ and $m'$ satisfy $U_m(\eta_m^{m'}) \geq U_m(\eta)$ and $U_{m'}(\eta_m^{m'}) \geq U_{m'}(\eta)$ and $\Gamma_{m,k'}(t) \geq \beta$ and $\Gamma_{m',k}(t) \geq \beta$ **then**
20:         **if** $U_k(\eta_m^{m'}) \geq U_k(\eta)$ or $U_{k'}(\eta_m^{m'}) \geq U_{k'}(\eta)$ **then**
21:             Update matching: $\eta \leftarrow \eta_m^{m'}$.
22:             Update offloading decision: $\boldsymbol{f}(t) = \boldsymbol{f}'(t)$.
23:         **else**
24:             Do not update $\eta$.
25:             The computation resource allocation $\boldsymbol{f}(t)$ remains.
26:         **end if**
27:     **end if**
28: **until** Matching $\eta$ satisfies **Definition 4**.
29: Let $\boldsymbol{\alpha}^*(t) = \eta$, $\boldsymbol{f}^*(t) = \boldsymbol{f}(t)$.

---

The above problem is non-convex due to the objective function, thus we further transfer problem $\mathcal{P}3.1$ into:

$$\tilde{\mathcal{P}}3.1: \quad \max_{\boldsymbol{f}(t)} \sum_{m \in \mathcal{M}_t} \frac{1}{T_m^{com}(t)}, \tag{20}$$

$$s.t. \quad (9), C4, C5.$$

Now, $\tilde{\mathcal{P}}3.1$ is a convex optimization problem, which can be solved directly through existing solving tools like CVX. Based on the above analysis, the proposed offloading decision and computation resource allocation (ODRA) algorithm is summarized in Algorithm 2.

## 3.2  Optimization of IRS Phase Shift Coefficients

After obtaining the optimized offloading decision $\alpha^*(t)$ and computation resource allocation $f^*(t)$, we now focus on optimizing the phase shift of IRS. It is evident that we can obtain the total computation latency $\sum_{m \in \mathcal{M}_t} T_m^{com}(t)$ after executing Algorithm 2. So, in order to get the max value of $\sum_{m \in \mathcal{M}_t} \mu_m(t)$, we only need to minimize the total transmission latency $\sum_{m \in \mathcal{M}_t} T_m^{trans}(t)$. Furthermore, minimizing $\sum_{m \in \mathcal{M}_t} T_m^{trans}(t)$ is approximated as maximizing the overall transmission rate of each vehicle. Therefore, the original problem $P2$ can be transferred to

$$P4: \quad \max_{\boldsymbol{\theta}(t)} \sum_{m \in \mathcal{M}_t} \sum_{k \in \mathcal{K}} R_{m,k}(t) \tag{21}$$

$$s.t. \quad (1) - (8), \; C2, C3.$$

Since the objective function of $P4$ is non-concave, we try to introduce the slack variables $V = \{V_{m,k}(t) = \frac{p_m \, |\mathbf{g}_k^H(t)\boldsymbol{\Theta}(t)\mathbf{h}_m(t) + h_{m,k}(t)x_{m,k}(t)|^2 \alpha_{m,k}(t)}{\sum\limits_{\substack{m' \in \mathcal{M}_t \\ \pi_{m'} < \pi_m}} p_{m'} \, |\mathbf{g}_k^H(t)\boldsymbol{\Theta}(t)\mathbf{h}_{m'}(t) + h_{m',k}(t)x_{m',k}(t)|^2 \alpha_{m',k}(t) + \sigma^2}, \; \forall m, k, t\}$ and then transform it into a feasibility-check problem and solve it iteratively until converge. And the variables $V$ satisfy that

$$\frac{p_m \, |\mathbf{g}_k^H(t)\boldsymbol{\Theta}(t)\mathbf{h}_m(t) + h_{m,k}(t)x_{m,k}(t)|^2 \alpha_{m,k}(t)}{\sum\limits_{\substack{m' \in \mathcal{M}_t \\ \pi_{m'} < \pi_m}} p_{m'} \, |\mathbf{g}_k^H(t)\boldsymbol{\Theta}(t)\mathbf{h}_{m'}(t) + h_{m',k}(t)x_{m',k}(t)|^2 \alpha_{m',k}(t) + \sigma^2} \geq V_{m,k}(t), \tag{22}$$

$$\forall m \in \mathcal{M}_t, k \in \mathcal{K}, t \in \mathcal{T}.$$

Thus, problem $P4$ can be reformulated to

$$\bar{P4}: \quad \text{Find} \quad \boldsymbol{\Phi}(t) \tag{23}$$

$$s.t. \quad (1) - (8), (22) \; C2, C3.$$

Due to the non-convexity of constraint $C3$ and (22), we will do the following transformation. The combined channel gain in (6) of each vehicle can be reformulated as

$$|\mathbf{g}_k^H(t)\boldsymbol{\Theta}(t)\mathbf{h}_m(t) + h_{m,k}(t)x_{m,k}(t)|^2 = |\mathbf{H}_m(t)\boldsymbol{\Phi}(t) + h_{m,k}(t)x_{m,k}(t)|^2, \tag{24}$$

where $\mathbf{H}_m(t) = \mathbf{g}_k^H(t)\text{diag}\{\mathbf{h}_m(t)\}$ and $\boldsymbol{\Phi}(t) = [e^{j\theta_1(t)}, e^{j\theta_2(t)}, \cdots, e^{j\theta_N(t)}]^T$. We then introduce two slack variables $\kappa_m(t)$ and $\zeta_m(t)$, which are defined as [31]:

$$\kappa_m(t) = \mathrm{Re}(\mathbf{H}_m(t)\boldsymbol{\Phi}(t) + h_{m,k}(t)x_{m,k}(t)), \ \forall m \in \mathcal{M}_t, \forall t \in \mathcal{T}, \tag{25}$$

$$\zeta_m(t) = \mathrm{Im}(\mathbf{H}_m(t)\boldsymbol{\Phi}(t) + h_{m,k}(t)x_{m,k}(t)), \ \forall m \in \mathcal{M}_t, \forall t \in \mathcal{T}. \tag{26}$$

The variables $\kappa_m(t)$ and $\zeta_m(t)$ stand for the real part and imaginary part, respectively, and they satisfy the relationship $\kappa_m(t)^2 + \zeta_m(t)^2 = |\mathbf{H}_m(t)\boldsymbol{\Phi}(t) + h_{m,k}(t)x_{m,k}(t)|^2$. To this end, problem $\tilde{\mathcal{P}}4$ can be rewritten as below

$$\tilde{\mathcal{P}}4: \quad \text{Find} \quad \boldsymbol{\Phi}(t) \tag{27}$$

$$
\begin{aligned}
s.t. \quad &(1)-(8),(24)-(26),\\
&C6: |\boldsymbol{\Phi}_i(t)| \le 1, \ \forall i \in \{1,\cdots,N\}, \forall t \in \mathcal{T},\\
&C7: \frac{p(\kappa_m(t)^2+\zeta_m(t)^2)\alpha_{m,k}(t)}{\displaystyle\sum_{\substack{m'\in\mathcal{M}_t\\ \pi_{m'}<\pi_m}} p(\kappa_{m'}(t)^2+\zeta_{m'}(t)^2)\alpha_{m',k}(t)+\sigma^2} \ge \beta, \forall m \in \mathcal{M}_t, \forall t \in \mathcal{T},\\
&C8: \frac{p(\kappa_m(t)^2+\zeta_m(t)^2)\alpha_{m,k}(t)}{\displaystyle\sum_{\substack{m'\in\mathcal{M}_t\\ \pi_{m'}<\pi_m}} p(\kappa_{m'}(t)^2+\zeta_{m'}(t)^2)\alpha_{m',k}(t)+\sigma^2} \ge V_{m,k}(t),\\
&\forall m \in \mathcal{M}_t, \forall t \in \mathcal{T}.
\end{aligned}
$$

$\boldsymbol{\Phi}_i(t)$ represents the $i$th component in $\boldsymbol{\Phi}(t)$.

Note that, problem $\tilde{\mathcal{P}}4$ is still non-convex due to the constraint $C7$ and $C8$. So, we decide to adopt the successive convex approximation method to deal with the non-convexity [32]. At given initial point $(\tilde{\kappa}_m(t),\ \tilde{\zeta}_m(t))$, according to the first-order Taylor expansion of $\kappa_m(t)^2 + \zeta_m(t)^2$, we can get

$$
\begin{aligned}
\kappa_m(t)^2 + \zeta_m(t)^2 &\ge \tilde{\kappa}_m(t)^2 + \tilde{\zeta}_m(t)^2 + 2\tilde{\kappa}_m(t)(\kappa_m(t) - \tilde{\kappa}_m(t))\\
&\quad + 2\tilde{\zeta}_m(t)(\zeta_m(t) - \tilde{\zeta}_m(t)) = \Gamma_m^{low}(t).
\end{aligned} \tag{28}
$$

Therefore, problem $\tilde{\mathcal{P}}4$ can be further formulated as

$$\hat{\mathcal{P}}4: \quad \text{Find} \quad \boldsymbol{\Phi}(t) \tag{29}$$

$$
\begin{aligned}
s.t. \quad &(1)-(8),(24)-(26),(28),\\
&C6: |\boldsymbol{\Phi}_i(t)| \le 1, \ \forall i \in \{1,\cdots,N\}, \forall t \in \mathcal{T},\\
&C9: \frac{p\Gamma_m^{low}(t)\alpha_{m,k}(t)}{\displaystyle\sum_{\substack{m'\in\mathcal{M}_t\\ \pi_{m'}<\pi_m}} p(\kappa_{m'}(t)^2+\zeta_{m'}(t)^2)\alpha_{m',k}(t)+\sigma^2} \ge \beta, \forall m \in \mathcal{M}_t, \forall t \in \mathcal{T},\\
&C10: \frac{p\Gamma_m^{low}(t)\alpha_{m,k}(t)}{\displaystyle\sum_{\substack{m'\in\mathcal{M}_t\\ \pi_{m'}<\pi_m}} p(\kappa_{m'}(t)^2+\zeta_{m'}(t)^2)\alpha_{m',k}(t)+\sigma^2} \ge V_{m,k}(t),\\
&\forall m \in \mathcal{M}_t, \forall t \in \mathcal{T}.
\end{aligned}
$$

Problem $\hat{\mathcal{P}}4$ is a convex optimization problem, and can be solved effectively through CVX. The detailed steps involving in phase shifts optimization (PSO) algorithm is summarized in Algorithm 3.

---

**Algorithm 3.** The PSO Algorithm

---

**Input:** $\mathcal{M}_t$ : The set of vehicles in slot $t$, $\mathcal{K}$ : The set of RSUs, $\boldsymbol{\theta}^0(t)$: Initial phase shift coefficient in slot $t$, $\boldsymbol{\alpha}^*(t)$: Optimal offloading decision in slot $t$, $\boldsymbol{f}^*(t)$: Optimal computation resource allocation in slot $t$.
**Output:** $\boldsymbol{\theta}(t)^*$.
1: Set $r = 0$.
2: Compute $\boldsymbol{\Phi}^0(t)$ according to $\boldsymbol{\theta}^0(t)$.
3: **repeat**
4:     $r = r + 1$.
5:     Update $\tilde{\zeta}_m(t)$ and $\tilde{\kappa}_m(t)$ based on $\boldsymbol{\Phi}^{r-1}(t)$ according to (25) & (26).
6:     Solve problem $\hat{\mathcal{P}}4$ to obtain $\boldsymbol{\Phi}^r(t)$, $\zeta_m^r(t)$, $\kappa_m^r(t)$.
7: **until** $\boldsymbol{\Phi}^r(t)$, $\zeta_m^r(t)$, $\kappa_m^r(t)$ coverage.
8: Let $\boldsymbol{\theta}^*(t) = \boldsymbol{\Phi}^r(t)^T$.

---

# 4   Numerical Results

In this section, simulation results are presented to verify the effectiveness of the proposed optimization algorithm. To begin with, we consider a two-way lane road where RSU and IRS are arranged on opposite sides. Under a three-dimensional Cartesian coordinate system, the IRS is loacted at $(0, 0, 20)$, while two RSUs with 200m coverage radius locate at $(20, -300, 20)$ and $(20, 300, 20)$, respectively. So, the interval between two RSUs is 200 m. To generate vehicles, we use the traffic flow dataset "MIDAS Site - 19542 at A2260 southbound between A2 and B262", which is from a freeway in Untied Kingdom. And the vehicles' coordinates are in the region between two RSUs, with the y-axis coordinate from $-400$ to 400. The x-axis coordinate is 0 to 5 and the z-axis coordinate is fixed as 0. Then, the path loss at the reference distance $d_0 = 1$m is configured as $-20$ dB, and the Rician factor is set as 3 dB. The path loss exponents for vehicle–RSU link, RSU–IRS link and vehicle–IRS link are set as 3.5, 2.2 and 2.2 [29], respectively. Other simulation parameters are shown in Table 1.

In addition, the length of each time slot is set as 1 s, and the overall number of time slots is 10. The task is reckoned as succeed only when the total delay of the task is less than or equal to the maximum tolerable delay, otherwise the task executed fails. All the experimental results are averaged from 50 groups of corresponding experiments.

In the simulations, the following three schemes are involved into the comparison:

- **Without IRS:** In such method, the IRS will not be placed in the considered VEC network, so the total successful number of tasks will only be maximized through optimizing offloading decision and resource allocation
- **With PSO without ODRA:** The ODRA algorithm that relates to offloading decision and resource allocation are not included in such method, but the phase shifts of IRS will be optimized.

**Table 1.** Simulation parameters

| Symbol | Simulation parameter | Value |
|--------|----------------------|-------|
| $s_m$ | Task data amount for each vehicle | $[4 \times 10^5,\ 6 \times 10^5]$ bits |
| $D_m$ | Delay constraint of each task | $[0.5, 1]$ s |
| $F$ | The computing capability of two edge servers | 15 GHz, 20 GHz |
| $C$ | Number of CPU-cycles needed by executing tasks per bit | 800 cycles/bit |
| $p_m$ | The transmission power of each vehicle | 1 W |
| $B$ | Uplink bandwidth of each vehicle | 10 MHz |
| $\beta$ | The threshold for SINR | 0.1 |
| $\sigma^2$ | The Gaussian white noise power | −100 dBm |

- **With ODRA without PSO:** The phase shifts of IRS will not be optimized in such scheme, but the ODRA algorithm will be adopted to optimize offloading decision and computation resource.

We first present detailed results of our algorithm under different number of total tasks during the 10 time slots, and compare it with other three schemes. Then, we show the effect of the number of reflection elements on the result of all methods. At last, we indicate the relationship between the location of IRS and the number of total successful offloading tasks.

In Fig. 2, the number of successful offloading tasks versus the various number of total tasks during the 10 time slots is illustrated. These results are presented considering the number of reflecting elements $N = 30$ and the interval between RSUs is 200 m. Notably, all three schemes that incorporate IRS exhibit substantial performance advantages compared to the scheme without IRS, and our proposed algorithm is always the most superior. This outcome effectively showcases the capability of deploying IRS to expand the service coverage of RSUs, as well as the efficacy of our proposed algorithm. Moreover, when the number of generated tasks during 10 slots is below 300, the outcome for all schemes increases with the number of generated tasks rises. In such condition, the three schemes adopting IRS have the similar results. However, when the number of tasks surpasses 300, the results for all schemes consistently grow, except for the "without IRS" scheme. This is because the "without IRS" scheme has a longer average transmission time than other methods. As the number of tasks increases, the average computation time also rises, leading to an increasing number of tasks exceeding their time constraints. Besides, the "with ODRA without PSO" scheme has slightly better performance than the "with PSO without ODRA" scheme, which indicates the importance of correct offloading decisions.

In the second simulation, we investigate the impact of the number of reflection elements while keeping the number of generated tasks fixed. The total number of generated tasks is set at 500, and the RSU interval is maintained at 200m.

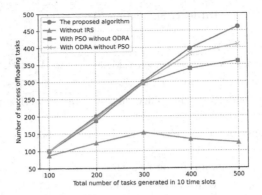

**Fig. 2.** The number of successful offloading tasks versus the number of tasks generated in 10 time slots, interval = 200 m, $N = 30$.

Subsequently, we set the number of reflecting elements $N$ ranging from 2 to 10 and then from 10 to 50. As shown in Fig. 3 (a), it can be observed that the number of successful offloading tasks under three IRS-assisted schemes increase with the augmentation of $N$ and eventually remains unchanged. Notably, the proposed algorithm and the "with PSO without ODRA" algorithm achieves converge with $N = 6$, while the "with ODRA without PSO" algorithm achieves converge until $N = 8$. This outcome indicates the effectiveness of phase shift optimization method, which helps to obtain the best performance with relatively little number of reflecting elements. Similar to Fig. 3 (a), the situation in Fig. 3 (b) also prove the completion above, as the two schemes employing phase shifts optimization get the maximum performance quicker. However, when the number of reflecting elements exceeds 50, the proposed algorithm and the "with PSO without ODRA" algorithm rises their performance again. In addition, combining both figures, the results for all three IRS aided schemes first remain stable from $N = 8$ and $N = 10$, then rising again. This phenomenon is attributed to a significant reduction in transmission latency when $N = 20$.

In the final simulation experiment, we explore the influence of intervals between RSUs. In this simulation, we keep the reflecting element number $N = 30$ and the total number of generated tasks as 500. To alter the interval, we adjust the y-axis coordinate of the two RSUs from 200 to 400 and −200 to −400, respectively. As shown in Fig. 4, one can observe that as the interval between two RSUs increase, the amount of successful offloading tasks corresponding decreases. Nevertheless, the proposed algorithm remains its maximum performance unchanged until interval surpasses 200 m. In contrast, neither the other two IRS-assisted schemes nor the without IRS scheme manage to achieve similar effects. Furthermore, the performance of without IRS scheme equals our proposed algorithm at the beginning, but experiences a significant drop when the interval is 100 m, being outperformed by other schemes. This simulation result demonstrates that the efficacy of our proposed algorithm in enhancing communication quality and expanding the service range of RSUs. Notably, the "with ODRA without

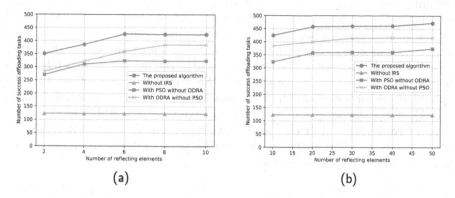

(a)                                        (b)

**Fig. 3.** The number of successful offloading tasks versus the number of reflecting elements, interval = 200 m.

PSO" always outperforms the "with PSO without ODRA" algorithm until the interval between two RSUs reach 400 m. This outcome demonstrates that the phase shifts optimization is more important with the increasing interval.

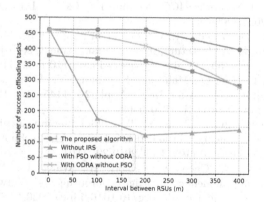

**Fig. 4.** The number of successful offloading tasks versus the interval between RSUs, $N$ = 30.

## 5    Conclusion

In this paper, a roadside IRS aided VEC network is proposed, where the IRS is positioned between two RSUs but outside the coverage area of either. Moreover, in order to explore IRS's potential ability on expanding the service range in the considered model, we aim to maximize the number of tasks completed during a certain period. Since the formulated problem is challenging to cope with, we first decouple the original problem into two subproblems and then propose a heuristic algorithm to jointly optimize the offloading strategy, the computation resource allocation and the phase shifts of IRS. Simulation results show that the proposed algorithm can effectively maximize the overall success offloading tasks, especially compared to the scheme without IRS. It is also notable that the proposed algorithm can maintain its performance even there is interval between two RSUs. Since the positive impact of IRS in extending the RSU's service range has been proved, we will further investigate its potential benefits of enhancing energy efficiency. Additionally, cooperation between multiple IRSs and partial vehicle offloading will be considered.

# References

1. Munawar, S., Ali, Z., Waqas, M., Tu, S., Hassan, S.A., Abbas, G.: Cooperative computational offloading in mobile edge computing for vehicles: A model-based DNN approach. IEEE Trans. Veh. Technol. **72**(3), 3376–3391 (2023). https://doi.org/10.1109/TVT.2022.3217323
2. Slamnik-Kriještorac, N., Peeters, M., Latré, S., Marquez-Barja, J.M.: Analyzing the impact of vim systems over the mec management and orchestration in vehicular communications. In: 2020 29th International Conference on Computer Communications and Networks (ICCCN), pp. 1–6 (2020). https://doi.org/10.1109/ICCCN49398.2020.9209636
3. Meneguette, R., De Grande, R., Ueyama, J., Filho, G.P.R., Madeira, E.: Vehicular edge computing: Architecture, resource management, security, and challenges. ACM Comput. Surv. **55**(1) (2021). https://doi.org/10.1145/3485129
4. Liu, L., Chen, C., Pei, Q., Maharjan, S., Zhang, Y.: Vehicular edge computing and networking: a survey. Mob. Netw. Appl. **26**, 1145–1168 (2019). https://api.semanticscholar.org/CorpusID:201070569
5. Zhang, J., Guo, H., Liu, J., Zhang, Y.: Task offloading in vehicular edge computing networks: a load-balancing solution. IEEE Trans. Veh. Technol. **69**(2), 2092–2104 (2020). https://doi.org/10.1109/TVT.2019.2959410
6. Lin, H., Zeadally, S., Chen, Z., Labiod, H., Wang, L.: A survey on computation offloading modeling for edge computing. J. Netw. Comput. Appl. **169**, 102781 (2020). https://doi.org/10.1016/j.jnca.2020.102781, https://www.sciencedirect.com/science/article/pii/S1084804520302551
7. Jaiswal, N., Purohit, N.: Performance analysis of NOMA-enabled vehicular communication systems with transmit antenna selection over double nakagami-m fading. IEEE Trans. Veh. Technol. **70**(12), 12725–12741 (2021). https://doi.org/10.1109/TVT.2021.3119979
8. Geng, L., Zhao, H., Wang, J., Kaushik, A., Yuan, S., Feng, W.: Deep-reinforcement-learning-based distributed computation offloading in vehicular edge computing networks. IEEE Internet Things J. **10**(14), 12416–12433 (2023). https://doi.org/10.1109/JIOT.2023.3247013
9. Yu, H., Liu, R., Li, Z., Ren, Y., Jiang, H.: An RSU deployment strategy based on traffic demand in vehicular ad hoc networks (VANETs). IEEE Internet Things J. **9**(9), 6496–6505 (2022). https://doi.org/10.1109/JIOT.2021.3111048

10. Ghosh, S., Misra, I.S., Chakraborty, T.: Optimal RSU deployment using complex network analysis for traffic prediction in VANET. Peer-to-Peer Network. Appl. **16**, 1135–1154 (2023). https://api.semanticscholar.org/CorpusID:257435229

11. Leung, V.C.M., Dong, Y., Pan, H.: Editorial recent techniques of green information and communications technologies. IEEE Trans. Green Commun. Netw. **5**(4), 1649–1652 (2021). https://doi.org/10.1109/TGCN.2021.3125232

12. Chen, R., Liu, M., Hui, Y., Cheng, N., Li, J.: Reconfigurable intelligent surfaces for 6g IoT wireless positioning: a contemporary survey. IEEE Internet Things J. **9**(23), 23570–23582 (2022). https://doi.org/10.1109/JIOT.2022.3203890

13. Liao, Y., Xia, S., Zhang, K., Zhai, X.: UAV swarm trajectory and cooperative beamforming design in double-IRS assisted wireless communications. In: 2022 18th International Conference on Mobility, Sensing and Networking (MSN), pp. 594–600 (2022). https://doi.org/10.1109/MSN57253.2022.00099

14. Wu, Q., Zhang, S., Zheng, B., You, C., Zhang, R.: Intelligent reflecting surface-aided wireless communications: a tutorial. IEEE Trans. Commun. **69**(5), 3313–3351 (2021). https://doi.org/10.1109/TCOMM.2021.3051897

15. Gong, S., Lu, X., Hoang, D.T., Niyato, D., Shu, L., Kim, D.I., Liang, Y.C.: Toward smart wireless communications via intelligent reflecting surfaces: a contemporary survey. IEEE Commun. Surv. Tutorials **22**(4), 2283–2314 (2020). https://doi.org/10.1109/COMST.2020.3004197

16. Zheng, B., You, C., Mei, W., Zhang, R.: A survey on channel estimation and practical passive beamforming design for intelligent reflecting surface aided wireless communications. IEEE Commun. Surv. Tutorials **24**(2), 1035–1071 (2022). https://doi.org/10.1109/COMST.2022.3155305

17. Chen, N., Liu, C., Jia, H., Okada, M.: Intelligent reflecting surface aided network under interference toward 6g applications. IEEE Network **36**(4), 18–27 (2022). https://doi.org/10.1109/MNET.001.2100675

18. Cao, Y., Xu, S., Liu, J., Kato, N.: Toward smart and secure v2x communication in 5g and beyond: a UAV-enabled aerial intelligent reflecting surface solution. IEEE Veh. Technol. Mag. **17**(1), 66–73 (2022). https://doi.org/10.1109/MVT.2021.3136832

19. Chu, Z., Xiao, P., Shojafar, M., Mi, D., Mao, J., Hao, W.: Intelligent reflecting surface assisted mobile edge computing for internet of things. IEEE Wirel. Commun. Lett. **10**(3), 619–623 (2021). https://doi.org/10.1109/LWC.2020.3040607

20. Li, Z., et al.: Energy efficient reconfigurable intelligent surface enabled mobile edge computing networks with NOMA. IEEE Trans. Cogn. Commun. Netw. **7**(2), 427–440 (2021). https://doi.org/10.1109/TCCN.2021.3068750

21. Mao, S., et al.: Reconfigurable intelligent surface-assisted secure mobile edge computing networks. IEEE Trans. Veh. Technol. **71**, 6647–6660 (2022). https://api.semanticscholar.org/CorpusID:247689318

22. Chen, X., Xu, H., Zhang, G., Chen, Y., Li, R.: Secure computation offloading assisted by intelligent reflection surface for mobile edge computing network. Phys. Commun. **57**, 102003 (2023). https://doi.org/10.1016/j.phycom.2023.102003, https://www.sciencedirect.com/science/article/pii/S187449072300006X

23. Wang, Z., Wei, Y., Feng, Z., Yu, F., Han, Z.: Resource management and reflection optimization for intelligent reflecting surface assisted multi-access edge computing using deep reinforcement learning. IEEE Trans. Wirel. Commun. **22**, 1175–1186 (2023). https://api.semanticscholar.org/CorpusID:252963387

24. Salem, A.A., Rihan, M., Huang, L., Benaya, A.: Intelligent reflecting surface assisted hybrid access vehicular communication: Noma or OMA contributes the

most? IEEE Internet Things J. **9**(19), 18854–18866 (2022). https://doi.org/10. 1109/JIOT.2022.3162787

25. Chen, Y., Wang, Y., Zhang, J., Li, Z.: Resource allocation for intelligent reflecting surface aided vehicular communications. IEEE Trans. Veh. Technol. **69**(10), 12321–12326 (2020). https://doi.org/10.1109/TVT.2020.3010252

26. Jiang, W., Schotten, H.D.: Intelligent reflecting vehicle surface: a novel IRS paradigm for moving vehicular networks. In: MILCOM 2022–2022 IEEE Military Communications Conference (MILCOM), pp. 793–798 (2022). https://doi.org/10. 1109/MILCOM55135.2022.10017691

27. Huang, Z., Zheng, B., Zhang, R.: Transforming fading channel from fast to slow: intelligent refracting surface aided high-mobility communication. IEEE Trans. Wireless Commun. **21**(7), 4989–5003 (2022). https://doi.org/10.1109/TWC.2021. 3135685

28. Li, S., Duo, B., Yuan, X., Liang, Y.C., Di Renzo, M.: Reconfigurable intelligent surface assisted UAV communication: Joint trajectory design and passive beamforming. IEEE Wirel. Commun. Lett. **9**(5), 716–720 (2020). https://doi.org/10. 1109/LWC.2020.2966705

29. Bai, T., Pan, C., Deng, Y., Elkashlan, M., Nallanathan, A., Hanzo, L.: Latency minimization for intelligent reflecting surface aided mobile edge computing. IEEE J. Sel. Areas Commun. **38**(11), 2666–2682 (2020). https://doi.org/10.1109/JSAC. 2020.3007035

30. Liu, Z., Wang, K., Zhou, M.T., Shao, Z., Yang, Y.: Distributed task scheduling in heterogeneous fog networks: a matching with externalities method. In: 2020 International Conference on Computing, Networking and Communications (ICNC), pp. 620–625 (2020). https://doi.org/10.1109/ICNC47757.2020.9049775

31. Yang, Y., Zheng, B., Zhang, S., Zhang, R.: Intelligent reflecting surface meets OFDM: protocol design and rate maximization. IEEE Trans. Commun. **68**(7), 4522–4535 (2020). https://doi.org/10.1109/TCOMM.2020.2981458

32. Razaviyayn, M.: Successive convex approximation: analysis and applications (2014). https://api.semanticscholar.org/CorpusID:59834031

# Collaborative Task Processing and Resource Allocation Based on Multiple MEC Servers

Lei Shi[1,2], Shilong Feng[1,2(✉)], Rui Ji[1,2], Juan Xu[1,2], Xu Ding[1,3], and Baotong Zhan[4]

[1] School of Computer Science and Information Engineering,
Hefei University of Technology, Hefei 230009, China
fsl@mail.hfut.edu.cn
[2] Engineering Research Center of Safety Critical Industrial Measurement
and Control Technology, Ministry of Education, Hefei 230009, China
[3] Institute of Industry and Equipment Technology, Hefei University of Technology,
Hefei 230009, China
[4] Taian Hualu Metalforming Machine Tool Co., Ltd., Taian 271000, Shandong, China

**Abstract.** Mobile Edge Computing (MEC), an emerging computing paradigm, shifts computing and storage capabilities from the cloud to the network edge, aiming to meet the delay requirements of emerging applications and save backhaul network bandwidth. However, compared to cloud servers, MEC servers have limited computing and storage capabilities, which cannot meet the massive offloading demands of users during high-load periods. In this context, this paper proposes a multi-ENs collaborative task processing model. The model aims to formulate optimal offloading decisions and allocate computing resources for tasks to minimize system delay and cost. To solve this problem, we propose an online algorithm based on Lyapunov optimization called OKMTA, which can work online without the need for predicting future information. Specifically, the problem is formulated as a mixed-integer nonlinear programming (MINLP) problem and decomposed into two subproblems for solution. By using the Lagrange multiplier method to solve the computing resource allocation problem of tasks, and by using matching theory to solve the offloading decision problem of tasks. The simulation results show that our algorithm can achieve near-optimal delay performance while satisfying the long-term system average cost constraint.

**Keywords:** Mobile Edge Computing · Lyapunov Optimization · Collaborative Task Processing · Resource Allocation

## 1  Introduction

With the development of the Internet of Things(IoTs), an increasing number of resource-intensive tasks are being deployed on user devices, such as mobile

The work is supported by the Key Technology Research and Development Project of Hefei, NO. 2021GJ029.

H. Gao et al. (Eds.): CollaborateCom 2023, LNICST 561, pp. 385–402, 2024.
https://doi.org/10.1007/978-3-031-54521-4_21

games, video analysis, and virtual/augmented reality (VR/AR). However, the limited computing and storage resources of these devices are often difficult to meet the processing demands of user tasks [1]. Cloud computing becomes an effective solution for offloading tasks from local devices to remote clouds for processing. However, the large data transmission volume and long backhaul distances between users and remote clouds can lead to large communication overhead, resulting in prolonged system delay and high offloading cost [2].

To solve this problem, mobile edge computing (MEC) technology as a new computing paradigm has attracted much attention in academia [3,4]. By offloading tasks from terminal devices to nearby MEC servers, it provides users with low-delay and high-bandwidth services [5,6]. In [7], Ren et al. proposed a latency-optimized method for resource allocation, aiming to minimize the communication delay between mobile devices and MEC servers. Chen et al. discussed the problem of energy efficient dynamic offloading in MEC for internet of things, aiming to minimize the average transmission energy consumption and guarantee the performance of devices [8].

However, compared to remote cloud servers, MEC servers have limited communication and computing capabilities, which cannot satisfy a large number of offloading demands from users during high-load periods. Therefore, to effectively process tasks, the collaboration between cloud computing and edge computing has become a new research trend. Delay-sensitive tasks can be offloaded to the edge for processing, while delay-tolerant tasks can be offloaded to the remote cloud server for processing [9]. Concurrently, optimizing task offloading decisions and resource allocation to minimize task processing delay and cost has become a crucial aspect of cloud-edge collaborative processing for computing tasks [9–11]. Ren et al. proposed a cloud-edge collaborative computing framework, aiming to minimize task processing delay by combining remote cloud and edge resources [9]. In MEC networks with limited communication capabilities, [10] detailed a scheme for cloud-edge-end collaborative task offloading to improve system performance and user experience. Dai et al. considered the cooperation scenarios of cloud computing and MEC, and designed an iterative heuristic MEC resource allocation algorithm to solve the problem of multi-user computing offloading in [11]. However, the above articles only consider the scenario of collaborative task processing between a single MEC server and a remote cloud server, ignoring the collaboration among multiple MEC servers. Therefore, it is necessary to consider the collaboration among multiple MEC servers to allocate reasonable computing resources to users, thereby improving the quality of user experience [12,13]. Aiming at the problem of task offloading in vehicle edge computing networks, [14] proposed a load balancing scheme. Through the collaboration among multiple MEC servers and the cloud servers, tasks are jointly processed, thereby reducing task processing delay.

As one of the rapidly developing technologies, edge caching is getting more and more attention from people [15]. The edge caching technology can store different types of services that users require on MEC servers during off-peak periods, thereby reducing both the delay and energy consumption of user tasks

[16,17]. Recently, several studies have proposed to use edge caching technology in the MEC system to minimize task processing delay or energy consumption [18–20]. In [18], the authors proposed a cooperative content placement problem to minimize the delivery delay of location-based content and the service cost of two types of content. The authors proposed an energy-efficient task caching and offloading scheme in [19]. This scheme takes into account both the resource utilization of MEC servers and user experience. By storing part or all of the task data on the MEC server can improve task execution efficiency. [20] integrated three computing layers of vehicle, network edge and high-altitude platform station to build an intelligent transportation system framework. By considering the computing offloading strategy of the vehicle, planning the caching strategy of the basic data at the edge of the network, and coordinating resource scheduling to improve the delay performance of the application.

Due to the limited storage capacity of MEC server, it must store the services required by users while meeting the capacity constraints. This makes us still face huge challenges when solving the above problems. Some current research mainly focuses on a single MEC server for caching services to minimize task processing delay [21]. However, the research on mutual collaborative caching service among MEC servers is not deep enough. Therefore, we need to design a method for multiple MEC servers to collaborative service caching to meet task requests.

Against this background, we proposes a multiple servers collaborative task processing model. The aim is to minimize system delay and cost by making optimal offloading decisions and computing resources for tasks. The main contributions of this paper are as follows:

1) Under the constraint of satisfying the long-term average system cost, the system delay is minimized by making optimal offloading decisions and computing resources for tasks.
2) To solve the above problems, this paper based on Lyapunov optimization proposes an online algorithm(OKMTA), which is executed in an online manner without predicting future information.
3) By using the Lagrange multiplier method to solve the computing resource allocation problem of tasks, and by using matching theory to solve the offloading decision problem of tasks.
4) The simulation results show that the scheme proposed in this paper not only achieves the near-optimal delay effect, but also keeps the system cost low.

The rest of the paper is organized as follows: Section 2 presents the system model and formulates the optimization problem. Section 3 designs the OKMTA algorithm to solve the optimization problem. Section 4 compares the performance through simulation results. Finally, Sect. 5 concludes the paper.

## 2   System Model and Problem Formulation

In this section, we will introduce the system model. Suppose the whole network consists of one remote cloud server, multiple edge nodes (EN) and multiple users (as shown in Fig. 1). Suppose these users have many different types of task requests that need to be executed in the whole network. For each user's task request, it may need the execution of several services, which are stored on ENs and cloud servers. Suppose the cloud server has all services for all task requests, while for each EN, it randomly has part of these services. Based on the location feature, each user can only communicate with its associated EN, while ENs can communicate with each other. This means that when a user sends a task request to its associated EN, the required services may not be stored on this EN. Then this EN may need to send this request to other ENs or request downloading services from the cloud server. Our optimization goal is to minimize the system delay and system cost by formulating optimal offloading decisions and computing resources for task requests. Next, we will introduce the network and service models, communication model, computing model and system cost model in this paper, respectively.

## 2.1    Network and Service Models

Suppose there are $N$ ENs in the whole network, and denote $\mathcal{N}$ as the set of ENs. For each $EN_j(\in \mathcal{N})$, denote $B_j$, $F_j$ and $G_j$ as the communication resource, the calculation capability, and the storage capacity respectively. Suppose there are $K$ services in the whole network, and denote $\mathcal{K}$ as the set of services. Denote $c_k$ as the required storage space for service $k$. When initializing, each EN will randomly download services from the cloud server. Denote $\mathcal{K}_j$ as the service set of $EN_j$, we have

$$\sum_{k \subseteq \mathcal{K}_j} c_k \leq G_j. \tag{1}$$

Suppose there are $M$ users in the network model, and denote $\mathcal{M}$ as the set of users. For each user $i(\in \mathcal{M})$, it may have a computationally intensive task needed to be processed during the scheduling time. Denote $U_i$ as the task for user $i$, and we use the quadruple $\{D_i, C_i, K_i, T_i^{max}\}$ to represent resource requirements of $U_i$, where $D_i$ is the workload data volume, $C_i$ is the required computing resources, $K_i$ is the set of required services, and $T_i^{max}$ is the threshold of time delay.

## 2.2    Communication Model

Suppose we use the Orthogonal Frequency Division Multiple Access (OFDMA) technology for wireless communication, thus we can ignore the interference between users. Denote $R_{i,j}$ as the uplink transmission rate between user $i$ and $EN_j$, we have

$$R_{i,j} = B_j log_2(1 + \frac{p_{i,j} h_{i,j}}{\sigma^2}), \tag{2}$$

where $B_j$ is the available spectrum bandwidth, $p_{i,j}$ is the uplink transmission power, $\sigma^2$ is the noise power and $h_{i,j}$ is the state of the uplink channel between

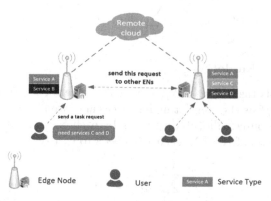

**Fig. 1.** Multi-ENs collaborative task processing model

user $i$ and $EN_j$. Denote $T_{i,j}^{up}$ as the uplink transmission delay for task $U_i$ to $EN_j$, we have

$$T_{i,j}^{up} = \frac{D_i}{R_{i,j}}. \tag{3}$$

In our scheduling scenario, we only consider the uplink transmission delay and thus ignore the downlink transmission delay.

Denote $x_{i,j}^t \in \{0,1\}$ as a binary decision variable on whether task $U_i$ is executed on associated $EN_j$ in time slot t. $x_{i,j}^t = 1$ means task $U_i$ is executed on the associated $EN_j$, otherwise $x_{i,j}^t = 0$.

Denote $z_{i,j,j'}^t \in \{0,1\}$ as a binary decision variable on whether task $U_i$ is executed on other $EN_{j'}$ in time slot t. $z_{i,j,j'}^t = 1$ means that task $U_i$ is sent to $EN_{j'}$ for execution, otherwise $z_{i,j,j'}^t = 0$. When the user $i$ sends task request to $EN_j$, $EN_j$ needs to send a task request to $EN_{j'}$ if $EN_j$ doesn't have the required service $k$. Based on this situation, $x_{i,j}^t = 0$ and $z_{i,j,j'}^t = 1$.

Denote $R_{i,j,j'}^{round}$ as the transmission rate of the task $U_i$ between $EN_j$ and $EN_{j'}$. Denote $T_{i,j,j'}^{round}$ as the round trip delay of task $U_i$ between $EN_j$ and $EN_{j'}$, we have

$$T_{i,j,j'}^{round} = \frac{D_i}{R_{i,j,j'}^{round}}. \tag{4}$$

When $EN_j$ executes task $U_i$, if the required service $k$ is missing, it needs to download this service from the cloud server to $EN_j$. Denote $R_{c,j}^{down}$ as the download rate between the cloud server and $EN_j$. Denote $T_{c,j}^{down}$ as the download delay for the required set of services from the cloud server to $EN_j$. We have

$$T_{c,j}^{down} = \sum_{k \in K_i \cap k \notin K_j} \frac{c_k}{R_{c,j}^{down}}. \tag{5}$$

Thus the total transmission delay mainly consists of three parts: uplink transmission delay, round trip delay and download delay. Denote $T_i^{trans}$ as the total transmission delay, we have

$$T_i^{trans} = T_{i,j}^{up} + x_{i,j}^t T_{c,j}^{down} + \sum_{j' \in \mathcal{N}} z_{i,j,j'}^t (1 - x_{i,j}^t)(T_{i,j,j'}^{round} + T_{c,j'}^{down}). \qquad (6)$$

## 2.3   Computing Model

When user $i$ sends task $U_i$ to $EN_j$, $EN_j$ will allocate computing resources for user $i$. Denote $f_{i,j}^{mec}$ as the computing resources allocated by $EN_j$ to user $i$. Since the computing resources allocated to users by each EN cannot exceed the total computing resources of the EN, each EN needs to satisfy

$$\sum_{i=1}^{M_j} f_{i,j}^{mec} \le F_j, \qquad (7)$$

where $M_j$ is all users who execute tasks in $EN_j$. Denote $T_{i,j}^{exe}$ as the computing delay for $EN_j$ to execute task $U_i$, we have

$$T_{i,j}^{exe} = \frac{C_i}{f_{i,j}^{mec}}. \qquad (8)$$

Denote $T_i^{exe}$ as the computing delay for EN to execute task $U_i$, we have

$$T_i^{exe} = x_{i,j}^t T_{i,j}^{exe} + \sum_{j' \in \mathcal{N}} z_{i,j,j'}^t (1 - x_{i,j}^t) T_{i,j,j'}^{exe}. \qquad (9)$$

The total delay mainly consists of transmission delay and computing delay. Thus denote $T_i^t$ as the total delay for EN to execute task $U_i$, we have

$$T_i^t = T_i^{trans} + T_i^{exe} \qquad (10)$$

## 2.4   System Cost Model

User renting EN resources to execute task will incur additional costs, mainly including communication, computing, and storage costs. The communication cost is the overhead generated by the bandwidth resource used for data transmission between the user and the EN, determined by the transmission energy consumption. The computing cost is the overhead incurred in executing task in EN, determined by the amount of task data. The storage cost is the cost of using EN and remote cloud storage services, which is determined by the storage resources occupied by the services. Furthermore, denote $Q_i^{avg}$ as the long-term average system cost for user $i$. Denote $Q_i^t$ as the system cost incurred by user $i$ renting the resource of EN in time slot $t$. We have

$$Q_i^t = \frac{\alpha_j p_{i,j} D_i}{B_j log_2(1 + \frac{p_{i,j} h_{i,j}}{\sigma^2})} + \beta_j C_i + \sum_{k \subseteq K_i} \nu_j c_k + \sum_{k \subseteq K_i} \mu_c c_k, \qquad (11)$$

where $\alpha_j$ and $\beta_j$ are the unit cost of energy consumption and task execution in $EN_j$ respectively. $\nu_j$ and $\mu_c$ are the unit cost of the storage service in $EN_j$ and cloud server respectively.

## 2.5  Problem Formulation

In this section, we formulate multiple ENs collaborative processing and resource allocation problem for tasks. Minimize system delay and keep cost low by designing optimal solution. Based on the previous discussion, we can express the problem as follows:

$$
\mathbf{P1}: \min_{x^t, z^t, f^t} \lim_{T \to \infty} \frac{1}{T} \sum_{t=0}^{T-1} \left( \sum_{i=1}^{M} T_i^t \right)
$$

$$
\text{s.t. } C1: \lim_{T \to \infty} \frac{1}{T} \sum_{t=0}^{T-1} Q_i^t \le Q_i^{avg}
$$

$$
C2: T_i^t \le T_i^{max}
$$

$$
C3: \sum_{k \subseteq \mathcal{K}_j} c_k \le G_j \tag{12}
$$

$$
C4: f_{i,j}^{mec} > 0
$$

$$
C5: \sum_{i=1}^{M_j} f_{i,j}^{mec} \le F_j
$$

$$
C6: x_i^t \in \{0,1\}
$$

$$
C7: z_{i,j,j'}^t \in \{0,1\}
$$

Constraint C1 represents the long-term average system cost threshold for each user. Constraint C2 is the maximum threshold constraint imposed on the total delay of executing tasks. Constraint C3 is the constraint that the storage space of EN is limited. Constraint C4 and C5 are the computing resource constraints allocated by EN to tasks. Constraints C6 and C7 represent binary offloading decision variable constraints that determine whether the task is executed on the associated EN or $EN_{j'}$ respectively.

Through the analysis of the above problems, we can conclude that $\mathbf{P1}$ is a mixed-integer nonlinear programming problem. It contains constraints of two discrete binary variables and continuous variables C4-C5, making the problem an NP-hard problem. Therefore, it is impractical to solve $\mathbf{P1}$ directly. In addition, solving $\mathbf{P1}$ requires a large amount of future network state information, but predicting such future information is difficult or even impossible. Therefore, in the absence of complete information, it is necessary to propose an online optimization algorithm to solve the problem.

## 3  An Online Optimization Algorithm

To solve $\mathbf{P1}$ efficiently, we propose an online distributed optimization algorithm (OKMTA for short). The algorithm mainly includes two parts: (1). Based on Lyapunov optimization, we propose an online algorithm to reformulate $\mathbf{P1}$, decomposing the long-term optimization problem into a series of one-slot optimization problems. (2). For the one-slot optimization problem, we propose a distributed solution based on Lagrange multiplier method and matching theory.

## 3.1   Restate the Problem by Lyapunov Optimization

The idea of Lyapunov optimization is to decompose an optimization problem with long-term constraints into each time slot. And then we can directly optimize the problem in each time slot while ensuring the stability of the system [22]. Denote $q(t) = \{q_1(t), q_2(t), ..., q_i(t)\}$ as a virtual cost queue and set the initial value to 0 for solving the long-term average cost constraint. The virtual cost queue constructed for user $i$ can be expressed as

$$q_i(t+1) = max\{q_i(t) + Q_i^t - Q_i^{avg}, 0\}, \tag{13}$$

where $q_i(t)$ is the queue backlog of time slot $t$, representing the deviation between the system cost and the threshold under the current time slot $t$.

To stabilize $q(t)$, we denote $L(q(t)) = \frac{1}{2}\sum_{i=1}^{M} q_i^2(t)$ as quadratic Lyapunov function, representing the "congestion level" of the virtual cost queue length [23]. A small value of $L(q(t))$ means that the backlog of all virtual cost queues is small, so that the stability of all queues can be achieved. However, it is impractical to keep $L(q(t))$ small all the time. Therefore, to solve this problem, we further denote $\Delta(q(t))$ as a one-slot Lyapunov drift to keep the Lyapunov function low and thus keep the queue stable. we have

$$\Delta(q(t)) = \mathbb{E}[L(q(t+1)) - L(q(t))|q(t)], \tag{14}$$

where $\Delta(q(t))$ represents the change of the virtual cost queue within a single time slot in the Lyapunov function. We define a drift-plus-penalty function that integrates system delay and virtual cost queue stability via (15).

$$\Delta(q(t)) + V\mathbb{E}[\sum_{i=1}^{M} T_i^t|q(t)], \tag{15}$$

where V is a non-negative parameter controlling the trade-off between system delay and cost. The following **Lemma** 1 provides an upper bound on the drift plus penalty function.

**Lemma 1:** For all possible optimization variables satisfying C2-C7, there is an upper bound for the drift-plus-penalty function [24], as shown in (16). Where B is a constant, $B = \frac{1}{2}\sum_{i=1}^{M}(Q_i^{max} - Q_i^{avg})^2$. Where $Q_i^{max}$ is the upper bound of the one slot virtual cost for user $i$.

$$\Delta(q(t)) + V\mathbb{E}[\sum_{i=1}^{M} T_i^t|q(t)] \leq B + V\mathbb{E}[\sum_{i=1}^{M} T_i^t|q(t)] + \mathbb{E}[\sum_{i=1}^{M} q_i(t)(Q_i^t - Q_i^{avg})|q(t)]$$
$$\tag{16}$$

According to **Lemma** 1, our goal is to minimize the expression on the right side of (16) to determine the upper bound of the drift-plus-penalty function. This will help us transform the long-term optimization problem **P1** into a one-slot optimization problem **P2**. The offloading decision and resource allocation problems of tasks are determined by solving **P2**.

$$\textbf{P2}: \min_{x^t, z^t, f^t} \sum_{i=1}^{M} VT_i^t + q_i(t)Q_i^t \tag{17}$$

Algorithm 1 describes the implementation process of OKMTA algorithm. The algorithm runs online, using real-time network information and the current backlog status of the queue as input, and solves **P1** by solving the approximate optimal solution of **P2**. At each time slot $t$, by solving for **P2** we can obtain the values of the variables $x^t, z^t, f^t$. At the same time, each virtual cost queue is also updated for calculation in the next time slot.

---

**Algorithm 1:** OKMTA Algorithm
___

**Input:** $\mathcal{M}$: the set of users, $\mathcal{N}$: the set of ENs, task $U_i$, the set of services, non-negative parameter V and q(0)=0

**Output:** The offloading decisions $x^t, z^t$ and the computing resource $f^t$ for task for each time slot $t$

1 **for** $t = 0$ to $T\text{-}1$ **do**
2     According to Algorithm 2 and 3, the values of $x^t, z^t, f^t$ for each time slot $t$ are obtained.
3     Update the q(t+1) according to (13).
4     t = t + 1.
5 **end**

---

We can observe that (17) is a joint optimization problem. They are mutually constrained when the conditions are satisfied, so it is difficult to use mathematical methods to solve **P2**. The offloading decisions $x^t$ and $z^t$ are binary variables, and the computing resource $f^t$ is a continuous variable, so **P2** is a mixed-integer nonlinear programming problem. We can decompose the original problem **P2** into two sub-problems to solve: (1). Under the given conditions of $x^t$ and $z^t$, use the Lagrange multiplier method to solve the allocation problem of computing resources $f^t$. (2). On the basis of obtaining the $f^t$ solution, the optimal solutions of $x^t$ and $z^t$ are obtained by bilaterally matching the task set and the EN set. By alternately solving these two subproblems, we can gradually optimize **P2** and find the optimal solution finally.

### 3.2 Distributed Optimization Algorithm in Each Time Slot

**The Optimal Computing Resource Allocation.** When user $i$ sends a task $U_i$ to EN, assuming $x^t$ and $z^t$ are already given, we will ignore variables unrelated to $f^t$ in the optimization objective function. Therefore, we can express the optimization problem for allocating computing resources to tasks as follows:

$$\mathbf{P3} : \min_{f^t} F_1(f_{i,j}^{mec}) = \sum_{i=1}^{M} \frac{C_i}{f_{i,j}^{mec}}$$

$$\text{s.t. } C4 : f_{i,j}^{mec} > 0 \tag{18}$$

$$C5 : \sum_{i=1}^{M_j} f_{i,j}^{mec} \leq F_j$$

In order to prove that **P3** is a convex problem, we take the second derivative of $F_1(f_{i,j}^{mec})$ with respect to $f_{i,j}^{mec}$. we have

$$\frac{\partial^2 F_1(f_{i,j}^{mec})}{\partial(f_{i,j}^{mec})^2} = \frac{2C_i}{(f_{i,j}^{mec})^3}. \tag{19}$$

Due to constraint C4, we have $\frac{\partial^2 F_1(f_{i,j}^{mec})}{\partial(f_{i,j}^{mec})^2} > 0$, so **P3** is a convex problem. Therefore, the Lagrangian function can be used to solve **P3**. We have

$$L(f,\lambda) = \sum_{i=1}^{M} \frac{C_i}{f_{i,j}^{mec}} + \lambda(\sum_{i=1}^{M_j} f_{i,j}^{mec} - F_j), \tag{20}$$

where $\lambda$ is a non-negative Lagrangian multiplier associated with the computing resource constraints of EN. Then we use the Karush-Kuhn-Tucker (KKT) condition to obtain the optimal computing resource allocation $f^*$ [25]. Thus the partial derivative of (20) with respect to $f_{i,j}^{mec}$ is given as

$$\frac{\partial L(f,\lambda)}{\partial f_{i,j}^{mec}} = -\frac{C_i}{(f_{i,j}^{mec})^2} + \lambda. \tag{21}$$

Based on the KKT condition, we can obtain the approximate optimal solution of (21), we have

$$f^* = \sqrt{\frac{C_i}{\lambda}}. \tag{22}$$

Then we can obtain the optimal computing resource allocation scheme $f^*$ based on Algorithm 2.

**The Optimal Task Offloading Decisions.** Then we need to further transform **P2** into a problem of how to optimize the offloading decisions of task to reduce system delay and cost when the computing resource $f^*$ is determined. Therefore, we can express the problem as follows:

$$\mathbf{P4} : \min_{x^t, z^t} F_2(x_{i,j}^t, z_{i,j,j'}^t)$$

$$\text{s.t. } C2 - C7 \tag{23}$$

---

**Algorithm 2:** Optimal Computing Resource Allocation Algorithm

---

**Input:** $\mathcal{M}$: the set of users, $\mathcal{N}$: the set of ENs, task $U_i$, Maximum tolerance $\zeta = 1 \times 10^{-8}$, $\lambda_{min} = 0$ and $\lambda_{max} = 1$

**Output:** The optimal computing resource allocation $f^*$

1 **for** *all users* $i \in \mathcal{M}$ **do**
2     **while** $\lambda_{max} - \lambda_{min} > \zeta$ **do**
3        Denote $\lambda = (\lambda_{max} + \lambda_{min})/2$.
4        Compute $f^*$ according to substitute $\lambda$ into (22).
5        If $\sum_{i=1}^{M_j} f_{i,j}^{mec} < F_j$, update $\lambda_{max} = \lambda$, otherwise update $\lambda_{min} = \lambda$
6     **end**
7     $f^*$ can be obtained by substituting $\lambda$ into (22).
8 **end**

---

$$
F_2(x_{i,j}^t, z_{i,j,j'}^t) = \sum_{i=1}^{M} V[T_{i,j}^{up} + x_{i,j}^t(\frac{C_i}{f_{i,j}^*} + T_{c,j}^{down}) +
$$
$$
\sum_{j' \in \mathcal{N}} z_{i,j,j'}^t(1 - x_{i,j}^t)(\frac{C_i}{f_{i,j'}^*} + T_{i,j,j'}^{round} + T_{c,j'}^{down})] + q_i(t)Q_i^t \tag{24}
$$

To effectively solve **P4**, we propose a task offloading algorithm based on matching theory. This algorithm views the problem of task offloading as a two-sided many-to-one matching problem, aiming to find a stable optimal matching between task set and EN set. By establishing a stable two-sided matching, it can ensure that the task in the current matching can obtain the maximum system utility. When no "blocking pairs" are found during the matching process, the matching is considered stable [26].

In this paper, user tends to offload task to EN with required services and sufficient computing resources, while EN tends to process tasks with less demanding computing resources. To simplify the description, we denote $\mathcal{U}$ as a set of tasks and denote $\mathcal{N}$ as a set of ENs, which are two disjoint players. Then we need to match $\mathcal{U}$ and $\mathcal{N}$. Tasks can only select one EN for processing, and each EN can process multiple tasks. Denote $H(x)$ as the matching function between $U_i \in \mathcal{U}$ and $EN_j \in \mathcal{N}$. It needs to satisfy the following conditions: (1). $H(U_i) \in \mathcal{N}, \forall U_i \in \mathcal{U}$ means that any task matches any EN in the set $\mathcal{N}$. (2). $H(EN_j) \in \mathcal{U}, \forall j \in \mathcal{N}$ means that $\mathcal{U}$ contains any task processed by any EN in the set $\mathcal{N}$. (3). $H(EN_j) = U_i \Leftrightarrow H(U_i) \in EN_j$ means that the task $U_i$ to $EN_j$ processing is equivalent to $EN_j$ processing of tasks including $U_i$, but not only processing a task $U_i$. If there is a current matching $H$, the offloading decision of the task can be determined as

$$
x_{i,j}^t = \begin{cases} 1 , & \text{if } H(EN_j) = U_i; \\ 0 , & \text{otherwise.} \end{cases} \tag{25}
$$

$$z_{i,j,j'}^{t} = \begin{cases} 1, & \text{if } H(EN_{j'}) = U_i \text{ and } x_{i,j}^t = 0, \ j \neq j'; \\ 0, & \text{otherwise.} \end{cases} \quad (26)$$

Each player can build a preference list with other players by defining a utility function that is inversely proportional to the sum of the system's total delay and cost [27]. Then the utility function of EN for task $U_i$ can be expressed as

$$SU_{U_i}(EN_j) = \frac{1}{F_2(x_{i,j}^t, z_{i,j,j'}^t)}. \quad (27)$$

If there is the following definition $SU_{U_i}(EN_{j_1}) > SU_{U_i}(EN_{j_2})$, it means that the task $U_i$ prefers to be processed in $EN_{j_1}$ rather than in $EN_{j_2}$.

---

**Algorithm 3:** Based on Matching Theory Task Offloading Algorithm

---

**Input:** $\mathcal{M}$: the set of users, $\mathcal{U}$: the set of tasks, $\mathcal{N}$: the set of ENs and the set of services

**Output:** All tasks optimal offloading decisions $x^t$ and $z^t$

1　**Initialize Phase:**
2　All users and associated ENs are initialized to construct a matching $H$ that satisfies all constraints C2-C7.
3　Calculate the system utility under the current matching pair according to (27).
4　**Matching Phase:**
5　**while** *there exists unstable matching* **do**
6　　**if** *$EN_{j'}$ exists the services required by $U_i$* **then**
7　　　Obtain the parameters of $EN_{j'}$.
8　　　Calculate system utility of user $i$ to $EN_{j'}$.
9　　　**if** $SU_{U_i}(EN_j) < SU_{U_i}(EN_{j'})$ **then**
10　　　　$EN_{j'}$ accepts the matching request and calculates the system utility of user $i$ according to (27).
11　　　　If constraints C2-C7 can not be satisfied, user $i$ will be re-matched.
12　　　**end**
13　　**else**
14　　　　$EN_{j'}$ rejects matching request of user $i$, and user $i$ sends matching requests to other ENs.
15　　**end**
16　**end**
17　**end**
18　The system unility does not change, that is, tasks and ENs achieve an optimal and stable matching $H$.
19　According to the matching results and (25)-(26), we can obtain the optimal offloading decisions $x^t$ and $z^t$ of all tasks.

---

Based on the above definition of matching theory, we propose Algorithm 3 to solve **P4**. The algorithm includes two phases: an initialization phase and a matching phase. In the initialization phase, all users are matched with associated ENs and calculate the system utility. In the matching phase, all users continuously search for available ENs to process their tasks and establish stable matching relationships with ENs. If task $U_i$ has low system utility with the currently matched EN, user $i$ will send a matching request to other ENs. When other ENs receive this matching request, they calculate the system utility and make corresponding matching decisions: (1). If the EN accepts task $U_i$ to improve the system utility, it accepts the matching request of user $i$. (2). Otherwise, it rejects matching request of user $i$. If user $i$'s matching request is rejected by the EN, user $i$ will send a matching request to the next available EN. When no user initiates a matching request in the matching phase, the matching phase ends. During each round of matching between tasks and ENs, both parties can achieve stable matching with the maximum system utility. Finally, according to the matching results satisfying all the constraints, the optimal offloading decisions of all tasks can be obtained.

## 4    Simulation Results

In this section, we evaluate the performance of the proposed OKMTA algorithm through simulation results.

### 4.1    Simulation Setting

In the scenario of multi-ENs collaborative task processing, we can set the following parameters for simulation experiments. The coverage area size is 500m × 500m, in which there are 10 users and 4 ENs randomly distributed. The wireless channel gain from user $i$ to $EN_j$ can be expressed as $h_{i,j} = d_{i,j}^{-\vartheta}$, where $d_{i,j}$ denotes the distance between the user $i$ and the associated $EN_j$, the path loss factor $\vartheta = 4$, the noise power $\sigma^2$ is set to -100dBm, and the transmission power for user $i$ is set to $p_{i,j} = 30$dBm [28]. Considering the heterogeneity of EN, the channel bandwidth $B_j$, storage capacity $G_j$, and computing resources $F_j$ of $EN_j$ are set to [8, 12] MHz, [5, 10]GB, [30, 60]GHz respectively. The input data size $D_i$ of the task $U_i$ is set to [30, 50]MB [29]. The number of CPU cycles required to execute each bit task is set to 1200. To process tasks, various resources of EN need to be rented. The communication unit cost $\alpha_j$ and the execution unit cost $\beta_j$ of the task are set to $[2 \times 10^{-4}, 3 \times 10^{-4}]$ unit/J, $[0.4 \times 10^{-7}, 0.8 \times 10^{-7}]$ unit/bit respectively. The unit cost of the storage service on the remote cloud server and EN is set to [1.0, 1.2] unit and [0.54, 0.6] unit respectively [30].

Next, we conduct a performance research on the OKMTA algorithm proposed in this paper. We use 500 time slots for evaluation, and the time interval of each time slot is set to 10ms. Additionally, we introduce three benchmark algorithms to evaluate the algorithmic performance of OKMTA algorithm: (1). Non-Collaborative EN Processing Algorithm (NCEPA): ENs within the coverage area process tasks independently, and there is no collaborative relationship between them. Tasks can only be processed in their associated EN. (2). Optimal System Delay Processing Algorithm (OSDPA): When processing tasks, it only considers reducing system delay, without considering system cost constraints. (3). Random Processing Algorithm: tasks can be randomly offloaded to any EN for processing.

## 4.2  Performance Comparison

Figure 2 and 3 respectively show the average delay and cost performance of 4 ENs processing 10 tasks in the case of V = 4. As can be seen from the following two figures, the OKMTA algorithm achieves near-optimal delay performance while satisfying the long-term cost constraint. Although the OSDPA algorithm performs best in terms of delay performance, it can be clearly seen in Fig. 3 that using the OSDPA algorithm for task processing results in higher costs. In comparison, the random algorithm assigns tasks randomly to any EN without considering specific resource requirements, leading to inferior delay and cost performance. In addition, in the NCEPA algorithm, EN processes task requests sent by users independently, without considering the mutual collaboration relationship between ENs, resulting in poor overall system delay performance.

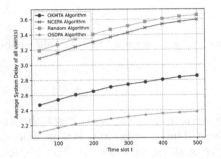 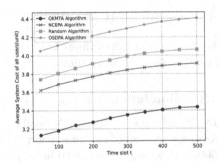

**Fig. 2.** Average system delay of all users      **Fig. 3.** Average system cost of all users

## 4.3  The Effect of Parameter V on System Performance

Figure 4 and 5 show the average system delay and cost of processing 10 tasks for OKMTA and OSDPA algorithms with different parameters V, respectively. It can be seen from Fig. 4 that as the parameter V increases, the average system delay of the OKMTA algorithm decreases significantly, and gradually approaches the optimal processing delay of the system. It can be seen from Fig. 5 that with the increase of the parameter V, the average system cost of the OKMTA algorithm gradually increases, and finally remains at a level lower than the cost of OSDPA algorithm. But the OSDPA algorithm achieves the best system delay at a higher system cost. The above two figures verify that the parameter V can flexibly adjust the trade-off between system delay and cost, and different parameters V can be set according to different situations to meet the needs of the system. Considering the long-term cost constraints, our algorithm outperforms the OSDPA algorithm.

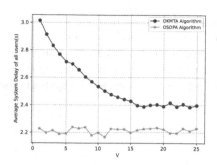
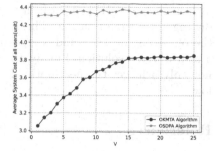

**Fig. 4.** The impact of different V        **Fig. 5.** The impact of different V

## 4.4 The Effect of the Number of Users on System Performance

Figure 6 and 7 show the total system delay and cost when using different schemes to process tasks with different numbers of users, respectively. As the number of tasks increases, system delay and cost increase for all scenarios. Specifically, the OSDPA algorithm achieves the lowest system delay, followed by our OKMTA algorithm with slightly higher system delay, while the NCEPA and random algorithms result in the highest system delay. Additionally, from Fig. 7, it can be observed that our algorithm has the lowest system cost. Although the OSDPA algorithm maintains low system delay, its cost is the highest, indicating that this algorithm consumes significant system cost to achieve the best system delay. In summary, under the condition that the constraints are satisfied, our algorithm closely approaches optimal system delay while maintaining lower system cost.

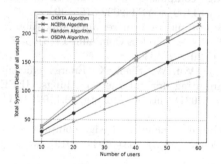
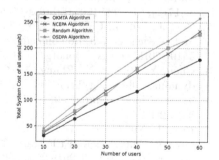

**Fig. 6.** System delay with different $M$        **Fig. 7.** System cost with different $M$

## 5 Conclusion

In this paper, we propose a multi-ENs collaborative task processing model. It mainly studies the collaborative task processing among multiple ENs, making optimal offloading decisions and computing resources for tasks to minimize system delay and cost. To solve this problem, we propose an online optimization algorithm (i.e., OKMTA), which is executed in an online manner without predicting future information. The algorithm is mainly used to jointly optimize the offloading decision and computing resource allocation of tasks, and obtain a near-optimal solution. Finally, the simulation results show that our algorithm not only achieves the near-optimal delay effect, but also keeps the system cost low.

# References

1. Elgendy, I.A., Zhang, W.-Z., Zeng, Y., He, H., Tian, Y.-C., Yang, Y.: Efficient and secure multi-user multi-task computation offloading for mobile-edge computing in mobile IoT networks. IEEE Trans. Netw. Serv. Manage. **17**(4), 2410–2422 (2020). https://doi.org/10.1109/TNSM.2020.3020249
2. El Haber, E., Nguyen, T.M., Assi, C.: Joint optimization of computational cost and devices energy for task offloading in multi-tier edge-clouds. IEEE Trans. Commun. **67**(5), 3407–3421 (2019). https://doi.org/10.1109/TCOMM.2019.2895040
3. Zhao, M., et al.: Energy-aware task offloading and resource allocation for time-sensitive services in mobile edge computing systems. IEEE Trans. Veh. Technol. **70**(10), 10925–10940 (2021). https://doi.org/10.1109/TVT.2021.3108508
4. Li, Q., Wang, S., Zhou, A., Ma, X., Yang, F., Liu, A.X.: QoS driven task offloading with statistical guarantee in mobile edge computing. IEEE Trans. Mob. Comput. **21**(1), 278–290 (2022). https://doi.org/10.1109/TMC.2020.3004225
5. Chen, Y., Zhang, N., Zhang, Y., Chen, X., Wu, W., Shen, X.S.: TOFFEE: task offloading and frequency scaling for energy efficiency of mobile devices in mobile edge computing. IEEE Trans. Cloud Comput. **9**(4), 1634–1644 (2021). https://doi.org/10.1109/TCC.2019.2923692
6. Zhou, T., Yue, Y., Qin, D., Nie, X., Li, X., Li, C.: Mobile device association and resource allocation in HCNs with mobile edge computing and caching. IEEE Syst. J. **17**(1), 976–987 (2023). https://doi.org/10.1109/JSYST.2022.3157590
7. Ren, J., Yu, G., Cai, Y., He, Y.: Latency optimization for resource allocation in mobile-edge computation offloading. IEEE Trans. Wireless Commun. **17**(8), 5506–5519 (2018). https://doi.org/10.1109/TWC.2018.2845360
8. Chen, Y., Zhang, N., Zhang, Y., Chen, X., Wu, W., Shen, X.: Energy efficient dynamic offloading in mobile edge computing for internet of things. IEEE Trans. Cloud Comput. **9**(3), 1050–1060 (2021). https://doi.org/10.1109/TCC.2019.2898657
9. Ren, J., Yu, G., He, Y., Li, G.Y.: Collaborative cloud and edge computing for latency minimization. IEEE Trans. Veh. Technol. **68**(5), 5031–5044 (2019). https://doi.org/10.1109/TVT.2019.2904244
10. Kai, C., Zhou, H., Yi, Y., Huang, W.: Collaborative cloud-edge-end task offloading in mobile-edge computing networks with limited communication capability. IEEE Trans. Cogn. Commun. Netw. **7**(2), 624–634 (2021). https://doi.org/10.1109/TCCN.2020.3018159
11. Dai, Y., Xu, D., Maharjan, S., Zhang, Y.: Joint computation offloading and user association in multi-task mobile edge computing. IEEE Trans. Veh. Technol. **67**(12), 12313–12325 (2018). https://doi.org/10.1109/TVT.2018.2876804
12. Xu, X., et al.: Secure service offloading for internet of vehicles in SDN-enabled mobile edge computing. IEEE Trans. Intell. Transp. Syst. **22**(6), 3720–3729 (2021). https://doi.org/10.1109/TITS.2020.3034197

13. Zhou, J., Zhang, X.: Fairness-aware task offloading and resource allocation in cooperative mobile-edge computing. IEEE Internet Things J. **9**(5), 3812–3824 (2022). https://doi.org/10.1109/JIOT.2021.3100253

14. Zhang, J., Guo, H., Liu, J., Zhang, Y.: Task offloading in vehicular edge computing networks: a load-balancing solution. IEEE Trans. Veh. Technol. **69**(2), 2092–2104 (2020). https://doi.org/10.1109/TVT.2019.2959410

15. Xia, X., et al.: OL-MEDC: an online approach for cost-effective data caching in mobile edge computing systems. IEEE Trans. Mob. Comput. **22**(3), 1646–1658 (2023). https://doi.org/10.1109/TMC.2021.3107918

16. Zhang, F., Han, G., Liu, L., Martinez-Garcia, M., Peng, Y.: Joint optimization of cooperative edge caching and radio resource allocation in 5G-enabled massive IoT networks. IEEE Internet Things J. **8**(18), 14156–14170 (2021). https://doi.org/10.1109/JIOT.2021.3068427

17. Song, C., Xu, W., Wu, T., Yu, S., Zeng, P., Zhang, N.: QoE-driven edge caching in vehicle networks based on deep reinforcement learning. IEEE Trans. Veh. Technol. **70**(6), 5286–5295 (2021). https://doi.org/10.1109/TVT.2021.3077072

18. Chen, J., Wu, H., Yang, P., Lyu, F., Shen, X.: Cooperative edge caching with location-based and popular contents for vehicular networks. IEEE Trans. Veh. Technol. **69**(9), 10291–10305 (2020). https://doi.org/10.1109/TVT.2020.3004720

19. Gupta, D., Moudgil, A., Wadhwa, S., Solanki, V.: Efficient data caching and computation offloading strategy for edge network. In: 2022 International Conference on Emerging Smart Computing and Informatics (ESCI), Pune, India, pp. 1–5 (2022). https://doi.org/10.1109/ESCI53509.2022.9758379

20. Ren, Q., Abbasi, O., Kurt, G.K., Yanikomeroglu, H., Chen, J.: Caching and computation offloading in high altitude platform station (HAPS) assisted intelligent transportation systems. IEEE Trans. Wireless Commun. **21**(11), 9010–9024 (2022). https://doi.org/10.1109/TWC.2022.3171824

21. Ning, Z., et al.: Intelligent edge computing in internet of vehicles: a joint computation offloading and caching solution. IEEE Trans. Intell. Transp. Syst. **22**(4), 2212–2225 (2021). https://doi.org/10.1109/TITS.2020.2997832

22. Tang, C., Zhu, C., Wu, H., Li, Q., Rodrigues, J.J.: Toward response time minimization considering energy consumption in caching-assisted vehicular edge computing. IEEE Internet Things J. **9**(7), 5051–5064 (2022). https://doi.org/10.1109/JIOT.2021.3108902

23. Xia, X., Chen, F., He, Q., Grundy, J., Abdelrazek, M., Jin, H.: Online collaborative data caching in edge computing. IEEE Trans. Parallel Distrib. Syst. **32**(2), 281–294 (2021). https://doi.org/10.1109/TPDS.2020.3016344

24. Chen, W., Wang, D., Li, K.: Multi-user multi-task computation offloading in green mobile edge cloud computing. IEEE Trans. Serv. Comput. **12**(5), 726–738 (2019). https://doi.org/10.1109/TSC.2018.2826544

25. Zhao, J., Li, Q., Gong, Y., Zhang, K.: Computation offloading and resource allocation for cloud assisted mobile edge computing in vehicular networks. IEEE Trans. Veh. Technol. **68**(8), 7944–7956 (2019). https://doi.org/10.1109/TVT.2019.2917890

26. Chen, D., et al.: Matching-theory-based low-latency scheme for multitask federated learning in MEC networks. IEEE Internet Things J. **8**(14), 11415–11426 (2021). https://doi.org/10.1109/JIOT.2021.3053283

27. Wu, H., et al.: Delay-minimized edge caching in heterogeneous vehicular networks: a matching-based approach. IEEE Trans. Wireless Commun. **19**(10), 6409–6424 (2020). https://doi.org/10.1109/TWC.2020.3003339

28. Feng, H., Guo, S., Yang, L., Yang, Y.: Collaborative data caching and computation offloading for multi-service mobile edge computing. IEEE Trans. Veh. Technol. **70**(9), 9408–9422 (2021). https://doi.org/10.1109/TVT.2021.3099303

29. Xu, J., Chen, L., Zhou, P.: Joint service caching and task offloading for mobile edge computing in dense networks. In: IEEE INFOCOM 2018 - IEEE Conference on Computer Communications, Honolulu, HI, USA, pp. 207–215 (2018). https://doi.org/10.1109/INFOCOM.2018.8485977

30. Zhao, J., Sun, X., Li, Q., Ma, X.: Edge caching and computation management for real-time internet of vehicles: an online and distributed approach. IEEE Trans. Intell. Transp. Syst. **22**(4), 2183–2197 (2021). https://doi.org/10.1109/TITS.2020.3012966

# Collaborative Cloud-Edge Computing with Mixed Wireless and Wired Backhaul Links: Joint Task Offloading and Resource Allocation

Daqing Zhang and Haifeng Sun$^{(\boxtimes)}$ (iD)

School of Computer Science and Technology, Southwest University of Science and Technology, Mianyang 621010, China
dr_hfsun@163.com

**Abstract.** Mobile Edge Computing (MEC) is a promising technology that provides computing services at the edge of wireless networks to reduce the latency and the energy consumption for Smart Mobile Devices (SMDs). Additionally, the Ultra-Dense Network (UDN) will play a key role in providing high transmission capacity for SMDs in 5G networks. In order to improve the edge cloud efficiency within limited communication and computing resources, this paper proposes a joint task offloading and resource allocation scheme collaborated between cloud computing and edge computing in the UDN. Since wireless backhaul is more economical than expensive wired backhaul deployments, we consider the mixed deployment of either wired or wireless backhaul between each Small Base Station (SBS) and the Macro Base Station (MBS) in UDN scenarios, then formulate an optimization problem to minimize the system-wide computation overhead, and apply the Linear Decreasing Weight Particle Swarm Optimization (LDWPSO) algorithm to solve the problem. Numerical experiments validate the effectiveness of our proposed scheme compared to other baseline schemes.

**Keywords:** Mobile Edge Computing · Ultra-Dense Network · task offloading · resource allocation · wireless backhaul

## 1 Introduction

With the rapid development of mobile communications and the Internet, the fifth generation (5G) communication technology has now entered the stage of full commercial deployment. The explosive growth of mobile data traffic, coupled with computation-intensive and delay-sensitive applications like augmented reality, face recognition and interactive games, poses a significant challenge for smart mobile devices (SMDs) with limited computation resources and battery capacity [1]. Traditionally, remote cloud centers have been relied upon to offload

This work was supported in part by NSFC of China under Grant 62261051.

H. Gao et al. (Eds.): CollaborateCom 2023, LNICST 561, pp. 403–420, 2024.
https://doi.org/10.1007/978-3-031-54521-4_22

resource-intensive applications from SMDs due to their high computing and storage capabilities. However, numerous SMDs and tremendous traffic load can result in network congestion and high latency. To address these challenges, the European Telecommunications Standards Institute (ETSI) proposed Mobile Edge Computing (MEC) to deploy cloud computing services at the edge of the mobile access network, allowing mobile devices to efficiently offload computing tasks to MEC servers deployed at wireless access points or base stations for quick response [4].

While MEC effectively reduces traffic pressure on the core network, the computing and storage capabilities of MEC become the main bottleneck compared to cloud computing. To address this challenge, a layered collaborative cloud-edge architecture can be adopted, where non-computing-intensive tasks are processed at edge servers to achieve high energy efficiency and low latency, while computing-intensive tasks are offloaded to cloud servers to utilize richer computing resources. Effective collaboration between the cloud and the edge is crucial for improving system performance [11].

The Ultra-Dense Network (UDN) is a dense network deployment that can provide wide-area coverage of local hotspots and enhance system capacity to achieve low latency and high reliability [7]. In the UDN, a large number of low-cost and low-power Small Base Stations (SBSs) for better wireless access links are deployed. Computing tasks generated from SMDs can be transmitted to the SBS through wireless access links, and continue to be transmitted to the Macro Base Station (MBS) integrated with an MEC server through either wired or wireless backhaul links. While wired backhaul links usually offer higher reliability and data transmission rates compared to wireless backhaul links, practical considerations such as difficulty in deployment and high maintenance costs must also be taken into account. Therefore, the choice of backhaul links depends on a variety of factors including the service requirements of mobile users, traffic load intensity, and the cost of building the backhaul links [10]. In scenarios where installing fiber optic backhaul links is not feasible, a mixed wired and wireless backhaul links approach can be employed, enabling the SBS to receive and send data traffic using the wired or wireless connection.

In this paper, we combine the layered architecture of cloud computing and edge computing as a collaborative cloud-edge system in the UDN, taking into account wired or wireless backhaul links between the SBSs and the MBS, and comprehensively consider factors affecting system performance, such as offloading decisions, bandwidth allocation, computing resource allocation, and transmission power allocation, to achieve optimal computation overhead in terms of both energy consumption and computing delay. We first establish a system model and introduce a collaborative offloading process between cloud computing and edge computing in the UDN, then formulate the energy consumption and the latency of each phase of the process on the local SMD, the SBS, and the MBS, respectively. Finally, we model the offloading problem as an optimization problem to minimize the system-wide computation overhead and solve the problem by applying the Linear Decreasing Weight Particle Swarm Optimization (LDW-PSO) algorithm. In summary, this paper makes the following contributions:

1) We study a collaborative cloud-edge system in the UDN with wide-area coverage, in which the SBSs provide relay services between SMDs and the MBS integrated with an MEC server, while the cloud servers are deployed at the cloud center for computing offloading services. Mixed wired and wireless backhaul links are deployed between the SBSs and the MBS, and the available spectrum is shared between the wireless access links and the wireless backhaul links.

2) Considering the varying performance and energy requirements of different SMDs, this paper models the computation overhead of each SMD as the weighted sum of energy consumption and computing delay, then proposes a joint optimization problem related to offloading decisions, bandwidth allocation, computing resource allocation, and transmission power allocation to minimize the system-wide computation overhead.

3) By applying the LDWPSO algorithm, we solve the non-convex optimization problem in our proposed collaborative cloud-edge scheme. Subsequently, we evaluate the scheme's performance against other baseline schemes through numerical simulations, which indicate that our proposed scheme outperforms the baseline schemes.

The rest of the paper is organized as follows. In Sect. 2, we review the related work. Section 3 describes the system model. In Sect. 4, we formulate the considered optimization problem. Section 5 describes the LDWPSO algorithm applied for solving the proposed problem. Section 6 performs the numerical experiments. We conclude our work in Sect. 7.

## 2   Related Work

In recent years, researchers have made significant strides in solving the problem of computing offloading in MEC, in order to allow users to fully experience the performance benefits of MEC in 5G networks. MEC is a versatile technology that can be applied to various rich application scenarios, and it can effectively overcome the limitations of centralized cloud computing. Optimizing task offloading and resource allocation has become a key area of research for both academia and industry.

Aiming at the task offloading and resource allocation problems of MEC, there have been many related studies. Tran *et al.* decomposed the resource allocation problem for multi-user and multi-server MEC systems into convex and quasi-convex problems, by using the KKT condition and the dichotomy method to solve it, maximizing the weighted sum of all users' offloading benefits [13]. Furthermore, The academic community has also conducted extensive research on collaborative offloading of MEC and cloud computing systems. Ren *et al.* studied the joint optimization of computing and communication resources for MEC and cloud computing systems, and formulated a multi-user, multi-relay, and multi-server scenario, aiming to minimize system delay [11]. In addition, in MEC networks, computing collaboration is considered as a technique to further improve users' quality of experience (QoE), and has been extensively studied by the academic community recently. Cao *et al.* proposed an offloading method for communication and computing collaboration based on MEC systems, and suggested a four-slot transmission protocol to improve energy efficiency under delay constraints [2]. The authors in [16] proposed a three-stage Time Division Multiple Access (TDMA) protocol to minimize delay in multi-assistant scenarios, and solved the relaxed convex problem using the Lagrangian dual decomposition technique with the ellipsoid method.

In the field of task offloading and resource optimization for the UDN combined with MEC, several related studies have been conducted. However, when a large number of users choose to offload tasks, bandwidth constraints severely limit the scalability of MEC. To address this problem, the authors in [8] jointly optimized offloading decisions, transmission power allocation, and sub-channel allocation to minimize the energy consumption, utilizing the coordinate descent method to update offloading decisions and allocating sub-channels with the Hungarian and greedy algorithms. In [10], the authors introduced a new wireless backhaul framework to achieve dense cell deployment and efficient data transmission, but did not dynamically manage limited transmission power and computing resources of local devices. Yang *et al.* considered a multi-cell MEC system based on Non-Orthogonal Multiple Access (NOMA) and proposed a hybrid genetic hill-climbing algorithm to minimize the weighted sum of energy consumption and delay, but they did not optimize communication and computing resources [17].

This paper differs from the aforementioned literature by studying a scenario that involves collaborative cloud-edge computing in the UDN and covers mixed wired and wireless backhaul. We analyze the joint optimization problem of offloading decisions, bandwidth allocation, computing resource allocation, and transmission power allocation and propose a solution using the LDWPSO algorithm to determine the optimal strategy.

## 3   System Model

The UDN under consideration in this paper consists of one MBS equipped with an MEC server and $S$ SBSs of the same type, as shown in Fig. 1. We assume that each SMD has already been associated with a SBS through user association strategies [9]. To facilitate the analysis, the link between the SMD and the SBS is called the wireless access link, while the wired and wireless links between SBSs and the MBS are respectively referred to as the wired backhaul link and the wireless backhaul link, and the link between the MBS and the cloud is referred to as the backhaul link. The set of all SBSs is denoted as $\mathbb{S} = \{1, 2, \ldots, S\}$. Let $\mathbb{S}_0 = \{1, \ldots, M\}$ and $\mathbb{S}_1 = \{M + 1, \ldots, S\}$ represent the subsets of SBSs connected to the wireless backhaul links and the wired backhaul links, respectively, and $M$ represent the total number of SBSs accessing the wireless backhaul link. Suppose $U_s$ SMDs locate in the $s$-th SBS cell, let $\mathbb{U}_s = \{1, 2, \ldots, U_s\}, s \in \mathbb{S}$ denote the set of SMDs, and $u_{s,k} \in \mathbb{U}_s$ represent the $k$-th SMD. The computing resources of the MEC server and the cloud server can be allocated to SMDs through virtual machine technology.

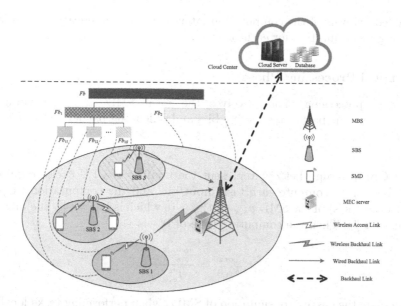

**Fig. 1.** System model.

Assuming that the SBSs and the MBS share the same frequency spectrum (as shown in Fig. 1), the system's total frequency band $Fb$ is divided into two parts: $Fb_1$ and $Fb_2$. $Fb_1$ is allocated for SBSs, and $Fb_2$ is allocated for the MBS. Notably, $Fb_1$ is equally allocated to each SBS, then each SBS's frequency band is evenly allocated to its associated SMDs, while the MBS's frequency band is evenly allocated to the connected SBSs by the wireless backhaul links. The widths of frequency bands $Fb$, $Fb_1$, and $Fb_2$ are $B$, $\lambda B$, and $(1 - \lambda)B$, respectively, where $0 \leq \lambda \leq 1$ is the frequency band partitioning factor. The model cancels out inter-tier interference, eliminates intra-tier interference, and completely avoids intra-cell interference [18].

Suppose each SMD has a computing task, and the input-bits of the task for the SMD $u_{s,k}$ is denoted as $L_{s,k}$. Assume that the computing task belongs to data-partitioned oriented tasks and can be divided arbitrarily, regardless of the internal content, such as virus scanning tasks and GZip tasks [14]. Tasks can be executed in three layers including the local device of the SMD, the MEC server, and the cloud server respectively. Let $l_{s,k}^{u}$, $l_{s,k}^{m}$ and $l_{s,k}^{c}$ respectively denote the task input-bits executed on the local SMD $u_{s,k}$, on the MEC server, and on the cloud server. Then we have

$$L_{s,k} = l_{s,k}^{u} + l_{s,k}^{m} + l_{s,k}^{c}, \quad \forall s \in \mathbb{S}, k \in \mathbb{U}_s. \tag{1}$$

The entire process of task computation and offloading in the system can be categorized into three phases: the local processing phase, the SBS processing phase and the MBS processing phase. In the upcoming sections, we will provide a detailed analysis of the computation latency, the communication latency, and the energy consumption for each phase.

## 3.1 Local Processing Phase

The local processing phase involves the local SMD $u_{s,k}$ performing self-computing on the partial task of $l^u_{s,k}$ bits and offloading partial task of $l^m_{s,k} + l^c_{s,k}$ bits to the SBS.

**Local Computing.** Let $c^u_{s,k}$ represent the number of CPU cycles required by the SMD $u_{s,k}$ to compute each task input-bit, and the computation frequency (in CPU cycles/s) of the SMD $u_{s,k}$ as $f^u_{s,k} \geq 0$, which is limited by the maximum frequency $F^u_{s,k}$. Then the computing time of $l^u_{s,k}$ is

$$t^{u,comp}_{s,k} = \frac{l^u_{s,k} c^u_{s,k}}{f^u_{s,k}}. \tag{2}$$

To calculate the energy consumption of SMDs when performing tasks locally, we use the widely adopted model of the energy consumption per computing cycle as $\varepsilon = \kappa f^u_{s,k}{}^2$, where $\kappa$ is the energy coefficient depending on the chip architecture [3]. Therefore, the energy consumption of the SMD $u_{s,k}$ to execute the $l^u_{s,k}$ bits locally is given by:

$$E^{comp}_{s,k} = l^u_{s,k} c^u_{s,k} \varepsilon = l^u_{s,k} c^u_{s,k} \kappa (f^u_{s,k})^2. \tag{3}$$

**Computation Offloading to SBS.** The SMD $u_{s,k}$ offloads the remaining $l^m_{s,k} + l^c_{s,k}$ task bits to the SBS $s$ through a wireless access link. The transmission power of the SMD $u_{s,k}$ is represented by $p_{s,k} \geq 0$, and the maximum transmission power is represented by $P_{s,k}$. The data transmission rate (in bits/s) from the SMD $u_{s,k}$ to the SBS $s$ is given by the equation:

$$r_{s,k} = \frac{B\lambda}{SU_s} \log_2(1 + \frac{p_{s,k} h_{s,k}}{N_s}), \tag{4}$$

where $h_{s,k} \geq 0$ is the channel gain from the SMD $u_{s,k}$ to the SBS $s$, $N_s$ is the Additive White Gaussian Noise (AWGN) power of the SBS $s$.

Using the equation (4), we can derive the offloading delay and energy consumption from the SMD $u_{s,k}$ to the SBS $s$:

$$t^{u,trans}_{s,k} = \frac{l^m_{s,k} + l^c_{s,k}}{r_{s,k}}, \tag{5}$$

$$E^{trans}_{s,k} = t^{u,trans}_{s,k} p_{s,k} = \frac{p_{s,k}(l^m_{s,k} + l^c_{s,k})}{r_{s,k}}. \tag{6}$$

## 3.2  SBS Processing Phase

After receiving the $l^m_{s,k} + l^c_{s,k}$ task bits from the SMD $u_{s,k}$, the SBS $s$ offloads the task segment to the MBS using a wired or wireless backhaul link in the SBS processing phase.

When the SBS $s$ accesses the MBS through a wireless backhaul link, the transmission power of the SBS $s$ is represented by $p_s$. The data transmission rate from the SBS $s$ to the MBS is given by:

$$r_s = \frac{B(1-\lambda)}{M} \log_2(1 + \frac{p_s h_s}{N_0}), \forall s \in \mathbb{S}_0, \tag{7}$$

where $h_s \geq 0$ represents the channel gain from the SBS $s$ to the MBS, $N_0$ represents the AWGN power at the MBS.

Since the transmission delay of the wired backhaul link is typically much smaller than that of the wireless backhaul link, the transmission delay of the wired backhaul link can be ignored [8]. Therefore, we can obtain the transmission delay for the SBS $s$ to send $l^m_{s,k} + l^c_{s,k}$ task bits to the MBS:

$$t^m_{s,k} = \begin{cases} \dfrac{l^m_{s,k} + l^c_{s,k}}{r_s}, & \text{if } s \in \mathbb{S}_0, \\ 0, & \text{if } s \in \mathbb{S}_1. \end{cases} \tag{8}$$

## 3.3  MBS Processing Phase

The processing phase of the MBS can be split into two parts. In the first part, the MEC server computes the $l^m_{s,k}$ task bits received from the SMD $u_{s,k}$. In the second part, the MBS offloads the remaining $l^c_{s,k}$ bits to the cloud server for computation.

**Computing at MEC Server.** Let $c^m_{s,k}$ denote the number of CPU cycles required by the MEC server to calculate each task input-bit from the SMD $u_{s,k}$, and let $f^m_{s,k} \geq 0$ specify the computing resources allocated by the MEC server to the SMD $u_{s,k}$. The execution delay of computing $l^m_{s,k}$ task bits on the MEC server can then be expressed as

$$t^{m,comp}_{s,k} = \frac{l^m_{s,k} c^m_{s,k}}{f^m_{s,k}}. \tag{9}$$

Given the limited resources at the edge, it is necessary to satisfy the computing resources constraint, which can be expressed as

$$\sum_{s=1}^{S} \sum_{k=1}^{U_s} f^m_{s,k} \leq F^m, \ \forall s \in \mathbb{S}, k \in \mathbb{U}_s, \tag{10}$$

where $F^m$ is the maximum computational frequency of the MEC server.

**Offloading to the Cloud Server.** The MBS is connected to the cloud server through a backhaul link, which is typically characterized by high bandwidth and shared by multiple SMDs. Following the assumptions made in [11], we consider a fixed resource scheduling policy. Accordingly, we can denote $W$ as the backhaul communication capacity for each SMD. Therefore, similar to the offloading delay in (5), the backhaul transmission delay $t_{s,k}^{m,trans}$ is proportional to the size of data to be offloaded, as

$$t_{s,k}^{m,trans} = \frac{l_{s,k}^c}{W},\qquad(11)$$

where $W^{-1}$ can be interpreted as the required time for the backhaul link to transmit one-bit data.

Since the cloud has abundant computing resources in comparison to the edge, we can neglect the delay of executing these offloaded task bits [6]. Furthermore, the size of the output is small enough, then the download delay can be ignored [5].

## 4  Problem Formulation

As the MEC server and cloud servers have a reliable power supply, this paper mainly focuses on analyzing the energy consumption of the SMDs. Using the Eqs. (3) and (6), the total energy consumption of the SMD $u_{s,k}$ can be computed as

$$E_{s,k} = E_{s,k}^{comp} + E_{s,k}^{trans}.\qquad(12)$$

Since the task of the SMD $u_{s,k}$ can be executed in parallel on the local SMD, the MEC server and the cloud server, the total time delay required for the SMD to complete the task is:

$$T_{s,k} = \max\{t_{s,k}^{u,comp}, t_{s,k}^{u,trans} + t_{s,k}^m + t_{s,k}^{m,comp}, t_{s,k}^{u,trans} + t_{s,k}^m + t_{s,k}^{m,trans}\}.\qquad(13)$$

In a mobile edge computing system, the users' QoE is primarily determined by the time and the energy consumption required to complete tasks. Therefore, we define the computation overhead of the SMD $u_{s,k}$ as follows:

$$Z_{s,k} = \alpha_{s,k}E_{s,k} + (1-\alpha_{s,k})T_{s,k},\qquad(14)$$

in which $\alpha_{s,k} \in [0,1]$.

Our objective is to minimize the system-wide computation overhead, which we define as a weighted sum of all SMDs computation overheads:

$$Z = \sum_{s=1}^{S}\sum_{k=1}^{U_s} \beta_{s,k}Z_{s,k},\qquad(15)$$

where $\beta_{s,k} \in (0,1]$ specify the resource provider's preference towards the SMD $u_{s,k}$. The minimization problem of the system-wide computation overhead is then formulated as

(P1):    $\min\limits_{\mathbf{L},\lambda,\mathbf{F},\mathbf{P}} Z$    (16a)

s.t.    $l_{s,k}^u \geq 0,\ l_{s,k}^m \geq 0,\ l_{s,k}^c \geq 0,\ \forall s \in \mathbb{S}, k \in \mathbb{U}_s,$    (16b)

$0 \leq \lambda \leq 1,$    (16c)

$0 \leq f_{s,k}^u \leq F_{s,k}^u,\ \forall s \in \mathbb{S}, k \in \mathbb{U}_s,$    (16d)

$f_{s,k}^m \geq 0,\ \forall s \in \mathbb{S}, k \in \mathbb{U}_s,$    (16e)

$0 \leq p_{s,k} \leq P_{s,k},\ \forall s \in \mathbb{S}, k \in \mathbb{U}_s,$    (16f)

$$\sum_{k=1}^{U_s} r_{s,k} \leq r_s,\ \forall s \in \mathbb{S}_0,$$    (16g)

(1) *and* (10),

where the task offloading decisions is denoted by $\mathbf{L} = (l_{1,1}^u, l_{1,1}^m, l_{1,1}^c, \ldots, l_{S,U_S}^u, l_{S,U_S}^m, l_{S,U_S}^c)$, the computing resource allocation policy by $\mathbf{F} = (f_{1,1}^u, f_{1,1}^m, \ldots, f_{S,U_S}^u, f_{S,U_S}^m)$, and the transmission power allocation by $\mathbf{P} = (p_{1,1}, \ldots, p_{S,U_S})$, where $U_S$ means the SMD locates in the $S$-th SBS cell. (16c) represents the lower and upper bounds of the frequency band partitioning factor. (16d) represents the constraints on the computational frequency of the SMDs. (16f) indicates the constraints on the transmission power of the SMDs. (16g) indicates that the total transmission rate of all SMDs associated with the SBS connected to the wireless backhaul link should be not greater than the transmission rate of the SBS.

## 5    Problem Solving

It is worth noting that the problem (P1) can be further simplified. The task size computed on the local device, on the MEC server and on the cloud server can be modeled as, respectively

$$l_{s,k}^u = \gamma_{s,k}^u L_{s,k}, \forall s \in \mathbb{S}, k \in \mathbb{U}_s,$$    (17)

$$l_{s,k}^m = \gamma_{s,k}^m (1 - \gamma_{s,k}^u) L_{s,k}, \forall s \in \mathbb{S}, k \in \mathbb{U}_s,$$    (18)

$$l_{s,k}^c = (1 - \gamma_{s,k}^m)(1 - \gamma_{s,k}^u) L_{s,k}, \forall s \in \mathbb{S}, k \in \mathbb{U}_s,$$    (19)

where $\gamma_{s,k}^u \in [0,1]$ and $\gamma_{s,k}^m \in [0,1]$. In addition, we define the vectors $\mathbf{\Gamma^u} = (\gamma_{1,1}^u, \ldots, \gamma_{S,U_S}^u)$ and $\mathbf{\Gamma^m} = (\gamma_{1,1}^m, \ldots, \gamma_{S,U_S}^m)$, so the original problem (P1) can be transformed into the following equivalent optimization problem (P1-Eqv):

(P1-Eqv):    $\min\limits_{\mathbf{\Gamma^u},\mathbf{\Gamma^m},\lambda,\mathbf{F},\mathbf{P}} Z$    (20a)

s.t.    $\gamma_{s,k}^u \in [0,1], \gamma_{s,k}^m \in [0,1], \forall s \in \mathbb{S}, k \in \mathbb{U}_s,$    (20b)

(16c), (16d), (16e), (16f), (16g) *and* (10).

The Particle Swarm Optimization (PSO) algorithm is a kind of swarm intelligent algorithm inspired by bird predation behaviors. It analogizes the optimization problem's search space to the birds' flight space and represents each bird as a particle. Each particle has its fitness value equals to the value of the objective function (20a), and particles follow the current optimal particle to search in the solution space.

## 5.1   Particle Encoding

To utilize the PSO algorithm to solve the problem (P1-Eqv), we represent the vector of particles as $\mathbf{I} = (1, 2, \ldots, I)$, and $\mathbf{\Gamma^u}$, $\mathbf{\Gamma^m}$, $\lambda$, $\mathbf{P}$ are encoded as $\mathbf{A_i}$, $\mathbf{B_i}$, $c_i$, $\mathbf{Q_i}$, $i \in \mathbf{I}$, where $\mathbf{A_i} = (a_{1,1}^i, \ldots, a_{S,U_S}^i)$, and $a_{s,k}^i$ represents the proportion of the task at the SMD $u_{s,k}$ to be computed locally found by the particle $i$; $\mathbf{B_i} = (b_{1,1}^i, \ldots, b_{S,U_S}^i)$, and $b_{s,k}^i$ represents the proportion dimensions of the task received by the MBS from the SMD $u_{s,k}$ to be computed on the MEC server found by the particle $i$; $c_i$ is the frequency band partitioning factor found by the particle $i$; $\mathbf{Q_i} = (q_{1,1}^i, \ldots, q_{S,U_S}^i)$, and $q_{s,k}^i$ is the transmission power of the SMD $u_{s,k}$ found by the particle $i$. $\mathbf{F}$ is further encoded as $\mathbf{D_i}$ and $\mathbf{E_i}$, where $\mathbf{D_i} = (d_{1,1}^i, \ldots, d_{S,U_S}^i)$, and $d_{s,k}^i$ represents the computation frequency of the SMD $u_{s,k}$ found by the particle $i$; $\mathbf{E_i} = (e_{1,1}^i, \ldots, e_{S,U_S}^i)$, and $e_{s,k}^i$ represents the computing resources allocated by the MEC server to the SMD $u_{s,k}$ found by the particle $i$.

## 5.2   Particle Velocity and Position Update

In the PSO algorithm, each particle has two attributes including the position and the velocity, where the position represents a solution found by the particle of the optimization problem, and the velocity shows how the solution evolves.

According to the constraint conditions (10), (16c)-(16f), and (20b), the initial position of the particle $i$ is described as follows:

$$
\begin{cases}
a_{s,k}^{i,0} = rand(1), \forall s \in \mathbb{S}, k \in \mathbb{U}_s, \\
b_{s,k}^{i,0} = rand(1), \forall s \in \mathbb{S}, k \in \mathbb{U}_s, \\
c_i^0 = rand(1), \\
d_{s,k}^{i,0} = rand(F_{s,k}^u), \forall s \in \mathbb{S}, k \in \mathbb{U}_s, \\
e_{s,k}^{i,0} = rand(\dfrac{\beta_{s,k} F^m}{\sum\limits_{s=1}^{S} \sum\limits_{k=1}^{U_s} \beta_{s,k}}), \forall s \in \mathbb{S}, k \in \mathbb{U}_s, \\
q_{s,k}^{i,0} = rand(P_{s,k}), \forall s \in \mathbb{S}, k \in \mathbb{U}_s,
\end{cases}
\tag{21}
$$

where $rand(a)$ randomly generates a number between 0 and $a$.

Then, the velocity of the particle $i$ can be updated by

$$
av_{s,k}^{i,t+1} = \omega^t av_{s,k}^{i,t} + c_1 \eta_{s,k}^i (aj_{s,k}^{i,t} - al_{s,k}^{i,t}) + c_2 \hat{\eta}_{s,k}^i (ag_{s,k}^t - al_{s,k}^{i,t}),
$$
$$
\forall s \in \mathbb{S}, k \in \mathbb{U}_s,
\tag{22}
$$

$$bv_{s,k}^{i,t+1} = \omega^t bv_{s,k}^{i,t} + c_1\eta_{s,k}^i(bj_{s,k}^{i,t} - bl_{s,k}^{i,t}) + c_2\hat{\eta}_{s,k}^i(bg_{s,k}^t - bl_{s,k}^{i,t}),$$
$$\forall s \in \mathbb{S}, k \in \mathbb{U}_s, \tag{23}$$

$$cv_i^{t+1} = \omega^t cv_i^t + c_1\xi_i(cj_i^t - cl_i^t) + c_2\hat{\xi}_i(cg^t - cl_i^t), \tag{24}$$

$$dv_{s,k}^{i,t+1} = \omega^t dv_{s,k}^{i,t} + c_1\eta_{s,k}^i(dj_{s,k}^{i,t} - dl_{s,k}^{i,t}) + c_2\hat{\eta}_{s,k}^i(dg_{s,k}^t - dl_{s,k}^{i,t}),$$
$$\forall s \in \mathbb{S}, k \in \mathbb{U}_s, \tag{25}$$

$$ev_{s,k}^{i,t+1} = \omega^t ev_{s,k}^{i,t} + c_1\eta_{s,k}^i(ej_{s,k}^{i,t} - el_{s,k}^{i,t}) + c_2\hat{\eta}_{s,k}^i(eg_{s,k}^t - el_{s,k}^{i,t}),$$
$$\forall s \in \mathbb{S}, k \in \mathbb{U}_s, \tag{26}$$

$$qv_{s,k}^{i,t+1} = \omega^t qv_{s,k}^{i,t} + c_1\eta_{s,k}^i(qj_{s,k}^{i,t} - ql_{s,k}^{i,t}) + c_2\hat{\eta}_{s,k}^i(qg_{s,k}^t - ql_{s,k}^{i,t}),$$
$$\forall s \in \mathbb{S}, k \in \mathbb{U}_s, \tag{27}$$

where $al_{s,k}^{i,t}$, $bl_{s,k}^{i,t}$, $cl_i^t$, $dl_{s,k}^{i,t}$, $el_{s,k}^{i,t}$ and $ql_{s,k}^{i,t}$ are the position coordinates of $a_{s,k}^i$, $b_{s,k}^i$, $c_i$, $d_{s,k}^i$, $e_{s,k}^i$ and $q_{s,k}^i$ at the $t$-th iteration; $av_{s,k}^{i,t}$, $bv_{s,k}^{i,t}$, $cv_i^t$, $dv_{s,k}^{i,t}$, $ev_{s,k}^{i,t}$ and $qv_{s,k}^{i,t}$ are the velocity vectors of $a_{s,k}^i$, $b_{s,k}^i$, $c_i$, $d_{s,k}^i$, $e_{s,k}^i$ and $q_{s,k}^i$ at the $t$-th iteration; $\omega^t$ represents an inertia weight at the $t$-th iteration; $c_1$ and $c_2$ denote the self-learning and social learning factors respectively; $\eta_{s,k}^i$, $\hat{\eta}_{s,k}^i$, $\xi_i$ and $\hat{\xi}_i$ are random numbers between $[0,1]$; $aj^{i,t} = (aj_{1,1}^{i,t}, \ldots, aj_{S,U_S}^{i,t})$, $bj^{i,t} = (bj_{1,1}^{i,t}, \ldots, bj_{S,U_S}^{i,t})$, $cl_i^t$, $dj^{i,t} = (dj_{1,1}^{i,t}, \ldots, dj_{S,U_S}^{i,t})$, $ej^{i,t} = (ej_{1,1}^{i,t}, \ldots, ej_{S,U_S}^{i,t})$ and $qj^{i,t} = (qj_{1,1}^{i,t}, \ldots, qj_{S,U_S}^{i,t})$ are the historical optimal position coordinates of the particle $i$ until the $t$-th iteration; $ag^t = (ag_{1,1}^t, \ldots, ag_{S,U_S}^t)$, $bg^t = (bg_{1,1}^t, \ldots, bg_{S,U_S}^t)$, $cg^t$, $dg^t = (dg_{1,1}^t, \ldots, dg_{S,U_S}^t)$, $eg^t = (eg_{1,1}^t, \ldots, eg_{S,U_S}^t)$ and $qg^t = (qg_{1,1}^t, \ldots, qg_{S,U_S}^t)$ are the historical optimal position coordinates in the solution space until the $t$-th iteration.

To balance the global and local search capabilities, a Linearly Decreasing Weight (LDW) strategy can be employed, which has better performance than using a fixed inertia weight [15]. Specifically, the update formula for the inertia weight is:

$$\omega^t = \omega_{max} - \frac{t(\omega_{max} - \omega_{min})}{T}, \tag{28}$$

where $\omega_{max}$ and $\omega_{min}$ are the maximum and minimum inertia weights, and $T$ is the number of iterations. After updating the velocities of particles, the position coordinates of the particle $i$ can be updated by

$$al_{s,k}^{i,t+1} = al_{s,k}^{i,t} + av_{s,k}^{i,t+1}, \forall s \in \mathbb{S}, k \in \mathbb{U}_s, \tag{29}$$

$$bl_{s,k}^{i,t+1} = bl_{s,k}^{i,t} + bv_{s,k}^{i,t+1}, \forall s \in \mathbb{S}, k \in \mathbb{U}s, \tag{30}$$

$$cl_i^{t+1} = al_i^t + cv_i^{t+1}, \tag{31}$$

$$dl_{s,k}^{i,t+1} = dl_{s,k}^{i,t} + dv_{s,k}^{i,t+1}, \forall s \in \mathbb{S}, k \in \mathbb{U}_s, \tag{32}$$

$$el_{s,k}^{i,t+1} = el_{s,k}^{i,t} + ev_{s,k}^{i,t+1}, \forall s \in \mathbb{S}, k \in \mathbb{U}_s, \tag{33}$$

$$ql_{s,k}^{i,t+1} = ql_{s,k}^{i,t} + qv_{s,k}^{i,t+1}, \forall s \in \mathbb{S}, k \in \mathbb{U}_s. \tag{34}$$

In summary, the specific process of using the LDWPSO algorithm to solve the optimization problem (P1-Eqv) is shown in Algorithm 1.

---

**Algorithm 1: LDWPSO**

---

1: **Initialization:**
2:    $t = 1$, and a large fitness value $N$
3:    Initialize the positions of $I$ particles using Eq.(21).
4:    Set the current position of each particle as its historical optimal position.
5:    Find the global best particle of current population.
6:    Initialize the velocities of $I$ particles.
7: **While** $t \leq T$ **Do**
8:    Update inertia weight using Eq.(28).
9:    Update the velocities of $I$ particles using Eqs.(22)–(27).
10:    Update the positions of $I$ particles using Eqs.(29)–(34).
11:    **For** each $i \in \mathbf{I}$ **Do**
12:        **If** the position of the particle $i$ satisfies the constraints of the problem (P1-Eqv) **then**
13:            calculate the fitness value of the particle $i$ using Eq.(20a);
14:        **else**
15:            set its fitness value to $N$.
16:        **End if**
17:        **If** its current fitness value is less than its historical optimal fitness value **then**
18:            the historical optimal position is updated by its current position.
19:        **End if**
20:    **End for**
21:    Find the global best particle of current population.
22:    Update the iteration index: $t = t + 1$.
23: **End while**
24: **Output:**
25:    $ag^T, bg^T, cg^T, dg^T, eg^T$ and $qg^T$ as the solution to (P1-Eqv)

---

# 6    Results and Analysis

In this section, we will evaluate the performance of the proposed joint task offloading and resource allocation scheme by setting corresponding simulation parameters. We consider an outdoor environment of 300m × 300m, where the MBS is located at the center, 15 SBSs and $K$ SMDs are randomly distributed within the area. Let $d$ denote the distance between the transmitter and the receiver. The path-loss between any two nodes is given by $\beta_0(d/d_0)^{-\xi}$, where $\beta_0 = -60db$ represents the path-loss at the reference distance of $d_0 = 10m$, and $\xi = 3$ is the path-loss exponent [12]. Table 1 lists other parameters in detail.

**Table 1.** Simulation Parameters

| Parameter | Value | Parameter | Value |
|-----------|-------|-----------|-------|
| $\omega_{max}$ | 0.9 | $\omega_{min}$ | 0.4 |
| $c_1$ | 2 | $c_2$ | 2 |
| $T$ | 800 | $I$ | 500 |
| $K$ | [15,120] | $L_{s,k}$ | [1,10] Mbits |
| $B$ | [5,50] MHz | $c_{s,k}^u$ | $10^3$ cycles/bit |
| $c_{s,k}^m$ | $10^3$ cycles/bit | $\kappa$ | $10^{-26}$ |
| $N_s$ | $-60$ dbm | $N_0$ | $-70$ dbm |
| $p_s$ | 20 dbm | $P_{s,k}$ | 20 dbm |
| $m$ | 4 | $W$ | 5 Mbps |
| $F_{s,k}^u$ | 1 GHz | $F^m$ | 50 GHz |
| $N$ | $10^{10}$ | $\alpha_{s,k}$ | 0.6 |
| $\beta_{s,k}$ | 1 | | |

Based on these parameters, we conducted simulation experiments to compare the performance of the proposed collaborative cloud-edge scheme with three baseline schemes:

1) Local-Computing-Only: Tasks are not offloaded, and all SMDs only use local computing to execute their tasks.
2) Full-Offloading: All SMDs offload all their tasks to the cloud and the MEC server at the MBS.
3) Computing-without-Cloud: Tasks are not offloaded to the cloud server and are jointly executed by SMDs locally and the MEC server at the MBS.

Figure 2 shows the relationship between the system-wide computation overhead (i.e., total computation overhead) and the total SMD number $K$ when $L = 5$ Mbits and $B = 30$ MHz. The experimental results demonstrate that the system-wide computation overhead of all schemes gradually increases with the increase of the number of SMDs. It was observed that the proposed collaborative cloud-edge scheme is superior to other schemes. This is because the collaborative cloud-edge scheme not only has local and edge collaboration, but also takes the advantage of the larger computing resources of the cloud server. Moreover, when the number of SMDs is less than 30, the computation overhead of computing-without-cloud is close to that of full-offloading. This is because when the number of SMDs is relatively small, the computing resources that SMDs obtain from the MEC server as well as the allocated bandwidth are sufficient, while when the number of SMDs is greater than 60, the performance of local-computing-only is better than that of full-offloading, and the gap between them gradually increases. This is because the computing resources of the MEC server and the system bandwidth are not enough to meet the needs of multiple devices simultaneously.

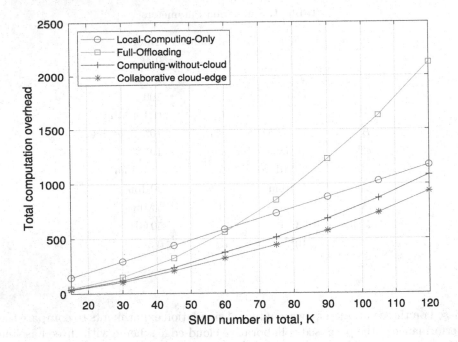

**Fig. 2.** Computation overhead versus SMD number.

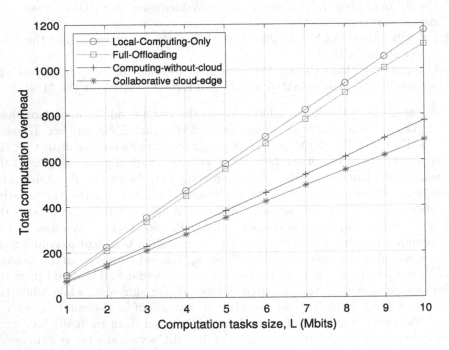

**Fig. 3.** Computation overhead versus computation task size.

Figure 3 illustrates the variation of computation overhead for the four schemes with the increase of the computation tasks size when $K = 60$ and $B = 30$ MHz. The results show that the overhead of all schemes increases as the computation task size grows. Among these schemes, the overhead of the proposed collaborative cloud-edge scheme is the smallest. This is because the proposed scheme support offload partial of the task to the MEC server and cloud server for execution. When the computation task size is small, the performance of local-computing-only is similar to the other schemes, as the CPU execution frequency of the local device is sufficient to complete the computation task. It can be observed that the overhead of full-offloading is higher than that of computing-without-cloud, and this gap gradually increases with the increase of the computation task size. This indicates that with the increase of the computation task size, the energy consumption and the latency required for communication (data transmission) will also increase.

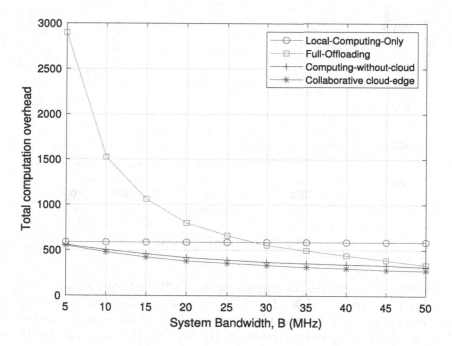

**Fig. 4.** Computation overhead versus system bandwidth.

Figure 4 illustrates the relationship between the system-wide computation overhead and system bandwidth when $K = 60$ and $L = 5$ Mbits. As can be seen, the computation overhead of local-computing-only remains constant as system bandwidth increases, while the overhead of other schemes decreases. This is because local-computing-only is independent of offloading. We can again observe that the proposed collaborative cloud-edge scheme generates the minimum overhead compared to the other baseline schemes. When the system bandwidth keeps low, full-offloading performs more worse than the other schemes for long offloading delay. When the system bandwidth is large enough (i.e., great than 28 MHz), full-offloading is better than local-computing-only. Especially, when the system bandwidth is relatively large enough, such as 50 MHz, the overhead of full-offloading is almost as low as that of the proposed scheme. This is reasonable because when the system bandwidth is large enough, the task offloading time is quite small.

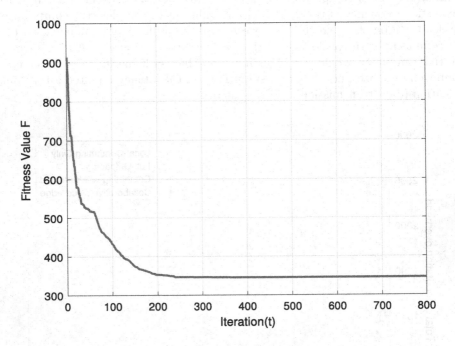

**Fig. 5.** Convergence analysis.

Figure 5 evaluates the convergence of the LDWPSO algorithm for the proposed scheme with $K = 60$, $L = 5$ Mbits, and $B = 30$ MHz by varying the number of iterations to observe the system-wide fitness value. It can be observed that the algorithm converges quickly in the first 150 iterations and the fitness value remains unchanged after 250 iterations with the global optimal solution found which means the LDWPSO algorithm can constantly search for the global optimal solution in the early stage of the algorithm and has good local search capabilities in the later stage.

## 7  Conclusions

With the advent of the 5G era, the requirements for delay and energy consumption in mobile communication networks have become increasingly strict.

To meet the QoE demands of SMDs, this paper explores the problem of task offloading and resource allocation based on collaborative cloud-edge system in the UDN. Under the deployment of mixed wired and wireless backhaul links, a system model for computing offloading is constructed, and the computation time, offloading delay, and energy consumption are given for the local processing, the SBS processing, and the MBS processing, respectively. Using the LDWPSO algorithm, the optimization problem including the computing offloading decision, frequency band partitioning factor, CPU execution frequency of the SMDs and the MEC server, and the transmission power of the SMDs is solved, and the optimal system-wide computation overhead is achieved in the entire task offloading process. Simulation results show that our proposed collaborative cloud-edge offloading scheme effectively reduces the system-wide computation overhead and improves the overall system performance compared to the other three baseline solutions.

# References

1. Abbas, N., Zhang, Y., Taherkordi, A., Skeie, T.: Mobile edge computing: a survey. IEEE Internet Things J. **5**(1), 450–465 (2018). https://doi.org/10.1109/JIOT.2017.2750180
2. Cao, X., Wang, F., Xu, J., Zhang, R., Cui, S.: Joint computation and communication cooperation for energy-efficient mobile edge computing. IEEE Internet Things J. **6**(3), 4188–4200 (2018)
3. Chen, X.: Decentralized computation offloading game for mobile cloud computing. IEEE Trans. Parallel Distrib. Syst. **26**(4), 974–983 (2014)
4. Dong, S., Li, H., Qu, Y., Zhang, Z.: Survey of research on computation unloading strategy in mobile edge computing. Comput. Sci. **46**(11), 32–40 (2019)
5. Elgendy, I.A., Zhang, W.Z., He, H., Gupta, B.B., Abd El-Latif, A.A.: Joint computation offloading and task caching for multi-user and multi-task MEC systems: reinforcement learning-based algorithms. Wireless Netw. **27**(3), 2023–2038 (2021)
6. Gao, Z., Hao, W., Han, Z., Yang, S.: Q-learning-based task offloading and resources optimization for a collaborative computing system. IEEE Access **8**, 149011–149024 (2020)
7. Ge, X., Tu, S., Mao, G., Wang, C.X., Han, T.: 5G ultra-dense cellular networks. IEEE Wirel. Commun. **23**(1), 72–79 (2016)
8. Haibo, Z., Hu, L., Shanxue, C., Xiaofan, H.: Computing offloading and resource optimization in ultra-dense networks with mobile edge computation. J. Electr. Inf. Technol. **41**(05), 1194–1201 (2019)
9. Oo, T.Z., Tran, N.H., Saad, W., Niyato, D., Han, Z., Hong, C.S.: Offloading in HetNet: a coordination of interference mitigation, user association, and resource allocation. IEEE Trans. Mob. Comput. **16**(8), 2276–2291 (2016)
10. Pham, Q.V., Le, L.B., Chung, S.H., Hwang, W.J.: Mobile edge computing with wireless backhaul: joint task offloading and resource allocation. IEEE Access **7**, 16444–16459 (2019)
11. Ren, J., Yu, G., He, Y., Li, G.Y.: Collaborative cloud and edge computing for latency minimization. IEEE Trans. Veh. Technol. **68**(5), 5031–5044 (2019)

12. Sun, H., Wang, J., Peng, H., Song, L., Qin, M.: Delay constraint energy efficient cooperative offloading in MEC for IoT. In: Gao, H., Wang, X., Iqbal, M., Yin, Y., Yin, J., Gu, N. (eds.) Collaborative Computing: Networking, Applications and Worksharing. Lecture Notes of the Institute for Computer Sciences, Social Informatics and Telecommunications Engineering, vol. 349, pp. 671–685. Springer, Cham (2020)
13. Tran, T.X., Pompili, D.: Joint task offloading and resource allocation for multi-server mobile-edge computing networks. IEEE Trans. Veh. Technol. **68**(1), 856–868 (2018)
14. Wang, Y., Sheng, M., Wang, X., Wang, L., Li, J.: Mobile-edge computing: partial computation offloading using dynamic voltage scaling. IEEE Trans. Commun. **64**(10), 4268–4282 (2016)
15. Xiaojing, Y., Qingju, J., Xinke, L.: Center particle swarm optimization algorithm. In: 2019 IEEE 3rd Information Technology, Networking, Electronic and Automation Control Conference (ITNEC), pp. 2084–2087. IEEE (2019)
16. Xing, H., Liu, L., Xu, J., Nallanathan, A.: Joint task assignment and resource allocation for d2d-enabled mobile-edge computing. IEEE Trans. Commun. **67**(6), 4193–4207 (2019)
17. Yang, L., Guo, S., Yi, L., Wang, Q., Yang, Y.: NOSCM: a novel offloading strategy for NOMA-enabled hierarchical small cell mobile-edge computing. IEEE Internet Things J. **8**(10), 8107–8118 (2020)
18. Zhou, T., Yue, Y., Qin, D., Nie, X., Li, X., Li, C.: Joint device association, resource allocation, and computation offloading in ultradense multidevice and multitask IoT networks. IEEE Internet Things J. **9**(19), 18695–18709 (2022)

# Dynamic Offloading Based on Meta Deep Reinforcement Learning and Load Prediction in Smart Home Edge Computing

Mingchu Li$^{(\boxtimes)}$, Shuai Li, and Wanying Qi

School of Software Technology, Dalian University of Technology, Dalian 116620, China
mingchul@dlut.edu.cn

**Abstract.** In the edge computing enabled smart home scenario. Various smart home devices generate a large number of computing tasks, and users can offload these tasks to servers or perform them locally. Offloading to the server will result in lower delay, but it will also require paying the corresponding offloading cost. Therefore, users need to consider the low delay and additional costs caused by offloading. Different users have different trade-offs between latency and offload costs at different times. If the trade-off is set as a fixed hyperparameter, it will give users a poor experience. In the case of dynamic trade-offs, the model may have difficulty adapting to arrive at an optimal offloading decision. By jointly optimizing the task delay and offloading cost, We model it as a long-term cost minimization problem under dynamic trade-off (DT-LCMP). To solve the problem, we propose an offloading algorithm based on multi-agent meta deep reinforcement learning and load prediction (MAMRL-L). Combined with the idea of meta-learning, the DDQN method is used to train the network. By training the sampling data in different environments, the agent can adapt to the dynamic environment quickly. In order to improve the performance of the model, LSTNet is used to predict the load level of the next slot server in real time. The simulation results show that our algorithm has higher performance than the existing algorithms and benchmark algorithms.

**Keywords:** Edge computing · Task offloading · Meta deep reinforcement learning · Smart homes · Dynamic trade-off

## 1 Introduction

With the rapid development of the mobile Internet and the popularity of smart devices, the demand for large amounts of data generation and processing is increasing [1]. The traditional method of transmitting data to the cloud center for processing has faced some limitations and cannot fully meet people's increasing real-time and responsiveness requirements. Especially for application scenarios

© ICST Institute for Computer Sciences, Social Informatics and Telecommunications Engineering 2024
Published by Springer Nature Switzerland AG 2024. All Rights Reserved
H. Gao et al. (Eds.): CollaborateCom 2023, LNICST 561, pp. 421–439, 2024.
https://doi.org/10.1007/978-3-031-54521-4_23

such as smart homes, high latency, strong dependencies, and privacy and security issues have become major challenges, and traditional cloud computing has been unable to solve these problems [2]. Edge computing has become a new paradigm to solve these problems. Unlike cloud computing, edge computing is closer to users and data sources, and can provide users with nearby services [3], process user data promptly, reduce costs, and reduce bandwidth pressure.

In smart homes, it is an inevitable trend to combine infrastructure with artificial intelligence (AI) [4]. The combination of the two will produce a variety of smart devices, such as smart shoe cabinets [5]. These smart devices involve AI functions in six key areas, namely activity perception, data processing, speech recognition, image cognition, decision making, and future prediction [6]. For example, in terms of image recognition, monitoring, and analyzing human activities and body characteristics to achieve facial, emotional, biological, and other recognition, and also to understand different scenarios. These tasks are usually latency-sensitive and computation-intensive, and require certain computing resources for processing. Long-term heavy computation can reduce the service life of Internet of Things (IoT) devices [7]. Offloading these tasks to edge servers is a more appropriate solution. This approach can effectively reduce not only the execution delay of tasks but also the maintenance cost of IoT devices. But it will also be accompanied by an additional increase in bandwidth delay [8] and a certain offloading cost [9].

This paper focuses on the joint optimization problem between delay and offloading cost when offloading tasks in edge computing-enabled smart home scenarios. Consider the user's dynamic trade-off between delay and offloading cost, as a dynamic parameter that can be changed by the user's input, rather than a fixed hyperparameter of the model. In reality, different users have varying measurement standards for delay and offloading costs at different times. For instance, freelancers at home might prioritize low latency, as they require efficient real-time task processing. For office workers outside, the delay requirements at home may not be so high. They just rest at home and do not need to perform frequent smart tasks. For the same user, when they are at home, the delay requirement may be higher, because they want to respond to smart home devices in a timely manner. Conversely, when they are outside, the latency requirements may be relatively lower since specific intelligent tasks continue even in their absence, such as smart security and energy management.

In this work, we focus on the joint optimization problem between latency and offload cost under user dynamic trade-offs. We reformulate it as a Markov decision process (MDP) and propose an offloading algorithm based on multi-agent meta deep reinforcement learning. Multi-agent meta deep reinforcement learning is an extended multi-agent deep reinforcement learning method whose goal is to allow agents to learn from multiple tasks and form a global policy for adapting quickly to new tasks. By combining meta-learning, the agent can learn the optimal strategy under different trade-off criteria, so that the agent can make decisions more flexibly and efficiently without retraining [14]. In this paper, a model-free meta-learning algorithm [15] is used to train the model, so that it has stronger adaptability and generalization ability in the face of different tasks and environments, and achieves the effect of rapid convergence. Ability to quickly make adaptive decisions based on the current task situation and user trade-offs. Such an approach can not only improve the efficiency and performance of agents but also bring better user experience to smart home systems (SHS). The algorithm in this paper runs on multiple edge servers and multiple SHSs. When each SHS can observe server information but cannot observe the other's information, it trains a deep reinforcement learning agent to offload tasks. The main contributions of this paper are as follows:

1) We formulate the long-term cost minimization problem under dynamic trade-offs. This problem considers the joint optimization between the delay and offloading cost of task offloading and proposes a dynamic weighted sum to minimize the delay and offloading cost.
2) We propose the offloading algorithm MAMRL-L. The algorithm is based on multi-agent deep reinforcement learning, and uses DDQN to train agents, so that each agent can perform efficient task offloading when only server information can be observed, but other agents cannot be observed. At the same time, combined with the meta-learning method, it is proposed to use probability sampling to train the meta-policy to improve the adaptability of the agent in the dynamic environment. To improve the performance of the algorithm, we combine LSTNet [39] to predict the future server information to optimize the offloading decision.
3) Through simulation experiments, we compare the DMRO and the benchmark algorithm. The results show that our proposed algorithm achieves efficient offloading of computing tasks, significantly reduces the long-term cost of users, and can adapt quickly to the new environment.

The other parts of this article are arranged as follows. Section 2 discusses the related work, and Sect. 3 introduces the system model and problem description. In Sect. 4, the offloading algorithm based on multi-agent deep reinforcement learning and LSTNet is introduced in detail, and the optimal offloading scheme of computing tasks is obtained by this algorithm. In Sect. 5, the performance of the proposed algorithm is evaluated based on simulation experiments, and other algorithms are compared. Section 6 summarizes the work of this paper and looks forward to future research.

## 2   Related Works

In the current research, a wealth of research results have emerged for the problem of task offloading in the mobile edge computing (MEC) environment. From different perspectives, these studies are dedicated to solving multiple challenges in MEC systems.

### 2.1   User Experience

In terms of guaranteeing user experience (QoE). Based on traditional algorithms, Jiang et al. [16] proposed an online joint offloading and resource allocation method under long-term MEC energy constraints to solve the problems of increased energy consumption and poor resource allocation caused by task offloading. At the same time, Lyapunov is used to pursue the optimization of long-term user experience (QoE). Luo et al. [17] solved offloading decisions by allocating communication and computing resources jointly. The offloading problem and deep reinforcement learning (DRL) have become research hotspots in recent years. Zhou et al. [19] redefined the QoE metric and used the DRL algorithm to make optimal offloading decisions. Considering that in the limited experience in the distributed environment, the time state of the fully connected layer is not considered by the existing DRL method, Park et al. [18] proposed a calculation offloading scheme based on distributed DRL.

## 2.2   Delay and Energy Consumption

Delay and energy consumption constraints are the focus of many researchers. Reference [10–12] focused on minimizing system delay and energy consumption in task offloading. Huang et al. [13] studied joint task offloading decision and bandwidth allocation optimization to minimize the overall offloading cost in terms of energy cost, computing cost, and delay cost, and proposed an MEC task offloading and resource allocation algorithm based on Double Deep-Q network (DDQN). To minimize the task computing delay of single-user multi-edge server system and balance the workload between edge servers, the optimization algorithm based on downlink NOMA is studied in [20]. To solve the problem of limited battery capacity and low computing power of IoT nodes, Seo et al. [21] used a deep neural network (DNN) and corresponding exploration and training strategies to learn near-optimal wireless power transmission (WPT) duration. In the task offloading scheduling in dynamic MEC systems, Wang et al. [22] combined energy harvesting technology with IoT devices to provide a hybrid energy supply model, which minimizes the cost of the system.

## 2.3   Pricing Strategy

Some papers focus on solving the problem of MEC server pricing in edge environments. Considering the imbalance of information availability, Chen et al. [23] introduced the Stackelberg game to describe the relationship between the MEC server and the end users (EUs) to obtain a reasonable pricing scheme. In terms of differential pricing, Chen et al. [24] determined the unit price according to the actual usage of computing resources. According to the obtained unit price and execution delay, the Stackelberg game method is developed to obtain the user's optimal offloading strategy and the server's equilibrium pricing strategy. In addition to static pricing, dynamic pricing is also a problem worth studying. Xu et al. [25] studied the dynamic pricing problem that meets the computing needs of users that change over time, to minimize the scheduling cost of servers and maximize the service pricing utility of service providers. Developed a decentralized online optimization framework. Considering the task offloading needs of resource-poor users, Qu et al. [26] proposed a DNN combined with a baseline neural network BNN as a policy network to design price policies.

## 2.4  Dynamic Offloading

To bring higher performance and lower latency in various scenarios. In [27], a dynamic task offloading (DDTO) algorithm based on deep reinforcement learning (DRL) was proposed considering the rapidly increasing problem size and solution space size under changing channel conditions and task generation. In order to incorporate renewable resources into mobile edge computing while efficiently managing resources, Yan et al. [28] proposed a reinforcement learning-based algorithm that can dynamically learn offloading schemes and optimal provisioning strategies for edge servers. In order to quickly adapt to a dynamic environment, Dabin et al. [29] proposed a meta deep reinforcement learning-based offloading (DMRO) algorithm. The algorithm aggregates the perception ability of deep learning, the decision-making ability of reinforcement learning, and the rapid environment learning ability of meta-learning. Cai et al. [30] proposed a training method for meta-reinforcement learning, including local training based on a specific task policy and meta-policy-based training on MEC.

These studies consider the problems existing in edge computing systems from different perspectives. However, in the process of task offloading, the dynamic trade-off between delay and offloading cost has not been considered. This question mainly studies and solves this problem.

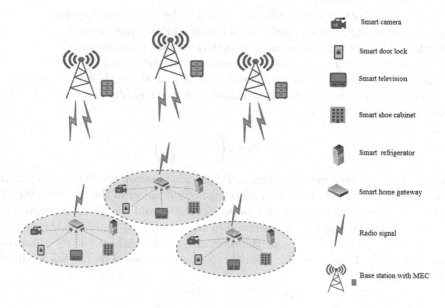

**Fig. 1.** Model diagram of smart home combined with edge computing.

## 3   System Model and Problem Formulation

We consider that in a multi-smart home system with multiple edge servers, $\mathcal{N}$ = { 1,2,..., N } is used to represent the set of N smart home systems (SHS), and $\mathcal{M}$ = { 1,2,..., M } is used to represent the set of M base stations (BS) equipped with edge servers. The BS, edge server, and server mentioned later in this article have the same meaning. As shown in Fig. 1, each SHS has multiple smart devices (SDs) and a smart gateway (SG). SG can bridge the internal and external networks of the home, transform different communication methods, and collaboratively manage various SDs equipped in the smart home [31]. In this paper, SG is responsible for processing data generated by various SDs and decides to compute locally or offload to BS for processing. We assume that the rate of receiving a task in the SG is R, and the length of the time slot $\tau$ is defined as 1/R, that is, each time slot generates a task. Then $\mathcal{T}$ = { 1,... T } is used to represent the set of T time slots. Task V is represented by a tuple { d, c }, where d represents the data size of the task (in bits as a unit), and c represents the number of CPU cycles required to process per-bit data. p represents the price to be paid for each time slot occupied by the server. In addition, we define $n \in \mathcal{N}$ to represent the $n^{th}$ SG, $m \in \mathcal{M}$ to denote the $m^{th}$ BS, and $t \in \mathcal{T}$ to denote the $t^{th}$ slot. The t time slot and the $t^{th}$ time slot have the same meaning. Table 1 shows the main notations.

When transmitting over a wireless channel, the signal will experience effects such as signal attenuation and channel gain during transmission [32]. Signal attenuation means that the signal strength decreases with the increase of transmission distance, while channel gain means that the signal is affected by the channel during transmission, and the signal may be strengthened or weakened. In order to better describe the transmission rate between devices, we express the transmission rate of SG as:

$$r_m = B \log_2 \left( 1 + \frac{Ph_m}{\sigma^2} \right) \tag{1}$$

Among them, $r_m$ represents the transmission rate between the SG and the BS m. B and P represent the bandwidth and transmission power of the SG, respectively, and $h_m$ represents the channel gain between the SG and the BS m. $\sigma^2$ represents the noise power. If the task is executed locally, $c_t$ and $d_t$ represent the number of CPU instructions per bit and the data size of the task in the $t^{th}$ time slot, respectively, the local execution delay of the task processed by the SG in the $t^{th}$ time slot is as follows:

$$D_t^{ex} = \frac{c_t \cdot d_t}{f_{local}} + D_{local,t}^{wait\_ex} \tag{2}$$

Here, $D_{local,t}^{wait\_ex} = \sum_{i=1}^{u'} \frac{c_i \cdot d_i}{f_{local}}$ represents the time that the task at time t is waiting for execution locally, and $u'$ represents the number of tasks to be executed in the current local execution queue. If the task is offloaded to the BS for execution, the task data needs to be uploaded to the BS. The transmission delay of the task in the t slot is as follows:

**Table 1.** Notations.

| Notations | Definition |
|---|---|
| $\mathcal{M}=\{1,2,...M\}$ | Set of the MEC |
| $\mathcal{N}=\{1,2,...N\}$ | Set of the SHS |
| R | The generation rate of task |
| $\mathcal{T}=\{1,2,...T\}$ | Set of the time slot |
| $\tau$ | Length of time slot |
| $\lambda_t$ | The weight of the $t^{th}$ time slot |
| $\Lambda = \{\lambda_t, t \in \mathcal{T}\}$ | Set of the weight of each time slot |
| V(d,c) | The data size of the task and the number of CPU cycles required per-bit of data |
| $r_m$ | The transmission rate between the SG and the $m^{th}$ base station |
| B | The bandwidth of SG |
| P | The transmission power of SG |
| $\sigma^2$ | The noise power |
| $D_{ex}^{local,t}$ | The local execution delay of the task in $t^{th}$ time slot |
| $D_{local,t}^{wait\_ex}$ | The local execution wait delay of the task in $t^{th}$ time slot |
| $D_t^{tr}$ | The transmission delay of the task in $t^{th}$ time slot |
| $D_t^{wait_{tr}}$ | The local transmission wait delay of the task in $t^{th}$ time slot |
| $D_{m,t}^{wait}$ | The server wait delay of the task in $t^{th}$ time slot |
| $D_{m,t}^{ex}$ | The server execution delay of the task in $t^{th}$ time slot |
| $f_{local}$ | CPU frequency of local device |
| $f_m$ | CPU frequency of the $m^{th}$ server |
| $x_t$ | Indicates whether the task is offloaded. 0 or 1 |
| $y_t \in \{1, 2, ..., M\}$ | Offload to which server to execute |
| $D_t^{total}$ | The total delay of the task in $t^{th}$ time slot |
| p | The price to be paid to occupy a server time slot |
| $cost_t$ | The cost of the task in $t^{th}$ time slot |
| s | The environmental state observed by the agent |
| a | The action given by the agent |
| r | The reward for the action given by the agent is by state s |

$$D_t^{tr} = \frac{d_t}{r_m} + D_t^{wait\_tr} \tag{3}$$

where, $D_t^{wait\_tr} = \sum_{i=1}^{q'} \frac{d_i}{r_m}$ represents the waiting delay in the transmission queue, and q' represents the number of tasks to be transmitted in the current transmission queue. Since the calculation result of the task is usually much smaller than the task data size, the downlink delay of the calculation result is ignored [33]. The main frequency of the server is generally much higher than that of the local device, and it is multi-core and multi-threaded. Under the default CPU trade-off [34] tuning scheme, the task can be run on multiple cores. Using $f_m$ to represent the CPU frequency of server m, the execution delay of the task on server m is as follows:

$$D_{m,t}^{ex} = \frac{c_t \cdot d_t}{f_m} \tag{4}$$

Without considering the task priority, the waiting delay of the task on the server m is equal to the sum of the execution delay of the tasks to be executed in the server m, and n′ is used to represent the number of tasks currently to be executed in the server, then the waiting time of the task Extension is expressed as:

$$D_{m,t}^{wait} = \sum_{i=1}^{n'} \frac{c_i \cdot d_i}{f_m} \tag{5}$$

Then the total delay of the task on the server is: $D_{m,t}^{total} = D_{m,t}^{ex} + D_{m,t}^{wait}$. Define $x_t$ as an indicator, $x_t \in \{0,1\}$. 0 represents local execution, and 1 represents offloading to BS. The total delay of the task as:

$$D_t^{total} = (1 - x_t) \cdot D_t^{ex} + x_t \cdot (D_t^{tr} + D_{m,t}^{total}) \tag{6}$$

Under the traditional billing method, there will be problems such as waste of resources, lack of flexibility, and difficulty in estimating costs. Pay-as-you-go has gradually become a more reasonable payment model [35], which has the advantages of flexibility, cost reduction, and changing business needs [36]. We use p to denote the price to be paid per slot of server, then the offloading cost of the task generated by $t^{th}$ time slot can be expressed as:

$$cost_t = D_{m,t}^{ex} \cdot p \cdot x_t \tag{7}$$

If the task is executed locally at $x_t = 0$, the $cost_t$ of offloading is 0. We consider the long-term cost minimization problem under dynamic trade-offs, that is, the dynamic weighted sum problem of joint optimization of delay and offloading cost. Then the optimization objective is expressed as:

$$DT - LCMP : min \sum_{t=1}^{T} ((1 - \lambda_t) \cdot cost_t + \lambda_t \cdot D_t^{total}) \tag{8}$$

This is an NP-hard problem. We use $\Lambda = \{\lambda_t, t \in \mathcal{T}\}$ to represent the user's weight set, where $\lambda_t \in [0, 1]$ and represents the weight of $t^{th}$ time slot. Without loss of generality, we take the step size of $\lambda$ to be 0.1.

## 4    Algorithm Based on Meta Deep Reinforcement Learning and Long-Term and Short-Term Time Series Networks

In this section, we describe the establishment of MDP in detail and propose a task offloading algorithm based on multi-agent meta deep reinforcement learning and a load forecasting algorithm based on LSTNet, Combining MLP with LSTNet improves the performance and convergence speed of model training.

## 4.1    MDP Description

For the long-term cost minimization problem under dynamic trade-offs proposed in this paper, we transform it into a partially observable Markov decision process. Multiple smart home systems (SHS) with multiple base stations (BS) equipped with edge servers, each SHS agent observes the state of the local device and the state of the edge servers, and takes action to enter the next state, which is expressed as a multi-agent Markov decision process (MAMDP) [37], using tuples $(\mathcal{U}, \mathcal{S}, \{A_n\}_{n\in\mathcal{U}}, \mathcal{P}, \{R_n\}_{n\in\mathcal{U}}, \gamma)$. Where $\mathcal{U}$ represents the set of agents, $\mathcal{S}$ represents the set of state of all agents, $A_n$ represents the set of actions of agents, $\mathcal{P}$ represents the probability of transferring to the next state, $R_n$ represents the set of rewards after the agent takes action, and $\gamma$ represents the discount factor. Each SHS trains an agent in the SG, and the agent interacts with the environment to continuously learn and optimize offloading decisions. The agent state, action, and reward at time slot t are defined as follows:

- State: $s_t$ is defined as $\{d_t, c_t, SG_t, \{r_m, I_t\}_{m\in\mathcal{M}, t\in\mathcal{T}}\}$. Among them, $d_t$ and $c_t$ represent task information, and $SG_t$ represents local device information, including transmission queue information, load information (the current time slot being processed number of tasks), and CPU frequency. $r_m$ indicates the transmission speed with the edge server, and $m_t$ indicates the CPU frequency and load information of the edge server. $s_{t+1}$ represents the state at the next moment.
- Action: $a_t$ represents the action chosen for time t. The action space $a_t \in \{0, 1, ..., M\}$. Among them, 0 means to offload to the local, $\{1, 2, ..., M\}$ means to offload to which server.
- Reward: $r_t$ represents the reward for the agent to take actions in state $s_t$. For the convenience of exposition, we transform DT-LCMP into the reward maximization problem R-DT-LCMP, where R-DT-LCMP is expressed as

$$R - DT - LCMP : max \sum_{t=1}^{T} -((1 - \lambda_t) \cdot cost_t + \lambda_t \cdot D_t^{total}) \qquad (9)$$

## 4.2    Task Offloading Based on Multi-agent Meta Deep Reinforcement Learning

Multi-agent meta deep reinforcement learning is a method that combines meta-learning and multi-agent deep reinforcement learning to improve the agent's ability to use in dynamic environments. The meta-strategy improves the rapid adaptability in dynamic environments by collecting samples from each environment to train the model. In this paper, we use meta-policy gradients to implement meta deep reinforcement learning and use the DDQN method for training. Meta deep reinforcement learning includes inner and outer loops:

- Internal loop: We use DDQN [38] as the training method of the internal loop. DDQN is a value function optimization method, which optimizes the strategy by learning an action-value function (Q function). The update of Q function is expressed as $Q'(s, a_t) = Q(s, a_t) + \gamma \max_{a_t} \hat{Q}(s_{t+1}, a_t) \cdot done_t$, where $Q'$ represents the updated Q function, $\hat{Q}$ represents the target Q function, $\gamma$ represents the discount factor, $done_t$ represents whether the last time slot is reached, and the arrival $done_t$ is equal to 0, otherwise, it is 1. For each agent, we use MLP to build a neural network model, use the DDQN algorithm to update the parameters of the MLP network and select actions based on the $\epsilon$-greedy strategy, as shown in formula 10. In order to improve the sample efficiency, the experience playback mechanism is used to reuse the previous data for sampling training. The structure and training process of the DDQN model are shown in Fig. 2

$$a_t = \begin{cases} \operatorname{argmax}_{a_t} Q(s_t, a_t), & \text{random number} > \varepsilon \\ \text{random action } a_t, & \text{random number} \leq \varepsilon \end{cases} \tag{10}$$

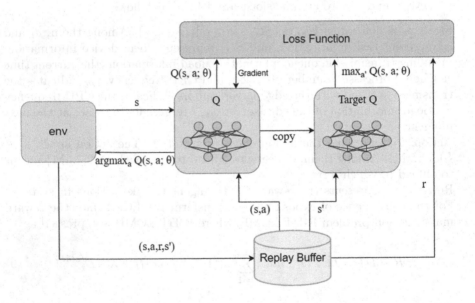

**Fig. 2.** DDQN model structure and training process.

- Outer loop: Consider establishing the task offloading process by each weight as an MDP, and the meta-policy treats each MDP as a training task. Assuming that all MDP tasks obey the distribution L, the meta-policy designed in this paper samples MDP according to the probability $\mathcal{P}(i)$ of the distribution L, and performs training to obtain the loss. $\mathcal{P}(i)$ represents the MDP sampling frequency corresponding to the $i^{th}$ weight. This allows the model to learn more about the MDP with higher probability. Specifically, we train the $i^{th}$ MDP according to the probability $\mathcal{P}(i)$ and calculate the loss, such as the formula 11.

$$loss'_i = \begin{cases} 0, & \text{random number} > \mathcal{P}(i) \\ loss_i, & \text{random number} \leq \mathcal{P}(i) \end{cases} \tag{11}$$

If the random number is less than the frequency, the sampling is successful, and the loss of the $i^{th}$ MDP is obtained. Otherwise, the sampling fails and the loss is 0. On this basis, the loss of the outer loop is calculated using the average error and Loss is expressed as formula 12.

$$\text{Loss} = \frac{1}{N} \sum_{i=1}^{N} loss_i' \tag{12}$$

---

**Algorithm 1.** Multi-agent Deep Reinforcement Learning Algorithm

---

1: Initialize the number of agents, M; environment, env; model parameters; time steps, T; the number of episode, E; replay buffer rb with size M; Sampling probability, P.
2: **while** e from 1 to E **do**
3:     Reset env
4:     Observe the state of the environment, get the state
5:     Initialize $loss_{set}$
6:     **while** t from 1 to T **do**
7:         **while** m from 1 to M **do**
8:             According the formula 10, choose the action at
9:             Execute at, observe $next_{state}$ st, reward rt and $done_t$.
10:             store $D(s_t, a_t, r_t, s_{t+1}, done_t)$ in $rb_m$
11:         **end while**
12:         **while** m from 1 to M **do**
13:             sample batches of tuples uniformly from $rb_m$, called Db
14:             According to the formula 11, using Db to calculate, get the loss
15:             **if** random number $< p_m$ **then**
16:                 push loss to $loss_{set}$
17:             **else**
18:                 push 0 to $loss_{set}$
19:             **end if**
20:         **end while**
21:         Calculate the average error of the $loss_{set}$, called Loss
22:         Update model with Loss
23:     **end while**
24: **end while**

---

In the training phase, the inner loop is trained on the SG, and by collecting the samples of the inner loop training process, the model on the BS performs probability sampling on each SG sample to perform the outer loop training. In the test phase, the meta-policy parameters trained on the BS are updated to each SG, and each SG generates a weight set that obeys the beta distribution by setting different beta distribution parameters. In a dynamic environment where weights change over time, evaluate the model's performance and convergence rate by observing how the total reward changes. According to the description of the inner loop and the outer loop, we express the training process of the multi-agent meta deep reinforcement learning model as Algorithm 1.

### 4.3   Load Forecasting Based on Long-Term and Short-Term Time Series Networks

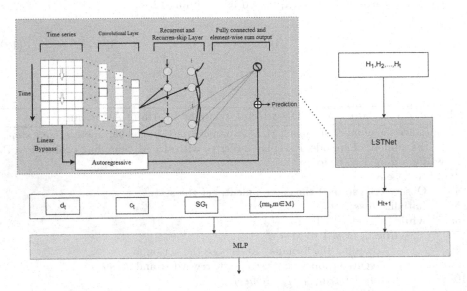

**Fig. 3.** The Network Model of MLP combined with LSTNet.

When the agent makes an unloading decision, predicting the future load situation through the historical information of the edge server can effectively improve the performance and convergence speed of the model [11]. Considering the mutual influence between servers and the long-term dependence of individual server information, the LSTNet [39] model based on a spatiotemporal attention mechanism is a good choice. The self-attention mechanism adaptively weights different positions in the input sequence, so as to better handle long-term dependencies and avoid information loss in the process of information transmission. The LSTNet model includes a Convolutional Layer, Recurrent and Recurrent-skip Layer, and fully connected and element-wise sum output. The Convolutional Layer extracts information in the time dimension and local dependencies between variables. Recurrent and Recurrent-skip Layer can effectively process time series data, capture long-term dependencies, and improve the training efficiency and generalization ability of the model. The final prediction result is obtained by element-wise summation through fully connected and element-wise sum output, and the autoregressive model is used as a linear component to solve the problem that the output scale of convolution and loop components is not sensitive to different input scales.

The combined model of MLP and LSTNet is shown in Fig. 3. We use the server's historical load information $H = \{H_1, H_2, ... H_t\}$ to predict the load information $H_{t+1}$ at the next moment. Replace the server information in the input state $s_t$ of DDQN with the prediction information $\{H_{m,t}\}, m \in \mathcal{M}, t \in \mathcal{T}$ of multiple servers. Therefore, LSTNet takes the input H and gets the output $H_{t+1}$. Since LSTNet must have certain historical data to start prediction, we define that when the amount of data reaches the input width of LSTNet, start training and forecasting.

## 5   Simulation Results

In this section, we first introduce the setting of experimental parameters. The performance of the proposed algorithm is evaluated by simulation experiments. And compared with other algorithms.

### 5.1   Parameters Setting

We consider a simulation experiment in a system consisting of multiple smart home systems (SHS) and multiple edge servers, each SHS contains an SG and other multiple smart devices. The tasks of all smart devices are uniformly processed at the SG. Considering that different smart devices generate different tasks at the same time, we set R to represent the generation rate of tasks, and the length of the time slot $\tau$ is set to $1/R$. The parameter settings of this experiment are shown in Table 2 with reference to the parameter settings of [40–42].

### 5.2   Performance Evaluation

We study the performance and convergence speed of the proposed MMRL-L algorithm under different parameters. Considering 1000 episodes, each episode contains 100 slots, our evaluation index is to evaluate the long-term rewards for each 100 slots.

In Fig. 4, we show the convergence speed of the model by different batch sizes and learning rates. In Fig. 4(a), with the increase of Episode, the model by the three parameters begins to converge at 300 episodes. When the Batch Size is 16, the final effect of the model is slightly higher than in the other two cases. In Fig. 4(b), we show the convergence of the model by different inner loop learning rates. It is not difficult to find that when the Inner Learning Rate is 0.01, due to the high learning rate, the model oscillates at the local optimal point, and the effect is lower than the other two cases. Finally, the inner Learning Rate is 0.001. Figure 4(c) shows the different performance and convergence speeds of the model by different outer loop learning rates. Among them, the total reward of Outer Learning Rate of 0.001 is the largest, and it reaches near -35 when it converges.

**Table 2.** Algorithm Parameters.

| Parameters | Values |
| --- | --- |
| M | 4 |
| N | 50 |
| T | 100 |
| R | Generate 5 tasks per s |
| $\tau$ | 1/R |
| $\lambda$ | 0–1 Bera distribution,step is 0.1 |
| d | 300–500 KB uniformly |
| c | 100–300 cycle/Bit uniformly |
| $f_{SG}$ | 1.0–1.5 GHz uniformly |
| $f_{server}$ | 4.0–6.0 GHz uniformly |
| the number of SG'CPU | 4 |
| the number of BS'CPU | 8 |
| B | 20 MHz |
| p | 0.2 |
| $\gamma$ | 0.9 |
| Batch size of Double Dqn | 32 |
| Learning rate for inner loop | 0.001 |
| Learning rate of outer loop | 0.001 |

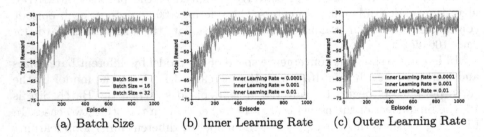

(a) Batch Size     (b) Inner Learning Rate     (c) Outer Learning Rate

**Fig. 4.** Model diagram of smart home combined with edge computing.

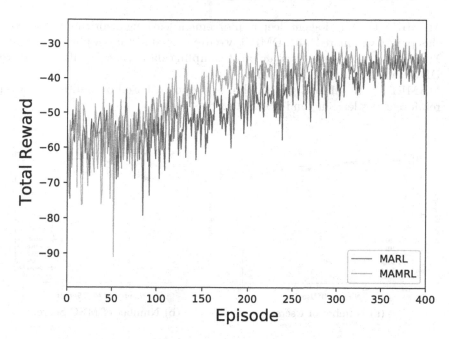

**Fig. 5.** Convergence of MARL and MAMRL.

In Fig. 5, we observe the convergence of the multi-agent deep reinforcement learning model (MARL) and the multi-agent meta deep reinforcement learning model (MAMRL) in the dynamic environment. It is not difficult to find that the model converges faster after combining meta-learning.

### 5.3  Method Comparison

To verify the performance of the MAMRL-L algorithm, we compare it with the DMRO and four benchmark algorithms in a dynamic trade-off environment. All algorithms are as follows:

- Local-all: All tasks are executed locally without uninstalling
- Greedy-all: All tasks are offloaded to the server for execution. According to the greedy strategy, the server with the lowest load is selected according to the current observation state of the server by the local device.
- DDQN: DDQN(Double DQN) algorithm improves DQN, reduces overestimation problems, enhance performance and convergence speed, and more accurately evaluates action value.
- DMRO: An offloading algorithm based on meta deep reinforcement learning. When the proposed algorithm trains the meta-policy, it randomly selects a sample of one environment from multiple environments for learning at a time. After the learning is completed, the sample of another environment is selected for learning. The initial parameters of the model are obtained.

- MAMRL: The multi-agent deep reinforcement learning algorithm proposed in this paper. Compared with DMRO, we use probabilistic sampling for various MDP tasks, use the average error of sampling data for calculation, and use DDQN method for model training.
- MAMRL-L: An offloading algorithm is proposed based on multi-agent deep reinforcement learning and LSTNet in this paper.

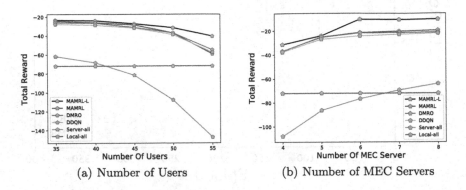

(a) Number of Users    (b) Number of MEC Servers

**Fig. 6.** The impact of the number of users or the number of MEC Servers.

We show the impact of the number of users or servers, as shown in Fig. 6. In Fig. 6(a), We show the total rewards for different numbers of users. As the number of users increases, the pressure on the server increases, resulting in a backlog of tasks and an increase in the execution delay of subsequent offloading tasks. The Local-all algorithm performs all tasks locally, so when the server increases, there will be no change. Other algorithms reduce the final total reward due to the increase in delay, especially Server-all. This is because only offloading tasks to the server will lead to an increase in the waiting delay of tasks, and will affect the waiting delay of all tasks that are later offloaded. It can be seen that the performance of DDQN, DMRO, and MMRL algorithms is similar. Citation meta-learning does not directly improve the performance of the model but improves its environmental adaptability. Because MAMRL-L combines the LSTNet algorithm, has the load information of the future server and optimizes the offloading decision, and the final effect is the best.

Figure 6(b) shows that as the number of edge servers increases, the total reward gradually increases, because the increased servers share the pressure of other servers and reduce the waiting delay of tasks. When the number of servers increases from 7 to 8, the waiting delay for tasks is very small, and adding more servers can not significantly reduce the waiting delay. It can be found that MAMRL-L has better results than other algorithms.

# 6   Conclusion

In this paper, we study the scenario of edge computing-enabled smart homes, considering the dynamic weighted sum of task execution delay and offloading cost by dynamic trade-offs. Based on this, the long-term cost minimization problem by dynamic trade-off is formulated. To solve this problem, an offloading algorithm based on multi-agent deep reinforcement learning and long-term and short-term time series network is proposed, which can quickly adapt to different environments and obtain the optimal task offloading strategy. Compared with other algorithms, our algorithm effectively reduces the long-term cost of task offloading in a dynamic trade-off environment.

In future work, we will consider more factors that have an impact on the offloading algorithm, including energy consumption, pricing mechanisms of different service providers, and bandwidth allocation issues. Furthermore, we will focus on the optimization problem of combining task offloading and task caching.

**Acknowledgments.** This paper is supported by the National Nature Science Foundation of China under grant number: T2350710232.

# References

1. Naeem, M., et al.: Trends and future perspective challenges in big data. Smart Innov., Syst. Technol. **253**, 309–325 (2022)
2. Durao, F., et al.: A systematic review on cloud computing. J. Supercomput. **68**(3), 1321–1346 (2014)
3. Cao, K., et al.: An overview on edge computing research. IEEE Access **8**, 85714–85728 (2020)
4. Kopytko, V., et al.: Smart home and artificial intelligence as environment for the implementation of new technologies. Path Sci. **4**(9), 2007–2012 (2018)
5. Huh, J.H., Seo, K.: Artificial intelligence shoe cabinet using deep learning for smart home. In: Park, J., Loia, V., Choo, K.K., Yi, G. (eds.) Advanced Multimedia and Ubiquitous Engineering. Lecture Notes in Electrical Engineering, vol. 518, pp. 825–834. Springer, Singapore (2019). https://doi.org/10.1007/978-981-13-1328-8_108
6. Guo, X., et al.: Review on the application of artificial intelligence in smart homes. Smart Cities **2**(3), 402–420 (2019)
7. Jeon, Y., et al.: Mobility-aware optimal task offloading in distributed edge computing. In: International Conference on Information Networking, 2021-January, pp. 65–68 (2021)
8. Wu, Y., et al.: Noma-assisted multi-access mobile edge computing: a joint optimization of computation offloading and time allocation. IEEE Trans. Veh. Technol. **67**(12), 12244–12258 (2018)
9. Zhang, T.: Data offloading in mobile edge computing: a coalition and pricing based approach. IEEE Access **6**, 2760–2767 (2017)
10. Huang, X., et al.: Vehicle speed aware computing task offloading and resource allocation based on multi-agent reinforcement learning in a vehicular edge computing network. In: Proceedings - 2020 IEEE 13th International Conference on Edge Computing, EDGE 2020, pp. 1–8 (2020)

11. Tu, Y., et al.: Task offloading based on LSTM prediction and deep reinforcement learning for efficient edge computing in IoT. Future Internet **14**(2), 30 (2022)
12. Zhou, H., et al.: Energy efficient joint computation offloading and service caching for mobile edge computing: a deep reinforcement learning approach. IEEE Trans. Green Commun. Netw. **7**(2), 950–961 (2023)
13. Huang, L., et al.: Deep reinforcement learning-based joint task offloading and bandwidth allocation for multi-user mobile edge computing. Digit. Commun. Netw. **5**(1), 10–17 (2019)
14. Beck, J., et al.: A survey of meta-reinforcement learning (2023)
15. Finn, C., et al.: Model-agnostic meta-learning for fast adaptation of deep networks (2017). https://proceedings.mlr.press/v70/finn17a.html
16. Jiang, H., et al.: Joint task offloading and resource allocation for energy-constrained mobile edge computing. IEEE Trans. Mob. Comput. (2022)
17. Luo, J., et al.: QoE-driven computation offloading for edge computing. J. Syst. Architect. **97**, 34–39 (2019)
18. Park, J., Chung, K.: Distributed DRL-based computation offloading scheme for improving QoE in edge computing environments. Sensors **23**(8), 4166 (2023)
19. Zhou, Z., et al.: QoE-guaranteed heterogeneous task offloading with deep reinforcement learning in edge computing. In: Proceedings of 2022 8th IEEE International Conference on Cloud Computing and Intelligence Systems, CCIS 2022, pp. 558–564 (2022)
20. Zhu, B., et al.: Efficient offloading for minimizing task computation delay of NOMA-based multiaccess edge computing. IEEE Trans. Commun. **70**(5), 3186–3203 (2022)
21. Zhang, S., et al.: DRL-based partial offloading for maximizing sum computation rate of wireless powered mobile edge computing network. IEEE Trans. Wirel. Commun. **21**(12), 10934–10948 (2022)
22. Chen, Y., et al.: Dynamic task offloading for mobile edge computing with hybrid energy supply. Tsinghua Sci. Technol. **28**(3), 421–432 (2023)
23. Tong, Z., et al.: Stackelberg game-based task offloading and pricing with computing capacity constraint in mobile edge computing. J. Syst. Architect. **137**, 102847 (2023)
24. Seo, H., et al.: Differential pricing-based task offloading for delay-sensitive IoT applications in mobile edge computing system. IEEE Internet Things J. **9**(19), 19116–19131 (2022)
25. Wang, X., et al.: Decentralized scheduling and dynamic pricing for edge computing: a mean field game approach. IEEE/ACM Trans. Netw. **31**(3), 965–978 (2023)
26. Chen, S., et al.: Dynamic pricing for smart mobile edge computing: a reinforcement learning approach. IEEE Wirel. Commun. Lett. **10**(4), 700–704 (2021)
27. Chen, Y., et al.: Dynamic task offloading for internet of things in mobile edge computing via deep reinforcement learning. Int. J. Commun. Syst., e5154 (2022)
28. Xu, J., et al.: Online learning for offloading and Autoscaling in energy harvesting mobile edge computing. IEEE Trans. Cogn. Commun Netw. **3**(3), 361–373 (2017)
29. Qu, G., et al.: DMRO: a deep meta reinforcement learning-based task offloading framework for edge-cloud computing. IEEE Trans. Netw. Serv. Manage. **18**(3), 3448–3459 (2021)
30. Wang, J., et al.: Fast adaptive task offloading in edge computing based on meta reinforcement learning. IEEE Trans. Parallel Distrib. Syst. **32**(1), 242–253 (2021)
31. Yan, W., et al.: Survey on recent smart gateways for smart home: systems, technologies, and challenges. Trans. Emerg. Telecommun. Technol. **33**(6), e4067 (2022)

32. Dabin, J.A., et al.: A statistical ultra-wideband indoor channel model and the effects of antenna directivity on path loss and multipath propagation. IEEE J. Sel. Areas Commun. **24**(2), 752–758 (2006)

33. Cai, J., et al.: Deep reinforcement learning-based multitask hybrid computing offloading for multiaccess edge computing. Int. J. Intell. Syst. **37**(9), 6221–6243 (2022)

34. Wang, W., et al.: Trade-off analysis of fine-grained power gating methods for functional units in a CPU. In: Symposium on Low-Power and High-Speed Chips - Proceedings for 2012 IEEE COOL. Chips. XV. (2012)

35. Chen, E., et al.: SaaSC: toward pay-as-you-go mode for software service transactions based on blockchain's smart legal contracts. IEEE Trans. Serv., Comput. (2023)

36. Chargebee, what is pay as you go pricing model, on-line webpage (2022). https://www.chargebee.com/resources/glossaries/pay-as-you-go-pricing/

37. Zhao, N., et al.: Multi-agent deep reinforcement learning for task offloading in UAV-assisted mobile edge computing. IEEE Trans. Wirel. Commun. **21**(9), 6949–6960 (2022)

38. Van Hasselt, H., et al.: Deep reinforcement learning with double Q-learning. In: Proceedings of the AAAI Conference on Artificial Intelligence, vol. 30, no. 1, pp. 2094–2100 (2016)

39. Lai, G., et al.: Modeling long- and short-term temporal patterns with deep neural networks. In: 41st International ACM SIGIR Conference on Research and Development in Information Retrieval, SIGIR 2018, pp. 95–104 (2018)

40. Liu, Z., et al.: Computation offloading and pricing in mobile edge computing based on Stackelberg game. Wirel. Netw. **27**(7), 4795–4806 (2021)

41. Li, F., et al.: Stackelberg game-based computation offloading in social and cognitive industrial internet of things. IEEE Trans. Industr. Inform. **16**(8), 5444–5455 (2020)

42. Liao, L., et al.: Online computation offloading with double reinforcement learning algorithm in mobile edge computing. J. Parallel Distrib. Comput. **171**, 28–39 (2023)

# Author Index

**A**

Angelis, Ioannis   I-18
Antonopoulos, Christos   I-3

**B**

Besimi, Adrian   III-154
Bi, Zhongqin   III-134
Blasi, Maximilian   III-229

**C**

Cang, Li Shan   II-265
Cao, Bin   II-437
Cao, Cong   II-205
Cao, Dun   III-79
Cao, Wenwen   II-414
Cao, Ya-Nan   II-321
Chang, Jiayu   II-131
Chen, Hui   II-115
Chen, Juan   II-173, II-375, III-100
Chen, Kaiwei   II-79
Chen, Liang   II-242, II-392
Chen, Mingcai   II-20
Chen, Peng   II-173, II-375, III-100, III-118
Chen, Shizhan   II-281
Christopoulou, Eleni   I-18
Cui, Bo   I-207
Cui, Jiahe   III-23
Cui, Jie   II-414

**D**

Dagiuklas, Tasos   III-41
Deng, Shaojiang   II-495
Di, Qianhui   II-514
Ding, Weilong   III-329
Ding, Xu   I-187, I-365, I-385
Ding, Yong   I-167, I-243, II-301, II-321
Du, Miao   I-54
Duan, Liang   II-458
Duan, Yutang   III-134

**F**

Faliagka, Evanthia   I-3
Fan, Guodong   II-281
Fan, Jing   II-437
Fan, Yuqi   I-187
Fan, Zhicheng   II-20
Fang, Cheng   I-54
Feng, Beibei   II-341
Feng, Lin   III-308
Feng, Shilong   I-385, III-273
Feng, Xiangyang   III-291
Feng, Zhiyong   II-281, III-208
Fichtner, Myriel   III-249
Fu, Jianhui   II-205

**G**

Gan, Yanglan   III-291
Gao, Chongming   III-191
Gao, Jinyong   III-365
Gao, Min   III-191, III-365
Guo, Linxin   III-191
Guo, Meng   II-474
Guo, Ming   II-20
Guo, Zhenwei   II-321

**H**

Han, Dingkang   III-347
Han, Jianghong   III-308
Hao, Junfeng   III-100
He, Hongshun   II-474
He, Hongxia   II-173, II-375
He, Yunxiang   III-23
Henrich, Dominik   III-249
Hu, Bowen   II-96
Hu, Haize   I-284, I-303, I-343
Hu, Qinglei   III-23
Hu, Zekun   I-128
Huang, Jie   I-225
Huang, Jihai   III-329
Huang, Kaizhu   III-3
Huang, Xingru   II-96

Huang, Yakun   II-474
Huang, Yi   III-3

**I**
Idoje, Godwin   III-41
Iqbal, Muddesar   II-265, III-41

**J**
Jablonski, Stefan   III-249
Jelić, Slobodan   I-38
Ji, Rui   I-385, III-273
Jian, Wenxin   I-93
Jiang, Qinkai   II-437
Jiang, Xinghong   I-93
Jiang, Yujie   III-173
Jiao, Liang   III-347
Jin, Yi   I-265
Jin, Zhifeng   I-187
Ju, Zixuan   I-225

**K**
Keramidas, Giorgos   I-3
Knežević, Milica   I-38
Kraft, Robin   III-229
Kuang, Li   I-265, II-131

**L**
Lei, Nanfang   III-79
Li, Baoke   II-205
Li, Bing   I-54
Li, Dongyu   III-23
Li, Fan   I-77
Li, Jiaxin   II-39
Li, Min   II-281
Li, Mingchu   I-421, II-3
Li, Peihao   I-225
Li, Peisong   III-3
Li, Qi   I-323
Li, Shuai   I-421, II-3
Li, Wenwei   II-474
Li, Xi   II-173, II-375
Li, Xiang   II-341
Li, Yang   II-96, II-414, II-474
Li, Yantao   II-495
Li, Yin   I-77, III-118
Li, Yixuan   II-96
Li, Youhuizi   II-514
Li, Yu   II-514
Li, Zhehao   I-365, III-273

Liang, Hai   I-167, I-243, II-321
Liang, Qingmi   I-265
Liang, Tian   II-131
Liang, Tingting   II-514
Liang, Weiyou   I-167
Liao, Jie   II-392
Liu, Donghua   III-208
Liu, Feng   I-365
Liu, Jianxun   I-284, I-303, I-323, I-343
Liu, Jinyuan   I-243
Liu, Lingmeng   II-79
Liu, Peiyu   II-39
Liu, Qingyun   III-347
Liu, Ruiqi   III-365
Liu, Xiangzheng   I-284
Liu, Xu   I-207
Liu, Yanbing   II-205
Liu, Yi   I-284
Liu, Yilin   II-301
Liu, Yumeng   II-223
Long, Teng   I-303
Lu, Tong   II-458
Luo, Huaxiu   II-495
Lyu, Zengwei   III-308

**M**
Ma, Jingrun   II-341
Ma, Yong   I-77, I-93, II-79
Mei, Tianyu   I-207
Mihaljević, Miodrag J.   I-38
Mo, Dikai   III-347

**N**
Nanos, Nikolaos   I-3
Ni, Mingjian   II-96
Niu, Xianhua   III-100

**O**
Oikonomou, Konstantinos   I-18
Ouyang, Zhaobin   III-118
Ouyang, Zhenchao   III-23

**P**
Peng, Chao   III-208
Peng, Qinglan   I-77, II-79, III-118
Peng, Xincai   II-265
Peng, Yang   I-225
Pryss, Rüdiger   III-229

**Q**

Qi, Chufeng I-149
Qi, Wanying I-421, II-3
Qi, Zhiwei II-458
Qian, Shuwei II-20
Qiao, Xiuquan II-474
Qin, Huafeng II-495
Qiu, Houming II-357

**R**

Reichert, Manfred III-229
Ren, YongJian III-59
Riedelbauch, Dominik III-249

**S**

Schickler, Marc III-229
Selimi, Mennan III-154
Ševerdija, Domagoj I-38
Shan, Meijing III-134
Shao, Shiyun II-79
Sheng, Yu I-265
Sherratt, Robert Simon III-79
Shi, Lei I-187, I-365, I-385, III-273
Shi, Yukun III-385
Shkurti, Lamir III-154
Shu, Xinyue I-111
Song, Qihong I-343
Song, Weijian II-173, II-375
Song, Yi II-115
Song, Yulun II-96
Spournias, Alexandros I-3
Su, Jiajun II-79
Su, Majing II-205
Sucker, Sascha III-249
Sun, Haifeng I-403
Sun, Maoxiang III-329
Sun, Yong III-347

**T**

Tchernykh, Andrei III-3
Todorović, Milan I-38
Tsipis, Athanasios I-18
Tu, Jiaxue I-77

**V**

Voros, Nikolaos I-3

**W**

Wan, Jian II-151
Wan, Zihang II-223

Wang, Bin II-39
Wang, Bo II-115
Wang, Chongjun II-20
Wang, Chunyu II-189
Wang, Fan II-39
Wang, Gongju II-96
Wang, Hongan II-223
Wang, Huiyong I-167, II-301
Wang, Jiaxing II-437
Wang, Jin III-79
Wang, Peng II-57
Wang, Pengwei I-128
Wang, Quanda II-96
Wang, Shiqi III-191
Wang, Shunli II-189
Wang, Xi II-341
Wang, Xiaowen I-225
Wang, Xin III-59
Wang, Xinheng III-3
Wang, Xu III-118
Wang, Yang III-100
Wang, Yongjie II-57
Wang, Yujue I-167, I-243, II-301, II-321
Wei, Zhen III-273
Wei, Zhenchun III-308
Wen, Baodong I-243
Wu, Hongyue II-281
Wu, Quanwang I-111
Wu, Ruoting II-242, II-392
Wu, Shouyi II-474
Wu, Yujiang III-365

**X**

Xi, Qinghui II-173, II-375
Xia, Yunni I-77, I-93, II-79, II-375, III-100, III-118
Xiao, Wang III-208
Xiao, Wanzhi II-131
Xiao, Ziren III-3
Xie, Qi I-265
Xie, Qilin I-93
Xie, Yibin I-365
Xing, Weiwei I-149
Xiong, Jiasi III-79
Xiong, Xinli II-57
Xu, Chaonong III-173
Xu, Fuyong II-39
Xu, Jie II-151
Xu, Juan I-385
Xu, Junyi III-308

Xu, Lei   III-100
Xu, Peiran   III-385
Xu, Xiaolin   II-341
Xue, Meiting   III-385
Xue, Xiao   II-281, III-208


**Y**
Yan, Cairong   III-291
Yan, Long   II-96
Yan, Xiangpei   III-208
Yang, Changsong   I-167, I-243, II-301,
    II-321
Yang, Ke   II-115
Yang, Peng   I-54
Yang, Yuling   II-205
Yao, Qian   II-57
Yao, Xinwei   I-149
Yi, Chen   II-301
Yi, Meng   I-54
Yin, Yuyu   II-514
Yu, Qi   III-329
Yuan, Fangfang   II-205
Yuan, Xiaohui   III-308
Yue, Kun   II-458
Yue, Lupeng   III-385


**Z**
Zang, Tianning   II-341
Zeng, Jie   III-365
Zeng, Kaisheng   III-385
Zeng, Yan   III-59

Zeng, Yanguo   III-385
Zhan, Baotong   I-385
Zhang, Beibei   III-59
Zhang, Changjie   III-23
Zhang, Daqing   I-403
Zhang, Jia   III-365
Zhang, Jilin   III-59, III-385
Zhang, Jun   I-187, II-189
Zhang, Lihua   II-189
Zhang, Lu   II-281
Zhang, Qingliang   I-111
Zhang, Qingyang   II-414
Zhang, Shuai   II-265
Zhang, Weina   III-134
Zhang, Xiangping   I-303, I-323
Zhang, Xin   II-151
Zhang, Yiwei   III-291
Zhang, Yuanqing   II-514
Zhang, Yuedong   III-347
Zhang, Yuxin   II-242, II-392
Zhang, Zhaohui   I-128
Zhao, Han   II-79
Zhao, Peihai   I-128
Zhao, Yijing   II-223
Zheng, Haibin   I-243
Zheng, Hui   III-59
Zhong, Hong   II-414
Zhou, Mingyao   III-59
Zhou, Sirui   I-225
Zhu, Dongge   I-77
Zhu, Kun   II-357
Zhu, Yujia   III-347

Printed in the United States
by Baker & Taylor Publisher Services